This work is the second in a three-volume series on significant studies of the 1813 campaign to appear si over a century ago. Unlike the majority of other Er using French archival and published sources, as wo sources. It discusses every battle and significant action in all parts of Germany various sieges. Detailed color maps support the major battles and a large collection of orders of battle drawn from the French Archives, as well as period-published documents, support the discussion of the campaign, complemented by a wide selection of images. Both images and maps are new to this edition of the work.

ry few
a little
epared
blished

George F. Nafziger, PhD, Captain USNRRet. earned his BA and MBA at Miami University, Oxford, Ohio, and his PhD From the Union Institute, Cincinnati, Ohio. His first book, *Napoleon's Invasion of Russia*, was published in 1988 and was the first of a series of works on the Napoleonic era. He has served as a Director of the Napoleonic Society of America and the Napoleonic Alliance. He is a fellow of the Le Souvenir Napoléonienne Internationale, and runs the Nafziger Collection, Inc., a publishing house specializing in military history. He served in the US Navy for 4 years and a further 20 in the US Navy Reserves. He did two tours to Vietnam and experienced combat firsthand.

NAPOLEON AT DRESDEN

My father and his father,
both of whom instilled in me a love of history.
George Andrew Francis Nafziger
Adolph Andrew Nafziger

NAPOLEON AT DRESDEN

The Battles of August 1813

George Nafziger

Helion & Company

Helion & Company Limited
Unit 8 Amherst Business Centre
Budbrooke Road
Warwick
CV34 5WE
England
Tel. 01926 499619
Email: info@helion.co.uk
Website: www.helion.co.uk
Twitter: @helionbooks
blog.helion.co.uk/

Originally published by Emperor's Press 1994
This new edition published by Helion & Company 2018. Reprinted in paperback 2021
Designed and typeset by Mach 3 Solutions Ltd (www.mach3solutions.co.uk)
Cover designed by Paul Hewitt, Battlefield Design (www.battlefield-design.co.uk)

Text © George Nafziger 1994
Images open source
Maps drawn by George Anderson © Helion & Company Limited 2018

Front cover: The battle for the churchyard at Gross-Beeren, by Röchling.

ISBN 978-1-914059-60-5

British Library Cataloguing-in-Publication Data.
A catalogue record for this book is available from the British Library.

For details of other military history titles published by Helion & Company Limited contact the above address, or visit our website: http://www.helion.co.uk.

We always welcome receiving book proposals from prospective authors.

Contents

List of Illustrations

List of Maps

Sketch Maps

Color Maps

* Map has key. Map keys can be found at the end of the color section.

Acknowledgements

I would like to acknowledge the assistance of a few people, without whom this work could not have been what it is. The first is Mr Peter Harrington, curator of the Anne S. K. Brown Military Collection, Brown University. He most graciously received me on numerous occasions, opening the collection to me and giving me access to anything that he could to assist my researches.

The second is Mr J.J. Slonaker of the U.S. Army Military History Institute who opened the doors to the Army's historical library to me, allowing me to have copies made of numerous rare and obscure works that have contributed significantly to this work.

It is with special pleasure that I acknowledge the assistance of my friend, Mr Peter Hofschröer, who selflessly opened up his library, providing copies of the artwork, editorial comments, and other assistance for which I am much in his debt.

A special acknowledgement and most humble thanks goes to Mr Warren Worley, who continues to act as a technical editor, catching various discrepancies, helping to flesh out the text with technical details, catching discrepancies in the various source documents that slipped past me, and providing an extra comma here and there.

Abbreviations and Terminology

For simplicity's sake some abbreviations are used for many officer's ranks. In some instances, the full title is used where it is not particularly long. The ranks and their equivalents in current ranks are:

French

Maréchal	Field Marshal
Général de division	Major General (GD)
Général de brigade	Brigadier General (BG)
Colonel	Colonel
Major	Lt. Colonel
Chef d'escadron	Major (cavalry and horse artillery)
Chef de bataillon	Major (infantry and foot artillery)
Capitaine	Captain
Lieutenant	1st Lieutenant
Sous-lieutenant	2nd Lieutenant

Prussian, Russian, and Most German States

Feldmarschall	Field Marshal (FM)
General der Kavallerie	Lieutenant General (GdK)
General der Infanterie	Lieutenant General (GdI)
Generallieutenant	Major General (GL)
Generalmajor	Brigadier General (GM)
Oberst	Colonel
Oberstleutnant	Lt. Colonel (OBL)
Major	Major
Rittmeister	Captain (cavalry)
Hauptman, Kapitän	Captain (infantry)
Leutnant	1st Lieutenant
Unterleutnant	2nd Lieutenant

Austrian

Feldmarschall	Field Marshal (FM)
General der Kavallerie	General "of Cavalry" (GdK)
General der Infanterie	General "of Infantry" (GdI)
Feldzeugmeister	Lieutenant General (FZM)
Feldmarschal-lieutenant	Major General (FML)
Generalmajor	Brigadier General (GM)
Oberst	Colonel
Oberstleutnant	Lt. Colonel
Rittmeister	Captain (cavalry)
Hauptman, Kapitän	Captain (infantry)
Leutnant	1st Lieutenant
Unterleutnant	2nd Lieutenant

Note: The term used for an infantry captain in German has changed over the years and varies from source to source. All of the following terms are common forms of the German for "captain": Hauptman, Kapitain, Kapitän, and Capitain.

Introduction

The 1813 fall campaign was one of the major turning points in history. The wheel of fate had already turned against Napoleon in Russia, but it swung back in his favor in the spring of 1813. In the fall of 1813 it was to swing again.

Napoleon had rebuilt his shattered armies and, though their ranks were filled with recruits, they had served him well in the spring. Since January 1813 he had lost the territories conquered in 1806-7 to the advancing Russians. Prussia, a weak and questionable ally, had first deserted him, then joined his enemies. The Grand Duchy of Warsaw was lost to him as a source of troops and horses, though the shattered remains of its army still fought with him. His German allies were no longer totally reliable, but still provided significant contingents to his armies. The Austrians had signed a secret agreement neutralizing their army to the benefit of the allies.

Major portions of Napoleon's army were trapped in various garrisons throughout eastern Germany and Poland. Though they held important positions and held large numbers of allied troops away from the main armies, they also drained Napoleon of many of his veteran troops.

The Russian army was, itself, trying to shake off the losses of the 1812 winter campaign and had rebuilt itself to a significant degree. The Prussian army was reformed with the krumper system and had expanded dramatically from its pre-war strength. Where there had once been only 12 infantry regiments, there now stood nearly 30, soon to be supported by innumerable landwehr battalions. However, though they were drilled and trained, they were not battle hardened veterans. The dragon's teeth that Napoleon had planted with the Treaty of Tilsit had sprung from the ground as fully armed warriors.

During the spring of 1813 not everything had gone Napoleon's way, but once the serious campaigning had begun French arms had met with one victory after another in Germany. There were minor setbacks in small clashes, but so far in Germany all the chips were in Napoleon's corner.

To the south, in Spain, it was a different story. In June Joseph, Napoleon's older brother, had lost the Battle of Vitoria. By August the British had begun to lay siege to San Sebastian and by November 1813 they would invade France proper.

The two great spring battles in Germany, Lützen and Bautzen, were both French victories, but the lack of horses had crippled Napoleon's cavalry arm and had prevented him from gaining victories like those he had known in 1805 and 1806. The month of May and early June saw Napoleon's armies pushing a shattered Russo-Prussian army eastwards.

The Russians were worried about their lines of communications with the homeland and fell back due east. The Prussians were worried about a French move to re-capture Berlin, because the allied line of withdrawal was south of their capitol, leaving it open. The Austrians, though sympathetic to the allied cause, were still on the side lines, half-heartedly acting as the mediator in an effort to bring about a negotiated settlement of the war.

Though the allies were, seemingly, on the ropes, Napoleon was worried about the state of his army. He had taken heavy casualties, both from combat and the attrition of green and young troops thrust suddenly into a campaign. The weakness of his cavalry had cost him the fruits of his two victories and left him helpless against the Cossacks and streifkorps that roamed freely in his rear areas striking his communications. Napoleon needed time to rest and refit his army.

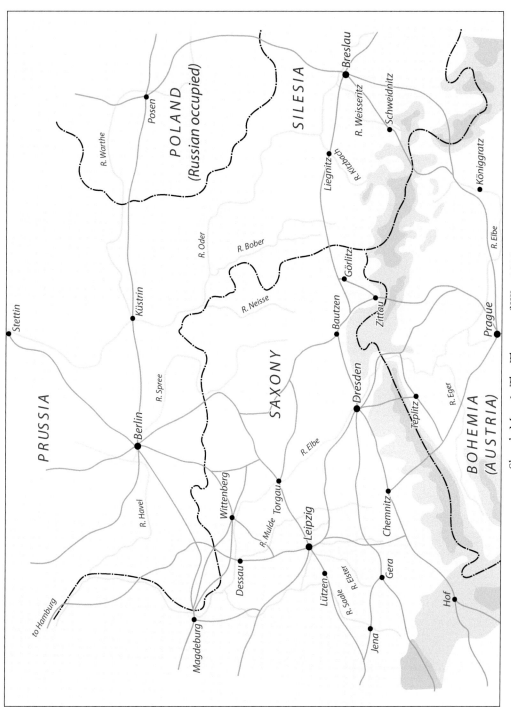

Sketch Map 1 The Theater of War 1813.

The summer armistice was a gamble. Perhaps Napoleon feared that if he were unable to refit his army, it would be so weakened from the process of destroying the Russo-Prussian armies that, once it had advanced into Poland and eliminated them, he would find a large, fresh and hostile Austrian army in his rear. That would have spelled defeat and ruin.

The gamble of an armistice would allow him to rebuild and expand his army. True, he threw away the momentum of victory and the psychological superiority it gives over one's enemies, but to offset that he would be able to consolidate his hold over his wavering German allies, replace his losses of the spring campaign, further train those troops he already had in the field, and find more horses to mount his sadly depleted cavalry.

The wild card in this gamble was Austria. Napoleon's attitude towards them was, from the modern perspective, incomprehensible. He continually bullied and threatened them. Certainly he knew from his espionage system that they were rebuilding and were everything but openly hostile to him and his goals. It is possible that he felt his marriage to Marie-Louise would be sufficient to keep the Austrian armies from joining the allies. Whatever his thoughts were, they are lost, and so was the gamble. Austria was to declare for the allies and join their cause against Napoleon.

When the negotiations finally collapsed and the war in Germany was resumed, Napoleon was to find himself facing the armed might of Austria, Prussia, Russia and Sweden, underwritten by British financial and material support.

1

The Summer Armistice
8 June–10 August 1813

Austria, The Balance of Power

With the signing of the armistice, Austria stood in the unusual position of holding the balance of power in Europe. It was a traditional enemy of the French, but it was also as the domain of Napoleon's father-in-law. The Austrian Emperor Franz, guided by the skilled diplomat Metternich, walked a difficult path. It is apparent that he and Metternich had no intention of negotiating a peace that would allow Napoleon to remain in power, but it is also must be realized that Austrian arms had never fared well against the French.

Metternich had played a significant role in the preliminaries that led up to the signing of the armistice. Von Bubna, another Austrian diplomat, had played a significant role in its signing.

The political situation at the beginning of the armistice was dominated by the mediation of Austria. Both Prussia and Russia had accepted it. Napoleon, however, made no precise response to the propositions that were made to him. Both the allies and Napoleon were playing a diplomatic game, in which neither side sincerely wanted peace. Napoleon did not wish to relinquish any of his conquests or the economic domination of the continent that French industry had established, nor did he wish to abandon the buffer between France and the east, that he had established with the Confederation of the Rhine. Both parties to the armistice danced a carefully orchestrated waltz of diplomatic warfare, while their armies refitted and prepared for the next round.

Metternich, under the direction of the Austrian Emperor, moved to Dresden to begin negotiations directly with Napoleon. His initial interviews were with the Minister of Foreign Affairs, the Duke de Bassano, and he reiterated the statements presented by von Bubna earlier. Austrian considered itself as free of all alliances and sought to provide mediation between the belligerents.

When Metternich arrived, he brought with him answers to the many questions posed to him by the Duke de Bassano, the French Minister of Foreign Affairs. Metternich had told the Duke de Bassano that he did not feel that Austria's alliance with France made it impossible for Austria to serve as a mediator in the current war. However, he did state that, under these circumstances, the alliance was not broken, only "suspended."[1]

With the alliance so lightly disposed of by the Austrians, the Duke de Bassano continued to insist to Metternich and von Bubna that Napoleon's goal was the simple negotiation of a peace through the use of plenipotentiaries who could gather and speak frankly.

On 28 June, Metternich was received by Napoleon, and presented Napoleon a letter from the Austrian emperor. Napoleon's reactions were brisk, if not sarcastic. His response to Metternich was, "You have arrived, Metternich. Welcome, but if you want peace, why have you come so late. We have already lost a month and by its inactivity your mediation has nearly become hostile."[2]

Napoleon declared to Metternich that he was aware of the terms of the Treaty of Reichenbach signed on 14 June 1813, by which the English had undertaken to provide subsidies of £1,333,344 to support the Prussians and the Russians in their war with France. He went on to say that his sources indicated to him that there was a third power involved in this treaty, but Monsieur Metternich "you are better informed than I in this regard."

After a pause, and while reviewing a series of maps of Europe, Napoleon declared to Metternich that he had offered Austria the return of the Illyrian provinces for her neutrality. He went on to say that Austria not only wanted the return of Illyria, but "the bulk of Italy, the return of the Pope to Rome, Poland, the abandonment of Spain, and of Holland, and of the Confederation of the Rhine, and Switzerland. That, therefore is what you call the spirit of moderation which you animate? You think of nothing but profiting from circumstances and you are occupied solely with transporting your alliances from one camp to the other so as to always be in the side with the spoils, and you come to speak with me of your respect for the rights of the independent states? So it is, you want Italy, Russia wants Poland, Sweden wants Norway, Prussia wants Saxony, and England wants Holland and Belgium. In one word, peace is but a pretext: you aspire to nothing but the total dismemberment of the French Empire."[3]

Francis I of Austria, by L. Kupelwiser.

Napoleon's bluntness continued as he declared that Austria was all but his declared enemy and that only the allied defeat at Lützen had stopped them. He spoke of the 200,000 men under Schwarzenberg that were massing in Bohemia and demanded to know why the Austrians, if they proposed to be mediators, were so uneven in their actions.

The attack upon his person and his government's actions was overwhelming. Metternich did not respond, even to the point of not picking up his hat when it fell from his head. When the conversation cooled and became formal, negotiations between Metternich, Napoleon, and the Duke de Bassano resumed. Metternich engaged himself, in the name of his government, to achieve the goal of establishing a prolongation of the armistice to 10 August.[4]

When Metternich returned to Vienna, he found himself struggling to convince the Austrian emperor that the extension of the armistice was in their best interest. A congress was convened in Prague for Metternich to speak with the allies. Though the Russian and Prussian delegates arrived on 8 July, they did not begin discussions until 12 July. The allies also expressed considerable displeasure with the idea of an extension. Barclay de Tolly was absolutely against such a prolongation, feeling that it was only to Napoleon's advantage. The negotiations lasted several weeks until the convention of 30 June was finally signed on 26 July.[5]

The plenipotentiaries were: The Duke de Vincenze and Count de Narbonne, who represented France, von Humboldt for Prussia, and von Anstett for Russia. These men began their negotiations with little hope of reaching an agreement.

Unfortunately, the French position was being steadily undermined by problems in Spain. Most notably was the disaster at Vitoria on 21 June 1813, where Wellington's victorious British savaged the withdrawing French army. In addition, Napoleon's 1805 and 1809 victories over Austria had built up such a thirst for vengeance in Austria, that they were determined to make Napoleon pay dearly for any settlement. In these circumstances the chances of permanent peace were almost nil.

The situation in Spain was becoming critical. Napoleon decided to send Maréchal Soult, Duc de Dalmatie, to Spain in an effort to recover the strategic situation from the victorious British.

Napoleon and Metternich at Dresden, 26 June.

His arrival in Spain on 12 July immediately caused Wellington to resume his previous course of prudence and caution.

Austria was actively arming itself. It had signed an agreement with England and was receiving half a million pounds of subsidies in return for its imminent hostilities with France.

Metternich had established himself in Prague on 12 July. The congress began with the various ambassadors and a cloud of "English voyagers." Initially, little happened beyond the exchanging of their powers to negotiate. The first action occurred on 29 July when Metternich issued a note on the form of the pending negotiations. Each belligerent was to submit to the mediator in writing what they wished to transmit to an opposing belligerent. The allies supported this method, but the French were greatly opposed to it. Further meetings occurred on 30 July and 1 August, but the diplomatic dancing consumed much time with little of substance being achieved.

Napoleon knew that while this farce of negotiations proceeded, the Austrian provinces of Moravia were providing supplies to the Russian and Prussian troops and that Austrian muskets were being shipped to the Prussian landwehr. Even the French negotiators in the congress realized that "Russia's goal was not to open negotiations with the goal of peace, but with the view of compromising Austria with France."[6]

The Cost of Peace

On 7 August Austria finally spoke out. Austria demanded, as the cost of peace, the following points.

1. Dissolution of the Grand Duchy of Warsaw.
2. The reestablishment of the free cities of Hamburg, Lubeck, etc.

3.   The reconstruction of the Kingdom of Prussia with a formal border on the Elbe.
4.   The cession to Austria of the Illyrian provinces and Trieste.

Napoleon had flatly refused to accept the conditions put forward by Austria. Though these conditions would strip France of many of Napoleon's conquests, France and most of its conquests would remain intact. This proposal left Italy, Switzerland, and western Germany under French domination, as well as leaving Belgium and Holland as part of greater metropolitan France.[7]

Napoleon responded to the proposal by proposing:

1.   The dissolution of the Grand Duchy of Warsaw, but Danzig was to become a free city with its fortifications demolished, and the King of Saxony would be indemnified by the cession of territories in Silesia and Bohemia that border Saxony.
2.   The Illyrian provinces would be returned to Austria, including the port of Fiume, but Trieste would not be returned.
3.   The German Confederation would extend only to the Oder River.
4.   Danish territories would be guaranteed.

Unfortunately, this counter proposal was not received until 11 August and the congress had already been dissolved. That same morning, Austria had publicly declared its alliance with France dissolved and announced its alliance with the allies.

On 12 August, Napoleon's ambassador to the Vienna Court, de Narbonne, was notified of the breaking of relations between Austria and France. He was told that not only had Austria decided to break relationships with France, but to strip France of all the conquests made during the Empire and Revolution.

Though the congress had dissolved, these proposals were passed to Metternich that day. He stated that the cession of Illyria without Trieste was inadequate. He stated that the other counter proposals were equally unacceptable.

Napoleon recalled Bubna to him in Dresden, Metternich being in Prague, and responded by an acceptance of all the allied conditions as pronounced by Metternich, but insisted on holding Holland and the Hanseatic cities until peace and compensation had been obtained from England. This offer reached Metternich during the morning of 14 August, and so it would seem Metternich, being intent on war, stated that it was too late to consider such offers, and that this proposition should be retransmitted to the allied sovereigns then in Prague.

On 15 August, the last hour of the armistice sounded. Austria had completed its rearmament, and though superficial, the Austrian government felt that it had made a sufficiently good effort at mediation that it could now openly drop its nominal neutrality.

Napoleon found himself facing the combined armies of Austria, Prussia and Austria, which were soon to be joined by the Swedes under Bernadotte. He also learned that Moreau, one of the finest French Republican generals, had joined the allies in their headquarters. Moreau had been exiled to the United States, and despite his former popularity with the army, had been nearly forgotten. His return was probably an effort to recover his position in France and to participate in the destruction of his enemy, Napoleon.[8]

Agreement of Trachenberg

Though Austria was nominally an ally of France, her generals were throughout the period of the peace congress negotiating with the Russians and Prussians over a military strategy with which to face Napoleon. The allies had the problem of coordinating three widely scattered main armies.

They had years of experience fighting Napoleon and realized that his unified command would give him a significant advantage over them, should any one of their armies consider engaging him personally.

The leaders of the armies held a long series of conferences in an effort to determine how to deal with this military dilemma. Every possible plan was put forward and rejected for various national and personal reasons. Eventually, based on the universal recognition that Napoleon was too dangerous for any of them to face alone, on 15 August, just as hostilities commenced, they agreed on a common strategy for dealing with Napoleon.

They had agreed that Bernadotte, commanding an army of Russians, Prussians and Swedes, was to operate so as to cover Berlin and to threaten Hamburg. His eventual objective was to be Leipzig, deep in Saxony to the south. Blücher was to command the Army of Silesia. He was to advance through Lusatia against the French. The Austrians were to move through Bohemia and strike at the French flank by Dresden.

Czar Alexander had proposed that Blücher operate in Bohemia and cover Prague while the main force advanced down the left bank of the Elbe. Though possibly a better plan, the Austrians opposed it. It is probable that they did not want Bohemia ravaged by the presence of an allied army and even less by the appearance of a ravenous French army seeking to engage that army. The Prussians opposed it because they felt that it exposed Berlin and Silesia to Napoleon's attack.[9]

Next, the Czar insisted that the main allied army, the Army of the Sovereigns, should have part of Blücher's army with it. It was finally agreed that 100,000 Russians and Prussians should move from Silesia to Bohemia, under Barclay de Tolly, Wittgenstein, and Kleist, where they would cooperate with an equal number of Austrians. This force would then advance down the left bank of the Elbe on Dresden. Blücher's army would then consist of the corps belonging to Langeron, St. Priest, Sacken, and Yorck.

This established the allied army with one principal army, under the direct supervision (and interference) of the three monarchs (Austrian, Prussian, and Russian), and two secondary armies under Blücher and Bernadotte.

In addition, another strategical agreement was reached in Trachenberg, hence its name, stating that under no circumstances should any one of the three allied armies incur the risk of a decisive action against Napoleon in person.[10] Though, apparently, this policy applied more to Blücher and Bernadotte than it did to the main allied army.

The allied commanders agreed that, whichever army should find Napoleon advancing against it,

Czar Alexander I of Russia, by F. Kruger.

should fall back while the other armies should then advance to take advantage of the less capable French marshals commanding whatever forces faced them.

So armed, the allied generals returned to their forces and began their initial maneuvers of the 1813 fall campaign. No doubt, if Napoleon had known of the allied agreement not to engage him personally, he would not have wasted much time with Blücher.

The French Strategic Situation

Napoleon had, even prior to the armistice, realized that Austria was one of his enemies and took wise precautions against a probable strike by them in his rear. He realized that the allied manpower gave them the potential to raise armies outnumbering him. He also realized that his strategic situation would allow him to use his internal lines of communications to the utmost. Recognizing that the Elbe River was the most important strategic geographical feature in the territory he controlled, Napoleon immediately set about strengthening his hold on it. He strengthened his middle Elbe fortresses of Torgau, Wittenberg, and the great fortress of Magdeburg. On the upper Elbe stood Hamburg, entrusted to his finest subordinate, Davout, and a sizable garrison.

Hamburg had both political and military significance which, to Napoleon, merited the attention of his most trustworthy and capable marshal. Napoleon ordered Davout to make the city as strong as possible. He established the XIII Corps to defend the entire region and shipped significant numbers of men and supplies north to defend the city.

To the south, also on the Elbe, stood Dresden. Dresden was to be the key to the early campaign and it was to be defended by the main French army. To prepare his position in Dresden, Napoleon established an entrenched camp in Neustädt to cover his westward communications. On the left bank he made only modest preparations to prevent against a *coup de main* by the allies.[11]

The city of Dresden had its fortifications largely dismantled during 1810, and during the armistice this process was reversed. The city walls were largely restored, and the suburbs were defended by an enceinte with thirteen redoubts.

Conclusions

It can be argued that Napoleon's acceptance of the June armistice was probably the worst mistake of his military career. He had, in an incredible string of powerful blows, driven the allied armies back to Poland. The Prussians were still mobilizing their army, and the Russian army was a tattered remnant of what had faced Napoleon 10 months before, when he advanced into Russia. Admittedly, the French army was overflowing with green troops and in desperate need of cavalry, but it was still an effective weapon.

Though his desire for an armistice may be attributed to many causes, not the least of those causes was his age and health. He was 44 years old and had been campaigning almost constantly for 18 years. During the 1809 campaign he had begun to show a certain lassitude, and despite the almost constant bleeding of his resources in Spain, he had preferred to embark on his Russian adventure rather than finish the old business of Spain. Similarly, during the retreat from Russia he had fallen into a great depression that was only occasionally broken.

Though victorious at Lützen and Bautzen, he had not shown the old command, timing, and decisiveness that earlier, would have during Bautzen, sent Ney crashing into the allied rear to complete their destruction.

Like any machine, the human body wears out after constant use and so too was the genius of Napoleon beginning to wear and crack. It is possible that, on an instinctive plane, the allies perceived this. Why would Austria, after seeing Napoleon's new army thrash the allied armies, suddenly feel impelled to join what appeared to be the losing side? It is true that all of the allied nations, Prussia, Russia, and Austria, had long standing grievances against France. They had their own national goals, but Austria was strongly linked with Napoleon through the marriage of Maria Louise to Napoleon in 1810. By remaining neutral Austria could have stood to gain territories in the Balkans, and perhaps, even at the expense of Russia. If it had actively allied itself with Napoleon, it is possible that he would have been quite generous with his father-in-law when it came time to divide up the spoils. It is almost certain that such an able diplomat as Metternich realized that the benefits from, and chances of, success against the French armies were slim, if Napoleon was still the man who vanquished them at Austerlitz.

2

The Armies Refit
8 June–1 August 1813

It was hardly peace, but with the signing of the armistice on 4 June and its taking effect on 8 June, the war in Germany stopped. Both France and the allies were exhausted from their efforts of the spring and struggled to regain their balance. The allies were reeling eastward, pounded by the twin hammer blows of Lützen and Bautzen. Their soldiers' morale was near breaking, and their generals needed to gather their wits about them.

To the west, the French army also was in need of rest. It had been reborn, then immediately baptized by fire. The raw conscripts had their first taste of battle almost before they knew how to fire their muskets. Their exertions had been monumental and they too needed to recover their equilibrium. More importantly, Napoleon needed to outfit his cavalry and bring it up to strength. It was the lack of cavalry that had kept both Lützen and Bautzen from being the decisive victories he so desperately wanted.

The Allied Armies

The allied armies were in desperate shape. Most of the Russian infantry regiments consisted of a single half strength battalion. The Russian cavalry and artillery had taken similar losses and their horses desperately needed to recover from their year of campaigning. The Prussian infantry and cavalry regiments were filled with reservists and new levies. These levies had an average of less than three months under arms. They had one strength, they were fighting in their homeland for the survival of that homeland.

The Prussian Army

The Treaty of Tilsit had limited the Prussian Army to 42,000 infantry. Of these, about half had accompanied Yorck into Russia as an ally of Napoleon. The actual strength of the Prussian infantry arm, assuming 46 battalions at an assigned strength of 801 men per battalion, was 36,846 men on January 1813.

The cavalry stood at two Guard and 18 line regiments (7 heavy and 13 light), each of which had a nominal strength of 601 men per regiment, providing the Prussians with a further 12,020 men.

The artillery consisted of three brigades, each with three horse and twelve foot companies, or 45 companies, manned by approximately 6,000 men. By the fall, with the entire force mobilized, the Prussians could field 236 field pieces. This established the main force of the Prussian army at a strength of about 56,000 men.

Added to this, there were a series of reserve regiments organized as a result of Scharnhorst's Krumper System. In this system each infantry company and cavalry squadron began a process of putting trained veterans on leave. They then began filling those positions with new recruits, training them, and then in turn putting them on leave. When the spring of 1813 arrived and these reservists were called back to the colors, 52 reserve infantry battalions were organized. Though many participated in the spring campaign, during the armistice they were reorganized into one line and 12 reserve regiments. Some of these regiments had 3 battalions and some had 4. The 42 battalions so organized provided the Prussians with 33,642 additional trained infantry.[1]

In addition to the reservists, on 3 February, calls for volunteers had been sent out into the land. Each infantry and cavalry regiment was authorized to organize a "freiwilliger jäger" (volunteer sharpshooter) detachment. These volunteers numbered 5,000 with the infantry, 3,000 with the cavalry and 500 with the artillery and pioneers.[2]

Similar to the freiwilliger jägers were the various freikorps, which were organized both from foreigners and native Prussians. The most famous was the von Lützow Freikorps,[3] which eventually grew to 3 battalions, 5 squadrons, and 8 guns.[4] In addition there was the von Reiche Jäger Battalion, von Hellwig Freikorps (3 squadrons of hussars and a jäger detachment), the von Schill Freikorps (2 squadrons of hussars) and the Elbe Regiment (initially formed with two battalions).

The newest formation was the "landwehr," or militia. Austria had called up its landwehr for the 1809 campaign and it had added significantly to the strength of the Austrian army. The Prussians had followed suit themselves, and on 17 March issued a proclamation ordering the mobilization of the landwehr.[5]

The landwehr was initially organized into brigades that were redesignated as regiments on 27 June 1812. By the end of July, the Prussian landwehr was sufficiently trained to begin field operations, but it was miserably equipped and often almost unarmed. The great Friedrich II would have scorned their unmilitary appearance, but they provided 37 regiments with 149 battalions for the Prussian army. As each battalion contained, in theory, 726 men, this provided nearly 108,000 infantry, though in fact 100,000 is a closer figure to what actually appeared.[6] The landwehr also supplied 116 squadrons or 10,000 cavalry. They were a force that would prove indispensable to the allied cause.[7]

The landwehr was amalgamated into the Prussian army in much the same manner as the French amalgamated their national guard battalions into the line army during the French Revolution. However, instead of blending landwehr and line battalions to organize new regiments, the blending was done on a brigade level. Each infantry brigade was organized with a line regiment, a reserve regiment, and one or two landwehr regiments, except for the forces assigned to the IV Corps, which were nearly entirely landwehr.

The artillery and pioneers were increased as well. Forty-five provisional artillery companies were raised from krumper reservists, and by fall they were organized into 45 more field batteries with 8,000 men and 378 guns. Of these, 43 companies were immobile and remained in fortresses or served as replacements. Two companies, however, would accompany the army into the field, joining the 45 field batteries. The six fortress pioneer companies were reorganized and expanded with the addition of seven field pioneer companies.

The Prussian army was as follows:

Line Infantry

2 Guard Regiments	4,822 men
1 Guard Jäger Battalion	801
6 Grenadier Battalions	4,830
1 Jäger & 1 Schützen Battalions	1,602
12 Line Infantry Regiments	28,836
	40,891 Total

Reserve Infantry

3 Regiments (4 bns ea)	9,612 men
9 Regiments (3 bns ea)	21,627
	31,239 Total

Foreign Volunteers

Elbe Infantry Regiment (2 bns)	1,716 men
Thüringian Battalion[1]	623
von Reiche Jäger Battalion	859
von Lützow Freikorps Infantry	2,421
Lucadou Battalion	200
Hellwig Freikorps	250
	6,069 Total

Freiwilliger Jägers

28 Detachments with infantry bns	5,000 men
von Rochow Land-Jäger-Battalion	400
	5,400 Total

Landwehr Infantry

37 Regiments with 149 battalions	101,320 Total

Garrison and Ersatz (Depot) Battalions

2 Guard Reserve Battalions	1,202 men
13 Ersatz Battalions	9,612
3 Ersatz companies for Jägers & Schützen	600
6 Ersatz companies for the Grenadiers	1,200
25 Garrison Battalions	20,400
Landwehr Reserve Battalions	10,000
	43,014 Total

Line Cavalry

2 Guard Regiments	
18 Line Regiments	12,020 men
Mecklemburg Hussar Regiment	601
	12,621 Total

National Cavalry

3 National Cavalry Regiments	954 Total

Freiwilliger Jäger

20 Sqns with Line Cavalry	3,000 men
von Lützow Jägers (5 sqns)	427
von Schill Hussars (2 sqns)	243
von Hellwig Hussars (2 sqns)	200
	3,870 Total

Landwehr Cavalry

30 Regiments with 116 sqns	10,500 Total
Depot Squadrons	
20 Depots for the Line	2,000 men
2 Depots for National Cavalry	200
	2,200 Total

Artillery

47 Field Batteries	8,000 men
von Lützow	118
Garrison Artillery	3,000
7 Field Pioneer Companies	560

6 Fortress Pioneer Companies	745
Freiwilliger Jägers	500
	12,923 Total
Total Strength	271,001

Note
1. The same Ducal Saxon battalion that defected to the Prussians in the Spring campaign.

The Army was organized as follows:

In Silesia	Battalions	Squadrons	Guns	Men
The Guard	6½	8	16	7,091
I Corps (Yorck)	45	44	104	38,484
II Corps (Kleist)	41	44	112	37,816
In Brandenburg				
III Corps (Bülow)	40½	42	80	41,135
IV Corps (Tauentzien)	48½	29	42	33,170
Freikorps	4	7	8	4,068
Siege Forces				
At Küstrin	9	5	8	7,122
At Stettin	15	7	8	10,548
At Danzig	10	6	8	8,000
At Glogau[1]	9	4	16	5,000
Totals	288½	196	402	192,434

Note
1. Friederich, *Geschichte 1813*, pp.45-48.

The Russian Army

The Russian army did not undergo the rapid growth that the Prussian army experienced. In the beginning of 1813 it consisted of:

> 170 Guard and Line Infantry Regiments
> 66 Guard and Line Cavalry Regiments
> 159 Field Artillery Companies
> 20 Pioneer Companies
> 10 Battalions of Technical Troops

The infantry nominally fielded the 1st and 3rd Battalions. The 2nd Battalion served as a depot and remained in Russia training new recruits. A line regiment in the field with its two battalions had a theoretical strength of 1,476 men. The Guard Regiments, in contrast to the line regiments, normally fielded all three battalions. However, after the Battle of Bautzen, the regiments serving in Germany generally consisted of a single battalion and had strengths ranging from 150 to 200 men each.

This deficiency was made up by the influx of 70,000 new levies that flowed into the main armies in Germany during the summer. This effort to bring the units up to their normal war strength still left most regiments with only a battalion, but it now numbered 500–600 men.[8]

There were very few new infantry units raised. Only the Borodino and Tarutino Infantry Regiments were newly organized. In addition, the Leib and Pavlov Grenadiers were transferred to the Russian Guard and the Kexholm and Pernau Infantry Regiments were redesignated as grenadier regiments.[9]

The Russian cavalry, in the field, was in a similar state to the infantry. New levies, totalling about 14,000 trained cavalry, were brought in to raise the regiments back to near normal strengths. There were no new cavalry regiments raised, nor were any redesignated.

The Russian army, at the end of the June Armistice, stood as follows:

	Battalions	Squadrons	Cossack Regiments	Guns	Men
In Silesia					
Langeron's Corps	47	15	10	139	34,551
Sacken's Corps	18	30	12	60	18,353
Wittgenstein's Corps	45	38	5	92	34,926
St. Priest's Corps	20	22	3	36	13,586
Guard Corps & Reserves	47	71	10	182	44,347
In Brandenburg					
Winzingerode's Corps (including Voronzov and Czernichev)	29	44	20	92	29,357
Attachments to:					
Prussian III Corps	0	0	3	22	1,160
Prussian IV Corps	0	0	1	0	318
In Mecklenburg under Wallmoden					
Tettenborn	0	0	4	0	1,495
Russo-German Legion	6	0	4	16	4,838
Dornberg's Division	0	8	0	0	1,192
2nd Line Troops					
Polish Reserve Army	70	67	10	198	59,000
Zamoscz Siege Force	21	5	3	36	15,000
Modlin Siege Force	?	?	?	?	9,000
Danzig Siege Force	58	12	11	59	29,100
Total Strength					296,223

The Austrian Army

The Austrian Army was a new antagonist in the war in Germany. Though Schwarzenberg had led an Austrian contingent into Russia as an ally of Napoleon, he had successfully neutralized himself and withdrew into the northeastern Austrian provinces. Though the Austrian government had remained superficially neutral, it had in fact, begun a very active program of rearming itself.

At the end of the 1812 campaign, Schwarzenberg commanded a corps of four divisions. His corps contained 25 infantry battalions and 44 squadrons, totalling 29,000 men and 7,000 horses. A second corps, under FZM Reuss, was similarly organized with four Divisions. It contained 28 battalions and 42 squadrons, with a total of 30,807 men and 5,129 horses.

By the end of January, a further 40,000 men were ordered mobilized and an "Observation Corps" was formed in Bohemia with 22 battalions and 34 squadrons. It totalled 27,740 men and 5,359 horses.[10]

As May came to an end, the Austrian Emperor ordered the expansion of the Bohemian Observation Corps to a strength of 120,000 men, which was done by drawing units from the forces commanded by Schwarzenberg, Reuss, and from elsewhere within the Empire. By mid-June it stood with 80 battalions, 98 squadrons, 22 batteries and 18 reserve batteries, as well as various auxiliary and technical forces.

On 15 June the Austrian Emperor ordered the raising of two more reserve corps, one with 43 battalions and 44 squadrons under the command of FZM Reuss and the second with 31 battalions and 40 squadrons under FZM Hiller. In addition, 22 landwehr battalions were ordered to arms, and they began service in various fortresses. By the time the armistice ruptured a total of 48,982 landwehr had been called to arms.

When the war resumed, the Austrian army consisted of:

Bohemian Army	107 Battalions	
	117 Squadrons	127,345 men
	290 Guns	
Between the Ens and Traun under FZM Reuss		30,079
Army of Inner Austria under FZM Hiller		36,557
Garrison of Prague		7,320
Garrison of Königgrätz		9,424
Garrison of Josefstadt		10,800
Total		221,525 men

The Swedish Army

The Swedish army was not a large army. It consisted of a national army, plus a number of German regiments raised in Vol Pommerania and Rügen Island. The latter consisted of two landwehr infantry regiments, which were not for field service, and two small detachments of volunteer infantry and cavalry that were much like the Prussian freiwilliger jägers.

At the rupture of the armistice, Sweden's army in Brandenburg consisted of 23,449 men organized in 33 battalions, 27 squadrons, and crews for 54 cannon. Another force was in Mecklenburg under the command of the Hanoverian Wallmoden. This single brigade consisted of 6 battalions, 5 squadrons, and a single 8 gun battery, totalling 3,814 men.

A further garrison was established in Stralsund, the Swedish stronghold on the coast and Bernadotte's seaport link to Sweden. This consisted of 2,452 men.[11]

The Swedish field army was organized into 3 divisions and six brigades, with an artillery reserve. The 50 Jagers assigned to each infantry battalion were converged into a single battalion for service with the brigade.

The Swedish army had not been engaged in any combat since the 1808–1809 Russo–Swedish war, but in its ranks were, as a result of that conflict, a large number of veterans, though they were not well versed in the type of war that they would encounter facing Napoleon.

An unusual aspect of the army was that its commander, Crown Prince Bernadotte, had been elected and had ascended to the throne, because of his predecessor's failure in the 1808–9 war with Russia. Bernadotte knew that if he failed in the field, or if his leadership resulted in the Swedish army suffering a crushing defeat, he would suffer the fate of all elected rulers that so fail. As a result, the part taken by the Swedish army would always be one of caution.

The Anglo-German and Mecklenburg Corps

In northern Germany the English fielded and funded, a small force formed mostly of German troops from Hanover, Lubeck, and Hamburg under the command of the Hanoverian General Wallmoden. This Anglo-German force consisted of a half battalion, a cavalry regiment, and six guns drawn from the KGL (King's German Legion), and the Hanseatic Legion, which had 2 battalions, 8 squadrons, and a single 8 gun battery (3,043 men).[12] There were no English troops in this force until much later in the campaign. The English that later joined it were limited to an infantry battalion, a small cavalry force and a few guns. This force was, during the course of the campaign, also to be joined by a Swedish division and the Russo-German Legion, formed of Germanic troops, that the Russians had captured from the Grande Armée during the 1812 campaign, and convinced that service in an anti-French Legion was superior to rotting in a prisoner of war camp.

The Mecklenburg corps was quite small. It consisted of 6,149 men, organized into four battalions, a single hussar regiment with four squadrons, and two guns. Only the Mecklenburg Grenadier-Garde-Bataillon was a veteran formation. The other forces were newly raised volunteers, there being very few survivors of the forces sent with the Grande Armée into Russia the year before.

The entire allied army stood at half a million men. In it, Napoleon found himself facing his old enemies commanding a mixed bag of veterans and new recruits. The entire combined allied armies in the field were as follows:[13]

	Bns	Sqns	Guns	Cossack Regts	Strength
Russian Field Army	212	228	639	68	184,123
Prussian Field Army	185½	174	362	–	161,764
Austrian Field Army	107	117	290	–	127,345
Swedish Field Army	39	32	62	–	23,449
Anglo-German Troops	9	17	26	–	9,283
Mecklenburg Contingent	4	4	2	–	6,149
Total	556½	572	1,381	68	512,113

The Allies' Overall Status

The condition of the allied armies at the signing of the armistice was exceedingly poor. Most of their infantry battalions were at half strength because of the privations of the spring campaign.

The Russians had fed a continuous stream of recruits forward from their depots to their army in the field. Despite their efforts the Russian army continued to be far below its mandated strength. Though seldom only at half strength, few of their regiments fielded two battalions and none were at full strength. Though seriously weakened in the spring campaign, its losses were made good, and it was as ready as any of the armies for a renewal of the fighting.

The principal Prussian advantage lay in the fact that they were fighting in their homeland, and the nationalistic fervor that swept the land had given them the strength to continue fighting, despite their string of losses in the spring.

The Prussians had, during the armistice, expanded their army at a frantic pace. The landwehr, called up in the spring, was drilled and trained until they were able to undertake an active military role. They were still short of weapons and proper uniforms, and in some cases they were armed only with pikes. A total of 37 regiments, 149 battalions of landwehr infantry was raised.

The landwehr also had a cavalry arm. Despite being superior to the infantry, it appears to have fallen far short of the caliber of formation desired by the officers of the active army. They were quick to charge, slow to rally, and always an undependable weapon that might break at the most inopportune moment. However, like the infantry, they added weight to the Prussian army. They often found themselves in garrisons and sieges, where they could function satisfactorily, releasing regular troops for more important actions against the French army. It would appear that the landwehr provided 116 squadrons of cavalry to the Prussian army.

The Austrian army's problem was not with manpower, but with finances. The result of the Austerlitz and Wagram campaigns had been to ruin the Austrian treasury and national economy. The lack of funds limited the Austrian ability to arm and equip its abundance of manpower. In contrast to the Prussians, who were defending or attempting to liberate their homeland, the Austrians were still safe behind their mountains, and their generals were unwilling to take to the field without a well equipped army.

The Austrian army consisted of 221,525 soldiers, two-thirds of which were recruits, with only three months service. When they found they were to engage the French, thoughts of revenge for their past humiliations rose in their breasts. Their generals' thoughts were tempered with the knowledge that this herd of conscripts was about to face the greatest general alive in Europe, the same general who had smashed every other army the Austrians had sent against him.

The Swedes, like the Austrians, were new players in the game. They had not engaged in the spring campaign, though they had been slowly building up their forces in Stralsund and the surrounding territories. Despite its military potential, its leader would never let the Swedish Army display its prowess because of his fear for his crown in the event of a defeat.

The French Army

Like his enemies, Napoleon had spent the summer of 1813 building his army up to full strength, or as nearly so as he could. By the end of the armistice, he had made considerable strides in the strength and size of his field armies. The numbers of added manpower are significantly higher than are indicated, since the 15 June strengths include many troops still en route to join the army. This tabulation includes only those troops present with the various corps on 15 June and not those indicated as scheduled to arrive in July.[14]

Corps	Bns	Sqns	Guns	August Strength	June 15 Strength
Guard	62	59	218	58,237	50,415
I	42	4	76	32,018	31,386
II	43	6	76	25,471	32,456
III	62	11	122	37,017	28,384
IV	36	8	72	20,867	20,587
V	37	7	74	27,740	22,973
VI	42	8	84	16,685	18,202
VII	33¼	13	68	25,200	14,807
VIII	10	6	44	7,573	unknown
XI	38	7	90	24,720	15,326
XII	30	14	58	19,359	20,511
XIII	47	15	76	35,161	21,615
XIV	51	12	92	31,434	not formed

Corps	Bns	Sqns	Guns	August Strength	June 15 Strength
Girard's Corps	16	16	28	15,000	not formed
37th Division				11,735	
50th Division				10,741	9,938
Artillery & Engineer Park	–	–	–	6,708	unknown
Margaron's Corps in Leipzig	10	8	10	7,323	not formed
IX (Corps d'observation de Bavarie)				39,131	
Total				401,254	
1st Cavalry Corps	–	78	36	13,376	8,726
2nd Cavalry Corps	–	52	18	9,043	6,944
3rd Cavalry Corps	–	27	24	5,730	11,751
4th Cavalry Corps	–	24	12	3,947	unknown
5th Cavalry Corps	–	20	6	3,930	not formed
Total Cavalry				36,026	
Total known present 15 June 1813					364,887
Total Disposable Field Forces August				437,280	

The IX Corps was originally intended to be Wrede's Bavarians, but the number was transferred to Augereau's corps, which was forming at this time. The X Corps was Rapp's forces, which formed the Danzig garrison.

Garrisons			
Hamburg	12,116 men	Zamoscz	4,000
Bremen	1,500	Modlin	5,690
Magdeburg	11,015	Stettin	7,583
Wittenberg	3,456	Ki strin	3,740
Torgau	4,248	Glogau	5,869
Dresden	7,500	Erfurt	1,924
Danzig	23,500	Würzburg	954
Garrison Total			93,095

2nd Line Troops:	
Lemoine's Division in Minden	6,297
Augereau's Corps	17,303
Milhaud's Cavalry Corps	3,842 forming
Wrede's Bavarian Corps[1]	25,000
	52,442

Total Disposable Field Forces	437,280
Besieged Garrisons	93,095
Second Line Troops	52,442
Total Strength of the Grande Armée	582,817

Note
1. French Archives, Cartons C²-537, 538, 539, 540, 541, 542, 543, 544, and C²-708.

Napoleon reviewing the Imperial Guard at Dresden, 10 August, after a painting by Thost.

This breakdown of forces indicates that Napoleon had something close to 582,817 men at his disposal. Admittedly 93,095 were locked in various garrisons, many behind the allied front lines. Though these garrisons were not available, they tied down greater allied numbers in the blockading forces.

This force had been built up over the summer by a stream of "bataillons de marche" that poured from France into Germany. Each battalion was formed from "compagnies de marche" that were organized in each regimental depot for the transporting of the newly trained recruits to the parent regiment. Several companies were organized into a battalion, which exercised the new recruits in battalion evolutions as it marched into Germany. These "bataillons de marche" were not intended as combat formations and were generally dismembered upon their arrival at the parent regiment. The company cadres were then sent back to their depots to get more recruits.

When the "bataillons de marche" arrived in Germany and the parent regiment was not available for them to join, they were broken up and distributed among units that needed the personnel.

In addition, these "bataillons de marche" were used to provide infantry escorts for the various artillery, munitions, and supply columns entering Germany, from the potential marauders and Cossacks.

Foreign Contingents in the Grande Armée

Napoleon's Grande Armée was heavily supported by a large number of allied armies, though those armies were neither of the strength or quality that his allies had supplied in earlier campaigns. These allies had sent their armies into Russia where they were almost entirely destroyed. Only small fragments remained that consisted of the lucky ones who had not gone into Russia and those who had survived the ordeal. The spring of 1813 had been spent reorganizing and rebuilding these armies. Some allies worked diligently to reorganize and others carefully resisted building a force that they perceived might continue their enslavement.

The largest and most devoted of these contingents was the now homeless army of the Grand Duchy of Warsaw. This was divided into two because of a political conflict between Dombrowski and Poniatowski. The 27th Division, under Dombrowski, contained 1,442 infantry, 1,246 cavalry, and 166 artillerists and train. Poniatowski commanded the VIII Corps, which contained the Polish 26th Division. It contained 4,467 Polish infantry and 413 Polish artillerists. This force was organized from the remains of the corps that Poniatowski had taken with him into Russia and had been interred in Austria during the spring campaign. As part of the summer armistice it had been permitted to march through Austrian and re-join Napoleon.

The last major forces of Poles were the 7th and 8th Light Cavalry Divisions. The 7th Light Cavalry Division contained 1,326 officers and men. The 8th Light Cavalry Division contained 2,642 officers and men. Supporting them was a single horse battery with 168 men. A further 993 cavalry were to be found in the VIII Corps.

Of the other Poles scattered about, the 17th Polish Uhlan Regiment, with 62 officers and 319 men, was assigned to the 30th Cavalry Brigade, part of the garrison of Hamburg. In addition, the garrison contained 5,049 Polish infantry. The garrison of Modlin contained about 3,000 infantry and another small infantry force was in Wittenberg with a total of 56 cavalry and 2,065 infantry.

The second largest allied army supporting Napoleon was the Saxon army. Their king had not shown himself to be particularly staunch in his support of Napoleon during the spring of 1813 and had tried to keep his treasured heavy cavalry away from the French. The King of Saxony's heart was not in the war, but his home would be its principal battleground. His force was to be substantial, but its contribution questionable. The VII Corps contained the Saxon 24th and 25th Divisions. Between these two divisions there was a total of 11,041 infantry, 1,255 artillery and train, supported by the 26th Light Cavalry Brigade with 1,522 cavalry. In addition, the Saxons provided a force of 1,262 excellent heavy cavalry and 80 artillerists to the cavalry reserve of the Grande Armée. There were two other small Saxon detachments. Modlin had 416 Saxon infantry and a Saxon battery of 95 was in Glogau.

Bavaria had historically been a strong French ally, but that alliance was now rather threadbare. Its army had been obliterated in Russia and was rebuilt almost from scratch. None of it had been ready to participate in the spring campaign. For the fall campaign the Bavarian army was placed in the 29th Division, part of Oudinot's XII Corps. On 10 August 1813 the Bavarian army was still struggling to rebuild, but it took to the field.

Formed with two infantry brigades and a force of artillery, the 29th Division contained 4,770 infantry and 602 artillerists and train. The Bavarians were able to field only a single combined cavalry regiment. It was assigned to the 29th Light Cavalry Brigade, part of the XII Corps and contained 410 troopers and 421 horses. In addition, the very large 13th Infantry Regiment, part of the Danzig garrison, had 41 officers and 1,132 men.

Italians from the Kingdom of Northern Italy provided the 15th Division, assigned to IV Corps. It contained 7,638 infantry and 496 artillery and train. In addition, in the cavalry reserve were 2,091 cavalry and 94 artillery. The XI Corps contained the 31st Infantry Division, which had 2,220 Neapolitan infantry and 2,589 Italian infantry and 562 artillerists. The 28th Light Cavalry Brigade had 687 Neapolitan cavalry and 298 Italian cavalry.

The IV Corps also contained the Württemberg 38th Division. This division contained 3,479 infantry and 115 artillerists. The assigned 24th Light Cavalry Brigade had 763 cavalry and 117 artillerists. The VI Corps contained a Württemberg cavalry brigade with 803 cavalry and 103 artillerists.

The once powerful Westphalian army had been destroyed in Russia and a strong anti-French sentiment prevented any substantial recruitment and rebuilding. Much of the army was to remain in Westphalia and did nothing of note during the war except desert. Westphalians were sprinkled about. They were to prove most unreliable, but they provided 2,578 infantry for the XI Corps and another 1,038 for the Danzig garrison. The II Corps was to have the notorious 1st and 2nd Hussar Regiments, with a total of 781 officers and men. These two regiments, however, deserted so rapidly and en masse that, if anything, they were a negative contribution to the war effort.

In contrast, the armies of Baden and Hesse-Darmstadt were to not only provide new contingents of nearly the same strength as sent into Russia, but their troops were fully equipped, trustworthy and valued soldiers. These two nations formed the 39th Division in III Corps. Baden provided 2,281 infantry, 398 cavalry and 123 artillerists. Hesse-Darmstadt provided 3,162 infantry, 260 cavalry, and 232 artillerists.

The contingent of tiny Anhalt, two cavalry squadrons, was assigned to the I Corps cavalry brigade. It contained 19 officers, 276 troopers, and 500 horses. Equally tiny Würzburg provided a single squadron with 11 officers and 158 men to the 31st Division, XI Corps.

There was also the Danish Auxiliary Division under Prince Frederick von Hesse, which contained 17,094 men. However, it had no major role in the principal theater.[15]

Allied contingents were to provide 57,235 infantry, 14,884 cavalry, 5,085 artillery and train, or 77,204 men, plus the 17,094 Danes, or 94,298 men. The Grande Armée had a total of 582,817 men. Excluding the Danes, over 13% of the Grande Armée was not French. This is not the proportion that was found in the 1812 Grande Armée, but it was still a very respectable force and much of it was to make very major contributions to the campaign. Certainly, Napoleon was most happy to have the nearly 15,000 cavalry that they provided. If the allies can be said to have made any significant contribution, it must surely be in the cavalry arm. His five cavalry corps had only 36,026 men and another 20,591 were found in his various infantry corps, excluding the Danes. His cavalry arm totalled 56,617 men, of which 14, 884, or 26% were not French. It is here that Napoleon's allies made a tremendous contribution to the 1813 campaign.

The Grande Armée in the Fall Campaign

The quality of the force that Napoleon had at his disposal was higher than that which had won the battles of Lützen and Bautzen. The spring conscripts had their metal tested in the fire of battle and hardened by a summer of incessant drill and training in their art.
The newer conscripts filled the ranks around this core of hardened veterans. Even amongst the newer conscripts, the weakest elements had been winnowed out. The major problem with Napoleon's army was still his cavalry. The quality of horses was poor, and their numbers insufficient to rebuild this once magnificent corps, the brigades and divisions that had once been the terror of Europe.

In contrast his artillery had done nothing but improve. Though it was somewhat handicapped by the lack of quality horses to draw its weapons, its skill at gunnery still surpassed that of the allies. Napoleon also had his magnificent staff of skilled officers, generals, and marshals. This force was fighting on familiar terrain where they had fought the 1805, 1806, and 1807 campaigns. The logistical problems were non-existent when compared to Russia, and atop the entire military machine sat the greatest strategic genius of the century, Napoleon himself.

During the interim of the armistice, Napoleon had paid close attention to the finest details of his military machine. Aside from the efforts to bring reinforcements, supplies, and equipment to his forces, he worked on their strategic and tactical positions.

Between Magdeburg and Hamburg Napoleon had a new "place de guerre" or fortified position raised in the town of Werben, near Havelberg. It dominated the confluence of the Havel and the Elbe. Capitaine Lamenza, an imperial aide, was charged with supervising the work and preparing it to receive its guns. Other aides visited the main cavalry depot in Brunswick, surveyed the communications through Erfurt, reconnoitered the Bohemian frontiers and attended to the hundreds of other tasks Napoleon assigned them.[16]

3

Blücher Advances: The Battles on the Bober 18–23 August 1813

The French Positions

The French armies facing Blücher were under the command of Maréchal Ney. On 6 August they were disposed such that Ney (III Corps) was in Liegnitz and Haynau, Lauriston (V Corps) was in Goldberg, Macdonald (XI Corps) was in Löwenberg, and Marmont (VI Corps) was in Buntzlau. In essence, it was deployed such that the III and V Corps were on the Katzbach, and the VI and XI Corps were on the Bober.

Blücher Strikes Westward

Blücher's assigned task was to distract Napoleon and draw him into Silesia. The Army of Silesia, under Blücher, contained 96,277 men. This figure included 66,202 infantry, 13,758 cavalry, 9,200 Cossacks, and 7,117 artillerists manning 356 guns. It was formed by the Prussian corps of GL Yorck and the Russian corps of GdI Count Langeron, GL St. Priest, and GL Baron Sacken.

	Infantry Battalions	Cavalry Squadrons	Artillery Batteries	Pioneer Companies	Cossack Regiments
Yorck's Corps	45	44	13	2	–
Sacken's Corps	24	20	5	–	11
Langeron's Corps	48	14	13	1	8
St. Priest's Corps	20	26	3	–	4
Total	137	104	34	3	23
	Infantry	Cavalry	Artillery	Cossacks	
Yorck	29,738	6,038	1,917	–	
Sacken	9,600	2,000	2,000	3,600	
Langeron	18,464	2,800	2,600	4,400	
St. Priest	8,400	2,920	600	1,200	
Total	66,202	13,758	7,117	9,200	

On 13 August, the Army of Silesia was positioned with Yorck's forces in lager by Wernersdorf am Zobtenberge. Sacken's forces were in Hunsfeld near Breslau, and those of Langeron were by Jauernick.

With the rupture of the armistice, Blücher began to execute the orders given to him earlier. His first actions were to send patrols into the neutral zone established by the armistice, in an effort to locate the French forces opposing him. Then his forces began to maneuver. On 14 August Sacken began to execute the allies' plans by moving on Breslau and Liegnitz. Langeron began moving his forces towards Löwenberg and Lähn, and Yorck began his movements from Breslau towards Goldberg.[1]

On 15 August, Yorck was in lager by Sara am Striegauer Wasser, with his advanced forces in Mertschütz. Langeron's corps was in lager by Striegau, with its advanced troops in Jauer. Sacken was by Lissa, with his advanced troops in Hirschberg.

When Blücher began to move into the neutral zone he was facing Ney (III Corps) and Sébastiani (II Cavalry Corps) in Liegnitz, Lauriston (V Corps) by Goldberg, and Macdonald (XI Corps) by Löwenberg.[2]

Blücher.

On 15 August, the Army of Silesia remained in its positions, sending patrols towards Liegnitz and Goldberg, where it found the French still in their lagers. On 16 August, Blücher sent his forces forward. General von Sacken advanced by Ober-Moys and Eisendorf, while Yorck moved through Jauer, and Langeron moved through Bolkenhayne. Sacken was, on the following day, in Kloster Wahlstadt, while the middle and left wings were still by Jauer. Graf von Pahlen was in Hirschberg in order to cover the left flank of the army.[3]

Blücher's advanced guard was commanded by Oberstleutnant von Lobenthal.[4] On 17 August, while under special instructions from General von Gneisenau, it undertook a special reconnaissance against Goldberg, while supported by the Prussian cavalry reserve under Oberst von Jürgass. The French were on the west side of the Katzbach, and a skirmish erupted suddenly. In the village of Röchlitz, the Fus/1st East Prussian Infantry Regiment was stopped cold, suffering 2 officers and 32 men wounded and 7 men killed. The French remained in their positions behind the Katzbach, and the allied advanced guard withdrew to the heights by Hennersdorf.

On 18 August Sacken moved to Liegnitz, the Prussians stood in Goldberg, and Langeron moved into Schönau. Yorck's advanced troops, supported by the cavalry reserve, followed the French down the road from Haynau to Adelsdorf. Sacken took 200 prisoners in a short encounter with the French at Siebeneichen.

GM Grekov had discovered a ford to the left of Siebeneichen and led his Cossacks to the heights between Hellau and Schmotseiffen, while the 12th and 22nd Russian Jagers passed over the river and attacked the village. Siebeneichen was defended by three companies of Italian soldiers. When the Russians appeared, GB Vachot (1st Brigade, 17th Division) sent forward the 2/134th Line Regiment to support them. GD Lauriston saw the Russian cavalry turning the position and sent the 1/134th Line forward to support the other forces. The two battalions were thrown back, losing the village after a hard fought battle.[5]

Having taken Siebeneichen, Rudsevich sent his cavalry into the French rear where they raided the baggage trains. The French withdrew from Lähn to Greiffenberg. The word of the French retreat was sent to Blücher, who decided that the French left was not going to undertake an offensive. He ordered Yorck to resume his march west.

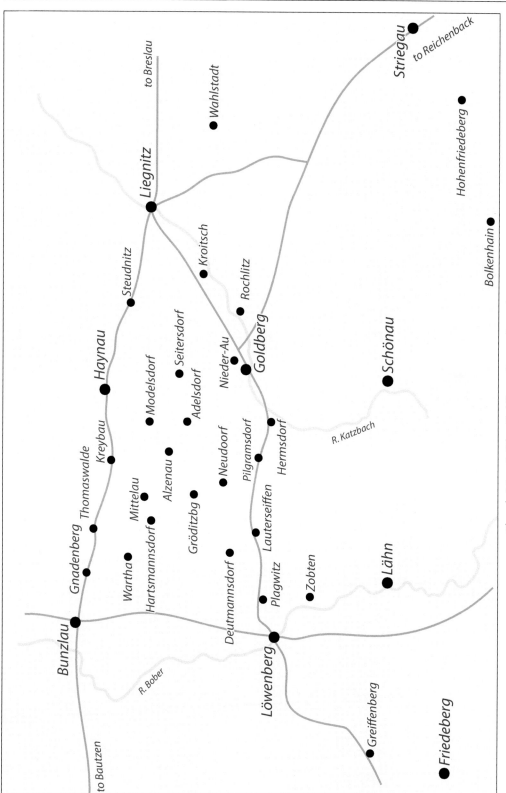

Sketch Map 2 The Goldberg-Löwenberg Area.

Napoleon's Response

On 15 August Napoleon departed Dresden with the Imperial Guard and advanced on Görlitz, where he arrived on 18 August. Having no positive information on the situation of the allies and operating on the assumption that the Army of Silesia would attempt to join the Army of Bohemia, he had moved the Guard to Görlitz and moved his headquarters to Zittau with Poniatowski (VIII Corps). It was his intention to cut the communications between Blücher and Schwarzenberg so that he could turn on which ever presented the best opportunity for a French victory, defeat it, then deal with the other army. He was, however, ignorant of Blücher's advance on the Katzbach and Bober. The allies, however, had established Bubna's division in Georgenthal and a detachment in Rumburg, in order to maintain liaison between the two armies.

Napoleon dispatched the VIII Corps to Gabel and sent Uminsky's 27th (Polish) Light Cavalry Brigade to Reichenberg and Friedland to cover his left flank, to hold the defile located there and to assure his communications with Görlitz and Löwenberg.

While Poniatowski (VIII Corps) moved on Gabel, a Guard infantry, and a Guard cavalry division, under the orders of Lefèbvre-Desnoëttes, arrived in Rumburg, pushed out the Austrian forces in the village, and advanced on Georgenthal, where they dislodged Bubna's division.

At the same time Vandamme (I Corps) moved on Rumburg and Victor (II Corps) moved on Zittau. The movement of these two corps cut through the defiles of the Lusace Mountains and provided Napoleon with information that the corps of Barclay de Tolly and Wittgenstein, detached from the Army of Silesia to join the Army of Bohemia, had arrived in Prague where the allied headquarters and the Russian Guard were posted.[6]

This news brought to Napoleon the realization that a reinforced Army of Bohemia was about to move on Dresden and attack his lines of communications to the Rhine. At the same time, he also learned of Blücher's move out of Silesia. Napoleon decided that he would move to the east, push back Blücher, and then swing to the south to face Schwarzenberg and the Army of Bohemia. He calculated that he had sufficient time to cover Dresden before this move occurred.

Contact on the Bober

On 18 August Langeron's advanced guard, under GL Rudsevich, moved down the road to Löwenberg and encamped by Pilgramsdorf. GM Kaisroff, commanding a brigade of Pahlen's cavalry, moved to Lähn am Bober and found himself in a brief skirmish with Zucchi's Italian 2nd Brigade, 35th Division, XI Corps. Kaisroff was forced back across the Bober to the village of Grünau.

The French detachment sent down the road from Greiffenberg to Hirschberg got as far as Bertelsdorf. In the center the French took and occupied the villages of Seifersdorf, Haynewald, and Lauterseiffen.[7]

The corps of Macdonald (XI Corps), Ney (III), Marmont (VI), Lauriston (V), and Sébastiani (II Cavalry Corps) had a total of 130,387 men facing Blücher. They faced him across the Bober River at Löwenberg, and opposite Buntzlau. Blücher gave every indication, as he deployed his forces, that he was ready to give Napoleon the battle he so desired.

On 19 August GL Rudsevich marched with the advance guard of the left wing of the Army of Silesia from Lauterseiffen towards Zobten, going over a branch of the Bober, and seized the village of Siebeneichen from a small French garrison. Rudsevich remained master of the village and the French withdrew down the road to Löwenberg. Count Scherbatov pursued them with the Lithuanian and Kiev Dragoons, taking 260 prisoners and capturing much of the French baggage, including a payroll chest from the XI Corps and some of Maréchal Macdonald's personal possessions.

In reaction, GD Lauriston sent Rochambeau's 19th Division against Zobten, to support the French garrison of the village. Lafitte's brigade, six battalions of the 150th and 155th Line Regiments, struck GL Rudsevich in Hellau, driving him back to Siebeneichen. At the same time Zucchi's brigade, moving down the road from Lähn struck Grekov's Cossacks, driving them back.[8]

Langeron advanced at the head of his column from Schönau towards the Bober River. He dispatched the Moscow and Libau Infantry Regiments to support the advanced guard as it crossed the Bober. A French column of Puthod's 17th Division stood in Siebeneichen and was engaged by Langeron's advanced guard. The 1st and 3rd Ukrainian Cossack Regiments, under Général de Witte, drove the French back.

Langeron, by G. Dawe.

Langeron was uncertain of the French positions and decided that the Russian 22nd Division should assault Siebeneichen frontally and directed the forces of GL Kapzevich (10th Corps) and GM Turtshaninov (Russian 22nd Division) to strike the flanks of the village. Colonel Durnov, with the 29th Jager Regiment, struck the left, while Colonel Vassil'shikov led the Viatka Infantry Regiment against the right. Colonel Szapsky held the Staroskol and Olonetz Infantry Regiments behind to support Lieutenant Colonel Prigara as he led the 45th Jager Regiment around the village. This three pronged attack drove the French out of the village with great loss.[9]

GL Rudsevich (Russian 15th Division) moved onto the Hopfenberges Heights near Mertzdorf in the night and then moved down a path by Dippoldisdorf back over the Bober. The troops in Siebeneichen also withdrew back across the Bober, leaving the village lightly held.

In the middle of Blücher's army was the 1st Prussian Corps, formed in two columns and advancing from Goldberg. The advanced guard, under Oberst von Katzeler and Oberstleutnant von Lobenthal marched through Gröditz and Wilhelmsdorf and took positions on the heights by Deutmannsdorf. There they established an advanced post and were supported by the reserve cavalry under Oberst von Jürgass. They faced a portion of the French V Corps located on the Hirschberg before Löwenberg.

The Prussian advanced guard and some of the cavalry passed through the defiles before Deutmannsdorf, but the greatest portion of the reserve cavalry remained behind.

Oberstleutnant von Lobenthal advanced with the sharpshooters of fusilier battalions of the 1st and 2nd East Prussian Infantry Regiments,[10] as well as the Leib Fusilier Battalion in an attack on the French positions on the Hirschberg. The sharpshooters of the 1st East Prussians occupied Deutmannsdorf, while those of the Leib Regiment moved to the left and those of the 2nd East Prussians moved against the middle.[11]

Lobenthal learned that the church in Ludwigsdorf was strongly held by the French. He then moved the sharpshooters of the 2nd East Prussian Regiment into the edge of the woods, and on a hill by Deutmannsdorf, he placed a few horse guns covered by a squadron of the Brandenburg Uhlans.

The French faced him with three battalions and a substantial mass of infantry in reserve. On the plain before Braunau the French also had 10 squadrons of cavalry posted to support the Hirschberg position. Oberst von Katzeler led his portion of the reserve cavalry against them in an effort to keep them away from Lobenthal's attack on the Hirschberg.

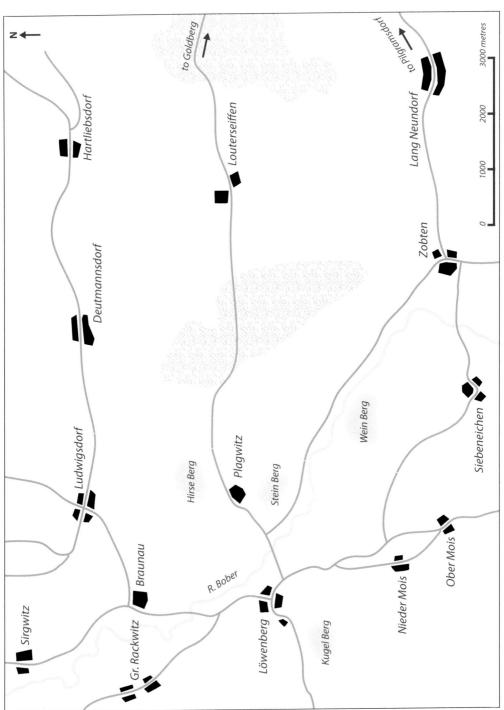

Sketch Map 3 The Battlefield of Löwenberg.

The French infantry began a lively fire. The skirmishers of the Leib Fusilier Battalion, under Lieutenant von Beyer, advanced and slipped to the right side of the Hirschberg as they advanced against the French, supported by the Brandenburg Fusilier Battalion and four horse guns.[12]

As they advanced a French column moved from Gröditz and advanced against the Prussian advanced guard. Oberstleutnant von Lobenthal led the Leib-Fusilier-Batallion, both landwehr battalions, and a foot battery forward to face the attack. Oberst von Katzeler remained before Braunau with his cavalry, facing the French cavalry. He then detached the Brandenburg Uhlans and two horse guns to the Prussian left flank, by the Hirschberg, to cover the infantry standing there. Being heavily pressed, the Prussians withdrew back across the Bober, burning the bridge behind them.[13]

During this day Maréchal Ney moved into Haynau with the III Corps and II Reserve Cavalry Corps. He established his headquarters in Wartha. The 10th (Albert) and 39th (Marchand) Divisions and the corps light cavalry were in Wolfshayn, the 11th Division (Ricard) was in Thomaswalde, the 8th Division (Souham) was in Mittelau, and the 9th Division (Delmas) was in Hartmansdorf. The II Reserve Cavalry Corps was in Alt-Jescwitz. Exelmans' 4th Light Cavalry Division was detached from the II Reserve Cavalry Corps and sent to Gröditzberg, where it encountered Yorck's advanced guard.[14]

GL Yorck, who was traveling with the second column of his corps along the road from Ulbersdorf to Neudorf on the Gröditzberg mountain, encountered French forces on the Gröditzberg that had cut him off from his advanced guard. This French force proved to be the 9th Division (Delmas) and Exelmans' 4th Light Cavalry Division. Yorck quickly contacted Blücher, advising him of the French force, and made preparations to strike it from all sides in the morning. That evening he contented himself with leaving his 1st and 2nd Brigades to watch the French.

Yorck, by Ernst Gebauer.

III Corps

On 19 August the III Corps stood with the 39th Division still in Nischwitz. The 11th Division occupied a position behind Thomaswalde, with the Klein-Bober on its front. The reserve battery and a company of light artillery stood with the 11th Division. The 10th Division moved behind Wolfshayn, with the exception of the 4th Provisional Regiment, which remained with the light cavalry. The 9th Division moved to Ober-Mittelau, behind the Klein-Bober while the 8th Division moved through Steinsdorf and Mertzdorf to take a position at Gross-Hartmansdorf, behind the Klein-Bober. The corps cavalry, supported by the two battalions of the 4th Provisional Regiment,[15] stood behind Kreybau.[16] The II Reserve Cavalry Corps covered the movement of the 8th Division's left flank. The 3rd Heavy Cavalry Division stood in Alt-Jescwitz and the 2nd Light Cavalry Division stood in Seitendorf, Deutmannsdorf, Graditzberg and Altzenau to maintain liaison with the III Corps.

The III Corps was in these positions when at 11:00 a.m., several Cossacks appeared on the heights in front of Wolfshayn, heralding the arrival of the Russian 27th Division, under GM

Neverovsky. They closed on the 10th Division and gave every appearance of intending to attack. GD Albert prepared to receive them warmly. The 139th Line Regiment rested its right on the road from Wolfshayn to Kreybau near the windmill and its left on the woods. The 140th Line and the 1/,2/141st Line Regiment formed a single line at the foot of the heights that dominated Kayserwalde. The 3/141st Line stood behind them, filling the interval between the two woods above the division's position.[17]

The French artillery began bombarding the Russians and did so for an hour. At 4:00 p.m., the Russians renewed their attack with forces very superior to the French, being estimated at 9,000-10,000 infantry and 5,000-6,000 cavalry.

After sustaining enemy fire for nearly two hours, the 139th had lost a large number of men and was obliged to fall back on the 2nd Brigade. GD Albert began to fear that he would be pushed back and sent a message to Marmont (VI Corps) for some cavalry support, but the VI Corps was moving to support the V Corps, which was also engaged and on the point of being turned. It became necessary for Albert's 10th Division to hold out until the 11th Division could arrive.[18]

At the same time, however, Maréchal Ney arrived on the battlefield, and at 5:00 p.m., ordered the II Reserve Cavalry Corps to move to Wartha to move, as necessary, on the right of Thomaswalde, and turn the Russian left. The 8th and 9th Divisions were to move up and place themselves between Wartha and Thomaswalde.

The musketry and cannon fire continued with unrelenting intensity, and by 6:00 p.m., the Russians had occupied the woods on the right, by the village of Wolfshayn. The Russians, supported by several heavy guns, descended from the windmill's hill in a limited attack, but the Russians who approached the French did not push their attack very hard.

By 9:00 p.m., the French stood with the 2nd Light Cavalry Division of GD Roussel in Wolfshayn covering the 10th and 11th Divisions. The 8th and 9th Divisions stood between Wartha and Thomaswalde. A brigade of the 39th Division stood to the right of the 10th Division, in a position that had been occupied by the 11th Division earlier in the day. The other brigade stood in echelons between Thomaswalde and Wolfshayn, to cover the 10th Division. Though nightfall brought the clash to an inconclusive end, it had cost the III Corps 544 men hors de combat.[19]

On the morning of 20 August, the French pushed the V and XI Corps across the Bober and took up positions in Löwenberg. The III Corps and the II Reserve Cavalry Corps took positions on the heights by Buntzlau. The VI Corps passed over the Bober, destroyed the bridges, and took up positions behind the Bober.

Napoleon Arrives

Reacting to Blücher's advance, Napoleon left Poniatowski (VIII Corps) at Gabel, Reichenberg, and Friedland. Victor (II Corps) was in Zittau, Vandamme (I Corps) stayed in Rumburg and Léfèbvre-Desnoëttes (Guard) in Georgenthal. Napoleon directed Latour-Maubourg to lead the I Reserve Cavalry Corps from Löbau and Görlitz to Löwenberg, where he arrived during the morning of 21 August. After arranging these dispositions,

Maréchal Victor.

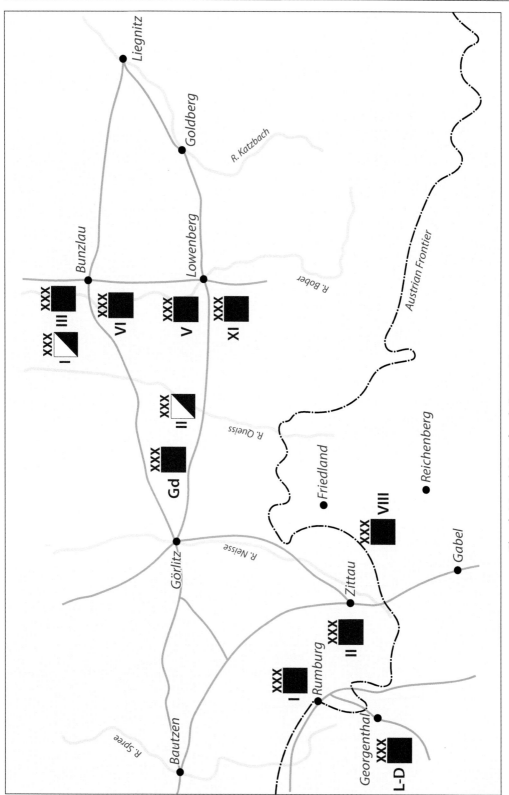

Sketch Map 4 Napoleon's Dispositions on 21 August.

Napoleon learned that Ney had wisely concentrated his forces behind the Bober. Napoleon decided to take the offensive immediately.

On 21 August Napoleon ordered Macdonald (XI Corps) and Lauriston (V Corps) to move their corps and attack the allied positions on the Bober. Marmont (VI Corps) was to move to the left, towards Löwenberg. The Guard infantry, the Guard cavalry and the I Reserve Cavalry Corps were to continue their march. Ney (III Corps) was to cross the Bober at Buntzlau at 10:00 a.m., and to move against Alt-Giersdorf.[20]

Napoleon ordered the repair of the bridges destroyed during the 21st, and at noon, Lauriston led his V Corps, Maison's 16th Division leading, across the Bober. The V Corps was followed shortly by Macdonald's XI Corps.

The Army of Silesia was distributed on the morning of 21 August such that Langeron's Corps stood with its main body in Pilgramsdorf. Its advanced guard, the 10th Corps under Kapzevich, was in Neuwiese. General Yusseffovich, with two cavalry regiments, was in Schönau. Yorck's Corps was arrayed with the 1st, 2nd and 8th Brigades and the reserve cavalry in Neudorf am Gröditzberg. The 7th Brigade and his advanced guard were in Wilhelmsdorf-Gröditz. Sacken's Corps was in Modelsdorf and his advanced guard was in Altzenau. Pahlen's corps was in Hirschberg. The Army of Silesia had two partisan formations working on its flanks.[21]

Major Boltenstern's partisans operated to the south and those of Major Falkenhausen operated to the north. Boltenstern was directed to move through

Lauriston

Kupferberg, Schreiberhau and Flensberg. Falkenhausen was to march on Haynau in order to cut the road between Buntzlau and Glogau. That evening Falkenhausen crossed the Bober at Nieder-Leschen and moved on Niesky to threaten the Buntzlau-Berlin road.

The III and VI Corps crossed the Bober in the afternoon and drove back Sacken's corps. Sacken had taken up a position by Gnadenberg and held Bunyan with light troops.

As the 8th Division stood on the heights behind Tillendorf, it was ordered to attack. The 6th Provisional Regiment,[22] commanded by Major Delaunay, moved forward at 10:00 a.m., against the Bober bridges. The 19th Provisional Regiment,[23] commanded by Colonel Bony, was also ordered to move against Tillendorf. His regiment pushed into the suburbs, scaled the wall, and seized the Saxe Gate. A house to house battle began and lasted for an hour, until the allies were forced out of the village and rallied on the right bank of the Bober.[24] Sacken withdrew under the cover of his cavalry, which made several counterattacks. Sacken then took up a position behind a branch of the Bober near Modelsdorf.

The 8th Division (Souham) crossed through the village and the 1st Brigade deployed on the plain outside the Wartha suburb. The 2nd Brigade moved through and deployed before the Haynau suburb. Both brigades formed themselves in masses by battalion, covering themselves by what terrain features best suited the defense.

The Allied left hung in the open, covered only by a skirmish screen. GD Souham profited by the houses and villages to move a strong force of his 2nd Brigade into contact with his 1st Brigade, reuniting his division. Once this maneuver was complete, he ordered the attack. The 1st Brigade moved forward at the "pas de charge" and the allies took to their heels, reeling before the advancing French.[25]

The 9th Division appeared on the field and supported the advance of the 8th with its artillery. The 10th and 11th Divisions moved on to the left of the plain, along the road to Haynau, and demonstrated as if to turn Gnadenberg.

The II Reserve Cavalry Corps, which had followed the movements of the III Corps after passing through Buntzlau, was charged by an allied light cavalry division and was pushed back to the Thomaswalde plains. The day's action cost the French about 60 killed and 350 wounded. The allies lost 400 prisoners and 700–800 killed and wounded.

The French pursuit lasted until 11:00 p.m. The 8th Division and two light cavalry divisions moved towards Gross-Hartmansdorf, where they stopped at midnight. The 9th and 10th Divisions moved towards Alt-Giersdorf where they bivouacked with the 10th Hussar Regiment, the 3rd Heavy Cavalry (Cuirassier) Division, and the reserve battery. The 11th Division moved behind Giersdorf with its left on the village and its right on Gross-Hartmansdorf.[26]

Blücher, reacting to the attack of the III Corps, moved the 1st and 7th Brigades, the Cavalry Reserve, and the artillery from Ludwigsdorf through Wilhelmsdorf towards Neudorf. The 8th Brigade moved through Lauterseiffen. Oberstleutnant von Lobenthal, supported by Prinz Carl von Mecklenburg, covered this movement. He took his forces to Deutmannsdorf, and the 2nd Brigade moved on Lauterseiffen.

The rearguard was heavily attacked repeatedly, but fought off the French and allowed Yorck to bivouac his forces between Neudorf and Gröditzberg. His advanced posts were in Wilhelmsdorf. GdI Langeron moved behind Pilgramsdorf, where Blücher had his headquarters.[27]

The 39th Division and the Baden Dragoons, which were already in Naumburg when the order to march on Buntzlau arrived, moved forward and arrived at noon. Two battalions and a squadron were installed in Buntzlau as a garrison, two others were left to guard the bridges, and a fifth was placed on a strategic hill, which dominated the road from Thomaswalde to Wartha. The rest of the division and the Baden Dragoons assumed a position on the Tillendorf heights, where they could cover the park and equipage assembled there.[28]

At 4:00 p.m., the Baden brigade moved towards Loschwitz where it took up positions. Two battalions were placed behind the village to maintain contact with the battalion placed on the heights watching the Thomaswalde-Wartha road. Three other battalions stood before the village, straddling the road to Wartha, and guarding the exits from the forests. The brigade sent forward patrols that evening to chase the Cossacks and allied skirmishers out of the forests.

The VI Corps stood in Sirchwitz. The V Corps had Puthod's 17th Division in Zobten watching the roads from Hirschberg and Schönau. Rochambeau's 19th Division was to the rear and Maison's 16th Division stood on the road from Löwenberg to Lauterseiffen with a brigade of Chastel's 2nd Light Cavalry Division.

The XI Corps had the 31st Division (Ledru) echeloned between Greiffenberg and Grosseiffen. The 35th (Gérard) and 36th (Charpentier) Divisions stood between Löwenberg and Lauterseiffen.

Action at Plagwitz

Faced by the Prussians, Lauriston moved his V Corps aggressively forward and attacked Yorck's combined corps before Löwenberg. During the day Yorck had reinforced his advanced guard with two 12pdr batteries. They stood in Weinberg, facing Löwenberg. The 2nd Brigade, under Prinz Carl von Mecklenburg, supported these two batteries. In Plagwitz stood the Brandenburg Fusilier Battalion and to the left of it, on a low ridge, stood the Russian 7th Jager Regiment (10th Corps).[29]

The French began the assault with skirmish fire on the town bridge of Plagwitz. It was solely to draw the attention of the Prussian defenders, while to the left a French force pushed across the

The contest for Plagwitz during the Battle of Löwenberg, by Knötel.

Bober. They advanced at a run in an effort to seize the middle of the city. Reinforcements poured across and the allies were unable to hold their position and withdrew. In order to cover the road to Goldberg and maintain contact with the Russians, the 2nd Brigade moved to the left and held their position until 5:00 p.m.

Langeron let GL Kapzevich bring the 10th Corps forward. The 37th Jager Regiment moved to support the 7th Jagers, which had been thrown back. Two French cavalry regiments struck at their flanks, but GM Denissiev with two squadrons of the Sieversk Chasseur à Cheval Regiment and four light field guns stopped them and drove them back. Langeron dispatched Prussian Oberstleutnant von Ende, with four squadrons of Ukrainian Cossacks, forward along the Bober to take the French cavalry in the right flank.[30]

During the night a new advanced guard was organized under Oberst von Katzeler and it stood between Lauterseiffen and Deutmannsdorf where it watched for the French. It consisted of the 1st West Prussian Dragoon Regiment, the 2nd Leib Hussar Regiment, and the landwehr cavalry brigade of Major von Bieberstein.[31]

Blücher, learning from a spy that he was personally faced by Napoleon, and observing the vigor of the V Corps attack, immediately decided that he should withdraw, conforming to the agreements made at Trachenberg. Since Sacken and Yorck were thrown back, Langeron's position in Zobten and Lakin was now compromised.

Sacken.

Blücher rallied Yorck's corps behind Graditzberg and awaited Langeron's arrival. Langeron, who had been ordered to withdraw on the Goldberg, arrived shortly and the two corps assumed a position with their right supported on Adelsdorf and their left on the main road. When Sacken arrived, he established his corps between Haynau and Wolfshayn.

Napoleon no doubt learned that he was facing Yorck and Sacken. On his left Maréchal Ney informed him at 10:00 p.m., on the evening of 21 August, that he was facing Sacken's corps, which, "according to the reports of prisoners, contained 3 divisions of infantry, estimated at 10,000 men each. His cavalry consists of three dragoon regiments, three hussar regiments, and two Cossack regiments. He has 75 guns. According to the prisoners, the Russian army is formed of three corps with a combined strength of 80,000 men. The Czar Alexander is to the left, GdI Langeron is in the center, and GL Sacken is on the right."[32]

At 6:30 a.m., the next morning, Napoleon ordered Ney to "push the enemy energetically towards Haynau, and following the direction which he takes." Ney was also to push a column between Haynau and Goldberg, towards the point where Macdonald was directed and where the enemy has retired.

Macdonald was to pursue the enemy energetically in the direction of Goldberg. The XI Corps was to move on the left of the route and the V Corps on the right. The two corps and Chastel's 3rd Light Cavalry Division were placed under Macdonald's command.

GD Ledru signalled the presence of a corps to the south. At 8:30 a.m., Napoleon directed Ornano's Guard Cavalry Division, supported by two battalions of the V Corps, to move between Löwenberg, Goldberg, Hirschberg, and Friedeberg. Once they were there, they were to ensure that there was no enemy force between the mountains and Löwenberg.

The Guard arrived in Löwenberg that morning, and the I Reserve Cavalry Corps arrived in Plagwitz. Reports gave Napoleon little indication of the presence of the allies or the directions in which they had withdrawn.

The French on the Morning of 22 August

Early on 22 August the French push began again. At 9:00 a.m., Ricard's 11th Division and a brigade of light cavalry arrived behind Thomaswalde. Souham's 8th Division was in Gross-Hartmansdorf with a brigade in Wartha, and a light cavalry brigade watching the passes at Mittelau.

GD Sébastiani was in Gross-Hartmansdorf with a brigade of light cavalry. GD Marchand, with the 39th Division, was in Buntzlau and to the east of the village. The divisions of Delmas (9th), Albert (10th), the 10th Hussars and Saint-Germain's 3rd Heavy Cavalry Division were in Alt-Giersdorf.

To the east the allies occupied Wolfshayn, with what appeared to Ney, as a very small force. Nonetheless, Ney acted to push them back and secure his position from any threat from that quarter. Fearing attack by superior forces from either Thomaswalde or Wartha, he drew his forces together by Gross-Hartmansdorf and Mühlstein-Bruch and maneuvered to his right to cover Löwenberg. Napoleon's order to energetically pursue the allies no doubt did not arrive until later in the afternoon.[33]

Maréchal Macdonald received, around 9:00 a.m., in Lauterseiffen, a dispatch from Berthier. He responded by announcing that the "Russians had moved either towards Schönau or Hirschberg." "Yorck's corps", he said, "was following the main road to Goldberg." It was certain that Blücher was facing Ney.

The French were in a difficult situation. Not only did the V Corps and XI Corps not have contact with each other, but Maison had no contact with his corps commander (Lauriston – V Corps) and did not know where to find him. Macdonald was equally ignorant of the movements of the III and VI Corps.

Napoleon had directed Ornano to cover the right of the army, but Macdonald was not informed. About 9:00 a.m., Macdonald was about to have his two flanks uncovered, but nonetheless he began his movement. Montbrun's 28th Light Cavalry Brigade and Charpentier's 36th Division formed the advanced guard. Gérard's 35th Division followed, but Macdonald awaited the arrival of the V Corps before he began a vigorous advance.[34]

Gérard.

Blücher's Dispositions on the Morning of 22 August

The cavalry of GL Sacken had operated very poorly on 21 August, and in the morning of 22 August. They announced the French had evacuated Thomaswalde and that they were advancing against the center of the allied army. This information caused Sacken to move to the south, so as to close with Yorck's corps. His advanced guard remained in Modelsdorf.

Sacken's movement came as the French began their attack and Blücher quickly ordered him to withdraw by Seifersdorf and Giersdorf towards Schmogwitz. Yorck was ordered to withdraw on Dohnau and Kroitsch, while Langeron was ordered back to Röchlitz and Goldberg.[35]

The Battles of 22 August

Macdonald's column advanced out of Lauterseiffen around 10:00 a.m. It attacked Langeron's advanced guard, formed by the 10th Corps (Kapzevich). Kapzevich withdrew leisurely before the French, profiting from all the advantages of the terrain. His forces fell back to the heights by Pilgramsdorf, where they joined part of the Russian reserve cavalry.

At 10:30 a.m., the French attacked Kapzevich's advanced forces before Pilgramsdorf. His orders were to withdraw slowly. Oberst von Katzeler withdrew his forces towards Ulbersdorf. The 7th and 37th Russian Jager Regiments and the Schusselburg Infantry Regiment took up positions in Pilgramsdorf and held it until the allied forces had cleared the Goldberg defile. In the defile stood six Prussian battalions under Major Golz.[36] Golz held this position until Kapzevich was able to pass behind him, on the main road to Jauer. Oberst von Katzeler remained with two landwehr regiments and the Leib Hussar Regiment behind the stream, by Nieder-Au on the Katzbach.[37]

These attacks were by the V and XI Corps (Lauriston and Macdonald), who had assumed the offensive and obliged Yorck and Langeron to withdraw behind the Katzbach. Langeron's withdrawal had uncovered the left of the Army of Silesia, obliging Blücher to renounce his intention of holding the Katzbach line. He then dispatched an urgent order to Yorck and Sacken ordering them to hold Goldberg and calling forward the right column's advanced guard under Katzeler, which was the only force available to him. This occurred about 6:00 p.m.

Yorck established himself at Röchlitz and Langeron in Wolfsberg, leaving a division in Ober-Au and Nieder-Au, before Goldberg. The Russian and Prussian cavalry was posted between Wolfsberg and Jauer. While Yorck and Langeron positioned themselves, Sacken was being driven back by Ney's III Corps on Liegnitz.

During the pursuit of the 22nd, Lauriston (V Corps), on the French left, constantly moved against the allied right, while Macdonald (XI Corps), moved directly against the allied forces before him. At the same time Marmont (VI Corps) stood on the right of Ney's III Corps and slowly crept towards the V Corps so as to be able to move against the Allied flank. Thus, Napoleon's forces kept contact between themselves, while pushing between the two portions of the Army of Silesia that faced him, Sacken on one hand and Yorck and Langeron on the other.

Blücher's troops withdrew quickly, and except for the brief halt of Yorck's in Adelsdorf, they were in constant withdrawal towards Goldberg. Their movement was precipitous, but orderly.[38] The allies fell back and took up positions to defend Goldberg. The village of Goldberg was occupied by seven battalions and two guns under the command of Major von der Glotz.[39]

The 2nd Leib Hussar Regiment and a landwehr regiment stood in Hohberg, where they covered the entire plain, six other squadrons with Katzeler were behind Flensberg, the 7th and 37th Jagers stood behind the Russian rear guard cavalry and to the east of Goldberg.[40] The northern column of Katzeler's advanced guard re-joined Yorck's corps.

During the evening of 22 August, Napoleon learned from Maréchal Gouvion St-Cyr that the Army of Bohemia had begun moving through the Erzgebirg passes, and was moving on Dresden.

Napoleon responded by stopping the Imperial Guard, VI Corps and the I Reserve Cavalry Corps. The Guard withdrew to Görlitz, while Marmont's VI Corps and Latour-Maubourg's I Reserve Cavalry Corps (less one light brigade) moved on Dresden. This move was necessary because only the XIV Corps was in the Dresden area, and the garrison of Dresden consisted of only eight battalions under General Durosnel.

Before moving himself to join St-Cyr (XIV Corps), Napoleon directed Vandamme (I Corps) and Victor (II Corps) to withdraw from Rumburg and Zittau towards the Elbe. Poniatowski (VIII Corps) was to remain in the defiles of the Lusace Mountains. Napoleon also directed the III, V, and XI Corps and the II Reserve Cavalry Corps to continue their offensive eastward against Blücher.

At 5:30 a.m., Blücher received word from Major von der Glotz that his position was in danger of being turned to the south. Blücher ordered Kapzevich to move in that direction. Yorck was ordered to place a brigade by the Katzbach and to support his left wing on Zittau to prevent the French from moving between Goldberg and Röchlitz in the Katzbach valley.

Latour-Maubourg.

Yorck sent the 2nd Brigade, Prinz von Mecklenburg, to hold that position. He was told to establish his left on Nieder-Au and his right on Hohberg. If he was obliged to retreat, he was to withdraw slowly and cross over the Katzbach in such a manner that Goldberg would be covered from any turning movement that might come up the Katzbach valley, as well as to protect Langeron's right flank. The 2nd Brigade began to move about 7:00 a.m.[41]

Blücher then decided to hold this position until he could confirm the reports of the French withdrawing down the Buntzlau-Haynau road. Spies brought him confirmations at 7:00 a.m., and at 8:30, he ordered the following preparatory dispositions.

Sacken's light cavalry was to push from Haynau to Buntzlau. Sacken was to march from Schmogwitz via Adelsdorf against Gröditzberg. He was to remain on the defensive and stop any enemy coming out of Löwenberg or Buntzlau, which might attempt to fall on the rear of Yorck via Neudorf-am-Gröditzberg.

Yorck was to move against Ulbersdorf. He was to detach his cavalry with some horse artillery from Ulbersdorf against Neuwiese, in order to stop any French who might come from that direction. He was to move against the French left wing or if possible their rear as soon as Yorck's right arrived in Pilgramsdorf. A 12pdr battery and a brigade were to remain in reserve on the heights to the east of Pilgramsdorf. The remainder of the corps was to attack the French without losing time in a prolonged bombardment.

As soon as the cannonade showed that Yorck's corps was in possession of the heights, Langeron was to move against the French right. Blücher was to remain on the Goldberg heights with Langeron.

Blücher ordered that Katzbach was to remain the base of operations. All of the wounded and prisoners were to be sent to Jauer or march with the eight battalions, twelve squadrons and two batteries coming from Liegnitz.

As a result of this order, Yorck ordered his corps to begin its advance at 11:00 a.m., and to move against Ulbersdorf in two columns. The left column was to consist of the 1st and 7th Brigades, the Cavalry Reserve, and the artillery reserve. It would pass over the Katzbach and advance on Dohnau. The right column, the 8th Brigade, would advance on Kroitsch.[42]

The III Corps

On 23 August Ney began to move his corps forward. At 6:00 a.m., the 8th Division (Souham) was sent through Woitsdorf, Baudmansdorf and Göhlsdorf towards Steudnitz. The 8th Division took a position and was to serve as the pivot around which the III Corps was to execute a conversion. A brigade of light cavalry formed the advanced guard and covered the right flank. The cuirassiers followed behind.

The 9th Division (Delmas) left Kreybau at 8:00 a.m., and marched on Michaelsdorf. After passing through Haynau, it was covered by a light cavalry brigade. The general staff and the 10th Hussars marched with it. The 39th Division (Marchand) set out at 5:00 a.m. When the head of its column appeared, the 10th Division (Albert) departed its camp followed by a reserve battery and the grand park. Both of the latter moved on Haynau, where the 11th Division (Ricard) was posted. The 8th Light Cavalry Brigade of Roussel's 2nd Light Cavalry Division covered their right. The 11th Division followed behind the 10th Division as they passed through Haynau.

That evening the 8th Division was formed in two lines with its right behind Pahlwitz and its left towards Liegnitz. The 9th Division stood behind Neudorf on the road to Jauer. The 10th Division was in Waldau, the 11th Division stood to the left of the 8th Division with a regiment forming the garrison

Marchand.

of Liegnitz. The 39th Division was in Fellendorf. A light cavalry brigade occupied Neudorf and pushed reconnaissance detachments towards Jauer, Neumärk and Goldberg. A cavalry division, established in Fellendorf, detached six squadrons to Pfaffendorf and Gross-Beckern. The cuirassiers were in Schmogwitz with the 10th Hussar Regiment.[43]

The V and XI Corps

During the night of 22 August Macdonald and Lauriston believed that Goldberg was abandoned by the allies. Their reconnaissance on the morning of 23 August indicated, however, that it was still occupied. Lauriston decided to attack. Instead of a frontal attack, Lauriston chose to maneuver on both flanks of the village. He sent Puthod's (17th) and Rochambeau's (19th) divisions towards Wolfsberg, while Gérard's 35th Division, the 3rd Light Cavalry Division (Chastel) and 28th Light Cavalry Brigade (Montbrun) moved on Nieder-Au. Maison's 16th Division remained in reserve in Steinberg, to watch the roads from Falkenhayn .and Schönau. One brigade from Maison's 16th Division was posted in Grimmenberg, while the other stood on the Hermsdorf defile and attacked the Goldberg suburb.

The Battle of Goldberg

Blücher's forces had taken a position to face the French. Langeron was in Röchlitz. Yorck was in Wolfsberg, but had distributed the Prussian brigade of Prinz Karl von Mecklenburg along the right bank of the Katzbach from Ober-Au to Nieder-Au. Blücher's cavalry stood behind Yorck's corps and Sacken's forces were in Ober-Au.

Both of the allied wing corps were maneuvered so as to cover Yorck's flank, as it crossed over the Katzbach and moved over the Ulbersdorf heights, so it could strike the French flank as they moved on Goldberg. Prinz Karl of Mecklenburg's brigade was ordered to cross the Röchlitz and move against Nieder-Au in an effort to join Langeron's corps. Langeron had reinforced his posts in Conradswalde, where there had only been four squadrons, with the Moscow and Libau Infantry Regiments and two guns commanded by GM Tallisin II (7th Division). The entire force in Conradswalde was then placed under the command of GL Count Pahlen II. At the same time Count Pahlen III was sent over the Hirschberg towards Bolkenhayne and Landshut.[44]

Lauriston, who in the absence of Macdonald, commanded both the V and XI Corps, directed the XI Corps towards Goldberg covered by a light cavalry brigade drawn from the I Reserve Cavalry Corps. At the same time he ordered the V Corps to pass over the Katzbach above Seiffenau to fall on the left flank of Langeron's corps.

At 7:00 a.m., Prinz Karl von Mecklenburg moved his 6,400 men from their cantonments. He detached Fisher's Battalion (2/6th Silesian Landwehr) to Röchlitz, where it assumed a position in the cemetery to cover any retreat, and posted the Fus/1st East Prussian Infantry Regiment in Nieder-Au,[45] where it would provide an anchor for the Prussian line. The Fus/2nd East Prussian Infantry Regiment stood in a valley behind the village as a reserve. The 1/, 2/Brandenburg Uhlan Regiment formed an advanced guard and covered their deployment.

Mecklenburg had deployed his battalions slightly behind Nieder-Au, in an old French bivouac where a number of huts still stood. His right wing reached towards Hochberg, which was filled with skirmishers from the 1st East Prussian Regiment supported by the 2nd Leib Hussar Regiment. The cavalry, consisting of 300 men of the 3/, 4/Mecklenburg-Strelitz Hussar Regiment, 1/, 2/ Brandenburg Uhlans, and one landwehr squadron, stood behind the wing. The last three squadrons were in the Reissig farm.

Duke Charles of Mecklenburg at Goldberg, by Knötel.

Mecklenburg deployed his brigade in two lines. The first line was formed by Dobrowolski's (3/6th Silesian) and Rosteken's (4/6th Silesian) Landwehr Battalions and the 1/, 2/2nd East Prussian Regiment. The second line was formed with Kempsky's (1/6th Silesian) Landwehr Battalion and the 1/, 2/1st East Prussian Regiment.[46]

Mecklenburg hoped that the two cavalry regiments from the cavalry reserve would support his right, but their commander, fearing an attack by the French coming out of Seifersdorf, refused. The 1/, 2/Mecklenburg-Strelitz Hussars were swung over to the right to cover that flank in Hohendorf.

Mecklenburg sent forward the skirmishers of the Fus/2nd East Prussian Regiment and Kempsky's (1/6th Silesian) landwehr to clear the old barracks of French skirmishers, but Gérard's skirmishers bested them, driving them back. They withdrew under the cover of a squadron of the Brandenburg Uhlans.[47]

As Mecklenburg's dispositions were made, the scouts from the Mecklenburg Hussars returned with word that three strong French columns from Gérard's Division were moving from Goldberg and Neudorf-am-Rennewege against Nieder-Au.[48] After a careful preparation with 24 to 30 guns, Gérard led his division forward in a bayonet attack. It was 9:30 a.m.[49]

The French artillery fire quickly dismounted three guns from Prussian Battery #1 and set Hohberg afire. The skirmishers in Hohberg evacuated the village under the protection of the Mecklenburg Hussars. A quick attack against the Prussian left was repulsed.[50]

The French artillery then concentrated on the Prussian center, decimating the landwehr standing in dense columns. The French infantry then moved directly against the middle of the Prussian position where the landwehr battalions stood. Mecklenburg had reportedly ordered that the landwehr not operate together, but in this instance all four battalions were together in the middle of his position. The French artillery had shaken them and Dobrowolski's (3/6th Silesian)

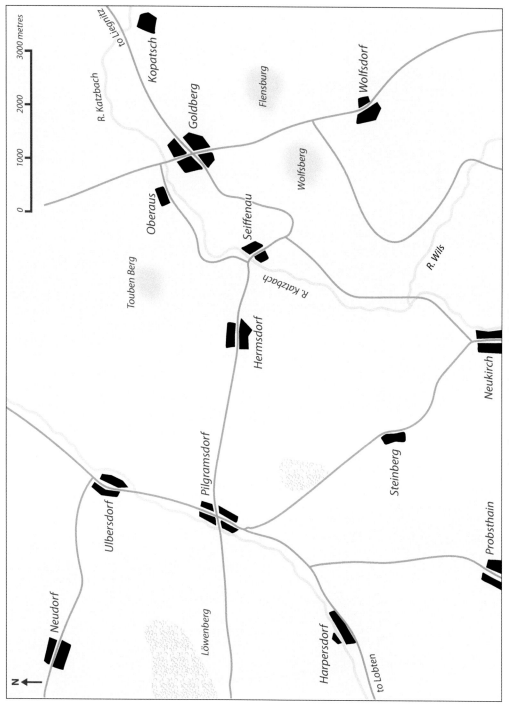

Sketch Map 5 The Battlefield of Goldberg.

The Battle of Goldberg, by Royer.

battalion fell back, disordering the other two landwehr battalions and the line battalion in the first line. Kempsky's (1/6th Silesian) landwehr battalion acted quickly and stabilized the situation, while Dobrowolski's (3/6th Silesian) battalion totally disintegrated and fled the field. The three landwehr battalions forming the center of the Prussian line were to suffer incredible losses during this engagement.

Though mortally wounded, Oberstleutnant von Grumbkow ordered Kempsky's (1/6th Silesian) Landwehr Battalion forward with bayonets to meet the advancing French. The landwehr battalion advanced without firing a shot. Its advance was supported by the Fus/2nd East Prussian Regiment. The Brandenburg Uhlans, under Major von Wulfen, advanced to support the attack, but was met by the 9th Chasseur à Cheval Regiment, and driven back.

To the south, the French skirmishers penetrated to the Katzbach. A French battery took a Prussian half battery under fire from the flank, dismounted a gun, and forced the rest to retire. Major Sjoeholm, who commanded the two fusilier battalions, stopped their advance and requested two landwehr battalions to support him as he drove the French skirmishers out. The landwehr was sent and his attack was successful for a time, but withdrawal he was soon driven back by a larger French force. His retreat was covered by a charge of the Brandenburg Uhlans, reinforced by the Issaev II Cossacks.[51]

At the same time, to the north of this action, the Prussian right flank was struck by two French infantry battalions formed in column. The French totalled about 1,000 to 1,200 men. Oberst Lobenthal pulled the 1/, 2/2nd East Prussian Regiment from the second line. He deployed the 1/2nd in line, while the 2/2nd remained in column. The 2/2nd East Prussian Infantry Regiment counterattacked with bayonets, pushing the French back.[52]

However, the withdrawal of those two battalions opened a hole in the middle of the Prussian line, through which the French quickly sent a force of cavalry. At a distance of 800 paces from the Prussian lines, the 2/2nd East Prussian Regiment found itself surrounded by French cavalry, and began a desperate withdrawal back to the safety of its lines. Only the quick thinking of Oberst von Warburg, who led the 3/, 4/Mecklenburg-Strelitz Hussars forward in a counter-charge, saved the regiment. As the hussars swung "rechts-um-kehrt" by zügen,[53] a French cannon ball ripped into the 4th Zug of the 4th Squadron, killing a man and his horse.[54] Despite the heavy fire and an unrelenting fire from French skirmishers, the hussars advanced to engage the French cavalry assaulting the 1/1st East Prussian Infantry Regiment. They were met by the French cavalry, and though they withdrew, they allowed the 2/1st East Prussians to escape.

The French counter battery had pounded the Prussian artillery. Only 3 Prussian guns remained. Though they continued their fire, they were unable to slow the assault by 24 squadrons of French cavalry against the 1/,2/1st East Prussian Infantry Regiment. Mecklenburg put himself at the head of the 2/1st East Prussian Infantry Regiment, and carrying the regimental flag in his own hands,[55] pushed back the French in an effort to allow those three guns to escape.

Mecklenburg reformed his brigade on the Bruckenkretscham heights. His brigade had lost 1,780 men. As he withdrew, his forces were covered by the 1/2nd East Prussian Regiment and supported on the left by the 7th and 37th Jagers and a number of Cossack regiments under GL Kapzevich. Finally he received an order from GL Yorck to withdraw to Röchlitz and Lasnig, passing over the Katzbach.

Battle Around Wolfsberg

Puthod's 17th Division attacked Wolfsberg early in the morning. As the French moved into Wolfsberg, Oberst von Katzeler ordered a withdrawal, but this order was suddenly counter-manded, as a new order came to hold the city against the French. He stood there with three battalions and ten guns.[56] Another French column from the V Corps had appeared, coming from Seiffenau and moved against the Wolfsberg. It was Rochambeau's 19th Division with the 135th Line Regiment in the lead. GM Kornilov, with the Russian 10th Division, was sent forward to support GL Rudsevich's Russian 15th Division. The remainder of the 10th Corps remained on the heights by Kopatsch, with the objective of preventing the French from passing between the advanced guard and the village.[57]

These two generals engaged in an intense battle with the French. Around 10:00 a.m., the French advanced again. The 29th and 45th Russian Jager Regiments, Archangel and Ingermanland Infantry Regiments, as well as the 15th Russian Division, found themselves being pounded by an intense French assault. Unfortunately, the Russian defense was not enough and the French captured the village, filling it with artillery. The situation became serious and Oberst von Katzeler sent the Gfug (4/14th Silesian) Landwehr Battalion and four cannons to support the Russian 22nd Division.

GM Emanuel and Colonel Paradovski moved to the left and Count Scherbatov and Obolenski moved to the right of Goldberg, leading a successful cavalry attack.[58] Despite this the French moved out onto the plain. However, their efforts to seize Flensberg were checked by the two Prussian battalions, and the Prussian artillery on a hill that intervened and stopped the advance.

The Assault on Goldberg

The city of Goldberg was defended by the Zeplin and Gfug (4/14th Silesian) Landwehr Battalions, six 3pdr guns and four 6pdr guns, which stood in Flensberg. The remaining four battalions of the advanced guard were distributed between the suburbs and the various gates. The city of Goldberg had four gates and a crenelated wall. The troops of GL Kapzevich stood on the Kopitz

The French storming the Russian-held Wolfsberg at the Battle of Goldberg, by Knötel.

heights, behind the city, acting as a reserve. Four light Russian guns stood to the right of the Nikolai-Kirchhof.[59]

GdI Langeron stood between Prausnitz and Goldberg. He dispatched GL Rudsevich to his left flank with his advanced guard, where he took up positions around Wolfsberg and Wolfsdorf.

At 8:30 a.m., the French advanced guard moved against Goldberg, passing over the stone bridge that spanned the Katzbach. Heavy fire poured into the column from the surrounding houses filled with Prussian marksmen. Quickly the battle devolved into an artillery duel supporting a skirmish battle that raged from house to house. About 2:00 p.m., with the suburbs in flames, the Prussians withdrew to the main part of the city, behind the walls. This move, however, was prompted by the pending fall of Flensberg, which would have left the Goldberg garrison surrounded.[60] The battle around Goldberg cost the Prussians 10 officers and 487 men as casualties.[61]

The Battle at 2:00 p.m.

At 2:00 p.m., the allied army stood with Mecklenburg retreating, Major von der Glotz still holding Goldberg, and Kapzevich having lost Wolfsberg, but was holding Lauriston in check before Flensberg. Blücher felt certain that major French forces stood behind the hills, and all of the French prisoners attested to the presence of Napoleon on the battlefield.

Blücher saw that his right wing[62] was under attack while another French column, the V Corps, was moving against Seifersdorf, which was defended by Langeron. This column was to attack Langeron three times before Langeron found himself obliged to withdraw. Yorck reported that yet another strong French column was moving in the direction of Neudorf-am-Rennewege. The situation was becoming serious and Blücher decided it was time to withdraw.

GdI Langeron moved GL Olsufiev's Russian 9th Division to the defile by Prausnitz to cover the withdrawal of Rudsevich and Kornilov. The 6th Corps, under Scherbatov, stood before Seichau. Kapzevich and the defenders of Goldberg withdrew down the main road towards Jauer. The Russian 15th Division and the advanced guard moved down the road to Seichau via Prausnitz. General Korff covered the withdrawal with the allied reserve cavalry and engaged in a running battle with the French cavalry of the XI Corps.[63]

The Russian detachment in Ober-Au was, in its turn, pushed back by the XI Corps.

On his side, Ney advanced with the III Corps and the II Reserve Cavalry Corps (Sebastian) taking up a position before Liegnitz. Lauriston moved after Langeron, but very feebly. Langeron withdrew in echelons, little pressed by the French. Sacken's corps had crossed the Katzbach and withdrew on Pinkendorf. That evening Yorck took up a strong position in Hennersdorf and his advanced posts were in Seichau.

The 2nd and 8th Prussian brigades united by Lasnig, and then moved to the heights behind Nieder-Crayn and Weinberg. The other brigades that had been by Dohnau, also moved to the Nieder-Crain and Weinberg area. Sacken had withdrawn to Maltisch. The 1st Corps and the right wing were ordered to withdraw to Jauer and to the village of Profen. The 1st Brigade of the Cavalry Reserve and the Reserve Artillery reached this point that evening. The remaining three brigades bivouacked on the Galgenberg ridge, by Jauer, and GL Sacken stood on their right wing.

Prinz Carl had suffered heavy losses from the 1st, 3rd and 4th Battalions of his brigade's 6th Landwehr Regiment. These forces were reformed into a single battalion under the command of Major von Fischer.[64]

Finally, on the 24th, Blücher's three corps left their positions by Kohlhohe and Gross-Rosen and moved to Striegau. The advanced troops of GdI Langeron remained by Peterwitz, in front of Jauer. The Reserve Cavalry, under General Korff, moved into Jauer. The entire Army of Silesia was now united in and around Jauer. The battles of the previous two days had cost Blücher about 8,000 men and the French about 5,000.

The Battle of Goldberg was executed by the V and XI Corps using classic methods. The allied side had defended their position very passively; the only aggressive action was Langeron's pushes to retake the Wolfsberg heights. Their cavalry, which was badly placed, was not employed, and there were no reserves. The allied retreat was not significantly different from their earlier withdrawal.

Assured that Blücher intended not to fight, Napoleon departed on 23 August and went to Dresden, to face the advancing Army of Bohemia. He had GD Souham relieve Ney as III Corps commander and took Ney with him for the pending battle at Dresden. Macdonald was given overall command of the III, V, and XI Corps, and the II Cavalry Corps. GD Gérard assumed command of the XI Corps, while Macdonald acted as overall commander.

4

Macdonald goes to War: The Battle of the Katzbach 24–26 August 1813

The Battle of Katzbach

Napoleon had ordered Macdonald to throw Blücher back, towards Jauer, and then to establish himself strongly on the Bober, between Löwenberg and Buntzlau, in such a manner as to hold the Army of Silesia away from Dresden, as well as to prevent the Army of Bohemia from pushing detachments towards Berlin, through Lusace. Napoleon recommended to Macdonald that he position the bulk of his forces on the right bank of the Bober. He was to have communications posts along the mountains of Bohemia and to the left in the plains of Lusace. Finally, he was to keep Napoleon continually updated on the actions of the allies before him.

On 24 August Macdonald's forces stood on the Katzbach. The III Corps stood near Rathkirch (left bank), with two battalions in Liegnitz. The V Corps was between Wolfsberg and Röchlitz (right bank). The XI Corps and II Cavalry Corps were between Goldberg and Seifersdorf (left bank).

Not seeing an attack on the 24th, Blücher deduced that Napoleon, and a portion of the forces that had been facing him, had withdrawn to face Schwarzenberg's movement on Dresden. This opinion was reinforced when a French courier was captured, who carried dispatches ordering Ney to accompany Napoleon to Dresden. Blücher assumed that this meant that the III Corps was also leaving. This was reinforced by the misinterpretation of the III Corps movement on Rathkirch, which was perceived as a withdrawal of the corps. Blücher decided that it was a propitious time to resume the offensive, profiting from Napoleon's absence and the reduction of the forces facing him.

Blücher reorganized his advanced guard under Oberst von Katzeler. Major von Hiller commanded the infantry. It now consisted of the Silesian Grenadier Battalion, 1/Brandenburg Infantry Regiment, Thüringian Battalion,[1] the Seydlitz (3/5th Silesia) and Kempsky (1/14th Silesian) Landwehr Battalions,[2] two companies of East Prussian Jägers, 4 squadrons of the Brandenburg Uhlans and the 5th Silesian Landwehr Cavalry Regiments, 6pdr Foot Battery #24, and Horse Battery #2.[3]

Langeron's forces were arranged with Rudsevich's advanced guard, 4 battalions, 6 squadrons, 2 Cossack regiments, and 10 guns, between Seichau and Hennersdorf. Between Hermannsdorf and Weinberg stood the Russian 9th Corps of Generallieutenant Olsufiev with 11 battalions and 24 guns.[4] Behind them was Korff's cavalry reserve with 7 squadrons, 2 Cossack regiments and 6 guns. Along the Kirchberg-Breiteberg-Schlaupe line stood the 6th Corps of Scherbatov, with 15 battalions and 24 guns and behind him stood the 10th Corps under GL Kapzevich, with 8 battalions and 24 guns. Yorck's Corps stood with its advanced guard between Bellewitzhof and Christianshöhe.

On 25 August, Blücher's knowledge of the French dispositions was slim. He understood that the III Corps was by Waldau. At 9:00 a.m., he learned that the French in Liegnitz were moving to Buntzlau. The 25th (Saxon) Division was also withdrawing to Liegnitz, and the divisions remained between Waldau and Buntzlau were remaining echeloned. The 25th Division had joined with the 10th Division, under Albert, and 39th Division, under Marchand, by Waldau with orders to withdraw to Haynau. Later it became apparent to him that only the 8th Division (Souham) remained by the Katzbach.

Blücher believed that the V Corps was before Goldberg, with its advanced posts by Prausnitz. The XI Corps and Sébastiani's II Cavalry Corps were behind Goldberg on the Kreuzberg, between Rothbrüning and Hohendorf. Blücher's orders for the attack were as follows:

> The detachment of General Count Langeron, which stands by Schönau and Conradswalde, shall advance down the road against Goldberg, following this order from the beginning, attacking the enemy, and drawing the enemy's attention to him.
>
> The advanced guard of General Count Langeron shall remain on the defensive, the Corps of General Count Langeron shall march to the right, pass over the Katzbach by Weinberg, and where possible, by Röchlitz, and form itself on the heights between Kosendau and Hohendorf in column, and drive away the French cavalry standing by the Dieschel [the stream which ran through Pilgramsdorf].
>
> Yorck's Corps shall go by Kroitsch and Dohnau and cross over the Katzbach, moving to the right of Rathkirch and against Steudnitz in order to cut off the French corps by Liegnitz from Haynau and to strike the French rear.
>
> The corps of von Sacken shall stop before the French corps by Liegnitz as Yorck's corps stops, and shall then follow Yorck's corps over the Katzbach so as to be able to strike the French right flank. Yorck shall send his light cavalry over the Katzbach in order to strike the French left flank and cut the French withdrawal on Glogau in case that General von Sacken finds himself strong enough.
>
> I shall remain on the point of Yorck's column. I await the withdrawal of the French knowing that our cavalry shall act with boldness and prevent his reorganizing once his withdrawal begins.[5]

On 25 August Blücher sent Sacken's corps to Malitick and Langeron's corps to Hermannsdorf, where it deployed. Yorck's corps remained in Jauer. The advanced guard, under Oberst von Katzeler, moved with the cavalry to Kroitsch, where it encountered, with no success, a force of French cavalry.

During the night von Katzeler was ordered to annoy the French with his light cavalry. He detached Major von Stutterheim with the Brandenburg Uhlans and one cannon, supported by two squadrons of the Lithuanian Dragoons under Oberstleutnant von Platen.

They advanced against the French posts at Rathkirch and started a small fight, that stirred up the French camp and disturbed their sleep until daybreak.

Between 1:00 and 2:00 p.m., Langeron shifted the position of his corps and it now stood with Rudsevich's advanced guard between Monchswalde and Hermannsdorf. The 9th Corps stood with its advanced troops in Hennersdorf and the bulk of its forces between Hermannsdorf and Weinberg. The 6th Corps stood with its forces between Kirchberg and Breitenberg. A small detachment of three battalions was moved to Schlaupe. The 10th Corps moved from Weinberg west to Peterwitz and faced Pombsen and Jägendorf.[6]

On 26 August, Blücher set his plan in motion. Sacken and Yorck were to move towards Liegnitz and attack the French III Corps. Langeron was to advance through Prausnitz towards Goldberg, where Blücher assumed he would find and hold the V and XI Corps.[7] The 1st Prussian Corps advanced in two columns. The right column consisted of the 1st and 2nd Brigades. The left column consisted of the 7th and 8th Brigades. These two columns moved on Brechtelsdorf, where they stopped.

Sketch Map 6 The Area East of the Katzbach.

Macdonald, under the impression that Blücher's forces were still in Jauer, had resolved to advance on that city on 26 August, to fulfil his instructions from Napoleon.

Macdonald had weakened his forces by detaching two divisions. He did so because he learned that Hirschberg, on the banks of the Bober and near the mountains, was occupied by an allied force. He detached Ledru's 31st Division, XI Corps, to move up the Bober and eliminate this force. The second division, Puthod's 17th Division, V Corps, moved to Schönau to support this maneuver.

At 2:00 a.m., on 26 August, Puthod received an order to depart with his division and 100 horse from Steinberg at 7:00 a.m., on the 26th. As soon as he arrived in Schönau, he was to send two companies to Deppelsdorf, before Lähn, with instructions for

Maréchal Macdonald.

the 134th Regiment, then occupying Lähn, to depart at 4:00 a.m., on the 27th for Hirschberg.

At the same time, Puthod was to detach the 146th Regiment and 3rd Foreign Regiment (Irish Legion) to Hirschberg with three 6pdrs and a howitzer. Puthod's division was then to march in two columns from Lähn and Schönau on Hirschberg, to support Ledru's 31st Division, XI Corps, in its attack on Hirschberg.

As Puthod's first brigade moved on Hirschberg, the second brigade (147th and 148th Regiments) and the rest of his artillery was to advance against Jauer.

Puthod was to accompany the advance on Jauer personally and to take a position on the Jagersdorf heights. Once there he was to send an officer to Macdonald for further instructions.[8]

Macdonald then marched with the remainder of his forces on Jauer. Though his path was not cut by any major rivers, it was cut by numerous ravines of significant depth. Macdonald directed Souham to cross the Katzbach at Liegnitz and move through Neudorf and Malitick with the III Corps. The XI Corps, around Seifersdorf, was to cross the Katzbach by Schmochwitz, and to move towards Jauer via Dohna, Jänowitz, and Bellewitz, along the right bank of the Wuthende-Neisse. Sébastiani's II Cavalry Corps was to cross between Kroitsch and Nieder-Crayn and to advance along the left bank of the Wuthende-Neisse. Finally, the V Corps was to march via Seichau and Hennersdorf. Each corps had a single route allocated to it for this maneuver and all were to converge on Jauer, two attacking it frontally, while one attacked each flank.[9]

At 7:00 a.m., on the morning of 26 August, Lauriston had directed Maison's 16th Division to move on Prausnitz, and Rochambeau's 19th Division to move between Prausnitz and Felnsberg. Dermoncourt's 6th Light Cavalry Brigade remained with them, while Puthod's 17th Division departed for his separate mission.[10]

During the 26th, there were rain and thunderstorms, which lasted most of the day, flooded the streams and rendered the roads almost impassable. The Neisse was considerably flooded. By Schönau it was normally nine paces wide and one foot deep, by Parschwitz it was normally 24 paces wide and at its effluence it was normally four feet deep. With the rain, it was now eight feet deep at Schönau and eighteen feet deep at its effluence. Macdonald began moving his troops despite the rain. At the same time the allies began moving theirs. Puthod and Ledru also began their movement on Hirschberg. Puthod was to move towards Jauer by passing through the mountains and take a position where he could strike the left flank of the Army of Silesia.[11]

Around 2:30 p.m., Macdonald was informed that GD Souham was at Nieder-Crayn and was moving in the direction of Kroitsch because the bridge over the Katzbach at Liegnitz had been destroyed. To Macdonald it was clear, that as Souham attempted to pass his corps over the Katzbach at Kroitsch, it would become entangled with Sébastiani's corps. The resultant traffic jam would take many hours to clear the village. Souham observed the same problem and responded to it by swinging his corps to the south to prevent the congestion. The hindmost division would have to remain in reserve. Only Brayer's 8th Division had been able to pass through Kroitsch, but in doing so it had been obliged to leave behind its artillery.[12]

The Allies

At daybreak on 26 August, around 5:00 a.m., the Prussian 1st Army Corps stood in lager by Jauer. It was organized in two columns. The first column consisted of the 1st and 2nd Brigades and marched from Alt-Jauer to Weinberg. The second column consisted of the 7th and 8th Brigades and the reserve artillery. It moved from Alt-Jauer, through Bellewitzhof, to a position behind the heights between Brechtelshof and Bellewitzhof in closed columns. The advanced guard, under Oberst von Katzeler, stood by Nieder-Crayn, and had its forward pickets in the Katzbach valley. Behind Katzeler stood the Prussian Reserve Cavalry of Oppen.[13]

Sacken, marching on Eichholz, and Yorck, marching on Brechtelsdorf, found themselves in a meeting engagement with the French. Langeron, moving towards Goldberg, found himself under heavy attack by Lauriston.

Blücher's reaction was instantaneous. He ordered his corps to deploy and prepare for battle. Sacken was to move behind and to the west of Eichholz, where he would be supported by a strong battery of artillery. Another Prussian 12pdr battery was soon dispatched to reinforce this.

The advanced guard reported the passage of the French over the Katzbach by Nieder-Crayn and onto the plateau. A break in the weather permitted Müffling to make a personal reconnaissance. To his surprise he found that the steady downpour had masked the advance of heavy columns of French cavalry and several batteries across the Blüchersfelde plain. There were only a few infantry battalions passing through Nieder-Crayn towards the plateau. The attention of the French appeared on to be directed on Eichholz.

Müffling immediately realized that if Yorck were to advance immediately, he could probably force the French back. Even if a further French column advanced through Dohna, Yorck and Sacken's force would suffice for the action. However, no time could be lost if the opportunity were to be seized.

Müffling rode back and proposed to the Blücher that Yorck's main body, – 2½ brigades – immedi-

Müffling.

ately advance between Christianenshohe and Streilrand and throw the French back on the Neisse and Katzbach. A brigade was to remain in reserve, with Langeron's assistance the movement would surely be successful.[14]

The first forces seriously engaged were Oberst von Katzeler's advanced guard. Around 10:30 a.m., he found himself being attacked by a cavalry column with 6-8 cavalry regiments moving against Wültsch and Kroitsch. Major von Klüx, whose infantry was inside the villages in prepared positions, had his infantry take the cavalry under skirmish fire. As they closed to within 50 paces of his infantry, he issued the orders for volley fire.

The Prussian vanguard was forced back and retreated to Bellewitzhof, pursued only by French insults as their artillery was unable to advance fast enough. The Prussian reserve cavalry under Oberst von Jürgass marched to their assigned position to the north of Christianshöhe. Later, some French batteries moved up on the high plateau and with their fire threw the landwehr battalions of the Prussian vanguard into some confusion. The commander of the von Kempsky Landwehr Battalion, Major von Hiller, stated that:

> some cannon shot struck the battalion, throwing it into disorder. It tried to push in a wild mass through the other battalions. My officers attempted to stop the rout but they were not successful until I had some cannons directed at them and gave my men my word of honor, that I would have fire on them if the rout continued. This worked, and from that moment the battalion returned to order despite a single cannon shot that killed 14 men and later stood solidly in square while hostile cavalry swarmed about them.[15]
>
> In contrast, the von Seidlitz Landwehr Battalion behaved like a veteran unit throughout the entire battle combat.

During this phase of the action, Blücher rode along the front of his men and addressed them. He described his deliberate act of permitting the French to cross the Katzbach so that he could strike them and throw them into the Katzbach, completing their destruction. He harangued his men to ignore the rain, which prevented their muskets from firing, but to go at the French with cold Prussian steel.

Blücher at the Katzbach, by Röchling.

When in front of the 2/Brandenburg Infantry Regiment Blücher turned and said "Well, old Brandenburgers! Today we shall seize the French properly. I have enough before me now!"

The battle developed more quickly, as one could expect. Sacken was the first engaged. He recognized the importance of holding Eichholz, and occupied it, while his vanguard pushed past Hochkirch and Schlotting. He then pushed his heavy artillery onto the Taubenberg from where it took the French lines under heavy fire.

To Sacken's left, as a result of the 11:00 a.m., orders, Yorck advanced with his forces in two columns across the Blüchersfelde, towards Schlauphof and Nieder-Crayn. The Fus/Brandenburg Infantry Regiment, under Major von Krosigk, occupied the village of Schlaup. Two further battalions of the 8th Brigade, under the brigade commander Hünerbein personally, reinforced the Prussian position in Schlaupe as strong French columns appeared on the left bank of the Neisse

The advance Yorck's infantry and their deployment between Christianenshohe and Bellwitzhof went slowly because of the deep mud, which sucked the shoes off the landwehr, and also because of changes in orders. There was also some disagreement as to how Yorck was to deploy his forces. Yorck wanted to have his battalions deployed in line before engaging in combat, but Sacken requested he remain in column because of the limited room on the battlefield and his need to maneuver in the same area. Blücher finally had to intervene personally to resolve the situation.[16]

Because of a misunderstanding in orders the 7th Brigade (Horn) had moved to the right wing of the first rank of the attack instead of the 2nd Brigade (Prince von Mecklenburg). This obliged the 2nd Brigade to follow in the second wave of the attack. The main body of the 8th Brigade, under the command of Oberstleutnant von Borcke, had reached his assigned positions near Bellewitzhof early in the formation change. As Horn's Brigade extended more to the right, a gap emerged between it and the main body of the 8th Brigade emerged. This gap drew the battalions of Oberstleutnant von Lobenthal into it. Further to the west the infantry vanguard fell back to the advancing brigades and Steinmetz's brigade was held as a reserve behind the middle of the allied line.

The problems resulting from the displacement of the corps during the process of changing formation could well have allowed the course of the battle to be changed.

During this period Blücher said to General Yorck, he wished to "permit as many French as he thought he could vanquish onto the high plateau". This order annoyed Yorck who, answered Blücher with the remark that because of the heavy rain he could no longer see his fingers to count the French.[17]

The advanced troops of General Langeron stationed in Seichau were the first of his troops attacked by the French. They found themselves under infantry assault. Blücher took this as the main French attack and dispatched his forces forward to strike the head of the French column.[18]

The Russian infantry of the right wing stood between the village of Eichholz and the front of Christianshöhe. Sacken's 11th Corps deployed with the Russian 27th Infantry Division, under General Neverovsky, forming the first line, and the Russian 10th Division, under General Lieven III, forming in the second line. The Kurland and Smolensk Dragoons stood on the left flank by the village of Eichholz, which was occupied by the 8th and 39th Jager Regiments of the 10th Division. On the heights next to Eichholz stood 12pdr Battery #13, forming the right flank. The Okhotsk and Kamtchatka Regiments, from GM Reppninsky's brigade, stood behind Eichholz to support that flank . The Russian 2nd Hussar Division, under GM Lanskoy, stood on the extreme left of Sacken's right wing and the corps Cossacks were on the far right.[19]

Langeron's left wing stood on the left bank of the swollen Neisse by the village of Hennersdorf. His advanced troops were in front of the village, on the Plinse stream.

The center of the left wing's advanced guard was formed with the Archangel and Old Ingermanland Infantry Regiments on the left; the 45th Jager Regiment occupied the ravine behind Plinse, and the 29th Jager Regiment stood to the right of the Jauer-Goldberg road. On the right wing of the advanced guard was the 2nd Ukrainian Cossack Regiment. On the left wing of the infantry was the Lithuanian Chasseur à Cheval Regiment (2 squadrons), then the Kiev Dragoons (5 squadrons), and somewhat further, the 3rd Ukrainian Cossack Regiment.[20] The Don Cossack Battery #2 was to the left on a small hill. General Uschakov stood with the Tver and Kinbourn Dragoon Regiments as a reserve behind the advanced guard.[21]

The center, Yorck's Prussian I Corps, stood on the heights of Weinberg and Hirschberg. Yorck's Corps was arranged in two lines. The 8th Brigade, under Hünerbein, stood on the left The 7th Brigade, under von Horn, was on the right, on the Steinberg Heights, with Russian 12pdr Position Battery #34 in Breitenberg, and the Russian 18th Division was on the Hirschberg Heights. The 11th and 36th Jager Regiments (Russian 7th Division) were in Schlaupe. The 28th and 32nd Jager Regiments (Russian 18th Division) were on the heights between Schlaupe and Hennersdorf. The corps artillery was deployed in front of the infantry.[22]

The Russian 9th Corps was arranged with the Russian 9th and 15th Division behind the Weinberg Heights in two ranks. The 10th and 38th Jager Regiments (Russian 9th Division) were in Hennersdorf. The 22nd Jagers were in Hermannsdorf and the 12th Jagers (Russian 15th Division) were left on the stream northwest of the village. The 12th Jagers later withdrew to the second line. The cavalry stood in the third line as a reserve.

The Russian 10th Corps was, initially, in column behind the right wing serving as a reserve, but later it was sent to the left to Peterwitz and took up a position to watch the French approach from Schönau.

French batteries were set up on the heights before the village of Weinberg, as the Prussian 1st Corps moved into position. The 7th and 8th Brigades formed the first line, the 7th to the right and the 8th to the left. The 2nd and 1st Brigades moved behind the first line to form a second line. The 2nd Brigade stood to the right and the 1st stood to the left. The infantry battalions were in columns formed on the middle. The reserve cavalry formed up behind the first line, in front of the 2nd Brigade. The infantry advanced guard, under Major von Hiller, with the Silesian Grenadier Battalion, moved to the left of the 7th Brigade, with the Jager Company in reserve. The cavalry of the advanced guard joined that of the main cavalry reserve.

Behind the right wing stood Sohr's 1/, 2/Brandenburg Hussar Regiment and the Osarowsky (5th Silesian) Landwehr Cavalry Regiment. The 3rd Silesian Landwehr Cavalry Regiment was sent off. The Fus/Brandenburg Regiment and the Brixen (3/14th Silesian) Landwehr Battalion, as well as the 3/, 4/Brandenburg Hussar Regiment, also from the 8th Prussian Brigade, were posted behind the Silesian Grenadier Battalion behind Schlaupe, around Bellewitz, in order to maintain communications with the left wing. A squadron of the East Prussian National Cavalry Regiment was also posted there, with another squadron covering an artillery battery nearby.

Oberst von Hünerbein was the commander of the forces around Schlaupe. His command included the 11th and 36th Russian Jager Regiments that stood by the Fus/Brandenburg Infantry Regiment. Oberstleutnant von Borke commanded the remaining six battalions of the 8th Brigade. In the first line, on the right wing was the 2/Brandenburg Infantry Regiment, the Thiele Landwehr Battalion (2/14th Silesian), and the 2/12th Reserve Regiment. In the second line stood the 4/14th Silesian Landwehr Regiment and the 1/, 3/12th Reserve Regiment.[23]

Macdonald began to deploy his troops as well. The XI Corps began moving about 6:00 a.m., and deployed between Weinberg and Klein-Tinz. The II Cavalry Corps was on its left and the V Corps was on its right.

The II Cavalry Corps passed through Biersdorf at 9:00 a.m., and moved on Kroitsch. Roussel's 2nd Light Cavalry Division advanced in column by squadrons on the right of the road, Exelman's 4th Light Cavalry Division moved on the left, and the 2nd Cuirassier Division was behind and in the center of the two light cavalry divisions. The cavalry column did not have a skirmish screen or scouts out and as it closed within 50 paces of the village of Kroitsch, it received a volley of fire from the Prussian advanced guard under Katzeler.

Katzeler had occupied all the villages to the north of the Katzbach in an effort to support the cavalry screens. In Kroitsch and Wildschutz, he had one or two companies of East Prussian Jägers, and 100 skirmishers from the Brandenburg Regiment. In Schimmelwitz he had 50 skirmishers and a detachment of jägers from the Silesian Grenadier Battalion. In Nieder-Crayn he had 50 skirmishers from the Silesian Grenadiers and 100 from the Thüringian Battalion. The 1/Brandenburg Regiment was distributed with its 4th Company occupying the Nieder-Weinberg mill, the 2nd and 3rd Companies guarding the bridge over the Niesse at Nieder-Crayn, and the 1st Company occupying the bank below the bridge. The Thüringian Battalion had its 1st and 3rd Companies to the right and left of Nieder-Weinberg, its 2nd Company before the village and its 4th Company in Schlauphof.[24] The two landwehr battalions and the Silesian Grenadier Battalion stood as a reserve on the heights to the east of Weinberg and 6pdr Foot Battery #24, Barenkampf, stood on the right of the road from Nieder-Crayn to Jänowitz.[25]

The French Arrive on the Battlefield

The first French to appear on the battlefield was the 7th Light Cavalry Brigade, under GB Gérard,[26] 2nd Light Cavalry Division, consisted of the 4th Lancer and the 5th and 9th Hussar Regiments, supported by some light artillery.

As he came onto the field, GD Gérard observed about a dozen squadrons of Katzeler's cavalry on the plain. He sent three battalions from Charpentier's 36th Division and two guns to chase them off the field and after 40 shots the Prussian cavalry departed, moving on Weinberg.[27]

Macdonald then ordered GD Gérard to open the Weinberg-Ober-Crayn road and he ordered Sebastian to form his forces before Kroitsch and to pass through the Weinberg defiles as soon as Charpentier had mounted to the plateau with Meunier's infantry brigade and artillery. The bulk of the XI Corps, supported on the right by the V Corps, was already engaging Langeron.

Gérard moved in line between Weinberg and Klein-Tinz covering the infantry that followed them. The infantry was Meunier's 2nd Brigade, 36th Division, which consisted of five battalions of the 3rd and 14th Légère Regiments, supported by a 12pdr battery from Charpentier's 36th Division.[28] They moved to strike the Prussian advanced guard and clear the way for Sébastiani's corps to cross the Neisse by Nieder-Crayn.

GD Gérard sent three battalions forward to attack the villages of Nieder-Crayn and Weinberg. Barenkampf's 6pdr Foot Battery #24 fired on the advancing French, but with little success. The Prussian infantry surrendered both villages with little resistance.

Around 1:30 p.m., the remaining two battalions of Meunier's brigade joined the first three and they moved to within musket range of the Bellewitzhof woods, facing Brechtelshof. A French 12pdr battery was emplaced on the plateau and the two divisional batteries took up positions in front of Meunier.

The 2nd Cavalry Corps, Roussel's 2nd Light Cavalry Division leading, moved through the defile in a column of twos after Charpentier's 36th Division seized a position on the plateau. As each squadron was organized, it was placed to the left of the infantry. Roussel established his division in three lines just west of Klein-Tinz. The first line, the 8th Light Cavalry Brigade (GB Dommagnet), contained the 11th and 12th Chasseurs and the 2nd Lancers. The 7th Light Cavalry Brigade (GB Gérard) formed the second and third lines. The second line contained the 4th Lancers and the 5th Hussars. The third line contained the 9th Hussars. They were supported by 24 horse guns from Sébastiani's corps, which were organized in a battery between the cavalry and Charpentier's 36th Division.[29]

It is advocated by some historians that the passage through the defile was delayed because of the traffic jam caused by Charpentier's infantry passing through the defile, but it is more likely that the delay was due to Katzeler's combined arms advanced guard and the effectiveness of its delaying actions.

The Thüringian Battalion had defended the villages of Nieder- and Ober-Weinberg, while Katzeler's advanced guard formed itself in two lines on the plateau. It then withdrew by echelons 100 paces on Bellewitzhof, with its left wing forward, in a manner to support itself on the ravine. Barenkampf's 6pdr Foot Battery #24 placed itself on both wings of the infantry. The French artillery did engage Barenkampf's battery with some success, dismounting one gun and a howitzer in the action on the right.[30]

General Jürgass, upon hearing the first cannon shot, formed the cavalry reserve between Christianshöhe and the road from Weinberg to Bellewitzhof. It protected, on the right, Katzeler's retreat and merger with the cavalry reserve. Its two horse batteries deployed and engaged the French artillery.

During these preliminaries Macdonald remained near the road from Liegnitz to Jauer, awaiting the arrival of the III Corps. On the plateau the few allied battalions rapidly with-

Sébastiani.

drew, while to the south Gérard and Sébastiani were engaged in a lively fight. Macdonald believed that the main battle would be on that side and moved to the right. On the road he encountered Souham, who announced the arrival of the III Corps.[31]

The III Corps

An officer, carrying an order, arrived at the III Corps headquarters during the evening of 25 August. The order directed that the departure of the III Corps be delayed from 9:30 to 11:30 a.m., on 26 August.

Though the III Corps had two battalions in Liegnitz since the 25th, it had taken no steps to search for usable fords or to repair the bridges. This was to prevent the III Corps from crossing at Liegnitz, which would have made a significant difference in the evolving battle. As a result, Souham decided to march down the west bank of the Katzbach to Kroitsch, leaving the 39th Division in Liegnitz as a garrison. He ordered them to build a bridge, but that was too late to affect the battle or his maneuvers.[32]

At noon, on 26 August, the III Corps began its movement towards Jauer, via Kroitsch. Though ordered to move through Liegnitz, the engineer commander, Cossigny, noted that the bridges over the Katzbach were broken and Souham chose to reroute his forces through Kroitsch, in an effort to recover the lost time.[33]

The 8th Division (GD Brayer) formed the head of the column. It arrived at the Kroitsch defile about 2:30 p.m. The II Cavalry Corps, which marched with it, embarrassed and slowed its march considerably. Macdonald directed Souham to send the 8th Division up to the plateau, while turning the plateau with two other divisions, and holding the fourth in reserve.

The clutter of baggage so blocked the road that it was necessary to delay the passage of the division's artillery. The infantry, however, soon broke into a marshy valley. At the instant that the infantry broke clear, the XI Corps' park was struck and captured by a swarm of Prussian lancers.

About 2:00 P.m., Yorck ordered his corps to begin movement. The sound of cannon fire and musketry convinced Langeron that a serious engagement was unfolding. Blücher moved to Yorck's corps and Gneisenau and Müffling joined the advanced guard. They concentrated their infantry at Christianshöhe, on a plain where they could see 800 to 1,000 paces.

Katzeler, who had withdrawn all of his skirmishers, was unable to provide the Prussian staff officers with any information other than that the French were on his heels. The French, on their part, had not pushed any scouting forces forward and were obliged to either advance in their dense masses or withdraw.

Müffling rode forward personally to observe the French positions. He saw nothing on the plain between Jänowitz and Klein-Tinz, though he did hear cannon fire in the valley towards Ober-Weinberg. He continued and arrived to the south of the village of Jänowitz, where he encountered a line of 3,000 French cavalry deployed in line, followed by a few batteries and a stream of infantry flowing up the defile. The head of the infantry had already reached the plateau.

Müffling hurried back to Blücher and proposed that he advance with the two brigades of Yorck's corps, one brigade serving as a reserve and standing with its left on the ravine. Part of the 8th Brigade would hold the west edge of the ravine and the other would occupy Schlaupe, Schlauphof, and ensure Yorck's liaison with Langeron. Sacken was to move on Eichholz.

Blücher agreed and directed Müffling to conduct the deployment of Yorck's corps. As his orders were given a battery on the Taubenberg began firing.[34]

The Battle at the Weinberg Defile

The battle began when Sacken opened fire with Brams' 12pdr battery, which stood on the Taubenberg, in front of Christianshöhe. This ridge dominated the entire battlefield and General von Gneisenau, who stood nearby, gave the same order to the Prussian 6pdr Foot battery #3, which also opened fire.

Yorck's corps advanced down the roads as prescribed with the 7th and 1st Brigades on the right and the 8th and 2nd on the left. Upon arriving at the ridge running from Bellewitzhof and Christianshöhe, Yorck ordered his corps to deploy into battle formation. The maneuver was badly handled and resulted in the 7th and 2nd Brigades becoming somewhat entangled. However, when they sorted themselves out the corps had arranged itself such that the first line consisted of the 7th and 8th Brigades. The second line consisted of the 2nd Brigade, while the 1st Brigade remained in reserve. Each brigade was placed in two lines with its battalions standing in column formed on the center.[35]

About the time that Yorck's corps was deployed, Blücher learned from the garrison of Schlaupe that the French had appeared before the village with two strong columns, and were advancing against it. He also learned from Major Oppen, of his staff, that the French force facing him consisted of no more than four battalions, a battery of eight guns, and some cavalry.

Yorck became concerned with holding the village of Schlaupe, and sent successively the 3/14th Silesian Landwehr and the Silesian Grenadier Battalion, joining the Fus/Brandenburg there to hold the village. Hünerbein, believing he would encounter strong resistance on the plateau, took personal command of these three battalions. To support his infantry, 6pdr Foot Battery #3 stood by Brams' 12pdr battery.

Oberstleutnant von Schmidt, Chief of artillery, strengthened this battery by bringing up 12pdr Battery #1, 6pdr Battery #15, and Horse Battery #2. The French responded by bringing up five batteries to return the allied fire. It was about 3:00 p.m., and a heavy thunderstorm began.[36]

Based on the report of Major von Oppen, Blücher ordered his forces to attack in column, believing it would gain him time. Müffling vainly tried to convince Yorck to comply, but Yorck, concerned about the increased casualties such an assault would cause, ordered his corps to advance in line.

The Prussian 8th Brigade advanced by itself and was the first to engage the French. The 7th Brigade, retarded by the movement of the 2nd Brigade, was no longer in column and had the reserve infantry on its left. The cavalry passed through the intervals in the artillery and placed itself with the 5th and 10th Silesian Landwehr Cavalry Regiments covering the right of the artillery. The Brandenburg Uhlan Regiment was ordered to maintain liaison with Sacken and the rest of the cavalry formed behind the infantry lines. Barenkampf's 6pdr Foot Battery #24 and Horse Battery #1 assumed positions to the left of the artillery line.[37]

The 8th Brigade soon found itself isolated. Its cavalry, 3/, 4/Brandenburg Hussars, stood to the south of Bellewitzhof, ready to support Hünerbein in case of need. The 8th Brigade stood in two lines. The first line contained, from left to right, 2/12th Reserve Regiment, 3/14th Silesian Landwehr Regiment and 2/2nd Brandenburg Regiment. The second line contained the 3/12th Reserve Regiment, 1/12th Reserve Regiment, and 2/14th Silesian Landwehr Regiment. Their skirmisher platoons were deployed forward of their lines, but they remained in formation. The rain was so heavy that they could not see the French.

Three French battalions of Meunier's Brigade and four guns standing on the Kreuzberg heights by Weinberg, found themselves engaged in a pitched battle against the Prussians of the 8th Brigade. Major von Othegraven led the 2/Brandenburg Infantry Regiment,[38] forward in a successful bayonet attack, with the von Thiele Landwehr Battalion (2/14th Silesian) in support, throwing back a French battalion. They captured 7 officers and 165 men, but lost 3 officers and 188 men.

The 2/12th Reserve Regiment threw back the other two French battalions. Major von Golz, leading the 3/12th Reserve Regiment, was also successful and captured 4 guns.

Then, however, the brigade found itself threatened with an attack by the French cavalry and the wide gap separating them from the other brigades of the corps and was obliged to form squares on the Kreutzberg.[39]

The French 12th Chasseur à Cheval Regiment, supported by a force of infantry, moved to attack the Prussian battalions. A squadron caught the right flank of a battalion dispersed in skirmish formation and drove it back. Because of the rain, the Prussians were unable to fire their muskets and had little recourse against the cavalry striking them. The Prussians, despite their best efforts, were pushed back to the heights, where the battalions of the second line had formed square.

At the time of this engagement, the Russians reinforced their artillery on the Taubenberg and the Prussians reinforced their battery by the addition of 12pdr Battery #2 and 6pdr Battery #12.

The four battalions of the advanced guard stood in a line to the rear of these batteries, having the 7th Brigade to their right and its cavalry extending to the extreme right. The reserve cavalry stood behind them and the 2nd Brigade formed the last echelon.

During the attack of the 8th Brigade, the 7th and 2nd Brigades had stood stationary. The 7th Brigade formed the first line and the 2nd Brigade stood behind them. When they finally advanced, the infantry of the advanced guard and the reserve cavalry passed through the artillery line, which had been reinforced by three horse batteries.[40]

The advanced guard placed a battalion on the left flank of the 7th Brigade and two were left to support the artillery. A regiment was also positioned to form a link with Sacken's Corps as well as to link the 7th and 2nd Brigades. The Reserve Cavalry did not pass through the artillery line with the advanced guard. However, Oberst Jürgass now believed that the moment for it to charge was at hand. He organized his cavalry as it stood, placing four squadrons in the first rank, the left three squadrons echeloned forward.[41] These three squadrons did move forward to engage the

French passing out of the defiles in an effort to support the 8th Brigade. They struck two French chasseur squadrons and drove them back.[42] It is also reported that a French battery was overrun and four guns were taken.

The French, having received reinforcements, organized Wathiez's 10th Light Cavalry Brigade on the plateau. It had passed through the defile in a column of squadrons with Maurin's 9th Light Cavalry Brigade behind it. Exelman's 4th Light Cavalry Division, however, had encountered considerable difficulty in attempting to pass through the defile. In an effort to slow the progress of the Russian columns menacing the French left towards Eichholz, General Roussel established a second line facing that village. At the same time, the head of the 8th Division column began to reach the top of the plateau.

The 8th Division appeared on the road from Schmmelwitz by Schmochwitz. Commanded by Brayer, it was supported by the 10th Hussar Regiment and the Baden Dragoon Regiment. Sebastian called the 8th Division to his assistance. The 1st Brigade, formerly under General Brayer,[43] supported the cavalry, while the 2nd brigade remained behind, to the left of the ravine. They advanced in a vigorous attack, attempting to seize the initiative for the French.

The 1st Brigade, 8th Division, quickly formed itself into battalion masses. One of them, the 4/34th Line Regiment, fired on the attacking Prussian cavalry and the park. It had rained all morning and the musketry was not very effective. Perhaps one sixth of the muskets discharged properly. However, the cavalry was not in an advantageous position and the 4/34th Line charged them with bayonets and recaptured the park.[44]

GD Sebastian ordered the 1st Brigade, 8th Division, to move forward to support his cavalry. Though less than 100 of their muskets were in a condition to fire, they advanced resolutely onto the battlefield. Isolated and denuded of artillery, they stood on the edge of a vast plain filled with Prussian and Russian cavalry. The 1st Brigade was subjected to repeated attacks, but held firm.

The 2nd Brigade, motivated by the spectacular efforts of the 1st Brigade, sent forward a battalion to hold the defile and prevent any further passage of allied cavalry on that flank. The remainder of the brigade marched forward to cover the rallying of Sébastiani's cavalry. The cavalry was pushed back to 40–50 paces from the 1st Brigade, but the weather prevented the French muskets from providing any assistance to them.

The 7th Brigade and its advanced troops lay quietly behind the heights by Christianshöhe, watching the 8th Brigade fight. Before they could intervene, however, Major Brandenburg arrived and announced the success of the attack of the 8th Brigade. Oberst von Jürgass, with the Cavalry Reserve, advanced. It was about 3:00 p.m. He advanced with the 1st East Prussian Dragoons and 3/, 4/Lithuanian Dragoons in his first line.[45] In echelon to his left were the 1/, 2/Lithuanian Dragoons and a detachment of the East Prussian National Cavalry Regiment. Oberstleutnant von Below led the first wave and Oberstleutnant von Platen led the second. The infantry of the 7th Brigade followed in his wake.

Behind them followed the 1st Neumärk Landwehr Cavalry Regiment and the Brandenburg Uhlan Regiment. The 3/, 4/Brandenburg Hussars from the 8th Brigade later had the occasion to strike at the French as well. The Prussian cavalry passed in column between the woods and the right of Charpentier's infantry to attack Wathiez's brigade.

The East Prussian National Cavalry Regiment struck at the head of a French column, the 4/34th Line Regiment, coming out of the Weinberg defile. The 4/34th Line fired and a few squadrons of Wathiez's Chasseurs à Cheval counterattacked. The French drove the East Prussian National Cavalry Regiment, back and succeeded in deploying. Behind the French cavalry, an infantry column appeared, but so too did the 1st West Prussian and Lithuanian Dragoons with some artillery.

The French were pushed back again, and the Prussians temporarily overran four batteries of French artillery before the remainder of Wathiez's 10th Light Cavalry Brigade appeared and drove

The East Prussian National Cavalry Regiment during the Battle of the Katzbach, by Knötel.

them back. Wathiez's cavalry drove forward and obliged the left of the Prussian artillery to withdraw, abandoning nine guns. The 23rd and 24th Chasseurs and the 11th Hussars, who executed this charge, captured 200 prisoners.

Soon more and more French infantry began to appear. Three battalions were pushed to the left and sought to move against the Prussian cavalry's flank. All the while, a continuous stream of French light cavalry flowed onto the battlefield.

Wathiez's cavalry, supported by its own artillery, was taken under fire by half of Horse Battery #1, but charged against Major Hiller's infantry and the artillery on the heights. The 1/Brandenburg Infantry Regiment and Thüringian Battalion, though covered by artillery fire, were heavily attacked. Despite the force of the French attack, they stood firm. As the two Prussian battalions were under attack, the Brandenburg Uhlans, Brandenburg Hussars and a Russian hussar regiment struck the French cavalry, driving it back.[46]

As this occurred, however, the rest of Exelmans' 4th Light Cavalry Division arrived on the plateau and deployed in three lines facing Brechtelshof. The regimental history the Brandenburg Uhlan Regiment describes this process.

As Oberst Katzeler observed the withdrawal of the reserve cavalry, about 6:00 p.m., he brought his regiment immediately to the attack, simultaneously with his attack the Russian Achtyrsche Hussar Regiment, which stood in some distance to the right of the uhlans, also attacked. The regiment went ahead in line. As it came to the gallop, it extended its line and made a "half right" turn to more directly oppose the French. A regiment of French Chasseurs faced the uhlans and had a small ditch approximately on thirty paces in front of them. As the uhlans leaped over the ditch the French chasseurs greeted them with a volley of carbine fire.

"However in the same moment" – according to an eye witness account, "we also struck them with our lances in the back."

As they saw that neither the ditch nor their fire stopped our attack, they immediately turned about and fled. The allied loss was insignificant. It would have been greater, if they had engaged us with their sabers instead of firing a volley.

Rittemeister von Stülpnagel was with the 4th Squadron which attacked the French elite squadron of the chasseurs regiment. The French squadron commander stood before his squadron and called a challenge to us in German, 'Now come here!' At this Stülpnagel gave his horse the spurs, raised his saber and responded: 'Wait a moment, I'm coming!' However, at this moment the French officer, found his men withdrawing from behind him, turned himself and withdrew before his adversaries could reach him.[47]

Slowly another brigade of the III Corps moved from Liegnitz, cleared the defiles, and arrived in Nieder-Crayn. It moved onto the Jänowitz plateau with a 12pdr battery, where it was slowly joined by Souham's corps cavalry, which took up a position behind its left. St. Germain's 3rd Cuirassier Division moved into Kroitsch, but did not take part in the action.[48]

After this charge, Exelmans formed his division in three lines facing Bellewitzhof. The allies returned with and attacked Wathiez with 30 squadrons, and Roussel with another 40 squadrons. A further 20 allied squadrons appeared by Gross-Jänowitz, and the French cavalry found itself being attacked from three sides.

The left wing echelon of the Prussian Reserve Cavalry, which consisted of three squadrons, advanced against a French battery protected by two chasseur squadrons and stood on the road to Ober-Weinberg. The French horsemen were thrown back by their attack. The battery swung around and tried to withdraw down the narrow road, but overturned and blocked the road entirely. The Prussian horsemen then encountered three French battalions, which were deployed on the Kuhberg. However the French musketry was too severe and the Prussian cavalry was forced back behind the shelter of its own infantry.

The allies supported this attack with their infantry. The Russians marched against the square formed by the 14th Légère Regiment and engaged it in a bayonet fight. The 14th Légère succeeded in fighting off both the cavalry and the Russian infantry.[49]

The allies were repulsed twice, but at 6:15 p.m., more than 12,000 line cavalry and 2,000 to 3,000 infantry attacked, driving the French back.[50]

Sacken's Arrival

As Exelman's division arrived on the field, Sacken's infantry arrived in Eichholz. General Vassil'shikov ordered General Lanskoy[51] to fall on the left flank of French XI Corps who stood before Klein-Tinz, with Eichholz on their left. General Karpov was to move against their rear from Klein-Tinz with his Cossacks. GM Jurovich was to charge them frontally with Landskoy's other brigade.[52] Neverovsky's 27th Division was to support the attack and it was to be replaced in Sacken's front line by Lieven's 10th Division.[53]

Yorck's Corps

The French countered after the first Prussian cavalry attack and launched their own cavalry against the flank of the 8th Brigade, though without success. The allied Reserve Cavalry was then ordered forward to defend the infantry of the 8th Brigade. It had completed rallying behind the 2nd

Brigade after its earlier, failed attacks. It was reinforced by the arrival of the 5th and 10th Silesian Landwehr Cavalry and the 1st Neumärk Landwehr Cavalry. It moved out between the 8th and the 7th Brigade. Prinz Karl von Mecklenburg then advanced with four battalions of his 2nd Brigade straight ahead to support the cavalry attack. Four more battalions, under Oberstleutnant von Lobenthal, moved to the left to cover the left flank of the attack.

The French XI Corps had supported its right on Weinberg, but its left hung in the air. Blücher profited from this by attacking that open flank with Sacken's cavalry and part of Yorck's under the command of Oberst von Jürgass. With the French stopped to face this attack, Yorck deployed himself between Weinberg and Tribelwitz.

The French II Cavalry Corps was attacked on three sides by superior forces. The II Cavalry Corps did not receive any real support from the supporting French infantry. Though GD Gérard observed the allied cavalry moving on his left and profited from it by firing on their rear, the rain, which continued to fall, had ruined many powder charges and only one musket in four fired. Only his artillery, whose powder was in prepared charges, was not hurt by the rain, and poured shot and canister into the allied cavalry.

Brayer's position was very difficult. His left was uncovered and his right was being pounded by fifteen guns. Two strong columns of Prussian infantry and a dozen guns advanced against his front. He organized his old brigade on the crest of a hill and attempted to cover the retreat of the II Cavalry Corps, but the two Prussian columns continued closing. When they were within musketry range, his forces received several rounds of canister. According to Prussian sources, this fire drove his shattered forces off the plateau. However, Souham stated that the withdrawal was quite orderly. Gérard's report repeats that the withdrawal was done in good order.[54]

Sébastiani, despite his efforts, was unable to resist the Prussians and withdrew. What remained of Charpentier's infantry on the ridge, found itself obliged to withdraw, once its flank was uncovered. It pulled back across the woods and the ravine by Ober-Crayn and reorganized itself on the nearby hills, where a division of Souham's Corps had positioned itself.

The French were trapped up against the Wuthende-Neisse and the Katzbach Rivers. They had become quite deep, with strong currents, and were difficult to cross other than at bridges.

A Prussian period report describes the movement of the French towards the bridges most vividly.

> The (French) enemy fled. It was every man for himself. As the fleeing crowd of French arrived at the cliff, which contained the angry Neisse, a terrible confusion arose in the narrow road. The horsemen rode down infantrymen. In response the infantry used their bayonets against the horses to open space for themselves. Then a column of guns and munition wagons entered the roadway at a gallop, crashing into the crowd and forming an impenetrable tangle. With terrible cries those in the rear called on those in front to move out of the way. Wheels collapsed, horses panicked, guns drove into each other, and orderly movement, if it had ever existed, ceased. In a second road down the slopes horsemen and train soldiers with and without guns raced down the hill side. The infantrymen climbed down the cliffs and over the fences of Nieder-Weinberg, because it was faster than using the roads. The sound of a single allied "Hurrah!" would rouse the crushing crowd horrible cries of panic.
>
> The fields were filled with wounded and dead soldiers and horses, littered with cast off muskets, shakos, knapsacks and bullet pouches. Here and there lay overturned carts and abandoned guns. Whole housefuls of fleeing infantrymen were taken prisoner by individual horsemen. The confusion in the narrow valley road was an impassable tangle of wagons, horses, and corpses. In one of the roads the allies found 4 guns, 2 howitzers and 39 caissons. That part of the French rout which could not pass over the Niesse at Nieder-Crayn, fled further downstream through Gross-Jänowitz.

Yorck was quick to take advantage of the panic and advanced Horse Battery #12, the howitzers from 12pdr Battery #2 and a Russian 12pdr Battery, to fire into the mass of trapped Frenchmen. Two French battalions attempted to take a stand on the heights by Weinberg, to cover the French withdrawal across the flooded Wuthende-Neisse, but Prince Karl von Mecklenburg led forward the 1/1st and 1/, 2/2nd East Prussian Regiments from Nieder-Crayn, driving them back and bringing the battle to an end.

The defile remained clogged with the equipment of the II Cavalry Corps, and this prevented any of the equipment that the French had taken up onto the plateau from escaping. As a result, the artillery assigned to Meunier's brigade and the 12pdr battery that had moved onto the plateau were lost.

A part of the French army passed through the defile by Dohnau. Sacken's corps advanced to Schweinitz and put its batteries on the edge of the Katzbach valley. The 1/, 2/Brandenburg Regiment and the 2nd Leib Hussar Regiment pushed into Nieder-Crayn, but stopped there as night fell.[55]

Other French Forces

Around 5:00 p.m. the remaining divisions of the III Corps arrived on the battlefield. Delmas' 9th Division arrived with orders to cross by Kroitsch and Dohnau. However, he chose to withdraw towards Kroitsch, when he saw the overwhelming allied forces facing him. Albert and Ricard (10th and 11th Divisions) crossed by Schmochwitz. They quickly encountered Sacken's corps. Ricard learned of the disaster that had struck the French middle, and withdrew both divisions back through Schmochwitz to the left bank of the Katzbach.

The Attack on Langeron

On the left bank of the Wuthende-Neisse, Langeron fought on against the French V Corps and its supporting cavalry.

About 7:00 a.m., the V Corps began to move out. Its scouts encountered a line of Cossacks in the village of Seichau and chased them out. Around 1:00 p.m., Rochambeau's 19th Division deployed before the Plinse ravine and Maison's 16th Division deployed to the south. Around 2:00 p.m., Lauriston began by an attack across the ravine. He placed a foot battery of six 12pdrs cannons and two 6 inch howitzers to support his advance. This battery's fire took the Russian's forces with oblique fire. Other batteries were deployed to support the attack.

About 13:00 p.m., Maison advanced several columns of infantry against General Rudsevich. Two battalions and two guns occupied the forest by the Buschmühle mill. This threatened the advanced positions of Langeron's corps, so he ordered Rudsevich to withdraw with the left wing of the corps, back to a position by Hennersdorf. General Pahlen II was ordered back to Conradswalde to cover the road to Jauer.

Successively, the greater part of the XI Corps deployed to the left of Rochambeau's division on Macdonald's orders. Gérard overran Hennersdorf and occupied the Steinberg. The Russian 32nd and 28th Jager Regiments withdrew behind the stream by Schlaupe. The 10th, 12th and 38th Jagers formed a second line behind Weinberg.[56]

The French advanced over the Plinse stream and marched forward in line. The attack had problems from the beginning. To the right, Maison's 16th Division had great problems attempting to push through the defiles.

Because of the force and direction of the French attack, Langeron sent the entire Russian 10th Corps to Peterwitz and gave General Kapzevich orders to move to Moysdorf. The 10th Corps stood in column behind Langeron's left flank.

About 2:30 p.m., Maison directed two columns against the Russian left and towards the origin of the Plinse stream, so as to fall on the enemy line and a third column marched on Hermannsdorf.

General de Witt threw back the column attacking Hermannsdorf with the 4th Ukrainian Cossacks. The other two columns were stopped by General Emanuel and Colonel Paradovski with the Kiev Dragoon Regiment and the Lithuanian Chasseur à Cheval Regiment.[57] At this time the French had passed to the right bank of the Wuthende-Neisse, as Langeron's center, was struck by the heaviest French assault, Maison's entire 16th Division plus a brigade of Rochambeau's 19th Division. A grand battery was organized between Seichau and Hennersdorf, containing 40 guns. It pounded the Russian center. Perhaps this was a diversion against Langeron, as the French moved to disengage their left flank. It was 4:00 p.m.; Lauriston sent all his reserves forward against Hennersdorf and Steinberg, between Dorfe and Schlaupe.

Under the support of the heavy artillery, Gérard advanced and captured Weinberg. Unfortunately the same did not occur on the far right, where Lauriston's troops failed to capture Buschhauser. Without the support of Lauriston's troops, Gérard was obliged to halt his advance.

It was 5:00 p.m., and Macdonald found himself on the spot. On the left, his forces were beaten and Macdonald had just learned of their disaster. His center has been thrown back, though the Prussians were not pressing their advantage and the III Corps was just arriving, night was beginning to fall. His right was still gaining ground. However, his left was being shattered by a superior cavalry and the weather would negate his infantry, leaving his inferior cavalry to face the more numerous allied cavalry.

While Macdonald evaluated the situation, Lauriston directed more heavy batteries to the heights by Hennersdorf and attempted to silence the Russian artillery. Under the cover of their heavy fire, the French sent their attack columns forward from Hennersdorf. From their vantage point on the Hennersdorf Heights, the French artillery overlooked the entire Russian line.

General Langeron ordered GL Alsusiev to retake the heights. The Nacheburg, Riajsk, and Iakout Infantry Regiments went forward under the orders of General Udom. The heights were stormed and the French were driven back from the position, into Hennersdorf. However, by this time it was a fighting withdrawal, as Macdonald had already decided to cede the field to the allies.

The Russian 7th and 18th Divisions, under Generals Tallisin and Bernodossov, were ordered forward, but a French battery kept them at bay. The 28th and 32nd Jager Regiments, under General Mescherinov, then moved to attack the French from the ridge to the right of Hennersdorf. Once they cleared the ridge, Count Scherbatov moved his artillery, under Lt. Colonel Nesterovsky, to the ridge to fire on the French battery's flank, raking it.

At this time, the 1st Prussian Brigade moved to support General Langeron at Schlaupe. Oberst von Steinmetz, who led this brigade, had seen the force of their attack on the Russian center and moved to support them. He moved to the left, to cross over the Wuthende-Neisse by Schlaupe, and take the French V Corps in the flank and rear. He sent four battalions to Schlauphof, three battalions to Schlaupe, and sent the Leib-Grenadier Battalion and the Rekowsky Landwehr Battalion (3/13th Silesian) to wade the Neisse below Schlaupe, where an artillery battery, covered by the East Prussian Grenadier Battalion, stood. This battery, with its fire, covered their passage and held the French cavalry at arm's length. With the passage of these troops over the Neisse, the battle on the left flank was over.

After the Battle

During the night, Macdonald withdrew the III and XI Corps back across the Katzbach, abandoning to the Prussians nearly the entire park and baggage of the XI Corps.

The retreat of the French army after the Battle of the Katzbach, 26 August, by Knötel.

To the south, Lauriston had attacked Langeron and obliged him to withdraw. But when he learned of the actions on the Jänowitz plateau, he withdrew back towards Goldberg via Prausnitz, where he bivouacked his troops in the ongoing rain.

During the morning of the 27th, Lauriston found himself attacked by Langeron, as he effected his withdrawal, and lost a number of guns to the allies. The state of the roads did not allow him to drag them with him.

That evening Langeron entered Goldberg and Lauriston arrived in Löwenberg. During the evening Souham (III Corps) and Gérard (XI Corps) arrived in Buntzlau. The V Corps had attempted to cross the Bober at Löwenberg, but the bridge approaches were flooded, forcing Lauriston to move to Buntzlau, where he crossed on the 28th, re-joining the III and XI Corps.

The III Corps, which had suffered the least in the engagement, covered Macdonald's retreat and on 4 September, Macdonald's forces found themselves near the battlefield at Bautzen. The rearguard was in Görlitz.

Results of the Battle

The Battle of Katzbach cost the French 10,000 men, including Puthod's 17th Division.[58] A further 9,000 to 10,000 men quietly deserted after this disaster, reducing Macdonald's forces to around 50,000 men, from the 70,000 he had led to the Katzbach. A total of 30 cannons were lost as well.[59]

The allies reported capturing 36 cannons, 110 caissons, 2 medicine wagons, 4 field forges, and between 1,200 and 1,400 prisoners.[60]

The battle won for Blücher the title of prince. It also won for him the laurels of the victor and it gave a significant victory for the allies. His handling of the battle was not without its flaws, but victory on the battlefield shrinks all other faults. His most significant fault was his failure to use

Blücher and Gneisenau on the night after the Katzbach, by Rocholl.

his still significant superiority in cavalry, to more thoroughly scout out the French positions, and take advantage of the French movements. The direct result of this failure was his blundering into the French, and finding himself in an unplanned meeting engagement.

As for Macdonald, he failed to maintain the impetus of Napoleon's advance, allowing Blücher time to stop, regroup and turn back to the offensive. He failed a second time by assuming that the allies would remain stationary on 24 August, while he dawdled slowly forward. His orders redirecting the III Corps once the engagement began, cost him half of his army and probably the battle. His staff failed him, by not allowing Sébastiani to clear the defiles first, and then send the III Corps through after the cavalry was clear of the defiles. Finally, on the tactical level, he blundered by not finding a better position from which to defend himself against the superior numbers of allied cavalry. Leaving his left flank hanging in the air, invited a cavalry attack and Blücher graciously obliged him. The impact of the rain is not something that can be overlooked, but such acts of God fall on both sides. Had the allies not had such superiority in cavalry, the battle would probably have reduced itself to an angry cannonade with a few bayonet charges. But the allied cavalry was present in overwhelming numbers and quite able take advantage of the embarrassment of the French infantry.

5

Macdonald's Flanking Corps: The Battle of Löwenberg 22 August-4 September 1813

Marchand's Actions

On the extreme left of the French army, Marchand's 39th Division left the 1/Hessian Leib Regiment in Haynau and moved the rest of his division towards Liegnitz, stopping in Waldau. The 2/Hessian Guard Regiment was detached to Liegnitz. Then, for a reason that remains unknown, Marchand withdrew his entire division towards Haynau. It was impossible that he was aware of Macdonald's defeat, but may have learned that Falkenhausen's partisans had been joined by 300–400 Cossacks, under the command of Colonel Nachmanov, that had been detached from Sacken's Corps.[1]

On 22 August, Falkenhausen had attempted to seize Waldau, capturing four officers and a few men in Waldau's castle. In the following days his partisans had moved along the left flank of the French army. On 23 August, they came close to capturing General Marchand and his staff, as they stood between two parts of his division.

During the night of 26 August, Falkenhausen moved around Thomaswalde and appeared before Haynau, where it summoned the 1/Hessian Guard to surrender. Its commanding officer, Prince Wittgenstein, refused and prepared the city for the assault. His response convinced Falkenhausen that an attack would not be wise, and he withdrew when the 39th Division appeared.

That night Prince Madatov's partisans joined those of Falkenhausen and Nachmanov. They continued to operate in the area between Liegnitz and Haynau, harassing the 39th Division.

The French Withdrawal

On the 27th, the V Corps moved through Goldberg. General Langeron sent his advanced troops after them, collecting the spoils of war that littered their line of withdrawal. General Rudsevich sent General Grekov with his Cossacks through Prausnitz and sent General Emanuel down the main road. By Pilgramsdorf, Emanuel encountered the French rearguard and a quick skirmish with the disheartened French yielded six guns and 1,200 prisoners. General Grekov captured five cannon and 700 prisoners near Prausnitz.

Another French column of 1,500 men was encountered near Wolfsberg. It was Colonel Morin with two battalions of the 150th Line Infantry.[2] General Grekov, using three Cossack regiments cut their withdrawal, while GL Kapzevich, with the Russian 10th Corps, advanced with two light field guns. The French column was taken, with Colonel Morin, 30 officers, and 950 men being captured.[3]

The pursuit by the 1st Prussian Army Corps was led by the 7th Brigade. Yorck ordered it to cross the Katzbach at 2:00 a.m., at Kroitsch. They crossed in dense columns in total silence. No soldier was permitted to smoke. The battalions moved with sufficient interval so that they would not crowd one another or transmit disorder from one battalion to another. If they encountered the French, they were to attack with bayonets, without firing.[4]

Oberst von Katzeler followed the infantry with his advanced guard consisting of 12 squadrons and Horse Battery #2, von Borowsky. They moved through Kroitsch, finding it clogged with wagons and various other abandoned equipment. On the far side of the village, they encountered a force of French cavalry supported by three horse guns. After an exchange of shots, the French withdrew. In Röchlitz, the 2nd Leib Hussar Regiment captured a colonel, 19 officers, and 500 men.

For the rest of the day, Langeron moved into and remained in Goldberg. General Sacken advanced into Liegnitz and the Prussian middle moved over the Katzbach. General Rudsevich occupied Pilgramsdorf and Lauterseiffen.

GM von Horn marched towards Haynau with Sacken's advanced forces. Oberst von Katzeler drove the French from Kreibau, through the Thomaswalda forest, to the Little Bober and bivouacked in Königshayn. The 2nd Leib Hussar Regiment occupied Adelsdorf, where they captured six guns, but had to drive out a small force of Polish uhlans and about 150 infantry holding the villages.

The Death of Puthod's Division

Macdonald had detached Puthod's and Ledru's Divisions (17th and 31st) to attack an allied force in Hirschberg on 26 August. Ledru had learned of Macdonald's defeat, as he advanced down the left bank of the Bober, and withdrew without difficulty, but Puthod's fate was very different.

On 26 August, Puthod stopped for the evening in Alt-Schönau, after chasing out a few squadrons of allied cavalry. His forces had marched all day in the torrential rain. When they crossed the stream at Falkenhayn, they had waded in the water up to their waist. His division was fatigued. Two companies of voltigeurs and 50 Chasseurs à Cheval from the 6th Regiment occupied the village. A company of voltigeurs from the 146th Line Regiment and a detachment of the 134th Line Regiment departed at 4:00 a.m., on the 27th for Hirschberg.

Puthod learned of Macdonald's defeat when he arrived at Mochau, one third of the way to Hirschberg, and found himself isolated. Still, conforming to orders, he sent the 147th and 148th Regiments towards Jauer, and the 134th and 146th Infantry Regiments and 3rd Foreign Regiment,[5] which were in Lähn, moved towards Hirschberg, in order to contact Ledru's 31st Division, XI Corps.[6] He continued on towards Hirschberg more in hopes of finding the bridge intact, rather than advancing up the Bober, into the waiting arms of Blücher's victorious army. When Puthod arrived at Hirschberg he found the bridge destroyed and the ford defended. He chose to move back down the Bober in an effort to find another ford.

On the morning of 29 August, at 7:00 a.m., Puthod began to move out of Höfel. He observed some allied cavalry supported by some infantry that stood by a ravine. It moved to the right of Plagwitz. Puthod detached two companies of the 147th Line and the 1/148th Line Regiment to flank the allied forces. The allies occupied the village of Plagwitz, but the French drove them out. They were the cavalry of General Jusseffovicz, part of Langeron's Corps.

Puthod realized he was about to be trapped and decided to cut a path through them towards Buntzlau. Unfortunately, it was too late and his path was blocked at the Euftenberg heights. He quickly found his tiny division completely encircled and trapped against the flooded Bober River. He moved his division to the best defensive position he could find, the Plagwitz heights before Löwenberg, and awaited his fate.

Puthod arranged his force with the 146th Line supported by the 2/, 3/148th Line and five guns on his left. Two companies of voltigeurs and the 3rd Foreign Regiment were sent to Plagwitz and

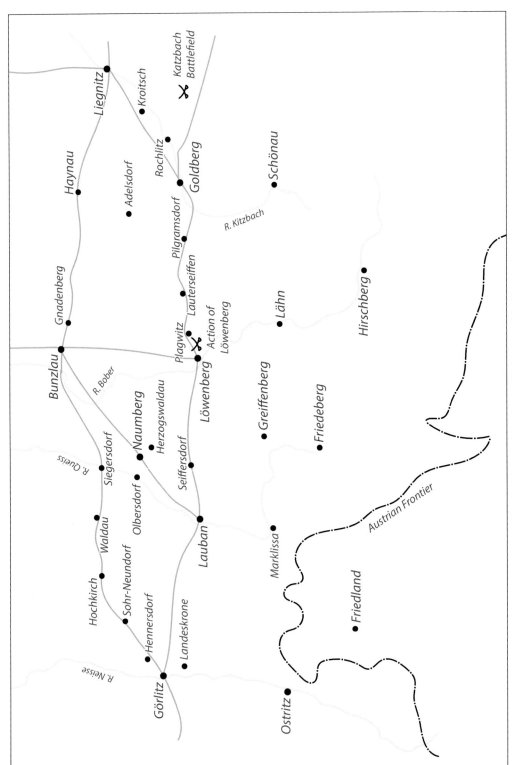

Sketch Map 7 The Area of Macdonald's Retreat.

told to defend it to the death. A battalion of the 147th Line occupied the center, while the two others were formed in square on the center of the ridge to act as a reserve.[7]

The allies swarmed forward, attacking him with three infantry divisions and a large force of cavalry. Count Scherbatov brought forward part of his artillery, six guns of Light Battery #34, to pound Puthod's division. Oberst Dietrichs advanced with the 11th and 36th Jager Regiments (7th Division), while General Mescherinov led the 28th and 32nd Jagers (18th Division) up a gully in a two pronged bayonet attack. Korff's cavalry supported the attack. Count Scherbatov led the attack of these two brigades in person. GM Rudsevich brought the 15th Division around to Puthod's flank so as to close the ring around him.[8]

The 146th Line, charged with the defense of the left, held as long as possible, but eventually had to abandon its position and the battery. Puthod threw himself twice into the mass of fugitives and rallied them, leading them back to attack the advancing allies.

The 147th and 148th Line Regiments were also pushed back. The 134th was struck by Rudsevich's 15th Division and overrun.

Puthod's valiant division fought until its ammunition was expended. Unable to resist further it was crushed and its survivors fled into the swollen Bober. General Puthod and his brigadiers were taken prisoner and his division was completely destroyed. Only a few hundred men survived and escaped the allied attack.

The allied records indicate that of the 11,800 men in the division, 100 officers, 4,000 men and 16 cannon were taken. The captured officers included General Puthod and 13 battalion commanders.[9] On a more emotional level, the French lost the eagles of the 134th, 146th, and 148th Line Regiments. Lieutenant Kalinin and Fähnrich Bogdanov of the 28th Jager Regiment are given credit for taking eagles of the 146th and 148th Line Regiments, respectively.

The 134th and 147th Regiments and the 3rd Foreign Regiment were thrown back into the Bober. General Sibuet drowned trying to swim the Bober, but about 400 men did escape. On 7 September, Berthier wrote to the Minister of War, the Duc de Feltre, advising him that the 9 officers and 30 non-commissioned officers and soldiers of the 3rd Foreign Regiment that escaped from Löwenberg would be returning to their depot in Bois-le-Duc.[10]

Maréchal Berthier, by Pajou.

The Allied Advance Continues Westward

As Puthod's 17th Division died, General St. Priest assumed command of Pahlen's Corps and Pahlen I was dispatched to the Army of Bohemia. St. Priest drew his forces through Schmiedeberg and Hirschberg moving towards Greiffenberg, where his advanced guard, under General Bistram, had a small skirmish with the French on 30 August.

GM von Horn advanced on the 29th in union with Sacken's advanced guard, commanded by GL Vassil'shikov, in the direction of Gnadenberg. Gnadenberg was occupied by the French and it formed part of their line extending from Loschwitz to Neu-Schonefeld that defended Buntzlau. General von Horn left two battalions in Haynau and one in Thomaswalda as garrisons, which weakened his infantry force.[11]

Despite that, he continued his march on Buntzlau. On the following day he was joined by Oberst von Katzeler with the Brandenburg Uhlans and Borowsky Horse Battery #2, on the left of the city, on the Eckersdorf Heights. Leading his force were the freiwilligerjägers of the Leib Regiment, the skirmishers of the Fus/Leib Infantry Regiment, a Russian 12pdr battery, and 3 Russian jager battalions.

The Skirmish at Buntzlau

The attack down the main road was to be executed by the Fus/Leib Infantry Regiment and the Sommerfeld Landwehr Battalion (1/15th Silesian) under Oberst von Katzeler. The Leib Infantry Regiment, the remaining four landwehr battalions, Ziegler's 6pdr Foot Battery #3, and the cavalry remained in reserve.[12]

Oberst von Katzeler moved quickly from Kesselberg. His forces descended from the heights and encountered the French skirmishers moving across the bridge and a French brigade formed in mass on his side of the bridge. Buntzlau was abandoned by the French without a fight. Lieutenant von Uklansky, with the jägers of the Leib Regiment, and Captain von Zastrow, with the skirmishers, moved down the mill run, where they encountered a French battalion covering the French retreat. The skirmishers took this force in the flank, forcing them back across the bridge.

The French quickly abandoned their post and set a small magazine afire, as well the small bridge. The skirmishers and jägers moved across a larger bridge on the Bober and quickly extinguished the fire. Oberst von Katzeler then sent his uhlans across the bridge and into the city.[13]

General Souham ordered the 11th Division to retake the bridge, as it was the only point on the Bober where passage was possible. General Ricard stopped his division and advanced with the 50th Line Regiment to throw back the Prussian skirmishers. The skirmishers fell back, the bridge was set afire, and the 50th Line held its position.[14]

The Russian artillery on the heights fired on the French. The Fus/Leib Regiment, the Sommerfeld (1/15th Silesian) and Reichenbach (3/4th Silesian) Landwehr Battalions, and the 4th Company, Guard Jäger Battalion, under Captain Neuhaus, moved forward in an effort to seize the bridge and extinguish the flames. General von Horn sent Captain von Ziegler with two guns from 6pdr Foot Battery #3 to assist. The Sommerfeld (1/15th Silesian) Landwehr Battalion then moved up the stream to observe a small bridge towards Nieder-Mühle.

Horn continued to feed combatants into the battle. He sent forward 1/, 2/Leib Regiment and some artillery. Lieutenant Milewsky, with a cannon and a howitzer, moved to the bridge to engage the French. The French artillery fire quickly dismounted

Souham.

the howitzer and wounded Milewsky. A second lieutenant with another cannon was sent forward. In short order he too was lost, as were two guns.

The Sommerfeld (1/15th Silesian) Landwehr Battalion found its ammunition useless and was replaced by a battalion of the Leib Regiment. The 7th and 8th Companies, Leib Regiment, moved across the main bridge into the battle there, while the 5th and 6th Companies moved to the left into houses on the Bober. The Pottinghofer (2/15th Silesian Regiment) and Wedell (4/15th Silesian) Landwehr Battalions remained in reserve.

About 10:30 a.m., as the battle continued, Sacken's corps appeared, and a large force of Cossacks was sent across the Bober. General von Horn then sent the Courbiere and Knorr Landwehr Battalions (1/, 4/4th Silesian Landwehr Regiment), with the skirmishers from the Leib Regiment, against Tillendorf. The Fus/Leib Regiment was pulled back as a reserve, its ammunition being expended.[15]

Learning of the steady increase in allied forces, Macdonald diverted the III Corps, ordered the 11th Division to turn and face the river, the 8th Division placed itself by the woods before Buntzlau to support the 11th Division, the 9th Division assumed a position straddling the routes to Löwenberg and Görlitz, and the 10th Division continued on towards Siegersdorf, escorting the grand park.[16]

After two hours of combat, the French 11th Division drove back the Cossacks, advanced against the village of Tillendorf, overwhelmed the infantry posted there, and recaptured the bridge. Two voltigeur companies engaged in a lively firefight with the Prussian skirmishers. As they advanced, pushing back the Prussians, they were supported by a French battalion. They arrived at the bridgehead and pushed the Prussians back to the mill. There they began an hour long skirmish fight. However, further progress was impossible because the bridge was in flames and falling apart.

On the Prussian side, the 7th Brigade was running out of ammunition and contented itself with stopping any continued French advance. Then allied reinforcements arrived. General Uschakov advanced the Ochotsk and Kamchakta Regiments (a total of two battalions),[17] to support the Prussian attack on the bridge, and to drive the French from Tillendorf, where they supported two landwehr battalions attempting to reoccupy the village. With this reinforcement, the French found their situation untenable, and withdrew across the Queis, and moved to Naumburg.

Yorck's Advance

In the meantime, on 28 August, General von Yorck crossed over the Neisse and the Katzbach. Only the Reserve Cavalry under Oberst von Jürgass remained on the far side of the Katzbach, by Neudorf on the Gröditzberg Heights. The 1st Brigade remained in Seifersdorf, the 7th Brigade in Ulbersdorf, and the 2nd Brigade with the Reserve Artillery stood in Leissersdorf.

The main headquarters of Blücher were now in Goldberg. The casualties had been heavy in many units and Blücher authorized the merging of two battalions of the 6th Silesian Landwehr Regiment (2nd Brigade) into a single battalion under Major von Fischer. This particular battalion was to remain in Goldberg until 2 September.[18]

On 30 August the Army of Silesia's advanced guard moved before Buntzlau. The 1st Prussian Corps broke into two columns and lagered on the heights before Buntzlau, left of the main road. General Sacken moved in from Haynau and put himself to the right of the main road. That evening Yorck sent a message to Blücher advising him that the French had passed through Buntzlau with the III Corps forming the rearguard. A report later that night from Captain Schwanenfeld, posted near Görlitz, that the commander of Görlitz had closed his gates to the refugees and that "7,000 refugees had passed by the city in chaotic disorder."[19]

General Langeron, who was in Pilgramsdorf, erected two pontoon bridges on the Bober, one in Löwenberg and the other in Dippoldisdorf. His advanced guard, supported by his infantry, moved forward on 31 August. Langeron moved his forces towards Lauban-am-Quies, where he took up position on the Bertelsdorf Heights.

The French Retreat

On 31 August the 10th Division stood by Naumburg, the 9th between Naumburg and Siegersdorf, and the 8th and 11th Divisions stood behind Siegersdorf. Four battalions and a squadron were dispatched to Klitschdorf to destroy the bridge. The 39th Division (Marchand) had moved to the Neisse. The Hessian Guard Fusiliers were in Zadel, the 2nd Hessian Regiment and two guns were in Rothenburg, and the Hessian Leib Regiment garrisoned Görlitz. The 1st (Baden) Brigade moved to Seichwitz and Ostritz to destroy the bridges in those villages as well as to maintain contact with the VIII Corps.[20]

The V Corps moved into Lauban with the 35th and 36th Divisions of the XI Corps and Lageon's Brigade, 31st Division. Lageon's Brigade had abandoned its position in Seifersdorf that morning at 6:00 a.m., The brigades of Fressinet and Macdonald (also 31st Division) left Greiffenberg at 3:30 a.m., and re-joined the corps during the day.

Generals von Yorck and Sacken passed through Buntzlau, over the Bober. Yorck took up positions by the Herzogwalde before the city of Naumburg and Sacken assumed positions by Hermannsdorf. Naumburg was garrisoned by the French and von Yorck sealed it off from communications with the French armies. A small, unimportant skirmish began around the bridge.

Blücher moved his main headquarters to Löwenberg and began to contemplate his next moves. So far he had captured 20,000 men, 105 cannons and 300 caissons.[21]

The VIII Corps

The Poles under Poniatowski had not been engaged during Macdonald's actions on the Bober. The forces opposing it consisted of Neipperg's 2nd (Austrian) Light Division with 3,600 infantry and 2,500 cavalry. Neipperg, doubting a French invasion of Bohemia, decided on 22 August to concentrate his forces on the upper Iser, to menace the French lines of communication and support the army of Silesia.[22]

On 23 August he dispatched part of the Liechtenstein Hussars, three companies of the 1/ Peterswardeiner Grenz and a half horse battery towards Neuschloss. In order to monitor the operations of the Army of Silesia, he placed a post of 90 men in Ober-Polan.

Poniatowski's orders were to watch the mountain defiles to Bohemia. Limited probing actions were executed in order to keep track of the Austrian activities, but no major offensive action was undertaken. The first major occurrence was the evacuation of Reichenberg during the morning of 23 August, when General Bruno (22nd Light Cavalry Brigade) was obliged to withdraw because of the defection of the 2/, 3/1st and 1/, 3/2nd Westphalian Hussar Regiments. His withdrawal was harried by Austrian forces and covered by a small detachment under General Uminski consisting of part of the Krakus Regiment and a few of the 14th Polish Cuirassiers.[23]

Poniatowski sent Bruno 500 men and four guns and ordered him to retake Reichenberg to cover the left of the VIII Corps.

The IV Cavalry Corps moved to the south on a reconnaissance sweep towards Niemes, Hunnerwassser, and Hirschwasser, which revealed that the allies had nearly totally abandoned

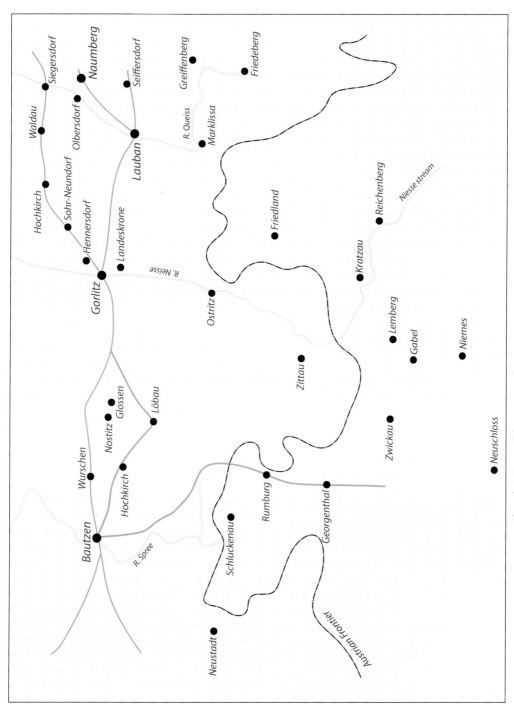

Sketch Map 8 The Region between Bautzen and Naumberg.

Bohemia. On 25 August General Uminski sent two columns towards Reichenberg and reoccupied the city without firing a shot.

Neipperg frequently changed the positions of his small forces to prevent the French from cornering and destroying him, but he did not forsake all aggressive moves either. On 26 August he detached a party of Austrian hussars supported by 60 infantry that attacked and carried the 70-man Polish post at Kratzau. To the south four squadrons of the Liechtenstein hussars, two companies of 1/Peterswardeiner Grenz and a half battery under Oberst Zichy left Neuschloss on 25 August, to make a demonstration the city of Gabel. They established their pickets a league from those of the VIII Corps.[24]

These small movements and attacks by Neipperg disquieted Poniatowski, who sent two companies to retake Kratzau. Zichy's moves obliged him to protect Friedland and Georgenthal from a coup de main. During the night of 26/27 August, Uminski retired from Neisse to Kratzau, and detached 350 men to watch Friedland and Reichenberg.

On 27 August Poniatowski wrote Berthier to advise him that Neipperg had probably received reinforcements in the form of Russian troops. However, the Austrians had made no aggressive moves. He reported his positions as follows: On the right was General Weyssenhoff with a cavalry regiment, nine companies of infantry, and half of a light battery. This force occupied Rohldorf and Rumburg, with an advanced post in Zwickau. The center was under General Sulkowski with three cavalry regiments, three companies of infantry and half a light battery. They were in the entrenched camp at Gabel, as well as occupying Gabel and the posts before Lemberg. In the entrenched camp there were three infantry regiments and three batteries. In Luckendorf were two more infantry regiments and one and a half batteries. The Polish left was under General Uminski with 800 horse, 500 infantry, and half a light battery. He occupied Kratzau, Reichenberg and Pankratz. A reserve was formed under General Sokolnicki with two cavalry regiments and a horse battery. They stood on the right of the road to Gabel.[25]

This movement encouraged Neipperg, whose forces assaulted Gabel in the morning of 28 August, and aroused its garrison of 2,000 infantry and 1,400 cavalry. The Austrians withdrew after destroying what they could.[26]

When Poniatowski learned of Macdonald's defeat, he held his ground, even when he heard that three Russian divisions had appeared near Rumburg. This was, in fact, the 2nd Russian Grenadier Division of GM Tchoglokov, which had been detached to watch the Melnik bridge, not Rumburg. Schwarzenberg had ordered that a corps of landwehr from Moravia and Prague be formed at the Melnik bridge.

Poniatowski understood that he had been ordered to guard the Gabel and Georgenthal mountains and that the French success at Dresden allowed him to act without fear of other consequences. As a result, Poniatowski decided to hold his ground, but moved his forces into Lieckendorf and established the IV Cavalry Corps in Zittau, Lieckendorf and Hirschfeld.

The troops under his command began moving to Rumburg on 1 September, with the goal of reaching it that evening. The IV Cavalry Corps was moving to the Neisse heights to observe the allied movements on Gabel Mountain.[27]

The allies did not act aggressively against Poniatowski on 1 September. The 1st Polish Uhlans engaged a squadron of Russian dragoons on a reconnaissance mission, to determine the location of the VIII Corps. The Poles captured an officer and two men, who informed Poniatowski that they were from Pahlen's brigade, consisting of the Mitau, Kargopol, and Little Russian Dragoons and four regiments of jagers.

Poniatowski was beginning to suspect that he was the object of some major maneuvers and decided on 3 September to move the VIII Corps to Neustädt and to hold the IV Cavalry Corps in Schluckenau. He felt that if Macdonald was to continue his withdrawal, he would be obliged to follow his movement.[28]

During the evening of 4 September, Poniatowski received a letter from Berthier. Berthier had written that Napoleon would be concentrating his forces in the vicinity of Bautzen, and that he expected to give battle. He ordered Poniatowski to hold himself ready to act against the Allied left and to arrive in Bautzen at daybreak.[29] In response to Berthier's orders to move, Poniatowski organized a column of two infantry regiments, a cavalry regiment, and four guns under General Malachowski, and dispatched them to Neusaltza. The VIII Corps and the IV Cavalry Corps were to march united, but would be unable to leave until the morning. The two corps would march with strong forces of cavalry and infantry on their flanks under General Uminski.[30]

Macdonald's Retreat from 1-4 September

Macdonald's forces were not aggressively pursued by the allies. During the day of 31 August, he was followed only by allied cavalry. Nonetheless, he felt it desirable to impose a night march on his troops. The III Corps departed at midnight with Macdonald's park leading the march. They were followed by the reserve battery, Macdonald's equipage, and the 9th and 11th Divisions. The 10th Division marched on the Naumburg-Görlitz road and the 8th Division formed the rearguard. The III Corps arrived in Görlitz around noon, and its passage over the Neisse was covered by the 11th Division. Once across, it organized itself into two lines of squares, by divisions, on the right of the suburbs, towards Ludwigsdorf.[31]

The 11th Division arrived around 10:00 p.m. About 3:00 a.m., the 39th Division departed Görlitz and arrived in Ostritz. The XI and V Corps moved directly to Görlitz, resulting in a concentration of the entire army.

To the south Poniatowski maneuvered to cover Macdonald's right. The VIII Corps moved to Rumburg and Georgenthal. The IV Cavalry Corps continued to watch the Gabel defiles. On 2 September Poniatowski moved to Schluckenau and the IV Cavalry Corps moved to Rumburg and Löbau.

The Allied Pursuit

Blücher had given his army a day of repose, leaving only his cavalry in contact with Macdonald. The advanced guards followed at a respectful distance. At 7:00 a.m., Sacken reported to Blücher that the French were withdrawing on Görlitz and that he no longer had contact with them.[32]

Mandatov's partisans reported that the French were moving in a continuous stream towards Bautzen. He also reported that Poniatowski's VIII Corps was entrenched in Zittau, and that his forces had burned all the bridges on the Neisse below Görlitz.

Karpov's Cossacks resumed the pursuit of the French III Corps and reported that the French were passing through Hennersdorf. GL Vassil'shikov moved his advanced guard to Sohr-Neundorf and held his reserve in Hochkirch. The Brandenburg Uhlans and the 2nd Leib Hussars moved across the Queiss by Naumburg. Three companies of jägers and the Fus/1st East Prussian Regiment crossed, using a bridge. Around 10:00 a.m., a pontoon bridge was in place and Yorck's advanced guard crossed with the 2nd Brigade occupying Olbersdorf.[33]

Oberst von Katzeler caught up with the French rearguard a half a league from Naumburg and at 8:30 a.m., he joined Karpov's forces before Waldau. Despite the increase in his forces, he was unable to inflict much damage on the retreating French.

The pursuit increased its tempo slightly and Macdonald continued his withdrawal. He abandoned the line of the Queiss without resistance, writing to Napoleon that many of his forces were without arms or ammunition, and that he feared they would disband themselves. Lauriston's letters of the same period contradict that, stating that the III Corps and the II Cavalry Corps were in good condition. The XI Corps was also strong, because the 31st Division had re-joined it with 8,000 men. He stated that the 36th Division was in good shape, but that the 35th Division was weakened. Only the V Corps was significantly reduced. It had only 9,831 men present.[34]

Nonetheless, the withdrawal on Bautzen continued. On 2 September Blücher directed his army on Görlitz. Sacken moved down the main road through Siegersdorf, Waldau and Görlitz. Langeron moved down the Lauban-Görlitz road, and Yorck used an intermediary road. To protect themselves against the possibility of the French holding Görlitz, the advanced guards were pushed way ahead to provide adequate warning.

However, during the morning of 2 September, Prince von Liechtenstein arrived at Blücher's headquarters with news of the Battle of Dresden. He also bore an order from Schwarzenberg, ordering Blücher to send 50,000 men to the Army of Bohemia via Theresienstadt. The rest of his army, about 30,000 men, was to join Bubna's Division and take a position on the left flank towards Georgenthal or Zittau.[35]

Needless to say, Blücher was distressed. His triumph was snatched from him and he was to be reduced to a subordinate role. Blücher ordered his forces to stop, and the pursuit of Macdonald ended. Orders were sent out and at 11:30 p.m., Katzeler learned he was to stop. Though he stopped his active pursuit of the French, he continued gathering what intelligence he could.

GL Vassil'shikov received an order at 7:00 a.m., to continue to hold contact with the French. He was to be the commander of all the advanced guards of the three allied corps. Blücher then decided to bring them forward and to establish them before Görlitz. His left wing was to be at Landskrone, the river Schops would be before his front.

Bubna.

Blücher learned, however, that the French had abandoned the river line and decided to press forward. Sacken crossed the Neisse on a pontoon bridge below Görlitz and turned towards Ebersbach. Langeron crossed above Görlitz and Yorck used both bridges. The army moved between Landskrone and Ebersbach that night.

The Skirmishes at Hochkirch and Pitschenberg

Vassil'shikov was informed of the French resuming their withdrawal at 4:30 a.m., and ordered Katzeler to follow the French with two regiments and inflict as much damage on the French as possible, in the defiles before Bautzen.

Katzeler departed with the Brandenburg Uhlans, two squadrons of the Brandenburg Hussars, two squadrons of "black uhlans",[36] and a battery and moved towards Hochkirch. The remainder of his advanced guard and its infantry followed as best they could.[37]

They encountered a force of French skirmishers to the west of Hochkirch, who took the Prussians under fire. Katzeler withdrew his cavalry and sent his jägers, the Fus/1st East Prussian Regiment, and his skirmishers forward to occupy the French, while he waited for orders from Vassil'shikov.

Vassil'shikov was, at that time, moving his advanced guard forward to the west of Würschen. At 8:00 a.m., he judged that his flank was uncovered by the elongation of St. Priest and requested Blücher order him to move forward to watch Rumburg.

In order to cover his left Vassil'shikov ordered Major Hiller to occupy Pitschenberg and to defend the heights. Hiller placed the 1st East Prussian Grenadiers and a few of Barenkampf's guns on the right facing Spikel. In the center he placed three battalions of landwehr and on the left, behind Breitendorf, he placed the 3/12th Reserve Regiment, the Leib Grenadiers, and the remainder of Barenkampf's 6pdr Foot Battery #24. The 10th Silesian Landwehr Regiment covered the extreme left.[38]

Oberst Katzeler was briskly attacked by a force of French, he estimated at 10 battalions, supported by a force of artillery. They threw him out of Hochkirch and he withdrew from the field. He placed his right by Kupritz and his left on the road to Löbau. Even though he brought forward Borowsky's Horse Battery #2 and four howitzers, the French artillery maintained its superiority.

To the north things remained quiet until about noon. About 12:30 p.m., Vassil'shikov reported French forces moving from the left to the right towards Hochkirch. About 1:00 p.m., the head of the Prussian I Corps reached Nostitz and its right established contact with Sacken's Corps.

At the same time, Yorck learned that the French rearguard had received a major reinforcement of infantry and cavalry from Bautzen. Yorck stopped his corps and began drawing it together.

Langeron, on hearing the cannon fire, moved to his advanced guard. He thought he saw about 50,000 men near Bautzen, and that he saw other strong columns coming from Weissenberg. He had no doubt that Napoleon had arrived from Dresden with superior forces.

In fact, Napoleon had arrived in Bautzen at noon, and the tables were about to turn once again.

The Master's Hand

Napoleon called Macdonald and Sébastiani to him and reviewed the actions of the last few days. Once he felt he understood the situation, he turned to his generals and ordered the offensive be resumed in one hour. Murat's cavalry passed on the two sides of Hochkirch with the III Corps on his right. The XI Corps moved against Pitschenberg. The V Corps moved down the road to Löbau. The attack was to begin at 6:00 p.m.

Fearing an attack, Yorck formed his corps with the 2nd Brigade on the right of Stromberg in column. The 8th Brigade stood on the right of the Pitschenberg road. The 1st and 7th Brigades remained in reserve.

The French attack did not surprise Blücher, who had received several hints of its imminent occurrence. Lieutenant Scharnhorst reported at 5:15 p.m. that three enemy columns, each of 3,000 to 4,000 men, were on the heights above Hochkirch, and that one of them was moving on the Hochkirch-Löbau road. He also reported that 5,000 to 6,000 French cavalry were to be seen on both sides of Hochkirch.

Blücher decided to withdraw and ordered Yorck to recross the Löbauer-Wasser. His army began its movement at 10:00 p.m. It was his intention to avoid any serious contact, but if Napoleon moved into Bohemia via Zittau, and left a weak force facing him, Blücher would attack that force and then advance into Bohemia after Napoleon.

The 1st and 7th Brigades moved through Nostitz. The 8th Brigade crossed the ford at Glossen, leaving the Fus/Brandenburg Regiment as a rearguard, while the 2nd Brigade crossed at Maltitz.

The Fall of Pitschenberg

Macdonald directed Gérard's 35th Division on Breitendorf. His attack was supported on the right, by part of the XI Corps that moved on Pitschenberg, and a force of French artillery that took the Prussian batteries located there, under an oblique fire. The Prussian artillery withdrew quickly after a short cannonade, accompanied by their cavalry. The French forces then moved against Pitschenberg from the north. Oberst Hiller, with both his wings turned, abandoned his position after a serious fight. Oberst Katzeler covered his retreat with numerous attacks by the 1st East Prussian Dragoons. Hiller's forces withdrew through Krappe and Glossen. At 10:00 P.m., the entire allied army had returned to the vicinity of Landskrone, after a hard night's march.

The French army followed the withdrawing allies. The V Corps was in Esinroda with Maison's 16th Division in the first line and Rochambeau's 19th Division in the second. The XI Corps had Gérard's 35th Division between Pitschenberg and the V Corps. The 31st and 36th Divisions, plus the 28th Light Cavalry Brigade stood behind Breitendorf. Exelmans 4th Light Cavalry Division was in Sarck, and Sébastiani's II Cavalry Corps was in Lehna.

The III Corps was in the woods before Lauske, and Murat's cavalry was on its left. Behind them the VI Corps was in Bischofswerda.

The fires of the allied army were arrayed before the French along the horizon that night. To the south, General St-Priest marched until 4:00 a.m., when he reached Possewitz. It is understood that he did not receive Blücher's order to withdraw until 8:00 a.m., but the error was quickly corrected.[39]

Poniatowski, who faced St-Priest, had intended to withdraw that day, but received an order from Berthier and decided to wait where he was. Nonetheless, Uminski evacuated Rumburg that day. The remainder of the corps began its movement in the morning and advanced via Kottmarsdorf. The two corps were flanked on their right by a force of cavalry, infantry, and some artillery under the orders of Uminski.

Conclusions

A comparison of the force of Macdonald's army at the beginning of the August campaign and on 1 September provides a very quick indication of what happened to this force.

	15 August Officers	1 September Officers	15 August Men	1 September Men
III Corps	1,499	1,426	37,073	29,348
V Corps	995	443	26,723	10,483
XI Corps	877*	833	22,386*	19,071
II Cavalry Corps	523	483	8,988	6,622

* Figures as 1 August.

The losses of the French army between 15 August and 1 September were about 35,000 men. Nearly 27,000 men were lost in the III Corps, V Corps, and II Cavalry Corps. Indications are that another 6,000 were lost in the XI Corps. These losses were tremendous, but not crushing. They did, however, indicate that the French army was not what it had been in the spring. They speak of a disintegration in the morale of the army, both before the battle and after the disaster at Katzbach. They also reflect the lack of the vigor and aggressiveness that had once been the hallmark of the French general staff.

6

Oudinot's Advance on Berlin: The Prelude to the Battle of Gross-Beeren 20–23 August 1813

To the north of Saxony, Bernadotte commanded an army of about 156,000 men, of whom about 46,000 were on detached duties. These forces consisted of the Swedes under Stedingk, two Russian divisions under Winzingerode and Voronzov, the Prussian corps of Bülow and Tauentzien, and a corps of about 28,000 Germans and British under Wallmoden. Wallmoden's force was placed behind the Mecklenburg canals and its function was to block any movement by Davout, who occupied Hamburg.

At the time the armistice collapsed, 17 August, Bernadotte's Army of the North, except for Wallmoden's force, stood between Berlin and Spandau. Its headquarters were in Charlottenburg.

Facing Bernadotte were Maréchal Oudinot's three army corps and one cavalry corps. The XII Corps, which Oudinot commanded, contained GD Pacthod's 13th Division, GD Guilleminot's 14th Division, and GL Raglovich's 29th (Bavarian) Division. Oudinot was ordered to concentrate the XII Corps around Baruth on 17 August.

The second force under Oudinot, the IV Corps, was commanded by GD Bertrand and consisted of GD Morand's 12th Division, GD Fontanelli's 15th (Italian) Division, and GL Franquemont's 38th (Württemberg) Division. This force was to concentrate at Luckau on 17 August.

Reynier's VII Corps, containing Durutte's 32nd (French) Division and the Saxon 24th and 25th Divisions of Lecoq and von Sahr, also moved towards Luckau. The III Cavalry Corps of Arrighi contained three divisions of cavalry, about 6,000 men and was moving on Dahme for a rendezvous slated for 17 August. From there he was to proceed towards Baruth. In total, Oudinot had about 64,000 men facing 110,000 allies.

The French Plans

Napoleon had ordered Oudinot to move immediately towards Berlin and attempt to take it by 21 or 22 August. He had no time to waste. As he made that movement, a corps under Girard, formed with a single division with 12 battalions of French, Croatians and Germans, under Lanusse, and a smaller division formed with four battalions and eight squadrons of Poles under Dombrowski, was to march from Magdeburg (GD Lanusse) and Wittenberg (GD Dombrowski) directly on Berlin, while Davout also was to leave Hamburg and converge on Berlin, cutting the lines of communication between Berlin and Stettin. Once these forces had taken Berlin, Davout was to take overall command of all the forces.

The combined march of these three forces moving from Magdeburg, Hamburg, and Luckau on Berlin was filled with problems, the greatest of which was that the three cities are separated by great distances making coordination difficult.

In addition, Oudinot had never exercised much authority and found himself fighting with his subordinate corps commanders when he attempted to enforce his will.

Oudinot had to cross terrain heavily cut with rivers and woods that divided his forces into isolated pockets. Coordination and mutual support was a problem, even for a single corps traveling in smaller columns, let alone for actions between involving several corps.

On 18 August Oudinot arrived in Baruth and concentrated his three corps there. He found that the scheduled three days march to Berlin did not allow him time to engage in combat along the way. Another problem arose when Defrance's 4th Heavy Cavalry Division did not arrive on time. Oudinot did not have time to wait and decided to leave without it.

Oudinot's Army of Berlin started its movement by crossing through the Lückenwalde Forest with a flanking movement. This is normally dangerous in the face of an enemy and it cost Oudinot more time, but allowed Defrance's 4th Heavy Cavalry Division time to join him on 20 August.

Maréchal Oudinot.

Fortunately, for Oudinot, Bernadotte's army did not move. Despite seeing that the French were not moving forward there was little Bernadotte could or would do. The Army of the North lacked supplies. Watching the situation, Bernadotte moved his headquarters to Potsdam on 20 August. That same day his forces redeployed themselves between Saarmund, Belitz, Treuenbrietzen, Trebbin, Zossen, Mittenwalde, GrossZiethen, Zehrensdorf, and Potsdam. His line of advanced posts extended from Treuenbrietzen, Trebbin, Schulzendorf, and Mollen.[1]

Bülow's III Corps was in Trebbin and Gross-Beeren. Tauentzien's IV Corps was in Blankenfelde. The Swedish Corps and the Russians stood to the rear between Ruhlsdorf and Heinersdorf.

After completing his movement through the Lückenwalde, Oudinot moved his army towards the north and began his movement towards Berlin on 21 August. The XII Corps advanced along the road from Trebbin, the IV Corps (GD Bertrand) moved down the road to Blankenfelde, and the VII Corps (GD Reynier) advanced to Nunsdorf.

Prince Bernadotte, Crown Prince of Sweden.

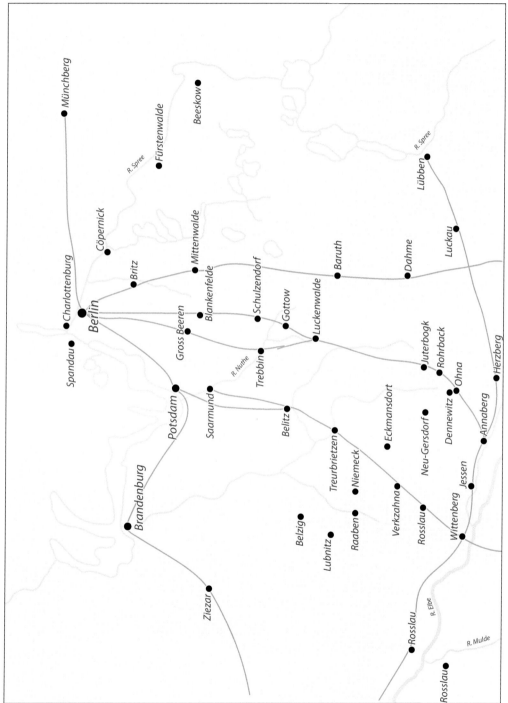

Sketch Map 9 The Region between Berlin and the Elbe River.

Actions of 21 August

After a weak resistance, the allied advanced posts fell back on Trebbin, Nunsdorf, and towards Zossen. Pacthod's 13th Division moved to attack Trebbin, which was prepared to withstand a French assault. Around 10:00 a.m. the 11th Company, 4th East Prussian Regiment and the 9th and 10th Companies of the 3/5th Reserve Regiment (under Major von Meyern), after a fire-fight with the advancing French, withdrew into Lowendorf, which was occupied by a company of the East Prussian Jägers. The entire advanced guard was under the command of Major von Clausewitz.[2]

The gullies that lined the southwest and west of the village were impregnable, but the south was favorable to an attack. There was a raised fleche before the southern gate facing Cliestow. Maréchal Oudinot knew that Trebbin was occupied by infantry, and around 12:30 p.m., ordered his artillery to assume a position on the heights south of the village, from which they could bombard the village while his cavalry moved past its right.

GM von Thümen rushed to Trebbin when he heard the guns of Oudinot's bombardment. At v4:00 p.m. he wrote Bernadotte reporting the movement a French column through Scharfenbrück and Neuendorf on Trebbin and the movement of another column through Cummersdorf towards Wendisch-Wilmersdorf. Thümen reported that his advanced posts before Trebbin had been thrown back, that there was a large cavalry force before Trebbin that covered the front of a large mass of infantry, and that Major Hellwig had been in Cummersdorf and Lüdersdorf, but that he too had been thrown back and then stood behind Wilmersdorf. Hellwig was sending patrols towards Mittenwalde.

The Saxons

Sahr's 25th Division moved out early that morning, moving through the Cummersdorf Forest. Von Hellwig had his force in those woods, but withdrew in front of von Sahr without offering any resistance. Around 8:00 a.m., von Sahr arrived at the edge of the forest, and to the north, on the heights between Judersdorf and Gadsdorf, they saw a body of Prussian cavalry.

The 25th Division formed itself into regimental columns, moved out onto the plains, and advanced towards the heights. Once again Major Hellwig withdrew without offering combat. The Fus/4th East Prussian Regiment placed its 11th Company in Cliestow, its 10th Company in Schulzendorf, and the 9th and 12th Companies in Christinendorf.

The 25th Division stopped between Judersdorf and Gadsdorf to await the arrival of the other corps. Shortly later, the IV Corps arrived on the right with its columns ready to continue the advance.

The rest of Reynier's VII Corps, the 24th and 32nd Divisions, arrived in Schönweide that morning, where they stopped until the arrival of the XII Corps in Gottow. After the XII Corps arrived, they advanced into Scharfenbrück to support the 25th Division.

The Skirmish of Nunsdorf

Sahr's 25th Division attacked Christinendorf and drove out the two companies standing before the village. The Prussians fled back to Nunsdorf. The 11th and 12th Companies, 3/5th Reserve Regiment occupied the village of Wendisch-Wilmersdorf and all four companies of the 4/5th Reserve Regiment occupied Nunsdorf.[3]

When the garrison of Wendisch-Wilmersdorf learned that the French were about to arrive they took up defensive positions behind the defile. The 4/5th Reserve Regiment remained in Nunsdorf, but sent a half a company to the northern end of the Gadsdorf dike. The two companies of the 4th Reserve Regiment that had withdrawn from Christinendorf arrived in Nunsdorf around noon and assumed the function as a reserve in the city.

The detached company of the 5th Reserve Regiment, by the Gadsdorf dam, found itself under heavy artillery fire from a Saxon battery posted on the heights to the south of the dam. After having delayed the Saxon progress for some time, it withdrew to a hill to the southeast of the

Sketch Map 10 Roads to Gross Beeren.

village where it re-joined its battalion, which was in a dense column formation. There the battalion was engaged by Saxon skirmishers, but withdrew in good order to Wendisch-Wilmersdorf to join two more companies of the 3/5th Reserve Regiment.

GM Thümen began to worry about his left flank and detached the 1/5th Reserve Regiment towards Weinberg, near Wendisch-Wilmersdorf, after withdrawing his other two battalions. However, Reynier did not pursue them. The 11th and 12th Companies, 5th Reserve Regiment joined the 1/5th Reserve. The 4/5th Reserve moved back to Thyrower-Berg with the 9th and 12th Companies/4th East Prussian Infantry Regiment, while its 10th Company remained in Schulzendorf.

The VII Corps bivouacked by Nunsdorf and Christinendorf. A light infantry battalion was sent to occupy Nunsdorf, while Devaux's Brigade, a horse battery, and three squadrons were posted near the city. A battalion from the Saxon Löw Regiment camped on the dam, while the rest of the division was posted on the heights to the north of the defile.

The 24th Division supported its right on GL von Sahr's 25th Division and its left on Christinendorf. Its advanced posts were pushed a great distance to the north of this line, with a battalion holding a position on the road to Christinendorf in Wendisch-Wilmersdorf.[4]

The Saxon VII Corps, after occupying Nunsdorf, moved on Wilmersdorf and attacked Trebbin from the east. The French artillery bombarding Trebbin did so at a range of 1,500 paces with no visible result. Nonetheless, at 4:00 p.m. Oudinot called on the defenders of Trebbin to surrender. It was refused. At 5:00 p.m., Oudinot sent Jarry's brigade, XII Corps, forward in a violent assault, supported by heavy artillery fire. His skirmishers stopped 100 paces from the city's walls by the Prussian skirmish fire. As a result, the skirmishers shifted to the right, towards the mills, and began to threaten Trebbin from the north. Around 5:30 p.m., Major Clausewitz evacuated the city and withdrew to Klein-Beuthen that night, and on to Thyrow the following day. The French did not pursue him.

The IV Corps Advances

Guilleminot's 14th and Fontanelli's 15th Divisions, IV Corps, marched on Saalow. They covered their east flank with a separate column that advanced on Wünsdorf via Jachzenbrück and Col-Neuhof.

Bertrand's IV Corps had on its flank some small Prussian detachments. They consisted of the Fus/1st Pomeranian Regiment posted in Nächst-Wünsdorf, the 9th Fusilier Company/1st Pomeranian Regiment and two other companies posted in Mellen, the 3/2nd Neumärk Landwehr Regiment in the Zossen castle to the north, and the 3/2nd Reserve Regiment in Zehrensdorf.

The Prussians had a force in the village of Mellen, under the command of Captain Kuylenstjerna. He had prepared for a French assault by destroying the wind mill, breaking the bridge and raising a parapet behind the broken bridge. A peloton of the 9th Company occupied the parapet. The two other companies remained in reserve to the east of the village. The jägers were dispersed along the river bank.

When GD Bertrand arrived before Mellen, his first action was to send forward an Italian brigade. The two Prussian companies in the village resisted three attacks between 1:00 and 6:00 p.m. However, with the appearance of a French column on the Prussian right, the defenders detached a company to watch them.

After the combat Major Cardel estimated that the French had 15,000 men present and reported that figure to Borstell. This resulted in Borstell's withdrawing that battalion to Telz and the one in Zehrensdorf to Machnow.

The French IV Corps resumed its march during the combat, side stepping the village and camped that evening between Schunow and Dergischow.[5]

However, when Bertrand began to advance again, the IV Corps found its communications with the VII and XII Corps was cut by the difficult terrain that did not permit lateral communications.

Actions of 22 August

In preparations for the day's events, Thümen ordered the 4/5th Reserve Regiment and two guns from 6pdr Foot Battery #6 to occupy the pass by Wittstock. He ordered three companies of the Fus/4th East Prussian Regiment and three squadrons of the Pomeranian National Cavalry Regiment to support them. In addition, there already stood one and a half battalions on the Wilmersdorfer Weinberg Heights, and the 1/Elbe Regiment and a cannon stood to the right in Jütendorf. This put five battalions, two squadrons and nine guns by Thyrow.[6]

At 3:00 a.m., GM Oppen ordered three dragoon regiments and the horse batteries to gather at Blankenfelde and to move to Jühnsdorf where they were to join the other squadrons. When they arrived the Brandenburg Dragoon Regiment and two guns remained by Blankenfelde until the Reserve Division was in position, the dragoons moved to Gross-Beeren. The Kurmärk Brigade moved to Genshagen. The two other dragoon regiments and 14 guns moved through Gross-Beeren towards Ludwigsfelde.

In the early morning Borstell sent the 1/2nd Kurmärk Landwehr from its encampment by Mittenwalde to Jühnsdorf and the 3/2nd Reserve Regiment and the 1/West Prussian Uhlan Regiment to the edge of the woods by Dabendorf.

On the French side, Maréchal Oudinot began his preparations. Lebrun and Arrighi began to move from their positions by Trebbin to a position by Thyrow. An early morning council was held between these generals and Reynier. It was decided that the XII Corps, instead of the VII Corps should march in the middle of the French formation. This would put Reynier on the flank and give him more maneuvering room.

It was decided that a division of the XII Corps would march to the right, against Christinendorf and take up a position in Wilmersdorf and on the Wilmersdorf heights. The VII Corps would support the attack on Wilmersdorf from the direction of Nunsdorf as well as seize the passes from Wittstock over the upper channel of the Nuthe. A division of the IV Corps would strike west from the Rangsdorf Lake against Jühnsdorf in order to seize Blankenfelde. Raglovich's 29th (Bavarian) Division and Lorge's 5th Light Cavalry Division, followed by the artillery park, were to move through Gottow and Scharfenbrück to Trebbin. The

Arrighi, Duke of Padua.

Württembergers (38th Division) were to move from Baruth through Speerenberg and Gadsdorf, towards Nunsdorf.[7]

That morning Reynier had inspected his advanced lines, on the Nunsdorf heights, which were manned by Lecoq's 24th Division. He directed that they be ready for combat. However, they were obliged to wait until 11:00 a.m., when the head of Guilleminot's 14th Division reached Christinendorf. When GD Reynier's advance began, he left only two batteries (one 12pdr battery and one 6pdr battery), covered by a single battalion to hold the Nunsdorf dike.

GD Durutte's 32nd Division marched against Wittstock in a column of regiments, supported by GL von Sahr's 25th Division that marched to the left rear in open column. On the right Durutte was flanked by a brigade of cavalry. In addition, skirmishers covered the column. Bardet's Brigade was ordered against Wilmersdorf and Brause's Brigade was ordered to attack Weinberg from the north. The two Saxon batteries stood on the Nunsdorf heights to cover their movement.

Bertrand sent Fontanelli's 15th Division forward from Schunow towards Gross-Schulzendorf and left a detachment of GB Wolf's brigade by Glienick to watch his flank. Pacthod's 13th Division moved out of Trebbin.

GM Brause's Brigade advanced with a jäger company and the Lecoq Regiment at the head of its column. The terrain forced the column to diverge towards Weinberg. Part of its forces were deployed as skirmishers to the north of the hill and their right flank was always covered by the valley of the Nuthe.

Reynier.

Bardet's brigade's skirmishers were stopped by the eastern edge of the village. The two Saxon batteries fired in support, but the distance rendered their fire ineffective.[8]

Thümen judged it necessary to reinforce his left flank posts to resist the French assault and sent the 2/Elbe Infantry Regiment to Kerzendorf to cover the west of the Wittstock position. Major Clausewitz was given the order to move his three battalions back about 10:00 a.m. The 2/5th Reserve Regiment and an additional company moved to cover the Nuthe bridge.

The advanced position of Weinberg had prevented the Prussians from posting any artillery in it, should the village be lost and the guns would have to be abandoned. Nonetheless, the advance of the French and Saxon infantry was very slow.

Around 5:00 p.m., a cloud of Saxon skirmishers, from the 1st (Lecoq) Light Regiment and the Saxon Schützen of Brause's Brigade, covering seven French and Saxon columns, moved forward to assault the Prussian position on the heights by Wilmersdorf. They were supported by the fire of a Saxon and a French 6pdr battery. Clausewitz, having completed his mission and seeing no point in being swept over by a greatly superior enemy, evacuated his position. The French and Saxons swept up to the crest Clausewitz had just abandoned.

Once in possession of the heights the French established a battery of twelve guns there, four Saxon 12pdr cannon and a French 6pdr battery.[9] They fired on the retreating Prussians as they withdrew towards their main lines.

The Skirmish at Wittstock

The terrain between Kerzendorf and Wittstock consists of damp prairies cut by a ditch that carries water to the Nuthe. The inundation flowed out of the river's normal banks, forming an obstacle 800 paces wide. A dam, 500 paces long, crossed the ditch with a wooden bridge that led from Wittstock to Ludwigsfeld. A hill dominated its exit to the north and overlooked the route. This position was quite strong and compromised any defender in the village.

On the other hand, the marshes and the positions of the houses of Wittstock prevented an assailant from deploying to the north of the village and limited the effectiveness of artillery.

Major Wedell, commanding the 4/5th Reserve Regiment and two guns from 6pdr Foot Battery #6, stood in Wittstock. He detached his schützen platoon under the command of Kapitän von Francois to engage the French as they advanced. The two guns under the command of Lieutenant Lemke stood by the dike. The Pomeranian National Cavalry Regiment remained behind the crest of the hill.

As the fight over Wittstock began the Fus/4th East Prussian Regiment (Kemphen's Battalion) was marching on Kerzdorf and Thümen had not yet sent forward the 2/Elbe Regiment. In addition, Oppen's Reserve Cavalry was not yet appeared.[10]

Around 1:00 p.m. Durutte's 32nd Division arrived before Wittstock and moved against the wind mill heights. Von Sahr's 25th Division and Gablenz's 36th Light Cavalry Brigade remained in the second line. Durutte sent Devaux's brigade to assault Wittstock and the bulk of his skirmishers occupied the village covered by a battery positioned on a hill to the north of the church.

The 4/5th Reserve Regiment withdrew from the village because of the problems in defending the position. Instead, it moved to be accessible to its only line of retreat, the bridge over the dam, was accessible to it. Major Wedel put his skirmishers along the water's edge and two guns were placed on the hill. His cavalry was placed to the north of a small hill and dispatched a peloton to a position before Wittstock.

The Fus/4th East Prussian Regiment arrived in Kerzendorf at 1:00 p.m. The skirmishers and the jägers of the fusilier battalion were barely deployed in a skirmish line in the field when they found themselves under a heavy attack. They expended 120 rounds per man.[11]

Seeing the attack, GL von Bülow detached GM von Oppen with two horse batteries and four cavalry regiments to support the Wittstock garrison.[12]

GM Oppen established himself on the road from Ludwigsfelde and Löwenbrück. His two batteries relieved the guns placed in the redoubt.[13] The 2/Elbe Regiment arrived at 1:00 p.m., to the west of Wittstock and moved to the right, where it deployed in skirmish formation, holding two companies in reserve.

Reynier had contented himself with a skirmish battle and the Weinberg hill fell into the French hands. Once held, a battery moved up and took a position in Wittstock. It engaged the Prussian artillery, but soon found Wittstock burning around it, obliging it to move. The bulk of Durutte's 32nd Division stood to the south of the village, having in its right rear Gablenz's 26th Light Cavalry Brigade. Von Sahr's 25th Division stood with its right in contact with the 24th Division.

Between 5:00 and 6:00 p.m., Reynier decided to execute a frontal assault. He drew two battalions from von Sahr's Division, one from the Anton Regiment and a battalion from the 2nd Light (von Sahr) Regiment. They moved across the swamp, towards Kerzendorf with the objective of supporting the march of Devaux's brigade. Devaux's brigade was formed in *colonne serrée*.[14] The 1/35th Légère Regiment, leading, was assigned the frontal assault. The first attack was checked by the Prussian artillery firing canister into its dense ranks.[15] The 1/35th broke and fled. Two further attacks were mounted, but also failed.

Then the 4/133rd Line Regiment, passing through the swamp behind a heavy force of skirmishers, arrived on the bank and obliged the battery to withdraw. As the Prussian battery withdrew, the Prussian defenders received the order to fall back on Ludwigsfelde.[16]

Devaux, seizing on the opportunity presented by the withdrawal of the artillery, threw his brigade forward again, across the dike. His leading battalion, after pulling out of the village on the north, formed square with remarkable discipline and marched to the heights where the brigade formed itself in two lines. GM Oppen threw the 2nd and 4th Kurmärk Landwehr Cavalry Regiments (Sydow's Landwehr Cavalry Brigade) and the Pomeranian National Cavalry Regiment at them without formally preparing to attack.[17] His attack threw back a few ranks of infantry on the French right, but having no reserve, he was checked before the second line. Then, some of the men of the first rank, who had thrown themselves to the ground, rose up and fired on the Prussian cavalry from the rear.

GM Oppen, not being discouraged, threw a dragoon brigade forward. Oberst von Treskow, believing his orders ill understood, stopped his brigade under the French artillery and called a conference with his officers, explained his intentions, then ordered the charge again. This stop allowed Devaux's brigade time to reassemble and prepare to receive the attack. Rarely was such a perfect charge executed. The cavalry regiments advanced with decisiveness and with great order. Nonetheless, they were checked before an infantry that was prepared to receive them and they withdrew, rallying behind the 4/East Prussian Dragoon Regiment. This squadron had been placed to support a battery and had not taken part in the charge. It now threw forward its 3rd and 4th Zügen as skirmishers to keep the French skirmishers at bay.[18]

Durutte's forces rushed forward and seized the Schanzen Heights and positioned their artillery there. Once in position the French artillery began to bombard the retiring Prussians.

Durutte's offensive was so rapid that it cut the Prussian infantry off from the Ludwigsfelde road. At 8:00 p.m., these three Prussian battalions threw themselves towards Kerzendorf.[19] The Prussian artillery moved to the Weinberg farm, but its fire was masked by Oppen's cavalry. Oppen's cavalry withdrew by echelons towards Ludwigsfelde under heavy French artillery fire and arrived there about 8:00 p.m. Two battalions joined it there. The third, 2/Elbe Regiment, was scattered in skirmish order. As the infantry lined the southern edge of the woods to await Thümen, Oppen's cavalry withdrew towards Gross-Beeren, which it reached at 10:00 p.m. GL Bülow ordered it from there to Heinersdorf, where it bivouacked around midnight.

Shortly after the overrunning of the hill by Durutte, von Sahr's 25th Division and Gablenz's 26th Light Cavalry Brigade crossed the dam and formed up on Durutte's right. A horse battery pushed down the road to Berlin and fired on the retiring Prussian cavalry.

During the evening the VII Corps bivouacked with the 15th Division and Gablenz's 26th Light Cavalry Brigade near Löwenbrück, between the forests. Durutte's 32nd Division stood on its right, near Kerzendorf, where Reynier established his headquarters. The 24th Division stood on the Wind Mill Heights, to the north of Wittstock. The divisions called back its two batteries that had engaged the Prussians during the assault on Wilmersdorf and the entire train moved into Schoneweide and the park to the north of Wittstock.

It had been a serious fight. The Prussian losses for that day were 23 officers, 334 men and 221 horses. Their fourteen guns had fired 335 round shot, 107 howitzer shells and 115 canister rounds.[20] The French lost about 568 men.[21]

Engagement at Jühnsdorf

The road from Gross-Schulzendorf to Jühnsdorf crossed an inundation on a causeway raised one meter above the water. To the west, it passed at the foot of the Lindenberg Heights. To the east, the land parting the water between the Rangsdorfer lake and the canals, was practical.

The 1/2nd Kurmärk Landwehr Regiment (Closter's Battalion) that was sent from Mittenwalde arrived in Jühnsdorf around 8:00 p.m., joining the dragoon squadron that had been there. It established a position on the Lindenberg Heights where it stopped Bertrand's first scouts. One of its companies was detached and moved 1,200 meters to the south of the village. Dobschütz's Division, which arrived at midnight, had not left its encampment before Berlin until 9:00 a.m. Tauentzien withdrew it from the Lindenberg Heights after watching the French and determining that the heights would not be the point of a decisive attack. Dobschütz was sent to the east, in the direction of Mittenwalde, via Dahlwitz and towards Klein-Kienitz. He left only two battalions, two squadrons and two guns in Blankenfelde. Of these, a battalion and two guns, under Major Hiller, were sent to Jühnsdorf.[22] The 3/2nd Neumärk Landwehr Regiment and the guns later moved to Jühnsdorf. Tauentzien rejoined Dobschütz at 2:00 p.m.[23]

Major Hiller posted the guns in Lindenberg, by Closter's Battalion (1/2nd Kurmärk), and ordered Steinmetz's Battalion to withdraw into the village. Around 3:00 p.m., the village was taken under fire from Wittstock, as Fontanelli's 15th Division, IV Corps, moved out of Gross-Schulzendorf.

Fontanelli established a battery on a hill to the north of the village. This battery fired on the Prussian artillery, but the Prussians remained concealed and did not respond. The first Italian attack began around 4:00 p.m. One column moved against the dike. As soon as they arrived within 1,000 paces of it, Lieutenant Wilke pushed his pieces out into the open and fired two salvos.

Bertrand sent two brigades, one behind the other, forward. One moved against the dike and the other moved to the left to turn the Prussian position. The left column appears to have been led by GB Martel. Three companies of the 3/2nd Neumärk Landwehr Regiment (Steinmetz's Battalion) moved to the west of the Lindenberge hill to oppose this movement. Its commander, Captain von Steinmetz, led it forward in at least one bayonet attack, driving the Italians out of Jühnsdorf after their first assault.[24] The fourth company occupied the woods situated between the hill and the village. One of the Prussian guns, a howitzer, was given the mission to defend the dam and the cannon was placed to the west, on a hill.

The attack ran from 5:00 to 6:00 p.m. A battalion of the 4th Italian Line, Martel's brigade, succeeded in turning the hill. Major Hiller was

Bertrand.

forced to withdraw and withdrew towards Blankenfelde. The 4th Italian Line Regiment swung into line and advanced against the Prussians, covered by a screen of skirmishers. The Prussian skirmishers were driven back, taking fire from the closed companies of Italians and canister fire from their supporting cannons.

Hiller was unable to withstand the assault and withdrew with Martel's Brigade pursuing him. Hiller attempted to take a position behind the village of Jühnsdorf, but the Italians began to turn his right flank.[25]

GL Tauentzien heard the sound of the battle and stopped Dobschütz's brigade between Klein-Teinitz and Brusendorf. Tauentzien then sent five battalions, two squadrons, and two guns to Jühnsdorf. At that time he had the intention of retaking the initiative with a battalion moving from Blankenfelde. His counterattack stopped the Italian troop's progress, but the attack was too weak and the Prussians continued to withdraw towards Blankenfelde. Dobschütz's entire brigade reorganized and reunited that evening.[26]

This action was not particularly bloody, the Prussians losing only one officer and 56 men. Their two guns fired 16 rounds, including four rounds of canister. The Italian losses were about the same.

The Württembergers

In response to orders received on 21 August, GL Franquemont directed a battalion towards Speeremberg. This battalion arrived at 1:00 a.m. on 22 August, after a very hard march. The battalion established a barricade between two lakes and posted itself behind it. A half company was detached down the road to Saalow. The rest of the night passed quietly.

New orders were received to re-join the main body, so the brigades of Döring and Spitzenberg started moving at 5:00 a.m. Stockmayer's brigade followed behind them at 6:00 a.m. The cavalry brigade detached 100 men to a convoy as an escort and another 100 with the two infantry brigades. The rest marched with Stockmayer's brigade.

During the next day, Bertrand's IV Corps left Jühnsdorf and moved towards Blankenfelde, completely isolated from the other two corps. That evening the XII Corps established its advanced guard, a single brigade, in Thyrow. The VII Corps moved to Wittstock.

That day Bernadotte had assumed a position in Ruhlsdorf with his Russian corps forming the right flank standing behind Jüterbogk. GL von Bülow's III Corps formed the left wing between Ruhlsdorf and Heinersdorf. The 5th Brigade was ordered to a position between Zossen and Wusterhausen. GM von Hirschfeld stood behind the Nuthe and held the fords between Saarmund and Potsdam. GM Wobeser stood by Gruben. The Prussian light troops watched the main road between Belitz and Treuenbrietzen and the area between Treuenbrietzen and the Nuthe near Lückenwalde.[27]

7

Oudinot's Advance on Berlin: The Battle of Gross-Beeren 23–25 August 1813

During the day of 22 August, Bernadotte concentrated his forces. He recalled the detachments in Saarmund and Mittenwalde and took a position near Heinersdorf.

On 23 August Maréchal Oudinot resumed his march on Berlin with the IV Corps moving down the Blankenfelde road, the VII Corps moving through Gross-Beeren, and the XII Corps detouring through Ahrensdorf. The VII Corps was ordered to stop in Gross-Beeren and the other two corps were told to join it there. But this disposition had a fundamental flaw, each corps having to move via a separate route, separated from the others by a distance of about 4 kilometers and lacking all lateral communications. A military check on one corps would check the progress of the others. It allowed Bernadotte to concentrate his forces on one of the French columns and not fear finding himself struck by a coordinated counterattack of the other two.

Oudinot was unaware of Bernadotte's dispositions, and he knew that he was running a major risk by dividing his forces as he did. He could have easily moved to the allied left and passed through Heinersdorf with the IV and XII Corps, if he wished solely to move on Berlin.

During the morning of 23 August, Maréchal Oudinot's forces continued their advance, with the VII Corps, in the center, marching on Gross-Beeren. The XII Corps, on the left, was moving towards Arensdorf and the IV Corps, on the right, was moving towards Blankenfelde.

The ground before Blankenfelde and Gross-Beeren was covered by a heavy forest that was filled with sharp undulations and was cut by a few roads. Any wheeled traffic advancing towards Gross-Beeren was, as a result, confined to the roads.

The Fight at Blankenfelde

The route from Jühnsdorf to Blankenfelde passed through a wood that closed to the southern edge of Blankenfelde. An open field approximately one kilometer by 1,500 meters surrounded the rest of the village, except on the east where the Blankenfelde lake stood.

GL Tauentzien decided to hold this position, but did not wish to have his inexperienced landwehr engaged in a battle in the village or in the woods. He gave Major Creilsheim command of a small advanced guard, formed with three battalions of the 3rd Reserve Regiment, two squadrons, and two guns. He placed this force at the southern exit of Blankenfelde with the mission of warning him of a French attack.

Tauentzien then posted his division, ten battalions with twelve guns, to the west of the village and organized them into two lines. They stood between the village and the windmill hill. Another four battalions, three squadrons, and six guns were posted to the east of the village. These troops were also formed in two lines. In order to train the landwehr, which had yet to be under enemy fire, the only veteran unit, the 3rd Reserve Regiment, was deployed forward to receive the initial French attacks.[1]

About 10:00 a.m., Bertrand sent forward the brigades of GB Santa-Andrea and GB Moroni, the 2nd and 3rd Brigades of the 15th Division.[2]

Tauentzien.

To slow their advance, Creilsheim sent forward the skirmishers of the three battalions of the 3rd Reserve Regiment. These skirmishers, under Major von Schmalensee, were forward in the woods. They were supported by the 3/3rd Reserve Regiment and the two musketeer battalions of the 3rd Reserve that stood to the right of the village on the edge of the woods. Behind the village stood two squadrons of the 2nd Neumärk Landwehr Cavalry Regiment in column. To the left of Blankenfelde stood the 1/, 2/1st Kurmärk Landwehr Regiment with 2 guns of half 6pdr Battery #20 in the interval between the two battalions, and 6pdr Foot Battery #17.

Behind them stood the second line consisting of the 1/, 2/1st Silesian Landwehr Regiment with four cannons. Behind them stood the 3rd East Prussian Landwehr Cavalry Regiment.

To the right of the village, on the Windmühlberg stood the other battalions of the first line, the 1/, 2/, 3/, 4/5th Kurmärk Landwehr Regiment, 6pdr Foot Battery #17 standing in the middle of that regiment, and on the left wing half of 6pdr Foot Battery #27 – von Matthias.

In the second line, stood the 1/,2/,3/,4/2nd Neumärk Landwehr Regiment and the 5/1st Silesian Regiment. A few paces behind them, under the cover of the terrain, stood the cavalry in two columns. On the right was the 1st Kurmärk Landwehr Cavalry and the 3rd Pomeranian Landwehr Cavalry Regiment and on the left was the 7th Kurmärk Landwehr Cavalry Regiment and the two squadrons of the Berlin Landwehr Cavalry Regiment.[3] The village of Blankenfelde remained unoccupied.

Tauentzien's forces held a strong position. His artillery lined the northern edge of the fields, but were in the woods. The Blankenfelde lake covered his left against any turning movement from the east.

The Italian skirmishers spent several hours pushing back the Prussian skirmishers. They made five efforts before they finally succeeded and pierced through the forest to the east of Blankenfelde. They were followed by three infantry columns and an artillery battery. The Italian battery took a position in the woods and supported the attack by three columns, which was aimed against the left of the Prussian line. Major Kleist held that position with four battalions and six guns.

The Italian battery moved to the edge of the woods and began to fire on the Prussians, at a range of 700–900 paces with canister fire. The Prussian artillery was surprised by this and responded by firing canister back at them. However, the Prussian artillery appears to have lost this exchange and it withdrew.[4]

Tauentzien brought his second line to the heights to stop the Italian attack. The Italian infantry and battery soon withdrew.

After regrouping in the forest, the Italians sent forward several hundred skirmishers, supported by artillery. The Prussian artillery, under Lieutenants Papendick and Blankenburg,[5] held its fire and at a range of 400 paces stopped them cold with canister. A patrol of 22 horsemen from the 7th Kurmärk Landwehr Cavalry Regiment, followed them along the length of the lake and brought back news of a new attack being prepared.

The 1/1st Kurmärk Landwehr Regiment, on the extreme left, sent its skirmishers forward to assist the cavalry. This combined force threw back the third Italian attack. Major Dullack supported the skirmishers with three companies of his battalion (1/1st Kurmärk). The Italian skirmishers withdrew into the forest after a two hour battle. The Italians did not fight particularly aggressively and withdrew without seriously engaging Tauentzien.

GL Tauentzien had engaged three battalions and six guns. His losses were about 200 men. For this minimal loss, he had held the 15,000 men of Bertrand's IV Corps at bay for several hours, and captured 11 officers and 200 men. The Prussian artillery fired 123 round shot and 51 rounds of canister.[6]

The VII Corps

GD Reynier started the VII Corps advancing about noon, on 23 August. His advanced guard, formed from Saxon light infantry, encountered the Prussian skirmish line about a mile before Gross-Beeren. The Prussians, however, did not attempt to prevent his advance.

As the road exits the woods before Gross-Beeren, there is a large, slightly rising plain that extends to the village. To the southwest of Gross-Beeren, the terrain is a long hill that runs parallel to the edge of the woods at a distance of a mile. Though not a steep or high rise, it rises 30 or more feet and is sufficient to dominate the terrain below it. The Saxon advanced guard, as it advanced onto the plain, observed columns of Prussian cavalry and a battery on this hill.

Major Cardel had assigned the defense of the village to the 1/9th Reserve Regiment. Its 1st and 2nd Companies were at the eastern exit of the village towards Genshagen. The 3rd Company was to the east, towards Klein-Beeren. The 4th Company was in the woods by the northern exit from the village and the schützen (skirmishers) were along the south and west edge of the village. A second battalion, Fus/Colberg, stood in the interior of the village as a reserve, and the 1/1st Neumärk Landwehr Regiment stood outside the village, as a further support. Four guns were on the hill, covered by the 1st Leib Hussars.[7]

Reynier decided quickly to attack the village. His Saxon horse artillery and a foot battery set up and began a counterbattery designed to eliminate the Prussian half battery. The gunfire set the village afire. GL von Sahr's 25th Division moved forward a line of skirmishers and organized itself behind them. Bose's 1st Brigade deployed to the right of the road and Ryssel's 2nd Brigade to the left. They were organized in four lines, in columns by battalions. Reynier ordered them forward to seize Gross-Beeren.

The Prussian infantry detachment facing Reynier reformed itself to the north of Heinersdorf. The 1st Leib Hussars returned to their brigade. Major Sandrart, commander of the advanced guard and the 1st Leib Hussars, estimated that the French were advancing with 8,000 men.

Sandrart's advanced guard consisted of the Fus/Colberg, 1/9th Reserve, 1/1st Neumärk Landwehr, 1st Leib Hussars, and 4 guns from 6pdr Foot Battery #19 (Liebermann).[8] At 4:00 p.m., these forces, standing in Gross-Beeren, were attacked by Saxon troops of the VII Corps moving from Wittstock. At the same time the XII Corps and the French cavalry was moving from Ahrensdorf and Sputendorf.

The Saxon Sperl Grenadier Battalion, commanded by Major Sperl, pushed to the right of the dirt road, where it broke from the northern point of the woods and moved to the southern part of the village. The battalion was supported by 2/König Infantry Regiment, which straddled the road. The division's battery assumed a position on the heights to support the attack and to fire on the village.

The Saxons deployed 16 to 20 guns and covered them with a large swarm of skirmishers. The half of Prussian 6pdr Foot Battery #19, under Lieutenant Arnhold, attempted to stem the tide of advancing Saxons and French, but was out gunned, lost a gun and several horses, and was forced to withdraw. A slight rain was falling, that impeded the ability of muskets to operate, but Sperl led his grenadier battalion forward. A half company of grenadiers took up positions in the village, while the rest established itself in the woods between Gross-Beeren and Klein-Beeren. The infantry entered the village from the side where the road from Holzecke enters the village. The Prussians pulled back and the Saxons moved through the village.[9] Once they moved out of the village, they saw the Prussian skirmishers on the plain.

Reynier thought that the day's action was finished and did not bother to send his light cavalry after the retiring Prussians. He indicated the positions where the VII Corps was to bivouac. The 25th Division moved to the right of Gross-Beeren and to the left of the wind mill. The 32nd Division (GD Durutte) was to its left and rear. The 24th Division was on the left end the line these divisions formed. GD Reynier established his headquarters in a manor house. GD Defrance's 4th Heavy Cavalry Division had not yet arrived and Reynier may well have felt that he could not risk the Saxon cavalry brigade against the obviously superior allied cavalry.[10]

Before Reynier lay the entire Army of the North, except for Tauentzien's corps. To the east of Ruhlsdorf stood Bülow's 3rd Prussian Corps. To the west of Ruhlsdorf, stood Stedingk's Swedish corps and on his right stood the Russians of Winzingerode and Voronzov, extending towards Gutergotz.

Bernadotte, observing the French dispositions, decided he had the opportunity to destroy the French central column, Reynier's VII Corps, before the other two corps could effectively intervene. However, instead of seizing the opportunity, he hesitated, yielding to the Prussian desire that they lead the advance. This necessitated a reshuffling of his forces and gave precious time to the French and Saxons. Bülow's 3rd Corps attacked without the support of the rest of the army, at 6:00 p.m. Bülow massed his corps into a single column and advanced quickly against Reynier's isolated corps.

Winzingerode, by G. Dawe.

Bülow had the 3rd Brigade on his right, the 6th Brigade on the left, and the 4th Brigade behind the 6th Brigade. The 5th Brigade stood behind the 4th Brigade. All of the regiments were formed in *battalionsmasse*. Treskow's cavalry brigade, of the cavalry reserve, stood behind the Prussian right. Sydow's cavalry brigade stood behind the left wing. The Fus/4th East Prussians and a squadron of the 1st Pomeranian Landwehr Cavalry stood in Klein Beeren.[11]

Reynier stood with GL von Sahr's 25th Division in the first line. Bose's 1st Brigade formed his first line with the 2nd (von Sahr) Light Regiment on the left and 2/König Regiment on his right next to Gross-Beeren. Ryssel's brigade formed the second line with the two battalions of the von Löw Regiment to the left and the two battalions of the Prinz Anton Regiment to the right, next to Gross-Beeren. The Sperl Grenadier Battalion[12] stood on the far side of Gross-Beeren, across the stream with its back to Gross-Beeren. Deployed in front of von Sahr's brigade were, left to right, the 1st Horse Battery, the 3rd 6pdr Foot Battery and the 4th 6pdr Foot Battery, which stood nearest Gross-Beeren.

Durutte's 32nd Division would shortly stand to the left rear of von Sahr. Once there, he deployed in three lines with the four battalions of his first line deployed in line, the four battalions of his second line held in column and the two battalions of his third line deployed in line.[13] He held his artillery, the 12/1st Foot Artillery and the 13/8th Foot Artillery, behind the infantry.[14]

GL Lecoq's 24th Division would appear later on the road to Neu-Beeren and assume a position behind the left flank of the first line. Brause's brigade would be on the right and Mellentin's would be on the left. The cavalry stood in columns of squadrons between the two lines of infantry and on the road from Gross-Beeren to Neu-Beeren. The Saxon Hussars stood on the left and the Prinz Clemens Uhlan Regiment stood on the right. The 1/Prinz Maximilian Infantry Regiment (GM Brause's brigade, 24th Division) stood in Luckau and the 1/Niesmeuschel Infantry Regiment (GM Bose's Brigade, 25th Division) were detached to Wittstock.[15]

The Armies Collide

Bülow, seeing an opportunity to strike the isolated Saxons, chose to advance against the them. The Prussian example was quickly followed by Stedingk, who moved his corps on Neu-Beeren, in order to be able to strike Maréchal Oudinot's corps in the flank.

The Prussian 3rd Corps advanced in two lines. The first was formed by the 3rd and 6th Brigades of GM Hessen-Homburg and GM Krafft. The second line was formed by GM Thümen's 4th Brigade, which was to serve as a reserve.

The forces that had engaged the French earlier during the fall of the village of Gross-Beeren, remained as a reserve by Heinersdorf. They were the 1/9th Reserve Regiment, 1/1st Neumärk Landwehr Regiment, part of 6pdr Foot Battery #19 (Liebermann), Hellwig's detachment, two companies of the East Prussian Jager Battalion, and 12pdr Foot Battery #5 (Conradi).

Bülow's first line was formed with intervals between the battalions sufficient for them to deploy. The second line was formed in columns on the center, each brigade being equally disposed on two lines.

The lines were, right to left as seen by the Prussians, as follows:

> Hessen-Homburg's 3rd Brigade:
> First line: 2nd East Prussian Grenadier Battalion, 1/, 2/3rd East Prussian Regiment, 1/, 2/, 3/4th Reserve Regiment.
> Second line: Fus/3rd East Prussian Regiment, 1/, 2/, 3/, 4/3rd East Prussian Landwehr Regiment, 6pdr Foot Battery #5 (Glasenapp) before the right wing.

> Krafft's 6th Brigade:
> First Line: 2/1st Neumärk Landwehr Regiment, 1/, 2/Colberg Regiment.
> Second Line: 4/1st Neumärk Landwehr Regiment, 2/, 3/9th Reserve Regiment, 6pdr Foot Battery #16 (Spreuth) before the left wing. Sandrart's advanced troops stood as a reserve. In addition, the 3/1st Neumärk Landwehr Regiment was detached before Stettin.

> Thümen's 4th Brigade:
> First line: 1/, 2/4th East Prussian Regiment, 2/5th Reserve Regiment.
> Second line: 2/Elbe Regiment, 1/, 4/5th Reserve Regiment
> Third Line: 3/5th Reserve Regiment.

The 1/Elbe Regiment had been sent to Saarmund, the day before and was operating with GM Hirschfeld. Thümen's two companies of East Prussian Jägers and the half 12pdr Foot Battery #5 (Conradi) had remained behind in Heinersdorf. The other half of Conradi's battery was with Tauentzien's Corps.

In addition, part of 6pdr Foot Battery #6 (Ludwig) stood to the left rear. The reserve artillery was deployed as follows. To the right of Thümen stood Russian 12pdr Battery #21 (Schlueter), part of 6pdr Foot Battery #19 (Liebermann). Before and to the left of Hessen-Homburg stood Russian

12pdr Battery #7 (Dietrichs), and 12pdr Foot Battery #4 (Meyer) stood in front and to the right of Krafft.

> Borstell's 5th Brigade:
> First line: Pomeranian Grenadiers, 1/, 2/, 3/2nd Reserve Regiment, 2/2nd Kurmärk Landwehr Regiment.
> Second line: 1/, 2/, Fus/1st Pomeranian Regiment, 4/2nd Kurmärk Landwehr Regiment.
> To the rear: 6pdr Foot Battery #10 (Magenhöfer), half of Horse Battery #11 (Bouchardt), West Prussian Uhlans, Pomeranian Hussar Regiment (2 squadrons).[16]

Borstell.

> Cavalry Reserve:
> The cavalry stood in columns of squadrons. Treskow's Brigade stood with the Königin Dragoons on the right and the 2nd West Prussian Dragoons on the left. The second line was formed by two squadrons of the Brandenburg Dragoon Regiment and Horse Battery #5 (Niendorff). Sydow's Brigade stood with the 2nd Kurmärk Landwehr Cavalry Regiment on the right and the 4th Kurmärk Landwehr Cavalry Regiment on the left. One squadron of the 2nd Pomeranian Landwehr Cavalry Regiment stood behind them with Horse Battery #6 (Steinwehr) being on the right rear. The two squadrons of 3/,4/2nd Silesian Hussars were posted behind the left wing. The West Prussian Uhlan Regiment of Borstell's brigade was attached.[17]

The Artillery Duel

At the moment when the corps began to move forward, Oberst Holtzendorf observed to GL Bülow that the terrain was very level and that the French had already established a strong battery on the Windmühlberg. He proposed that the Prussians bring forward the greatest part of their batteries and form a battery to face them. Bülow consented and the battery was formed, right to left, from 6pdr Foot Battery #6 (Ludwig), Russian 12pdr Battery #7 (Dietrichs), 12pdr Foot Battery #4 (Meyer), 6pdr Foot Battery #16 (Spreuth), and part of 6pdr Foot Battery #19 (Liebermann). Russian 12pdr Battery #21 (Schlueter), and Horse Batteries #5 (right) and #6 (left) remained in the reserve behind the infantry.[18]

Between 5:00 P.m., and 6:00 p.m., the 12pdr batteries began to fire on the Saxons at a range of 1,800 paces. The Prussian infantry stood 300 paces behind the guns. After their fire had continued for about a half hour, the 6pdr batteries advanced to a range of 1,300 paces and began to fire on the Saxon first line. After suppressing the Saxon artillery, Holtzendorf moved forward the other part of 6pdr Battery #19 (Liebermann) and the Russian 12pdr Battery #21 (Schlueter). They moved between the other two 12pdr batteries already in position. Horse Battery #5 (Niendorff), escorted by the Freiwilliger Jäger Squadron, Königin Dragoon Regiment, moved to the right where it fired on the left flank of the Saxon artillery. At the same time, Horse Battery #6 (Steinwehr) moved against the Saxon left.[19]

Later, Colonel von Cardel led forward a small Swedish force consisting of Captain Mühlenfels' battery and two squadrons of the Smaländ Dragoon Regiment, to join the grand battery. This battery took up a position to the right of Horse Battery #5 (Neindorff) and began firing canister at a range of 600 paces. It drew the attention of the Saxon artillery and suffered a number of casualties as a result.

The weather was very advantageous for the use of artillery. Rain fell heavily and made observations easier, as the clouds of smoke from the guns was immediately knocked down, where normally smoke obscured the battlefield completely after a few minutes. On the other hand, the sodden ground prevented the ricochet effect of the round shot from having its usual effectiveness. The battle was, like those at Dresden and on the Katzbach, to be one of saber, bayonet, and cannon.

The Saxon batteries of the VII Corps fired back on the Prussians with some success. They were disposed, right to left, as follows: The two batteries of the 25th Division were to the north of a small wood to the northwest of Gross-Beeren. Two Saxon horse batteries and the two batteries of GD Durutte's 32nd Division stood across the front of Durutte's line.

The Saxon infantry supported the artillery, which stood in front of the infantry. Sperl's Converged Grenadier Battalion, too weak to occupy the entire edge of Gross-Beeren, stood in the cemetery. The 1/, 2/2nd (von Sahr) Saxon Light Infantry Regiment stood in the small woods to the west, having on its left the battalions of the 1/, 2/Anton and 2/König Infantry Regiments and all the rest of von Sahr's 25th Division.

During the battle, the artillery of the VII Corps dismounted five guns from the Prussian Horse Battery #5 (Niendorff) and four from 6pdr Foot Battery #5 (Glasenapp). Glasenapp's 6pdr Foot Battery #5 was, as a result of this punishment, obliged to withdraw from the battle. In view of the poor reputation of the Saxon artillery, their success in this artillery duel is quite surprising.

After about a half hour, the half 6pdr Foot Battery #6 (Ludwig) and 6pdr Battery #19 (Liebermann) advanced to within 900 paces of the village. The entire line followed their example. Twelve pounder Foot Battery #4 (Meyer) and 6pdr Foot Battery #16 (Spreuth), protected by Gross-Beeren, had suffered very little from the artillery duel. They advanced and took the village under fire.

The Prussian infantry marched to a range of 300 paces behind its artillery. When they did, the batteries of the VII Corps turned their fire on them, forcing them to deploy from battalion column to line, so as to minimize their casualties from the artillery fire.

GM Borstell had received the general instruction to follow Thümen's 4th Brigade, and to act according to circumstances, to cover the left flank of the army. Borstell began to believe that the movement of the 3rd Corps to the right threatened to cut communications with Tauentzien's 4th Corps and decided to move towards Klein-Beeren, by a conversion to the right and to occupy the village.

The Attack on Klein-Beeren

Reynier was unaware of Borstell's movement and made no effort to anticipate it. Borstell, ignorant of the Prussian garrison of Klein-Beeren, ordered the 1/, 2/2nd Reserve Regiment, two squadrons of the Pomeranian Hussar Regiment and four guns from Horse Battery #11, under Major Knobloch, to take the village.[20] The two battalions advanced in column, having the skirmishers of the 1/2nd Reserve deployed across their front. The battalions advanced with their artillery in the center. Oberst Knobloch, directed Captain Wins, who had earlier reconnoitered Klein-Beeren, to cover his left with two squadrons of the Pomeranian Hussar Regiment. Captain Wins found the woods to the north of the village unoccupied, but beyond stood the 4/3rd East Prussian Landwehr Regiment. The East Prussians passed through the village of Klein-Beeren, with the 2nd Reserve Regiment behind it as a reserve.

At the same time the rest of the brigade moved against the heights. The first line consisted of the Pomeranian Grenadier Battalion, Fus/1st Pomeranian Infantry Regiment, and the three battalions of the 1st Reserve Regiment. Behind them came the 1/, 2/1st Pomeranian Infantry Regiment and 2/, 4/2nd Kurmärk Landwehr Regiment in the second rank. The West Prussian Uhlans stood on their right flank and the remaining Pomeranian Hussar squadrons stood on the left. Foot Battery #10 (1st Lt. Magenhöfer) and half Horse Battery #11 (1st Lt. Bouchardt) took positions before the wooded entrance into Gross-Beeren, where they could fire into the Saxon lines.[21]

On hearing the cannonade towards Gross-Beeren, Major Knobloch decided to attack, in order to facilitate the march of Krafft's 6th Brigade. He sent a report to his commanding general, Borstell. The artillery and cavalry advanced in front of the infantry and took up a position on the heights to the east of Gross-Beeren, facing it across the stream.

The artillery bombarded the village until the moment when the infantry joined it. The skirmishers of the 2/2nd Reserve moved forward, while those of the 1/2nd Reserve advanced only to the road running from Klein to Gross-Beeren.

Major Knobloch, having observed that the Saxon cavalry supported the Saxon artillery, moved his artillery to the right of the Klein-Beeren-Gross-Beeren road where it bombarded them with some success. The Saxon cavalry, to escape the fire, withdrew into Gross-Beeren. Shortly after this, 6pdr Foot Battery #10 (Magenhöfer) relieved Horse Battery #11 (Bouchardt). The horse battery moved to a position on the heights to the east of the village. From here it was could fire on any troops entering or leaving Gross-Beeren.

Knobloch ordered the skirmishers of the two battalions to attack the village, supported by the 1/2nd Reserve. The 2/2nd Reserve advanced to the left in column, to cover the Prussian artillery. Soon 82 Prussian guns were firing on the Saxons in Gross-Beeren.

Reynier was finally aware of the danger to his right. Lecoq's 24th Division stood in the woods while the cannonade went on. Reynier had given Lecoq the mission of covering the left and the division was deployed in column, while forming a large square that was open in the rear. The 1/ Grenadier Guard Regiment, von Spiegel's Grenadiers, and the regiments of 1/, 2/Prinz Friedrich and 1/, 2/Steindel formed the square. The 1st Brigade placed a chain of skirmishers on the north edge of the Genshagener-Heide. The remainder moved into Neu-Beeren and on towards the forest to the north west to observe the Prussians. The Saxon skirmish fire, probably from the 2/Prinz Friedrich Regiment, struck the flank of the Swedish battery and obliged it to withdraw into a small forest occupied by five Swedish battalions.[22] A Saxon battery stood before the square and the other remained in reserve, in front of the skirmishers from Brause's brigade.

Reynier, hearing action to his right, sent Colonel Charlet to investigate the situation. He found all of von Sahr's 25th Division engaged, with no reserve left. Reynier sent von Sahr the order to arrange his forces so they could charge the first troops that advanced against him. Von Sahr responded by withdrawing from his line two battalions, the 2/Anton and 2/König Regiments, as well as half of Zandt's battery to reform a reserve.

The Attack on Gross-Beeren

The Saxon artillery inflicted enough casualties on Hessen-Homburg's infantry that he was forced to form them into line, to diminish the effectiveness of the Saxon artillery fire. The process of deploying them into line disordered them and they returned to column formations.

They stood in echelon in two lines. The left flank, also the closest to Gross-Beeren, being forward. That exposed position was held by the 3/4th Reserve Regiment. To its left stood the 2/, 1/4th Reserve Regiment. Further to the left stood the 2/, 1/3rd East Prussian Regiment and the 2nd East Prussian Grenadier Battalion, which stood on the extreme right flank.

The second line, left to right, consisted of the 4/, 3/, 2/, l/3rd East Prussian Landwehr Regiment and on the extreme right flank stood the Fus/3rd East Prussian Regiment. Slightly further to the right and rear stood the 1st Leib Hussar Regiment covering that flank.[23]

The rain had fallen heavily and the soaked uniforms of the soldiers emitted clouds of water vapor, as the rain evaporated out of them. The Prussian columns resembled great clouds of steam.

The Prussian corps advanced in an oblique order. The left was forward. Krafft's 6th Brigade was obliged, as it closed on Gross-Beeren, to pull several battalions out of the first line and put them behind it, because of a stream that ran parallel to the Heinersdorf-Gross-Beeren road. The battalions formed a third echelon. Thümen's 4th Brigade detached two battalions of the 5th Reserve Regiment to search the woods that stood to the north of the village, to the east and parallel to the Heinersdorf road. They found the woods unoccupied and returned to Krafft's brigade where they became a reserve.

The 1/, 2/Colberg Infantry Regiment and the 2/5th Reserve Regiment, preceded by the skirmishers drawn from those three battalions, formed the first line. The second line consisted of the 2/, 4/1st Neumärk Landwehr Regiment and the 3/5th Reserve Regiment. The 2/4th East Prussian Regiment formed the third line.[24] The 2/4th Reserve Regiment, drawn from Thümen's 4th Brigade, formed the general reserve for the second line. All of the battalions were formed in column on the center.

This formation indicates that GL Bülow had, by this time, judged it necessary to support the landwehr battalions with regular line regiments in order to bolster their morale and to hold the line should they break.

The Prussian attack advanced against Gross-Beeren at the same time as the 1/, 2/2nd Reserve Regiment, supported by two squadrons of the Pomeranian Hussar Regiment and four guns, struck from the east. Sperl's Grenadier Battalion defended the village. The 131st Line and 36th Légère Regiments sent two battalions to support the Sperl Grenadiers. The 1/2nd Reserve Regiment struck the Sperl Grenadier Battalion and one of the French battalions, throwing them out of the village. As they withdrew, they suffered under the fire of the four guns of Horse Battery #11.

The battle for the churchyard at Gross-Beeren, by Röchling.

The Attack on the Gross-Beeren

The 1/Colberg Regiment, covered on the left Gross-Beeren by the 2/Colberg and the right by the 2/5th Reserve Regiment, attacked Gross-Beeren frontally. The 1/Colberg was deployed in line, while the other two battalions advanced in columns of companies. The Saxons of the Prinz Anton Regiment and the Sperl Grenadier Battalion attempted a volley, but only five or six guns fired.[25] The rest misfired. The Prussians charged forward with a bayonet assault, capturing and bayoneting many. The remainder of the Saxons withdrew hastily. Captain Roell's company, 1/Colberg Regiment captured two Saxon cannon. The 2/5th Reserve Regiment, under Major von Puttlitz, captured three cannon. The road down which the Saxons withdrew crossed a wooden bridge, which was blocked, and many of the Saxons were captured.

At the same time as the 1/, 2/Colberg and 2/5th Reserve Regiment advanced, Oberst Krafft decided that he no longer required the two battalions of the 5th Reserve Regiment and left their commanding officer, Major Gagern, directions to move then to the battery, placed to the right of the village, and do what he deemed proper. The two battalions then advanced into the woods to the west of Gross-Beeren, while Oberst Krafft moved his second echelon to close the gap that had formed between himself and GM Hessen-Homburg's brigade.

As the Fus/Colberg and 1/2nd Reserve Regiments advanced out of Gross-Beeren, they saw the Saxon battalions of the 2/König and 1/, 2/Prinz Anton Regiments standing in column. GL von Sahr had placed Anton's battalion on the right wing of the ravine and the 2/König to the left. Zandt's battery was between them, but its support was short lived, as the fire from the Prussian Horse Battery #11 quickly silenced it.[26]

Reynier Counterattacks

In order to disengage his right, Reynier ordered Lecoq's 24th Division to advance against the Windmühlberg and to stop the advance of Hessen-Homburg's brigade there. From there it was to cover the road to Wittstock. GD Durutte's 32nd Division was to support von Sahr's attack towards Gross-Beeren.

It is reported by various German sources that Durutte's 32nd Division disbanded itself in a most shameful manner. Though they had fought well at Kalisch, it is not overly surprising that they did not perform well here. These regiments had been heavily reinforced and were nearly two thirds new conscripts.

Reynier, however, had less to say and stated only that the 32nd Division advanced to the edge of the woods to guard the exits through it. Devaux's brigade, which marched in the lead, accidentally crossed in front of the formation and became disordered, but Jarry's brigade marched in good order to its allocated position.

Whatever account may be the more factual, Reynier ordered von Sahr to attempt a counterattack. This counterattack was executed with great energy. The von Löw Regiment advanced its two battalions in battalion columns. The 1/von Löw Regiment threw back the 2/1st Neumärk Landwehr Regiment, but it was promptly counterattacked frontally by the 2/5th

Durutte.

Reserve Regiment, while the 3/5th Reserve Regiment attacked its flank. The result was that the 1/von Löw was annihilated, losing 330 prisoners.[27]

The 2/von Löw was attacked by the 3/4th Reserve Regiment, led by Prince von Hessen-Homburg personally. When the 3/4th Reserve Regiment was within 70 paces of the Saxons, the 2/von Löw made a half turn and sought to withdrew behind a small copse. The 3/4th Reserve had its skirmishers deployed before it and they followed the fleeing 2/von Löw. The 3/4th Reserve then advanced with an aggressive bayonet attack while Major von Siöholm led the 1/3rd East Prussian Regiment against its flank. The combined attack drove the 2/von Löw back 500 paces beyond the woods. During the attack the Prussians captured the 2/von Löw's standard and their skirmishers captured a howitzer.[28]

Grand Duke Prince Hessen-Homburg.

At the same time the 3/Pomeranian Hussar Regiment attacked a French square and captured a few prisoners. The Prussians stopped their attack, when they saw three squadrons of the Prinz Clemens Uhlan Regiment and half of Probsthayn's foot battery facing them. The 3/4th Reserve withdrew back behind the hill with the rest of the brigade.

The 1/Colberg and the two battalions of the 5th Reserve Regiment stopped their advance and assumed defensive formations. The 2/, 4/2nd Neumärk Landwehr Regiment advanced to support them. The 1st Pomeranian Landwehr Cavalry Regiment counterattacked the Prinz Clemens Uhlans, capturing the Saxon regimental commander and pushing them back. The Saxon Hussar Regiment advanced, engaged the Pomeranians and forced them back, covering the uhlans' withdrawal.[29]

On the right flank of this battle, Prince von Hessen-Homburg sent his forces forward to engage von Sahr's left, standing to the west of Gross-Beeren.

The rest of Hessen-Homburg's 3rd Brigade formed into line. The batteries of Glasenapp (#5), Ludwig (#6), the half Battery of Liebermann (#19), and later the Russian 12pdr Position Battery #21 of Dietrichs assumed a position before them. Treskow's cavalry brigade, including the Brandenburg Dragoon Regiment, assumed a position on the left flank, forming in columns of squadrons. Darkness was beginning to fall.

The Fus/3rd East Prussian Regiment (von Gleisenberg) and the 2nd East Prussian Grenadiers (von Beckendorf) began to advance. They were supported on their right by the 1st Leib Hussar Regiment.[30] Major von Sandrart, commander of the 1st Leib Hussars, sent forward their frei-williger jäger squadron, but it was countered by the Saxons and driven back. Sandrart then led forward his entire regiment and the West Prussian Uhlan Regiment. They struck at the right flank of the first Saxon line. The two left squadrons of the 1st Leib Hussars struck the second Saxon line forcing them into square.

The Advance of Fournier & Guilleminot

Fournier's 6th Light Cavalry Division was at this time moving up the main road, north from Ahrensdorf towards Sputendorf, with Guilleminot's 14th Division behind it. Fournier heard the sound of artillery at Gross-Beeren and turned east in Sputendorf to close on Gross-Beeren.

The XII Corps had reached Ahrensdorf during the day, but stopped there for the evening. Around 6:00 p.m., it heard the sounds of Bülow's artillery and GD Guilleminot's 14th Division, led by Oudinot, moved towards Spitendorf.

At this phase of the battle, GL von Bülow brought his cavalry across the Gross-Beeren stream and ordered them to charge the debris of the French and Saxon divisions that remained on the battlefield by Gross-Beeren.

GD Fournier, leading the 6th Light Cavalry Division, advanced with GB Ameil's 15th Light Cavalry Brigade in the lead. Ameil came through the woods by Neu-Beeren about 8:00 p.m., in time to save the Saxon 12pdr battery. A quick attack drove the 1st Leib Hussars back, behind its supporting battalions of Gleisenberg and Beckendorf. The Prussians then withdrew in square to the Windmühlberg, leaving their skirmishers in the woods.

Oberst Sandrart, finding himself in a dangerous situation, formed the 1st Leib Hussars into line and threw them against Ameil's flank. The Leib Hussars were organized with three squadrons in their first line and the fourth in a second line serving as a reserve. Ameil's 15th Light Cavalry Brigade was thrown back, but the 1st Leib Hussars were then struck by GB Mouriez's 14th Light Cavalry Brigade and thrown back towards Heinersdorf where they were fallen upon by the 29th and 31st Chasseur à Cheval Regiments.

To meet the advancing Prussians the Saxon Prinz Clemens Uhlan Regiment moved forward to stem their advance. The 2nd Kurmärk Landwehr Infantry Regiment, seeing the advancing Saxon cavalry, withdrew and did not rally until it was behind Gross-Beeren. As the landwehr re-established itself on behind Gross-Beeren, it formed itself into battalion squares. The Saxon cavalry, meeting the prepared infantry and having no support, stopped and withdrew back to its original positions.

Attack of the 1st Leib Hussar Regiment under Major von Sandrart against Fournier's Division at Gross-Beeren, by Knötel.

Mouriez's brigade overran Neu-Beeren, but the Prussian pressure was so great, that it was unable to maintain its position in the village. Despite that, its timely intervention probably saved the VII Corps from complete disaster. With this, Guilleminot's 14th Division withdrew, with Pacthod's 13th Division towards Thyrow and Trebbin.

The Prussian force found fatigue beginning to tell very heavily on them. They had passed the previous night without sleep, on the wet ground. They had then marched most of the morning and had fought all afternoon in a heavy rain. They were in little condition to do anything, let alone pursue a beaten enemy.

After the destruction of the von Löw Regiment, Oberst von Bose, commander of the 1st Brigade, 25th Division, found his right and rear covered with Prussian skirmishers. He was in danger of being cut off, even though the effectiveness of the skirmishers was greatly diminished by the rain. He decided to withdraw on Lowenbrück, and while moving there, he was joined by the grenadier battalions and 2/König Infantry Regiment. Among his ranks as he bivouacked that night, were three eagle bearers from French regiments, who had become separated from their regiments.[31] Shortly afterwards the rest of the 25th Division joined him, and the 24th Division, which was covering the retreat, arrived at 10:00 p.m., that evening.[32]

At the end of this action GM Krafft's 6th Brigade was in position, to the left and 200 paces in front of Gross-Beeren. The battalion of his extreme right was on the Windmühlberg. GL von Bülow now stopped all forward movement.

Reynier Retreats

To the Saxon left, GL Lecoq's 24th Division had been unable to execute its orders. Mellentin's brigade's forward movement had started against Hessen-Homburg. The 1/3rd East Prussian Infantry Regiment stood before Neu-Beeren, having on its right the 2nd East Prussian Grenadier Battalion. The Saxon attack was serious. Part of the Saxons moved towards the small woods to the west of Neu-Beeren, to turn the Prussian right with their artillery. Major Sióholm observed this movement and sent the Fus/3rd East Prussian Regiment from the second line to the right of the grenadiers and extended his line towards two Swedish battalions that were approaching from the Ruhlsdorf forest.

A landwehr battalion was thrown back, but it was joined by the 1/3rd East Prussian Regiment, which drove back its assailants.

After the check of the 32nd Division, Reynier decided it would be an error to engage his last reserve, Brause's brigade. He ordered Lecoq to withdraw down the road from Neu-Beeren, while Jarry's Brigade and the 2nd (von Sahr) Saxon Light Regiment were to defend the road from Gross-Beeren to Wittstock. During this action, the Saxon Hussar Regiment was sent to Wittstock, to cover the bridges. The Saxon withdrawal was covered by Oberst von Brause using the 1st (Lecoq) Saxon Light Infantry Regiment, 2/Rechten, the Prinz Friedrich Regiment, the jägers and Rovray's 12pdr Battery.[33] The progress of the Prussians was stopped by the Saxon 2nd 6pdr Foot Battery and Rovray's 12pdr Battery.

The 2nd East Prussian Grenadier Battalion and the Fus/3rd East Prussian Infantry Regiment pursued the 24th Division, with their right covered by the 1st Leib Hussars, which threw their freiwilligerjägers towards the west. The infantry skirmishers pushed through and captured a small wood to the south of Neu-Beeren, capturing the Saxon 12pdr battery. Only the appearance of a strong force of French cavalry kept them from holding the battery. The Prussian skirmishers, now totally disorganized, withdrew back to their brigade, rather than face annihilation by the French cavalry. The Saxons re-manned their battery and withdrew it.

Oudinot's Actions during the Battle

The presence of the Prussian cavalry to the west caused Oudinot to be concerned about his left, so he directed Guilleminot's 14th Division towards Ahrensdorf, via Siethen, and moved with the rest of the XII Corps through Nunsdorf, towards Christinendorf, Trebbin, Gross-Beuthen, and Siethen where Pacthod's 13th Division bivouacked.

Once in Siethen, Maréchal Oudinot indicated the intention to send to Guilleminot the two divisions of the III Cavalry Corps, but the appearance of a large force of Prussian cavalry by Klein-Beuthen, caused him to retain Lorge's 5th Light Cavalry Division with him. Fournier's 6th Light Cavalry Division was detached to join Guilleminot's 14th Division.

The Prussian cavalry withdrew towards Saarmund. The direction of their withdrawal caught Oudinot's attention, and distracted him with more concerns for this left. The 1st Bavarian Brigade was left in Trebbin with a battery. The 2nd Bavarian Brigade was left in Gross-Beuthen, because of his preoccupations with this force of Prussian cavalry.[34]

That evening Oudinot was informed that Guilleminot's 14th Division was in Ahrensdorf, and that advanced forces had been sent as far as Sputendorf, without encountering the Prussian cavalry. He knew nothing of his right, but heard a strong cannonade in that direction, and concluded that the VII Corps was engaged.

Pacthod.

Despite his apparent understanding that the VII Corps was engaged, he did not issue orders for a rapid move to support them. Indeed, he made no decision as to what the XII Corps would do the following day.

The cannonade renewed on his right about 6:00 p.m., and further disquieted him. He dispatched a number of officers to the right to reconnoiter and report to him. They returned at 8:00 p.m., and reported that Reynier was engaged and withdrawing in great disorder.

Though one corps was beaten, he still had two that were in good order. Nonetheless, Oudinot decided to withdraw. He sent his chief of staff to locate Reynier and Bertrand and give them the order to withdraw. His chief of staff returned at 1:00 a.m., with Reynier's report of the battle and news that Reynier was withdrawing on Gottow, in no state to assume the offensive.

The Battle of Gross-Beeren had, in fact, consisted of three disjointed and isolated battles. The defeat of the VII Corps obliged the IV and XII Corps to withdraw, but with insignificant losses. Reynier's losses were not overwhelming. The Saxons lost 28 officers, 2,096 men and 7 guns.[35] The von Löw Regiment was so punished and reduced in strength that its two battalions were merged into one. Durutte's 32nd Division, including the 133rd Line and Würzburg Regiment, lost 16 officers and 1,122 men, including about 600 prisoners. Fournier lost about 400 men. Reynier's VII Corps was reduced by 3,662 men out of slightly over 23,000 men, or about 16% of his strength. Not a crippling loss, but most assuredly substantial. As a gage of the severity of these losses, there are indications in the French archival records that these losses were significant enough to result in the complete reorganization of the two Saxon divisions into a single division. However, it is not clear if the losses forcing this change were the result of losses during the battle or further losses suffered from the withdrawal from the battlefield. The Prussians reported capturing 14 cannons,

52 caissons, two field forges, and six other wagons. The Prussians lost 159 dead, 662 wounded, 228 missing, and six dismounted guns.

The French Withdraw

The morning after the battle found the French withdrawing to their positions of the previous day, in Trebbin and Wittstock. Reynier decided to withdraw behind Wittenberg and to seek cover behind the Elbe. On 24 August his forces reached Baruth and Gottow.

On the allied side, the pursuit was leisurely at best and did not threaten or push Oudinot's forces significantly. The small force at Luckau was attacked by von Wobeser's landwehr.

8

Oudinot's Withdrawal and the Other Northern Corps 25 August–5 September 1813

Wobeser's Attack at Luckau

Wobeser, after being ordered to take Luckau, moved through Golsen and Giesmannsdorf. The city of Luckau was garrisoned by 100 French, the Saxon 1/Prinz Maximilian Regiment, 30 cavalry, and a battery of 8 6pdr guns.

Wobeser sent Colonel von Jeanneret to attack Luckau, with three battalions and four squadrons. Von Jeanneret moved in from the east with his infantry, as the 2nd West Prussian Landwehr Regiment attacked from the west. The battalions of Berg, Poblotzki and Lewinsky[1] advanced against the New and Sandower Gates.[2]

The Poblotzki Battalion (3/3rd West Prussian Landwehr) drove the Saxons back from the Sandower suburbs, inflicting several casualties on them. As the battle developed, Wobeser sent forward Wegener's 6pdr Battery #22. The battery bombarded the city with howitzer shells and the walls and works with round shot. Some houses were set afire and at 5:00 p.m., the city was stormed. That evening, 25 August, the 700 man garrison capitulated.

The Skirmish at Stulpe

During the morning of 25 August, the French IV Corps was moving down the road from Neuhof to Linow, but found the road impassable. The corps then moved towards Baruth, but this movement delayed the dispatching of Franquemont's 38th (Württemberg) Division to the east. It did not begin its movement until about 11:00 a.m. When it did, the Württembergers moved in the following order:

> Advanced Guard: one squadron of the Herzog Louis 3rd Chevauléger Regiment and two companies of the 1/4th Line Regiment.

> Main Body: The remainder of the Herzog Louis 3rd Chevauléger Regiment, two companies of the 1/4th Line, the 2/4th Line, 2nd Foot Battery, the 2/6th Line, 2/2nd Line, 1/1st Line, the Park and the 1/1st Line.

> Rear Guard: The brigade of GB Stockmayer and a light artillery battery. GB Briche moved along the right and the column moved by the road from Gross-Ziescht and Schenkendorf.[3]

The remainder of the IV Corps withdrew, with the Italian 15th Division forming the head of the column, and being sheltered by the two other divisions. Bertrand was following the direct road through Baruth, Holbeck, Linow, and Stulpe, but feared the appearance of the Prussians on his flank. When he reached Schenkendorf, he took the road to Jüterbogk and moved to the north.

Franquemont was ordered to occupy Holbeck, or a position near the village on 25 August. Not finding Holbeck, he chose to assume a position with his two brigades by Stulpe, such that he could be supported by a French division if necessary. He posted the 1/4th Line and three squadrons of the Herzog Louis 3rd Chevauléger Regiment near Holbeck, facing to the west a large force of Cossacks, which were moving in the direction of Lückenwalde. The 1/4th Line Infantry Regiment occupied the village and the Chevauléger positioned a line of pickets between the forest and the lake, on some open terrain facing towards Lückenwalde.

Two regiments of Cossacks, supported by a jager battalion,[4] descended on the Württembergers shortly after they took up their positions, galloping directly through the defile. The three squadrons of the Herzog Louis 3rd Chevauxlegers sent a troop forward in skirmish formation that chased the Cossacks back. After reforming their pulk, the Cossacks charged twice more without success and finally withdrew.

Franquemont.

The Skirmish at Kemlitz

GB Stockmayer received orders to take his rearguard to a position to the south of Baruth. Stockmayer responded by detaching the 1/10th Light Regiment and the 1/7th Line Regiment with five guns to the south of the village and posted the 1/9th Light Regiment to the north of it. As the terrain was impassable on the two sides of the road, this regiment executed its withdrawal very easily. It placed two companies behind a dike and the rest, with a gun, stood in the village. The 2/7th Line Regiment withdrew and joined the rest of the brigade.

Stockmayer held this position until 2:00 p.m., as ordered, without being disturbed by the allies. At 2:00 p.m., he began his move towards Kemlitz in the following order: 1/10th Light Regiment, 5 guns, 1/, 2/7th Line Regiment, 2 companies of the 9th Light Regiment, a gun, the rest of the 9th Light Regiment.[5]

As Stockmayer's force approached Kemlitz, it was approached by three strong columns of allied cavalry, about 1,500 Cossacks, and a battalion of Russian infantry coming out of the forest to the north of the village.[6] Stockmayer deployed his artillery and began to bombard these columns. The 1/9th Light Regiment deployed behind the guns and the rest of the brigade moved to the right and left of the road. The battery and the 1/9th Light Regiment withdrew slowly.

The attacking forces belonged to Wobeser's brigade. Prussian Oberst Jeanneret commanded three battalions, four guns, and two squadrons.[7] Jeanneret had sent 50 cavalry towards Baruth at the break of day. This detachment reported a force of Württembergers covered by cavalry and a battery. The Württemberger advanced posts were thrown back, but shortly afterward the force of 4,000 Württembergers moved up onto the windmill hill. Jeanneret withdrew behind a rearguard and fell back on Glashütte. Jeanneret called for reinforcements and soon received the 1st and 3rd West Prussian Landwehr Cavalry Regiments, and the 1/, 2/Pomeranian Hussar Regiment. With these reinforcements Jeanneret advanced again.

One of the Prussian regiments moved towards his right and Stockmayer sent the 1/10th Light Regiment and four guns to face them. The two other regiments and two guns stopped Oberst Jeanneret as he moved directly against the Württemberg position.

Because he had no artillery, Oberst Jeanneret was unable to effectively engage Stockmayer's brigade. As a result, he withdrew to Baruth, where Wobeser arrived at 8:00 p.m., with part of his brigade.

Stockmayer, for his part, withdrew from Kemlitz and re-joined Franquemont in Stulpe without being pursued. The contact between the French formations was so bad that very few of them knew where the XII Corps was. Stockmayer, wishing to know if Jüterbogk was occupied by the French sent a small force from the Herzog Louis 3rd Chevauléger Regiment under a lieutenant to make a reconnaissance of the village.

The Württemberg reconnaissance force had gone only a few miles when it encountered Oudinot's pickets. It continued and arrived in Jüterbogk between 3:00 and 4:00 a.m. A quick survey of the city revealed a small force of Cossacks, which were quickly chased away. They also learned that there were about 400 Cossacks camped in the vicinity of the village. They then returned to Holbeck without losses.

VII Corps

Reynier set the 25th Division en route to Linow the morning of 25 August. He found himself obliged to follow the route of the XII Corps. The 24th and 25th Divisions advanced with flank guards out, constantly apprehensive of the possibility of a cavalry pursuit by the allies or strikes at their flanks by other allied formations. That night the VII Corps arrived in Werbig, where it bivouacked.

Allied Pursuit

The lack of activity by Bülow during the 24th had allowed Tauentzien's forces to become somewhat separated from the rest of his forces. Bernadotte ordered him to stop his advance, rather than permit himself to become too far advanced and isolated, where he might be subjected to an attack by the larger French forces he was pursuing. In order to make up lost time, Bernadotte ordered the 4th Corps to not pass beyond Zossen and to align itself with the 3rd Corps. GM Wobeser was ordered to cover the left flank of the French, with the goal of harassing them, and taking every prisoner he could, during their retreat. As the ordered alignment between the 3rd and 4th Corps occurred, Tauentzien reported about 3:00 p.m., that the French retreat was a veritable rout, with the road being covered with abandoned arms and dead horses.

The advance of the 3rd and 4th Corps resumed and that evening the 3rd Corps arrived in Kerzendorf. The allied pursuit was so leisurely that Oudinot allowed his army to profit from it and spent 26 August reorganizing and reequipping itself. He had, however, lost contact with Bertrand's IV Corps and did nothing, until he heard the noise of the cannonade during the skirmish at Holbeck. It was the beginning of a series of rearguard actions fought by the Italians and Württembergers.

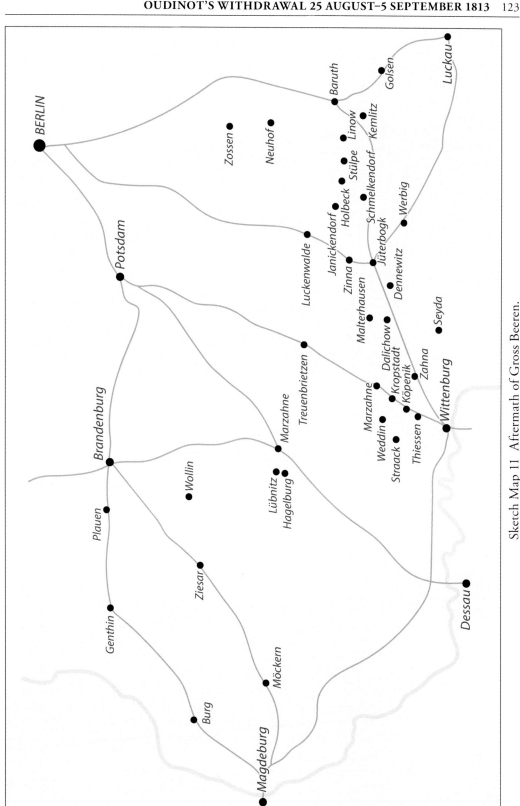

Sketch Map 11   Aftermath of Gross Beeren.

The Skirmish at Holbeck

GB Stockmayer's forces stood before Holbeck. He relieved the 1/4th Line Regiment with the 1/9th Light Regiment.[8] On its right the 1/7th Line was posted along the forest that extended from Holbeck to Stulpe. The 1/10th Light Regiment took a position before Stulpe and extending towards Dümpe. The 2/7th Line Regiment extended itself towards Linow.

The 1/9th Light Regiment had observed Cossacks from its advanced posts. About 8:00 a.m., two Cossack regiments and a Russian jager battalion appeared before Jänickendorf, and threw back the Württemberg half company that stood in front of the village. A total of three companies of the 1/9th Light Regiment defended the village against the Russians. The 4th Line Regiment moved to the gap between the village's southern exit and the lake. The Herzog Louis 3rd Chevaulégers stood to the east of the lake. The 1/9th Light Regiment was obliged to withdraw and fell back to the heights to the north where they were joined by the 1/1st Line Regiment on the left and the 1/4th Line Regiment on the right. The 2nd Line Regiment positioned itself behind this force and the formation advanced against the Russians with the support of a half battery. The Russians were thrown out of the village.[9]

The Russian GM Orurk, who commanded four brigades of cavalry, some infantry, and three horse batteries, advanced to the position and decided not to renew the battle. He maintained an observation force consisting of the battalion, two squadrons, and two guns, while sending his main body towards Jüterbogk, where he learned there was a body of Poles (four companies of voltigeurs and a squadron), which had thrown the Cossacks out of the village on the 25th. Orurk overran Jüterbogk quickly, with four Russian squadrons, Hellwig's two squadrons, and two guns. The Poles were pursued as far as Rohrbeck and Bochow, losing 300 men in the process.

The French division on the extreme right of the French army, had not been disturbed by these activities. Wobeser concentrated his division during the morning around Baruth, which he occupied with a single battalion. The bulk of his force stood on the wind mill heights. Colonel Galathi, of the Cossacks, informed him that a combined arms column was in Linow. Wobeser sent him a force of three battalions, four guns, and two squadrons.

A small rearguard action developed with these forces and Fontanelli's 15th Division, but it was of no significance. Both the Württemberg and Italian divisions bivouacked around Smielkendorf that afternoon.

Borstell's Attack

At 7:00 p.m., Borstell learned that there were about 7,000 Italians and Württembergers in Smielkendorf. He decided to attack them that evening. He dispatched a battalion to guard the defile and started the bulk of his 5th Brigade en route to Holbeck at 7:00 p.m. A flanking column moved through Dümpe.

As he arrived before Smielkendorf his landwehr mistook his flanking patrols for French and began firing, causing great disorder. One battalion broke and threw away its equipment in an effort to escape. The French were now aware of the Prussian presence and leapt to arms.

Borstell organized the 5th Brigade into a square of six ranks, the artillery in the center. At the break of day he discovered the Württembergers 600 paces in front of him and also learned that he was facing a far superior force. He decided to establish contact with the Russians at Zinna. He pulled his brigade back into a forest, to the north of the village of Smielkendorf.

The Württemberg advanced guard in the village pushed forward, and shoved back the skirmishers of the 3/2nd Reserve Infantry Regiment and the squadron of the Pomeranian Hussar Regiment facing them.

At 5:00 a.m., a Württemberg patrol, going for water, stumbled into a Prussian force and drove them back. They attacked the skirmishers from the 9th and 10th Companies, 2nd Prussian Reserve Regiment. The two last companies, which were held behind in reserve, and a few more companies of the 2nd Battalion moved forward to support their fellows, but they did not become engaged, as the Württembergers were not interested in sustaining a major skirmish and withdrew.

GD Franquemont had no goal other than to mask his corps' withdrawal, but the two Prussian companies were sufficient to draw his attention and stop his movement. After an hour, he broke the combat. Two squadrons drove back the advanced Prussian forces and a few rounds of artillery gave the Prussian skirmishers cause to pause.

The French withdrawal resumed. Small skirmishes of no significance continued until 28 August, when the IV and XII Corps were on the plateau to the north of Jüterbogk.

Skirmish at Jüterbogk

Though the VII Corps had begun its movement westwards, Oudinot remained stationary with the XII Corps. He pushed the 38th (Württemberg) Division onto the plateau north of Jüterbogk. Franquemont left the 2nd Württemberg Regiment, (Herzog Wilhelm), in the city and advanced the 1st Württemberg Regiment, (Prinz Paul), and the 2/7th Württemberg Regiment onto a heights north, near Weinberg.[10] He sent the 1/10th Light Regiment into the woods to the south of Dorf-Zinna, with the mission of chasing the Cossack posts from the heights, between the village and the woods. After completing this task, its commander Major Bequignoll, occupied the northern edge of the village with three companies and held the fourth in reserve. He had cavalry on the plain covering his right flank. Döring's Brigade and a foot battery occupied Kappan, which was to the left of Spitzenberg's Brigade. The other foot battery and horse battery, less two guns attached to the cavalry, were on the heights with the 1st Line Regiment. The Württemberg 24th Light Cavalry Brigade and two guns stood on the plain, to the north of Weinberg.

Morand's 12th Division was in Kappan. Fontanelli's 15th Division was in the Jüterbogk. At 3:00 p.m. Oudinot again began the withdrawal, by ordering the two French divisions of the XII Corps to move towards the left.

Orurk's advanced guard had continued all morning to skirmish with the Württemberg advanced posts. These advanced guards were joined by the 1st Leib Hussar Regiment, whose patrols announced that two strong columns were moving on Kaltenborn and Malterhausen.

Voronzov, commanding the Russian advanced guard, thought that a favorable moment had arrived to strike the Württemberg division, despite its superiority. He threw his forces against them, but the 2,000-3,000 Cossacks did not sustain the shock and dispersed to reform themselves. They were pursued by five platoons of Württemberg cavalry that caught and meleed with them.

The Württembergers stopped their pursuit when Russian infantry appeared. Four battalions began moving on Weinberg with the 1st Leib Hussars and two more moved against the forest. The Württemberg cavalry withdrew in the greatest order, falling back behind the 1st Line Regiment. At the same time, the Russians moved into the woods against the 10th Line Regiment and three battalions attacked it. GM Spitzenberg, reinforced by the 2/7th Line Regiment, which advanced to the right of the 1st Regiment, led his force forward and repulsed all of the Russian attacks.

The Russian 13th Jager Regiment, which had moved towards the forest, deployed two companies that were sent to the west. Four other companies moved to the east and the remaining two remained in formation.

Franquemont ordered Stockmayer to advance. Stockmayer sent the 1/9th Light Regiment to the right of the 1/10th Light Regiment and reinforced the center two companies of the 9th Light Regiment. The Russians were pushed out of the woods. The battle ended with a cannonade between the artillerists of both sides. The Württemberg artillery had moved onto a plateau to support the Württemberg line and was covered by the 1/4th Regiment.

During this battle, Oudinot stopped the withdrawal of the XII Corps, and a brigade of Pacthod's 13th Division executed a countermarch and arrived in Kappan, while Morand and Fontanelli's 12th and 15th Divisions moved to the right to support the Württembergers. The French 23rd Line Regiment advanced into the woods by Jüterbogk. Lorge's 5th Light Cavalry Division moved onto the field as well. The Bavarians (29th Division) stood with the park on the extreme left of the line, but none of these forces took any part in the battle.

Voronzov was quickly aware that he had gotten the attention of a force much larger than he had suspected, and stood a very real chance of being overwhelmed, if he pressed his attacks. He pulled back and Oudinot's forces again began their withdrawal. The withdrawal continued without significant incident until 3 September, when the corps returned to its original encampments.

Movements of the French Flanking Corps

Davout had also moved out of Hamburg with a corps of 30,000 men to support Oudinot. He moved on Schwerin and encountered the forces of Wallmoden, which he drove back. However, hearing nothing from Oudinot, he operated circumspectly so as to not find himself isolated and without support. Finally, Davout stopped.

Bernadotte's Advance to the West

Bernadotte, after his victory at Gross-Beeren began a slow pursuit of Oudinot. The first objective of his army was Wittenberg. His advanced guard reached Zahna and Kropstädt on 30 August where it contacted the VII and XII Corps standing on the right bank of the Elbe.

From there Bernadotte directed his forces towards Seyda. The Swedish army established itself on the right of Raben and to the left of Rödigke, while the other forces of the Army of the North remained stationary.

The Skirmish at Thiessen

During the morning of 3 September, Bülow sent a report to Bernadotte that the two Saxon divisions, with 10,000 men, were withdrawing towards Wittenberg. This report may have been tainted by Bülow's desire to resume a vigorous offensive.

At 6:00 a.m., the advanced guard of the Prussian 5th Brigade, four squadrons of the Pomeranian Hussars, the Fus/1st Pomeranian and 3/2nd Reserve Regiments and four guns from 6pdr Foot Battery #12 under the command of Major von Thümen, moved out of Marzahne on the road to Wittenberg. GM Borstell accompanied Bülow. Another column, under Major von Beier, with two squadrons of the East Prussian Uhlans, the 1/, 2/2nd Reserve Regiment and two guns from Horse Battery #11, was ordered to turn the forest to the east of Thiessen and then to advance through Wergzahna and Rahnsdorf, towards Woltersdorf. The bulk of the 5th Brigade was to follow the main road.

The advanced guard of the Prussian 3rd Corps followed Bertrand's rear guard, which stood on the south edge of the forest to the north of Thiessen. Bülow did not intend to start a serious engagement until he received an order from Bernadotte. He ordered the Fus/2nd Reserve to push through Bertrand's rearguard and ordered Krafft's 6th Brigade to move to Kropstädt and Dobschütz's Brigade to Zahna.

The fusilier battalions, after taking the edge of the forest, moved towards Thiessen. They succeeded, supported by two companies of skirmishers drawn from the Pomeranian Regiment, that had moved to their left to take a foothold in the northeast part of the village. Fontanelli, who attached great importance to the possession of the village, sent several battalions against their left. He supported their attack with a battery, whose howitzers had considerable effect in the forest. The Prussians were thrown out of the village. The Fus/2nd Reserve Regiment retreated in good order, while the skirmishers and six platoons were deployed in skirmish formation during the withdrawal.

During this the main body of the brigade stopped in Köpenik. Two battalions of the 1st Pomeranian Regiment were detached from the main body and moved to the left of the road. Their intention was to advance to the left of the line of fusiliers and assist them in the recapture of Thiessen. The 2nd Battalion was ordered to maintain liaison with Major Thümen's forces.

The Württembergers evacuated Woldersdorf at the approach of Major von Beier's forces. Von Beier then directed his two battalions, preceded by their skirmishers, into the woods between Thiessen and Euper. Oberst von Schön, commander of the 1st Pomeranian Regiment, heard the sound of the skirmish on his left and stopped his remaining battalion. After assuring liaison with Major von Beier, the two continued their movement on Thiessen. During this stop a gap occurred between the battalions of the 1st Pomeranian Regiment.

After these engagements, Bülow sent a report at noon, that the French were withdrawing. A dispatch came from Bernadotte, but did not contain any news of support. Left to his own devices Bülow resumed his advance. The 2/1st Pomeranian Regiment, carried away by its ardor, pushed out of the woods and into the plain. The Württemberg artillery had waited for such a target and immediately inflicted heavy casualties on it. Not being enough, the combined Bavarian cavalry regiment then charged and completed the job of pushing them back into the woods.

With the appearance of von Beier's detachment, Bertrand ordered Spitzenberg's Brigade to cover the right of Fontanelli, in occupying the heights to the north of Euper. This position allowed him to threaten to turn the left flanks of the two battalions of the Prussian 2nd Reserve Regiment, which immediately withdrew.

Borstell's 5th Brigade lost 8 officers and 227 men, while Spitzenberg's brigade lost 5 officers and 154 men.

The IV Corps did not pursue the Prussians, who after passing through the woods, reached Woldersdorf under the protection of two squadrons of uhlans. The position taken by Dobschütz contributed to Bertrand's decision to stop. Dobschütz had begun his movement towards Zahna at 2:00 a.m. It had been evacuated by the French and set afire by Cossacks. On hearing the sound of the battle, he turned the village and pushed on to the heights that dominated the valley of Abtsdorf. He positioned two battalions and two guns to face the French right. During the evening, he sent his troops between Bulzig and Woltersdorf.

After the battle, Stockmayer's Brigade moved into Euper, where it replaced Morand's 12th Division. Morand's division then passed into the second line. Stockmayer occupied the village and the small woods to the north of it with the 7th Line Regiment.

The 1/9th Light Regiment took a position on a wooded height to his right. The 1/10th Light Regiment remained in reserve. Bassewitz's squadron

Morand.

of the Herzog Louis 3rd Chevauléger Regiment was joined by a force of 90 Bavarian, Westphalian, and Hessian cavalry under Captain Korriger, and this cavalry patrolled the two flanks of the position. They waited for an attack that did not come.

Girard's Maneuvers

While Oudinot was moving towards Gross-Beeren, Girard's Division departed Magdeburg on 21 August and moved towards Belzig, where it sought to join Oudinot.

During the armistice, GM von Hirschfeld had been posted to the right wing of the Army of the North, to cover its flank, as well as to watch the Magdeburg Garrison. The main body of Hirschfeld's forces was posted by Brandenburg, while GM von Puttlitz, who commanded six battalions, three squadrons, two guns and a howitzer, maintained a closer watch on Magdeburg.

The 4/1st Reserve Regiment, 1/, 3/6th Kurmärk Landwehr Regiment, Finkenstein's squadron (2/3rd Kurmärk Landwehr Cavalry Regiment), and Puttlitz's guns were by Königsborn. Between Gerwisch and Buderitz stood the 4/3rd Kurmärk Landwehr Regiment, 4/6th Kurmärk Landwehr Regiment, and Erxleben's squadron (3/5th Kurmärk Landwehr Cavalry Regiment). The 2/6th Kurmärk Landwehr Regiment and Kreigsheim's squadron of the 3/6th Kurmärk Landwehr Cavalry Regiment stood by Pechau.[11]

In reaction to Girard's movement von Puttlitz sent Lieutenant von Kyckpusch with the 3/6th Kurmärk Landwehr Regiment, a few guns, and Finkenstein's squadron (2/3rd Kurmärk) forward to support the advanced posts, between Gabs and Alt-Königsborn, where Finkenstein's squadron found itself quickly involved in a small skirmish with a force of French cavalry.

However, the strong French column quickly pushed back the advanced posts and Lieutenant Kyckpusch's small force, first to Neu-Königsborn, then to the heights between Woldersdorf, Körblitz, and Büden. Here they found Kreigsheim's squadron (3/6th Kurmärk), which joined them. Puttlitz found himself able to assume the offensive and made a sharp attack against the French, as they passed out of Woltersdorf. The French paused long enough for Puttlitz to withdraw the two battalions he had in Buderitz. Rittmeister Erxleben had, earlier in the morning, harassed the French in their camp by Prester, by moving onto the glacis of that fortress.

GM von Puttlitz then began to move down the main road through Körblitz and Burg towards Genthin, and the following day he arrived in Plauen, without further contact with the French.

On the same day, the Poles found themselves in contact with Winzingerode, who sought to push them back and to strike Girard's flank. The Orurk Cossack Regiment patrolled around the Lückenwalde. GM Czernichev passed the village of Treuenbrietzen. His Cossacks attacked all of Dombrowski's advanced posts. Czernichev's main force, five regiments and four guns, under his immediate control, attacked Weddin, which was occupied by a squadron of the 4th Polish Lancer Regiment, three companies of the 14th Polish Infantry Regiment, and two guns under the command of Colonel Kostanecki.[12]

The ensuing battle lasted eleven hours. Kostanecki sustained ten attacks, and 500 Cossacks dismounted to combat as skirmishers, but to no avail. Dombrowski dispatched two squadrons and a

Czernichev, by G. Dawe.

battalion to reinforce his troops and this force tipped the scales in the Poles favor. The Cossacks withdrew in a skirmish line. As they withdrew, the Poles followed at a distance of about a mile.

To the east, two Russian columns attacked the Polish posts in Zahna and Kropstädt. To the west another column advanced against Straack. The Russian attacks were repelled.

On August 23 Puttlitz arrived by Brandenburg. He detached the 2/3rd Kurmärk Landwehr Regiment, with Finkenstein's squadron (2/3rd Kurmärk) and a few guns to watch the pontoon bridge over the Havel by Plauen. When he moved his force into Brandenburg, he left a single company of the 2/3rd Kurmärk Landwehr to guard the bridge.

Earlier, on 21 August von Puttlitz had detached Oberstleutnant von der Marwitz with the 1/, 3/3rd Kurmärk Landwehr Regiment and three squadrons of the 3rd Kurmärk Landwehr Cavalry Regiment to Rathenow. They were to act either as a reserve, or to form an Altmark Division. However, as von Puttlitz was pushed back to Brandenburg, this detachment withdrew, and on 23 August it joined again with Puttlitz.[13]

Girard moved his main force into Ziesar and had his advanced troops in Viesen. Von Puttlitz's forces were in Radkruge. Seeking information on the French strength von Puttlitz sent Oberstleutnant von der Marwitz to advance with his detachment and reconnoiter the French positions. Von Puttlitz reinforced him with two battalions of the 6th Kurmärk Landwehr Regiment, Erxleben's squadron (3/5th Kurmärk), and a few guns.

Marwitz moved out on 24 August, leaving two battalions and the cannon in an advanced work of the fortress, the two other battalions in Radkruge, and went forward with the cavalry. Lieutenant Lessing, 3rd Kurmärk Landwehr Cavalry Regiment, led 30 men on the point. As he advanced into the village of Viesen, he encountered a superior force of French hussars and was driven back over the Rogäsen.

Behind the Rogäsen stood a second Prussian squadron, which with the rest of Marwitz's force, went over the Fiener dam. Lt. von Bredow, with 30 men of Erxleben's squadron, was sent into the village of Zitz, where it reported a detachment of French cuirassiers. Rittmeister von Erxleben went into the village with his entire squadron to check the report, but encountered a company of the 26th Légère Regiment formed and waiting to receive him. A quick volley killed six Prussians, but the Prussians reportedly took 100 men prisoner and killed or wounded 22 more.

When Marwitz returned to Puttlitz, he reported French infantry in Ziesar, cavalry in Bückewitz, and in large numbers behind the Fiener dam.

The following day the French marched on Glienicke and Wollin. GM von Hirschfeld, with orders from Bernadotte, had moved out of Brandenburg on 22 August. He detached the 1/, 3/7th Kurmärk Landwehr Regiment by Potsdam and on 23 August was in Saarmund, and participated in the Battle of Gross-Beeren. Three battalions of the 1st Reserve Regiment were sent to Ruhlsdorf. On 24 August he marched with his entire corps. The 1/Elbe Infantry Regiment and a gun from the 4th Brigade were added to his force. On 25 August he joined Puttlitz's forces by Brandenburg.[14]

Hirschfeld had orders to seek out Girard and to engage him. He sent Puttlitz to Golzow and then followed him with the entire corps. Oberstleutnant von der Marwitz was sent to Wollin with two battalions and three squadrons. Once there von der Marwitz learned that the French were moving on Belzig. GM von Hirschfeld learned this news on 26 August, when he also received firm news that GD Girard was in camp by Lübnitz.

Hirschfeld quickly sent his forces forward towards Belzig. He arrived before the French and sent GM Czernichev with five Cossack regiments to a position opposite Belzig.

Once in Belzig, Girard found the city occupied by Czernichev's streifkorps. His advanced guard, of four battalions, four guns and some cavalry, encountered Czernichev's Cossacks and a quick skirmish resulted. Girard stopped and waited for orders.

9

The Battle of Hagelberg
27 August 1813

The Prussians Arrive

Hirschfeld's forces stood before the advancing French, which had lagered behind the village of Lübnitz. Hirschfeld divided his force into an advanced guard (Langren), two wing brigades (Puttlitz & Boguslavski), a reserve brigade (Marwitz), a small detachment under Oberstleutnant von Reuss, and a cavalry brigade (Bismark). His force contained approximately 10,350 infantry and 960 cavalry.

The 3/7th Kurmärk Landwehr Regiment and the 3rd Company, 2/1st Reserve Regiment were positioned in the Grebs earthwork, on the road from Brandenburg. A company from the 2/3rd Kurmärk Landwehr Regiment was posted in Plauen, and the 1st Company, 3/3rd Kurmärk Landwehr Regiment was sent to Drewitz. The 4/7th Kurmärk Landwehr Regiment had been detached to Spandau, as a garrison earlier.

On the left flank of the French stood a forest. Starting with his forces in Benken, Hirschfeld took his forces in a column to the left of his position, with his advanced guard (Major von Langen) leading the way, followed by Bismark's cavalry, then his guns, the skirmishers of the 1/1st Reserve Regiment, Boguslawsky's Brigade (left wing), Puttlitz's brigade (right wing), and finally Marwitz's brigade (reserve). His attack was to come from the Steindorf Forest. As they swung through the woods, they deployed in attack echelons at an interval of 150 paces.

Hirschfeld prepared his attack by issuing the following orders:

> The combined cavalry, except for von Bornstadt's squadron, shall march to the left under the command of Oberst von Bismark. The fusilier battalion [3/1st Reserve Regiment] shall lead, followed by the two musketeer battalions of the 1st Reserve Regiment. The fusilier battalion shall march formed on the middle, while the two musketeer battalions shall march formed on their left.[1] They shall be followed by the 11 cavalry squadrons, then the 10 guns of Captain Count Chamborand [Russian Light Battery #26]. The skirmishers from the 1/1st Reserve Regiment shall cover the right hand of the artillery. They shall be followed by three battalions of von Boguslawsky's Brigade, then the six battalions under the command of GM von Puttlitz, and then the two [and a half] battalions under Oberstleutnant von der Marwitz.[2]
>
> The march shall be made in the greatest quiet and tranquillity. Any noise or unauthorized discharge of weapons will be punished by six weeks arrest.
>
> These remaining battalions shall be formed on the left. When they are ordered to do so, the fusilier battalion shall march forward, both musketeer battalions shall swing into place, the cavalry shall trot behind the musketeer and fusilier battalions in mass and shall seek to strike the enemy as soon as possible.
>
> The artillery shall remain in formation and move according to the terrain.

The battalions of von Liewen [2/4th Kurmärk] and Schwerin [3/4th Kurmärk] shall march behind the infantry. When they arrive behind the 1/, 2/1st Reserve Regiment, they shall support its attack. Von Bornstedt's Battalion [4/3rd Kurmärk] and the remaining battalions shall swing in when Bornstedt's battalion is supported by the artillery.

The two battalions of the 1st Reserve Regiment von Langen shall advance forward. The battalions of Liewen [2/4th Kurmärk] and Schwerin [3/4th Kurmärk] shall follow 200 paces behind them. The battalions of Bornstedt [4/3rd Kurmärk] and Held [1/7th Kurmärk], as well as the artillery, shall follow a like distance behind them. The two battalion echelons shall follow at an interval of 150 paces. The position of the French and the terrain shall determine when the battalions on the right shall begin the attack.

The battalions under Oberstleutnant von der Marwitz shall swing against the middle of the enemy and remain in reserve.

Oberstleutnant Reuss, with the battalions of Ozorowsky [2/7th Kurmärk], Stutterheim [1/Elbe], Grolmann [1/4th Kurmärk], and Bornstedt's squadron [3rd Kurmärk Cavalry], shall march to the right, taking the way through the woods to Steindorf, where Reuss can deploy his forces to strike the enemy's flank and rear when the enemy falls back on Glien and Wiesenburg. Oberstleutnant von Reuss must not begin his attack too early, but only when the cavalry has advanced.[3]

Hirschfeld specifically ordered that his initial attack was to be made without firing. It was to be made with cold steel as done "by our brave comrades at Gross-Beeren."

Hirschfeld.

The Battles Begins

About 1:00 a.m., the Prussian advanced guard reached the woods. They noticed the French cavalry encampment by Lübnitz and its infantry pickets. Oberst von Bismark advanced at the trot with three squadrons of the 6th Kurmärk Landwehr Cavalry Regiment to engage them.[4] All three squadrons formed line and drove forward at a gallop. His move was quickly followed by the other two regiments, which moved against the French.

The French responded by bringing forward their infantry and artillery to the right side of the village. A quick fight began on the French right flank, as Kreigsheim's squadron, the 3/6th Kurmärk Landwehr Cavalry Regiment, countered a move by some French cavalry. As that cavalry skirmish began, Oberst von Bismark advanced with the 5th and 6th Kurmärk Landwehr Cavalry Regiments, leaving the 3rd Kurmärk Landwehr Cavalry Regiment to defend his battery.[5]

The French infantry was ridden down, except for two closed battalions that stopped the assault and drove back the three squadrons of cavalry.[6] The French cavalry was scattered and driven back on the main body of Girard's forces, about 1,500 paces behind Lübnitz.[7]

Girard.

The 2/3rd Kurmärk Landwehr Cavalry pursued the fugitives into the village of Lübnitz, while the 5th and 6th Kurmärk Landwehr Cavalry Regiments moved to the east side of Lübnitz, where two French battalions had taken a position behind a garden wall. The French defensive fire struck the 5th Kurmärk Landwehr Cavalry and killed three officers, but no troopers.

The three battalions of the advanced guard moved to the left. Their artillery was in echelon to the right with Boguslawsky's three battalions (4/3rd and 2/, 3/4th Kurmärk Landwehr) behind it. Oberstleutnant von Reuss was moving into the open fields between Steindorf and Lübnitz with the 2/7th Kurmärk, 1/Elbe and 1/4th Kurmärk.[8] He had his squadron, the 2/3rd Kurmärk Cavalry, (Bornstedt's) in Steindorf. The Prussian cavalry stood on the right wing, followed by the 2/7th Kurmärk Landwehr Regiment, 1/Elbe Infantry Regiment, the guns, and to the left was the 1/4th Kurmärk Landwehr Regiment. The French countered this attack with a single battery.[9] Reuss' goal was to strike the French flank and rear.

Reuss advanced behind the cavalry and moved into the woods in line, forming on the heights to the south of Steindorf. Once on the heights he began to receive fire from a French battery, located to south of the Lübnitz windmill. As soon as the first howitzer shell struck Ozorowsky's Battalion (2/7th Kurmärk), it turned around and refused to advance further. His two other battalions followed its example and stopped, but the French battery withdrew because of the approach of the main column.[10]

The main column, following the advanced guard, deployed the three battalions of the 1st Reserve Regiment into line and a battery of artillery to their right. The battalions of Schwerin (3/4th Kurmärk) and Liewen (2/4th Kurmärk) formed behind the infantry.

They advanced in the direction of the Belzig Woods in order to turn the French right. The village of Lübnitz was afire as the 4/3rd Kurmärk and the skirmishers of Langen's brigade advanced into it, capturing a cannon. The French were obliged to fall back towards Hagelberg and took up a

The 3rd Kurmark Landwehr Infantry Regiment attacking the French 19th Line Infantry at Hagelberg, by Knötel.

position on the heights by the village. Girard quickly called in his outlying troops, which included a battalion and two guns from Hüttenberg Hill on the right flank. His retreating forces were covered by two batteries south and southwest of Lübnitz. The Prussian cavalry had completely disbanded itself in its pursuit of the French cavalry and the 1/9th Westphalian Regiment, and was now called to reform. The 1/9th Westphalian Regiment was observed to be fleeing through Wiesenburg.[11]

Major von Langen directed the attack of the 1st Reserve Infantry Regiment against the French forces moving from Hüttenberg as they moved into the Belzig Woods. His attack was supported on the left by the 2/, 3/4th Kurmärk Landwehr Regiment, part of Boguslawsky's Brigade, which von Hirschfeld had brought forward from Lübnitz. The 1st and 2nd Companies, 2/4th Kurmärk Landwehr Regiment found themselves sorely pressed and bent back to the right, forming a hook.[12]

As Lübnitz burned, Czernichev's forces that were standing by Belzig, pulled back to their division and Hüttenberg. Then he extended them towards the Belzig Woods, so that the bulk of the first line moved in this direction. They remained by Hüttenberg through most of the battle in order to prevent the French from placing any artillery there.[13]

Lübnitz Falls

Lübnitz was occupied by a force of French artillery. The village of Lübnitz was afire as the Prussians advanced against it. Major Bornstedt, commander of the 4/3rd Kurmärk, advanced against Lübnitz preceded by the skirmishers of the 1st Reserve Regiment, reinforced by a detachment under Kapitän von Pochhammer. The battalions of Liewen (2/4th Kurmärk) and Schwerin (3/4th Kurmärk) followed closely behind them.

It was 3:00 p.m., Reuss stood before Steindorf. Bornstedt's Battalion (4/3rd Kurmärk) was passing through Lübnitz. The battalions of Liewen and Schwerin moved against the Hüttenberg so they could strike the right of Hagelberg. The Russian Light Battery #26 stood before Lübnitz. The cavalry stood with the 3rd Kurmärk Cavalry by Lübnitz to cover the left side of the Belzig Road. The remainder of the cavalry stood in the woods. Puttlitz had his six battalions in three echelons and the last was only just exiting from the woods. Marwitz marched behind Puttlitz and formed to the left with his three battalions in column, in order to move against the left.[14]

At this time the bulk of the French force stood united in their initial position on the Triftberg Hill, west of Klein Glien.[15]

Major von Bornstedt moved the 4/3rd Kurmärk through the burning streets of Lübnitz pursuing the retreating French. As he reached the heights of the Belzig Woods, the 2/, 3/1st Reserve Regiments joined him on the left. Reuss' brigade joined in on the right and this combined force swept forward towards the Birken Woods. The 3rd Kurmärk Landwehr Cavalry Regiment advanced on their right flank.

The seven Prussian battalions marched through the open field between the Belzig and the Birken Woods, with the 3rd Landwehr Cavalry Regiment on their right wing. Bornstedt's Battalion (4/3rd Kurmärk), still on the point, moved through Hagelberg. The French withdrew back towards Klein-Glien. The French were thrown from the Hagelberg heights and three Prussian battalions and the cavalry pushed them into Klein-Glien.

After Reuss' detachment was ordered to Steindorf, the battalions swung right and moved through the Steindorf Forest. As they passed through the southern edge of the woods, they saw the four Prussian battalions moving against Hagelberg. They were the Bornstedt Battalion (4/3rd Kurmärk) and the three battalions of the 1st Reserve Regiment, which had been relieved from the Hüttenberg position. Major Langen allowed Reckow's Battalion (1/1st Reserve) to follow in a second line. Reuss put Grolmann's Battalion (1/4th Kurmärk) with the howitzer by the windmill as a rallying point and moved with the two other battalions towards the Triftberg heights.[16] The Bornstedt Battalion (4/3rd Kurmärk) advanced through Hagelberg and then moved to the west of Klein-Glien in the direction of the Triftberg Hill. The six battalions of the second line followed to the right and left.[17]

Major von Langen prepared to strike at Klein-Glien, when he learned that the French left wing was closing from the Belzig Woods, where it had been. The French appeared in overwhelming numbers for Langen's small force and forcing him to withdraw into the Birken Woods.

Puttlitz had taken a half hour to deploy his brigade after it cleared the woods. As soon as Marwitz stood on his left, he directed his brigade to march towards the Hüttenberg, where he heard artillery fire.

Girard withdrew his forward units as the Prussian right flank advanced, Puttlitz's brigade advanced in three echelons through the Steindorf Forest. Each echelon consisted of two battalions, with the left wing forward. Marwitz's brigade stood to the left and extended right, where it stood in Battalionsmasse to cover the flank. The three battalions of Puttlitz's brigade, the 1/7th and 3/, 4/6th Kurmärk Landwehr Regiments, moved against the Belzig Woods as the reserve, three battalions under Oberstleutnant von der Marwitz (1/, 2/, 3/3rd Kurmärk), moved to the left and advanced against the Hüttenberg Hill to support the battalions of Liewen (2/4th Kurmärk) and Schwerin (3/4th Kurmärk) that had been pounded by French artillery.[18]

These two battalions had been under the fire of two French guns, 900 paces away on the Hüttenberg for about a half hour and had lost a number of men and officers without being able to respond.

With the arrival of the new battalions, the entire force advanced against the French. Oberstleutnant von der Marwitz, with his three battalions and his cavalry, advanced to the right. The 2/, 3/4th Kurmärk Landwehr were ordered forward, with the reserve brigade behind them. They were to move to the right and form line.

On the right wing the three battalions closed with the left wing of Puttlitz's brigade. The 1/7th and 4/6th advanced against Hagelberg. They engaged a French line, which was posted behind the Hagelberg heights, and a general firefight began. Major von Rohr ordered the other battalions forward and led them into line. The 3/6th Kurmärk moved to the right, so that a total of eight battalions now faced the French in the Belzig Woods. The 1/, 2/6th Kurmärk moved towards Lübnitz and the 4/1st Reserve Regiment remained behind to cover the guns.

It was 4:00 p.m. Of the seven battalions on the right wing, Bornstedt was even with Triftberg. Left at the same level stood the two battalions of the 1st Reserve opposite Klein-Glien. To the right of them, by Hagelberg and on the Windmühlberg, stood two of Reuss' battalions and the Prussian howitzer. The 3rd Kurmärk Landwehr Cavalry Regiment stood on the right wing in the Schmerwitz Thiergarten.

The left wing, eight battalions strong, stood a quarter of a mile to the rear. Five of Marwitz and Boguslawsky's battalions and two guns faced Hüttenberg, three of Puttlitz's battalions were engaged in a fight in the Belzig Woods. Two of Puttlitz's battalion were moving into Hagelberg, one stood with the eight undeployed guns by Lübnitz, and the eight squadrons of Bismark's cavalry stood on the left wing, facing Belzig.[19]

Oberstleutnant von der Marwitz found his troops beginning to suffer under French cannon fire. He ordered two guns forward to engage the French artillery. Quickly a French cavalry column appeared on the road from Belzig to Gross-Glien, which was on the French right flank. The French advanced from the Belzig Woods and Puttlitz swung his first echelon to support his forces there. One powerful volley stopped their advance and drove the French back.[20] GM Czernichev, with his Cossacks, marched to the right side of the Belzig forest, where a French battalion stood supporting their cannons. Oberstleutnant von der Marwitz sent his brigade forward and engaged the guns with his skirmishers, forcing the French to withdraw.

The Prussian Right

At 4:00 p.m., the three battalions of the Prussian right were in battle, pushing to reach the Triftberg Hill, two of the battalions of Reuss' detachment followed to the left in echelon, two stood before Hagelberg and below the Windmühlberg. The cavalry regiment stood on the right wing in Tiergarten.[21]

The battalions marching on Triftberg were led by the Bornstedt Battalion (4/3rd Kurmärk). They were about 1,000 paces in front of the French position as the French infantry moved into the Grützdorf earth works. As the Prussians advanced, a French battery on Triftberg fired on them. Bornstedt moved his battalion to the left of the 1st Reserve Regiment towards Klein-Glien and moved behind the Hagelberg Windmühlberg. The remaining battalions closed behind Bornstedt (4/3rd Kurmärk) and prepared for a bayonet assault against the battery. They advanced to within 200 paces of the hill, lowered bayonets, and charged forward.

The assault passed through the French skirmish fire and the volleys of the French battalion standing behind them. The Prussians deployed and began to exchange fire with the French line. After 3-4 minutes, the leading Prussian battalion, Bornstedt (4/3rd Kurmärk), was disordered and fell back, carrying the other battalions back with it.[22]

Girard took advantage of this and advanced his forces, reoccupying Klein-Glien, Hagelberg, and the Windmühlberg again. Thrusts and counter thrusts began between the Birken Forest and the Belzig Woods. One of the French batteries that had been on the Windmühlberg advanced again and resumed firing on the Prussians from its old position.[23]

The Prussian Left

As this was going on GM von Hirschfeld ordered Marwitz and the left wing to march to the right flank, where he was to attack the French. The left wing, 10 battalions, was 1/4 mile to the rear and had five battalions and two guns under Marwitz (1/, 2/, 3/3rd and 2/, 3/4th Kurmärk) moving to Hüttenberg Hill. Three more battalions, under Puttlitz, moved against the Belzig Woods. Two more battalions marched against Hagelberg and one supported eight guns that stood by Lübnitz. Eight squadrons stood on the left wing by Belzig.[24]

Von der Marwitz marched behind the battalions of the left wing, while engaging the French with his skirmishers. He began his march with the 3/4th Kurmärk, which was on his left flank. They were followed by the 2/4th, the 1/7th and the 3/, 4/6th Kurmärk Landwehr Regiments. He was moving against the Hüttenberg Hill. It was 4:00 p.m.

The 2/4th Kurmärk was obliged to remain in the woods because of a force of French hussars facing it. However, as the French cavalry withdrew, the 2/4th Kurmärk advanced to follow the rest of its brigade. The 1/7th received the order to move behind the battle line and move to the right flank where it was to move to the battle by Thiergarten and Schmerwitz.

Oberstleutnant von der Marwitz, by the Belzig Woods, swung his battalions to the left and put them between the Belzig Woods and on the right the Birken Forest. He even withdrew the battalions of the right wing. The French, instead of following, remained on the Hagelberg heights.

Three squadrons from the 3rd Kurmärk Landwehr Cavalry Regiment now moved to the left of von der Marwitz, while to the right stood the 3/1st Reserve Battalion. Somewhat behind this line stood Bornstedt's Battalion and Reuss's brigade. The 1/, 2/1st Reserve Regiment and Finkenstein's Squadron, 3rd Kurmärk Landwehr Cavalry Regiment, stood on the far right wing, where they had been sent as a result of some false information. The 6th Kurmärk Landwehr Cavalry Regiment moved to the Lübnitz windmill in order to watch Steindorf and Benken.

The artillery working with Marwitz moved to the left on a small hill, where the remaining guns soon moved. The 4/1st Reserve Regiment moved out to the left behind Reuss' brigade. Oberst von Bismark advanced with the 5th Kurmärk Landwehr Cavalry behind the infantry, facing the Belzig Woods.

The French stopped on the heights by Hagelberg and chose to engage the allies with their artillery. GM Czernichev continued his move towards Gross-Glien from Belzig. He detached a regiment into the forest and sent Oberst von Benkendorf forward with two regiments to the left, while he took the rest of his force through the woods. GM Czernichev, however, was unable to join the battle before it ended.

During the cannonade on the right wing, the French pushed out of the Belzig Woods. The 3/4th Kurmärk advanced, supported by the 3/6th Kurmärk, against Hagelberg. The 4/6th Kurmärk remained in the woods covering the flank. This flank was soon covered by the battle line. On the left were the skirmishers of Marwitz's brigade, which swarmed over the French positions, capturing a dismounted howitzer.[25]

Major von Rohr sent his two battalions forward in an attack. However, as they overran Hagelberg, they found that the French had established a battery on the Windmühlberg and began to take his force under canister fire. One of his battalions turned and returned fire. Despite its efforts, however, both battalions were driven back. Two French battalions pursued them into the Grützdorf Woods. On the other side, the French had established the 1/, 3/, 4/13th Hussar Regiment and a battery. These were attacked by a Cossack regiment and the skirmishers from Marwitz's brigade.

At the same time, the 2/4th Kurmärk Landwehr came out of the Belzig Woods and moved towards Hagelberg, driving the two counterattacking French battalions back. The 2/4th Kurmärk Landwehr then joined the approximately 300 skirmishers from the other battalions and moved against the Grützdorf Woods, which this force completely surrounded. The French in the woods lowered their arms and surrendered.[26]

The 2/4th Kurmärk Landwehr then moved towards Hagelberg and was sent to the right flank. On the way, it was ordered to move on Lübnitz, where it assumed a position behind the 6th Kurmärk Landwehr Cavalry Regiment. Bismark's cavalry brigade took up positions around Lübnitz. The 6th Kurmärk Landwehr Cavalry Regiment stood to the right of the village, the 5th to the left and the 3rd Kurmärk Landwehr Cavalry stood before the village.

GM von Hirschfeld then ordered a general advance by the right wing. It moved forward in echelon. Major von Grolmann led his 1/4th Kurmärk Landwehr forward with the 4/1st Reserve, under Major Rembow, moving on his left. Major von Bornstedt's landwehr battalion (4/3rd Kurmärk) followed on the left of the battle in skirmish formation.[27]

As the Prussian attack advanced, the two French battalions again appeared before Hagelberg and advanced against the Prussian middle. GM von Hirschfeld ordered the 1/3rd Kurmärk Landwehr to counterattack. The three squadrons of the 3rd Kurmärk Landwehr Cavalry Regiment were sent against the second French battalion. Oberstleutnant von der Marwitz, on the right wing, came back and sent the 3/3rd and 2/3rd Kurmärk Landwehr forward to support the attack.

The battalions of Grolmann (1/4th Kurmärk) and Rembow (4/1st Reserve) stormed the Hagelberg village heights. Major von Grolmann followed the French into the village, while Major von Rembow occupied the high ground. The French battle line was broken and its wings pushed back.

As the 1/, 2/3rd Kurmärk Landwehr advanced, so did the 3rd Kurmärk Landwehr Cavalry. Major von Zschi schen (1/3rd Kurmärk) captured two guns and pushed a force of French back into an enclosed garden in the village where they were surrounded and captured. The skirmishers from another Prussian battalion moved into the village and a bloody house to house battle began.

The 2/3rd Kurmärk, led by Major Schönholz, encountered another French battalion by the village, supported by a troop of cavalry. Major Schönholz advanced and the French, already shy because of the other losses around them, withdrew back towards Hagelberg.

The 3rd Kurmärk Landwehr Infantry Regiment advanced into a plowed field surrounded with a stone wall, which stood next to the village. The French exchanged volleys with the landwehr and withdrew into the village.

The Prussian Left

While the French were engaged in the battle to their front, Marwitz's forces on the left marched forward, striking the French skirmishers in the Belzig Woods and, pushing them aside, advanced to the Kiehnberg Heights. The three battalions following them moved to the northwest of the woods.

GM Puttlitz had been struck from his horse and overall command was assumed by Oberst von Borstell. His first action was to send a battalion from the Belzig Woods against the east side of Hagelberg. Hagelberg was only lightly held and fell quickly.[28] The battalions of Liewen (2/4th Kurmärk) and Held (1/7th Kurmärk) moved behind the Russian battery and the three others, Schwerin, Woisky and Delitz (3/4th and 2/, 4/6th Kurmärk respectively), moved through the woods in dispersed order against Hagelberg.[29] At the same Czernichev arrived on the battlefield with his four Cossack regiments.

On the left flank Major von Rohr led the 1/, 2/6th Kurmärk Landwehr against Hagelberg, while on the right the 2/7th Kurmärk Landwehr moved to the attack. The entire French right wing, 5-6 battalions, was thrown back into the village, with only a few escaping. The Windmühlberg was taken by storm and the French battalion standing there fled, abandoning two guns. The French middle was broken as well and the French began withdrawing.[30] GD Girard was wounded in this action.[31]

At 5:00 p.m., the frontal battle consisted of a cannonade. Girard pulled his forces behind the heights to the northwest of Hagelberg to unite them. He saw that his right flank and rear were threatened. However, to clear this threat he had first to throw back the threatening Prussian left wing. He sent four battalions against Hagelberg to throw out the Landwehr that had just captured the village.[32] In addition, he needed to recapture the Kiehnberg Heights. Soon the 13th Hussar Regiment and two French battalions moved forward to attack the withdrawing Prussian skirmishers. The Prussians moved back to Grützdorf. In this critical moment two of Czernichev's Cossack regiments appeared south of Grützdorf. They charged the hussars and broke them. The two French battalions, however, took up positions to the north of Petersberg.

The Prussian skirmishers pursued these two battalions. The Russian guns, supported by the Vlastov Cossack Regiment, struck at the two French battalions. Having no other chance the French surrendered about 30 officers and 1,000 men to 300 Prussian schützen and 500 Cossacks.[33]

Von Marwitz had advanced by Hagelberg in an attack with the battalions from the center. Grolmann's Battalion led the attack, supported on the left by Rembow's Battalion. The battalions of the right wing also advanced. Grolmann (1/4th Kurmärk) and Rembow (4/1st Reserve) pushed into the middle of the French position, breaking their line. The sharpshooters of these two battalions, under Kapitän von Sacken, pushed forward and captured two limbered guns before they could escape.

The Zschüschen Battalion (1/3rd Kurmärk) stood in column on the Windmühlberg near Hagelberg. About 250 men from Bornstedt's Battalion (4/3rd Kurmärk), deployed as skirmishers, covered Zschüschen's Battalion. They advanced over a wall, suffering heavily from French musketry, but continued to advance. They stormed forward into Hagelberg and engaged a battalion of the French 3/19th Line Regiment with bayonets. The French were forced to withdraw.[34]

The French left began its withdrawal, as did the force in Hagelberg. Initially only the 1/, 2/1st Reserve Regiment and the 1/Elbe Regiment pursued the French, but they were joined shortly by the 3/1st Reserve Regiment with two guns. The remainder of the Russian guns moved to the Windmühlberg by Hagelberg, under the cover of the 3/3rd Kurmärk Landwehr and, shortly after, the 4/6th Kurmärk Landwehr.

The French moved through Klein-Glien, where they stopped awhile, but the close pursuit of the 1/6th Kurmärk Landwehr obliged them to resume their movement. The 1/, 4/6th Kurmärk Landwehr and the 1/7th Kurmärk Landwehr moved past Klein-Glien. Oberst von Bismark moved forward with the 5th Kurmärk Landwehr Cavalry to support the pursuit, as the French withdrew from Gross-Glien in two columns. One moved towards Wiesenburg and the other moved towards Schlammau, through Wittenberg and towards Magdeburg.

The Prussians lost 9 officers and 229 men killed, 28 officers and 831 wounded, and 662 men missing. Their total losses come to 1,759 men and 49 horses. Out of the 8,900 men, this is a casualty rate of about 20%, which is quite high. It is, however, more probable than the figures Plotho provides – 2 officers, 14 non-commissioned officers, and 218 men dead, 30 officers, 53 non-commissioned officers, and 695 men wounded.[35]

In contrast, the Prussians claimed to have taken 5,000 prisoners, five cannons, two howitzers, 20 caissons, and the entire wagon train of Girard's division, for a loss of only 1,700 infantry and 45 horses. They also claim to have recovered 6,000 French muskets from the battlefield.[36] Though no doubt exaggerated, these figures must not be far from the truth. Boppe quotes a letter from Colonel Joly, speaking of the division after the battle, says, "I saved the debris of the division, which I brought into Wittenberg."[37] Sauzey states that when the division returned to Wittenberg after the battle, it contained no more than 3,500 men and had lost 5 cannons and 2 howitzers.[38] Sauzey's statement would make an estimate of 6,000 casualties and prisoners quite within reason.[39]

The Battle of Hagelberg is unusual, not in that the French were defeated, but that the defeat was at the hands of a force consisting largely of Prussian landwehr that had only recently abandoned its pikes for muskets. This suggests that the Landwehr was hardly what one would call veterans. Theoretically Girard was leading first line troops. It is true that they were mostly recent conscripts, yet it was conscripts that had defeated the allies at Lützen and Bautzen. It was also new French conscripts facing Prussian landwehr which had little difference in its overall training.

As the campaign progressed and other French generals faced the Prussians repeatedly, but they were not again to face a force so heavily composed of landwehr. And yet the French prevailed over the Prussians frequently. In addition there were about 10,350 Prussian infantry and 960 Prussian cavalry facing a French force of 8,000 infantry and 900 cavalry. The Prussians had a superiority of only 29% in infantry. There was no significant difference in cavalry strengths, though the French force was largely regular cavalry and the Prussians consisted entirely of landwehr and Cossacks. The French should have had a qualitative superiority. In addition, Girard had a potentially crushing superiority in artillery. Girard had 23 guns to Hirschfeld's 11 guns.

This strongly suggests that the problem at Hagelberg for the French was not particularly the quality of the troops, but more the quality of the general. It was Girard's first independent command and he failed. His dispositions were poor, he apparently had no plan of battle, he did not reconnoiter the Prussian forces with his light cavalry, his employment of his troops in combat was uncoordinated, and the precautions he did not take to prevent surprise were criminally negligent.

This is most surprising in light of Hirschfeld not being a first line Prussian general and a general who almost completely vanishes from the pages of history after his one victory. There is one other element that can be brought into the examination of why Girard lost and that is the morale of the French troops when compared to that of the Prussian troops. It is probable that the landwehr were motivated by a desire to liberate their homeland and had not yet experienced enough of the campaign to discover that war is not a pleasant experience. In contrast, the French were not motivated by any similar passion, a large number were new conscripts with little desire to be there, and even the veterans must have been tired of war by then.

10

The Army of Bohemia Advances on Dresden 12–25 August 1813

On 12 August Barclay de Tolly began to move the Russo-Prussian army into Bohemia, to join the principal allied army, under the Austrian general, Fürst Schwarzenberg. Initially, the principal allied army was to move up the Elbe towards Leipzig. Once he joined it, the principal allied army became known as the Army of Bohemia. Blücher, with the Army of Silesia, advanced into the neutral zone and seized the Katzbach crossings, pushing the French back onto the Bober River.

Napoleon was caught off guard by these moves, as he expected the main allied army to advance through Lusatia, while he assumed that no more than a covering force of 100,000 would operate in Bohemia.

By 14 August Blücher was in Strigau. Bernadotte, commanding only two thirds of the Army of the North, stood near Berlin. The remainder of his forces were scattered about northern Germany, in various garrisons.

Napoleon had positioned his army in a roughly triangular disposition. His base was on the middle Elbe, while the sides of the triangle stretched from the mouth of the Katzbach to Wittenberg and Königstein. The allied armies faced two sides of this disposition in a roughly semi-circular formation.

Napoleon's Plans

Napoleon planned to seize the initiative. The day before the end of the armistice, he left Dresden to re-join his army. First he moved to the camp at Lilienstein, near Königstein. From there he moved on to Bautzen, where he stayed until 17 August. The Imperial Guard served as his escort and accompanied him on his travels.

His intelligence sources had advised him of rumors that the Russians had left Silesia to join the Army of Bohemia. In reaction, he increased his forces around Zittau, sending Victor (II Corps) to meet the expected advance there.[1]

Napoleon estimated that Blücher had no more than 50,000 men and planned to strike swiftly at him. Napoleon felt that once he had destroyed the Army of Silesia, he could, from his central position, strike at either of the other two armies, now totally isolated from the other, and defeat them separately. He anticipated Blücher's army would be engaged at Buntzlau, where he was poised to concentrate 180,000 men.

Earlier, on 16 August, Napoleon had written Maréchal Macdonald:

> When I shall be assured that Blücher, with Yorck, Kleist and Sacken, which does not make 50,000 men, is advancing on Buntzlau, and that Wittgenstein and Barclay de Tolly are in Bohemia, to move on Zwickau or Dresden, I will march in force to destroy Blücher. As soon as you have information, advise me what you have before you. Of the rest, I have good hopes for this. It appears to me that the enemy is opening himself to heavy blows.[2]

139

With this as his plan, Napoleon directed Vandamme (I Corps) to move to Bautzen, where he could pull him to Zittau, or send him back to support St. Cyr (XIV Corps) in Dresden, should the Army of Bohemia advance up the Elbe. Napoleon was not particularly worried about St. Cyr's position, because he believed that the allies had only about 40,000 Russians around Glatz in Bohemia.

In the event St. Cyr was faced by the supposed 40,000 man Army of Bohemia, Napoleon directed St. Cyr to dispute every foot, to hold Dresden, and to maintain contact with Vandamme to ensure his communications with the main army.

Oudinot, to the north, was to maneuver on Berlin. Davout's headquarters were in Bergdorf, before Hamburg, but he had begun to move on 15 August. Girard's division, with 8,000 to 9,000 men, was to be dispatched to Magdeburg. Dombrowski's 27th (Polish) Division of 5,000 or 6,000 men stood in Wittenberg. Including those forces covering his flanks, there were about 120,000 men involved in Oudinot's march on Berlin.[3]

In addition, Davout was ordered on 18 August to move across the Stettnitz and seize Lauenburg. On 20 August Girard was ordered to move against Brandenburg. Napoleon's headquarters were in Görlitz, where he had drawn to him the five Imperial Guard Divisions, the III, V, VI, and XI Corps, and the I and II Cavalry Corps.[4]

If the Russians and Austrians were to advance out of Bohemia towards Zittau and Gable, causing Poniatowski (VIII Corps) and Kellerman (IV Cavalry Corps) to find their position untenable, Victor (II Corps) was to advance to their assistance. Vandamme (I Corps) was positioned so that he could join them in a day and a half, and should that happen, St. Cyr (XIV Corps) was to dispatch Mouton-Duvernet (42nd Division) to replace Vandamme's forces at Neustädt and Rumburg.

This would give Napoleon about 70,000 men at Gabel, and if the Guard was not engaged, Napoleon would personally led 50,000 of them to Gabel.[5]

As Napoleon reviewed the situation, he felt confident that he had envisioned every contingency. He felt that the allies on the right bank of the Elbe must pass by way of Zittau, which was the only good road. If they used the left bank they must pass through Teplitz and Peterswalde, as they moved on Dresden. Here St. Cyr would meet them with 60,000 men, and in four more days a total of 150,000 would be concentrated to face them.

If the allies were to move against Nürnberg or Munich, Napoleon would have all of Bohemia exposed before him and available for his maneuvers. If, instead, the allies had detached large forces to the Army of Bohemia, Napoleon could invade Silesia with 200,000 men.

Assuming that Schwarzenberg would cross the Elbe, Napoleon planned to move to Königstein, so that when the allies closed on Dresden, he would have them between two armies. If they chose to avoid battle and withdraw by Commotau, Napoleon felt he could reach Prague before them.

The Army of Bohemia

The main Austrian army was under the command of Karl, Fürst zu Schwarzenberg.[6] Its 130,850 men had stood, during the armistice, between the Elbe, Moldau, and Eger Rivers waiting for the political decisions to be made.[7] It had been agreed at Trachenberg that the Austrian army would be reinforced by a force of Russians and Prussians. To effect this reinforcement, the Russo-Prussian forces under Barclay de Tolly marched south in six columns. On 19 August Barclay joined the Army of Bohemia in the camp by

Prince Schwarzenberg.

Bubin, behind the Eger. His arrival brought the Army of Bohemia to a total strength of 237,770, including 172,000 infantry, 43,500 cavalry, 7,200 Cossacks, 14,900 artillerists and 698 cannon.

Along the Bohemian border with Saxony, stood a line of Austrian posts formed by the Austrian 2nd Light Division of FML Graf Bubna. This screen extended from Rumburg to the right bank of the Elbe. The 1st Light Division of FML Fürst Moritz Liechtenstein stood with the main body at Brix, with advanced posts by Nollendorf, Zinnwald, and Kloster Grab. The 3rd Reserve Division of FML Graf Crenneville extended from Kloster Grab across Sebastiansberg and Commotau.[8]

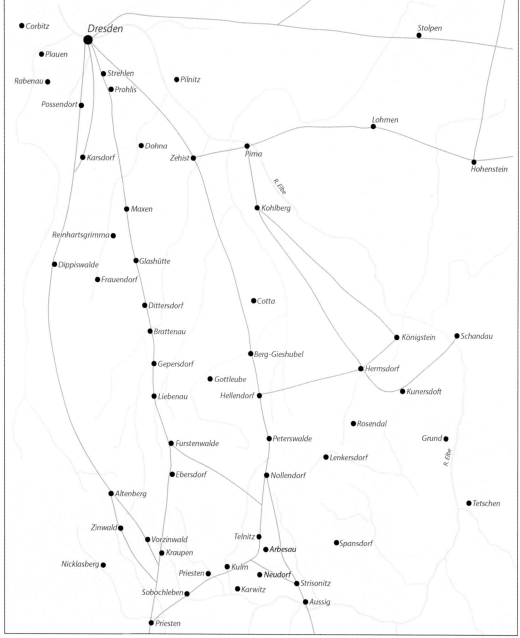

Sketch Map 12 The Region between Dresden and Teplitz.

On 20 August the Army of Bohemia was poised to strike. GM Count Kudaschov stood with a light streifkorps in Zinnwald. GM Roth stood with a line of pickets extending from Dorn to Nollendorf.

Zeithen's Advanced Guard Corps stood in the Jörgenthal, from Freiberg to Grünthal, watching Streck with his advanced posts. His advanced guard stood in Creutzberg. The 1st Austrian Light Division (Moritz Lichtenstein) was ordered, at daybreak, to move through Commotau, and to move down the Grünthal-Gestadt road.

The 3rd Austrian Reserve Division (Crenneville) marched its main force to Reichshöhe, and had its advanced posts extending from Gestàdt to Wiesenthal. Meszko's 3rd Light Division, acting as the advanced posts for Klenau's corps, stood by

Barclay de Tolly.

Schlackenwerth and watched the Streck, from Wiesenthal to Haus Georgenstadt.[9]

Bubna's 2nd Austrian Light Division (Neipperg) was reinforced by the addition of St.-Priest's Russian corps in Landshut and was scheduled to execute a diversionary attack against the right bank of the Elbe as well as to defend the Bohemia border.

During the day, Wittgenstein's wing moved to Teplitz, and Kleist's II Corps moved to Brix. The Austrian right wing moved into Commotau and lagered there. It consisted of the infantry divisions of Colloredo (1st Division), Civalart (3rd Division), and Chasteler (1st Reserve Grenadier Division), with Nostitz (1st Cavalry Division) and Schneller (3rd Cavalry Division).[10]

The Austrian left wing, under Graf Gyulai, marched into its lager by Caaden and consisted of the divisions of A. Lichtenstein (4th Division), Weissenwolff (2nd Division) and Lederer (2nd Cavalry Division). Bianchi's 2nd Reserve Division marched through Saatz and lagered on the right wing of the Commotau encampment. Klenau's corps marched from Caaden and encamped on the left wing of the Commotau lager.

The fifth column of the Russian Reserve (Raevsky) marched to Sinutz, the sixth column of the Russian Reserve (Gallizin V) moved into lager by Budin. The first Austrian artillery reserve moved into Klein Kerbitz, and the second Austrian artillery reserve was in Wissoezin. The first and second munition reserves were in Postelberg and Liboschann.[11]

The first movement of the Army of Bohemia began, when Oberst Graf Mennesdorf, with a few cavalry squadrons and two Cossack regiments, crossed the Eger on 21 August and began acting as a streifkorps.[12] The honor of being the first to engage the French was to fall to Bubna's division.[13]

French Plans

On 19 August, in an effort to verify his concept of the allied attack, Napoleon detached Poniatowski (VIII Corps) with a strong reconnaissance force towards Gabel to confirm the allied advance. Napoleon learned that Schwarzenberg had passed through Melnik on the 17th, and Schlan on the 18th, with the Russians in support. This led Napoleon to believe that he was marching west, and he ordered Berthier to fortify the Zittau gap. Vandamme (I Corps) had relieved all the posts of the 42nd Division (Mouton-Duvernet) in Schluckenau, Neustädt and Rumburg. The 42nd Division stood so it could move on Hohenstein and Schandau, ready to support Vandamme if the need arose. Vandamme was to keep himself ready to move on the Eckartsberg camp, a few miles behind Zittau, and join Poniatowski's 7,573 men.[14]

The Allied Advance into Saxony

The Army of Bohemia was deployed in five columns. They were organized as follows:

	Bns	Sqns	Guns	Men
1st Column Wittgenstein	45	19	72	28,000
2nd Column Kleist	41	44	112	37,000
3rd Column Hessen-Homburg	54	61	86	56,000
4th Column Gyulai	25	18	36	36,000
5th Column Klenau	25	20	48	24,000

Part of the Russian Guard and the reserve stood by Zinutz, while the rest was posted in a lager by Budin. The various trains and columns stood with the reserve south of the Eger.[15]

On the morning of 21 August, the day before the Army of Bohemia began its march northwards into Saxony, Poniatowski's VIII Corps stood on the Austro-Saxon border in three columns. The middle column stood in Gabels, the right column under GD Léfebvre-Desnouëttes stood in Rumburg and extended to the passes of Georgenthal. The left column was under the Polish GB Uminsky and extended from Friedland and Reichenberg.

To the west of Poniatowski, St. Cyr stood with his XIV Corps spread along the Austro-Saxon border between Königstein and Annaberg, though the bulk of his forces were between Königstein and Altenberg. Little did he know, that he was about to face the advance of 237,770 Austrians, Russians and Prussians with his single corps and l'Heritier's V Cavalry Corps.

Graf Wittgenstein began the assault by leading his column down the main road from Teplitz towards Dresden. He was supported by the Russian and Prussian Guard. Kleist led the second column from Brix, across Jöhnsdorf, towards Sayda. His reserve consisted of the 1st Grenadier Division, while the Russian Cuirassier Division and the Guard Light Cavalry Division were organizing by Minitz. The third column, under GdK Erbprinz von Hessen-Homburg, advanced from Commotau towards Marienberg. The fourth column, under FZM Graf Gyulai, advanced from Caaden towards Marienberg. Klenau's Corps served as Gyulai's reserve.[16]

The first column, under Wittgenstein, moved through the passes of Gieshübel, moving forward to observe Königstein and Pirna, and if the French withdrew, it was to follow them as far as Pirna. Their right flank was secured by a strong detachment that advanced from Schneeberg, over the Rosenthal,

Wittgenstein, by G. Dawe.

towards Königstein. To cover its left flank, a similar detachment advanced from Geiersberg over the Fürstenwalde and on to Breitenau. Weaker detachments watched the roads through the Eichwalde forest, towards Altenberg and over the Nickelsberg, towards the Kreuzwald forest. These detachments linked Wittgenstein's forces to those of Kleist.

The second column, Kleist, stood as the right wing of the main army. Kleist was to seize the Sayda heights. If enemy forces were encountered by Wittgenstein's column and a battle begun, Kleist's column was to maneuver against the French right flank.

Hessen-Homburg, in the third column, was to advance on Marienberg as quickly as he could. He was to maintain communications with Kleist through three detachments that were strung between them. The fourth column, under Gyulai, was to move from Karlsbad towards Annaberg. Klenau's column was to follow behind Gyulai as a reserve for him, and the army Reserve was to maneuver behind Wittgenstein's column.

The main allied advance began at 5:00 a.m. on 22 August, though an hour previously the 3rd Light Division of GM Meszko moved from Joachimsthal over the Gottesgabe and into Saxony, in an effort to quickly seize Annaberg. The streifkorps under Oberst Graf Mennesdorf moved against Schlettau. Once Meszko's 3rd Light Division crossed and reorganized itself, it joined with the advanced guard of the fourth column, Crenneville's 3rd Reserve Division, in Bärenstein, and both divisions moved against Jöhnstadt. Crenneville's division extended itself to the east in an effort to join with the advanced guard of the third column, M. Liechtenstein's 1st Light Division. Facing little opposition, the allied advance wheeled clockwise towards the north east and Dresden.[17]

In contrast to the other allied columns, Wittgenstein was opposed by the 18,000 man XIV Corps, of Maréchal St. Cyr. St. Cyr's headquarters were in Pirna. His left wing was secured on the Elbe River with Mouton-Duvernet's 42nd Division and Claparède's 43rd Division in lager by Königstein. On the main road from Prague to Dresden, by the village of Oberfedlitz, stood the divisions of Berthezène (44th) and Razout (45th). Berthezène's 44th Division stood by Herbergen and Razout's 45th Division stood by Dippoldiswalde. The narrow paths between Gieshübel and Marienberg were patrolled by mounted troops and supported by posts in Cottaberg and Zehist.[18]

The Skirmish at Gieshübel

The first engagement between the Army of Bohemia and the French occurred when Wittgenstein's forces, under GM Roth, encountered part of the 43rd Division (Claparède), the 2/, 3/27th Légère Regiment supported by two 12pdr cannons.

Roth's advanced guard, consisting of the Grodno and Soum Hussars, the Radinov, Illowaisky XIII and half of the Ataman Cossack Regiments under GM Seslavin, the Seleginsk Infantry Regiment, the 20th, 21st, 24th, 25th and 26th Jagers, and 18 cannons, including 12 from Horse Battery #6,[19] moved with Württemberg's 2nd Corps and two squadrons of the Loubny Hussars in support. Württemberg advanced with the Loubny Hussars and six guns from a light battery in the lead. The 3rd Russian Division, under GM Prince Schachafskoy followed with Wolf's brigade[20] leading, and Chelvinski's brigade[21] behind it. Then came Puschnitzki's 4th Division with Treuffurt's brigade[22] leading and Mamonov's brigade[23] in the rear. The 13th and 27th Light Batteries, with 18 guns, followed in the rear.[24] Württemberg's corps contained about 12,500 men.

The 1st Corps, under GL Gortschakov, remained behind Peterswalde until the battle began. It consisted of the 5th and 14th Divisions. The 5th Division, under GM Mesenzov, and contained four infantry and two jager regiments.[25] The 14th Division was under GM Helfreich had only two regiments at this time.[26] The 1st Corps Artillery consisted of Position Battery #3 and Light Battery #6. The Russian cavalry, fourteen squadrons, consisting of two squadrons of the Loubny Hussars, the Tartar and Tschougouiev Uhlan Regiments under GM Millesinov, stood behind the 1st Corps.

At 10:00 a.m., Roth advanced down the main road with the 26th Jagers and eight horse guns supported by the 20th and 24th Jagers, the Seleginsk Infantry Regiment, the cavalry and eight foot guns. On his left was Lieutenant Colonel Lutzow with the 21st Jagers, four horse guns, two squadrons of the Grodno Hussars and 25 Cossacks, went down the valley by Hellendorf. A third column, under Colonel Witoschkin, with the 25th Jagers and 60 Cossacks advanced by Ölsen and Gottaleube.[27]

The 2/, 3/27th Légère Regiment supported by two 12pdrs, part of the French 43rd Division, held a position before Gottleube, on the hill before Gieshübel. They engaged Lützow's and Witoschkin's columns. The allied attack pushed the French back to the Gieshübel heights, opening the passage to Wittgenstein's forces. At the same time, the leading French elements were reinforced by the 3/65th Line Regiment. A strong firefight began between the French and the jagers of GM Roth, who attempted to trap the French. The Russian army deployed on the opposite plateau with infantry, artillery and cavalry.[28] However, the wooded slopes were not suitable for cavalry.

Württemberg directed GM Roth to maneuver his forces against the French right flank, while he led the 2nd Corps up the Gottleube valley. Once the head of Württemberg's column reached Hohenstein, he directed Wolf's brigade to strike the French flank, while his artillery and cavalry continued to march against the rear of the French position. A battalion of the Tschernigov Regiment engaged the French and threw them out of the rocks that supported their right. Not losing a moment, the French quickly withdrew to Gross Cotta.[29]

Though stripped of his cavalry and artillery, which could not maneuver well in the wooded terrain, Württemberg chose to continue his advance with just his infantry. The Russian infantry pursued the withdrawing French, until it arrived before the Ottendorf heights, where it encountered the bulk of the French forces. The French were withdrawing down the Gross-Seydewitz-Dresden road. The French force consisted of about ten squadrons covering the 2/, 3/45th Line Regiment. Württemberg deployed the head of his column and advanced the few guns that had finally joined him, but he lost precious time in the deployment. The two squadrons of the Grodno Hussars, under Lützow, joined him and were quickly sent forward to strike the right of the French cavalry. The Russian infantry advanced as well, serving to hasten the French withdrawal on Zehist. The French withdrawal was too quick and was covered by a successful cavalry attack. Württemberg, satisfied with his pursuit, stopped it in Torna.[30]

GM Roth had pushed the French down the main road to Zehist, where, during the evening, he was stopped by a strong force of French on Mount Kohlberg, near the city of Pirna.

GM Millesinov advanced with the Tenginsk and Estonia Infantry Regiments, the Loubny Hussars, and the Illowaiski Cossack Regiment #XII, to observe the passes to Königstein and hold that flank, while the Russian infantry under Roth stormed the French position at Kohlberg, driving the French back down the main road.[31]

Maréchal St. Cyr withdrew and concentrated his forces on the heights of Gross-Sedlitz, from which he later withdrew to Dresden.

The Allied Advance Continues North

The road to Dresden lay, for all intents and purposes, open to a coup de main by Wittgenstein. If the Russian attack had not been slowed by a French cavalry attack on their left during the affair at Gieshübel, as the 2nd Corps moved on Zehist, nothing would have kept the Russians out of Dresden.

As the affair at Gieshübel wound down, the Russian right was disturbed by the advance of a French force in the direction Gross Cotta, from Königstein. This force was trying solely to join St. Cyr, but Roth's timely intervention cut it off from this direction, forcing it back in the direction of Pirna. Helfreich sent a detachment of infantry and the Illowaiski XII Cossacks to Leopoldshayne and Nickolsdorf, to watch the bridges at Königstein, while GM Millesinov followed the withdrawing French through Gross Struppen.

The French XIV Corps of St. Cyr withdrew to Dresden, concentrating itself there for the defense of the city, against what appeared to be an overwhelming force of allies. Kleist's II Corps moved to Reichenau and Hennersdorf, while the Austrians moved to Rechenberg and Seyda, and the reserves of GdI Barclay de Tolly were distributed at several points to support Wittgenstein, i.e. Nassau, Kloster Grab, Hermsdorf, Jöhnsdorf, and Neuhausen. The Russian 1st Guard Division stood in Teplitz, under the orders of GL Yermolov.[32]

Wittgenstein stopped and spent the evening in Pirna, while Millesinov's advanced parties were in the Grossen-Garten (Great Garden), southeast of Dresden. After the day's events, there was a great conference between the sovereigns, Fürst Schwarzenberg and General Moreau in Commotau. There was considerable debate over the advisability of a continued march on Dresden. Some advocated a movement on Leipzig, to join with Bernadotte and the Army of the North.

In view of the pending withdrawal of the French army from Silesia, because of the allied movement on Dresden, it was realized that it would be possible to take Napoleon's army in the flank. However, if the allies were to advance too far forward, it might be them, taken in the flank, as well as having their communications along the great road from Dresden to Prague cut.

The decision was to keep advancing on Dresden. The allied lines of communication would not be so long that Napoleon could easily slip across and cut them. In addition, the Elbe River, which flows through Dresden, would give the allies a strong position behind which to face Napoleon.

Napoleon Reacts

On 23 August Napoleon left Macdonald facing Blücher's withdrawing army, and taking Ney with him, hurried back to Dresden. He had earlier detached the Imperial Guard, the I Cavalry Corps (Latour-Maubourg), and the I and VI Corps (Vandamme and Marmont) from the forces facing Blücher, and sent them hurrying westwards, towards Dresden.

On 25 August Napoleon arrived in Stolpen, a city equal distant from Dresden and Königstein. Murat met him there with a complete report on the situation. At the same time, Vandamme's I Corps was moving on Königstein. Part of Teste's 23rd Division had been detached and was between Königstein and Dresden.

Napoleon, master of the bridges on the Elbe, was able to advance on both banks of the Elbe, and developed his plans for the defense of Dresden around that ability. He decided to gather all the forces coming from Görlitz and send them across the Elbe at Königstein and Lilienstein, points held by Vandamme's I Corps. He hoped to allow the allies to establish themselves before Dresden and fall in their rear, driving them to the north and away from their lines of communication.

On 25 August he wrote to Vandamme. Vandamme's Corps had the 2nd Division (Dumonceau) in Neustädt, the 1st (Philippon) in Stolpen and six battalions (Quiot's Brigade) of the 23rd Division in Lilienstein, giving him a total of 34 battalions presently under his control. The 42nd Division (Mouton-Duvernet), XIV Corps, was to be assigned to him, if it had not already passed through his area. This would bring him to 42 battalions. With this force Napoleon directed Vandamme to move on Königstein during the 26th.

That night Napoleon sent orders to the 42nd Division and to the six battalions of Quiot's Brigade, 23rd Division. This force was to move onto the plateau behind Königstein, to deploy into battle formation in complete silence, and to be ready to accept battle, if necessary, at the break of dawn. If Quiot's Brigade, 23rd Division, was unable to bring its artillery, Vandamme was to detach two of his batteries to support the 42nd Division (Mouton-Duvernet).

Between his light cavalry, the forces of the 42nd Division and Quiot's Brigade, 23rd Division, Vandamme was to have approximately 10,000 to 12,000 men on the plateau. At daybreak this advanced guard was to seize the entire Pirna plateau. Dumonceau's 2nd Division in Neustädt was to then move onto the Königstein plateau immediately and was to be followed as quickly as possible by the 1st Division (Philippon).

Mouton-Duvernet, with the 42nd Division, Quiot's Brigade, and 24 guns, was then to move towards Pirna and take a position on the Pirna heights. Once Vandamme had ascertained that the Allies were not in a position to dispute the French possession of the plateau, he was to take a military position by Langen-Hennersdorf. Here he was to establish, as quickly as possible, a battery of 12pdrs to face any battery the allies might establish at Kohlberg.

The French bridging train was scheduled to arrive around noon in the Pirna area, with the rest of Teste's 23rd Division. The bridge was to be erected between 1:00 and 2:00 p.m., and the Pirna heights were to be occupied by the Young Guard Divisions. Teste was, at this point, to recover the six battalions operating with Mouton-Duvernet and reform his division. This would put 40,000 Guard and 8,000 to 10,000 cavalry on the left of Vandamme's I Corps. From there, Vandamme and his entire force were to advance northwestwards, seize the defiles, and fall on the rear of the enemy, supported by the Young Guard.

Mouton-Duvernet.

Corbineau was ordered to take his 1st Light Cavalry Division and join Vandamme in occupying the Pirna plateau. Corbineau commanded 4,000 cavalry and a horse battery.

The following evening the rest of the army was scheduled to arrive, and one corps was to arrive via Königstein and the other via Pirna. All of the baggage was to remain at Hohenstein, where Reuss' brigade, II Corps, was to stand guard. Reuss was to arrive that morning.

To support this passage of the Elbe, Napoleon gathered up all the boats on the left bank of the Elbe, in an effort to construct two supplementary bridges, giving him a total of five bridges over the Elbe, not including the bridge at Lilienstein.

To prevent the allies from passing the Elbe too easily, Napoleon also detached two battalions from the XI Corps and l'Heritier's (V Cavalry Corps) cavalry to Meissen, 30 kilometers north of Dresden.

Napoleon's plan was to hold Schwarzenberg at the Elbe, with the 40,000 men of the XIV Corps and to attack the allied rear on 27 August, by running the I Corps, VI Corps, part of the II Corps, and the Guard, approximately 120,000 men, through Pirna and Peterswalde. The only problem was that St. Cyr had to hold the allies for 48 hours, and prevent them from crossing the Elbe. St. Cyr stated that he could not guarantee that. Murat doubted the ability of the XIV Corps to hold its position and Gourgaud spoke to the restlessness of the Dresden populace.

Because of these negative perceptions by his generals, Napoleon found himself obliged to abandon his maneuver as being too risky. Instead he chose to send those forces slated for Königstein directly into Dresden, leaving only Vandamme to attack the allied rear. The graceful flanking slash of the rapier was to be replaced by the sledgehammer.[33]

The Allied Movements

Between 23rd and 25th of August the allies brought their forces forward. On the evening of 24 August Schwarzenberg's headquarters were in Reichstadt, with the head of the Austrian army in Dippoldiswalde and Freiberg. Kleist's II Corps was in Reinholdsheim and Wittgenstein's was before Königstein. The Austrian right wing stood between Dippoldiswalde and Beerwalde. The Austrian left wing stood before Gross-Waltersdorf, with its right by Zethau. Klenau's corps moved towards Freiberg, to cross over to the left bank of the Freiberger Mulde. From there they prepared to move against Dresden.[34]

On 25 August it was resolved to converge the allied army before Dresden. Schwarzenberg ordered that the 1st column, Wittgenstein, detach a corps to hold Königstein and observe the passes so as to prevent any French move against the allied rear. This corps was also to destroy any and all bridges it encountered.

The remainder of the column was organized into a single force that marched down the main road through Mügeln, towards Dresden, while a small detachment was sent down the Elbe by Tolkwitz to cover the flank. Wittgenstein took with him Russian Position Batteries #3 and #5 and had them march parallel to his line of march on his left flank, so that they could deploy on his left flank if he was attacked.

The second column, under Kleist, advanced with 18–20,000 men along the road to Maxen, by Lockwitz, towards Dresden with a direct link to Wittgenstein. This column took two position batteries and a howitzer battery with it. The rest of the corps formed a reserve near Maxen. The column marched by the left, so it could deploy to the right, again to face Napoleon's armies that would be coming from Silesia, to the east.

Colloredo commanded a third column, which marched by the center ready to deploy to either the right or left. It had at its head the 1st Light Division of Fürst M. Liechtenstein, which was followed by four position batteries. Colloredo's 1st Division marched at the army's rear. This column moved through Wendisch Carsdorf towards Kaitz.

A fourth column, under Chasteler, marched by its left so as to deploy the right if necessary. It had Crenneville's 3rd Reserve Division in the lead, followed by four position batteries. Chasteler's 1st Reserve Grenadier Division marched in the rear of the column. The column moved along the right bank of the Plauen valley, passing through Rabenau and Coschütz.

Bianchi's 2nd Reserve Division formed on the heights by Wendisch Carsdorf, to serve as a reserve for the two Austrian columns. The left wing of the

Colloredo-Mansfeld.

Austrian army and Civalart's 3rd Division were also placed in Dippoldiswalde to serve as a reserve.

This force began its movement at 4:00 p.m. on 25 August with a new marching order as ordered by Schwarzenberg. This directed that the advanced posts and advance guards of the first column move behind the Grossen-Garten, which was to be occupied by skirmishers, while other detachments of light troops were to move behind Striesen and Blasewitz.

The second column was to be behind Strehlen. The third column was to be before, and stretch between, Kaitz and Racknitz. The fourth column was to stand on the left wing near Plauen. Meszko's 3rd Light Division to move behind Lobda, with a detachment sent forward to Schuster Hauser to observe the French.

When that was complete, the first column of Wittgenstein stood on the road from Pirna to Dresden. It was to place its position batteries at the head of the column and wait for orders. GL Thielmann, who had defected from the Saxon army earlier in the year, was directed to accompany this column, to provide it his local knowledge.

Austrian cuirassiers, after Klein.

The second column was to occupy the road from Maxen with skirmishers, put its position batteries in the front and wait for orders.

The third column was to occupy the road to Dippoldiswalde. It too was to place its artillery at the head of the queue and wait for new orders. The fourth column was to occupy the road to Rabenau and the bridge at Löbtau. It sent a detachment up the Plauen valley. Its artillery was to be placed forward and was also to wait for orders.

Once its first dispositions were completed, Meszko's 3rd Light Division was ordered to move forward and occupy the road from Freiberg to Dresden. It was to send another smaller column towards its flank, along the road from Priesnitz to Dresden, putting it into communication with the fourth column. The cavalry of the first column was to maintain liaison with the second column, while that of the second touched the third column and the cavalry of the third column touched the fourth column.

Schneller's 3rd Cavalry Division was ordered to send a brigade to the third column and the other to the fourth column. These brigades were then to march at the heads of these columns. Erbprinz Hessen-Homburg was to follow the third column on the main road from Freiberg to Dresden, with the 1st and 2nd Cavalry Divisions of Nostitz and Lederer.[35]

When the order was given, most of the allied forces executed the actions at the prescribed hour. However, some of the Austrian troops were delayed and this was to have a significant effect on the allied assault on Dresden.

The Russian 1st Grenadier Division, the 2nd Guard Division and the Guard Light Cavalry Division found themselves united that evening under the orders of Miloradovich in Dippoldiswalde.

Grand Duke Constantine, with the bulk of the cavalry, and GL Yermolov, with the 1st Guard Division, marched by a different route towards Dresden. Barclay was in Leubnitz, near Kleist's corps.

Wittgenstein advanced on Dresden with Roth's advanced guard. The 3rd Division of the 2nd Corps was left in Zehist to observe Königstein, with eight regiments of infantry from the 2nd Corps, two squadrons of hussars and 16 cannons, and GM Helfreich, with five more battalions, a Cossack regiment and six more cannons.

Württemberg detached GM Wolf's brigade, two hussar squadrons, and two guns to the Pima plateau, where they took up positions in the village of Gross Struppen, facing the fortress of Königstein. Wolf's advanced pickets closed on Königstein and attempted to burn the bridges over the Elbe, but failed because of the fortress garrison's alertness.

Schwarzenberg planned to attack Dresden on 26 August, but he was plagued by hesitation and incertitude. Since that morning, the bulk of the allied forces moved to assume their positions. The allied advanced posts skirmished with the French pickets. On the extreme right, a French column was cannonaded as it passed through Neustädt, the Dresden suburb on the eastern bank of the Elbe.

The Battlefield

The city of Dresden sits on both banks of the Elbe River. The old city lies on the western or left bank. The newer suburbs lie on the eastern bank. The city sits in a natural amphitheater formed by a ring of hills that surround it.

The defenses of the city were in a semi-circle ring around the old city that rested on the Elbe at both ends. The left wing of the defense line was in the Pirna suburb and the right wing was in the Friedrichstadt suburb. There were five lunettes on the wall, separated by an abatis and other smaller defensive works. Behind this line stood an enceinte consisting of a ditch and palisade. Various major streets had barricades erected where they exited the city.

The XIV Corps, less the 42nd Division (Mouton-Duvernet) that was serving with I Corps under GD Vandamme, occupied the city's defensive works. The 43rd Division (Claparède) stood in the Pirna suburb in the lunette near the Dippoldiswalde. The 45th Division (Razout) stood to the right, by the Friedrichstadt lunette. The 44th Division (Berthezène) manned posts in the Grossen-Garten (Great Garden), and was held in reserve behind the garden. A further eight battalions, the Dresden garrison under GD Durosnel, occupied the city wall.[36]

Napoleon Arrives in Dresden

Napoleon arrived in Dresden on 26 August. He had left his forces to the east, facing Blücher, under the command of Maréchal Macdonald once he felt that things were well in hand, and returned to deal with the allied threat to his communications.

Once in Dresden, he made an immediate reconnaissance and approved the dispositions made by St. Cyr. The Old Guard arrived at 10:00 a.m., and detachments were immediately positioned in the city's barricades to provide a defense if the allied attack should be successful. The bulk of the Old Guard was posted in the new city, where it would serve as the last reserve. The four divisions of Young Guard were not to arrive in Dresden until that evening. The II and VI Corps would not arrive until later that evening either.

The I Cavalry Corps of Latour-Maubourg had been placed under the orders of Murat, who was overall cavalry commander. It was positioned before the Friedrichstadt suburb, on terrain

Napoleon enters Dresden, 26 August, after Philippoteaux.

appropriate for the use of cavalry. It was supported by O'Meara's brigade, Teste's 23rd Division, which had been recalled to Dresden.

The forces of the XIV Corps stood as follows on 25 August:

	Officers	Men[1]
42nd Division	165	5,464
43rd Division	162	5,165
44th Division	242	6,464
45th Division	242	7,568
10th Light Cavalry Division	109	2,122
V Cavalry Corps	153	3,202
Reserve Artillery	6	261

Note
1. Fabry, *Wurtemberg*, p.CXXIII.

The chessboard was set, the players were in place. All that remained was for the action to begin.

Vandamme and I Corps

It was 26 August. Napoleon ordered Vandamme to move against Königstein, but Vandamme's actions indicate that he either ignored the order or never received it. GD Mouton-Duvernet (42nd Division) remained in his position before Pirna, with one brigade, so Vandamme had with him only the eight or ten battalions belonging to the brigades of Quiot and Creutzer, without any guns. In order to cover this lack, he called on the fortress commander, to support him with fire from the fortress' artillery, in an effort to chase away small groups of isolated Cossacks.

Two battalions were posted in Neue Schenke, two in the paper mill. All four of these battalions sent forward their skirmishers against the Russian advanced posts between Struppen and Kriezschwitz. However, they did not move beyond the woods situated 1,600 meters from the fortress, because they were stopped by Russian artillery fire from Kriezschwitz.

Vandamme estimated that there were 8,000 to 10,000 Russians with eight to ten guns positioned around Kriezschwitz. Fortunately for the Russians, the bad roads had held up Vandamme's corps, and above all, the artillery. In Wartenberg, before Hohenstein, it had become necessary to double their teams in order to drag them through the mud.[37]

At 11:00 a.m., Vandamme learned of the approach of his corps and shortly after from a Russian prisoner, that he faced a Russian corps. A heavy skirmish fight continued between both sides and lasted all morning. By noon, there were already 300 to 400 wounded Frenchmen in the fortress.

The advanced posts of General Wolf raised the alarm at 8:00 a.m. He awaited Württemberg's arrival and sent him word that the French I Corps, with 50,000 men, had crossed the bridges over the Elbe and was en route. The Russian posts in Nollenstein confirmed this.

Württemberg's position was becoming very difficult. If he were to retreat, Vandamme had the facility to attack the right of the allied Army of Bohemia. If he stood his ground, he ran the risk of being defeated by a massively superior enemy.

He decided that it was more important to stop Vandamme and accepted his situation with grace, but chose a position that was as advantageous as possible to make his stand.[38]

He established his corps between Kriezschwitz and Struppen. His artillery was positioned on a plateau between the two villages, with it sighted on the road through which the French would have to advance.

He sent his aide de camp, Molostov, to Wittgenstein to advise him of his situation and to seek reinforcements. Meanwhile, the regiments of Krementchug, Volhynie and Tobolsk, formed in columns on the center, were formed in two lines between Kriezschwitz and Struppen. A battalion of the Minsk Regiment occupied Kriezschwitz, the 4th Jagers occupied Struppen and Klein Struppen. Four squadrons of cuirassiers and two of hussars formed the third line. Sixteen guns were placed in battery before the line. Württemberg placed another battery on the right, a little behind Kriezschwitz. Colonel Wolf formed the first line with the Mourmon and Tschernigov Regiments.[39]

Molostov found Wittgenstein in conversation with Ostermann-Tolstoy. After hearing his report, Wittgenstein ordered Ostermann-Tolstoy to join Württemberg. However, instead of reinforcements, Ostermann-Tolstoy took with him a note stating that Ostermann was to assume command of the right of the army. Württemberg was outraged, not only was he stripped of his command, but Ostermann-Tolstoy was not even a competent officer. Württemberg succeeded in limiting the damage, by confining Ostermann-Tolstoy with command of the siege forces in Poland.

The battle was already engaged when the Russian Reserve Cavalry, under Grand Duke Constantine, arrived in Gross-Cotta in the afternoon, some distance behind the Russian 2nd Corps. Württemberg requested that Constantine detach some cavalry to support him. Around 3:00 p.m., Constantine detached a reconnaissance that advanced into the battle area, and then withdrew at 4:00 p.m. He sent Württemberg the Empress Cuirassier Regiment, but it had specific orders to return to his corps during the night.

The Prussian Guard, moving from Kulm, had rested in Bergieshübel from 10:00 a.m. to 2:00 p.m. Three hours later it arrived, and set up camp with the Russian Guard in Ottendorf and Cotta. It took up a position facing the east, towards Königstein, with a line of pickets spread before it. During the night, the Prussian and Russian Guard was ordered to march on Dresden. This night march was marked by an icy cold, driving rain. The Russian 2nd Guard Division remained in Ottendorf.

Around 4:30 p.m., Corbineau's 1st Light Cavalry Division and Reuss's brigade arrived before the fortress of Königstein. The head of Dumonceau's column of the 2nd Division had reached Lilienstein, but his artillery did not join him until that evening, because the horses were too fatigued from the efforts of drawing the guns and caissons through the mud.

Vandamme perceived the allies being disposed as follows. At Kreizschwitz, there were 300 uhlans and Cossacks, with five battalions of infantry, and four squadrons of cuirassiers. Before Kriezschwitz there were four guns, with 400-500 uhlans and two battalions of infantry. Before Struppen there was another battalion of infantry, and on the main road, around the Himmelreich farm, were two more battalions of infantry. Towards Hermsdorf, he understood, there were three or four more battalions. Vandamme knew the Russian 4th Division was defending Kriezschwitz and that the 14th Division stood to its right.[40]

Vandamme stood with insufficient forces to strike the Russians, before the arrival of his main body. Quiot's brigade stood facing Hermsdorf and Creutzer's brigade faced Kriezschwitz. Reuss' brigade guarded the bridge. To strike the allies without sufficient artillery would be suicidal. He resolved, therefore, to march towards Pirna on the following day, but at 5:00 a.m. he heard the cannonade from Dresden.

As the guns boomed to the north west, the head of Dunesme's 1st Brigade, 2nd Division arrived. Vandamme felt that his duty and his honor required that he attack the enemy before him. Creutzer's brigade was directed against Struppen, Dunesme's brigade marched against Kriezschwitz, Quiot's brigade remained by the bridges over the Elbe, Reuss's brigade stood by the Königstein fortress and Corbineau's cavalry formed itself into three lines to support the attack. The French attack was executed without hesitation.[41]

The Russian skirmishers under Wolf were forced back across the plain. GM Helfreich was pushed out of Leopoldshayn to Roth-Wernsdorf.

Württemberg directed Wolf to send the Tschernigov Regiment and two guns to the heights between Gross-Struppen and the Elbe, and the Mourmon Regiment to Kriezschwitz. On the right, GM Helfreich retreated with his five battalions down the road from Leopoldshayne to Roth-Wernsdorf. Württemberg himself took up a position to the right of his main battery.

When Wolf's troops reached the line formed by the 2nd Corps, it became apparent to the French that the Russians had a large force of infantry posted behind Kriezschwitz and a large reserve of artillery. Vandamme's forces continued forward. Dunesme's brigade advanced in "colonnes serrées par division"[42] down the main road. The Russian artillery inflicted heavy casualties on these densely packed columns, forcing them to the left, into the woods. Despite the success of his artillery, Württemberg felt obliged to draw the Krementchug Regiment to his position.

Creutzer's brigade, after being pushed back from its first assault on Struppen, moved to the right, to overrun the village of Klein-Struppen. It slowly took over the village, but the Russian artillery posted by the angle of the ravine, prevented his forces from then moving against Struppen.[43]

A French column then attempted to fall on Struppen by turning it on the plateau to the east, while other French columns attacked it frontally. The turning column was discovered and heavily bombarded, taking many casualties. The frontal attack was also stopped.

Vandamme's two brigades had moved such that a large hole appeared in the French line. Corbineau's cavalry, formed in three lines, advanced to fill that hole. Württemberg was still mystified at the lack of French artillery.

Before Kriezschwitz, the situation had become stationary. The French had seized a few houses, but the rest remained under the control of the Tobolsk Regiment, Württemberg's only force in the area.

The first French guns began to appear on the ridge at night fall. Four were immediately engaged on the left flank, but night fall ended the battle. Vandamme advanced once more against the center and the Russian artillery, but a brilliant charge by the Empress Cuirassier Regiment stopped that assault. At the same time, as the charge was completed, the Empress Cuirassiers were ordered to return to their corps, and they withdrew from the field.

On the Russian extreme right, GM Helfreich had divided his forces into two portions. One consisted of Illowaiski's Cossacks and the Grand Duchess Catherine Battalion, which stood in Gieshübel. The other consisted of the Tenginsk and Estonian Infantry Regiments, with six guns, which were posted in the valley of Gottaleube, between Cotta and Gross-Wernsdorf, and covered the right of Kriezschwitz.

With the battle ended for the day, Württemberg faced a difficult situation. He was charged with covering the rear of the Army of Bohemia and guarding its lines of communications back to Bohemia. If he were to withdraw from Vandamme's growing strength, he would uncover those lines of communications and allow Vandamme to fall on the rear of the Army of Bohemia.

However, if he stood his ground, Vandamme was only growing stronger, and would soon be able to overwhelm Württemberg's forces, unless reinforcements were received. Those reinforcements were not likely, as a major battle was occurring in Dresden.

Württemberg had one choice, and that was to close towards the Army of Bohemia and Dresden. At midnight, he ordered the bulk of his forces, the Murmon, Tobolsk, Minsk and Tschernigov Infantry Regiments, to move behind Kriezschwitz, and to move on Zehist through Himmelreich, or other more rapid routes. The artillery and cavalry were to follow the main road to Pirna and establish a position on Kohlberg, to support the withdrawal of the rearguard. The rearguard was formed with the Volhynie and Krementchug Regiments, under GM Pischnitzky, who was ordered not to resist the French, but to force them to deploy their forces and to draw the French over the heights by Himmelreich. All of his mounted forces were to move to Pirna, which was guarded by the Revel Infantry Regiment. The 4th Jagers guarded Kohlberg.[44]

As Württemberg pulled back towards Dresden, the Czar was informed during the night of 26/27 August that Vandamme stood at Königstein with 50,000 men. The Czar responded by sending four successive officers from his staff, to contact Württemberg and determine the exact situation.

About the same time, the 1st Russian Guard Division re-joined Württemberg.[45] This reinforcement did not simplify the problem of command with Ostermann-Tolstoy, but Württemberg felt that Ostermann's health was sufficient to keep him out of the conduct of operations.[46]

At the break of dawn, on the morning of 27 August, Vandamme received a message from Napoleon written the day before. Napoleon ordered Vandamme to advance as quickly as possible on Pirna. Vandamme responded by issuing the orders to his corps to advance, despite the continuing rain that prevented clear observations of the allies.

Prince von Reuss' brigade marched to the extreme right against Pirna. Dumonceau's 2nd Division marched to the left, with Quiot's brigade behind it. The two remaining brigades of Corbineau[47] and the artillery formed in the center. Quiot's brigade, from Teste's 23rd Division, guarded Kriezschwitz. Philippon's 1st Division, with one brigade of the 1st Cavalry Division, moved against Langen-Hennersdorf, under the orders of GD Corbineau. This force was ordered to take Gieshübel, and to prevent any retiring allied forces from reaching Bohemia.

The Russians on the heights by Zehist, were formed in two lines. The first line consisted of the 2nd Corps, its battalions in columns by the center. The second line was formed by the 1st Guard Division. Part of the cavalry covered the left, while the remainder stood behind the infantry of the second line.

General Pischnitzky executed his withdrawal with skill. He covered it with skirmishers, and withdrew to the Kohlberg heights. General Haxo, Engineering Commander for the Guard, estimated that six battalions moved through Kohlberg, while the artillery and cavalry moved through Pirna, towards Seydewitz. GD Vandamme advanced four guns, which fired on the withdrawing Russians by Kohlberg, as they moved to re-join their main forces by Zehist.

A brigade from Dumonceau's division established itself on the Kohlberg heights. Its supporting artillery could fire on the road to Peterswalde, which passed by the foot of the hill. This effectively cut the allied line of withdrawal down that road.

On the right, Reuss moved with part of his brigade towards Pirna. Around 11:00 a.m., it encountered the Revel Infantry Regiment, which guarded the eastern side of the city, and forced it to withdraw with losses. Gobrecht's 21st Light Cavalry Brigade moved through Pirna, and moved down the road to Dresden, sabering the Russian fugitives.[48]

Vandamme chose not to attack Württemberg's central position by Zehist. Instead, his two primary objectives being completed, there remaining only to throw a bridge over the Elbe at Pirna, he chose to hold his position. This was probably the wiser choice, because if he had attempted to assault Württemberg and lost, he would not have been able to raise the bridge at Pirna, as required by Napoleon. In addition, he felt he was facing 60,000 Russians and Prussians under Yorck and Wittgenstein.

Vandamme pulled his brigades back together. The five brigades, having a maximum of 20,000 men, were no match for Württemberg. The brigades of the 42nd and 23rd Divisions still had no artillery and Teste had retained only one horse battery. The 12pdr reserve battery and the park, under General Baltus, had remained in Dresden. This left Vandamme only the two batteries of Dumonceau, the one of Prince von Reuss, and one reserve battery. Facing a minimum of 13,500 men supported by 52 guns, Vandamme had little choice but to await reinforcements.

11

The Battle of Dresden
26–27 August 1813

Dresden stands on a flood plain of the Elbe River. The old city is on the west bank and was surrounded by an old city wall in rather poor condition. Outside the wall lay several suburbs. The principal ones were the Pirna suburb, which stood on the road to Pirna and was adjacent to the Grossen-Garten. The central suburb was the Wilsdorf suburb, which was skirted to the west by the Weisseritz River. On the northwest of Dresden stood the suburb of Friedrichstadt. Friedrichstadt was cut off from the city by the Weisseritz River.

The French had erected five major redoubts around the city. The redoubts were all erected outside the suburbs where they had clear fields of fire across the open fields outside the city. Redoubt I stood to the south east of the Ziegel suburb, Redoubt II stood outside the Pirna suburb, Redoubt III stood in the Mosczinskischen Garten (garden), Redoubt IV stood in the Falken Garten, and Redoubt V stood outside Freiberg suburb.

The Neustädt suburb stood on the east bank of the Elbe and was connected to the old city by three bridges. Neustädt was surrounded by new fortifications, eight redoubts, a ditch, and a covered way. At a distance from the fortifications stood the suburbs of Neuer-Anbau and Scheunen.

The land to the west of the Elbe had been cleared of woods, except for a portion of forest around Blasewitz to the east, along the river. There were few major hills. To the south of Dresden and the west of the Grossen-Garten stood a ridge running from just to the west of Strehlen, through Zschernitz and Räcknitz and tapering down to the Weisseritz River. As the Weisseritz moves towards its source, starting about Plauen, it has carved a deep ravine ground that gradually rises from Räcknitz to the west.

The village of Doltschen stands on the edge of the ravine overlooking the Weisseritz River. A ridge that rises to the west runs north from Doltschen, through Ober-Nauslitz, Nieder Gorbitz, Wölfnitz, Burgstadtet and Leutewitz.

On 12 August Napoleon had issued orders for the fortification of Dresden. He directed that barracks, based on the model of those for the Young Guard, be erected in the eight redoubts on the right bank of the Elbe . They were to shelter their occupants not only from musketry, but also from canister.

A similar series of barracks were to be erected in the five redoubts on the left bank of the Elbe. The two battalions of Westphalians, and the battalions of the 11th Tirailleurs and 11th Voltigeurs were to do the work.

In addition, there was to be a field piece placed in each of the thirteen redoubts. The redoubt was to have a small magazine with 200 rounds and 5,000 infantry cartridges. The redoubts were to have a crew of 25 artillerists.

Napoleon also ordered that there be a supply of sandbags and gabions available to barricade the five streets entering the Wilsdorf suburb. Provisions were to be made to nail planks over the doors of all the houses near those entries into the city so that they might be sealed to enemy entrance. Napoleon also ordered that the Pirna gate be reinforced by a ditch filled with water.

Napoleon also ordered that all the gates in the garden walls, as well as the seven or eight gates to the suburbs be blocked up. He also ordered that, prior to 18 August, one field gun be posted at each city gate. In addition, barricades were to be raised and manned by crews of 25 men.

A wooden bridge over the ditch by the Wilsdorf Gate was to be covered with a barricade and *chevaux de frise*. Each night the planks of the bridge were to be raised and withdrawn into the suburb to prevent any attempt at a coup de main. By 18 August the city was also to have 80 guns in battery and a further 20 in reserve. The artillery of the garrison was to contain a Saxon artillery company and a 120 man French artillery company under the command of a colonel, a chef de bataillon, and five or six officers.

Should the city be approached by the allies, the bridges were to be raised every night and all prescribed precautions taken. The four houses that were on the counterscarp by the Pirna gate were either to be demolished or occupied.

By 18 August all of the boats in Königstein and Dresden, plus those below Meissen were to be locked up in Torgau. All of the loose military vehicles that were being repaired, French, Saxon, or whosoever, were taken into Dresden.

On 13 August the garrison was to begin cutting all of the trees around the redoubts on the right bank to a distance of 600 feet and *chevaux de frise* were to be placed by the gates.[1]

The Allied Plan of Attack

The allies were advancing in several columns. The Russians under Barclay de Tolly were advancing from Peterswalde, Wittgenstein's Russian I Corps was on the right and Miloradovich's Reserve Corps was en route to the left. They were maneuvering for an attack between the Grossen-Garten and the Elbe. Kleist's Prussian II Corps was moving directly at the Grossen-Garten.

The Austrians under Prince von Hessen-Homburg and Gvulai were moving to attack down the roads from Freiberg and Dippoldiswalde. The last column, Klenau's Austrians, was unable to arrive with the rest of the force and would not arrive until 27 August.

As the allies awaited Klenau's arrival, their general staff discussed how to go about attacking Dresden. The situation had changed because St. Cyr's three divisions (43rd, 44th and 45th) had not stood out on the plain before Dresden, as anticipated. Instead they withdrawn into the city's defenses. The allies' opportunity to overwhelm St. Cyr's inferior forces was lost and now they faced having to assault a fortified city.

Gouvion St Cyr, by Vernet.

Little did the allies know what was about to descend on them. Before the end of the battle Napoleon would have the following forces present in vicinity of Dresden:

42nd Division Mouton-Duvernet	5,500 men	16 guns
I Corps Vandamme	33,200	68
II Corps Victor	25,100	80
Imperial Guard	58,000	212
VI Corps Marmont	27,700	84
XIV Corps St. Cyr	20,000	76
I Cavalry Corps Latour-Maubourg	16,500	30
Total	186,000	566

Czar Alexander, Moreau, and Jomini argued against an attack that would cost the Army of Bohemia unnecessarily heavy casualties and advocated a withdrawal to Dippoldiswalde. Here they felt a strong, secure position could be found that would allow them to menace Napoleon's communications and minimize the risk to their army.

The King of Prussia did not support the idea of a withdrawal. He felt that the effect of a retreat on the morale of the allied troops would be devastating.

As the argument continued, it was learned that Napoleon had appeared personally in Dresden and that masses of French troops were approaching. This quickly swayed their sentiments to favoring the withdrawal and conformance with the Trachenberg Agreements. However, prior to the issuance of orders to effect that withdrawal, Schwarzenberg brought up the problem of Klenau's exposed position, but still promised to countermand the orders to attack.

The silence of the battlefield was then broken by a cannonade. Unfortunately for the allies, the earlier orders had directed that the battle was to begin at 3:00 p.m. and the signal to attack was to be a series of cannon shots. Chance had decreed that the attack begin, despite the changed allied plans, and the allied infantry began to roll forward to attack. Though orders were sent out to stop the battle, before they arrived, the allies were engaged on all fronts.

The allies were formed for the attack in six columns. They were, right to left:

1st: Wittgenstein's Russian I Corps to advance between the Grossen-Garten and the Elbe. Wittgenstein's forces stood between the villages of Blasewitz and Streisen. He was to advance in a demonstration and if possible, strike into the suburbs of Dresden.[2]

2nd: Kleist's Prussian II Corps faced Strehlen. He was to strike the Grossen-Garten. His 12pdr batteries were detached and joined to those of Wittgenstein's corps to pound the city.

3rd: Colloredo's Corps, which contained the 1st Light Division (M. Liechtenstein) and the 1st Division (Colloredo), was to attack via Rächnitz, to the left of Kleist, and move against the Schlossgarten, advancing in column.[3] Four 12pdr position batteries stood between Plauen and Rächnitz and were designated to fire on the city.

4th: Crenneville's 3rd Austrian Reserve Division was to attack Plauen. Four 12pdr position batteries were deployed near Plauen to support the attack of Bianchi's division.

5th: Bianchi's 2nd Reserve Division was to attack the village of Löbtau. He was to secure that flank as well as to push the French out of the area between the village of Löbtau, the Schutzenhausern and the Elbe. Once Löbtau fell, four 12pdr position batteries were to be positioned so they could fire on Friedrichstadt. Schneller's 3rd Cavalry Division was to support this column.

6th: The 1st Reserve Grenadier Division (Chasteler) stood in column and remained as a reserve to support the attack on Plauen. The 1st and 2nd Cavalry Divisions (Nostitz and Lederer) stood as a reserve between Koschitz and Kaitz.

In addition to these six principal columns, there was a column under Ostermann-Tolstoy/ Württemberg (Russian II Corps), which was moving against Pirna, where Vandamme had the I Corps. There was also Klenau's column and Bubna's cavalry that were advancing along the road from Freiberg, but they could not to arrive until the 27th.

A Cossack regiment was dispatched towards Bautzen and another light command under Colonel Seslavin was sent towards Priesnitz, across the Elbe, and from there it was to move against Radeberg.[4]

French Dispositions

St. Cyr had made the necessary dispositions to face the advancing allied armies during the prior day. Knowing the importance of defending the Grossen-Garten he placed the 44th Division behind the gardens. The 45th Division was placed in front of Friedrichstadt and the 43rd Division stood by the Pirna suburb. The troops of the Confederation of the Rhine, which formed part of the garrison of Dresden, were to form the reserve. Five companies were placed in the Anton field house, situated near the Elbe because it was judged suitable for a strong defense. A battalion was placed in the Hops Garden. These two positions were covered on the left flank by a battery placed on the right bank of the Elbe and were to be covered on their right by a horse battery placed by the wind mill. The artillery in the redoubts was completed and the surplus artillery pieces were spread about in the best possible positions, while others were placed in the intervals between the redoubts.

St. Cyr placed his cavalry on the right, in the plain before Friedrichstadt. Six battalions of the 42nd Division were guarding the gates, the gates in the city walls, and the entrenched camp at Lilienstein. The other six were distributed along the right bank of the Elbe from Wehlen to below Pillnitz to observe the major points where the allies might wish to cross their troops. Teste's 23rd Division should have been available on 25 August, but a series of contradicting orders had him marching and counter-marching to no use.[5]

At 9:00 a.m., on 26 August Napoleon arrived in Dresden. He directed that a battery be formed near Neustädt on the right bank of the Elbe that would provide flanking fire against the allied right. His next orders were for those troops passing into Neustädt to move as quickly as possible into Dresden and take positions in the line.

Napoleon then moved to the Dippoldiswalde barricade and began to tour the French lines to survey the allied dispositions. As he arrived in Redoubt #4, he chanced to find a post that St. Cyr had placed in a factory. From there they were able to observe the entire Weisseritz valley, but this post had been taken by the allies. Napoleon directed St. Cyr to retake the position. A French battalion was sent forward and retook the position, but could not maintain itself because a force of seven or eight allied battalions moved to retake it.[6]

Around 3:00 p.m., the French lines echoed with the sounds of four allied guns being fired from the heights by Räcknitz.

The Battle Begins

With the sounding of the fateful cannon, all of the Austrian columns moved to the attack. The Russians and Prussians were still en route. Approximately 50,000 men supported by 112 guns[7] lunged forward against Dresden.[8]

There was one other force of Austrians near the field. These 30,000 men stood near Zittau where they faced Poniatowski's VIII Corps.

Wittgenstein's Attack

Wittgenstein's forces and the reserve moved out between Striesen and the Elbe, moving to attack the two redoubts along the road to Pirna at that morning. Their advance was pounded by heavy artillery fire from the redoubts and from the horse artillery that was placed between them. In addition, the French had posted batteries on the far side of the Elbe that pounded their flank as they advanced. They continued, despite this fire, to close on the battlefield, but did not arrive until early that afternoon.

Wittgenstein began his attack at 4:00 p.m. The bulk of his forces stood north of the Pillnitz Road. He organized two attack columns. The northern most consisted of two battalions of the 23rd Jager Regiment and two guns under GM Lukov. The southern column consisted of the four battalions of the Sieversk and Kalouga Infantry Regiments under GM Millesinov. As a reserve, the Perm, Moghilev, Seleginsk Infantry and 24th Jager Regiments remained by Striesen. It is not known where he positioned his cavalry.[9]

The advanced troops under GM Millesinov moved against the Windmühlberg and Hops Garden, which was defended by artillery. Lukov's column moved between Striesen and the Blasewitz Woods, in the direction of Stückgiessers supported by the Soum and Loubny Hussars and a horse battery.

Two batteries supported this attack, one by the western side of the Blasewitz Woods, the second on the Windmühlberg, and the third arrived later, on the northern edge of the Blasewitz Woods. They sought to silence the French artillery by the Hops garden and on the right bank of the Elbe. Though inflicting heavy damage on the French, they received a significant counterbattery fire and the battery to the north of the Blasewitz Woods was obliged to withdraw.[10] The advancing Russian cavalry was thrown back by Doumerc's cavalry and the thrusts by Russian infantry were met by a counter attack of Young Guard, supported by a horse battery, which drove the Russians back.

Russian and French skirmishers exchange fire during the opening stages of the Battle of Dresden.

From Grünweise, GM Roth moved against the Grossen-Garten with the 20th, 21st, 25th, 26th, and 34th Jager Regiments,[11] supported by the Grodno Hussars. The first column consisted of a jager battalion supported by two horse guns that moved against Sandgruben. The second column consisted of two battalions of the Perm Infantry Regiment and four horse guns from Horse Battery #6, which stood by the Wirtshaus Engelhard.[12]

As this attack progressed, the French uncovered artillery in the Prinz Anton Gardens that fired into the Russian attack's flank. The artillery fire was reinforced by musketry from French infantry posted in the houses and gardens around the houses.

In order to overpower the French forces lying before Sandgruben, GM Lukov sent forward two further battalions. The French strength in this region lay in the thirty guns positioned on the right bank of the Elbe. As these two additional battalions formed in attack columns and advanced against Sangruben, they were taken under a murderous fire by those guns firing in their flanks, front and rear.[13]

Lukov's attack was supported on the north east by a force of cavalry and horse artillery, which moved from the Blasewitz Woods north of the Sandgruben. To the south, the attack was supported by the 24th Jager Regiment of Vlastov's brigade. The attack of the cavalry had little effect and both it and its supporting artillery were soon forced to retreat. The 24th Jagers moved from behind the cover of the Windmühlberg and found themselves subjected to a torrent of fire from the French guns in Redoubt I, and the Imperial Guard horse artillery that had taken a position on a knoll near that redoubt.

Wittgenstein then personally led forward four battalions of his reserve to the Windmühlberg, where they joined the two battalions of the 24th Jagers. They moved forward once again.

While this was going on the 3rd Young Guard Division (Decouz) moved from behind the Ziegel and Rammisch suburbs to a position behind Redoubt I. They waited for the arrival of Roguet's 4th Young Guard Division, which was then passing over the pontoon bridge on the Elbe. As Roguet appeared, both Young Guard divisions moved through the Pillnitz barricade and advanced towards the allied lines. At the same time, the Young Guard divisions of Dumoustier and Barrois (1st and 2nd) moved through the Pirna suburb.[14]

Roguet's 4th Young Guard Division initially moved against the Anton Gardens, and while the 3rd Young Guard Division (Decouz) moved against the Hops garden. The energy of their attack drove the Russians back. The 4th Young Guard Division's artillery advanced and inflicted heavy losses on the Russians as well.

Decouz.

Roguet's 4th Young Guard Division then turned south and struck the right flank of the Russians. The left flank was, at that time, under attack by Decouz's 3rd Young Guard Division, which pushed out of the suburbs.[15]

The Russians fell back, pursued by the French, who then attacked the Wirtshaus Engelhards. The French formed an artillery battery on the Windmühlberg, which began a heavy cannonade of the Russians in Striesen. The French then sent their infantry forward against the village.

The artillery fire became such that the village of Striesen was set afire and only with the greatest effort and losses did the Russian 5th Division retain its position between Striesen and the Blasewitz Woods. It was the timely arrival of Klüx's brigade that allowed them to hold their position.

Roth's Attack

Roth's attack against the Grossen-Garten started about 4:00 p.m., as he led the 25th and 26th Jager Regiments forward. A brigade of the Russian 14th Division, of four battalions, followed in support. They passed through the Grossen-Garten and about 5:00 p.m., were in a position to attempt a storm of Redoubt II. His first attempt failed, and as the French offensive was beginning on his right, Roth found himself obliged to withdraw his force to Grüna.[16] The 1st and 2nd Young Guard Divisions of Dumoustier and Barrois moved out of the Pirna suburb to attack him, in concert with the French attack to Roth's right.[17] They pushed into the Grossen-Garten, supported by the 43rd Division.[18] The French followed Roth's retreating forces and when the battle ended, each of the two forces occupied approximately half of the Grossen-Garten.

Kleist's Attack

Kleist's orders to his forces were quite detailed. The advanced guard was to push into the middle of the Grossen-Garten and to establish a half 6pdr battery to fire on the Pirna suburb. GM von Pirch's 10th Brigade was to advance to the rear entrance of the Grossen-Garten to support the advanced guard. Oberstleutnant von Jagow was to advance with the 11th Brigade, two 12pdr batteries, and a 7pdr howitzer battery, to the right striking against the suburb, occupying Strehlen with a battalion of the 8th Silesian Landwehr Regiment and the Rotehaus with another battalion of the 8th Silesian Landwehr. The 10th Reserve Infantry Regiment and the two other battalions of the 8th Silesian Landwehr were to stand to the right and left behind these battalions to support them. The 1st Silesian Regiment was to follow as a reserve. Behind the 11th Brigade, the 12th Brigade, under Prinz August, was to occupy the heights of Strehlen. The 9th Brigade, under Klüx, was to act as a reserve and stand between Strehlen and Grüna. The reserve cavalry was to stand behind the heights near Leubnitz. The cavalry of the 11th and 12th Brigades were to support the link between the right wing of Kleist's corps and the left wing of Wittgenstein's corps.[19]

About 4:00 p.m., the 10th and 11th Brigades moved out of Strehlen, with the 9th and 12th Brigades supporting them. The advanced troops of GM von Ziethen were divided in two groups. The 10th Brigade moved behind the Grossen-Garten, while the advanced guard moved into the Grossen-Garten. The 10th Brigade's infantry stood in battle order (line) 600 paces behind the garden, with their left behind the heights of Strehlen. On those heights, a 12pdr battery was also positioned. The reserve cavalry stood behind Torna, its right wing on Wittgenstein's corps and its left touching the Austrian right Wing.[20]

Ziethen was to capture the suburbs of Dresden that stood before him, not the garden, except as necessary. The 10th Brigade supported his advance. The 10th Brigade detached some troops towards the palace, but the bulk of the brigade remained behind the edge of the Grossen-Garten. A half 10pdr howitzer battery, a 7pdr howitzer battery, and a 12pdr battery advanced to the right of the Grossen-Garten, under the command of Oberstleutnant Braun. These batteries were to engage the French in the suburbs, as well as the earthwork in the palace gardens,

Ziethen.

Redoubt II. The French batteries in Redoubt II and in the Hop Gardens had the advancing Prussians under a heavy cross fire.

Ziethen advanced against the suburbs of Dresden as planned. The 2/10th Reserve moved through Strehlen and covered the artillery from there. Oberstleutnant von Jagow advanced with the bulk of his brigade to the foot of the Strehlen heights. The Neumärk Dragoons and the 1st Silesian Hussars stood between Strehlen, and Räcknitz to link the Prussian left with the Austrian right wing.[21] The Silesian Uhlan Regiment and the 8th Silesian Landwehr Cavalry Regiment stood between China and the Grossen-Garten. Two squadrons of the 2nd Silesian Hussar Regiment and a squadron of the Silesian National Cavalry Regiment served to cover Kleist's headquarters on the Räcknitz heights. The bulk of the reserve artillery stood on the heights to the south of Zschernitz.[22] The reserve stood about 100 paces behind the artillery.

Three battalions of the 10th Brigade went forward to reinforce the attack about 5:00 p.m., which was about the same time as Roth's abortive assault on Redoubt II. The Prussians advanced against the Dohnaer Suburb.

They advanced against the Grossen-Garten and quickly overran it. As the Prussians reached the end of the gardens, they found themselves about 500 paces from the edge of the city. The Fus/1st Silesian and 1/10th Reserve Regiment pushed through the northern end of the Grossen-Gartens. They quickly struck at Redoubt III lying before the Dohna suburb. Several battalions pushed forward. They formed themselves into two attack columns. The first column, formed by the battalions of Majors von Lettow and von Osseney, the Fus/1st Silesian and 2/10th Reserve Regiments, moved from the northwest of The Grossen-Gartens and advanced against Redoubt II. It suffered heavy casualties from the murderous canister and musketry coming from Redoubt II.[23]

The second column, three or four battalions, moved out of the main entrance to the Grossen-Garten against the Prinz Anton Gardens. A third Prussian attack, formed by the 2/7th Reserve

The 2nd West Prussian Infantry Regiment in action in the Grossen-Garten on the evening of 26 August, by Knötel.

and 1/2nd West Prussian Infantry Regiments, advanced out of the garden supported by Prussian artillery, that had been brought forward.[24] Despite its heavy casualties, this assault succeeded in gaining a foothold in the ditch around the redoubt. At the same time, a Russian battalion threw back a French line regiment to the right, and to the left two Prussian attack columns pressed into the Prinz Anton Gardens. The latter were quickly stopped, coming up against a wall in the Prinz Anton Gardens. The gardens were heavily defended by several battalions of French infantry and many guns.

Kleist's artillery, the two 12pdr batteries and the howitzer battery, moved forward to a position between Roten Haus and the Grossen-Garten. The Austrian artillery stood in two groups to the east of the Dippoldiswalde Road, their left wing on the Räcknitz-Plauen line. The Austrian artillery moved forward a few hundred paces at this time, with a few companies of the Warasdiner-St. Georger Grenz serving to cover them.[25] The big Austrian assault was well under way at this time.

The bulk of the Prussian 11th Brigade stood behind the village of Strehlen. As GL Kleist saw his attack succeeding in the Grossen-Garten and the Austrian attack against Redoubt III, he decided to send forward the 11th Brigade to support the Austrians. A column, three battalions strong, moved to the right of Strehlen. This was Oberstleutnant Jagow with a battalion of the 10th Reserve Regiment and the landwehr battalions of Graf Dohna (4/8th Silesian Landwehr) and von Borcks (1/8th Silesian Landwehr). The two battalions of the 1st Silesian Regiment remained back as a reserve. Yet another battalion moved left down the Dohna street against the Dohna suburb and the hospital garden. A half howitzer battery advanced behind them and took a posi-

tion on the west side of the Grossen-Garten. Both infantry columns moved behind the dike along the Kaitzbach to protect themselves against the enemy fire and advanced as far as they could. They held this position until the Austrian assault was driven back.

At this critical moment, the sounds of military music came out of the Dresden suburbs. The French 44th Division and a division of the French Imperial Guard advanced out of the suburbs in three columns under the command of Maréchal Mortier. One column marched down the Pirna Road against Roth's Russians. Its artillery moved to the north of Redoubt II, and began to fire on the Russian Jagers with canister. The second column moved into the ditch of the redoubt and threw the Prussians in the ditch back to the Grossen-Garten, with heavy casualties. The third column marched into the Prinz Anton Garden, throwing the Prussians there back into the Grossen-Garten.[26]

Maréchal Mortier.

The Austrian Attack

About 9:30 the Austrians advanced to their jumping off positions. They began establishing their artillery facing the Wilsdruff suburb about noon. They prepared for a heavy bombardment of the French positions in Redoubts III, IV and V, as well as around the paper mill.

The low level artillery duel that had started with the first assault lasted until about 4:00 p.m., when 72 Austrian guns erupted to life, firing on Redoubts III and IV.[27] A Russian battery joined the Austrian guns. Two French field batteries, one in the hospital gardens and the other in the Dohna suburbs, were driven back.

At the same time, the Austrians in the Köhler Garden advanced against the paper mill and those in Meisterei, marched against Redoubt V. One of the columns moving down the Tharandt Road moved left against Redoubt V, but its supporting column arrived too late to support its assault.[28]

Colloredo's column moved from Rächnitz against the central redoubt, Redoubt IV, which was equipped with a 12pdr battery. This attack was led by the Moritz Liechtenstein's 1st Light Division, supported by Colloredo's own 1st Line Division. The fourteen battalions advanced in five attack columns. Three columns moved between Rächnitz and Plauen, the other two moved down the Dippoldiswalde road.

As the Austrians pressed forward, St. Cyr's forces stood in the See suburb, subjected to a hail of Austrian howitzer shells. The suburbs were in danger of bursting into flames at any moment, from the intense fire. The Austrian fire also concentrated on the garden walls that surrounded the suburbs, in an effort to punch a hole in them.[29] Under the cover of this intense fire the Austrian attack columns advanced.

Colloredo personally led the 1st and 2nd Jäger Battalions forward to storm Redoubt III. Led by Oberstleutnants Luz and Schneider, the two battalions moved through a hail of canister and musketry fire, leapt into the ditch, climbed over the palisades and into the breast works, where they captured six cannons at about 5:00 p.m.[30]

By 5:00 p.m., a heavy musketry battle had begun from the barricades to the city spitting fire into the advancing allies. The French had been obliged to evacuate Redoubt III, after firing off all their cartridges and withdrew behind the Machzinsky garden. Four Austrian battalions had fired on this redoubt for an hour, killing or wounding all the gunners.[31] M. Liechtenstein's 1st Light

Austrian Jäger storming a redoubt at Dresden.

The assault on Dresden, viewed from the Austrian lines.

Division pushed forward to the Machzinsky Gardens and encountered an 8 foot high wall. The passage through the wall was defended by a ditch and palisade. The French stood in this strong position and fired volley after volley, into the advancing Austrians.

The Austrians fell back, regrouped and advanced again to storm the wall. A position battery was placed 200 paces from the palisade and began firing. The jägers pushed into the French position, but were pushed out before too long.

The fourth column, under Chasteler, moved against Plauen and the Freiberg suburbs, where the French had established a battery. The forces of Chasteler and Gyulai were enduring the artillery fire from the redoubts facing them. By 5:00 p.m., the redoubts were still holding out against Chasteler. Little by little, all the allied attacks were repulsed with by bayonet charges by the Grenadiers and Fusiliers of the Imperial Guard.

At 5:00 p.m., FML Meszko's 3rd Light Division passed by Gorbitz and moved to Schusterhäusern, Cotta and Löbtau. Its advance was supported by GM Greth, of the 3rd Austrian Reserve Division (Crenneville), who advanced with five grenz battalions. His advanced guard consisted of the 1/ Gradiscaner Grenz Regiment and two squadrons of the Klenau Chevauléger Regiment. They took up a position on the heights to the south of Plauen and began a skirmish fight with the French. On the Coschütz heights stood the bulk of the division, 21 grenz companies, 9 squadrons, and a 3pdr battery. Three companies of the 1/Warasdiner-St. Georger Grenz Regiment stood by Doltschen. Crenneville waited for news of the arrival of FML Meszko on the heights by Alt-Franken.[32]

Meszko had come forward the previous night with only five battalions of his division, plus seven squadrons and two batteries. The advanced guard was under GM Paumgarten and consisted of 2/Wallachian-Illyrian Grenz Regiment and five squadrons of the Palatinal Hussar Regiment. Meszko arrived by Alt-Franken at 6:00 a.m. Shortly after the word came for the attack to begin.

Crenneville's advanced guard, under Greth, advanced with the 1/Gradiscaner Grenz Regiment against the right bank of the Weisseritz. The 1/Warasdiner-Kreuzer Grenz Regiment moved over the bridge in Plauen to the left bank covered by three companies of the 1/Warasdiner-St.Georger Grenz Regiment standing by Doltschen. The weak French posts by the Reisewitzens Garden, were pushed back to the Jagdhaus by the Steinernen bridge.[33]

The powdermill, the customs house, the Holzhof and its adjacent stone bridge, and the field works were attacked by the 1/1st Gradiscaner Grenz Regiment and a violent fight erupted. The sheep pens were attacked by the 1/Warasdiner-Kreutzer Regiment, and the 1/Deutsch-Banat Regiment attacked the Schiesshofs.

About 8:00 a.m., as the 1/Warasdiner-Kreuzer Grenz Regiment occupied the Holzhof, Major von Simbschen, with the 1/Gradiscaner Grenz Regiment moved against the Türmchen and the Feldschlösschen. Behind them came the 1/Deutsch-Banat Grenz Regiment. Two companies stood as a reserve near Plauen while four companies moved east of Plauen. The bulk of the reserve stood to the south of Plauen.

A battery from Crenneville's division, led by Leutnant Müller, moved to the heights south of Plauen and from there forward, to support the attack against Trmchen.

About 11:00 a.m., a pause came to the battle. The 1/Gradiscaner, 1/Wallachian-Illyrian, and two companies of the 1/Deutsch-Banat Grenz found themselves completely mixed on the field. Two companies of the 1/Deutsch-Banat Regiment stood on the heights behind the Feldschlösschen, as a reserve. Oberst Benczek, with six companies of the 1/Warasdiner-Kreuzer Regiment and two companies of the 1/Deutsch-Banat Regiment moved against Redoubt IV in skirmish order. The three remaining companies of the 1/Warasdiner-St. Georger Regiment stood near Plauen as a reserve, as well as to maintain liaison with Chasteler's 1st Reserve Grenadier Division. In this position there also stood the Austrian cavalry.[34]

FML Meszko was ordered to send a brigade to Neissen, to destroy the bridge and to secure the allies' left flank. The force had departed at 11:00 a.m., under the command of GM Paumgarten. He commanded eight companies and two squadrons.[35]

Meszko sent the 1/Wallachian Grenz and a battalion of the Beaulieu Infantry Regiment forward towards Löbtau, Cotta, and the Drescherhäuser. Three companies of 1/Warasdiner-St. Georger Grenz Regiment, part of Crenneville's forces, closed the gap between Crenneville and Meszko's advanced guard. Cotta and the Drescherhäuser were weakly held and by 8:00 a.m., they were in Austrian hands. However, by Cotta a strong wall and the crossfire from the French artillery stopped the Austrian advance.

Crenneville found himself facing O'Meara's Brigade from Teste's 23rd Division, while Meszko found himself facing Razout's 45th Division.

The infantry of the Beaulieu Infantry Regiment, supported by two brigade batteries, moved forward at 9:00 a.m., to take Friedrichstadt, but had to withdraw after they fired off all their ammunition and had still not taken it.

Between 9:00 and 10:00 a.m., Paumgarten advanced with four companies of the Wallachian-Illyrian Grenz, 4 companies of the Deutsch-Banat Grenz and two squadrons of the Palatinal Hussar Regiment towards Meissen, as ordered by Schwarzenberg. With Meszko, there remained three battalions of the Beaulieu Regiment, two companies of the Deutsch-Banat Grenz, 4 companies of the Wallachian-Illyrian Grenz, five hussar squadrons, and two batteries. With the departure of these forces, Meszko's attack diminished significantly.[36]

In the meantime the advance of the other Austrian forces to the heights south of Dresden continued. Bianchi's 2nd Reserve Division moved from Wendisch-Carsdorf to its assigned position by Coschütz. By the Gittersee stood Chasteler's 1st Reserve Grenadier Division, where it contacted the 3rd Division of Civalart. The heavy cavalry of Erbprinzen von Hessen-Homburg and the bulk of Lederer's 2nd Cavalry Division had united by Kaitz. Nostitz's 1st Cavalry Division stood on the heights south of Kaitz and formed the right wing, Lederer formed the middle, Schneller's 3rd Cavalry Division stood south of Coschdtz behind Bianchi, who formed the left wing.

By Maxen, there remained part of the Prussian 2nd Army Corps, the 9th and 12th Brigades, the Reserve Cavalry and the Reserve artillery, which reached the battlefield at noon.[37]

At 5:00 p.m., the four divisions of Young Guard arrived in Dresden. The 3rd and 4th Young Guard divisions of Decouz and Roguet, under the orders of Ney, moved to the road to Pirna, while the 1st and 2nd Young Guard Divisions of Dumoustier and Barrois, under Mortier, moved into the See suburb against the Austrians. Murat's cavalry, to which a brigade of Teste's 23rd Division was attached, moved towards Friedrichstadt.

With these dispositions made, a thunderous roar of French artillery began and the troops of Ney, Mortier, and Murat moved out to engage the allies.

The Attack on the West of the Weisseritz

Around 4:00 p.m., FZM Graf Gyulai arrived on the left bank of the Weistritz, by the Rossthal heights, with Weissenwolff's 2nd Line Division, which advanced in three columns down the Freiberg road while Hessen-Homburg's Line Division occupied the heights along the Tharandt Road. From here,

Maréchal Murat.

the Austrian guns pounded Redoubt V. At the same time Crenneville's 3rd Reserve Division (five battalions) moved between Löbtau and Cotta, supported by Schneller's 3rd Cavalry Division (20 squadrons), which followed on his left flank. To the left stood FML Meszko's 3rd Light Division (five battalions). Three batteries stood to the right and left of the Drescherhäuser position and fired on Redoubt V as well as Friedrichstadt.[38]

At 4:00 p.m., the fifth column, under Bianchi and consisting of his 2nd Reserve Division and the 3rd Cavalry Division of Schneller, struck again. The Hessen-Homburg Regiment moved to the east towards the Weisseritz. The Simbschen Infantry Regiment moved against Löbtau, over the stone bridge, and against the flank and rear of Redoubt V.

The Hessen-Homburg Regiment and a detachment of Crenneville's division moved against the redoubt. The Hiller Regiment quickly occupied the Holzhof and the Simbschen Regiment struck at the Powdermill.[39]

At the same time Crenneville sent forward several companies of the 1/Deutsch-Banat Grenz, as skirmishers, leading the advance of the 1/Gradiscaner and 1/Deutsch-Banat Grenz Regiments. The French artillery showered them with canister, as they moved against Redoubt IV and the Powdermill. Two or three position batteries followed them and took up positions on the heights by Feldschlösschen, covered by three companies of the 1/Warasdiner-St. Georger Grenz Regiment. The combination of counterbattery fire by these guns and the musketry of the grenz, soon killed or wounded all the French gunners manning the redoubt. A fortunate howitzer shell landed in the redoubt and chased out the weak infantry garrison formed of French and Westphalian recruits. Only two officers and a few non-commissioned officers remained in the redoubt, as the grenzers entered.

However, the Austrians were not to remain there long. A company of Old Guard from the 2nd Chasseurs a Pied stormed into the redoubt and drove the Austrians out. Bianchi responded by bringing up his reserves, the Colloredo Infantry Regiment and Quallenberg's Brigade.[40]

It was 5:30 p.m., Chasteler sent forward the bulk of his forces to the heights, to the southwest of Plauen, and sent Portner's Grenadier Battalion into Holzhof. Rueber's Grenadier Battalion moved to Plauen and Fischer's Grenadier Battalion moved into Hahneberg, near the Feldschlösschen. G. Hessen-Homburg's cavalry brigade stood on the right wing of Crenneville and helped engage the French Chasseurs that were fighting the grenzers. Rothkirch's cuirassier brigade covered the allied headquarters.

Bianchi moved against Löbtau, and drove then the French out of the Schusterhäusern. In reaction, the French suddenly moved a large force of infantry and cavalry, out of the Friedrichstadt suburbs and over the Ostra Bridge.

Bianchi saw a weak spot and sent forward three columns. The columns were commanded by FML Colloredo. Their advance was covered by the 2nd Jäger Battalion and two companies of the 1st Jäger Battalion. The second line contained four jäger companies and the 1/Broder Grenz Regiment. Behind them came Chiesa's brigade, 1st Line

Bianchi.

Division. The 7th Jäger Battalion marched on Chiesa's left flank. The cavalry and both other brigades remained by Räcknitz as a reserve. The column from Bianchi's 2nd Reserve Division moved against the Freiberger suburb, along both banks of the Weisseritz to overrun the earthwork by the city. Schneller (3rd Cavalry Division) and Weissenwoiff (2nd Line Division) also attacked towards Löbtau and the Freiberger Schlag. They joined Meszko's 3rd Light Division by Schusterhäusern.

As Liechtenstein's forces struck at Redoubt III, they were met by the fire of the French 2/, 3/27th Légère. The first line of advancing Austrians was struck down. The advancing four companies of the 1st Jäger Battalion, two companies from both the Froon and de Vaux Infantry regiments and some of the 1/Broder Grenz Regiment drove forward. They plunged into the ditch and pressed up against the palisade, tearing it down as best they could. Once the palisade was breached the Austrians poured into the redoubt and a bloody hand to hand fight began. The French lost that fight, with the bulk of their number either killed or taken prisoner. The remainder fled into the Hospital Gardens, abandoning six guns to the Austrians.[41]

The Austrians brought forward two 12pdr guns to support their assault on the Hospital Garden walls and sent forward their infantry again. The 2/, 3/27th Légère, reinforced by two battalions from Berthezène's Division, held the Austrian advance and renewed the struggle for the redoubt.

FML Bianchi advanced his division to the earthwork before the Freiberger Schlag. The Simbschen Infantry Regiment drove the French back to Altona and Klein-Hahneberg. The Hiller Infantry Regiment defended Holzhof against a French counter attack aimed at the junction of Chasteler and Bianchi's corps. The H. Colloredo Infantry Regiment struck against the French flank and was followed by GM von Quallenberg's reserve brigade, which was formed in *battalionsmasse*.[42]

Gyulai left Weissenwolff's 2nd Line Division on the Rossthal heights in three lines. The 1/ Kaiser Infantry Regiment moved to and occupied the heights by the customs house, and covered a horse battery posted there. The 3/Kaiser Infantry Regiment stormed Löbtau inflicting heavy losses on the French. The remainder of Czollich's brigade followed behind them. The Kottulinsky Infantry Regiment then occupied the village and moved its supporting artillery to the heights to the left (south west) of the village. GM von Grimmer's brigade advanced to the right from Nauslitz. Between Nauslitz and Gorbitz stood a third line, the brigade of GM von Herzogenberg.[43] Schneller's 3rd Cavalry Division was positioned on the left flank of the same heights in battle line.

Part of the brigade formed to secure the flank and the other part to form a link with Meszko's 3rd Light Division.

As the first line of Czollich's brigade reached Löbtau, the Simbschen Infantry Regiment advanced into Klein-Hahneberg. At the same time, Weissenwolff's troops encountered a large force of French cavalry before Friedrichstadt. The timely arrival of the French cavalry prevented the Austrians from breaking through the Löbtau-Cotta line.

Schneller's 3rd Cavalry Division, acting as a fifth attack column, was pulled back at 6:00 p.m., to the left bank of the Weisseritz and placed under FZM Gyulai. It lost a half hour in this maneuver, as it waited for the lead brigade of Hessen-Homburg's division to enter Rossthal.[44]

FML Meszko advanced behind Czollich's brigade, into the battle with his forces moving against the French right flank. The Beaulieu Infantry and the grenz regiments of the division, advanced 500 to 600 meters beyond the Cotta-Schusterhäusern line. They were supported by three squadrons from the Palatinal Hussar Regiment, which marched with the horse batteries on the left wing of the division. Two further squadrons, from the Ferdinand Hussar Regiment, moved behind the right wing of the division.

As the Austrian attack rolled forward, it was taken under flanking fire by a French horse battery standing by Redoubt V. However, despite this, the advance of the left flank arrived in the vicinity of the Remise Forest and the Powder Magazine. Between 5:00 and 6:00 p.m., more French batteries were placed before the Löbtau Suburb, and around 6:00 p.m., Murat's forces began to appear before the suburb.

Murat's Attack

As Gyulai's forces took up these positions, the French deployed about 12,000 more infantry and cavalry, supported by 30 or 40 guns before Friedrichstadt. It was about 7:30 p.m. This was Murat and the 1st and 2nd Young Guard Divisions of Dumoustier and Barrois. The French holding Löbtau, heartened by the appearance of these reinforcements, redoubled their fight to hold the village as their cavalry moved between Löbtau and Cotta. GM Czollich, with the Kaiser and Kottulinsky Infantry Regiments, defended their position before Löbtau as Murat led his cavalry against them.

Teste's infantry and part of Razout's 45th Division struck from Löbtau Suburb towards Altona. To their left marched Pajol's 10th Light Cavalry Division and to the right was Latour-Maubourg's I Cavalry Corps. Before them, by the Powdermill, stood only a small force of Austrian infantry.

Gyulai.

A battalion of the 21st Line Regiment, Teste's 23rd Division, struck at the Kaiser Infan Regiment, holding the village of Löbtau. The French were thrown back.

Murat personally led forward the attack, guiding Stedmann's 31st Light Cavalry Brigade, Pajol's 10th Light Cavalry Division, and two other cavalry regiments between Dreschersdorf and Cotta against the juntion of Meszko's division and Gyulai's corps. The 7th Chevauléger Regiment led this assault.[45] The 7th Chevaulégers struck and drove back the two squadrons of the Palatinal

Hussars standing by Cotta. The Kienmayer Hussars counterattacked and drove the Chevaulégers back.[46] The hill by Löbtau was occupied by the 6pdr brigade battery from Grimmer's Brigade. It was supported by the Frölich Infantry Regiment.

While this battle occurred, Murat directed the bulk of Pajol's division to the northwest of Löbtau. They encountered four companies of the 3/Kaiser Regiment supported by a few squadrons of the Kienmayer Hussars. A bloody fight erupted in which at least one squadron of French cuirassiers took part.

Weissenwolff's division was hit hard, as was Meszko's. The Beaulieu Infantry Regiment stood in a position behind a ravine and fired several volleys into the French cavalry. At the same time, the O'Reilly Chevauléger Regiment moved forward to engage the French cavalry facing the Beaulieu Regiment and drove them back. The Saxon Zastrow Cuirassier

French hussars charging at Dresden, by Lalauze.

Regiment, defending its home country, was particularly ferocious. It inflicted grievous losses on the Manfredini Infantry Regiment and took many prisoners. The cannonade that accompanied the attack remained heavy until after nightfall. The battle on the allied left had been heavy. FZM Gyulai, FML von Schneller, and Oberst Fürst von Hohenlohe had horses killed under them. GM Prinz Philipp von Hessen-Homburg received a contusion from a shot and GM Mariassy was wounded.[47]

Mortier's Attack

On the allied far right, along the Elbe, Mortier prepared his attack. He had been ordered by Napoleon to take two divisions and advance down the Pirna road and strike the villages of Blasewitz, Streifen and Grüna, the allied right wing. The 3rd Young Guard Division (Decouz) moved to Rampischen and the Ziegel Suburbs. Roguet's 4th Young Guard Division, supported by three dragoon squadrons from Doumerc's 3rd Heavy Cavalry Division moved down the Elbe against the Hofgartens and Stückgiessers. A French battery quickly deployed in a position near Stückgiessers, two hundred meters in front of the Rampischen Suburb. It began firing on the Russian lines.

Surprised by Mortier's attack, the Russians stopped and withdrew to Landgraben. Dumoustier's 1st Guard Division moved to the right and attacked the Prussians in the Grossen-Garten, quickly overrunning it. The 43rd and 44th Divisions (XIV Corps) recaptured the central redoubt. As two companies of grenadiers of the 8th Légère and 34th Provisional Demi-brigade pushed into the redoubt, they found it filled with corpses, but still made 400 prisoners.[48]

Wittgenstein called for assistance and GM Klüx's 9th Brigade responded to the call, by sending forward the Silesian Uhlans and 8th Landwehr Cavalry regiment in three lines, formed in column on the middle. They passed over the Pirnau Road and moved behind Striesen, to join in the murderous battle between the Russians and French.

It was 9:00 p.m. The Russians moved behind Striesen and Klüx's 9th Brigade. The French contented themselves with occupying a few houses on the edge of Striesen.[49]

Ney's Attack

In the center, Moritz Liechtenstein's forces were pushing at the French, holding out in the Hospital Gardens. The French were reinforced by a Young Guard voltigeur regiment from Gros' brigade of Decouz's 3rd Young Guard Division. A French force then struck at the redoubt from the east. It was formed by 3/54th Line, 2/16th Légère and a Young Guard voltigeur regiment. Further French forces poured out of the city as these four battalions made short work of the Austrians in Redoubt III. The 2nd Young Guard Division of Barrois, part of Dumoustier's 1st Young Guard Division and a few battalions of Old Guard under the command of Maréchal Ney arrived and moved against Redoubt V and the Papermill. Part of Dumoustier's 1st Young Guard Division moved against Redoubt IV.

Ney's forces moved into the interval between Bianchi and Colloredo's forces. Seeing the very real threat to their positions, both Austrian generals reacted. Bianchi sent forward his reserve, the Hungarian regiment Hessen-Homburg and Quallenberg's entire brigade. Colloredo sent part of his reserve, Abele's Brigade,[50] in the direction of the Blinden Suburb and pulled Andrassy's Brigade back towards his central position. The French assault was not to be denied. The 1/Hessen-Homburg Regiment was surrounded and taken prisoner with its battalion flag.[51]

Ney's attack drove back the Austrians of Chasteler and Gyulai, while O'Meara's brigade (Teste's 23rd Division) seized Klein-Hahneberg, and Murat cleared the plain of Friedrichstadt with his cavalry.

The French attacks and victory on the allied right, plus Ney's assault had reversed the earlier Austrian successes against Redoubts III and IV.

Night fell, stopping the battle, which had so far cost the allies 4,000 dead and wounded, and 2,000 prisoners. The French casualties were about 2,000 men.

Wittgenstein withdrew between Blasewitz and Striesen. His left stood by the road from Dresden to Pillnitz. Kleist stood between Striesen and Strehlen, Colloredo's corps stood between Strehlen and Rächnitz, Chasteler's corps was between Rächnitz and Plauen, and Gyulai stood on the left bank of the Weisseritz between Plauen and Wölfnitz. On his left stood the advanced guard division of FML Meszko (3rd Light Division), from Klenau's corps. Meszko stretched his forces between Priesnitz and the road to Freiberg, covering Klenau's line of march.

During the night of 26 August, the Corps of Victor and Marmont (II and VI Corps), arrived in Dresden. Victor was placed under the orders of Murat and took positions facing Löbtau, with his right in Cotta. The I Cavalry Corps, Latour-Maubourg, also under Murat, was in reserve by Friedrichstadt. Marmont's VI Corps straddled the road to Dippoldiswalde, with his left at Roteshaus. The XIV Corps (St. Cyr) held the Grossen-Garten. The Old Guard (Grenadiers, Chasseurs and Cavalry) stood behind Roteshaus, in reserve. The two divisions of Young Guard,

Decouz and Roguet, commanded by Mortier, stood between the Grossen-Garten and the Elbe and the IV Cavalry Corps (Nansouty) stood behind Mortier's Young Guard as a supporting reserve.

Von Ziethen stood by Strehlen. He occupied the castle by the Grossen-Garten with the 1/2nd West Prussian Regiment and the 2/7th Reserve Regiment. The bulk of his advanced guard occupied the Strehlen heights with the 10th and 11th Brigades. The 12th Brigade also bivouacked on the Strehlen heights and occupied the village with two battalions.

At 10:00 p.m., A. Liechtenstein moved his 4th Line Division back. M. Liechtenstein's 1st Light Division and Colloredo's 1st Line Division stood on the heights south of Räcknitz. A battalion of the Argenteau Infantry Regiment occupied Räcknitz, and a detachment of the 7th Jäger Battalion occupied Zschernitz. Crenneville's 3rd Reserve Division stood south of Plauen. Chasteler (1st Reserve Grenadier Division) pulled back his scattered battalions and moved his division to a position on the left of Civalart's Division, by Kaitz. Behind the grenadiers stood Nostitz and Lederer's cavalry divisions.

Weissenwolff's light forces (2nd Line Division) spent the night around Löbtau. Schneller's 3rd Cavalry Division stood behind the hill by the Freiberg Road. Mezko pulled the 3rd Light Division back and established it by Ockerwitz, supporting it with a division of the Kienmayer Hussars and about 50 men from the Palatinal Hussar Regiment. His forward forces, three squadrons of the Palatinal Hussars and two companies of the Beaulieu Infantry Regiment, occupied the Schusterhäusern, Cotta, and the Löbtau heights.[52]

GdK Klenau marched with his corps towards the battlefield. He detached the Vacquant Infantry Regiment, a squadron of the Lothringen Cuirassiers, and a half battery to occupy Tharandt. The St. Julien Infantry Regiment, a squadron of the Lothringen Cuirassiers, and a half battery were sent forward to Kesseldorf to support Meszko's Division.

During the night, the allies did some reorganization. GL Graf Ostermann-Tolstoy was given command of an Observation Corps that consisted of the 1st Russian Guard Division (8 battalions), the 2nd Russian Corps (19 battalions), the 1st Brigade, 14th Infantry Division of GM Helfreich (5 battalions), and a cavalry force under GM Prinz Leopold von Sachsen-Coburg.[53] This force of about 15,000 men was engaged with Vandamme's I Corps to the south by Pirna. However, Ostermann's health was not good, and though he joined these troops, he did not take command.

Klenau.

The 1st Russian Guard Division stood by Ottendorf, and Württemberg's 2nd Corps stood before Königstein.

The Prussian Guard Infantry Brigade, under Oberstleutnant von Alvensleben, marched from Kulm to Cotta, where it lagered that evening. It received orders while there, to advance to Dresden and assume its position in the battle.[54] Czar Alexander of Russia and Schwarzenberg were in Nötnitz, the King of Prussia was in the village of Kausche, and Barclay de Tolly was in Nikkern.

The Second Day 27 August 1813

During the night of 26/27 August, the skies a torrential rain poured on Dresden. In the morning a thick fog covered the battlefield. The allies had spent the night aligning and preparing their lines for the French attack that was to come in the morning. Wittgenstein's corps now stood between Prohlis and Leubnitz, covering Strehlen and Grüna with its advanced posts.[55] On the road running from Grüna, stood six guns of Russian Horse Battery #6. It was covered to the rear by the Grodno and Loubny Hussar Regiments.[56] The right wing of the battle line was formed by the 5th Russian Division. It stood between the villages of Reieck and Leubnitz.

Between Prohlis and the road to Pirna, stood the Russian Reserve under Grand Duke Constantine. He had the 1st Grenadier Division on the Tschernitz heights between Leubnitz and Torna. The 2nd Russian Guard Division, the Prussian Foot Guard and the Prussian and Russian Guard Cavalry stood between Prohlis and Torna.[57]

The 1st Russian Guard Division and the Guard Hussars were detached to the Württemberg's 2nd (Russian) Corps to reinforce it for the day's battle near Pirna. Yermolov, who normally commanded the Guard Corps commanded the 2nd Guard Division personally.[58]

Kleist's 2nd Corps stood between Leubnitz and Rächnitz, supported by the Prussian Guard. Its advanced posts were between the Russian posts to the east and Strehlen. Colloredo's 1st Line Division and Chasteler's 1st Reserve Division stood between Rächnitz and Plauen. The allied grand headquarters were in Rächnitz. The Austrian grenadiers of Bianchi's 2nd Reserve Division, detached from Gyulai and stood against the Plauen ravine. Behind them, in Coschütz, stood the Austrian reserves under the Erbprinz von Hessen-Homburg. On the left bank of the Weisseritz, extending to Doltschen, stood the remainder of Gyulai's corps.

GM Czollich's brigade and a battalion of the Würzburg Regiment occupied Dölzchen and had their right wing on the Plauen ravine. Czollich's Brigade stood in two lines, in columns, stretched between Dölzchen, and Rossthal, where they touched A. Liechtenstein's 4th Line Division. A brigade of A. Liechtenstein's division occupied the villages of Rossthal and Nauslitz with the Kaunitz Regiment, and the villages of Wolfnitz and Gorbitz with the W. Colloredo Infantry Regiment. His two other brigades were posted as follows: The brigade of GM Mumb was on the Freiberger road to support Meszko's 3rd Light Division. The brigade of GM Meszerey remained in reserve between Pesterwitz and Alt-Franken.

The last allied force, FML Meszko's 3rd Light Division was strung out between Gorbitz and Bergstadel. This division had been reinforced by the addition of the Vacquant and St. Julien Infantry Regiments and two squadrons of the Lothringen Cuirassier Regiment.[59]

Shortly before 7:00 a.m., the brigades of Herzogenberg, Grimmer and Zechmeister moved from the heights to the south of Löbtau. Zechmeister's cavalry brigade (part of Schneller's 3rd Cavalry Division) moved to Plauen. The two infantry brigades (Herzogenberg and Grimmer) of Weissenwolff's 2nd Line Division moved towards Potschappel.

Though the allies were prepared for an attack, their position was flawed by the ravine of the Weisseritz, which cut off a significant portion of their forces from support of the reserves in Coschütz. Napoleon's sharp eye for enemy weaknesses, caught this flaw in their dispositions.

Standing in a bell tower during the morning of 27 August, Napoleon could view the entire battlefield and study the allied positions in detail. He resolved to profit from the isolation of Gyulai's forces from the rest of the allied army. His attack was to fall against the isolated allied wing between Doltschen and Gorbitz. That morning Murat commanded the I Cavalry Corps (68 squadrons, 30 guns), Victor's II Corps (36 battalions, 68 guns), and O'Meara's brigade of Teste's 23rd Division (8 battalions, 8 guns).[60]

The center was formed from Marmont's VI Corps (40 battalions, 78 guns), St. Cyr's XIV Corps (37 battalions, 76 guns), the 1st and 2nd Young Guard Divisions of Curial and Barrois (28 battalions, 48 guns),[61] Friant's Old Guard (10 battalions, 98 guns), and Walthier's 3rd Guard Cavalry Division (31 squadrons, 12 guns). The left wing was commanded by Maréchal Mortier and consisted of 3rd and 4th Young Guard Divisions of Decouz and Roguet (24 battalions, 48 guns) and the 1st and 2nd Guard Cavalry Divisions of Ornano and Léfèbvre-Desnoëttes (28 squadrons, 12 guns).[62]

Murat was to have the honor of the attack on the right, while Ney, commanding the left, would turn the Russian right wing. When the maneuvers of Ney and Murat were sufficiently

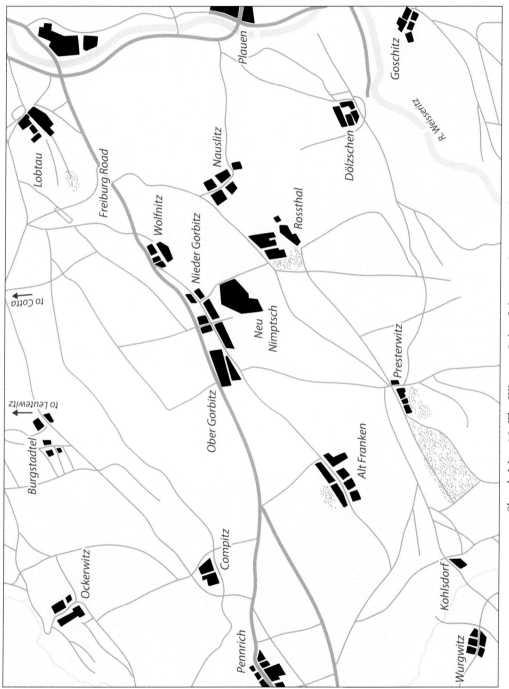

Sketch Map 13 The Western Side of the Dresden Battlefield.

Plauen

Goschitz

R. Weisseritz

Nauslitz

Dölzschen

Lobtau

Freiburg Road

Wolfnitz

Rossthal

Nieder Gorbitz

to Cotta

Neu
Nimptsch

Presterwitz

to Leutewitz

Ober Gorbitz

Burgstadtel

Alt Franken

Ockerwitz

Compitz

Kohlsdorf

Pennrich

Wurgwitz

developed, the entire French army was to advance and strike the allies, driving them down the road to Peterswalde, where Vandamme's I Corps, then en route from Pirna, would be waiting.

Napoleon's plans, it was hoped, would begin in time to destroy Schwarzenberg's left wing prior to Klenau's arrival. At 7:00 a.m., Napoleon issued the order to commence the attack and his artillery thundered to life. The allied artillery responded and the battle was begun.

The Allied Left

Between 6:00 and 7:00 a.m., Victor's II Corps moved to the junction of the Freiberg and Tharandt Roads. O'Meara's brigade stood between Löbtau and Klein-Hahneberg. Pajol's 10th Light Cavalry Division moved on the right of the II Corps, while Latour-Maubourg's I Cavalry Corps stood to the right of O'Meara's brigade. The II Corps artillery was posted before the II Corps, on the Löbtau Heights and was covered by a skirmish line.

As the French barrage began, P. von Hessen-Homburg struck at the French 21st Line Regiment by Löbtau and the stone bridge. The brigade batteries of Czollich and Hessen-Homburg fixed on the French artillery fire and the French skirmishers advancing against the Austrian line.[63]

The II Corps organized itself into four attack columns and moved against Gorbitz, Rossthal and Doltschen. On the left bank of the Weisseritz, Victor advanced by echelons to the right in advance. Marching on Gorbitz, Dubreton (4th Division) directed one of his brigades against Rossthal and his other brigade against Doltschen. Vial's 6th Division was held in reserve.

A battalion was pushed along the Weisseritz valley, into the Reischwitz Garden and palace. The Austrian 2/Kaunitz Infantry Regiment, which was posted in the garden, defended its position strongly, but was finally driven back to the palace.

Murat and his cavalry moved to the north of the Freiberg road and moved to his left, moving against the divisions of Meszko (3rd Light), A. Liechtenstein (4th Line) and Weissenwolff (2nd Line). At 9:00 a.m., Murat's cavalry was arranged in two lines. The first line had the 13 squadrons of Chastel's 3rd Light Cavalry Division on the right, near the Schusterhäusern. The left of the

A contemporary view of Dresden.

first line was formed by the 21 squadrons of Doumerc's 3rd Heavy Cavalry Division, which stood before Cotta. The second line consisted of the 22 squadrons of Bordesoulle's 1st Heavy Cavalry Division. Berkheim's brigade stood on the right in the wet ground to the south of Cotta with its left on the Drescherhäuser. Bessières' brigade stood before Löbtau. The five squadrons of the Saxon cuirassiers followed Murat as an escort.

Murat disposed his artillery with 12 horse guns standing before Cotta, 18 before Löbtau, and 36 before the Löbtau Jagdhaus. O'Meara's Brigade (Teste's 23rd Division), stood between the Drescherhäuser and Löbtau.[64]

The Austrians began a vigorous defensive artillery fire on Murat's forces, as soon as they became clearly visible. Meszko prepared his defense on the edge of the hill north of Nieder-Gorbitz and on the ground behind Gorbitz. He moved two squadrons of hussars forward and Mumb's brigade marched up in support of his position, putting its right against Gorbitz.

Murat sent his escort of Saxon cuirassiers through Cotta, behind the Leutewitz heights. Here they moved against the left flank of Meszko's line and struck the two squadrons of hussars supporting him. The hussars were completely overwhelmed and Meszko was obliged to fall back on Gompitz.

O'Meara's Brigade, Teste's 23rd Division, marched behind this advance and maneuvered to threaten the Austrian left wing. They moved past Drescherhäuser towards Burgstädtel about 10:00 a.m. Chastel's 3rd Light Cavalry Division moved through Cotta with a battery of horse artillery leading its advance.[65]

A. Liechtenstein had pulled his left wing back to Alt-Franken and Pesterwitz, so that the three brigades of his division stood in column. The village of Dölzchen was defended by GM Czollich with the 1/Kottulinsky Infantry Regiment. Two companies of the Kaiser Regiment stood in Nauslitz and between them stood the 2/Würzburg Infantry Regiment, part in *divisionsmasse* and part in line.[66] Seethal's Brigade, from A. Liechtenstein's 4th Division, occupied the villages of Rossthal, Wölfnitz and Gorbitz. Meszerey's Brigade stood on the heights between Alt-Franken and Pesterwitz, the cavalry brigade of G. Hessen-Homburg stood behind Rossthal. Mumb's Brigade stood between Gorbitz and Gompitz supporting Meszko's forces.

Shortly before 10:00 a.m., the Austrians moved a weak cavalry force from one flank to the other, and drew their forces together on the heights northwest of Gorbitz, in order to improve their communications with Freiberg. Meszko's cavalry, three squadrons of the Palatinal Hussars, six Züge of the Ferdinand Hussars, and the Lothringen Cuirassier Regiment, formed the advanced guard as they moved. Once in position, the cavalry assumed a position behind the left wing of the infantry. Mumb's Brigade stood as a reserve behind the middle. A half squadron of the Palatinal Hussars stood forward, to observe the French lines of advance. Paumgarten and a detachment of Meszko's forces that had been sent towards Nossen, were pulled back to Freiberg.[67]

O'Meara's brigade occupied the area between Löbtau and Cotta, as the Austrians withdrew onto the nearby heights. Between 8:00 a.m. and 10:00 a.m., Victor's II Corps marched onto the heights to the west of Löbtau. As a result of the absence of Reuss' Brigade, Dufour's 5th Division, had only two regiments standing on the right wing. They straddled the main Freiberg Road, while Dubreton's 4th Division stood to the left and extended to Weisseritz, Vial's 6th Division stood as a reserve behind the middle.

Murat advanced his cavalry through Gompitz. As soon as Murat held sufficient terrain to the right, about 10:00 a.m., Victor pushed his troops vigorously forward.

The first French column, which consisted of Estko's brigade of Dufour's 5th Division, moved down the Freiberg Road, striking at Wölfnitz, Klein- and Gross-Gorbitz. The second column, another brigade, moved between Nauslitz and Wölfnitz and directed their attack against the north side of Nauslitz and Weinberg. Later they moved against Rossthal and Neu-Nimptsch, in the wake of a cavalry column.

The third column, a brigade from Dubreton's 4th Division, moved frontally against the village of Nauslitz. From there it moved against Doltschen where it smashed the 1/Kottulinsky Infantry Regiment. The fourth column, another brigade of Dubreton's 4th Division, moved against the hill between Nauslitz and Doltschen. Here they encountered and attacked Czollich's Brigade.[68]

The Saxon Zastrow Cuirassier Regiment detached a force, under the command of Major Ziegesar, to occupy the Leutewitz Heights and serve as cover for the advance. It advanced and quickly chased Meszko's cavalry from the position. The main body of Latour-Maubourg's I Cavalry Corps held itself ready behind the Löbtau Heights. Bordesoulle's 1st Heavy Cavalry Division stood on the left, while Doumerc's 3rd Heavy Cavalry Division stood on the right wing.

The frontal assault by Victor's infantry and the flank attack by the cuirassiers of Bordesoulle's 1st Heavy Cavalry Division was more than Meszko's light troops could take and they fell back on A. Liechtenstein's 4th Line Division.

Murat took a squadron of the Saxon Guard Cuirassier Regiment as an escort and explored the Austrian position. His extravagant headdress was seen all across that front.

Murat ordered Victor's II Corps to occupy the villages of Wölfnitz, Gorbitz, Beerhut, Rossthal, Nauslitz and Doltschen. The artillery battle had already lasted several hours, when shortly before 11:00 a.m., the French infantry divisions burst forward with thousands of voices calling "Vive l'Empereur!"

Weissenwolff's 2nd Line Division stood before the village of Löbtau, straddling the Freiberg Road.[69] The Kaiser, Kottulinsky, Kaunitz, and Wenzel Colloredo Infantry Regiments stood in the first line. The position was heavily held, with troops behind all the walls, strong points loop-holed, and the village entrances barricaded. To the front, between the villages, the artillery was drawn up, its wheels sunk up to the axles in the mud.[70] The attacking French infantry column, Estko's brigade of Dufour's 5th Division, moved through Löbtau and Cotta, while Latour-Maubourg's cavalry passed by Priesnitz and struck at Nauslitz, Wölfnitz and Gorbitz.

Soon Austrian skirmishers fell back. Less than 100 paces behind them, half covered in the fog, the Austrian defenders caught glimpses of the massed and advancing French attack columns. The Austrian artillery took them under a heavy fire.

Dufour's 5th Division advanced through Wölfnitz towards Gorbitz, Dubreton's 4th Division, also in column, advanced before Nauslitz-Doltschen. Victor made his principal thrust between Nauslitz and Doltschen, in an effort to break through the Austrian line. The villages, thanks to their natural strength and the tenacity of their garrisons, would only be taken after a hard fight. The French chose instead to advance through the interval, and then, through a turning maneuver, to strike the rear of the villages and capture them.

The capture of Nauslitz quickly followed this maneuver. A frontal attack against Nauslitz foundered on the stubborn resistance from the two companies of the Kaiser Regiment reinforced by various detachments. The French then sought to push to the left and right of the village. A column endeavored to break through between Doltschen and Rossthal. The Kaiser and Kottulinsky Regiments, led by Czollich, threw themselves against the French and stopped the French attempt. Another column struck at them, trying to turn the west flank of Nauslitz and move between that village and Rossthal. The Kaunitz Regiment, which occupied Rossthal, turned to face the assaulting French and several detachments of Czollich's Brigade, moved to their left flank, breaking off from the battle to their front. The strong Austrian resistance succeeded in stabilizing the left flank of Czollich's Brigade and stopped the French advance. However, the village of Nauslitz was abandoned, its defenders falling back towards Rossthal. Around noon, Rossthal met the same fate.[71]Wölfnitz, which was held by a weak detachment of the Wenzel Colloredo Infantry Regiment, fell to a flanking movement by parts of Dufour's 5th Division, as they moved down the Freiberg Road.

The fall of Rossthal was a tremendous threat to the Austrian left flank. The French had moved their columns between the divisions of Weissenwolff and Alois Liechtenstein, and menaced the only practical line of retreat through Jagdhaus Juchhee. When G. Hessen-Homburg's Cavalry Brigade was still in its earlier position, it had only been lightly engaged. From that position it could have intervened in the present situation. Unfortunately, the brigade had been moved to the center of the line shortly before the fall of Rossthal. FML A. Liechtenstein shifted the 1/Vogelsang to stall the threat, menacing his line of withdrawal to Jagdhaus Juchhee. Meszerey's Reserve Brigade was ordered to attempt the recapture of Rossthal. Weissenwolff had no reserves left, as his last intact battalion, 2/Würzburg, had already been thrown into the battle, to retake Rossthal. The attack appeared to be successful. Part of the Würzburg Regiment had fought its way back into Rossthal, capturing a French captain with a few dozen men.

It was about 1:00 p.m., that the second battle for Rossthal took place. At the same time, around Doltschen and Gorbitz, another battle raged with neither side yielding. The Kottulinsky Infantry Regiment stood on the right and the Wenzel Colloredo Infantry Regiment stood on the left wing. Both units defended themselves tenaciously.[72]

As Murat waited for Victor's advancing forces, he ordered his cavalry to advance. Bordesoulle's 1st Heavy Cavalry Division advanced with a brigade of Victor's II Corps, into the gap between Neu-Nimptsch (Beerhut) and Rossthal. The Saxon Guard Cuirassier Regiment moved down the Freiberg Road as a reserve. To the north of the road, Doumerc's heavy cavalry moved against the Pennrich heights. Reiset's Dragoon Brigade formed the first line of Doumerc's advancing 3rd Heavy Division. Murat advanced with this force and was followed by a few of O'Meara's battalions.[73] The cavalry advanced over the ground very slowly, for the most part advancing at a walk. As a result, Meszko's Division saw itself under less pressure than the Austrian forces to the south of the road. It was soon reinforced by Mumb's brigade, which consisted of 10 companies of the Erzherzog Rainer Infantry Regiment and two battalions of the Lusignan Infantry Regiment. In addition, shortly before noon,

Bordesoulle.

the St. Julien Infantry Regiment was called forward from its position in the Herzogwalde. Meszko commanded, at this time, over 5,400 infantry and 620 cavalry.

Notwithstanding that, Meszko and his troops found themselves by no means in a confident mood. The heavy French cavalry massed before their front, whose movements and maneuvers were observed by Austrian hussar patrols, was unnerving. In addition, the Austrian cavalry present was so weak, that it was faced with withdrawal or annihilation by the overwhelming mass before it. The blow was coming.

FML Meszko personally strove to suppress his sense of alarm and that of his troops. He wrapped himself in a hussar's coat and plunged to and fro across the front, holding his troops steady. He chose not to withdraw, on the basis that his neighboring division was engaged.

To Meszko's right, A. Liechtenstein's Division fought its desperate battle by Gorbitz. However, against Meszko's front, the French advanced heavy masses of cavalry, and his left flank, bared by the French successes, was in grave danger.[74]

Around noon, as the French cavalry came even closer, Meszko sent a staff officer, Hauptman Oehm, to FML Alois Liechtenstein, to announce that he must withdraw, because of the pending attack of the French cavalry and artillery. Victor was sending forward his reserve, Vial's 6th Division, and the last of Weissenwolff's troops were chased from the village of Löbtau.

Allied Left After 1.00 p.m.

The Austrians in the villages of Wölfnitz and Gorbitz held strong positions and vigorously defended themselves against the French attacks, swirling past and crashing against them. The rain prevented the use of muskets and forced the attacks to be with bayonets alone.[75]

Between 1:00 p.m. and 2:00 p.m., Gorbitz fell to the French. Nearby, the Wenzel Colloredo Infantry Regiment, commanded by Oberst Laiml, found itself under heavy pressure. The French column, Estko's brigade, pushed into the village of Neu-Nimptsch and was stopped by a garden wall, defended by the Austrians. However, Estko's brigade pressed it closely from all sides. The Herrenhaus was set afire. A quick thrust quickly drove the Austrians back. The Austrian garrison moved to the heights, just south of the village, and from there back towards Meszerey's Brigade.[76] Oberst Laiml was concerned that some detachments of his unit had remained in Neu-Nimptsch, and were in danger of being cut off. In order to rescue them, Laiml led his regiment forward in an attack, hoping to save those brave troops from their probable demise. On the heights between Gorbitz and Rossthal, Bordesoulle's 1st Heavy Cavalry Division moved towards them. The Austrian artillery by Pesterwitz, attempted to defend the W. Colloredo infantry and fired on the French cavalry. Six French squadrons caught them in the open, though the battalions of the W. Colloredo Infantry Regiment formed squares. A French horse battery that had followed the attacking cavalry, unlimbered and began to fire on the helpless squares. The Austrian regiment was destroyed and many of its soldiers were killed and captured.[77]

With the fall of Ober-Gorbitz, the rest of A. Liechtenstein's division was completely separated from Meszko's Division and Mumb's Brigade. FML Weissenwolff was then obliged to order the entire wing to fall back.

The entire Austrian wing began to fall back on the Plauen ravine. The Austrian reserves watched helplessly as their left wing was about to be destroyed. It was about 2:00 p.m.

When Weissenwolff ordered his division to withdraw, he detached to Liechtenstein a battalion to hold the village of Zauckerode, and cover his withdrawal. His guns, the Kaunitz Infantry Regiment and the survivors of the W. Colloredo Infantry Regiment moved into the villages of Alt-Franken and Pesterwitz, followed by a brigade of FML Meszko that passed through the ravine by Pesterwitz. These Austrian columns then passed through Zauckerode and Döhlen and joined the lead elements of Klenau's corps by Gittersee.

When Ober-Gorbitz had fallen to the French, Pajol's cavalry drove down the Freiberg Road towards Wölfnitz and Nieder-Gorbitz.[78]

As Victor seized Ober-Gorbitz, the I Cavalry Corps moved north west of Gorbitz in two lines. Bessières' brigade moved past Ober- and Nieder-Gorbitz and assumed a position on the Freiberg Road, near where the road forks towards Alt-Franken and Pesterwitz.

About 3:00 p.m., Chastel's 3rd Light Cavalry Division and O'Meara's brigade of Teste's 23rd Division, which the Austrians had not seen because of the rain, arrived. Chastel's 3rd Light Cavalry Division moved past Pennrich, while O'Meara moved into the village. Meszko had occupied the village with only a single battalion. O'Meara's 23rd Division chased them out with little trouble.[79]

Meszko's Division and Mumb's Brigade fell back to a position to the north of the Freiberg Road in the area between Gompitz, Pennrich and Ziegelei. As Meszko defended his position he saw the withdrawal of Liechtenstein's division and ordered his division to once again withdraw. It did so in squares, as it was constantly attacked by Murat's cavalry.

The Saxon cavalry brigade, consisting of the Zastrow Cuirassiers and the 4/Garde du Corps Cuirassier Regiment, drove through Alt-Franken and broke two Austrian squares, capturing them entirely. The other three squadrons of the Garde du Corps Cuirassier Regiment captured two cannons.[80]

As Liechtenstein's division gathered itself together on the line from Juchhee-Pesterwitz-Alt-Franken, it saw the left wing of Czollich's Brigade forced, by the fire of the French batteries

The Saxon Cuirassier Regiment Jung-Zastrow assaults Austrian infantry during the Battle of Dresden, 27 August.

by Rossthal, to withdraw to the area around Plauschen. Major Arbter, with his battalion of the Kottulinsky Infantry Regiment, held the village of Plauschen against all the attacks of Dubreton's 4th Division.[81] He had turned this village into a pivot in the line. Between 2:00 p.m. and 3:00 p.m., Czollich's Brigade stood on the edge of the gorge, as the advance pushed past Plauschen.

Weissenwolff and A. Liechtenstein quickly realized that to linger longer on the heights would invite a catastrophe. Weissenwolff had already earlier detached Czollich's artillery, which was fully laden with munition, to the rear to take up positions by Potschappel. For the Austrians there now existed only the narrow pass down the Plauschen gorge, but it was impractical for the artillery.

Oberst Latour, Gyulai's staff officer, made his way to Weissenwolff, stating that speedy withdrawal was the sole possibility for salvation. The Zauckerode valley appeared to Weissenwolff to be the only practical terrain, especially since he feared that the French might be on the high road and advancing through Alt-Franken.

Oberst Latour relieved FML Alois Liechtenstein of his fears, and rode through Alt-Franken down the main Freiberg Road, where he encountered the Vacquant Infantry Regiment and the squadron of the Lothringen Cuirassier Regiment. This tiny force sat motionless, awaiting orders. The regiment's staff officer, Oberstleutnant Vukassovich, had gone ahead, seeking FML Meszko in order to ask him for orders.

Latour went to the regimental commander, Oberst Urmenyi, and directed him to immediately move in the direction of Gorbitz in order to cover the withdrawal of Liechtenstein's forces. Urmenyi set his forces in motion and Latour moved to the north to advise Meszko of Liechtenstein's withdrawal.

The appearance of this force changed Latour's opinion from that of A. Liechtenstein, and he felt that the situation of the troops to the north of the Freiberg high road, was much less worrisome than Liechtenstein had supposed. He presumed that Meszko's forces would cover the road and he then sent word of the actual disposition of Mumb's Brigade.[82]

In this situation I thought no more of it, and sent Mumb's Brigade orders. Also I thought, because of the favorable lay of the terrain and with a main road without defiles to the rear, the brigade was in no jeopardy and that they could withdrawal straight down the road to Freiberg.

Both Liechtenstein and Latour were deceived by this favorable judgment. When Latour later crossed Freiberg Road, he found Meszko's Division and Mumb's Brigade already in full retreat towards Kesseldorf.

On his return, it is certain that Generalstabshauptmann Oehm informed Liechtenstein of the fall of Gorbitz. By Oehm's account, Liechtenstein was west of the village Gorbitz and the withdrawing detachments of the W. Colloredo Infantry Regiment, when the French assault struck. Meszko's Division was already completely cut off from the bulk of the Austrian left wing and its only hope of salvation remaining was an immediate retreat.

The ground was slippery and wet because of the rains, which resulted in some losses. However, Meszko's troops were covered by an advanced guard formed from squadrons of the Palatinal Hussar Regiment, a battalion of the Lusignan Infantry Regiment, and a cavalry battery. They had advanced warning of the approaching French cavalry, which allowed the main body to form itself in squares, without particular haste. They began their withdrawal, stopping briefly on the Pennrich heights, then resuming their withdrawal.[83]

Oberst Illesy, who commanded the advanced guard, observed that the withdrawal went on in reasonable order. The French chose to bombard the retreating division heavily, until they suddenly struck the rear guard. Meszko ordered the withdrawal to Pennrich hastened. However, it was very clear that the French intended to and would soon pass the Austrians' two flanks, enveloping them. The position of Meszko's forces was hopeless. A successful French breakthrough with these forces on the flanks meant capture. Meszko rode past Illesy and shouted to the troops the word "Forward!" He then turned to the right and was seen no more. Shortly after, three of his staff officers came by with the news that the Meszko had been captured. Meszko had been captured by a troop of French dragoons from the 23rd Regiment, which he had mistaken for Austrian Chevaulégers.[84]

Oberstleutnant Hoditz drew two Zuge of Palatinal Hussars together and galloped in the direction where Meszko was last seen, hoping to free the general, only to be severely wounded and taken prisoner himself.

The French fell upon Meszko's now leaderless division, crushing together infantry, cavalry, guns, and wagons in their grasp. The crush of men, animals and equipment was tremendous as several soldiers were crushed to death. No one knew where to go.

As he watched the new advance of the Austrians, Murat ordered the greatest part of Reiset's brigade sent through Gompitz, to strike their right and placed d'Audenarde's brigade in his first line. Reiset urged Murat to seize the advantage and Murat drew d'Audenarde's Cuirassiers back somewhat, luring the Austrians over the Pennrich heights and into the open terrain, so that the planned French flank attack would succeed. The French horse artillery stood before d'Audenarde's front. Despite the devastating canister fire, the Austrian battalions continued to close. Infantry skirmishers drawn from the Erzherzog Rainier Infantry Regiment were sent between the hussar Hankers. Their effectiveness was limited because of the effect of the rain on their muskets.

The hussars knew they would be unable to stop the advance of the French heavy cavalry. Seeing the French cavalry closing, the Austrian infantry quickly formed square. Murat's cuirassiers rode over the advanced guard and struck the Austrian front. Reiset's dragoons slammed into the north flank of the Austrian squares. Part of the French broke into the Austrian masses and were repelled, while others succeeded in sabering the Austrians. Occasionally a small group of French cavalry men would pull back, to organize themselves again and renew the assault.[85]

Here and there small forces of Austrians detached themselves from the klumpen and desperately threw themselves against the French. Only a few of these brave men escaped with their lives. Many were killed or wounded by the hooves of the French horses.

Despite the fury of the French attack on the Gompitz heights, of the trapped Austrians on the northern wing, only a battalion of the Lusignan Infantry Regiment capitulated, and four guns of a cavalry battery were lost. All the others continued to stand, before the now breathless French horses and riders. The pause in the battle gave the Austrian battalions some chance to free themselves from the French grasp. As Murat rallied his strength for another assault on the Pennrich heights, the leaderless troops turned about and withdrew towards Kesseldorf.[86]

Meanwhile the Vacquant Infantry Regiment and its accompanying squadron of the Lothringen Cuirassier Regiment arrived. Oberst Urmenyi led a battalion against Gorbitz and succeeded in recapturing part of the village. Unfortunately, he was quickly forced to withdraw, because of the movement of a column of Bordesoulle's cuirassiers down the Freiberg High Road. At the head of this column, was the Saxon Zastrow Cuirassier Regiment of Doumerc's 3rd Heavy Division While the French cuirassiers attacked the Austrians frontally, the Saxons moved past the north flank of the Wacquant Infantry Regiment and swung in so that they could fully encircle the lone battalion and its cuirassier escort. The French commander offered Urmenyi the opportunity to lower his arms, but received "No" for art answer. Urmenyi then formed his unit in square and pushed through the tangle of infantry and cavalry between Alt-Franken, towards the high road running to the west.[87]

More than once the French, faced by the necessity to organize their spent forces, withdrew them from the battle, reorganized and renewed the assault. The Lothringen Cuirassiers responded to each such opportunity with another attack.

Fate and the French closed on the outermost left wing of the Austrians. Murat did not let loose his grip. Bessières' and d'Audenarde's brigades remained by Gompitz and Alt-Franken, as a reserve, leaving the Austrians no other way out other than to capitulate.

The Vacquant Infantry Regiment succumbed to this harsh fate. After a heroic resistance, Oberst Urmenyi allowed his men to lower their weapons and surrender. A Saxon staff officer rode up to him and took his hand, "Comrade, You have fought like lions, I am sorry at your fate."

Dubreton's 4th Division closed the trap by seizing and holding Dölzchen. At this time, the Erzherzog Rainer, Lusignan, Beaulieu Regiments, and a few dozen grenadier companies moved towards Kesseldorf, endeavoring to link with the battalions of the St. Julien Regiment and pass through Wurgewitz. These regiments pushed to reach the Zauckerode valley and escape their fate. However a regiment of Berkheim's brigade foiled their plan near Wurgewitz, hitting them from all sides and compelling them to capitulate. Only Major von Longueville succeeded in escaping with the middle division and 2/Erzherzog Rainer's battalion flag. The Erzherzog Rainer Regiment lost a total of seven officers and 1,083 men, of which over 900 remained in the hands of the French.[88] The other two regiments suffered similar fates. Little of this force succeeded in reaching Kesseldorf. What did, owed its escape to the six squadrons of hussars under Illesy. FML Baron Meszko and GM Seezenny were taken prisoners along with 16 guns.[89]

As Colonel Martigne advanced through Kesseldorf with the French 23rd Dragoon Regiment, Murat led the bulk of Reiset's Brigade north around the village and blocked the Austrians on the way to Freiberg. With cries of "Vive l'Empereur!" the dragoons drove the Austrians in, depriving them of their artillery, the last useful weapon they had. Again a bloody fight began. Illesy struck back with his two squadrons, pushing through the Tharandt Forest. A small force of Austrian infantry followed him. Oberst Leiningen of the Erzherzog Rainer Infantry Regiment, took his regiment's flags and fought his way through the French. The bulk of the Austrian forces, 10 companies of the Rainer Infantry Regiment, one battalion of the Lusignan, three battalions of the Beaulieu Infantry Regiment, and four grenz companies were trapped and forced to surrender.

In addition a cavalry battery, a brigade battery, a position battery, and the first detachment of the light reserve with forty wagons, were captured by the French.

The withdrawal of the other Austrian troops still fighting beyond the Weisseritz was abandoned. A. Liechtenstein's Division reached Pesterwitz, passing through the Zauckerode valley and moved from there to Döhlen, where four companies of the Vogelsang Infantry Regiment, under Oberst Graf Bentheim-Steinfurt, had formed themselves as a rear guard. French cuirassiers sought to harass the withdrawal from Kohlsdorf. They were stopped by a division of the Vogelsang Regiment near Zauckerode.[90]

The last glory waited Major von Arbter's battalion for its defense of the village of Dölzchen.[91] These heroic troops finally abandoned the village, when it was set on fire by French artillery. At the same time, a French battery moved to the left flank of Czollich's brigade and forced them to surrender the heights because of its heavy fire. Cut off from Jagdhaus Juchhee, by the Dubreton's 4th Division, the brigade was forced, under constant danger of being crushed, to move down the Weisseritz slope.

The 2/Würzburg Infantry Regiment and two companies of the Kaiser Infantry Regiment formed an advanced guard. As the Würzburg Infantry pushed to link with the brigade, it had to sacrifice the division of the Kaiser Infantry Regiment. The eastern column of Bordesoulle's 3rd Heavy Cavalry Division, followed by Victor's infantry, came across the two isolated Austrian companies and fell on them. Because of the constant rain no muskets could fire and this forced the Austrians to defend themselves with bayonets. They struggled to keep the French from penetrating their defense, and the clash of saber and bayonet continued for half an hour. The French dragoons loaded their pistols under their capes and fired them into the first rank, taking a fearsome toll. Soon the two Austrian companies were no longer able to defend themselves and surrendered.

The battalions of Czollich's Brigade were still climbing up the slopes of the Plauen to the Gittersee Lake, where they united with the bulk of Weissenwolff's division.

A. Liechtenstein's Division pushed its way through Potschappel and Burgk, towards the Gittersee Lake. As it passed through the vicinity of Potschappel, between 6:00 p.m. and 7:00 p.m., it encountered the lead elements of Klenau's Corps. Earlier, around noon, Major von Hartenthal had been sent back from the main army headquarters. He sought GdK Klenau and GM Rothkirch in Thrandt, where two hours earlier the leading brigade of Klenau's corps had arrived in a pitiful state.[92] It is understandable that their advance was delayed, when the Corps Commander and his Chief of Staff had the order from Schwarzenberg, "to above all, remain together."[93]

Nevertheless this did not hinder Hohenlohe's Division, which was half assembled by 2:00 p.m., in accordance with its orders. It marched through the Weisseritz valley and arrived by Deuben and Potschappel that evening. With regards to the movements of this corps, Oberst Tothkirch wrote in his operations journal:

> Some have testified too quickly, that there was nothing more to do, than direct the withdrawal of the remaining troops of the main army to cover at this time. It was with this intent they were placed by the Deuben Bridge and by Potschappel, and after the divisions of Weissenwolff and A. Liechtenstein had defiled, Klenau moved Hohenlohe's Division, while leaving a rear-guard under the command of GM Schaffer by the Deuben Bridge and Nieder-Häslich.

Around noon, Mayer's Division reorganized itself by Thrandt. At this time Meszko's cries of alarm were already being heard, for which reason Klenau pushed Mayer's troops through the valley, and over the heights to the right bank of the Weisseritz, to find Hohenlohe. Late that evening, the divisions in the Tharandt Forest moved to Somersdorf. Unfortunately, it was too late to save the Austrian left wing.

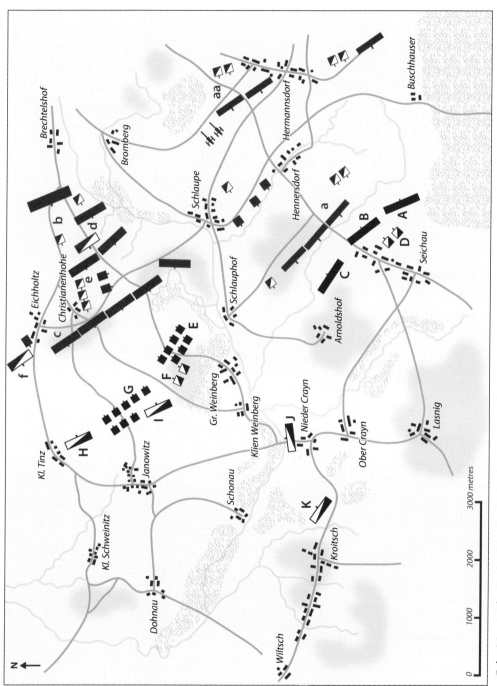

Color Map 1 The Battle of the Katzbach 26 August 1813, between the French Army of Maréchal Macdonald and the Army of Silesia under General der Infanterie Blücher, 26 August 1813. [Chapter 4]*

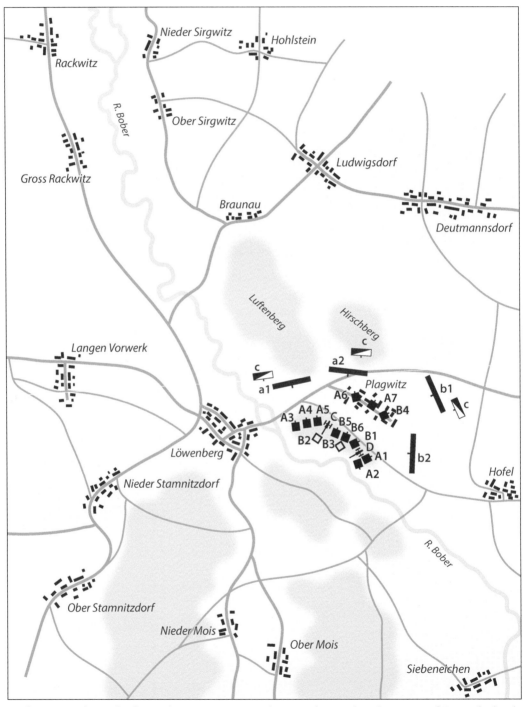

Color Map 2 The Battle of Löwenberg 29 August 1813, between the French 17th Division of GD Puthod and the Left Wing of the Army of Silesia under GdI Langeron. [Chapter 5]*

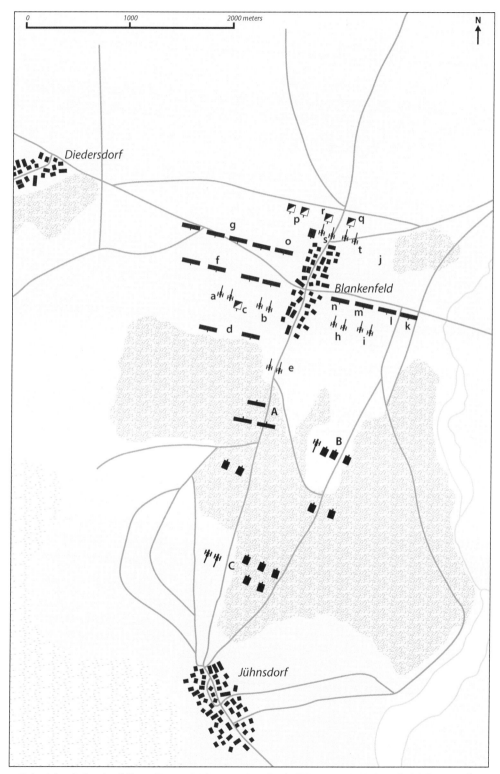

Color Map 3 Battle of Gross-Beeren 23 August 1813, Right-Wing 7:00 P.M. French IV Corps under GD Bertrand against the Army of the North under Prince Bernadotte. [Chapter 7]*

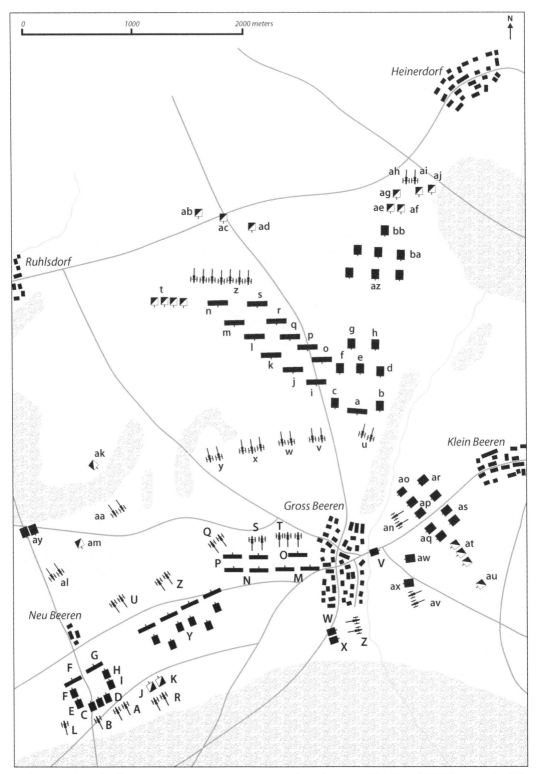

Color Map 4 Battle of Gross-Beeren 23 August 1813, Central Battle at 7:00 P.M. French VII Corps under GD Reynier against the Army of the North under Prince Bernadotte. [Chapter 7]*

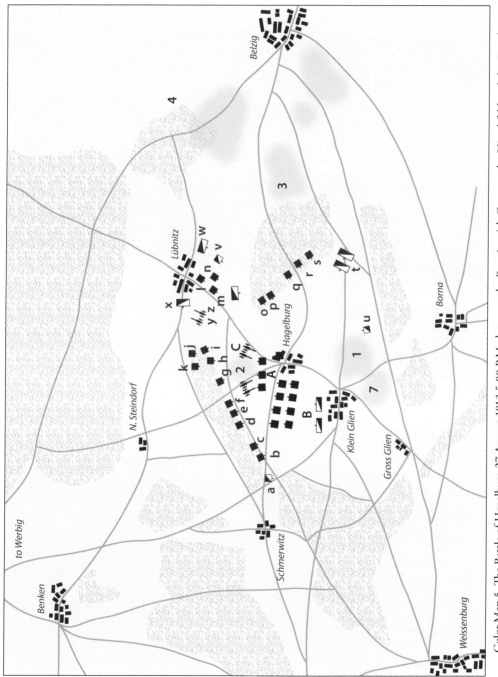

Color Map 5 The Battle of Hagelburg 27 August 1813 5:00 P.M., between the Prussian 4th Corps under Hirschfeld and the French Magdeburg Division under Girard. [Chapter 9]*

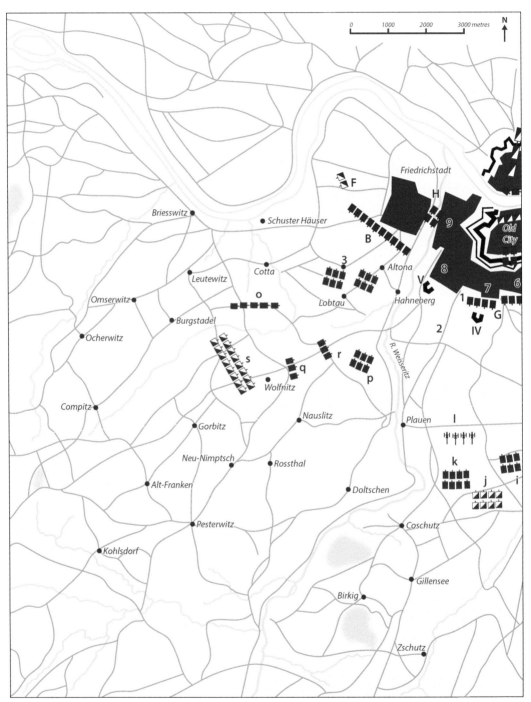

Color Map 6 The Battle of Dresden First Day, 26 August 1813, between the Grande Armée under Emperor Napoleon I and the Army of Bohemia under Fürst Schwarzenburg. [Chapter 11]*

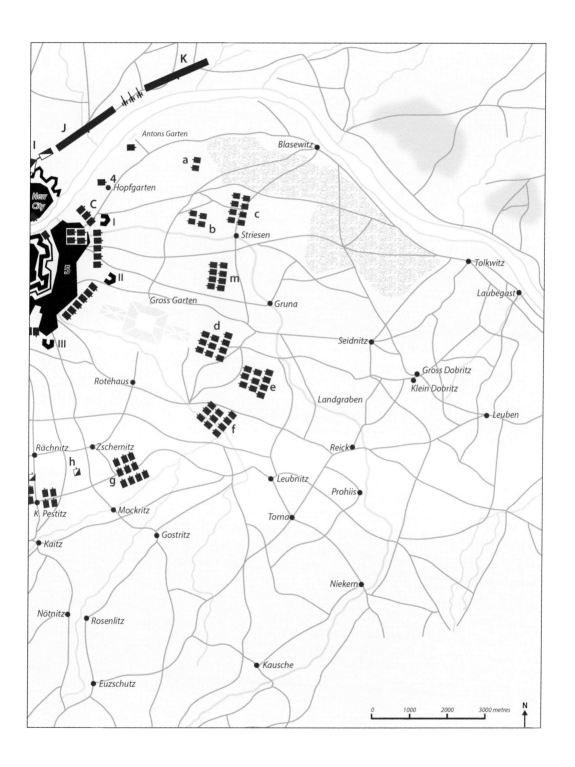

K

J

I

Antons Garten

Blasewitz

a

4

Hopfgarten

New City

C

I

c

b

Striesen

5

m

II

Gross Garten

Gruna

Tolkwitz

Laubegast

III

d

Seidnitz

Rotehaus

Gross Dobritz

Klein Dobritz

e

Landgraben

Leuben

f

Rächnitz

Zschernitz

Reick

h

g

Leubnitz

Prohiis

K. Pestitz

Mockritz

Torna

Kaitz

Gostritz

Niekern

Nötnitz

Rosenlitz

Kausche

Euzschutz

0   1000   2000   3000 metres

N

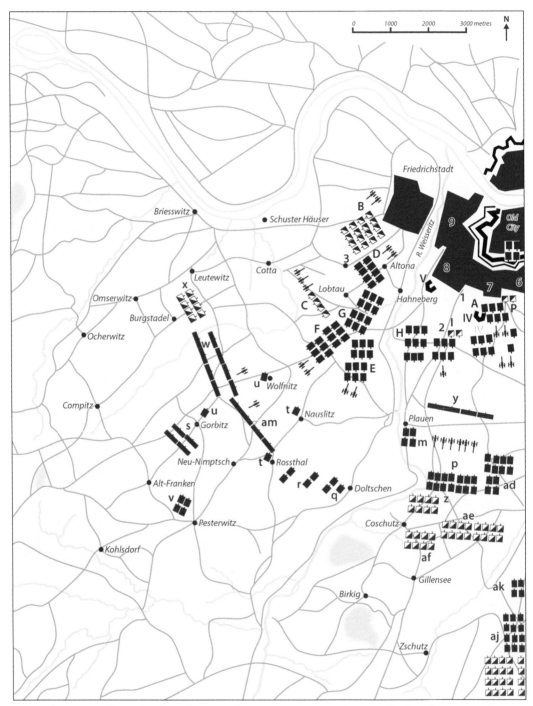

Color Map 7 The Battle of Dresden Second Day, 27 August 1813, between the Grande Armée under Emperor Napoleon I and the Army of Bohemia under Fürst Schwarzenburg. [Chapter 11]*

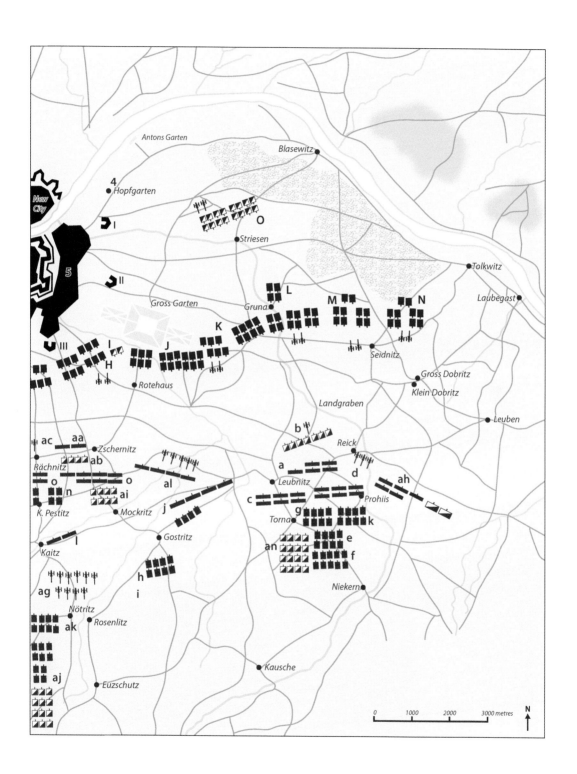

Antons Garten

Blasewitz

New City

4 ●Hopfgarten

Tolkwitz

I

●Striesen
O

Laubegast

II

Gross Garten
L
Gruna●
M N

5

III
I
H
K
J
Seidnitz

●Rotehaus
Gross Dobritz
Klein Dobritz

Landgraben
●Leuben

b
Reick●

ac aa
●Zschernitz
a
d
ah

Rächnitz
ab
al
Leubnitz●
Prohiis

o o
ai
c
g
k

n
j
e

K. Pestitz
●Mockritz
Torna●
an
f

l
●Gostritz
h
Niekern●

Kaitz
i

ag

Nötritz
●Rosenlitz

ak

aj
●Eüzschutz

●Kausche

0   1000   2000   3000 metres   N

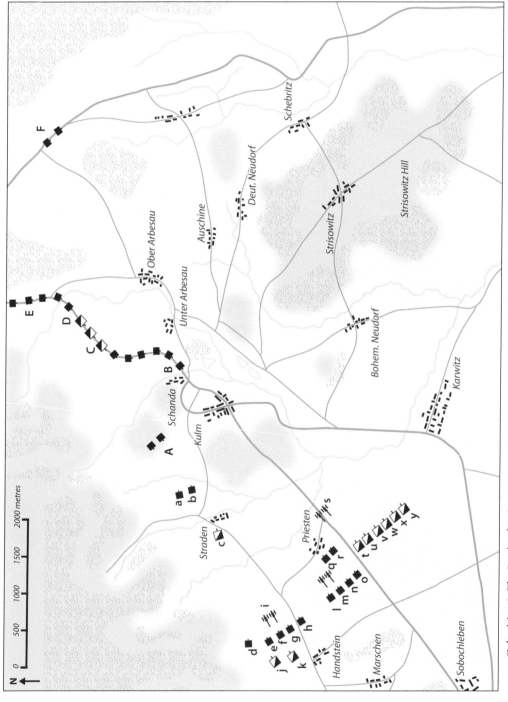

Color Map 8 The Battle of Kulm, 29 August 1813 1:00 P.M., between the Army of Bohemia and the French I Corps. [Chapter 13]*

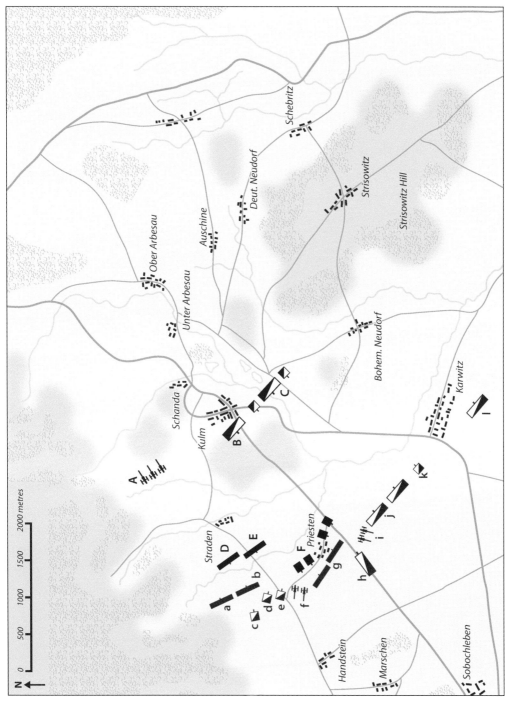

Color Map 9 The Battle of Kulm, 29 August 1813 5:00 P.M., between the Army of Bohemia and the French I Corps. [Chapter 13]*

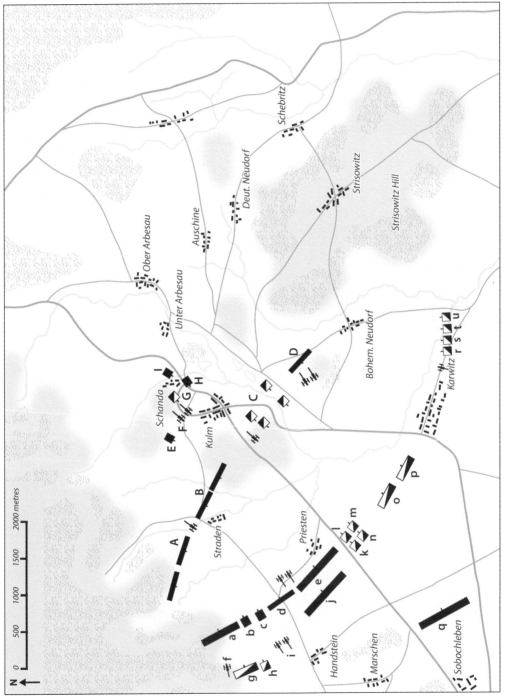

N

0 500 1000 1500 2000 metres

Ober Arbesau

Unter Arbesau

Auschine

Deut. Neudorf

Schebritz

Strisowitz

Strisowitz Hill

Bohem. Neudorf

Schanda

Kulm

Karwitz

r s t u

E F G H I

C

D

B A

Straden

Priesten

Handstein

Marschen

Sobochleben

f a b c d e j

g h i k l m n o p q

Color Map 10 The Battle of Kulm, 30 August 1813 7:00 A.M., between the Army of Bohemia and the French I Corps. [Chapter 13]*

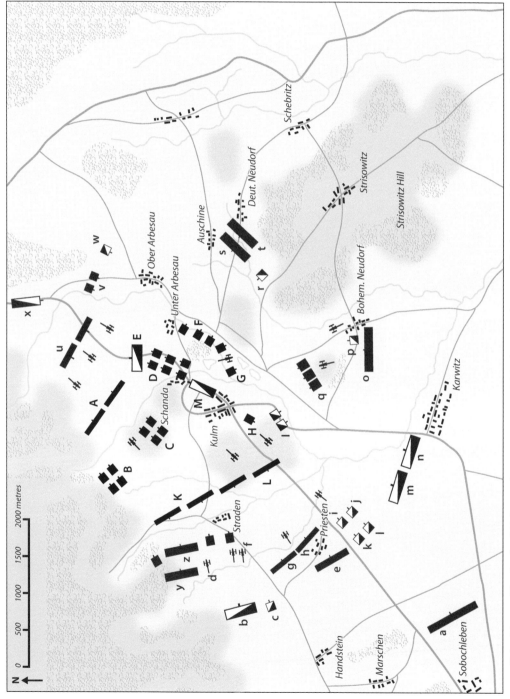

Color Map 11 The Battle of Kulm, 30 August 1813 12:00 P.M., between the Army of Bohemia and the French I Corps. [Chapter 13]*

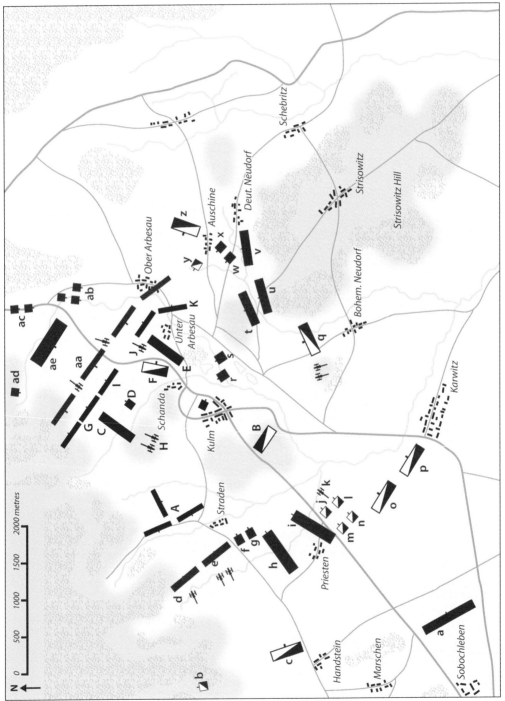

Color Map 12 The Battle of Kulm, 30 August 1813 1:00 P.M., between the Army of Bohemia and the French I Corps. [Chapter 13]*

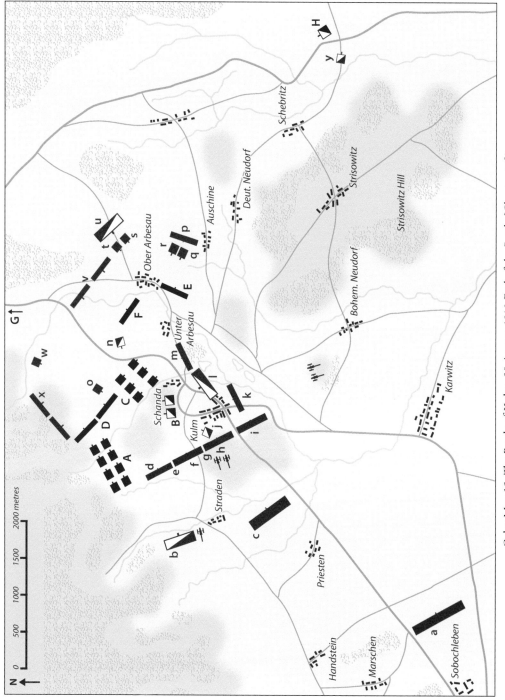

Color Map 13 The Battle of Kulm, 30 August 1813 End of the Battle [Chapter 13]*

N

G

0   500   1000   1500   2000 metres

Ober Arbesau

Unter Arbesau

Schanda

Kulm

Straden

Schebritz

Strisowitz

Strisowitz Hill

Bohem. Neudorf

Deut. Neudorf

Auschine

Karwitz

Priesten

Handstein

Marschen

Sobochleben

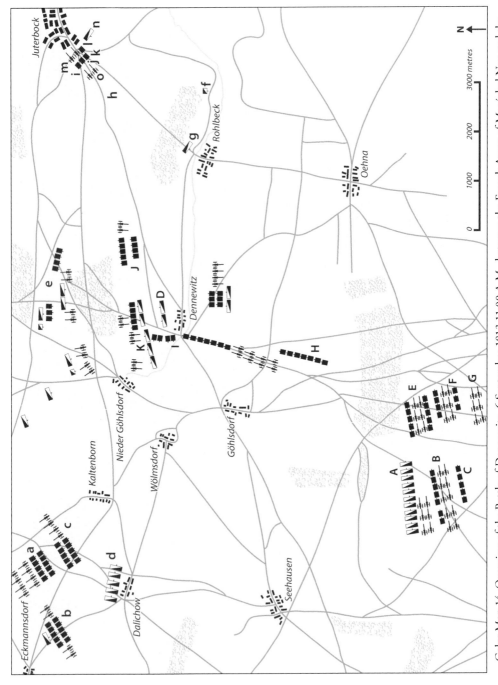

Color Map 14 Overview of the Battle of Dennewitz, 6 September 1813 11:00 A.M., between the French Army of Maréchal Ney and the Prussian 3rd Corps under Generallieutenant Bülow. [Chapter 14]*

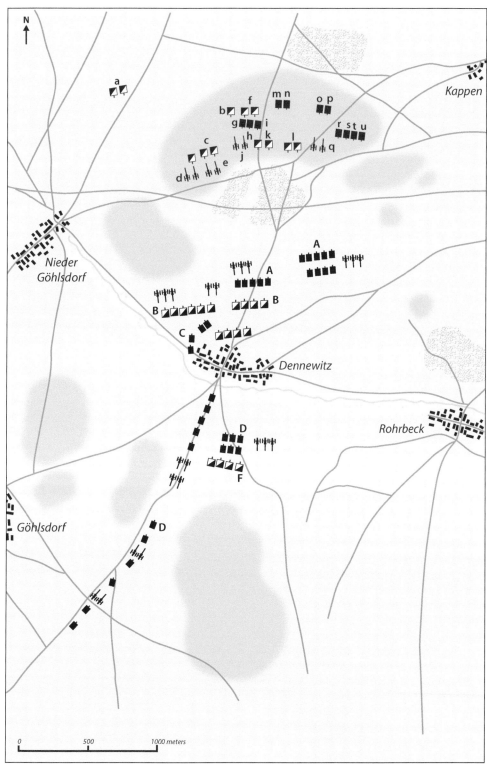

Color Map 15 The Battle of Dennewitz, 6 September 1813 11:00 A.M. , between the French Army of
Maréchal Ney and the Prussian 3rd Corps under Generallieutenant Bülow. [Chapter 14]*

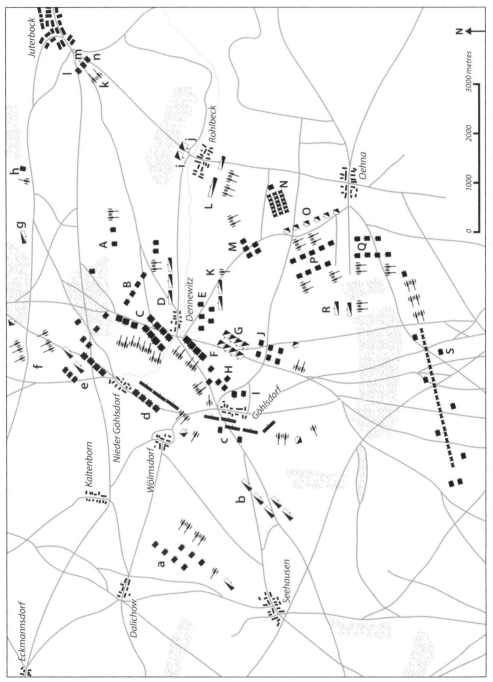

Color Map 16 Overview of the Battle of Dennewitz, 6 September 1813 3:30 P.M., between the French Army of Maréchal Ney and the Prussian 3rd Corps under Generallieutenant Bülow. [Chapter 14]*

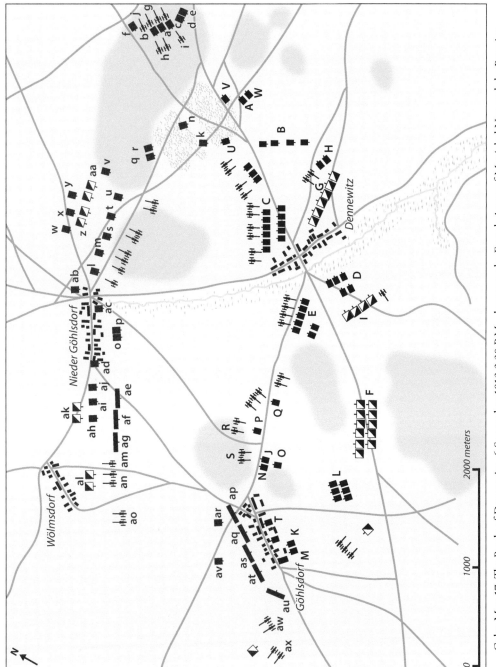

Color Map 17 The Battle of Dennewitz, 6 September 1813 3:30 P.M., between the French Army of Maréchal Ney and the Prussian 3rd Corps under Generallieutenant Bülow. [Chapter 14]*

List of Map Keys

Map 7 – Battle of the Katzbach 26 August 1813
French
A   19th Division – Rochambeau
B   16th Division – Maison
C   35th Division – Gérard
D   6th Light Cavalry Brigade – Dermoncourt
E   8th Division – Brayer (behind Roussel)
F   10th Hussar & Baden Dragoon Regiments
G   36th Division – Charpentier (by Exelman)
H   2nd Light Cavalry Division – Roussel
I   4th Light Cavalry Division – Exelman
J   2nd Cuirassier Division – Walthier
K   4th Cuirassier Division – St. Germain

Allies
a   1st Position of Left Wing – Langeron
aa   2nd Position of Left Wing – Langeron
b   1st Prussian Army Corps
c   Right Wing – Sacken
d   Prussian Cavalry Reserve – Jürgass
e   Russian Cavalry Corps – Vassil'shikov
f   Cossack Corps – Karpov II

Map 9 – Battle of Löwenberg 29 August 1813
French
A   1st Brigade – Penne
A1   1/134th Line Regiment
A2   2/134th Line Regiment
A3   1/146th Line Regiment
A4   2/146th Line Regiment
A5   3/146th Line Regiment
A6   1/3rd Foreign Regiment
A7   1/3rd Foreign Regiment
B   2nd Brigade Siblet
B1   1/147h Line Regiment
B2   2/147th Line Regiment
B3   3/147th Line Regiment
B4   1/148th Line Regiment
B5   2/148th Line Regiment
B6   3/148th Line Regiment
C   1/5th Foot Artillery
D   11/5th Foot Artillery

Allies
The Allied positions are estimations

a   6th Corps – Scherbatov
a1   7th Division – Tallisin
a2   18th Division – Bernodossov
b   9th Corps – Alsusiev
b1   9th Division – Udom II *(position unknown, presence uncertain)*
b2   15th Division – Rudsevich
c   1st Cavalry Corps – Baron Korff

Map 13 – Battle of Gross-Beeren 23 August 1813 Right Wing 7:00 p.m.
French
A   2nd Brigade, Saint-Andrea, 15th Division
B   3rd Brigade, Moroni, 15th Division
C   1st Brigade, Martel, 15th Division

Allies
a   1/2 6pdr Foot Battery #27 "Matthias"
b   6pdr Foot Battery #17 "Gleim"
c   2nd Neumärk Landwehr Cavalry Regiment (2 sqns)
d   1/, 2/, Fus/3rd Reserve Infantry Regiment
e   ½ 6pdr Foot Battery #27 "Matthias"
f   1/, 2/, 3/, 4/2nd Neumärk Landwehr Regiment
g   1/, 2/, 3/, 4/5th Kurmärk Landwehr Regiment I
h   ½ 6pdr Foot Battery #20 "Papendick" (4 guns)
I   ½ 6pdr Foot Battery #20 "Papendick" (4 guns)
j   3rd East Prussian Landwehr Cavalry Regiment
k   ?/1st Kurmärk Landwehr Regiment
l   ?/1st Kurmärk Landwehr Regiment
m   2/, 3/1st Neumärk Landwehr Regiment
n   2/, 3/1st Neumärk Landwehr Regiment

o   1/1st Silesian Regiment (Kosbach)
p   1st Kurmärk Landwehr Cavalry Regiment & 3rd Pommeranian Landwehr Cavalry Regiment
q   7th Kurmärk Landwehr Cavalry Regiment
r   Berlin Landwehr Cavalry Regiment (2 sqns)
s   Horse Battery #11 "Borchard"

Map 14 – Battle of Gross-Beeren 23 August 1813 Central Battle 7:00 p.m.
French & Saxons
A   Saxon 12pdr Foot Battery "Rouvroy I"
B   1st Saxon Foot Battery "Dietrich"
C   2/Rechten Infantry Regiment
D   1/,2/1st (Lecoq) Light Infantry Regiment
E   1/(Saxon) Guard Battalion Dressler
F   1/Maximilian Infantry Regiment
G   1/2/Prinz Friedrich August Inf. Regt
H   1/,2/von Steindel Infantry Regiment
I   1st Converged (Speigel) Grenadier Bn
J   Saxon Hussar Regiment
K   Prinz Clemens Uhlan Regiment
L   2nd Saxon Foot Battery "Zandt"
M   1/, 2/Prinz Anton Infantry Regiment
N   1/, 2/von Löw Infantry Regiment
O   2/König Infantry Regiment
P   1/, 2/von Sahr Infantry Regiment
Q   1st Saxon Horse Battery "Birnbaum"
R   2nd Saxon Horse Battery "Probsthayn" (1st Position)
S   2nd Saxon Foot Battery "Zandt"
S   3rd Saxon Foot Battery "Kühnel"
T   4th Saxon Foot Battery "Rouvroy II"
U   2nd Saxon Horse Battery "Probsthayn" (below Gross-Beeren?)
V   von Sperl Grenadier Bn (across river)
W   131st Line Regiment (1 bn) below Gross-Beeren
X   36th Légère Regiment (1 bn) below Gross-Beeren
Y   32nd Division – Durutte
Z   French Battery

Allies
a   1/Colberg Infantry Regiment
b   2/Colberg Infantry Regiment
c   2/5th Reserve Infantry Regiment
d   4/1st Neumärk Landwehr Regiment
e   3/5th Reserve Infantry Regiment
f   2/1st Neumärk Landwehr Regiment
g   1/,2/9th Reserve Infantry Regiment
i   Fus/4th Reserve Infantry Regiment
j   2/4th Reserve Infantry Regiment
k   1/4th Reserve Infantry Regiment
l   3/3rd East Prussian Infantry Regiment
m   1/3rd East Prussian Infantry Regiment
n   2nd East Prussian Grenadier Battalion
r   4/3rd East Prussian Landwehr Regt
q   3/3rd East Prussian Landwehr Regt
p   2/3rd East Prussian Landwehr Regt
r   1/3rd East Prussian Landwehr Regt
s   Fus/3rd East Prussian Infantry Regt
t   1st Leib Hussar Regiment
u   6pdr Foot Battery #16 "Spreuth"
v   6pdr Foot Battery #19 "Baumgarten/Liebermann"
w   12pdr Foot Battery #4 "Meyer"
x   Russian 12pdr Battery #7 (Dietrich)
y   6pdr Foot Battery #6 "Ludwig"
z   Russian 12pdr Battery #21 "Schleuter", Horse Batteries #5 (right) & #6 (left) (initial position)
aa   Horse Battery #5 "Neindorff" (deployed)
ab   Königin Dragoon Regiment
ac   2nd West Prussian Dragoon Regiment
ad   Brandenburg Dragoon Regiment
ae   2nd Kurmärk Landwehr Cavalry Regt
af   4th Kurmärk Landwehr Cavalry Regt
ag   2nd Pommeranian Landwehr Cavalry
ah   Horse Battery #6 "Steinwehr"
ai   3/,4/2nd Silesian Hussar Regiment
aj   West Prussian Uhlan Regiment
ak   Jager Sqn/Königin Dragoon Regiment

al   Captain Miihlenfels' (Swedish) Battery
am   Smaländ Dragoon Regiment (2 sqns)
an   6pdr Battery #10 "Magenhöfer"
ao   Pommeranian Grenadier Battalion
ap   Fus/1st Pommeranian Infantry Regt
aq   1/,2/, Fus/1st Reserve Infantry Regt
ar   1/,2/1st Pommeranian Infantry Regt
as   2/,4/2nd Kurmärk Landwehr Regiment
at   West Prussian Uhlan Regiment
au   Pommeranian Hussars
av   1/2 Horse Battery #11 "Borchardt"
aw   1/2nd Reserve Infantry Regiment
ax   2/2nd Reserve Infantry Regiment
ay   2 Swedish Battalions Ulfsparre (3 more to the east)
az   1/,2/4th East Prussian Regiment, & 2/5th Reserve Infantry
     Regiment
ba   2/Elbe Regiment, & 1/,4/5th Reserve Regiment

bc   3/5th Reserve Regiment

Map 16 – The Battle of Hagelberg 27 August 1813
French
A   Girard's Infantry
B   Girard's Cavalry
C   Girard's Artillery

Terrain
1   Petersberg
2   Windmühlberg
3   Hüttenberg
4   Belzig Woods
5   Thiergarten
6   Birken Woods
7   Weinberg

Prussians
a   3rd Kurmärk Landwehr Cavalry Regiment – Finkenstein
b   1/1st Reserve Infantry Regiment – Reckow
c   2/1st Reserve Infantry Regiment – Lemcke
d   1/7th Kurmärk Landwehr Regiment – von Osarowsky
e   1/Elbe Infantry Regiment – von Stutterheim
f   1/4th Kurmärk Landwehr Regiment – von Grolman
g   4/1st Reserve Infantry Regiment – Rembow
h   3/1st Reserve Infantry Regiment – Romig
i   2/3rd Kurmärk Landwehr Regiment – von Bornstedt
j   3/3rd Kurmärk Landwehr Regiment – Laviere
k   2/7th Kurmärk Landwehr Regiment – von Held
l   2/4th Kurmärk Landwehr Regiment – von Liewen
m   1/3rd Kurmärk Landwehr Regiment – von Zschüschen
n   4/3rd Kurmärk Landwehr Regiment – von Schönholz
o   1/6th Kurmärk Landwehr Regiment – von Bonigke f;.
p   2/6th Kurmärk Landwehr Regiment – von Streit
q   4/6th Kurmärk Landwehr Regiment – von Woisky
r   3/6th Kurmärk Landwehr Regiment – von Delitz
s   3/4th Kurmärk Landwehr Regiment – von Schwerin
t   Sisava #3, Grekov #18, Rebrejev & Pantelev Cossacks
u   Vlasov #3 Cossacks
v   3rd Kurmärk Landwehr Cavalry Regiment – Teschen
w   5th Kurmärk Landwehr Cavalry Regiment – Uckermann
x   6th Kurmärk Landwehr Cavalry Regiment – Jagow
y   Russian Light Battery #26 – Captain Chamboran
z   Prussian 6pdr Foot Battery #6 – Lt. Tiehsen

Map 18 – The Battle of Dresden 1st day, 26 August 1813
Geographical Points
I, II, III ,IV & V Redoubts
1   Paper mill
2   Feldschlössen
3   Drescherhäuser
4   Stuckgeisser
5   Pirna Suburb
6   Dippoldiswald Suburb
7   Blinden Schlag
8   Freiburger Schlag
9   Wilsdruffer Suburb

French
A   44th Division – Berthezène
B   45th Division – Razout
C   43rd Division – Claperède
D   3rd Young Guard Division – Decouz
E   4th Young Guard Division – Roguet
F   10th Light Cavalry Division – Pajol
G   1st & 2nd Young Guard Divisions – Dumoustier & Barrois
H   23rd Division – Teste
I   I Cavalry Corps – Latour-Maubourg
J   II Corps – Victor
K   VI Corps – Marmont
L   Old Guard – Friant
M   Guard Cavalry – Nansouty

Allies
a   23rd Jager Regiment & 2 guns
b   Sievsk & Kalouga Infantry Regiments
c   Penn, Mogilev, & Selenginsk Infantry Regiments & 24th
     Jager Regiment
d   10th Prussian Brigade – Pirch
e   9th Prussian Brigade – Klüx
f   11th Prussian Brigade – Jagow (replacing Zeithen)
g   12th Prussian Brigade – Prinz von Preussen
h   1st Light Division – M. Liechtenstein
i   1st Infantry Division – Colloredo
j   1st & 2nd Cavalry Divisions Nostitz & Lederer
k   1st Infantry Reserve (Grenadiers) – Chasteler
l   4 – 12pdr batteries
m   20th, 21st, 25th, 26th, & 34th Jager Regiments – Roth
n   2nd Reserve Division – Bianchi
o   Greth's Brigade, 3rd Reserve Division
p   Czollich's Brigade, Weissenwolf's Div.
q   Grimmer's Brigade, Weissenwolf's Div.
r   Herzogenberg's Bde, Weissenwolf's Div.
s   3rd Cavalry Division – Schneller
t   4th Division – Fürst A. Liechtenstein

Map 19 – The Battle of Dresden 2nd Day, 26 August 1813
Geographical Points
I, II, III ,IV & V Redoubts
1   Paper mill
2   Feldschlössen & Kohlgarten
3   Drescherhäuser
4   Stuckgeisser
5   Pirna Suburb
6   Dippoldiswald Suburb
7   Blinden Schlag
8   Freiburger Schlag
9   Wilsdruffer Suburb

French
A   Old Guard Division – Friant
B   I Cavalry Corps – Latour-Maubourg/Murat
C   10th Light Cavalry Division – Pajol
D   23rd Division – Teste
E   4th Division – Dubreton
F   5th Division – Dufour
G   6th Division – Vial
H   VI Corps – Marmont
I   25th Light Cavalry Brigade – Norman
J   XIV Corps – St. Cyr
K   2nd Young Guard Division – Barrois
L   1st Young Guard Division – Dumoustier
M   3rd Young Guard Division – Decouz
N   th Young Guard Division – Roguet
O   1st & 2nd Guard Cavalry Divisions – Nansouty
P   3rd Guard Cavalry Division – Walther

Allies
a   Russian 1st Corps – Wittgenstein
b   Russian Horse Battery #6, Loubny & Grodno Hussar
     Regiments
c   5th Russian Division – Menzentov
d   14th Russian Division – Helfrich
e   Prussian Guard
f   Russian Guard
g   11th Prussian Brigade – Zeithen

h	12th Prussian Brigade – Prinz August von Preussen
i	1st Silesian Hussar & 2nd Silesian Landwehr Cavalry Regiments
j	10th Prussian Brigade – Pirch
k	9th Prussian Brigade – Klüx
l	1st & 2nd Jäger Battalions
m	Murray's Brigade, 1stb Infantry Reserve
n	1st Division – Colloredo
o	Cilivart's Division
p	2nd Infantry Reserve – Bianchi
q	Würzburg Regiment (1 battalion)
r	Czollich's Brigade, Weissenwolf s Div.
s	Mumb's Brigade, Liechtenstein's Div.
t	Kaunitz Infantry Regiment (1 battalion)
u	W. Colloredo Infantry Regiment (1 bn)
v	Meszerey's's Bde, Liechtenstein's Div.
w	3rd Light Division – Mesko
x	Palatinal Hussars, six Züge of the Ferdinand Hussars & Lothringen Cuirassier Regiment
y	Greth's Brigade, 3rd Reserve Division
z	3rd Cavalry Division – Schneller
aa	Jäger Battalion #7 & Broder Grenz
ab	Kaiser & Vincent Chevauléger Regts.
ac	Russian 12pdr Battery
ad	Koller's Brigade, 1st Infantry Reserve
ae	1st Cavalry Division – Nostitz
af	Haecht's Brigade, 3rd Army Reserve
ag	Austrian Artillery Reserve: 8-1012pdr Batteries & Combined Brigade Batteries of the right wing
ah	20th, 21st, 25th, 26th, & 34th Jager Regiments – Roth
ai	2nd Cavalry Division Lederer
aj	1st & 2nd Russian Guard Divisions, & 1st & 2nd Russian Cuirassier Divisions
ak	2nd Russian Grenadier Division
al	1st Russian Grenadier Division
am	von Seethal's Brigade, Liechtenststein's Division
an	probable position of Russian Guard Cavalry & Prussian Cavalry Reserve

Map 22 – The Battle of Kulm 29 August 1813 1:00 p.m.

French

A	Revest's Brigade (5th Division, II Corps)
B	42nd Division – Mouton-Duvernet
C	1st Light Cavalry Division – Corbineau
D	21st Light Cavalry Brigade – Gobrecht
E	1st Division (1st Brigade – Pouchelon, followed by Corps Artillery & 2nd Brigade – Fezensac)
F	Detachment en route to Aussig

Allies

a	Guard Jager Regiment
b	Murmon Infantry Regiment
c	Guard Uhlan Regiment
d	Ismailov Guard Infantry Regiment
e	Semenovsky Guard Infantry Regiment
f	Preobragensky Guard Infantry Regiment
g	Estonia Infantry Regiment
h	Grand Duchess Catherine Battalion
i	Guard Foot Battery
j	Guard Hussar Regiment
k	Guard Dragoon Regiment
l	Tenguinsk Infantry Regiment
m	Tobolsk Infantry Regiment
n	Tschernigov Infantry Regiment
o	Minsk Infantry Regiment
p	Lt. Colonel Czeremissinov (Position Battery #14) left & Colonel Baikoff (Light Battery #27) on the right
q	Revel Infantry Regiment
r	4th Jager Regiment
s	1st Guard Horse Battery
t	Empress Cuirassier Regiment
u	Tartar Uhlan Regiment
v	Loubny Hussar Regiment
w	Serpuchov Uhlan Regiment
x	Erherzog Johann Dragoon Regiment
y	Illowaiski #12 Cossack

Map 23 – The Battle of Kulm 29 August 1813 5:00 p.m.

French

A	I Corps Artillery
B	21st Light Cavalry Brigade – Gobrecht
C	1st Light Cavalry Division – Corbineau
D	Revest's Brigade (5th Division, II Corps)
E	42nd Division (9 battalions) – Mouton-Duvernet
F	2nd Brigade – Fezensac

Allies

a	Russian Guard
b	Russian 14th Division
c	Guard Hussar Regiment
d	Guard Uhlan Regiment
e	Guard Dragoon Regiment
f	Russian 2nd Corps Artillery
g	Russian 2nd Corps
h	2nd Cuirassier Division
i	1st Guard Horse Battery
j	Russian Cavalry
k	Erherzog Johann Dragoon Regiment
l	Russian Cavalry

Map 24 – The Battle of Kulm 30 August 1813 7:00 a.m.

French

A	42nd Division – Mouton-Duvernet
B	1st Division – Philippon
C	1st Light Cavalry Division – Corbineau
D	1st Brigade, 2nd Division – Dunesme
E	2nd Brigade, 2nd Division – Doucet
F	Reserve Artillery
G	21st Light Cavalry Brigade – Gobrecht
H	2nd Brigade, 23rd Division – Quiot
I	1st Brigade, 5th Division – Revest

Allies

a	1st Grenadier Division
b	Krementchug Infantry Regiment
c	Volhynie Infantry Regiment
d	14th Division – Helfreich
e	2nd Corps – Württemberg
f	?? Foot Battery
g	3rd Cuirassier Division
h	Jagodin Cossack Regiment
i	Position Battery #5 & Light Battery #13
j	2nd Guard Division
k	Guard Uhlan Regiment
l	Guard Hussar Regiment
m	Loubny Hussar Regiment
n	Guard Dragoon Regiment
o	1st Cuirassier Division
p	2nd Cuirassier Division
q	1st Guard Division
r	Empress Cuirassier Regiment
s	Tartar Uhlan Regiment
t	Illowaiski #12 Cossack Regiment
u	Erherzog Johann Dragoon Regiment

The position around Priesten was greatly reinforced. The Russian 1st Grenadier Division relieved the Russian 1st Guard Division and the forces of the Russian 2nd Corps that had fought the previous day's battle, and now stood in the front line.

Map 25 – The Battle of Kulm 30 August 1813 12:00 noon.

French

A	2nd Brigade, 42nd Division – Creutzer
B	1st Brigade, 5th Division – Revest
C	1st Brigade, 5th Division – Revest
D	2nd Brigade, 23rd Division – Quiot
E	21st Light Cavalry Brigade – Gobrecht
F	2nd Brigade, 2nd Division – Doucet
G	Part of 1st Brigade, 2nd Div. – Dunesme
H	Unknown battalion, 2nd Brigade, 42nd Division – Creutzer
I	3rd Light Cavalry Brigade – Heimrodt
J	Reserve Artillery – Baltus
K	1st Brigade, 42nd Division – Mouton-Duvernet

L   1st Division – Philippon
M   2nd Light Cavalry Brigade – Montmarie

Allies
a   1st Russian Guard Division
b   3rd Russian Cuirassier Division
c   Jagodin Cossack Regiment
d   Russian Guard Foot Battery
e   2nd Russian Guard Division
f   Combined Artillery, Hessen-Homburg's Brigade, & 1st Grenadier Division
g   14th Division – Helfreich
h   2nd Corps – Württemberg
i   Guard Hussar Regiment
j   Loubny Hussar Regiment
k   Guard Uhlan Regiment
l   Guard Dragoon Regiment
m   1st Cuirassier Division
n   2nd Cuirassier Division
o   Mariassy's & Quallenberg's Brigades, Bianchi's Division
p   Knorring's Brigade; Empress Cuirassier Regiment, Tartar Uhlan Regiment (6), Illowaiski #12 Cossack Regiment, & Serpuchov Uhlan Regiment
q   Abele's Brigade, Colloredo's Division
r   Erherzog Johann Dragoon Regiment
s   Kolb's Brigade, Colloredo's Division
t   Chiesa's Brigade, Colloredo's Division
u   10th Prussian Brigade – Pirch
v   2nd West Prussian Infantry Regiment
w   Silesian Hussar Regiment
x   Prussian Reserve Cavalry
y   Hessen-Homburg's Brigade, Bianchi's Div.
z   1st Grenadier Division
aa Krementchug Infantry Regiment
ab Volhynie Infantry Regiment

Map 26 – The Battle of Kulm 30 August 1813 1813 1:00 p.m.
French
A   42nd Division – Mouton-Duvernet
B   3rd Light Cavalry Brigade – Heimrodt
C   1st Brigade, 1st Division – Pouchelon
D   3 Cos, 36th Line Regiment
E   2nd Brigade, 2nd Division – Doucet
F   2nd Light Cavalry Brigade – Montmarie & 21st Light Cavalry Brigade – Gobrecht
G   1st Brigade, 5th Division – Revest
H   Reserve Artillery – Baltus
I   2nd Brigade, 23rd Division – Quiot
J   2nd Brigade, 42nd Division – Creutzer
K   1st Brigade, 2nd Division – Dunesme

Allies
a   1st Russian Guard Division
b   Jagodin Cossack Regiment
c   3rd Russian Cuirassier Division
d   Hessen-Homburg's Brigade, Bianchi's Div.
e   Russian 1st Grenadier Division
f   Krementchug Infantry Regiment
g   Volhynie Infantry Regiment
h   14th Division – Helfreich
i   2nd Corps – Württemberg
j   Guard Hussar Regiment
k   1st Guard Horse Battery
l   Loubny Hussar Regiment
m   Guard Uhlan Regiment
n   Guard Dragoon Regiment
o   1st Cuirassier Division
p   2nd Cuirassier Division
q   Knorring's Brigade; Empress Cuirassier Regiment, Tartar Uhlan Regiment (6), Illowaiski #12 Cossack Regiment, & Serpuchov Uhlan Regiment
r   Argenteau Infantry Regiment, Abele's Brigade
s   Erbach Infantry Regiment, Abele's Brigade
t   Mariassy's Brigade, Bianchi's Division
u   Quallenberg's Brigade, Bianchi's Division
v   Chiesa's Brigade, Colloredo's Division
w   Czartoryski Infantry Regiment
x   de Ligne Infantry Regiment

y   Erherzog Johann Dragoon Regiment
z   Prussian Reserve Cavalry – Kleist
aa 10th & 11th Brigades – Pirch & Ziethen
ab 10th Silesian Landwehr Regiment
ac 2nd Silesian Infantry Regiment
ad 9th Reserve Infantry Regiment ?
ae Prussian 12th Brigade – Prinz August von Preussen

Map 27 – The Battle of Kulm 30 August 1813. End of the Battle
French
A   42nd Division – Mouton-Duvernet
B   3rd Light Cavalry Brigade – Heimrodt
C   1st Division – Philippon
D   1st Brigade, 5th Division – Revest
E   2nd Brigade, 2nd Division – Doucet & 1st Brigade, 2nd Division – Dunesme
F   2nd Brigade, 23rd Division – Quiot
G   2nd Light Cavalry Brigade – Montmarie & 21st Light Cavalry Brigade – Gobrecht
H   32nd Light Cavalry Brigade – Colonel Rosseau

Allies
a   1st Russian Guard Division
b   3rd Russian Cuirassier Division
c   2nd Russian Guard Division
d   Hessen-Homburg's Brigade, Bianchi's Div.
e   Russian 1st Grenadier Division
f   Krementchug Infantry Regiment
g   Volhynie Infantry Regiment
h   14th Division – Helfreich
i   2nd Corps – Württemberg
j   Russian Guard Light Cavalry Division
k   Abele's Brigade, Colloredo's Division
l   Russian 1st & 2nd Cuirassier Divisions
m   Bianchi's Division
n   Erherzog Johann Dragoon Regiment
o   Prussian 10th Reserve Infantry Regiment
p   Chiesa's Brigade, Colloredo's Division
q   de Ligne Infantry Regiment
r   Czartoryski Infantry Regiment
s   2nd Silesian Infantry Regiment
t   10th West Prussian Infantry Regiment
u   Prussian Reserve Cavalry – Kleist
v   10th & 12th Brigades – Pirch & von Preussen
w   6th Reserve Infantry Regiment
x   11th Brigade – Ziethen
y   Kaiser Cuirassier Regiment, 2 sqns

Map 29 – Overview of the Battle of Dennewitz 6 September 1813 11:00 a.m
French
A   4th Heavy Cavalry Division – Defiance
B   32nd Division – Durutte
C   1st Brigade, 27th (Polish) Division – Zoltowski
D   18th Light (Polish) Cavalry Brigade – Krukowiecki
E   24th (Saxon) Division – Lecoq
F   25th (Saxon) Division – von Sahr
G   26th Light (Saxon) Cavalry Brigade – Lindenau
H   38th Division – Franquemont
I   12th Division – Morand
J   15th Division – Fontinelli
K   5th Light Cavalry Division – Lorge

Allies
a   3rd Prussian Brigade – Hessen
b   6th Prussian Brigade – Krafft
c   4th Prussian Brigade – Thümen
d   Prussian Cavalry Reserve – Oppen
e   4th Prussian Corps – Tauentzien
f   3rd Pommeranian Landwehr Cavalry Regiment (1 sqn)
g   2nd Neumärk Landwehr Cavalry Regiment
h   Kleist's Command
i   1/1st Silesian Landwehr Regiment – Wins
i   2/1st Kurmärk Landwehr Regiment – Klöden
k   1/1st Kurmärk Landwehr Regiment – Dullack
l   5/1st Silesian Landwehr Regiment – Kosphoth
m   ½ 12pdr Foot Battery #5 – Lent

n   4th Kurmärk Landwehr Cavalry Regiment (2 sqns)
o   6pdr Foot Battery #27 – Mathias

Map 30 – The Battle of Dennewitz 6 September 1813 11:00 a.m

French
A   15th Division Fontinelli
b   5th Light Cavalry Division – Lorge
     Left: 13th Light Cavalry Brigade – Merlin
     Right: 12th Light Cavalry Brigade – Jacquinot
C   12th Division Morand
D   38th Division – Franquemont
E   18th Light Cavalry Brigade – Krukowiecki
F   24th Light Cavalry Brigade – Jett

Allies
a   Detachment Schmiterlow
b   Brandenburg Dragoons (2 sqns)
c   7th Kurmärk Landwehr Cavalry Regiment
d   ½ Horse Battery #6
e   ½ Horse Battery #11 – Borchard
f   1st Kurmärk Landwehr Cavalry Regiment
g   3/3rd Reserve Infantry Regiment – Rango
h   2/3rd Reserve Infantry Regiment – Welling
i   1/3rd Reserve Infantry Regiment – Wittich
j   6pdr Foot Battery #30 von Hertig
k   3rd Pommeranian Landwehr Cavalry Regiment
l   2nd Kurmärk Landwehr Cavalry Regiment
m   2/1st Silesian Landwehr Regiment – Bonin/Lemke
n   2/2nd Neumärk Landwehr Regiment – Grollman
o   3/2nd Neumärk Landwehr Regiment – Steinmetz
p   4/2nd Neumärk Landwehr Regiment – Paczkowski
q   6pdr Foot Battery #17 – Gleim
r   1/5th Kurmärk Landwehr Regiment Treskow
s   2/5th Kurmärk Landwehr Regiment Kamiensky
t   3/5th Kurmärk Landwehr Regiment – Mey
u   4/5th Kurmärk Landwehr Regiment – Mellersky

Map 31 – Overview of the Battle of Dennewitz 6 September 1813 3:30 p.m.

French
A   38th (Württemberg) Division – Franquemont
B   15th (Italian) Division Fontinelli
C   12th Division – Morand
D   5th Light Cavalry Division – Lorge
E   2nd Brigade, 32nd Division – Jarry
F   1st Brigade, 32nd Division – Devaux
G   4th Heavy Cavalry Division – Defrance
H   1st Brigade, 24th (Saxon) Division – Brause
I   2nd Brigade, 24th (Saxon) Division – Mellentin
J   25th (Saxon) Division – von Sahr
K   24th Light (Württemberg)) Cavalry Brigade – Jett
L   26th Light (Saxon) Cavalry Brigade Lindenau
M   3rd Brigade, 38th (Württemberg) Division – Döring
N   Niesemeuschel Infantry Regiment & Train Park
O   6th Light (Cavalry Division – Fournier
P   14th Division – Guilleminot
P   13th Division – Pacthod
P   29th Light Cavalry Brigade – Wolff
P   29th (Bavarian) Division – Raglovic

Allies
a   5th Prussian Brigade – Borstel
b   Prussian Cavalry Reserve – Oppen
c   3rd Prussian Brigade – Hessen-Homberg
d   6th Prussian Brigade – Krafft
e   4th Prussian Brigade – Thümen
f   4th Prussian Corps – Tauentzien
g   3rd East Prussian Landwehr Cavalry Regiment
h   5/1st Silesian Landwehr Regiment –Kosposth; 6pdr Foot
     Battery #17 – Gleim
i   2nd Neumärk Landwehr Cavalry Regiment
j   3rd Pommeranian Landwehr Cavalry Regiment
k   6pdr Foot Battery #27 – Mathias
l   1/1st Silesian Landwehr Regiment – Wins
m   2/1st Kurmärk Landwehr Regiment – Klöden
n   1/1st Kurmärk Landwehr Regiment – Dullack

Map 32 – The Battle of Dennewitz 6 September 1813 3:30 p.m.

French
A   2nd Brigade, 38th Division – Spitzemberg
B   15th Division – Fontinelli
C   12th Division – Morand
D   2nd Brigade, 32nd Division – Jarry
E   1st Brigade, 32nd Division – Devaux
F   4th Heavy Cavalry Division – Defrance
G   5th Light Cavalry Division Lorge
H   38th Division – Franquemont
I   24th Light Cavalry Brigade – Jett
J   1/Maximilian (Saxon) Regiment
K   2nd Brigade, 24th (Saxon) Division – Mellentin
L   25th (Saxon) Division – von Sahr
M   1, 2/Friedrich August (Saxon) Regiment
N   1, 2/1st "Lecoq" (Saxon) Light Regiment
O   1/Leib-Garde (Saxon) Regiment
P   2/von Rechten (Saxon) Regiment
Q   1/Anton (Saxon) Regiment
R   Saxon 12pdr Foot Battery
S   Saxon 2nd 6pdr Foot Battery
T   Converged Saxon Grenadier Battalion Spiegel & 1/, 2/
     Steindel Infantry Regt
U   2/4th (Württemberg) Regiment
V   1/2nd (Württemberg) Regiment
W   1/, 2/7th (Württemberg) Regiment
X   1/9th & 1/10th (Württemberg) Regiment

Allies
a   2/3rd Reserve Infantry Regt – Welling
b   3/3rd Reserve Infantry Regt – Rango
c   1/3rd Reserve Infantry Regt – Wittich
d   1/5th Kurmärk Landwehr Regiment – Treskow
e   4/5th Kurmärk Landwehr Regiment – Mellersky
f   2/1st Silesian Landwehr Regiment – Bonin/Lemke
g   6pdr Foot Battery #17 – Gleim
h   ½ Horse Battery #6 – Jenichen
i   ½ Horse Battery #11 – Borchard
j   ½ 6pdr Foot Battery #30 – von Hertig
k   3/4th Reserve Infantry Regiment
l   1/4th Reserve Infantry Regiment
m   2/4th Reserve Infantry Regiment
n   Fus/4th East Prussian Infantry Regiment
o   1/4th East Prussian Infantry Regiment
p   2/4th East Prussian Infantry Regiment
q   1/Elbe Infantry Regiment
r   2/Elbe Infantry Regiment
s   5th Reserve Infantry Regiment
t   5th Reserve Infantry Regiment
u   5th Reserve Infantry Regiment
v   5th Reserve Infantry Regiment
w   11/3rd East Prussian Landwehr Regt
x   12/3rd East Prussian Landwehr Regt
y   20/3rd East Prussian Landwehr Regt
z   Brandenburg Dragoons (2 sqns & jägers)
aa   1st Leib Hussar Regiment
ab   ½ East Prussian:. Jäger Battalion
ac   3/9th Reserve Infantry Regiment
ad   2/3rd East Prussian Infantry Regiment
ae   2/9th Reserve Infantry Regiment
af   1/9th Reserve Infantry Regiment
ag   2/Colberg Infantry Regiment
ah   2/1st Neumärk Landwehr Regiment
ai   3/1st Neumärk Landwehi Regiment
aj   4/1st Neumärk Landwehr Regiment
ak   1st Pommeranian Landwehr Cavalry Regiment
al   2nd West Prussian Dragoon Regiment (2 sqns)
am   2 howitzers from 6pdr Foot Battery #5
an   6pdr Foot Battery #16 – Spreuth
ao   ½ Russian Position Battery # 21
ap   1/Colberg Infantry Regiment
aq   Fus/Colberg Infantry Regiment
ar   1/1st Neumärk Landwehr Regiment
as   1/3rd East Prussian Infantry Regiment
at   2nd East Prussian Grenadier Battalion
au   Fus/3rd East Prussian Infantry Regiment
av   8/3rd East Prussian Landwehr Regiment
aw   6pdr Foot Battery #5 – Glasenapp
ax   Horse Battery #5 – Neindorff

For Victor's infantry, the battle was effectively over between 5:00 and 6:00 p.m. Dubreton's 4th Division occupied Dölzchen, Vial's 6th Division occupied Rossthal and Gorbitz, Dufour's 4th Division stood to the northwest of Vial, on the Freiberg high road. Victor left the pursuit to Bordesoulle's cuirassiers, which were more dangerous to the withdrawing Austrians than the infantry.

By evening's twilight, Murat's lead elements were in Kesseldorf. Doumerc's lead division camped there that evening. So as to have infantry on hand the next morning for the pursuit, Dufour pushed seven battalions forward into Kesseldorf that night.[94] Bordesoulle's 3rd Heavy Cavalry Division joined with Victor's main body in the area around Gorbitz-Rossthal-Doltschen. Late in the evening the returning forces of Chastel's 3rd Light Cavalry Division arrived and cantoned with one brigade in Wölfnitz and the second cantoned in Gompitz and Pennrich. O'Meara's Brigade (Teste's 23rd Division) stood watching the Tharandt Road and the stone bridge. Murat established his quarters in Wölfnitz and Victor in Gorbitz.

While Murat contented himself with the reaching of Kesseldorf, Oberst Illesy, with his squadrons, reached Naundorf around midnight, and established himself there for the night. The next morning he resumed his withdrawal towards Freiberg. About 10:00 a.m., GM Paumgarten also arrived, with just three squadrons of the Palatinal Hussars. They were by Meissen and had encountered no French there. After a short conference with GM Kudascheff, whose streifkorps the arrived around noon, on 27 August, Paumgarten resumed his withdrawal to Freiberg.[95]

With the withdrawal of the shattered remains of the Austrian army, it is no wonder that the French enthusiastically reported their success to Napoleon. In his report Murat wrote:

> Sire, the success of the arms of your Majesty this day is glorious. Your cavalry has made 15,000 prisoners and taken 12 cannons and 12 flags, one Generalleutnant, two generals, and a great number of senior officers and other grades are in our hands. I can verify to your Majesty that our enemy's casualties are at least 7,000 to 8,000 dead, wounded and missing. I hope, tomorrow also to seize their guns and baggage in the defile by Tharandt.[96]

Murat had, in his usual manner, exaggerated the situation slightly. Slightly more than 15,000 prisoners were taken. The only generals taken were Meszko and Szecsen.

The brilliance of the success achieved by the French right wing on 27 August cannot be overstated. The surrender of whole battalions and regiments of Austrians, on the field of battle represented a crushing blow to the morale of the Austrian army.[97]

The Center

At 4:00 a.m., the Austro-Prussian center was standing to arms. The 7th Jäger Battalion and the 1/ Broder Grenz stood on the Zschernitz-Räcknitz line. Behind them were the Kaiser and Vincent Chevauléger Regiments. The 1st and 2nd Jäger Battalions stood by Kaitz, where they were recovering from the previous day's battle. A Russian 12pdr battery stood between Zschernitz and Neu-Ostra, and covered the left flank of the 7th Jägers and the Kaiser Chevaulégers. Räcknitz was occupied by the Argenteau Infantry Regiment. Between Räcknitz and the Weisseritz, stood Greth's Brigade, part of Crenneville's 3rd Reserve Division. A single battalion was detached to the vicinity of Plauen, to act as an advanced post. Behind Räcknitz, on the Dippoldiswalde Road, marched the line divisions of the right flank. The first line was formed by Civalart's 3rd Line Division and the second line was formed by Colloredo's 1st Line Division. Murray's Brigade, from Chasteler's 1st Reserve Grenadier Division, moved to support Crenneville's division and assumed a position to the south of Plauen. Koller's brigade marched in four *battalionsmasse* to the left behind Colloredo's division. Bianchi's 2nd Reserve Division stood to the left of Koller's brigade. At 8:00 a.m., Zechmeister's cavalry brigade moved from Löbtau to a position behind the last line, as did that of G. Hessen-Homburg. Haecht's cavalry brigade, from Crenneville's division, moved to the left of the reserve cavalry. The bulk of the Austrian artillery, 8-10 heavy batteries and the combined brigade guns of the right wing, stood under the protection of the advanced guard, along the line from Zschernitz to Räcknitz and Plauen.[98]

Crenneville.

The right wing of the French center was formed by Marmont's VI Corps, and two Young Guard divisions that stood to the west of the Dippoldiswalde Road at 7:00 a.m. Their sole task was to hold the allied center in place, while the French left and right executed the principal attacks. As a result, the center began the battle with a heavy cannonade.

The left wing of the French center consisted of St. Cyr's XIV Corps. About 8:00 a.m., it began to advance against Strehlen. The Prussian 12th Brigade stood before St. Cyr. The weight of the French fire and the advance of St. Cyr, forced it to withdraw from the heights by Strehlen, to the village of Leubnitz. Here it engaged the French and was reinforced by the 5th Russian Infantry Division. The battle was very heavy and fought almost entirely with bayonets.

By 10:00 a.m., St. Cyr occupied Strehlen. The failure of the allies to hold it allowed the French to mass a large battery, including some Young Guard artillery, on the Strehlen Heights, where it pounded the middle of the allied line.[99]

St. Cyr reorganized his forces and began to threaten the allies with a renewed advance. FML Civalart threw the Albert Gyulai Infantry Regiment, of Quasdanovich's Brigade, into Räcknitz, and put the Argenteau Regiment behind it as a reserve. Lederer's 2nd Cavalry Division, which stood in front of the reserve cavalry, moved forward and took a position behind Hardegg's group.

From the Russian infantry reserve, the Russian 1st Grenadier Division was sent forward and its head stood by Nötnitz. The Finland Guard Infantry Regiment was sent from Kaitz towards Nordrand. The Russian 2nd and 3rd Cuirassier Divisions moved from Nötnitz towards Torna, and the bulk of the Russian 2nd Guard Division was moved to a position by Nothnitz, behind the 1st Grenadier Division.[100]

The Center 11:00 a.m. to 1:00 p.m.

St. Cyr's XIV Corps was pushing into and through Strehlen. Though his artillery was exceptionally strong, he found himself under a redoubled fire from the Prussian batteries in the center, as he tried to push out of Strehlen.[101] Napoleon stopped here about 12:00 p.m., and surveyed the situation. He ordered St. Cyr to resume the advance.

After a short burst of preparatory fire St. Cyr advanced out of Strehlen with three columns, moving towards Leubnitz in a massive bayonet attack. This attack threw back the two Prussian battalions defending the village.

Leubnitz was occupied by the Fus/1st and Fus/2nd Silesian Infantry Regiments, supported by the Russian Moghilev Regiment. This small force soon found itself facing an attack by a few battalions of Barrois' 2nd Young Guard Division. The French quickly took half the village from the allies, and faced an immediate counter attack.[102]

On the western part of the center, the battle consisted almost entirely of an artillery exchange. The village of Plauen had been set afire by French howitzer shells. About 1:00 p.m., Napoleon arrived in the Dohna Suburb from the left flank. He detached some horse artillery, and sent them forward with orders to silence an Austrian battery. After a short exchange, the Austrian artillery was silenced and the émigré French General Moreau, who was serving with the allies, was fatally wounded by a cannon shot.[103]

The Center after 1:00 p.m.

The battle in the center continued to be a massive artillery battle. St. Cyr had begun his third assault against Leubnitz shortly after 1:00 p.m. The allies had moved the Prussian reserve cavalry to a position behind the Torna Heights, in the hope of striking the French as they passed out of Reicks. Eventually two French battalions advanced out, chasing a few Russian jager battalions before them. GM von Röder brought forward his two horse batteries, unlimbered them, and began firing on the French battalions with cannister, as he brought his cavalry to a trot. Two squadrons of the 1st Silesian Hussars moved to the right flank of the French. The two French battalions, threatened by the hussars' advance, formed square and were attacked.

The Prussian reserve cavalry had its left flank taken under fire by a battery St. Cyr had posted by Strehlen, and was obliged to withdraw. They were then ordered to move to the right and join the Russian cavalry. They moved past Rickern towards Lockwitz, where a number of Russian cuirassier regiments stood under the orders of Grand Duke Constantine. Constantine's cavalry was ordered to withdraw shortly later.[104]

The Allied Right

Around 6:00 a.m., the two divisions of the Young Guard had taken up their positions. Decouz's 3rd Young Guard Division stood on the right of the Grossen-Garten, and extended to the village of Striesen. Roguet's 4th Young Guard Division extended from Striesen to the Elbe. The 1st and 2nd Guard Cavalry Divisions of Ornano and Lefèbvre-Desnoettes stood behind the middle of Roguet's 4th Young Guard Division. About 7:30 a.m., the entire line began its advance.[105]

Earlier, at 5:00 a.m., Kleist pulled the 1/2nd West Prussian and the 2/7th Reserve Regiments out of the Grossen Garten and sent them to Leubnitz. Strehlen was occupied by the 1/11th Reserve Regiment and behind them stood the 12th Prussian Brigade under Prinz August. The 10th and 11th Brigades stood between Leubnitz and Göstritz. The bulk of the Prussian artillery was on the heights to the west of Leubnitz.[106]

The Russians had small detachments in Blasewitz, Grüna, on the Grünen Wiese, and in the Landgraben. Behind the Grünen Wiese stood the Grodno and Lubnv Hussars. To the north of Grüna stood Roth's infantry and on the Pillnitz road stood the Soum Hussar Regiment, the Illowaiski #12, Ataman, and Rabinov #2 Don Cossack Regiments. Six Russian guns stood on the Grüna road, twelve more stood before the middle of the Russian line, and a few horse guns stood on the Pillnitz Road. Wittgenstein's infantry was dispersed between Leubnitz and Torna. Behind them stood Klüx's 9th Brigade, forming a second line.[107]

The French left, under Ney, defiled behind Grossen-Garten and advanced by echelons, left in advance. Decouz's 3rd Young Guard Division, reinforced by Vionnet's 1st Brigade of Barrois' 1st Young Guard Division, moved towards Grüna and Dobritz, then swung to the right towards Reick and Prohlis. As Decouz moved against Seidnitz, he was attacked by the Grodno Hussars.[108] The French cavalry on the flank were facing the principal danger, Roth's Russian infantry.

Mortier, directing Roguet's 4th Young Guard Division, moved against the Blasewitz Forest. Boyer de Rebeval's Brigade of Roguet's 4th Young Guard Division, the 4th and 5th Tirailleur Regiments, moved along the Elbe in the direction of Tolkewitz. Part of Ornano's and Lefèbvre-Desnoëttes' cavalry divisions moved to cover the Pillnitz Road. The remainder swung over the Striesen Heights and moved to the right to strike the Russians between Striesen and Grüna.[109] Roth's advanced guard stood above Reick, behind a strong force of skirmishers that stood along the Landgraben canal. He positioned cavalry on his right wing and his left wing was supported by the Prussian reserve cavalry.

Barrois.

It was at 11:00 a.m., when Napoleon arrived on this flank and ordered Pelet's Brigade to advance against Reick, supported by the rest of Roguet's 4th Young Guard Division.[110]

Decouz's 3rd Young Guard Division pushed past the Grossen-Garten, striking Roth's forces and pushing towards Striesen. The Young Guard crashed against the 24th Russian Jager Regiment, driving them back, despite the defensive canister fire. The 8th Voltigeurs were struck by the 1st Silesian Hussar Regiment, who drove them back sabering 60 men. The Loubny and Grodno Hussar Regiments attacked as well. The 5th Voltigeur Regiment immediately formed square. However, it was broken and lost 10 officers and 300 men killed, wounded and prisoner.[111] The Guard stopped and fought off that assault, but suffered heavily because of their inability to fire their muskets in the rain.

As the Young Guard moved out of the Grossen-Garten, they pushed the allied right back, into the villages of Klein- and Gross-Dobritz, which were occupied by the Russians. Despite the setbacks, the French attack steadily was to push the Russians back from Dobritz and Leuben towards Prohlis until an encirclement became possible.

Allied Right 11:00 a.m. to 1:00 p.m.

The Young Guard advanced vigorously against Klein-Dobritz, supported by a battery of 30 guns. They also veered right to close the gap between their right flank and St. Cyr's XIV Corps. Nansouty had directed the Guard cavalry divisions of Ornano and Léfèbvre-Desnoëttes down the Pirna Road, between Dobritz and Leuben.

About 11:30 a.m., the Russian Reserve Cavalry Corps of Galitzin moved between Lockwitz and Rickern, and the Guard Light Cavalry Division of Chevich moved south of Prohlis, between Lockwitz and Reick. These two divisions totalled 65 squadrons. In addition, between Reick and Torna, stood the 20 squadrons of the Prussian Reserve Cavalry. This put 85 allied squadrons facing the 28 French Guard squadrons on this flank. Despite this massive cavalry superiority, for some unknown reason, Barclay did not choose to unleash his cavalry against the French.

Allied Right After 2:00 p.m.

At 2:00 p.m., Ney attacked Reick and Prohlis. The Grodno Hussars again struck the left flank of the advancing Young Guard and reported breaking one of their squares.[112] The villages of Prohlis and Reick were heavily garrisoned by allied troops. The cavalry of Roth's advanced guard and eight guns of Horse Battery #6 stood to the right of Prohlis. Behind and to the right of them, stood the Reserve Cavalry of GM von Röder.

The French drove back the Russian right wing. The Corps of G. St. Cyr and Marmont began to cannonade the allied forces before them. Because of the rain, however, the battle so far had been one of the bayonet, saber and artillery. The rain had prevented the use of musketry to any significant degree.

Schwarzenberg, watching Ney's advance, decided to unite with Kleist's corps and counterattack towards Reick. His proper reserves stood in Coschütz, which was too far away to be of use in this project, and the Russians were too heavily engaged to spare any support. Unfortunately, Kleist's forces were heavily engaged by St. Cyr and were unable to execute a flanking march to attack Ney. As a result, Schwarzenberg was obliged to give up his proposed counterattack.[113]

Napoleon had established battery of 32 12pdr guns near Rächnitz, to hold the Austrian forces of Colloredo and Chasteler in place. Just as Marmont and St. Cyr were beginning their advance, Schwarzenberg learned from an officer coming from Peterswalde, that Ostermann-Tolstoy's Corps had fallen back before Vandamme and that Vandamme held the road to Kulm. Schwarzenberg's position had become critical and the allies risked being crushed in detail as well as being cut off from Bohemia.[114]

At 5:00 p.m., Schwarzenberg issued the order to his troops to retreat through Dippoldiswalda, towards Fürstenwalde, because the road to Peterswalde had been cut. As the retreat began, Klenau's Corps appeared on the battlefield by Kohlsdorf. He immediately withdrew down the Freiberg road, to move along the Leipzig road to Prague by Commotau.

At 6:00 p.m., the French occupied the allied morning positions. The allies had lost 26,000 men, including 16,000 prisoners. The French losses were about 8,000 men.

Vandamme's Actions

During the day of 26 August, Vandamme crossed the Elbe at Königstein and established himself on the Pirna plateau. Once there he began a long battle with Ostermann, on a battlefield drenched with rain, and his progress was slow. As a result, he was unable to completely cut the road to Peterswalde.

The Allied Withdrawal

Schwarzenberg withdrew his army in three columns towards Bohemia. The Russian Corps, under Barclay de Tolly, was joined by Ostermann-Tolstoy's Corps and moved along the road to Peterswalde. Kleist's Prussians, joined Colloredo and part of Chasteler's corps, moving down the road to Zinnwald and Teplitz. The remainder of the Austrians, including Klenau, moved down the road from Leipzig to Prague via Commotau.

As the allied columns began their withdrawal, the French began their pursuit, but because of the condition of the roads, the pursuit was not as close as Napoleon would have desired.

Barclay de Tolly, disquieted by the presence of Vandamme by Peterswalde, menaced in the rear by the French advancing from Dresden, ordered Ostermann-Tolstov to withdraw with him and to move to the west, along the road from Altenberg, followed by the Prussians. Prince Eugène von Württemberg, who was in Pirna, was the only general able to use the road to Peterswnwalde.

The Battle of Dresden is an example of the old allied style of battle. Their approach was not smoothly coordinated; instead, major formations straggled into combat only after the first day's battle was done. Still, such timing was always difficult, even for Napoleon. Their major flaw was that though the allies were on the strategic offensive the first day, their hesitation to use it allowed the initiative to pass over to Napoleon. They permitted him the precious time necessary to draw his forces together so as to erase the earlier allied numerical superiority. This, coupled with the terrible ground to the west of Dresden that split the allied forces, gave Napoleon the opportunity to use his interior position to concentrate superior forces on one part of the enemy who could not be reinforced because of the intervening Weisseritz ravine.

Napoleon's success to the east of Dresden is harder to explain, but the French troops involved were the Young Guard, backed up by the Imperial Guard Cavalry, both of whose fighting prowess was enhanced by the quality of their leadership and their inherent pride at being part of the Imperial Guard. It is also probable that the quality of the allied generalship on that flank was not equal to that of the opposing French generals.

Napoleon was certainly the finest general on the battle field and his generals were at their best when under their master's eye. On the other hand, the allies had one trump card to play, their cavalry advantage, but they played it in an appalling manner.

There are three possible explanations why the allies did not use their cavalry aggressively. The first is that the terrain around Dresden was not particularly well suited to cavalry action. True, there were parts where it was not, but then the French used their limited cavalry quite effectively. Cavalry is of little use in a city, but this excuse can only be used for the first day of the battle. Certainly on the second day there was ample open terrain for the allied cavalry. Heavy rains may have made the ground unsuitable for the use of cavalry, but then it does not seem to have bothered the French. No explanation can be found in the terrain.

A second explanation is that they chose not to commit it because of the large number of guns present and they did not wish to get it shot up. However, as the day was marked by heavy rain and, as musketry was largely unavailable, the battle became one of cold steel (bayonets and sabers) and artillery. It was a day when cavalry could close on infantry; a day when the infantry could not fire back to defend itself, but had to depend only on those tiny bayonets to keep charging eastern hordes at bay. Certainly if there was a battle in which cavalry would have the moral ascendancy over the infantry, it had to be this battle.

This leads to the third explanation, miserable generalship on the part of the allies. This is the same reason that Napoleon was able to take the initiative on the second day. It is also the reason that the allies deployed their Austrian forces to the west in such a manner as to allow them to be cut off by the Weisseritz ravine. Analysis of this situation reveals a commanding general, Schwarzenberg, who was operating under the impossible situation of having both the Czar and King of Prussia second guessing everything he said and did. His command situation could have only been worse if the Emperor of Austria were actually on the field too.

Any general who disliked an order could appeal directly to his sovereign. Any command or the commitment of any formation would undergo the scrutiny, direct or indirect, of its ruling sovereign. All of the "political creatures" and court dandies in uniform were present, engaging in their jockeying for power and royal favor at the expense of the soldiers in the field. The allied staff was unworkable for that reason alone. However, it was also far from the well developed and smoothly operating staff that Napoleon commanded.

It would appear that the failure at Dresden was a multi-fold failure of the allied command structure to function. Prior to Dresden the allied staff had never been very good and what little good it had was paralyzed into inaction by the presence of two sovereigns. There appears to have been little planning of what to do, poor execution of what was planned, no real sense of mission, and once the battle began it fell back to every corps commander and brigade commander doing what seemed right to him at the moment.

This paralysis would continue in the Army of Bohemia throughout the campaign and the final outcome of the campaign would be in the hands of the aggressive Blücher and of the equally aggressive Prussian and Russian generals in the Army of the North, who were eager to come to grips with the French.

12

The French Pursuit After Dresden 27–28 August 1813

The Pursuit Begins

The weather during the Battle of Dresden had made a pursuit on the scale of that in 1806 impossible. In addition, Napoleon did not have the cavalry to execute such an operation. Nonetheless, a pursuit was mounted as the allies withdrew towards Bohemia, and the French set off to reap the rewards of their victory. Despite the weakness of the French pursuit, the allies also suffered considerably from the hurried retreat. The Prussian Guard reported losing ten men per company and 400 were without shoes. The 1/7th Reserve Infantry Regiment lost 138 men through illness alone, the 2/7th also lost 214 men to illness.[1]

All of the Russo-Prussian reserves, as well as Wittgenstein's Corps and the 2nd Prussian Corps, under the orders of Barclay de Tolly, were retiring from Dresden via Dohna and Gieshübel on Peterswalde and Teplitz.

All the Austrians on the right bank of the Weisseritz or the right of the Plauen ravine retired down the two roads to Dippoldiswalde and via Eichwalde on Dux and Brix. The fragments of Gyulai's Corps and that of Klenau moved down the left bank of the Weisseritz and moved through Rabenau on Pretschendorf. The remnants of Gyulai's Corps, at this point, moved through Hermsdorf towards Dux. Klenau moved through Gross-Waltersdorf and Marienberg on Commotau.

Schwarzenberg's order for the Russians to move through Gieshübel and Peterswalde was the most difficult. It lay under the threat of Vandamme's I Corps and Barclay refused to execute the order. He ordered the Russian reserve to move, instead, on Dippoldiswalde. Kleist was ordered to move through Lockwitz and Maxen. Wittgenstein was ordered to form a rear guard supported by the 9th Prussian Brigade. The entire force was authorized to use the roads to Dippoldiswalde.[2]

After clearing the plains around Dresden main road and all of the minor roads south passed through narrow valleys whose slopes were heavily wooded. All traffic south would be confined to roads in these defiles for 15 to 20 miles when they eventually broke onto a high plateau of open alpine pastures. After crossing this plateau the roads once again plunged into narrow defiles and wove up the sides of the mountains to Zinnwald. These roads are quite steep and today they often have 12% grades. At Zinnwald the main road plunges down the equally steep southern flank of the Erzgebirg towards the narrow gorge of the Elbe River. There are few wide open spaces suitable for the deployment of large armies and many places where a small force could detain a much larger force for hours.

The French Pursuit

During the evening of 27 August the French army stood as follows: Doumerc's 3rd Heavy Cavalry Regiment and Dufour's 5th Division stood on the road to Freiberg, two leagues from Herzogwalde. Bordesoulle's 1st Heavy Cavalry Division stood in Berrhout and Rossthal observing the road to

Tharandt. Chastel's 3rd Light Cavalry Division had a brigade in Wolnitz and the remainder of the division stood in Compsen and Benerich at the fork of the roads to Freiberg and Nossen. The 4th and 6th Divisions of Dubreton and Vial stood in Wolnitz.

Teste's 23rd Division stood by the stone bridge in Weisseritz guarding the road to Tharandt. The VI Corps was in Strehla. The XIV Corps stood in Grune-Wiese. Mortier's Young Guard was engaging the allies around Reick. Decouz's 3rd Young Guard Division bivouacked in Gruhna, Roguet's 4th Young Guard Division stood with a brigade in Reick and in Dobritz. The two other Young Guard brigades stood in Seidnitz with some of Nansouty's Guard cavalry.

Maréchal Marmont.

Napoleon had assumed that the allies intended to resume the battle on the 28th. During the 27th, he wrote Murat stating that he doubted they intended to withdraw. He intended to hold the allies frontally with the VI and XIV Corps, and the Guard. Once fixed, he would turn their flank with the II Corps, Teste's 23rd Division, and the I Reserve Cavalry Corps.[3]

Marmont believed he heard the sounds of an allied withdrawal and reported that to Napoleon in Dresden. Napoleon ordered Marmont to follow the allies down the road to Dippoldiswalde and to take the heights between Leubnitz and Rackwitz, and put his advanced guard on the heights by Kaitza.

Wittgenstein's Withdrawal

Seven battalions of Klüx's brigade formed the rearguard of Wittgenstein's column. The Fus/1st West Prussian Infantry Regiment served as the ultimate rear guard. Marmont's pursuit of Wittgenstein was not particularly vigorous. The 9th Prussian Brigade had passed through Goppeln, Ruppgen, and Possendorf by day break. After passing through the Ruppgen defile they passed under the orders of FML Hardegg, who had been given command of the entire rearguard.

Hardegg took a position above the Possendorf defile, to slow the French pursuers, but lacking artillery, he felt obliged to call on the Prussian Guard Brigade to support him. The Prussian Guard had been ordered to withdraw at 2:00 a.m., but its columns had become so crossed that it had only just arrived in Possendorf.

Oberst Alvensleben detached the Fus/2nd Guard Regiment and a half battery. The 2/2nd Guard placed itself slightly to the right.

Two squadrons of the Berg Lancers advanced down the main road to Dippoldiswalde. They charged a skirmish line, but were thrown back by a charge by the Silesian Uhlans, a landwehr cavalry regiment and two squadrons of Austrian Chevauléger. Klüx moved to a new position, with the Russian jagers, and the Austrians moved into the village of Haselig, to facilitate the passage of the Russian artillery over the Lockwitz stream. Part of the village was held until 10:00 p.m., then voluntarily abandoned. The 9th Brigade reached Falkenheim that night.

The Prussian Guard Brigade found the road behind Dippoldiswalde completely blocked. Oberst Alvensleben sent the 1st and 2nd Battalions of his regiments on a detour through Behrenfeld and left the Fusilier Battalions on the road. The Fus/1st Guard Regiment became an advanced guard, while the Fus/2nd Guard Regiment became a rear guard. A battery stood between the two battalions. The Guard Brigade reached Altenberg during the 29th, at 1:00 p.m.

The VI Corps, to which had been added a brigade of guard cavalry under GD Ornano, pursued Wittgenstein. The VI Corps cavalry had been detached towards Hoyerswerda with GM Normann. After arriving in Wendisch-Carsdorf, Marmont wrote Napoleon, announcing that he had seen about 30,000 men withdrawing before him and that large forces were moving parallel to his line of march.

Marmont detached a division in Carsdorf and moved on Heselig with two columns. The Russian 5th Division had taken a position above Heselig and was supported by the Russian 2nd Guard Division and the Russian 3rd Cuirassier Division.

Lagrange's 21st Division followed the main road, while Compans' 20th Division moved through the forests, along a road that ran into the village from the west. The French cavalry remained behind Lagrange's 21st Division, ready to move as soon as the passages were open.

As Compans' column broke into the open, it found itself immediately engaged by the Russians. The 2/, 3/32nd Légère executed a bayonet attack against the foremost allied post and overran it. The 3/1st Marine Regiment supported it in this attack. The 1st Brigade formed to the right and left of the road, by battalions in dense columns, and marched forward to strike the Russians. They did so without artillery support, because their guns were still attempting to negotiate the defile. Only two guns had been moved forward to support the attack.

The 2nd Brigade was ordered to form identically to the 1st Brigade and to advance and form a second line behind the 1st Brigade. As they deployed, the Russians attacked, but the 4/, 5/1st Marine Regiment threw them back. Though the Russians fell back, they were quickly rallied by the growing number of infantry and artillery supporting them.[4]

Compans responded by marching the two unengaged battalions of the 1/, 2/1st Marines to the left in order to strike the Russians in the flank and rear. Compans quickly made himself master of the edge of the forest and turned the allies flank. However, he was unable to exploit his position, because the 1st Brigade had expended its ammunition and the 2nd Brigade was not yet in position.

And so it stood, while the allies passed Klüx's Brigade, Roth's Brigade, and the 1st Austrian Light Division behind the 5th Russian Division, that stopped Marmont's further advance.

Kleist's Retreat

In order to execute Barclay's orders, Kleist ordered his corps to retreat in the following order: The 11th Reserve Regiment, the Cavalry reserve with its artillery, the reserve artillery, the remainder of the 12th Brigade, the 11th Brigade, and the rearguard of GM Ziethen. GM Pirch led the withdrawal and the head of his column reached Hausdorf at 5:30 a.m. The rearguard, under GM Ziethen, followed the procession, operating as served its function best.[5]

The march passed through Glashütte, Dittersdorf, Liebenau, and on towards Fürstenwalde. The Neumärk Dragoon Regiment was passed to Ziethen's control. The 9th Brigade, under GM von Klüx, was placed directly under Wittgenstein's orders and moved via Dippoldiswalde.

Klüx's brigade formed the extreme rearguard on the two roads. At 1:00 a.m., Oberst Löbell received the order to occupy Leubnitz with the 1/, Fus/6th Reserve Regiment and the Fus/1st East Prussian Infantry Regiment in relief of the 11th Brigade.

At day break, GM Roth, who commanded that point, directed Löbell to not only occupy the village, but also the heights behind the village, and to hold that position until the allied columns had passed through the defile. The Russians, he said, were so fatigued, that he could count only on the Prussians. To which Oberst Löbell responded that his soldiers were also fatigued, but "I know their value, I know what I have in my battalion and to what point I can count on them."[6]

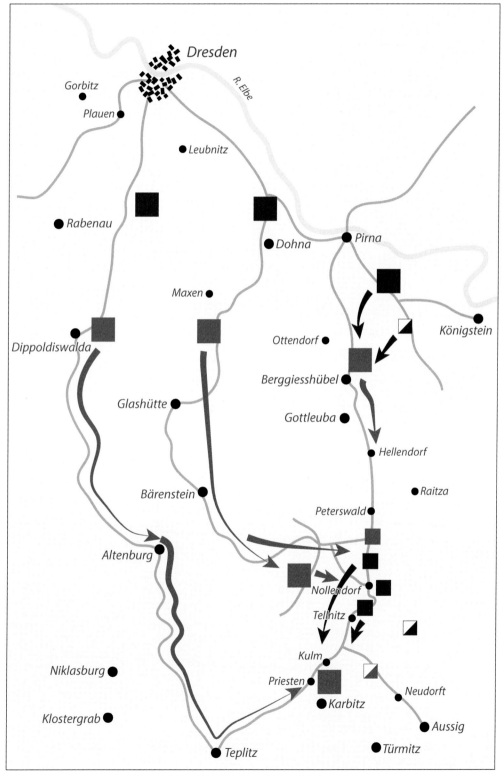

Sketch Map 14 The Road That Led to Kulm.

The Fus/ist East Prussian Regiment occupied the cemetery and the two other battalions moved to the heights, supported by a force of Russian artillery.

According to his habit, Maréchal Gouvion St. Cyr advanced with little vigor. He attacked Leubnitz solely about noon, when Napoleon arrived. Several attacks were pushed back, which allowed the Prussian 2nd Corps to withdraw without interference. The rearguard retired without being pursued to Hausdorf. St. Cyr had only advanced to between Kleba and Kreischa, when he received an order from Berthier to withdraw back to Maxen.

The Imperial Guard

Mortier, with the divisions of Decouz and Roguet, stood in Pirna. In front of him advanced the 2nd Dutch Guard Lancer Regiment. They bivouacked in Zehista. The 1st Guard Lancers bivouacked in Klein and Gross-Sedlitz. The 1st Guard Lancers sent out three reconnaissance patrols, one to Bohna, Blosewitz, and Schmorsdorf, one to Klein Rohrsdorf and Burgstadt, and the third to Welka, Lockwitz and Nickern. They were to determine the location of the enemy and ensure liaison with the XIV Corps. This precaution had been totally overlooked in the other French columns.

The first of these patrols reported that GM Tschernigov had been in Dohna for five days with 6,000 men, Cossacks and jagers, and GL Kleist had passed through Dohna on the 26th, with 12,000 men. Outside Schmorsdorf, the patrol encountered the vedettes of a Prussian cavalry squadron.

Württemberg's 2nd Corps

On 28 August, Württemberg and Ostermann-Tolstoy moved through Gieshübel, placed a covering force on the Kohlberg plateau, occupied by a battalion of Vandamme's corps, and succeeded in regaining the road to Peterswalde.

Vandamme was still unaware of the results of the battle at Dresden, but when he learned later that morning, he rapidly regrouped his forces and began his pursuit.

Württemberg took up a position by the village of Gross Cotta, south of Pirna. He prepared for a diversionary attack (*Scheinangriff*) with Knorring's Tartar Uhlan Regiment and the 4th Jagers of Ivanov's Brigade. The remainder of the 2nd Corps stood behind Gross-Cotta with GM Helfreich, and was to execute a false attack against Krietzschwitz.[7] As the French moved into Gross Cotta, they were attacked and driven back across the Gottaleubebach River towards Kreitzschwitz. Vandamme counterattacked and drove the Russians back in their turn.

Prince Eugène of Württemberg.

Yermolov supported Knorring's cavalry with the Russian Guard Jager Regiment under GM von Bistrom, holding the French back long enough to allow the Russian Guard and the 2nd Corps to withdraw towards Bohemia.[8]

After the violent clash with the allied rearguard under Württemberg, Vandamme moved his corps to Hellendorf, a short distance from Peterswalde, and stopped, awaiting orders from Napoleon.

The Main French Army

The main army in Dresden received its orders. Mortier, with the Young Guard, and St. Cyr were to take the road to Peterswalde and join with Vandamme. Marmont was to move down the road to Altenberg, and Murat, with Victor's Corps under his control, was to advance down the road to Freiberg.

Napoleon accompanied Marmont's corps, and as he arrived on the heights south of Dresden, watched the withdrawing allied columns. Noting that Barclay had quit the Dresden road and was moving to join Kleist, Napoleon sent orders to St. Cyr to leave the Peterswalde road and re-join Marmont near Dohna and Maxen.

Napoleon then moved to Pirna, to observe the allied activities in that area. At that time, he learned of the results of Macdonald's battle on the Katzbach and Oudinot's battle at Gross-Beeren.

When he arrived in Pirna, on 28 August, Napoleon was under the assumption that Vandamme had seized Gieshübel, and given St. Cyr and Mortier time to fall on the rear of the Russian columns moving down the road to Peterswalde, while Marmont, Murat, and Victor continued their pursuits down the roads to Altenberg and Freiberg.

Allied prisoners are marched through Dresden, 28 August.

The Action at Kohlberg

Vandamme had, through an incredible act of negli-
gence, placed a single battalion to hold the Kohlberg
position. It stood on a hill that overlooked the main
road south to Peterswalde, and as a result, was in the
way of the withdrawing Russian 2nd Corps. At the
beginning of the engagement, Yermolov sent forward
the Guard Jagers and Ismailov Guard Infantry
Regiment, to support GM Knorring. However, the
Ismailov Regiment was called off and replaced by a
battalion of the Semenovski Guard Regiment.

Kohlberg was taken and lost three times. The
Russians engaged successively, the 3/Semenovski
and the Guard Jagers. The Russians held the important hill after the third assault, executed by the 2/
Guard Jager Regiment.[9] The road now clear of
threatening French infantry, the withdrawal of the
allied columns continued undisturbed.

Württemberg, when he arrived at Gross-Cotta,
found the village already occupied by 3,000 French.

Yermolov, by G. Dawe.

He sent Helfreich forward, supported by Wolf's brigade, and recaptured the village. All of the
skirmishers of the division, led by Colonel Wolf, supported the attack, and turned the village to
the north, pushing on towards Krietzschwitz, which they were unable to capture.

Puschnitzki's division was deployed to the left, towards Gös. A 12-gun battery was established
to the north of the village, where it was able to strike Kohlberg, in addition to engaging the French
artillery established on the right bank of the Gottaleube. It contributed significantly to the repulse
of the attack of the 13th Légère Regiment.

Part of the guard stopped in Rothe-Schenke and prepared their noon meal, rather than pushing
rapidly towards the Gieshübel defile, under the protection of the covering efforts of the rearguard against Vandamme. Yermolov was sent an order by Württemberg to resume the retreat. The
Preobragenski Regiment led the withdrawal, followed by 24 guns.[10]

Württemberg's actions had confused Vandamme. Vandamme was ignorant that morning of
what was occurring on his left and sent an officer to generals Philippon and Corbineau, to direct
their efforts to cut the road to Bohemia, that ran through Peterswalde.

He drew together Mouton-Duvernet's 42nd Division and joined it with Dumonceau's 2nd
Division and Quiot's brigade, 23rd Division, supported by Reuss' brigade with their right on
Pirna and their left on Krietzschwitz, ready to move in whatever direction that struck Vandamme
as the most advantageous.

A reconnaissance advised him at 10:00 p.m., on the 27th, that a column of 5,000 to 6,000 men
was moving down the Zehista-Gieshübel road, with a large convoy of artillery. Part of this column
was at the Rothe-Schenke farm.

Learning of the Russian withdrawal past Gieshübel, Vandamme moved to intercept them,
supporting Philippon's 1st Division with Reuss' brigade around 9:00 a.m. With the Russians
retreating, Mouton-Duvernet established his 42nd Division at Kohlberg, with a few companies
thrown as far as Gös. These dispositions secured the Pirna bridge and Vandamme decided to move
to his left.[11]

The Action at Gieshübel

Around 2:00 p.m., the Russian Guard was passing Gieshübel. Simultaneously, the leading elements of Vandamme's column arrived. According to Bogdanovich, four French guns barred the road, though they are not mentioned in any other reports. The Preobragenski Guard Regiment led the Russian column. Its 1st Battalion was detached under Baron Rosen, to cover the road. The 2nd Battalion, led by Yermolov, moved to face to the east and throw back the French skirmishers. It was relieved by the Guard Jager Regiment, a battalion of which engaged in a skirmish fight with the French. The two other battalions of the Guard Jagers supported the first. The Guard Division passed behind them and reached the cover of Hellendorf. A battalion of the Semenovski Guard Regiment took up a position in the Markersbach valley, to strengthen the Russian hold on the passage.

The Russian 2nd Corps stood in a very difficult position because of the numbers facing it. On hearing the Russian Guard in combat, GM Helfreich and Schachafskoy moved into Gieshübel to support them. Colonel Wolf and his skirmishers, were supported by GM Pischnitzky in their efforts to stop the French before Krietzschwitz as long as possible, then withdrew on Geppersdorf and Schönewalde.[12]

GD Corbineau was ordered to lead his cavalry against Gieshübel. Corbineau then sent Fezensac's brigade against Gottaleube to support that attack. Corbineau's own division marched in a single column and deployed before Gieshübel about 3:00 p.m. Vandamme arrived just as Corbineau deployed and prepared for his attack. He was very excited and reproached Philippon for being so slow to attack. He stated that Napoleon was about to arrive and that it was up to them to win the victory. The 7th Légère of the 1st Brigade was thrown forward against Gieshübel.

The French attack cut through the Russian column, separating the Mourmon and Minsk Regiments from the rest and forcing into a hasty retreat. Württemberg, who had already passed through the village with the Tschernigov Regiment, turned the regiment around, despite its disorganization, and threw it back at the French.

The 7th Légère stopped and fired a volley into the charging Russians, stopping them abruptly. The Russians and French then broke out their skirmishers and began a skirmish duel, while the Russian regiment skirted towards the west to reach the Peterswalde road. Others passed through Gottaleube. The Tschernigov and Mourmon Regiments, engaged in the woods, suffered heavy casualties and were thrown back on the Guard Jager Regiment and those other forces behind Hellendorf.[13]

The first through were Helfreich's troops, then Schachafskoy's 3rd Division, Wolf's brigade leading Ivanov's brigade, and finally Treuffurt's brigade of Puschnitzki's 4th Division. The French were held at bay by the Guard Jager Regiment and a line regiment, until the road to Kunitz was reached and the Russians were once again free to move south.[14]

At 5:00 p.m., the 2nd Corps cleared Hellendorf. Pouchelon's 1st Brigade, 1st Division, continued the battle with the Russian rearguard, as it withdrew. Fezensac's 2nd Brigade, 1st Division, pushed to the right, towards Gottaleube, which was occupied by the 36th Line Regiment.

When Napoleon learned that Ostermann-Tolstoy and Württemberg had succeeded in escaping Vandamme, and reached the road to Kunitz, he felt that Vandamme could do little more than add to the pursuit directly to Teplitz. Under these conditions, he felt his personal command of the operation was no longer necessary, and turned the pursuit over to his lieutenants.

Despite everything, Vandamme still had the opportunity to arrive in Kulm and Teplitz before the allied columns, other than those of Ostermann-Tolstoy and Württemberg, and it would be advantageous for the French to profit from this opportunity. To this end, Napoleon sent to Vandamme the following order at 4:00 p.m., the afternoon of 28 August.

The Emperor orders that you direct your movements towards Peterswalde with the entirety of your corps, Corbineau's [cavalry] division, the 42nd Division [Mouton-Duvernet of the XIV Corps], and the brigade of the II Corps commanded by Reuss. This will give you an augmentation of 18 battalions. Pirna shall be guarded by the troops of the Duke of Trevise [Mortier], who shall arrive there this evening. The Marshal also has orders to relieve your positions in the Lilienstein camp. GB Baltus [I Corps artillery], with your 12pdr battery and your park, shall arrive in Pirna this evening. The Emperor desires that you unite all the forces that he has put at your disposition and that with them you penetrate into Bohemia and throw back Prince Württemberg, if he chooses to oppose you. The enemy that we have beaten is withdrawing on Annaberg. His Majesty thinks that you should arrive before him on his lines of communications with Tetschen, Aussig, and Teplitz, and take his equipment, his ambulances, his baggage, and, in the end, all that which marches in the tail of his army. The Emperor orders that the pontoon bridge at Pirna be raised so that another may be erected at Tetschen.[15]

In order to complete his assigned task, Vandamme had the divisions of Philippon (1st Division – 14 battalions) and Dumonceau (2nd Division – 14 battalions), Quiot's brigade (from Teste's 23rd Division – 6 battalions), all of which came from his corps, Reuss' brigade (II Corps, 5th Division – 6 battalions), and the three brigades of Corbineau's 1st Light Cavalry Division. This gave him a total of about 1,300 cavalry and 18,700 infantry, or approximately 20,000 men.

He was to vigorously push Ostermann-Tolstoy and Württemberg before him, and take positions around Kulm and Teplitz, while Mortier led the Young Guard to his support, less detachments sent to Pirna and Lilienstein. St. Cyr, Marmont, Victor and Murat's cavalry pursued the allies towards Teplitz.

As it was organized, the French pursuit had a good opportunity to annihilate Schwarzenberg's army if Napoleon's orders were fully executed. Unfortunately, that was not to pass.

After issuing his orders, Napoleon returned to Dresden with the Old Guard, leaving the pursuit to his marshals. There were rearguard skirmishes at Possendorf and Dippoldiswalde, where Marmont was heavily engaged. At Possendorf, Marmont overthrew the allied rearguard, taking 2,500 prisoners,

Dumonceau.

12 guns, numerous wagons and baggage. From there, he moved to the Windiskarsdorf heights, from which he could see the allies moving in several directions.

Heavy allied columns were viewed moving from Maxen, moving via Frauendorf along the road to Altenberg. Others were moving through Tharandt towards Frauenstein. Yet, before Marmont there stood a strong line of allied infantry supported by a large force of artillery.[16]

Marmont sent Lagrange's 21st Division down the main road to Dippoldiswalde to turn the allied position. He sent his cavalry behind Lagrange so it could support his attack. Friederichs' 22nd Division was then sent to Windiskarsdorf, to cover Marmont's left while supporting Lagrange's attack.

The fight was not a long one. The VI Corps threw back the allied forces facing them. Compans' 20th Division moved into Dippoldiswalde, and Lagrange moved through Kessenig and Bentholdheim. Ornano's 1st Guard Cavalry Division moved as quickly as possible, but night had almost fallen, and the plain was filled with allied cavalry. Ornano's movement was cut short.[17] Marmont claims to have taken a total of 20,000 prisoners in his advance.[18]

By 8:30 p.m., the night of 28 August, Vandamme had had little success. He reported to Napoleon, that he had before him 5,000 to 6,000 Russians and that he would attack them again at the break of dawn.

The Revel Infantry Regiment and the 4th Jagers withdrew via Geppersdorf towards Schönewalde and Peterswalde. Pischnitzky's division and Wolf's detachment continued to act as the rear guard, delaying and harassing Vandamme's pursuing forces. However, Vandamme's pursuit was not particularly aggressive.

Vandamme had ordered the bulk of his forces to march along a parallel route, because the Russians attacked Gross-Cotta again during the night. The Tartar Uhlan Regiment had been cut off by his movements, but it succeeded in piercing through his lines and moved through Gieshübel and rejoined Württemberg in Peterswalde.[19]

Murat's Pursuit

At 10:00 a.m., on 28 August Murat reported to Napoleon that the Austrians were in retreat on the road to Teplitz. He reported that they had passed all night through the village of Frauenstein. The 8th Chasseur à Cheval Regiment arrived in Tharandt at noon on 28 August and encountered a force of Austrians occupying the city. They were identified as belonging to Klenau's corps. In their move between Tharandt and Freiberg they had encountered no one. Murat had determined Klenau's line of retreat, but had no orders. He hesitated to throw his cuirassiers and the II Corps in pursuit, for fear of upsetting Napoleon's plans.

At 3:00 a.m., Murat sent GD Chastel forward with two regiments through Waltersdorf and on to Marienberg, to collect all the convoys that followed that road or that were coming through Chemnitz, Flohe and Oderan, or moving towards Waltersdorf or Marienberg. The 8th Chasseurs moved into Waltersdorf and the 19th Chasseurs moved to Chemnitz in pursuit of a major convoy, observed during the evening of the 28th in Oderan. As soon as the fifth regiment arrived in Nossen it was sent on Sayda.

Murat decided at noon, without consulting with Napoleon, to move towards Frauenstein. The II Corps was ordered forward in the following order: Reiset's Dragoon Brigade, the 5th Division, the cuirassiers, the light artillery, the 4th Division, the 6th Division, and the 23rd Division. The march was not particularly aggressive.

As he arrived on the Lichtenberg heights, Murat encountered an Austrian rearguard of 8,000 to 10,000 infantry with two cannons. They withdrew on Sayda. A strong reconnaissance force of 300 to 400 French cavalry was thrown forward against the village. It quickly reported back that a force 10,000 infantry, 2,000 cavalry and eight guns had arrived in the village that morning and had departed at 2:00 p.m., moving on Brux and Bohemia. The march was very disordered. Another reconnaissance force sent towards Frauenstein reported hearing cannon fire and presumed it to be the VI Corps.[20]

Murat's column pushed on. The 4th Division bivouacked that evening in Burkersdorf, the 6th and 23rd Divisions were in Weissenhorn, and the parks and the reserve remained in Freiberg.

Wittgenstein's Column

The Russian 5th Division departed Dippoldiswalde at 2:00 a.m., in order to move on Falkenhayn. GM Roth formed the rearguard of the column. Moritz Liechtenstein's 1st Light Division moved along the westerly route through Sillerhaus, Zaunhaus, and Grab. The infantry began moving at 8:00 a.m., the cavalry remained in Elend until noon.

Maréchal Marmont was also late in beginning his movement. Some of that tardiness was due to an effort to identify the direction of the allied retreat, but it was not a justified excuse. An incredible lack of motivation seems to have permeated the French general staff, and few of them showed any vigor or aggressiveness as the pursuit progressed.

As Roth arrived in Falkenhayn, he stopped to allow his strung out column to pull itself back together. He occupied the woods between Ober-Fraundorf and Falkenhayn with two battalions of jägers and sent the 9th Prussian Brigade to support them.

Maréchal Marmont arrived and began to attack those woods about 4:00 p.m.. He sent forward a single division over a wide front and seized the woods. Night fell as his forces came out the far side of the woods. Despite that a sharp skirmish occurred with Roth's rearguard and Klüx's supporting 9th Brigade. A French brigade seized Falkenhayn and threw the allies back through the defiles with considerable loss. The withdrawing forces of Roth and Klüx rallied on the Russian 5th Division posted in Altenberg. The 1st Austrian Light Division covered the road to Grab and the 2nd Russian Guard Division and the 3rd Russian Cuirassier Division occupied Dorn.

Kleist's Retreat

The Prussian 2nd Corps renewed its withdrawal at 2:00 a.m. They moved with the 11th Reserve Infantry Regiment leading, followed by the reserve cavalry, the 12th Brigade, the 11th Brigade, and the 10th Brigade. Oberst Löbell's detachment and Ziethen's rearguard brought up the rear.

Oberst Löbell departed Hausdorf at 9:00 a.m., and the rearguard abandoned it at around 10:00 a.m. At the defile at Glashütte, a sharp skirmish developed with Löbell supporting Ziethen's rearguard. However, the Prussians withdrew and all pursuit stopped as they departed the village. That evening the 2nd Corps was as follows: Ziethen was between Libenau and Glashütte. The 11th and 12th Brigades were behind Libenau, to the left of the main road. The 11th Reserve Regiment and the 1/1st Silesian Regiment stood with two brigade batteries on the right of the road. The 10th Brigade, the cavalry reserve, and the reserve artillery stood in Fürstenwalde.

The march had been difficult. The head of the column did not reach Fürstenwalde until 4:00 p.m., after covering 21 kilometers in six hours. The troops were exhausted and without food. Many of the weaker men fell out of ranks and died beside the road.[21]

At 3:00 p.m., however, Kleist received an order from the King of Prussia ordering him to move his force as rapidly as possible towards the Teplitz valley by way of the Erzgebirg defiles, to support Count Ostermann who was involved in a battle.

In view of the condition of his troops, Kleist wrote back stating that he would advance as rapidly as possible, but that his troops were desperately in need of rest. He stated that the head of his column had only just arrived (4:00 p.m.) in Fürstenwalde and that he would not arrive in Teplitz until long after dark, if he allowed his troops the desperately needed rest.

Because of the dangers of a night march down mountain roads cluttered with vehicles and the fatigue of his troops, Kleist decided to march on Nollendorf.

When the word of the condition of his troops and his intentions arrived at the main allied armies headquarters, Czar Alexander is reputed to have asked if Kleist felt it would be possible in some fashion, to fall on the French (Vandamme's) rear, but he did not mention Nollendorf. The

King of Prussia sent word that Kleist was free to seek his own route back to Bohemia, acting as seemed best.[22]

Oberst Schöler was dispatched back to Kleist with these messages. His progress was, however, considerably slowed because of the numbers of vehicles on the road. He was forced to abandon his horse and continue on foot, as he sought to return to Kleist. Once Schöler arrived, Kleist sent him back with the following message:

> The situation in which I find myself is desperate. I have learned that the Geiersberg defile is so completely blocked with baggage and broken down vehicles that it will take 24 hours to clear it. In this situation I have decided to march on Nollendorf in the morning so as to be able to cut my way through the French. I beg Your Majesty to assist my efforts by attacking at the same hour. If the combat is checked, I beg Your Majesty not blame me for the defeat, but to blame the people who have put me in this desperate situation.

A similar message was sent to Barclay de Tolly.[23]

At 9:00 a.m., Kleist informed his troops of the situation in which the corps stood and his plan to resolve it. He told them that an enemy corps stood on the road to Peterswalde.

> It is not possible to pass through the Geiersberg defile except with great losses. I have, as a result, resolved to fall on the back of the corps in Nollendorf, to attack them and to reestablish, by this means, our union with the Russian and Prussian forces that passed through Dippoldiswalde. The commanders are advised of this movement and will cooperate with it. In consequence, the troops present here shall assemble tomorrow morning at 3:00 a.m., by the marker that is near Fürstenwalde on the side of the road coming from Liebenau. The order of march shall be as follows: as an advanced guard, the 1st Silesian Hussar Regiment that GM Ziethen shall detach for this goal, the 10th brigade, the cavalry reserve, and the 11th and 12th Brigades. GM Ziethen shall follow as a rear guard at an appropriate distance and move from Streckenwalde to Peterswalde to watch the road from Pirna. The artillery reserve shall be divided amongst the brigades.[24] – The empty artillery baggage wagons and the empty caissons shall remain in Fürstenwalde. Their horses and harness shall be taken.[25]

Kleist's orders were well received and the morale of the corps improved markedly.

St. Cyr's Pursuit

On the morning of 29 August St. Cyr's forces stood with his cavalry in Burgstadt. His infantry was further to the rear. The Russian rearguard remained undisturbed in Maxen. As Pajol arrived in Reinhard-Grimma, he observed to the west, near Kunersdorf, a Prussian corps of 2,000 infantry and 1,500 cavalry, probably Klüx's brigade. Pajol pushed to the west to turn them, but the Prussians disappeared quickly by the road to Altenberg. St. Cyr was not doing anything to prevent the allies from reorganizing and preparing for the next fight, nor was he aggressively gathering in the spoils of the Battle of Dresden.

The Army of Bohemia

The main allied columns arrived on the Altenberg heights on 28 August. During the night of 28/29 August and on into the morning, they crossed the mountains in their movements to retire behind the Eger. The Russian Guard had started south about 5:30 a.m., moving towards Nollendorf, arriving there closely pursued by Vandamme. Prinz Leopold von Sachsen-Coburg led the advance with the Empress Cuirassier Regiment, supported by Knorring and the Tartar Uhlan Regiment. The two Russian cavalry regiments struck at the French, holding them back while the infantry rearguard moved south.

The Russian cavalry disengaged and moved into Nollendorf, where GL Yermolov had deployed Krapovitzki's Guard Brigade and a few guns. Ivanov's Brigade, Russian 2nd Corps, stood on the main road by Bergieshübel, holding the pass for the rearguard's withdrawal.

Württemberg pulled the rest of his corps onto the heights by the Nollendorf Church with Helfreich's forces, while Yermolov's Guard moved into the Kulm valley. Württemberg's forces stood here, holding the pass for 1½ hours, under intense French artillery fire.[26]

Knowing the importance of holding Teplitz, Ostermann-Tolstoy and Württemberg had stopped by Nollendorf and covered that position, holding it in an effort to allow Schwarzenberg time to escape. Schwarzenberg, knowing the importance of their position, ordered them to hold it to the last extremity and informed them that reinforcements were en route.

Vandamme's I Corps

During the night of 28/29 August the I Corps, according to GB Pelet, stood with Reuss' 2nd Brigade, 5th Division, in Hellendorf. Corbineau's 1st Light Cavalry Division and Gobrecht's 21st Light Cavalry Brigade, also stood in Hellendorf. The 1st Brigade, 42nd Division stood between Hellendorf and Gottaleube to the right and on the main road. Pouchelon's 1st Brigade, 1st Division, stood in Gieshübel and Giesenstein. Fezensac's 2nd Brigade, 1st Division, stood in Gottaleube. Dumonceau's 2nd Division stood in Gieshibel, with the 2nd Brigade towards Langenhennersdorf. Creuzer's 2nd Brigade, 42nd Division stood towards Gabel, to the right of BerGieshübel. Quiot's 2nd Brigade, 23rd Division, stood to the rear, between Bergieshübel and Langenhennersdorf.[27]

These positions are uncertain because Vandamme had with him, on the morning of 29 August, only the two brigades of Reuss and Pouchelon and his cavalry.

The village of Peterswalde stretched along the main road for approximately two miles, with many roads crossing the main road. Vandamme, wishing to avoid a direct assault, moved to turn the village. At nightfall, the previous night, he had sent part of his cavalry towards Kaitza.

Württemberg had noticed this, and the Russian Guard began to withdraw at 5:00 a.m., to move into the Teplitz valley. The provision of a rearguard was left to the Russian 2nd Corps. To prevent being surprised, Helfreich's forces were to take a position in the small woods to the south of Peterswalde. Schachafskoy was to take his Russian 3rd Division at 11:00 a.m., to a position to the north of the village and to post it behind the houses. GM Knorring was to remain in Peterswalde with the Tartar Uhlan Regiment. He was to keep patrols out on the flanks and rear of the withdrawing Russians. He was also ordered to depart at daybreak and to join Schachafskoy.

Württemberg established his headquarters in Peterswalde with his two brigades. On rising three hours later he moved to the edge of the village, where he discovered that Schachafskoy was not in the appointed position. Thinking that they had overshot the mark and joined Helfreich, Württemberg suggested to Yermolov that the Guard should also retire. They moved out at 4:30 a.m.

Schachafskoy's column did not re-join Helfreich until the break of day. He arrived, leading the Mourmon Regiment, and informed Württemberg that an officer had arrived the previous night ordering him to build large fires to impress the French and to not withdraw unless he was attacked.[28]

As Württemberg watched Schachafskoy's 3rd Division, he saw not a formed division, but a mass of fugitives, who had been struck repeatedly by the French cavalry in the flank and pressed frontally by French infantry, as they passed through Peterswalde. The earlier rout of the Tartar Uhlans by the French cavalry and their disorganized retreat through the division had caused the disorder and caused Schachafskoy's division to lose 1,040 prisoners.

Fortunately for Schachafskoy, Helfreich's forces remained firm, and his rabble was able to shelter behind Helfreich. The French cavalry were not strong enough to break Helfreich, and fell back before the Prinz Leopold's cuirassiers and Knorring's cavalry.

Yermolov detached Krapovitzki's Guard brigade to the Nollendorf chapel to support the Russian 2nd Corps. Colonel Ivanov, who passed through Schönewalde, waited there with the Revel, Tschernigov and Mourmon Infantry Regiments and the 4th Jager Regiment. Only GM Puschnitzki and Oberst Wolf had not yet re-joined Württemberg. They had become lost after crossing the Schönewalde and had taken the road to Teplitz through Graupen. They did not re-join Württemberg until the night of 29 August.[29]

Krapovitzki left his jagers in the village, while the rest of the brigade formed behind the chapel, with strong battery placed before them. Reuss' brigade was given the duty of pushing the Russians out of their position, and though it succeeded, the cost was high. The Prince de Reuss was killed and the French attack stopped.[30]

Württemberg profited by this halt of about two hours to draw in the Guard brigade. Once the fog had cleared, Württemberg evacuated his positions, and as he did so, he saw many columns of French moving to the attack.

Vandamme arrived before Kulm at noon. For Vandamme the situation was difficult. The forces disposable to him immediately consisted solely of his advanced guard, Reuss' brigade. The remainder of his forces were strung out along the mountain roads and it would take several hours for them to catch up.

13

The Battle of Kulm
29 August–5 September 1813

Kulm lies in a valley on the southern face of the Erzgebirg mountain chain. The two roads entering the valley pass down steep grades, 12% or more, along the heavily wooded slopes of the mountain ridge and burst rather suddenly into the valley where Kulm lies.

Across this undulating valley are a number of substantial hills. Three large circular hills lie around the village of Kulm, the largest of which is surmounted by a villa and surrounded by a heavy beech forest. This prominence rises about 100 feet above the valley floor and can be seen from all points of the valley. Before it are two more hills, rising to a height of no more than 60 feet from the valley floor. To the south, about two miles from Kulm lay a larger prominence, the rolling Strisowitz Heights which stretch in an oblong shape towards the Elbe. Its northern and southern ends were heavily wooded and quite steep, while its waist, along an east-west line, was a steep, yet open pasture. Across the top of the Strisowitz Heights stretched an open pasture.

The main road runs from the eastern defile past Arbesau, though Kulm, past Straden and Priesten, and on to the west. As it comes out of the defile it drops steeply, but once on the valley floor it is relatively level, passing over only a few gently rolling fingers that extend into the valley, towards the south.

Ostermann-Tolstoy and Württemberg had established their forces on a line from Straden, Priesten and Karwitz, with a rearguard detachment in Kulm. They had decided to delay the French advance until Schwarzenberg's forces had time to clear the mountains to their rear.

The middle of the Russian position, commanded by Duke Eugène of Württemberg, was built around the village of Priesten. Behind Priesten were the two battalions of the Tschernigov Infantry Regiment of Wolff's brigade, Treffurth's brigade, consisting of the Minsk and Tobolsk Regiments, and Ivanov's force from the advanced guard, consisting of the Revel Infantry Regiment and the 4th Jager Regiment, which had been detached earlier from Treffurth's brigade. This force was formed in columns and stood under the command of GM Schachafskoy, commander of the Russian 3rd Division.[1]

To the left of Schachafskoy stood Helfreich's detachment of the 14th Division, consisting of the Tenginsk and Estonia Infantry Regiments and the Grand Duchess Catherine Infantry Battalion. In front of Helfreich's forces stood the batteries of Colonel Baikov (Light Battery #27) and Lt. Colonel Czeremissinov (Position Battery #14), a total of 23 guns.

The left wing was under GL Yermolov. His forces were deployed on the mountain's edge. Yermolov's forces consisted of the bulk of the 1st Russian Guard Division under GM von Rosen. They were arranged with Potemkin's brigade (Preobragenski and Semenovski Guard Infantry Regiments) and Krapovitzsky's brigade (Ismailov Guard Infantry Regiment) in the front line. Before them stood the Guard Light Foot Battery #1 and the Guard Heavy Battery #2, 24 guns.

The Russian Guard Hussars, under Colonel Davidov (4 squadrons) were posted behind the Guard Infantry. The Guard Jager Regiment from Krapovitzsky's brigade, and the Murmon Infantry Regiment, from Wolff's brigade, 2nd Corps, stood with a few guns facing the main road, on a small hill by Priesten. They were commanded by GM Bistrom I.

The Russian Imperial Guard at Kulm, 29 August.

The right wing consisted mostly of cavalry, and included the Guard Horse Battery #1 of Lt. Colonel von Bistrom (12 guns). This wing extended from the Reichstrasse (Imperial Road) by Priesten to the Hafen Mill by Karwitz. Bistrom's battery stood straddling the road.

Next to Bistrom's guns stood Knorring's Tartar Uhlan Regiment (4 squadrons). Behind them, in a second line, stood two squadrons of the Austrian Erzherzog Johann Dragoon Regiment under Oberst Jakob von Suck. To the right of the Tartar Uhlans stood the Empress Cuirassier Regiment (4 squadrons) under the command of GM Prince Leopold von Sachsen-Coburg. Behind them were two squadrons of the Loubny Hussar Regiment and two squadrons of the Serpuchov Uhlan Regiment. On the extreme right wing stood the Illowaiski XII Cossack Regiment with five sotnias. The entire right wing was commanded by GL Prince Dimitri Galitzin.[2]

Ostermann-Tolstoy, by G. Dawe.

Shortly afterward the Russian Guard Uhlan and Guard Dragoon Regiments arrived from the hills by Priesten. The uhlans joined Bistrom's detachment and the dragoons joined the Guard Hussars behind the Guard Infantry.

On the afternoon of 29 August, the Russian Guard numbered about 6,700 men, while the line forces under Württemberg, totaled about 5,500 men. The artillery and cavalry, including the Guard Uhlans and Guard Dragoons, totaled about 2,000 men, giving the allies a force of around 14,000 men.

Colloredo's corps, which led the withdrawing allied columns moving from Ebersdorf, arrived in Geyersberg at 1:00 p.m. He was the first of the Austrian forces, which had been ordered to concentrate there, to arrive.

About 11:00 a.m., the Russian Guard Horse Battery #1 began to return fire from a French battery located on the heights before Kulm. Vandamme, seeing the steady stream of Austrians arriving believed that Victor, Marmont, and Murat were in hot pursuit, and assuming that he would shortly be supported by their forces, did not hesitate to attack with the troops at hand, that is to say Reuss' small brigade, now commanded by GB Revest. Revest's brigade moved forward against Straden, heavily attacking GM von Bistrom's forces.[3]

Corbineau's 1st Light Cavalry Division was sent to the left of the road, left near Karwitz, while Gobrecht's 21st Light Cavalry Brigade stood before Kulm, straddling the main road, to contain the Russian cavalry.[4] Despite documents that state to the contrary, Vandamme's 12pdr battery was not yet present.[5]

The French pressure against the Russian line was heavy. The Russian batteries of Bistrom (Guard Horse Battery #1) and Baikov (Light Battery #27) were attacked by one French column and were in

Vandamme.

serious danger of being overrun. Yermolov responded to Bistrom's distress by sending forward the Ismailov Guard Infantry Regiment, in two closed columns, to execute a bayonet counterattack that drove Revest's Brigade back momentarily. GM Krapovitzskv was wounded in this attack.[6] Once the French troops recovered their balance, they once again advanced on the now burning village of Straden driving Bistrom I from the village. The Semenovski Guard Infantry Regiment, which stood on the left of the village, was also struck again, but Yermolov sent forward 2½ battalions of the Preobragenski Guard Infantry Regiment to support them. The Russian Guard stood like a rock in the surf, with the French attacks dashing against it to no avail, and once again the French fell back. Two French battalions moved to the wooded Klöck Mill Heights, which stood behind the Russian position, and began firing on the Russians. Surrounded by enemy fire, the Russians found themselves obliged to withdraw, surrendering Straden to the French, but advancing through them with an unstoppable bayonet charge and the roar of a thousand enraged guardsmen.

Revest then sought to move through Priesten, which would allow him to overlook the Imperial Road. The attack came between the Klöck Mill and Priesten, striking a line formed by Russian line and Guard infantry. Schachafskoy counterattacked with the Revel, Minsk and 4th Jager Regiments, supported by the batteries of Baikov (Light Battery #27) and Czeremissinov (Position Battery #14).[7] Revest's attack on Priesten did not succeed and he was thrown back.

At 2:00 p.m., Revest's brigade fell back and reorganized. Shortly afterward, about 3:00 p.m., Philippon arrived with his two brigades. GB Pouchelon's 1st Brigade, 1st Division arrived and was immediately dispatched against the Russian line.[8] Part of his brigade, the 12th Line, advanced through Straden, against the Russian lines behind it to support Mouton-Duvernet's 42nd Division. The other part, Fezensac's 2nd Brigade, advanced against Priesten.

Not waiting for his entire force to be present, Philippon ordered forward the 1/17th Line Regiment. Fezensac complained in vain that it was futile to send forward such untried solders against a prepared enemy, but Philippon prevailed. All four battalions, which had finally arrived, of the 17th Line advanced and were pushed back, each in their turn. They pushed forward again and seized a toehold in the village of Priesten, but were counterattacked by the 4th Jagers, and the Minsk and Revel Infantry Regiments.

As the Russians counterattacked, the rest of GB Montesquiou-Fezensac's, 2nd Brigade, 1st Division, marched onto the field.[9] Unfortunately, this timely arrival of reinforcements was not enough to allow the French to seize Priesten. The 17th fell back again.[10]

Württemberg took advantage of this fight to move the batteries of Baikov (Light Battery #27) and Czeremissinov (Position Battery #14) to the west of Priesten. Here, protected by the terrain from the French guns in Kulm, they fired on the French columns attempting to turn the Russian left by skirting through the woods.

A grinding battle began between Priesten and the Klöck Mill. The French advanced again and overran Priesten, only to be driven back by murderous Russian artillery fire as they advanced out of the village. By 4:00 p.m., the village was in flames and once again stormed by the Russians.

To hold the village, Württemberg posted the batteries of Baikov and Czeremissinov by it. They quickly became involved in a counterbattery action with the French artillery posted between Straden and Kulm, under the command of General Baltus, the I Corps artillery commander.[11]

The battle in the center now settled down to an artillery duel. On the Russian left, the French sent forward a large force of skirmishers between Straden and the Sernitzbach stream, moving towards Karwitz. They pushed steadily forward, pushing the Russian cavalry before them. Eventually, around 4:00 p.m., they began a fight in the village of Karwitz and the village was set afire.[12]

As the day advanced, the Russian Guard Uhlans and Hussars, and the single Austrian regiment, two squadrons of the Erzherzog Johann Dragoon Regiment, were joined by the 1st and 2nd Russian Cuirassier Divisions.[13] This force of cavalry was posted on the right wing of the Russian line behind Karwitz. About 2:00 p.m., Ostermann-Tolstoy was struck and seriously wounded in the left arm by a cannon shot. His command then passed to General Yermolov.

At 5:00 p.m., Dumonceau's 2nd Division began to appear on the field. Vandamme was convinced, by this time, that he could not force the Russian left, and turned again to strike their center. He sent the 7th Légère forward against the batteries of the 2nd Corps. They marched into a storm of shot. Lt. Colonel Czeremissinov, the commander of Position Battery #14, was wounded. The battery itself came close to being captured, but was saved by the actions of part of a battalion from the Preobragenski Guard Infantry Regiment.

At this moment, GM Baron Diebitsch,[14] of GdI Barclay de Tolly's staff, arrived to announce that the 1st Russian Grenadier Division, the 2nd Russian Guard Division, and the Prussian Guard were about to arrive on the battlefield, as was Barclay himself.[15]

Shortly after this, two cuirassier regiments of the Russian 3rd Cuirassier Division, under the command of GM Schevich, moved through Priesten

Diebitsch.

and closed on the French lines. At the same time Diebitsch, at the head of the Guard Dragoon Regiment, charged directly at the French line. As the Russian Guard Dragoons ran down one French regiment, the Guard Uhlans, led by Prince Karl von Hessen-Philippstal, struck the French right in a combined attack with the cuirassiers. Though the attack succeeded and the French fell back, the cavalry suffered heavy losses. Prince Karl was knocked from his horse, 14 officers were either killed or wounded in the Uhlans. Diebitsch lost two of his adjutants.

The French infantry fired on the Russians, inflicting heavy casualties on the Guard Dragoons and the other two Guard cavalry regiments. The French withdrew slightly after the Russian Guard cavalry's attack, and began to prepare for a new attack.[16]

The Russian Chevalier Guard, the Horse Guard and the Leib Guard Regiments (1st Guard Cuirassier Division) arrived on the field and placed themselves to the right of the Russian 3rd Cuirassier Division. The Russians did not pursue their success. They were stopped by a battery of 24 guns that General Baltus established between Kulm and Straden, as well as by the fire of the French skirmishers in the edge of the wood to the north east of the Sernitz ravine.

Once the Russian 1st Grenadier Division was on the field it advanced into the front line and took the position of the Russian 1st Guard Division. The Russian Guard Light Cavalry Division took up a position behind their left flank. The Russian 2nd Corps and the 1st and 2nd Cuirassier Divisions held the Russian center. The remaining light cavalry and the two squadrons of the Erzherzog Johann Regiment stood under GM Knorring on the right flank. The Tenginsk Infantry Regiment occupied Karwitz.[17]

About 6:00 p.m., Barclay de Tolly and GdI Miloradovich arrived on the battlefield, relieving Württemberg of command of Ostermann-Tolstoy's force. A little later, Schwarzenberg, the army commander arrived in Priesten.

Vandamme, seeing his piecemeal attacks were failing, then decided that it would be preferable to wait until he could amass a larger force. He organized his line along the heights of Kulm, on a dominant position, from which his forces easily resisted the Russian counterattacks. The Russians had fully re-established their line between Straden, Priesten, and Karwitz.

Vandamme resolved to hold Kulm and became more and more convinced that the allies were soon to be attacked in the rear by the pursuing French corps. That evening he again received orders to continue his march on Teplitz and during the 30th he would execute that order.[18]

As the allied troops filed into the Kulm area, Schwarzenberg positioned them behind Priesten and Karwitz. He was concerned about Kleist, who had been cut off from Barclay's corps during the retreat and moved to the road to Fürstenwalde. Kleist commanded the only corps that remained north of the mountains and Schwarzenberg left him to cross the mountains, where he could.

Kleist.

The Second Day of Kulm

Except for Kleist, on the morning of 30 August, Schwarzenberg had his entire army at his disposal. The Austrian divisions of Colloredo-Mansfeld (1st Line Division) and Bianchi (2nd Reserve) arrived during the night and assumed positions between Dux and Teplitz. The troops they commanded were exhausted from their march over the Erzgebirg and would be of little value until they had rested.

Vandamme had his left in Bohmisch-Neudorf, covered by Corbineau. His center was in Kulm and his right was in Straden. He no longer had the strength to occupy Geyersdorf and left it unoccupied. Nollendorf was unoccupied, as was Tellnitz, for he was convinced that Mortier was coming from Pirna with the Young Guard.

During the night he too had received some reinforcements. Dunesme's 1st Brigade, 2nd Division, arrived.[19] Dunesme was followed by Doucet's 2nd Brigade, 2nd Division,[20] Creutzer's Brigade, 42nd Division,[21] and then the 42nd Division's artillery arrived.[22]

Vandamme had totally united his forces early during the evening of 29 August. The French position was arranged such that their center was on the heights between Kulm and Priesten, straddling the Reichstrasse. Quiot's brigade (6 battalions) formed the first line and Revest's Brigade (6 battalions) formed the second line. In Kulm were two battalions of Creutzer's brigade, 42nd Division.[23] Behind Kulm, between the Reichstrasse and the Erzgebirg, stood Doucet's Brigade, 2nd Division, with 5 battalions.

The right wing was formed by Philippon's 1st Division (14 battalions) and the remainder of Mouton-Duvernet's 42nd Division. The 42nd Division was to the right of Straden and in the Geiersberg woods. The 1st Division stood with the brigades of Pouchelon and Montesquiou-Fezensac closed in two ranks. They were behind Straden and very close to the woods.[24] Before them stood the mass of the I Corps artillery. To the right of the road, and somewhat forward, extending to the woods at the foot of the mountain, were three battalions from Creutzer's Brigade and four battalions of the other brigade of Mounton-Duvernet's 42nd Division.

The left wing was formed by Dunesme's brigade, 2nd Division (8 battalions), two brigades of Corbineau's 1st Light Cavalry Division (15 squadrons) and Gobrecht's 21st Light Cavalry Brigade (4 squadrons). Dunesme's brigade was dispersed across the Wappiage, the Schützenhohe Heights and behind Eisenberg. A horse battery stood on his extreme left.[25] Also, the western portion of the Strisowitz Hill was defended with infantry. Before Dunesme stood Corbineau's 1st Light Cavalry Division, formed in echelons on the level ground west of Karwitz. Gobrecht's 21st Light Cavalry Brigade stood behind Dunesme's brigade and guarded Vandamme's headquarters.[26]

The artillery of the 42nd Division stood behind the left wing somewhat pulled back. That of the 1st Division stood on the two hill tops south of Kulm. Dumonceau had left his artillery in the park, with the exception of four guns that remained with Doucet's brigade.

The reserve artillery park moved under the escort of a squadron of Gobrecht's brigade and arrived at 6:30 a.m. The 12pdr battery was dispatched to the position at Wappiage and the horse battery dispatched there earlier, moved to Horkaberg, while two 6pdr batteries moved north of Kulm to act as a reserve.[27] The French forces consisted of 48 battalions, 18 squadrons and about 11 batteries. In round figures, 39,000 men, 3,000 cavalry and 82 guns.

Earlier, during his advance on Nollendorf, Vandamme had detached a battalion of the 57th from Doucet's brigade, 1st Division, with 300 sappers and two guns to Aussig in order to establish a strong defensive position to support his rear. This was in conformance with orders from Napoleon to do so. It occupied the village without resistance, chasing out the two infantry battalions and two cannons that had garrisoned it. At 5:00 p.m., on evening of 28/29 August Vandamme had detached the 6/9th Légère and the 32nd Light Cavalry Brigade of 400 men under GB Creutzer to Aussig as well.[28] Also detached to Aussig from the 42nd Division were the 22nd Provisional Demi-Brigade with the 2/4th and 3/12th Légère, and the 2/, 3/76th Line Regiment.

Of the 14,000 Russian that had faced Vandamme the day before, 6,000, not including artillerists and train, were dead or wounded. The Semenovski Regiment had lost 900 men, Preobragenski had lost 700, Ismailov had lost 500 and the Guard Jagers had lost 600 men. Württemberg's corps had suffered similar losses, with Helfreich's force losing 2,400 infantry and 800 cavalry.[29]

The arrival of the two Austrian divisions would radically change the situation from the day before. They had a total of 25 battalions with 18,845 men. With them were approximately 534

Austrian cavalry and six batteries with approximately 45 guns. This would bring the total of the allied forces in the battle to 79 battalions, 82 squadrons and 14½ batteries, with approximately 41,000 men, 10,000 cavalry, and 136 guns.

As Schwarzenberg was present on the battlefield, he and his chief of staff, GM Count Radetzky, handled the disposition of the day's battle. The Austrian divisions of Colloredo (1st Line Division) and Bianchi (2nd Reserve Division), and Sorbenburg's cavalry brigade were placed under Barclay's orders.

The allies had reorganized their line such that their left flank stood on the mountain near the Klöck Mill and Juchtenkapelle. This flank was formed by the 1st Russian Grenadier Division of GL Raevsky's 3rd (Grenadier) Corps. They stood on the mountain, which ran from Eggenmuhle to Juchtenkapelle. On his right stood Mononoff's brigade,[30] 4th Division, 2nd Corps, under the orders of GM Pischnitzky. Behind them, in Theresienfeld, stood the Austrian 3rd Cuirassier Division under GM Duka, with part of the Austrian Kaiser Cuirassiers, and the Austrian infantry brigade of P. Hessen-Homburg.[31] The entire flank was commanded by Count Dimitri Galitzin V.[32]

The Russian center stood in and behind Priesten. The rest of the 2nd Corps, Helfreich's 14th Division and the Loubny Hussars held this position, supported by the 2nd Russian Guard Division under GM Udom, which stood behind them. In addition, behind the infantry was the Russian Guard Light Cavalry Division consisting of the Guard Hussars, Guard Uhlans, Guard Dragoons, with the Loubny Hussars, and the Serpuchov Uhlan Regiment attached.

To the right, between Priesten and Karwitz, stood the 1st and 2nd Russian Cuirassier Divisions under Grand Duke Constantine. GdI Miloradovich commanded the Russian center.

The right wing, which stood between Karwitz and Strisowitz Mountain was commanded by FZM Graf Colloredo-Mansfeld. The first line was formed by the Russian Emperor Cuirassier Regiment, Tartar Uhlans, Illowaiski XII Cossacks, and four guns from Horse Battery #3 under the command of GM Knorring. The second line was formed with Colloredo's 1st Line Division and Bianchi's 2nd Reserve Division formed the reserve or third line.[33] This force was supported by the Austrian Erzherzog Johann Dragoon Regiment, three batteries of Austrian artillery under Major Gepert (18 guns), which stood by Colloredo's division, and Bianchi's

Miloradovich.

divisional artillery. The 1st Russian Guard Division, because of its losses, had been pulled out of the line and stood to the rear, by Sobochleben as a reserve.[34]

The allied plan for the battle on the 30th was to hold the left flank on the defense, while the center was to pin the French in position and Colloredo, with the right wing, was to envelop the French left wing and strike towards the mountains. The battle was to begin when Kleist appeared in Tellnitz.

In the gray morning, Barclay's chief of staff Diebitsch and GM Toll reconnoitered the French positions and returned to have a war conference with Barclay and King Friedrich Wilhelm III. The result of this meeting was the decision to move around the French left wing and strike them from the mountain and then crush them against the slopes with the advancing Russian forces, who would advance frontally. They also believed there was a chance that they might join with Kleist's Prussian 2nd Corps that was moving in their direction from Nollendorf.[35]

The following orders were issued:

The arrival of von Kleist at Kulm, by Becker.

Colloredo's Division shall move from Sobochleben to the right and move behind the ridge to the heights to the right of Karwitz. Once behind these heights he shall conceal and organize himself. Bianchi's Division shall move a brigade behind the Sobochleben heights and estab-lish it there as a reserve to support Colloredo. As soon as Bianchi is in position, GM Knorring shall attack the heights between Neudorf and Karwitz with his cavalry and horse artillery. Colloredo's Division shall advance behind him in two columns, one moving to the far side of the heights, the other moving to the right up the Neudorf valley. Bianchi's division shall immediately place itself on the Karwitz heights and position its artillery there. Colloredo's artillery shall move to the point of high ground to support the advancing column, and to a position on the heights between Neudorf and Deutsch-Neudorf in order to take the road from Nollendorf under fire. As soon as the Austrian columns are in the rear of the French line, depending on the information received about the enemy's movements, the Russian troops shall strike the French from all sides and throw them into the defiles. GM Knorring will follow the orders of FML Colloredo.[36]

At 6:00 a.m., Colloredo's corps began moving against Sobochleben, as ordered, moving to the right behind the heights by Karwitz. At 7:00 a.m., the battle erupted on the Allied left wing. French had acted before the allies could fully form their defenses and assumed the offensive. Mouton-Duvernet pushed forward his guns on the right flank through the thickly wooded slopes. The French attack advanced with surprising vehemence and quickly turned into a close, bitter battle. The numerous wounded dragged themselves to shelter. Many pulled themselves to the closest solid building, which was the Klöck Mill. Unfortunately, the mill came under the fire of the French artillery, which set the mill afire, killing them and burying them under the mill's flaming ruins.[37]

Death gained a plentiful bounty, especially from the two Russian regiments, Volhynie and Krementchug. They suffered heavy losses from the fire of the French 42nd Division's artillery. The dead and wounded lay fallen in their ranks. The favorable posting of the French cannons allowed their enfilading fire to continue inflicting heavy losses on the Russians, until the Russians finally dragged a few cannon into position. The fire of these guns distracted the French artillery from firing on the Russian infantry. Despite this success, the battery of the Russian 1st Grenadier Division was able, only with the greatest effort, to hold its own against the French artillery.

The situation on the left wing was becoming critical, as the two regiments of the Russian 2nd Corps were scarcely able to hold their position. Help was coming.

About 8:00 a.m., the lead elements of the two Austrian divisions arrived at Sobochleben and began moving towards Karwitz. FML Bianchi detached P.Hessen-Homburg's Brigade, composed of the Hiller and H. Colloredo Infantry Regiments, by Sobochleben as a reserve for the weakening allied left wing.[38] P. Hessen-Homburg soon assumed a position nearer the mountain and advanced through the village of Marschen. During this march, the Austrian regiments passed under the fire of the French artillery posted by Straden. Hessen-Homburg quickly sent his brigade battery to a position by the Russian batteries, to return fire.[39]

The suffering of the Volhynie and Krementchug Regiments and the 1st Grenadier Division lasted from 9:00 and 10:00 a.m. About 10:00 a.m., Barclay de Tolly sought to prevent the French attack by executing a counterattack. This would be an attack by the Austrian brigade against the French right flank.

Prinz P.Hessen-Homburg immediately formed his brigade for the attack, in response to Barclay's orders. In his first line he posted the 2/Hiller Infantry Regiment. It was formed in three attack columns. Behind it was the 1/Hiller Infantry Regiment in support. The second line was formed by the H. Colloredo Regiment that formed the reserve. In addition, several detachments from both regiments were pulled together and sent up the wooded slope of the mountain in an effort to turn the French flank.

The Austrian attack moved against the French in *angriffskolonnen* or "attack columns" in an effort to gain ground and time. The Austrian attack, joined by the Russians, succeeded in driving the French back across the Straden stream. Contenting himself, for the time being, with this success on the left flank, Barclay returned to his original plan, and for the next few hours, allowed the left flank to devolve into a delaying battle.

The Austrian Flank Attack

About this time Colloredo's regiments began arriving in the positions from which they were to begin the attack against the French left flank. FML Colloredo moved his division to the east of Sobochieben and moved it forward in two columns over the plain towards Karwitz. Colloredo hurried in advance, in order to reconnoiter the French positions. He recognized immediately, the weakness of the French forces on the Strisowitz Heights. He decided to lead his attack against them, using a flanking maneuver to the east that promised an easy victory.

At this time GM Sorbenburg, with the Erzherzog Johann Dragoon Regiment, drew a division (2 squadrons) from the Kaiser Cuirassier regiment and sent it forward on a reconnaissance towards Aussig. The second division of the regiment had not yet arrived on the battlefield.[40]

This decision to attack essentially contradicted the overall battle plan, which Colloredo had received. Therefore he had to seek the approval of its execution from Barclay. Barclay sent GM Toll with his response. He approved the attack, but on the condition that at least one brigade must continue with the task originally assigned to the entire division and march behind the Russian cavalry over the plain against the "Wappiage."

As the French saw the advance of the Austrian troops against Karwitz, they became apprehensive that the position of the Corps would be cut off, by what was developing as an attack against their left wing. In order to gain time to shift reserves to the left, Vandamme ordered a demonstration designed to delay the advance of the allies. He ordered a horse battery, covered by a few battalions of the 13th Légère Regiment, to the high points south of the Wappiage and from there to move against Karwitz, to take the Austrian columns under fire.[41]

This demonstration reduced Colloredo's fears of a French counter attack against his march columns. However, in order to counter any such move, the leading regiment of the left column, the Czartoryski Infantry Regiment, was directed to occupy Karwitz. One battalion deployed on the northern edge of the burning village, the second was behind them as a reserve.[42]

The second regiment of Kolb's Brigade, the de Ligne Regiment, covered by the defense of Karwitz, continued its march against Hierbitz. It followed Abele's Brigade past Karwitz, marching to the heights, east of the village, so it could complete its task of serving the Russian cavalry as an infantry reserve. Chiesa's Brigade, on the other hand, marched farther on the same heights with the de Ligne Regiment.

Abele's Brigade and the eight battalions of Bianchi's division were now moved onto the rising ground by Karwitz, where they were to act as a reserve. With seven battalions and the Erzherzog Johann Dragoon Regiment, Colloredo passed over the Herbitz and moved against the Strisowitz heights from which they could take the French left from behind. Vandamme had not occupied these heights because of the weakness of his overall force. A heavy artillery duel began.

Austrian infantry storm the heights of Striesswitz at the Battle of Kulm, 30 August.

Behind Colloredo's 1st Line Division came two brigades of Bianchi's 2nd Reserve Division, those of Mariassy and Quallenberg. About 10:00 a.m., they assumed a reserve position southeast of Karwitz.

Having arrived by Hierbitz, Colloredo formed his seven battalions for the attack. The de Ligne Regiment climbed the Strisowitz Heights in three columns, behind a skirmish line formed from dispersed companies. Chiesa's Brigade followed as a reserve. The Erzherzog Johann Dragoon Regiment advanced along the Neudorf Stream, to assure the liaison between Abele and Colloredo.[43] The four battalions of Abele's Brigade marched in support of the cavalry between Karwitz and Bohmisch-Neudorf. Behind them, in reserve were the eight battalions of Bianchi's division.[44]

The rest of Bianchi's division marched behind Colloredo as a reserve. As soon as Bianchi was in position, Knorring's cavalry and horse artillery began to attack the heights between Neudorf and Karwitz. Colloredo's division followed quickly behind the cavalry, formed in two columns.

It was about 9:30 a.m., as both attacks groups began their advance. GM Knorring dispatched his cavalry and four horse guns to counter the French horse battery and its supporting infantry, to the northeast of Karwitz. This force consisted of the Russian Empress Cuirassier Regiment, under Prinz Leopold von Sachsen-Coburg, the Tartar Uhlan Regiment, and the Illowaiski #12 Cossack Regiment. The Russian horse artillery deployed and began firing on Dumonceau's flank.

The collision of the attacking Russian cavalry was so tremendous, that three guns were lost and a battalion of the 13th Légère was crushed, as it tried to cover the battery. The two regiments of Dunesme's brigade formed themselves in square to resist the cavalry. Unfortunately the allied attack lacked infantry, which would have allowed the position to be occupied and held. Soon Heimrodt's 3rd Light Cavalry Brigade (1st Light Cavalry Division), which stood in the French second line, threw itself against the Empress Cuirassier Regiment, driving it and its companion regiments back to Karwitz. The pursuit stopped as the French cavalry came within range of Knorring's horse artillery and Abele's infantry, which had advanced slightly.[45]

Bianchi's division then moved onto the heights by Karwitz and placed its artillery on the heights, while Colloredo placed his artillery on the heights between Bohmisch-Neudorf and Deutsch-Neudorf. At the same time, the Russian center launched a frontal assault on the French lines, pinning them in place.[46]

When Dunesme recognized the threat, he drew the 25th Line Regiment from his reserves, and sent it forward to counter the Austrian move. It did not stop to fully deploy for battle and immediately threw itself, with lowered bayonets, against Watterich's battalion. The Austrians were thrown back down the slope by the fury of the attack. The French reordered themselves and pulled back behind the "Wappiage." Kolb's Brigade battery advanced to Böhmisch-Neudorf and opened fire against Dumonceau's divisional artillery. The two other battalions of the de Ligne Regiment, and the Chiesa Brigade, advanced under Colloredo's leadership. They moved from the heights towards Auschine and took a position to the south of this village.[47]

In the center and right, the I Corps held firmly, resisting the allied advances, but remained immobile until the right wing had begun its move. A furious battle erupted with the main French attacks coming there. P. Hessen-Homburg's brigade, the Austrian brigade held in reserve, was called forward to stem the French onslaught.

Vandamme sent Quiot's brigade towards Deutsch-Neudorf, to slow the Austrian turning movement. They arrived in columns, but when they discovered themselves facing Russian cavalry, the six battalions formed themselves into three squares. These squares were supported by four guns. Quiot's brigade succeeded in stopping Colloredo's attack.

At the same time Abele's Austrian brigade moved out of Karwitz. The Austrian Erbach Regiment (#42) led the advance. Despite heavy losses, and with the support of the Argenteau Infantry Regiment, the Erbach Regiment waded through the Sernitzbach Stream, throwing the French back.

Vandamme had finally received word of the threatened envelopment of the left wing. To counter this he sent Doucet's brigade, which had earlier been northwest of Kulm, in the direction of the Strisowitz Heights. As the brigade arrived on the heights of the Kulm Castle Park, the 25th Line Regiment was thrown back in disorder to those heights, and at the same time strong allied columns were observed marching in that direction. Doucet feared being attacked at any minute. He quickly formed his five battalions into three strong columns, placing four guns in the intervals, and awaited the pending allied attack with his front facing southeast behind the Tellnitz Stream.

The withdrawal of the 25th Line Regiment and the fire of the Russian battery by Karwitz and the Austrian brigade battery by Böhmisch-Neudorf, steadily reduced the ability of Dunesme's brigade to hold its position on the Wappiage. Dunesme knew that he could not hold his position on these heights, once the Allies chose to push hard, and began slowly pulling his troops backwards. As this withdrawal began, about 10:00 a.m., GM Knorring seized the opportunity and renewed his cavalry attacks, this time attacking a French battery.[48]

Corbineau's 1st Light Cavalry Division counterattacked and drove him back. With Knorring driven back, the entire force of French cavalry moved against the Erbach Regiment.[49] The Erbach Regiment defended itself valiantly and drove the French cavalry back with devastating fire.

Despite this, the French position on the Wappiage was no longer tenable, as behind Knorring's cavalry, Abele's brigade advanced at the "*angriffschritt.*" Dunesme was pulled back from the heights, and withdrew his troops to the southeast of Kulm, where he occupied the small hill crest in the Castle Park. Dunesme then detached some of his guns to the left flank by Arbesau, which Colloredo's movement seemed to threaten the most.

Knorring, having regrouped his cavalry, advanced again against the French with Abele's Brigade. At the same time, the Austrian Erzherzog Johann Dragoon Regiment attacked from the right, taking the French counterattack in the flank and rear and driving the French back. An Austrian battery quickly unlimbered and began to take the French masses under fire with canister. Corbineau received a head wound and was taken from the battle during this exchange.

Corbineau was unable to stop the allied advance, and Vandamme's left wing was, little by little, enveloped by the Russian squadrons marching on Arbesau. The 3/, 4/85th Line Regiment, part of Quiot's Brigade, 23rd Division temporarily, attached to the 2nd Division, stood somewhat isolated. The 3/85th vanished in a mass of charging cavalry. Its commander, Chef de Bataillon Saint-Ange Chapuis, held his beleaguered battalion together, and with cries of "Vive l'Empereur" they drove the Russians away.[50] Vandamme moved to Arbesau to control the situation directly and brought with him the 8/2nd Foot Artillery.

The evacuation of the Wappiage by Dunesme allowed Abele's Brigade, screened by the Erzherzog Johann Dragoon Regiment, to occupy the position. They held the heights strongly. The assault had been supported by a half battery, held farther back and later pushed forward to a favorable position on the west to support Abele's attack.

Once the heights were occupied, the Russians sent some artillery to join Abele's half battery, and once combined, they opened a murderous fire against the new French position.

The capture of the Wappiage, released the Czartoryski Regiment from the requirement that it continue to occupy Karwitz. Since it was superfluous in its earlier position, Colloredo issued the order for it to advance and re-join its division.[51]

The two brigades of Bianchi's division still remained behind as a reserve. Schwarzenberg joined Bianchi, who defended Colloredo's actions in contravention of the original battle plan, which had bent him far to the east. Schwarzenberg was, however, apprehensive that Knorring and Abele's attack could fail. As a result, Feldmarschal Schwarzenberg ordered Bianchi "Follow Colloredo while he goes over the Strisowitz heights. GM Knorring will shortly succumb unless he has Colloredo's support. Your division shall, therefore, immediately attack Vandamme's left flank."

However, before the division received the order to advance, Kleist's Prussian 2nd Corps appeared in the French rear, changing the course of the battle dramatically.[52]

With the advance of the Austrians and Russians from Karwitz and Deutsch-Neudorf the situation of the French was critical, but Vandamme still hoped for the arrival of Mortier. He did, however, begin to worry about his line of retreat and sent a strong detachment from his center, towards Arbesau and Tellnitz.

At noon, Revest's brigade advanced against Schandau between the road and the woods. Quiot's brigade turned about and attacked the left, while Dunesme's brigade marched on Ober-Arbesau. The 42nd Division, the 1st Division, and Doucet's Brigade defended the center of the French position, facing south. The first gun shots from Kleist's cannons sounded and the French thought it was a French force arriving to support them. The French trumpets blared, drums rolled, and the entire French army advanced to the attack.

However, word soon came as to the truth of the guns and Vandamme moved to Horka, and with General Haxo, began issuing the orders for the withdrawal of his artillery and train.

Kleist's Advance

Kleist's corps had begun its march from Fürstenwalde through Rudolsdorf and Streckenwald towards Nollendorf at 5:00 a.m. He led the brigades of Klüx (9th Brigade), Pirch (10th Brigade), von Jagow (11th Brigade), and Prince August von Preussen (12th Brigade), plus a reserve cavalry brigade, a mass of landwehr infantry and cavalry, three horse batteries and eight foot batteries giving him a total force of about 30,000 men.

GM Ziethen had been sent with three fusilier battalions, half the schützen battalion, a hussar regiment, a dragoon regiment, one foot and a half horse battery to Peterswald in order to cover the corps from a possible French attack from the direction of Hellendorf.

Between 10:00 and 11:00 a.m., the Silesian Hussar Regiment, supported by the schützen of the 1/, 2/7th Reserve Regiment, began their march towards Kulm in a column of platoons. Behind them, the three battalions of the 9th Brigade advanced as follows: the 1/, 3/6th Reserve Regiment, straddling the main road to Nollendorf, the Fus/1st West Prussian Regiment covering the right flank of the corps and standing on the Nollendorf-Tellnitz road to the west of the main road.

The 2/Brandenburg Cuirassier Regiment remained in Nollendorf to watch the road to Peterswald and to seek contact with Ziethen's advanced guard.

Oberst von Blücher, son of the general, and Adjutant von Voss led Kleist's advanced guard between Streckenwald and Nollendorf. En route they encountered what they initially took to be a Russian transport column. It was French and in the ensuing skirmish they captured 26 wagons and 120 horses. From the prisoners that were sent back to Kleist, he learned that Vandamme's Corps was ahead and heavily engaged with the allies around Kulm. Kleist quickly dispatched a squadron of cavalry to a post between Nollendorf and Jungferndorf. From there it could watch the road to Peterswald while he accelerated the march of his corps.[53]

Kleist Arrives on the Field

About noon his lead elements began arriving in Tellnitz. They encountered a French battalion supported by two guns. The Prussians, under Oberst Blücher, charged in column and drove the French away, taking a position on the plateau to the right of the road. Horse Battery #7 established itself to the right. The schützen moved into the wooded heights to the west.

Vandamme, standing by Nollendorf, quickly heard about the raid against the munitions trans-port, and of the appearance of an enemy column being encountered on the Nollendorf road. Vandamme's situation was disastrous. He was encircled.

Vandamme weakened his line to send a force back to face the Prussians. Doucet's Brigade was ordered to cover the left flank as long as possible. Under its fire, Dunesme was to lead the portion of his brigade still by Kulm, against Arbesau, in conjunction with Gobrecht's cavalry brigade. In addition to defending Unter-Arbesau, he was to expel the Prussians from Ober-Arbesau. The battle was slowly breaking up as the retreat progressed. The withdrawal was supported by a grand battery south of Kulm formed from the batteries of the 1st and 2nd Divisions and part of the reserve artil-lery under General Baltus. Heimrodt's 3rd Light Cavalry Brigade remained to the south of Kulm and covered that flank.

Vandamme sent his adjutant, von Königsegg, to GB Gobrecht with the order to attack this column and to clear the road. Gobrecht stood his 21st Light Cavalry Brigade to the north of Kulm on the road. He sent the Anhalt Jäger zu Pferd up the road, while he personally led the 9th Chevauléger-lancier Regiment to the east to strike the Prussian flank. They caught the Prussian hussars shortly after they fell upon the train escort in Schanda.

As the hussar regiment was disordered from its attack, they were unable to withstand the impact of the Chevauléger-lanciers, when at the same time the Anhalt Jagers attacked them frontally through the village. The attack succeeded perfectly and 50 hussars were killed or wounded. The hussars were thrown back and aggressively pursued by the Chevauléger-lanciers.

Just as Horse Battery #7 began to deploy, it was struck by the 9th Chevauléger-lancier Regiment, who captured three guns and drove the survivors of the battery away. The commanding officer of the 9th Chevauléger-lanciers fell mortally wounded. Gobrecht then found himself facing a heavy column of advancing Prussians. He sent an aide de camp back to Vandamme, with the word of the Prussian advance, asking for a battalion and a few guns to support him, but stating that he would fight to the death.[54] Vandamme ordered Gobrecht to hold out and sent him a reinforcement. This battalion and a half battery quickly joined him.[55]

Pirch broke his forces into columns by section to traverse Tellnitz, and the 2/7th Reserve Regiment moved to the heights to the left of the 1/7th Reserve Regiment. They deployed at the exit of the village, on either side of the road. The 2/7th stopped the French cavalry. The infantry then took a position behind the numerous ditches that covered the road. The 2/7th was thrust forward. The 6pdr Foot Battery #8 established itself with two guns on the road and the others to the right of the road. Horse Battery #7 withdrew to reorganize itself, after its clash with the French cavalry.[56]

The French sent skirmishers forward to attempt to turn the Prussian right, so the 1/7th Reserve Regiment moved to cover the battery. The 7th Company crossed the road, but Oberst von Grolmann withdrew the 1/7th to its original position and dispatched the schützen of the 9th Silesian Landwehr Regiment to deal with the French skirmishers. Two battalions of this regiment were on the right of the 7th Reserve Regiment, while the other two stood in the second line.[57]

About 10:30 p.m., the first cannon shot thundered from the slopes of the Nollendorf moun-tain into the valley. The sound of these guns had many unusual effects on the battle in the valley below. The French troops in battle with the allies believed, naturally, that it was the anticipated reinforcements finally arriving and that the Emperor himself had come. They then redoubled their efforts, thinking deliverance had arrived. The gun shots had reverse effect on the Allies, who knew nothing of Kleist's movements, and believed that it meant the arrival of French reinforcements in Tellnitz.

Problems of interpretation also occurred in the headquarters of Czar Alexander I and King Friedrich Wilhelm III. Both monarchs had observed the battle since morning, from a position on the Teplitz Castle Hill. It is presumed that King Wilhelm transmitted Schölers announcement of Kleist's intentions to the Czar. However, The Czar and Barclay, had little faith in the potential appearance of Kleist by Tellnitz, and sent several adjutants in an effort to determine what was happening. Two things were clear to the Czar at this moment. The first was that the cannon shots by Tellnitz were important and that Vandamme would shortly know what it was. The second was that whatever was about to join the battle was a major force, as it had artillery with it. He was forewarned and began to prepare for what he feared was a major counterattack by the French.[58]

A violent fight had begun to the south of Vorder-Tellnitz. There GM Pirch had fully deployed the Prussian 10th Brigade. The 9th Silesian Landwehr Regiment was deployed, linking the 7th Reserve Regiment, on the right wing, to the foot of the mountain. On the right stood 6pdr Foot Battery #8 and 6pdr Foot Battery #11. The 12pdr Foot Battery #3 moved to the left of the road and assumed firing position. To the right stood the half Horse Battery #7. The fire of these guns was distributed between Gobrecht's half horse battery, a French 12pdr battery that stood on Horkaberg, and the advancing French infantry.

Favored by the terrain and failure of the French to take a position oblique to the Prussian position, the Prussian schützen zügen of the advanced guard pushed along the edge of the woods, and took the French under fire.[59] This move supported the right wing of the 9th Silesian Landwehr Regiment. However, sensing victory, the landwehr regiment advanced forward into a dangerously exposed position. Soon Revest's brigade marched onto the field. The Prussian landwehr was pounded with a heavy skirmish fire. The landwehr battalions turned heel and broke. The Prussian right wing found itself so endangered, that its line was obliged to bend into a hook. At the same time, 6pdr Foot Battery #8 was compelled to withdraw, because it had shot off its ammunition and the munition caissons could not come forward. The collapsing landwehr battalions pushed through the line and swept the 1/7th Reserve Regiment away with them. Consequently a confused mass moved to the western part of the battlefield. The battlefield was soon covered with small groups and individuals fleeing the battle.

The battle on the left wing was no less savage. GM von Pirch had sent the 2nd West Prussian Infantry Regiment, under the command of Major von Hopfgarten, to that wing with orders to occupy the village of Arbesau, to cover the advance of the other Prussian brigade to the southeast.

As the two battalions of the 2nd West Prussian Regiment passed by Arbesau in two columns, they found the village already occupied by the battalions of Dunesme's Brigade. Immediately the Prussians moved to the attack, struck without firing their muskets, and captured Ober-Arbesau. They captured about 300 prisoners. Despite all exertion they were not able to take Unter-Arbesau from its French defenders.[60]

The French withdrawal began on the left wing. The first portion to move was Dunesme's brigade, which withdrew from its position to the southeast of the Kulm Castle Park towards Arbesau. It was to be followed by Fezensac's lightly-engaged brigade from left wing of Philippon's 1st Division. Yet Fezensac was only able to pull six companies of the 36th Line Regiment out of the battle line. The 17th Line Regiment no longer responded to his orders. It remained defending the southern side of Kulm as the French artillery withdrew. During the march through Kulm, Fezensac detached three of his six companies to serve as cover for the Horkaberg where a French battery fired on the Prussians. With the small remainder of his brigade he began the withdrawal on to the west of Philippon's 2nd Brigade. Part of Mouton-Duvernet's 42nd Division followed.[61]

Revest's brigade was ordered to move to Tellnitz, Quiot's brigade was to follow him. Philippon's 1st Division and Mouton-Duvernet's 42nd Divisions were to cover the retreat between the Reichstrasse and the mountains. The artillery on the Kulm heights, under General Baltus, supported by Doucet's 2nd Brigade, 2nd Division, doubled its fire in an effort to allow the French line to disengage from the Russians and Austrians.

The allies finally recognized the fact that French were withdrawing and began a general advance. The Russian 2nd Corps moved in the direction of Straden, in order to strike the left flank of the 42nd Division, as it was uncovered by Philippon's withdrawal. This move supported a frontal attack by the Russian 1st Grenadier Division and P.Hessen-Homburg's Austrian brigade. The Russian Guard Hussar Regiment advanced with the infantry and succeeded in overrunning a French battery.

A little later the left flank of the allies finally began to make progress, as the 42nd Division's stubborn defense finally began to give way. As a final reserve, Heimrodt's 3rd Light Cavalry Brigade still stood by Kulm, ready to throw itself against the advancing allies.

On the right flank, the allies advanced Colloredo and Knorring's forces, pushing hard. Corbineau's cavalry formed the rear guard, keeping the advancing allies at bay, but they were steadily pushed back. Abele's Brigade moved to attack Kulm. The Argenteau Infantry Regiment moved into the castle's park with a bayonet assault, driving back the portion of the 17th Line protecting the French artillery, and captured a number of cannons. Despite this, the rest of the French artillery withdrew to the northwest of Kulm and took up a new position.

Bianchi advanced past the Kulm Park and Auschine, moving against the withdrawing French. Colloredo followed with Kolb's Brigade and Chiesa's Brigade, moving from Auschine and Tillisch against Arbesau.

At the same time, Miloradovich led his forces from the center forward against Kulm. Grand Duke Constantine led his two cuirassier divisions forward in support. The Russian 2nd Corps, formed in masses by battalion, moved forward in two lines and attacked the heights by Kulm from the south. The French artillerists fired their guns constantly up to the last minute and were sabered by their guns. Further resistance was impossible. The gunners strove to save their guns and mounted the draft horses on the limbers and caissons to ride them to the rear. The French artillerists fled, abandoning their equipment to the allies. A total of 20 guns and much other equipment was captured.

The Fight at Arbesau

As Kulm fell, the French and Prussians were engaged in heavy fighting around Tellnitz and Arbesau. The capture of Ober-Arbesau allowed the reserve cavalry to draw up behind Unter-Arbesau. The 11th Brigade was, at this time, marching in column towards Lucke. The 10th remained without support and could only with greatest effort hold its position. When the 11th Brigade arrived, the cavalry was in such disorder that it had to stop and reorganize itself.[62]

The 12pdr Foot Battery #3 took up a position to the left of the road, but left sufficient space for the remains of Horse Battery #7 to position itself to its right. The later rapidly used up its munitions and had to withdraw to replenish its supplies. Horse Battery #8 took its position.[63] Half Battery #7 resupplied its caissons and returned to the artillery line, but there was no room in the line and it joined two excess 12pdrs, that were following the cavalry.

The 9th Brigade was followed by the Cavalry Reserve. Pirch assumed a strong position around Tellnitz with his brigade, but left two squadrons of the 8th (Silesian) Landwehr Cavalry Regiment to hold Tellnitz. The rest of the brigade and the reserve cavalry moved to cover Ober-Arbesau. They formed themselves between Unter-Arbesau and Auschine where they joined with the Austrians under Colloredo. The 7th Landwehr Cavalry Regiment formed the first line, covered by two batteries. Four squadrons formed the second line.[64] Pirch's three regiments then formed the third line and the Austrians were to the left.

As soon as the order was issued to the 11th Brigade to support the wavering Prussian 10th Brigade, the 1st Silesian Infantry Regiment was directed to the extreme and most dangerous end of the right wing, where it was not only ordered to stop the French, but also to seize terrain.

King Frederick William III of Prussia encouraging an Austrian cuirassier regiment at Kulm, after Hofbauer.

The entire allied line, Russians and Austrians, began to advance. Vandamme moved with his staff to Kulm's gate in time to see the Argenteau Regiment, under Major Call, advance into the city. The city was, by this time, in flames.

The right wing, which stood between Karwitz and Strisowitz Mountain was commanded by FZM Graf Colloredo-Mansfeld. Colloredo's 1st Line Division with Bianchi's 2nd Reserve Division formed the infantry line. This force was supported by the Austrian Erzherzog Johann Dragoon Regiment, three batteries of Austrian artillery under Major Gepert (18 guns), that stood by Colloredo's division, and Bianchi's divisional artillery, three batteries.

Dunesme's Brigade marched against Unter-Arbesau in two squares. Vandamme ordered Philippon to send his 2nd Brigade shortly afterwards. Fezensac, who commanded the 2nd Brigade, found himself to the left of the division with the 36th Line Regiment, very exposed after the departure of Quiot's brigade. He hesitated to disengage himself. He sent for the 17th Line Regiment, but Philippon had charged this regiment with supporting his artillery. Upon the receipt of a new order from Vandamme, he sent six companies of the 36th Line. Three were detached and traversed Kulm behind the artillery. Vandamme sent them against the Prussians with Fezensac at their held. They threw back the Prussian skirmish line.[65]

After Kulm fell, Bianchi advanced between Kulm and Auschine in his march on Schandau. Two battalions from the Esterhazy and Davidovich Regiments moved into the village and took it by storm. The brigade of Prince P. von Hessen-Homburg and Raevsky's grenadiers moved between Horka and the mountain. There were 4,000 French standing between Horka, the mountain and Schandau in good order, waiting to receive them. After a few volleys, however, they had shot off what remained of their ammunition and threw down their arms. Those that could, fled, but most were taken into captivity.[66]

The 42nd Division, turned on the right by Hessen-Homburg's brigade and pressed in the front by Raevsky, had no choice but to throw itself through the forests to their right. A large part of this division succeeded in escaping through the mountains to re-join St. Cyr.

Vandamme's withdrawal was well under way, but as much of his force consisted of conscripts it quickly turned into a rout. His columns moved on Tellnitz, abandoning their artillery, but Kleist still blocked the way.

While Barclay was overrunning Kulm, Kleist's Prussians had their hands full. The passage of the cavalry reserve had slowed down the arrival of the 11th Brigade. It moved into line with the 1/, 2/1st Silesian Regiment and Donna's Battalion (4/8th Silesian Landwehr) moving to the right of the Prussian line. The 2/, 3/10th Reserve Regiment formed to the right of the main road. The battalions of Borcke (1/8th Silesian Landwehr) and Geisberg (2/8th Silesian Landwehr) formed to the left. Six pounder Foot Battery #11 took up a position to the right of 6pdr Batteries #8 and #14. However, 6pdr Battery #8 quickly shot off its ammunition and had to retire. It returned in a half hour.

The 2/, 3/10th Reserve Regiment arrived in time to help the hard pressed Prussian artillery. They threw back the French skirmishers to one of the walls situated parallel to the front of the attack, 120 meters from Schandau, and took several others. They could not maintain themselves in that position and the 3/10th Reserve was forced to withdraw back into the forest.

Horse Battery #8 advanced two guns, a few hundred paces forward to fire on the French infantry, but found themselves attacked by French cavalry and quickly withdrew to their original position. At the same time the 8th Silesian Landwehr Regiment crossed the artillery line, but was attacked by the French cavalry and the French skirmishers, who drove it back to the left of the 12pdr battery. Six pounder Foot battery #13 arrived as the landwehr fell back and placed three guns on the left of the artillery line, while the three others remained in reserve because of insufficient room to deploy.

Dunesme had moved his troops from Unter-Arbesau and united them with the rest of his brigade. He had begun to advance against Ober-Arbesau. The 7th Silesian Landwehr Cavalry Regiment, led by Oberst von Mutius, launched a desperate attack against Dunesme to block his advance, however, the terrain was too bad for a successful charge and the French response too stubborn. The Prussians were stopped and thrown back.

Dunesme established his brigade strongly in Unter-Arbesau and sent a force against the left of the Prussian artillery line. The remainder marched on Ober-Arbesau, where it threw out the 2nd West Prussian Regiment.

Prussian 6pdr Foot Battery #13 tried in vain to stop, with canister fire at 700 paces against the flank, a French column advancing out of Ober-Arbesau. At the same moment a cloud of French skirmishers appeared before the artillery line. Their advance had been hidden by the rolling terrain.

The constantly growing mass of French pressed the Prussian 10th and 11th Brigades harder and harder. The Prussian artillery had been in the line for a long time and its ammunition began to run out, so it was slowly rotating batteries in and out of the line. However, with the pressure of the French attack and the impassable ground, several guns were lost due to the lack of limbers and gunners. The two Prussian brigades were near collapse, when the 12th Brigade under Prince August von Preussen finally arrived. The support of the 12th Brigade allowed many of the guns and wagons of the first two brigades to safely withdraw. Prinz August had sent Generalstabsmajor Graf Dohna forward, in order to ask Kleist, where he wanted the 12th Brigade to position itself. The head came up in good order and soon began to support the two yielding brigades.[67]

The French Escape

Kleist threw forward, on his left, the 12th Brigade, which was beginning to arrive. The 11th Reserve Regiment advanced on the two sides of the road, having at its head Prince August of Prussia. Grolmann saw the failure of the 7th Silesian Landwehr Cavalry Regiment and advised Prinz August of the situation. Prinz August responded by sending the 10th Silesian Landwehr Infantry Regiment forward in column, It advanced with von Fritsch (1/10th Silesian Landwehr) and von Brixen Battalions (3/10th Silesian Landwehr) in the first line and the Frankenberg Battalion (4/10th Silesian Landwehr) in the second. They marched from the road, with orders to march to the east and attack Unter-Arbesau. The 2nd Silesian Regiment formed a reserve between the two groups. Then 12pdr Foot Battery #6 positioned itself near Vorder-Tellnitz, on the main road.[68]

The men of the 10th Silesian Landwehr Regiment advanced into fire for the first time. They were hungry from the lack of food, and very fatigued from the heavy marching of the last days. It is no wonder that they did not hold up like a hardened body of veteran troops.[69]

Quiot's and Revest's brigades moved forward with a detachment of cavalry. The three battalions of the 10th Silesian Landwehr stood in the way. The Prussian artillery pounded the advancing French. The only choice remaining open to Vandamme was to lower bayonets and advance with, as the French say, *"tête basse"* (a lowered head like a bull), in an effort to cut his way through the Prussian lines. This hell-for-leather infantry charge was supported by the limited cavalry still with Vandamme.[70] Despite the support of the 11th Reserve Regiment, the entire Prussian left was shattered and thrown in total disarray.

The 10th Silesian Landwehr Regiment's officers struggled to stop the panic and took heavy casualties. The regimental commander, Major Prince Christian von Anhalt-Köthen-Pless, was killed, while Grolmann, Dohna, and Prinz August were wounded as they tried to stop the rout. The three

Prince August of Prussia at Kulm, by Röchling.

landwehr battalions stampeded to the rear and threw themselves in their blind haste onto the 2nd Silesian Regiment. The Silesians began to break as well, when Prinz August threw himself from his horse, grabbed the flag of the 2/2nd Silesian Regiment and cried "Whoever has a true Prussian heart, follow me!" and advanced against the French. His cries worked and a few hundred men of the 2nd Silesian Regiment and a number of landwehr rallied under the flag. He then led them forward with a hurrah against the French. This renewed assault was also destined to be beaten back by the French assault.

After Prinz August launched this force back against the French, he moved back to the road to review the situation on the right flank. As he passed over the highway, he found a tangled mass of Prussian artillery and wagons heaped together, clogging the road. He struggled to bring some order in the chaos and the battle weary soldiers, when suddenly a French cavalry force moved up the road.

The French cavalry, which was followed by a crowd of escaping French artillery and train soldiers with their vehicles, took this opportunity to throw themselves on the Prussian artillery. The tangle of Prussian soldiers panicked, racing in every direction to seek shelter, abandoning their weapons in order to escape. It was Montmarie's 2nd Light Cavalry Brigade, and a collection of artillery limbers and crews, whose guns the Austrians captured by Kulm, and a mass of train horses. In desperation, this cavalry force had drawn itself together under Corbineau's personal command and was thrown against the allied infantry. Their advance was unstoppable, but desperate groups of Prussians stood as long as possible. One Prussian artillery officer discharged one last canister shot against the charging French cavalry and inflicted heavy casualties on them before he was ridden down.[71] The French cavalry drove past the few Prussian defenders and into the tangled mass of Prussian guns and wagons on the road, slashing soldiers and horses with their sabers, wrecking much of what stood before them, before they pushed through to their escape. The French captured 6pdr Foot Batteries #8, #11, #13, and #14, Horse Battery #8 and 12pdr Foot Battery #3. Only 12pdr Foot Battery #6 had time to withdraw into a position not far from the houses by the road, and escape the destruction of the Prussian artillery line. It unlimbered and began to fire on the French, but the enraged cavalry overran it and sabered its gunners. Part of Kleist's artillery reserve standing in column on the road, got the same treatment. Horse Battery #9, 6pdr Foot Battery #21 and 7pdr Howitzer Battery #1 were all sabered.[72]

The Prussian center was completely crushed. Everything that did not flee to the woods was sabered. The 1/1st Silesian Regiment and Dohna's landwehr battalion (4/8th Silesian) threw skirmishers into the streets and onto the foot of the mountain. The 2/1st Silesian Regiment, on their left in the plain, formed square. The entire Prussian line along this flank awaited the decisive French attack, but only a few stray French cavaliers struck at the square. Nonetheless, the square remained in place, not seeking information about what was occurring elsewhere on the battlefield.

Seeing the violence of the desperate French attack, the remaining Prussians threw themselves to the two sides of the road. The 11th Brigade moved towards the wooded mountain to the west, and the 10th and 12th Brigades moved to the east. Prince August von Preussen only barely escaped capture.

The three battalions of the 6th Reserve Regiment, 9th Brigade, standing to the south of Nollendorf, had been ordered to move to the right, and to follow the Prussian artillery on the road. Oberst Löbell was about to execute this maneuver, when a mass of French cavalry struck him. He quickly swung to the west and moved to a position on the foot of the hill, where he could fire on the valley.

As soon as the first mass of French cavalry passed by, Oberst Löbell sent the 3/6th Reserve to the east side of the road, in order to take whatever followed in a cross fire. This battalion was traversing the valley, when the second avalanche of French poured through. The disorder was incredible and the Prussian artillery was sabered. However, the fusiliers were able to move to a position to the east of the road and formed square.

They also temporarily captured GD Dumonceau, who was attempting to move with the debris of the 4th Légère. A second column passed in front of the 1/6th Reserve Regiment and received a volley that inflicted numerous casualties on it.[73]

Oberst Löbell vainly attempted to assemble his two battalions on the heights above Nollendorf, and ordered them to move from the woods to the left flank, to move to Tetschen. Unfortunately, the order was not heard and only the 4th Company, 1/6th Reserve Regiment headed as it was directed. En route it found the flag of the 2nd Silesian Regiment, around which were assembled a large number of fugitives. The three other companies regained the heights of Nollendorf. That evening, when the 3/6th Reserve Regiment assembled itself in the Kulm valley, it had only 300 men.

While the French that did escape were doing so, the Austrian Erzherzog Johann Dragoon Regiment attacked the French 12 gun battery covering the French retreat. Between the landwehr and the dragoons, 1,200 French were captured.

The Results of the Battle

Vandamme and Haxo were captured. Corbineau had remained at the head of his division, charging repeatedly in an effort to cover the French withdrawal.

The French lost between 15,000 and 17,000 men, including 7,000 prisoners. In addition, they lost three flags and 66 cannon. The debris of Vandamme's I Corps joined the XIV Corps in Dietersdorf, above Peterswald. Vandamme's disaster more than evened the score between the allies and the French for the last five days. On 31 August, the survivors of I Corps rallied.

General Vandamme is captured by Russian Jager at Kulm, 30 August, by Knötel.

The 42nd Division had slightly over 4,800 men remaining. A total of 4,000 was assembled at Pirna. Kreutzer's detachment, consisting of about 800 men from re-joined them later. Quiot's brigade had ceased to exist. Corbineau's cavalry division was also savaged. The 2nd and 3rd Light Cavalry Brigades ceased to exist and only the 1st Light Cavalry Brigade remained operational.

French I Corps After The Battle of Kulm 31 August 1813[74]

I Corps: Général de division Philippon (acting)
    1st Division: Général de division Corbineau (acting)
        1st Brigade: Général de brigade Pouchelon
            1/, 2/, 3/, 4/7th Légère Regiment (48/790)
            1/, 2/, 3/, 4/12th Line Regiment (53/921)
        2nd Brigade: Général de brigade Fezensac
            1/, 2/, 3/, 4/17th Line Regiment (39/956)
            3/, 4/36th Line Regiment (14/232)
    2nd Division: Général de division Dumonceau (absent)
        1st Brigade: Général de brigade Dunesme (killed)
            1/, 2/, 3/, 4/13th Légère Regiment (24/522)
            1/, 2/, 3/, 4/25th Line Regiment (10/292)
        2nd Brigade: Général de brigade Doucet
            1/, 2/, 3/, 4/57th Line Regiment (48/1,128)
            3/, 4/57th Line Regiment (27/500)
    23rd Division:
        2nd Brigade: Général de brigade Quiot (prisoner) (brigade is reorganizing)
            1/, 2/, 3/, 4/85th Line Regiment (nil)
            3/, 4/55th Line Regiment (nil)
    21st Light Cavalry Brigade: Général de brigade Gobrecht
            1/, 2/9th Chevaulégers-lanciers Regiment (8/83/97)[75]
            1/, 2/Anhalt Jäger zu Pferd (nil)
    Attached: Sappers (detached)
        Military equipage (8/112)

The allies were not without casualties from this battle. The 1st Russian Guard Division had been severely handled on the first day. It lost 2,800 men, the 2nd Corps lost about 2,400 men and the cavalry lost 800 men. Kleist's Prussians attempted to stop an avalanche and suffered accordingly. The 7th Reserve Regiment lost 492 men in its 1st and 2nd Battalions, the 3/6th Reserve lost 75% of their 219 man starting strength. The 1/, 2/6th Reserve lost 694 men, the Fus/1st West Prussian Regiment lost 162 men, the 1st Silesian Regiment lost 145 men, the 1/10th Reserve lost 199, while the 2/10th Reserve suffered about the same number. The Prussian artillery lost 17 officers, 44 non-commissioned officers, 521 men, and 580 horses. Nearly every battalion Kleist had, was reduced to two thirds of its original strength. His corps fell from 37,816 at the beginning of operations to 23,659 men by the beginning of September.[76]

Vandamme took a risk. He gambled that he could hold against the allied army and gambled that his fellow generals would aggressively push the allies. His gamble was for the big victory, and in doing what he did, he followed Napoleon's orders to the letter. The technique of using a portion of the French army to pin the main allied army in position and permit the rest of the French army to maneuver against it was very much Napoleon's method of warfare. Vandamme acted in that spirit and deserves praise at every level for his actions. If he had succeeded, Vandamme's actions would have resulted in the capture or destruction of the Army of Bohemia in the passes over the Erzegeberg and the almost immediate end of the 1813 Fall campaign.

Though Vandamme was not able to take and hold Teplitz, he did his best to fulfil those orders. The most probable reason for the failure, was the lack of communications between Vandamme and

Allied service of thanksgiving following the Battle of Kulm, at Teplitz, 2 September.

Mortier. If this had been maintained, Vandamme would have known that Mortier had received orders to stop and hold Pirna. What happened that this breakdown in communications occurred is something that will never be answered. If blame is to be laid for the French defeat it must be placed at the poor communications available to the generals of the day.

As for the allied victory, it was only due to overwhelming numbers and the merest chance that Kleist decided to maneuver as he did. Most assuredly it was not a thought-out allied plan that put Kleist in Vandamme's rear, but serendipity. The allied magnitude victory can only be ascribed to blind chance and superior numbers.

The debris of the I Corps withdrew. Philippon's 1st Division and Mouton-Duvernet 42nd Division moved to Libenau, occupied by the XIV Corps. Dumonceau's 2nd Division, with the four battalions of the 55th and 85th Line Regiments moved to Pirna, where they found Mortier with the Young Guard.[77]

After Kulm

On 29 August Murat arrived in Lichtenberg, Marmont in Falkenhain, and St. Cyr was in Reinhardtsgrimma. They had stopped their advance shortly, and as a result, had not caught up with the withdrawing allies, as directed by Napoleon. The immediate result was the destruction of Vandamme's forces at Kuhn.

On 31 August Murat was in Savda, Marmont was in Zinnwald and St. Cyr was in Libenau. On the day after the disaster at Kulm, only the VI Corps had passed through the mountains.

14

Ney Takes an Independent Command. The Battle of Dennewitz 2–7 September 1813

After Oudinot's failure at Gross-Beeren, Napoleon directed Ney to take command of the Army of Berlin on 2 September. Napoleon was troubled by the consequences of Oudinot's failure and began shifting much of his army to face the new threat and to cover the new threat to Macdonald's communications.

On 3 September, Ney took command of the III Cavalry Corps and the IV, VII, XII Corps, which were united in the camp at Teuchel, about four kilometers north of Wittenberg.

On the same day, the Polish Division of Dombrowski, which came from the Wittenberg garrison, had joined the left wing of the Ney's army. It consisted of the 2nd and 4th Polish Infantry Regiments, each with two battalions, the 2nd Uhlan and 4th Chasseur à Cheval Regiments, and two guns.[1] Dombrowski detached a battalion of the 2nd Polish Infantry Regiment and three squadrons of the 2nd Uhlan Regiment to support Ney.[2]

The VII Corps stood on the right of Dombrowski, by Reinsdorf. Extending to its right were the IV and XII Corps. Behind them stood the French cavalry. Their front and left flanks were covered by the Thiesener Wasser and it steep banks. The French cavalry's right wing stood on another stream. On the heights were two redoubts, an epaulement, two fleches, and an open work by Euper. While the French remained in lager around Wittenberg, they received 6,000 replacements to assist in replacing the losses from Gross-Beeren.[3]

Though ordered to put his army into "rapid" movement, Ney chose to spend 4 September, passing his troops in review. Though a useful action, it was not indispensable, and certainly, it was preferable that he should have conformed precisely to the orders he had received from Napoleon.

Ney Begins to Move

On 5 September, Ney put his army in motion, marching on Zahna and Jüterbogk. Once again the goal of this army was Berlin. To ensure liaison between Ney and Macdonald, as well as to cover Davout's movement on the left of Bernadotte's Army of the North, Napoleon directed a corps to Torgau.

As Ney began his movement, he quickly found himself in contact with the allied advanced posts. Voronzov's Division had been joined by Czernichev, Hirschfeld, and Tettenborn. It stood on the allied far right, in the direction of Roslau, where it prepared to cross the Elbe. Being light troops they easily broke contact with Ney and were to take no part in the Battle of 6 September.

The Prussians

Bülow's Prussian 3rd Corps stood on the road from Potsdam to Wittenberg via Marzahne. Borstell's 5th Brigade was in Kopnick. Tauentzien's Prussian 4th Corps was on the road to Jüterbogk, Dobschütz's brigade, 4th Corps, was in Zahna and Alt-Seyda, and Wobeser's brigade to the far left in Luckau, with various detachments reaching to Ohna. Finally, Winzingerode's Corps and Stedingk's Swedish Corps were united in Rödigke.

Bülow.

General von Dobschütz, of the Prussian 4th Corps, had engaged the French around Euper on 3 and 4 September. On 31 August, he was sent from Luckau to Woltersdorf with the 1/, 2/1st Kurmärk Landwehr Regiment, two battalions of the 1st Silesian Landwehr Regiment, two squadrons of the 1st Pomeranian Landwehr Cavalry Regiment, the 1/, 2/7th Kurmärk Landwehr Cavalry Regiment, and 6pdr Foot Battery #17 – Gleim. On 2 September, Bernadotte ordered him to join the left flank of the 3rd Army Corps. There he was assigned to the command of General Bülow along with 3/, 4/ Brandenburg Dragoons, 3/Königin Dragoons, 4/2nd West Prussian Dragoons, and 2/, 6/Berlin Landwehr Cavalry under the command of Major von Schmitterlöw and the half Horse Battery #6 under Lieutenant Jenichen.[4]

The 1/Elbe Regiment, which had been engaged in Trebgen on 22 August, had been withdrawn from Saarmund and returned to the wing corps of General von Hirschfeld. The 3rd Prussian Corps had risen to a strength of 37,800 men.

The 4th Prussian Corps, with a strength of 10 battalions, 13 squadrons, and 24 cannons stood by Luckau when Bernadotte ordered Tauentzien to lead it towards Dennewitz. On the following day it took up positions with two battalions, two squadrons, and a half foot battery being posted by Gudegast, on the heights facing Zalmsdorf. A further seven battalions, 11 squadrons, and 20 cannons were posted by Seyda. The 1/2nd Neumärk Landwehr Regiment stood in Luckau.

First Contact

On 5 September, at Jüterbogk, Ney found his advance blocked by a small allied force. He wished to maneuver and turn its position, by passing through Dahme, so as to bring the IV Corps behind Jüterbogk, put the XII Corps on the hill north of Ohna, and to put the VII Corps in Rohrbeck, but fate intervened and the marches did not occur as directed.

Maréchal Ney.

The Battle by Zahna

Earlier, after the review of 4 September, Oudinot made a demonstration against Zahna, but without a well-defined goal. It was 10:00 a.m., when he moved against General Dobschütz's forces. In Woltersdorf stood a detachment from the 5th Prussian Brigade under Major von Beyer. This force consisted of two battalions from the 3rd Reserve Regiment, two squadrons of the East Prussian Prussian Landwehr Regiment, and two guns from Horse Battery #11 (Borchard). Oudinot was to engage only five battalions in the battle.[5]

At 10:00 a.m., two companies of French pushed through the woods and engaged the Prussian skirmishers. Shortly afterward, about 10:30 a.m., a column under Gruyer, 1st Brigade, 14th Division, pushed through the woods. Gleim's 6pdr Foot Battery #17 and the two horse guns engaged them quickly. Shortly afterward, Lieutenant Jenichen (Horse Battery #6) with two more guns and the 2/1st Kurmärk Landwehr Cavalry Regiment, moved up on the right side of the French.[6]

Tauentzien reacted by organizing his forces in two lines and prepared to defend himself. His first line consisted of the 1/, 2/1st Kurmärk Landwehr Regiment, the 5th Kurmärk Landwehr Regiment, half 6pdr Horse Battery #6, Jenichen, on the right wing, half 6pdr Foot Battery #30, Hertig, on the left wing and all of 6pdr Foot Battery #17, Gleim, in the middle. Behind the first line stood Major von Schmitterlöw's cavalry – two squadrons 1st Kurmärk Landwehr Cavalry Regiment, the 1/, 2/7th Landwehr Cavalry Regiments, and the 2/, 6/Berlin Landwehr Cavalry Regiment.

In his second line stood the 1/, 2/, 5/1st Silesian Landwehr Regiment, the 3rd Reserve Regiment, three battalions of the 2nd Neumärk Landwehr Regiment, on the right wing half horse battery #11, in the middle there stood half 12pdr Foot Battery #5, Lent, and on the left stood all of 6pdr Foot Battery #27, Mathias. Behind them stood two squadrons of the Brandenburg Dragoons, four squadrons of the Pomeranian Dragoons, two squadrons of the 2nd Neumärk Landwehr Cavalry Regiment, and three squadrons of the 3rd East Prussian Landwehr Cavalry Regiment. The Illowaiski #3 Don Cossacks were on both wings.[7]

The French organized themselves behind a screen of the Westphalian Chevauxleger Regiment, who shortly after fell back at a trot behind the French lines. An artillery duel began. The Prussians brought up more guns, while Pacthod moved his artillery to the east. The artillery of Guilleminot and Beaumont's horse artillery stood before Euper. Under the cover of this artillery Brun de Villeret's 2nd Brigade, 14th Division, moved against Woltersdorf.[8]

Before Brun's brigade, in the vicinity of Woltersdorf, stood Beier's forces of Borstell's Brigade (2 battalions, 2 guns, and 2 squadrons). About 11:00 a.m., a French battalion moved down the road to Woltersdorf in column and attacked the 2/2nd Reserve Regiment. The fire of the Prussian battalion stopped the French, but four more battalions moved against the left side of the battalion. The Prussians were obliged to withdraw.

The French pushed through Zalmsdorf where they encountered Gleim's 6pdr Battery #17 again. The 1/2nd Silesian Landwehr Regiment (Bonin's battalion), covered the battery. The landwehr sent their skirmishers into the light woods to the right. The Prussian artillery pounded the French, inflicting a number of casualties. However, the superior numbers of the French obliged the Prussians to withdraw, ending the engagement.

The result of Oudinot's demonstration against Zahna was that Bernadotte, warned about a resumption of operations, concentrated his forces, principally those of his left wing. Bülow moved his corps to Kurz-Lipsdorf and Tauentzien moved towards Jüterbogk, except for Wobeser's division, and the remainder of the Army of the North moved towards Lobessen.[9]

The Army of the North had organized itself into three groups some distance from one and other. The group in Lobessen was the most important. It is probable that if Ney had acted quickly against the center, that is to say against Bülow, he could have dealt with Bülow before the wings of the Army of the North could have intervened. Having engaged and defeated the outnumbered Bülow, Ney could have proceeded to Berlin almost without interference.

Instead of this, on 5 September, Ney ordered Bertrand to make pinning attack directly ahead of him, and under the opening so formed, the XII Corps was to move to the right of the IV Corps, passing behind Bertrand, and moving towards Zahna, which would be taken from Tauentzien.

At the same time as the XII Corps, the VII Corps would move behind the IV Corps and to the left of the army, where it would support the move against Zahna. Bertrand's corps would then move behind the VII Corps and advance on Alt-Seyda.

The maneuver of 5 September has been admired by many tacticians and its execution was flawless, but took time to execute, time that could have been more profitably spent moving forward to deal with Bülow and swamping him with numbers, so as to inflict on him a defeat similar to the one Oudinot had suffered at Gross-Beeren.

As the maneuver was executed, Tauentzien learned that the campaign had become active again and discovered that he was the target of its first maneuver. He quickly withdrew towards Jüterbogk.

Prelude to a Battle

On 6 September, Ney set his forces in motion towards Jüterbogk. The IV Corps began its movement at 8:00 a.m., followed by the VII and then the XII Corps. The three corps marched, one behind the other, down a single route in echelons. They were to execute a flank maneuver if they encountered the enemy. As they marched, the three corps became separated by a distance of two

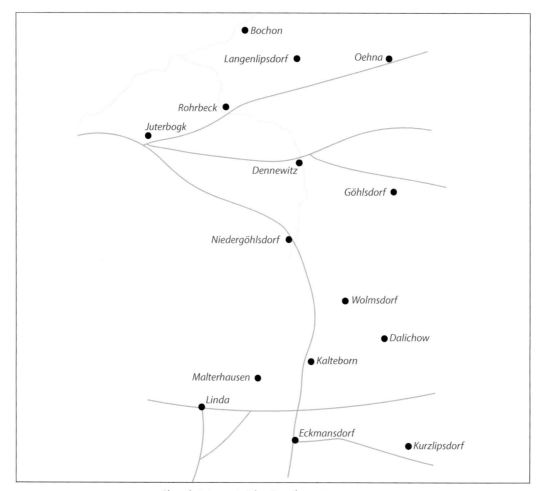

Sketch Map 15   The Roads to Dennewitz.

hours marching time. This was aggravated by the sandy roads which made the marching harder. In addition, the superiority in Prussian cavalry strength had shown itself early in the morning, and throughout the day no maneuvers were performed without a host of Prussian cavalry as witnesses.

After the battle, Ney stated in a letter to Berthier, that the battle line was be formed before 10:00 a.m., and at that hour he had only engaged the allied advanced guard, which had followed the movement of the IV Corps. The VII Corps did not arrive until 3:00 p.m., and it was not for four more hours that the XII Corps arrived and took part in the action. The strength of the XII Corps was:

13th Division Pacthod	4,263 men
14th Division Guilleminot	7,199
29th Division Raglovich	4,356
6th Light Cavalry Division Fournier	2,165
	17,983 Total[1]

Note
1   von Boyen, *Darestellung*, p.34.

Bertrand's IV Corps, which led the advance, encountered Tauentzien's advanced guard prior to arriving in Dennewitz. The IV Corps pushed them back and crossed the Agger River by Dennewitz. Bülow, who was in Kurz-Lipsdorf, withdrew towards Eckmansdorf and took a position behind that village and Malterhausen. Tauentzien, instead of straddling the road to Berlin, took up a position to the west, seeking to link up with Bülow.

Dennewitz is surrounded by open fields and gently rolling hills. There are no deep valleys that cut the battlefield and none of the rises are either steep or dominating in their height. Movement by troops and wheeled traffic throughout the area was relatively simple, with the only obstacles being the Agger and the tree lines that formed the boundaries of the various fields. Though the rolling rises across the entire battlefield may dominate significant parts of the landscape, movement up their gentle slopes would at no time impose a particular hardship on the attacker, nor an overwhelming advantage on the defender. There are several small woods scattered about the battlefield and one very large one to the south of the battlefield. These woods were sufficient to block wheeled traffic. As the land was of a relatively flat nature, these woods did not block or overly inhibit the movement of infantry or cavalry.

The Agger being the most significant military feature, Tauentzien had taken positions behind it. He posted the Illowaiski #3 Cossacks and a squadron of the 2nd Neumärk Landwehr Cavalry Regiment along the line of the stream to watch it for the advancing French. To watch his left flank, he posted the four squadrons of the 3rd Pomeranian Landwehr Cavalry Regiment under Rittmeister von Puttkammer to the east. The Silesian landwehr battalions of Wins (1/1st) and Kospoth (5/1st), the Klöden (2/1st) and Dullock (1/1st) Battalions of the 1st Kurmärk Landwehr Regiment, and Foot Batteries #5 (Glasenapp) and #27 (Mathias) were posted on and around the windmill hill by Jüterbogk.[10]

The remainder of Tauentzien's corps was deployed on the battlefield to face the French. Tauentzien's force, aside from the 3rd Reserve Regiment and the Brandenburg Dragoon Regiment, which was detached from the cavalry reserve of GM von Oppen, was formed entirely of landwehr. After detachments, he had a total of 11 battalions, 16 squadrons and 19 guns available to face the French. Tauentzien dispatched two half horse batteries, those of Jenichen (#6) and Borchard (#11), with a force of covering cavalry, to the northwest end of the small pine forest, which sat on the north of the battlefield, and had them deploy where they could direct their fire against the windmill hill by Dennewitz. On their right flank was Schmitterlöw's detachment from the reserve cavalry.[11] Hertig's 6pdr Foot Battery #30 was posted in the middle of the pine woods and Gleim's 6pdr Foot Battery #17 was posted on the left flank of the woods on a small hill.

Oppen's reserve cavalry was in Dalichow and advancing towards Dennewitz from the west. Further to the northwest, around Eckmansdorf, stood the brigades of Krafft (6th) and Prince von Hessen-Homburg (3rd). Thümen's 4th Brigade was slightly closer, being approximately one third of the way from Eckmansdorf to Kaltenborn. Major von Kleist's forces stood before Jüterbogk, facing south.

The Battle of Dennewitz Begins

Leading Ney's army was the IV Corps under Bertrand and Lorge's 5th Light Cavalry Division. Fontanelli's 15th (Italian) Division, IV Corps, was the first to deploy, taking up a position north of Dennewitz, on the south side of the woods behind which Tauentzien had deployed.

Seeing the French approaching, Tauentzien sent two battalions against Rohrbeck, supporting them with a force of cavalry and a battery. Then three columns appeared on the heights before Dennewitz. It was 9:00 a.m. Half Battery #30 was sent forward, covered by a squadron of the 3rd Pomeranian Landwehr Cavalry Regiment. Its goal was to slow the French and annoy them, as they tried to deploy.[12]

Fontanelli's 12 guns stayed with his division. To their left, the two 12pdr reserve batteries deployed for the coming battle, one near Dennewitz and the other between Dennewitz and Göhlsdorf.[13] Fontanelli was supported by Lorge's 5th Light Cavalry Division, which stood in the second line. Morand's 12th Division took up a position covering Fontanelli's western flank, and the approaches to Dennewitz. This maneuver was executed under the cover of the two 12pdr batteries.

Franquemont's 38th (Württemberg) Division was still marching north through Göhlsdorf, into Dennewitz. When it arrived, Spitzenberg's Brigade was sent to the right wing and assumed a position in the front line. The 2/4th Regiment and the Prinz Wilhelm Regiment #1 moved into the woods as ordered. The 7th Regiment assumed a position between them.[14] The second brigade retired to cover the French baggage. To the left of the woods occupied by Spitzenberg's forces stood the Italian division.

Defrance's 4th Heavy Cavalry Division and Durutte's 32nd Division were south of Franquemont, marching towards Dennewitz. To their right were the Saxons of Reynier's VII Corps, marching approximately due north.

Lorge's 5th Light Cavalry Division deployed towards Nieder-Görsdorf, covering the road and the juncture of Morand's and Fontanelli's divisions. The Polish 18th Light Cavalry Brigade, under Krukowiecki, moved towards Dennewitz.[15]

Despite the fire of the 28 Prussian guns of Tauentzien's corps, the 12th (Morand) and 15th Divisions (Fontanelli) completed their deployment about 10:00 a.m. A single battalion from Morand's division marched through Dennewitz towards the Wind Mill Hill (Windmühlberg). The Württemberg 38th Division and its artillery and cavalry, stood behind the Nuthe in reserve, supporting the attack of the Fontanelli's 15th Division.

Tauentzien's position was 300 paces north, behind the road from Nieder-Görsdorf. His left wing was formed principally of the 3rd Pomeranian Landwehr Cavalry Regiment and the 3rd East Prussian Landwehr Cavalry Regiment. His line extended left towards the city of Jüterbogk.

Italian artillery immediately began firing on the Prussian right wing, causing heavy loss. Two guns were lost by Borchard's Horse Battery #11 and one was lost by Hertig's Foot Battery #30. The skirmishers of the 5th Kurmärk Landwehr Regiment advanced quickly and began to pepper the

Italians with their fire. Steinmetz's (3/2nd Kurmärk) and Paczkowski's (4/2nd Kurmärk) Battalions stood in a second line behind them, supporting their advance. The advance did not succeed and the firing soon became an unregulated firing by file, until their ammunition was expended.

An Italian bayonet attack was possible, but did not occur because of the distance. However, the threat of a bayonet attack and the lack of ammunition caused the three battalions of the left flank to fall back precipitously, disordering the second line. The 2/5th Kurmärk Landwehr Regiment resisted the French stubbornly. Major Kamiensky, its commander, was wounded and unable to lead his battalion, so command fell to Captain von Hagen. Von Hagen was also wounded, as were four other officers and several men. Captain Gehlsdorf assumed command of the isolated battalion and moved it back behind the shelter of the skirmishers of the 3rd Reserve Infantry Regiment. In the process of this withdrawal, however, it took canister fire from four guns and in all suffered five officer and 100 enlisted casualties.[16]

Tauentzien's left wing was heavily assaulted and forced back to the Malter House, where it passed behind a small pine woods and found shelter.

On the right wing, the 3rd Reserve Regiment was driven behind the Dennewitz woods, but its skirmish line still held the leading edge of the woods. The Italians pursued the withdrawing Prussians. The 3rd Italian Brigade advanced in column into the brush before Dennewitz. The skirmishers of the 3rd Reserve Regiment took it under fire.

The Italians then dragged their artillery through the scrub and began to fire on the Prussians, driving them back another 800 paces. The Prussians were then struck in the right wing by Biernacki's Polish uhlan squadron operating on Morand's right. The 3/3rd Reserve Regiment, formed itself into column, but was caught off guard by the Polish cavalry. Part of the cavalry drove the Prussian skirmishers off, killing several, while the other part attacked the battalion proper. A third group of Poles remained in reserve. The Prussians were savagely handled and fell back with heavy casualties.

The 1/3rd Reserve Regiment and 2/2nd Newmärk Landwehr Regiment (Grolmann's battalion), were sent forward from the corps reserve with a detachment of cavalry. Despite this reinforcement, Tauentzien's right wing was forced back and had to reorganize itself. The Poles claimed to have broken three squares in this action.

In the Tauentzien's middle, the French infantry, supported by Jacquinot's 12th Light Cavalry Brigade, had moved to within 1,400 paces of the woods. The 4/Brandenburg Dragoon Regiment and the 1st Kurmärk Landwehr Cavalry Regiment, under the command of Oberstleutnant von Diezelsky, passed through the infantry and formed in line in front of them. They advanced against the French artillery, causing them to switch their fire, while the 7th Kurmärk Landwehr Infantry and Schmitterlöw's detachment organized itself into echelons and advanced. The 3/Brandenburg Dragoon Regiment followed.[17] Nine squadrons were gathered together and made an attack against the French.

During the attack, Oberstleutnant von Diezelsky's cavalry struck the 10th French Chasseur à Cheval Regiment in the flank and crushed it. The 4/Brandenburg and Schmitterlöw's detachment continued the advance and overran an Italian battery, but the fire of the 13th Line Regiment prevented them from carrying away more than a single wagon. The 2/, 4/8th Légère Regiment moved forward and recaptured the guns. At the same time, the 1st and 7th Kurmärk Landwehr Cavalry became embroiled with the 13th Chasseur à Cheval Regiment, which drove the Prussians back.[18]

Ney sent four battalions of Württembergers forward, down the road from Dennewitz and over the Nuthe. The Prussian cavalry, now reduced to 30 files, was sent forward again to face the Polish uhlans. It was between 12:15 and 1:15 p.m. The cavalry struck at the French again, falling back with little success, though the French line was disordered.

Tauentzien reformed his forces into two lines. On the right flank was half of Battery #20, covered by the 1/3rd East Prussian Landwehr Cavalry Regiment. To the left of the battery was the 1/, 3/, 4/5th Kurmärk Landwehr Regiment, 6pdr Battery #17 (Gleim), and the 2/2nd Neumärk Landwehr Regiment (Grolmann). The second line, right to left, consisted Horse Battery #6 (Jenichen), the 3rd Reserve Regiment, 1/1st Silesian Regiment, 2/5th Kurmärk Landwehr Regiment, and half Horse Battery #11 (Borchard). As a reserve, Tauentzien had the four squadrons of Major von Schmitterlöw (2nd West Prussian Dragoon Regiment), 2 squadrons of the Brandenburg Dragoons, 2 squadrons each from the 1st and 7th Kurmärk, 2 squadrons from the 3rd East Prussian, and 3 squadrons from the 3rd Pomeranian Landwehr Cavalry Regiments.[19]

It was also at this time, about noon, that the first Prussian cannon fire started from Nieder-Görsdorf, announcing to Ney that Thümen had arrived.

Bülow Arrives on the Battlefield

Bülow's 3rd Corps was advancing from the west. The 4th Brigade (Thümen) led, with the 6th Brigade (Krafft) behind it and the 3rd Brigade (Hessen-Homburg) acting as a reserve. Each Prussian brigade formed itself in echelon to the left. To the left of the infantry marched the 1st Leib Hussars. On their right marched the entire Cavalry Reserve.[20] The Cavalry Reserve consisted of 20 squadrons under the command of GM von Oppen.[21]

The cavalry moved towards Wölmsdorf and put their left wing behind the village. The Königin Dragoon Regiment formed its right wing. The 5th Brigade (Borstell) was ordered forward to assist the assault and provide a further reserve.[22]

To the north, facing Tauentzien, a Württemberg battalion, from Spitzenberg's 2nd Brigade, 38th Division, passed over the Nuthe as the Italians in the woods found themselves involved in a heavy fire-fight. It attempted to turn the Prussian position, but, without success, it fell back.

A renewed French assault began when Morand's 12th Division, which had been on the Wind Mill Hill, moved against Nieder-Görsdorf and the Denkmalsberg Heights.[23] The 13th Line and 8th Légère Regiments, of Toussaint's and Blair's brigades, were supported by a 12pdr battery firing canister into the Prussian lines.[24]

The Italians of Fontanelli's 15th Division took the middle of the forest, while four Württemberg battalions advanced into the eastern side of the pine forest, driving the Prussian batteries from their positions. With this success, Ney took the remaining Württemberg battalions and a horse battery and sent them forward to consolidate his gains.

Bülow, seeing the action around Nieder-Görsdorf and Dennewitz, had marched his forces forward in echelon, left in advance, and around noon, fell upon the flank of the IV Corps. Bertrand, who had held the terrain he had captured for about two hours, found himself being pressed to withdraw back towards Dennewitz.

The lead elements of Bülow's forces arriving in Nieder-Görsdorf about 12:45 p.m., consisted of Major von Sandrart with the 1st Leib Hussars and Ludwig's 6pdr Battery #6. Ludwig set up his battery east of the Agger's course and began to fire on the French on Denkmalsberg, at a distance of 800 paces. Thümen's battalions started appearing behind the battery very shortly thereafter. The first to arrive were the 1/, 2/4th East Prussian Infantry Regiment.[25]

Dietrichs' Russian 12pdr Position Battery #7 arrived shortly after, followed by more four battalions. The Prussian position began to take shape with 6pdr Foot Battery #6, Ludwig, forming the right wing. The first line was formed by the 2/, 1/5th Reserve Regiment and the 1/, 2/Elbe Regiment. The second line was quickly formed with the 1/, 2/, 3/4th East Prussian Infantry Regiment and the 4th Battalion (von Wedel) and the 3rd Battalion (von Meyern) of 5th Reserve Regiment. The 1st Leib Hussars formed behind the left flank, three squadrons of the Brandenburg Dragoons formed behind the middle and the 2/, 3/East Prussian Jager Battalion stood behind them.[26]

Krafft and his 6th Brigade moved from Kaltenborn, to a point between Nieder-Görsdorf and Wölmsdorf, to form the left of the Prussian main line.

As the 6th Brigade (Krafft) pulled into line, it organized itself with the Colberg Infantry Regiment on the right and the 9th Reserve Infantry Regiment on the left flank. Both regiments had their fusilier battalions on the flanks. In the second line stood the four battalions of the 1st Neumärk Landwehr Regiment and the 1/, 2/, 4/1st Pomeranian Landwehr Cavalry Regiment on the right flank. The 3/1st Pomeranian Landwehr Cavalry stood by Nieder-Görsdorf.

In front of his line stood Spreuth's 6pdr Foot Battery #16. The battery had ten guns and was posted close to Wölmsdorf. Half of 6pdr Foot Battery #19 (Baumgarten – from the reserve) was posted by Nieder-Görsdorf. Behind the latter stood the 3/1st Pomeranian Landwehr Cavalry Regiment.

Spreuth's 6pdr Foot Battery #16 had, somewhat earlier, moved up by Wölmsdorf, and deployed. It was to be detached and joined the 9th Reserve Regiment in its attack on the Göhlsdorf heights.

Thümen was to lead the first attack. Once his forces were organized Thümen led them forward, advancing in the direction of Jüterbogk. A skirmish fight began, supported by artillery, as Thümen pushed up against two battalions of Morand's 12th Division. The Elbe Regiment took them under fire at a range of 100 paces, throwing them back in great disorder.

The French counterattacked with three battalions supported by artillery. They struck the Prussians where they were not supported by their artillery, and the havoc wrought by the French canister fire was dreadful.

The pressure on Tauentzien's forces, to the left of Thümen, was too great. They began to fall back and as a result of the weakening of the left flank, the 2/5th Reserve Regiment (von Puttlitz's battalion) was taken in the left flank and rear and was itself thrown back in great disorder.

Major von Gagern kept the two battalions of the 5th Reserve Regiment deployed on the left flank, but they did not advance. The French closed to within 30 paces, engaging them with musketry. On the left flank, Major von Puttlitz, commander of the 2/5th Reserve Regiment,[27] rode up and dismounted, ordering his battalion to turn to the east and open fire. At the same time von Thümen drew the intact battalion on the right flank back behind the shelter of the rising ground, while sending forward his skirmishers.

At the same time the 1st Leib Hussar Regiment and a horse battery moved left to support the withdrawing Prussian infantry.

The Fus/3rd East Prussian Regiment, under Major Gleisenberg, provided the skirmish screen while the two other battalions of this regiment pulled back to the right of Nieder-Görsdorf where they were covered by Dietrichs' Russian 12pdr Position Battery #7. Majors Bentheim and Puttlitz (1/, 2/5th Reserve Regiment) pulled their battalions back as well. Here they were covered by Meyer's 12pdr Foot Battery #4 and Conradi's half 12pdr Foot Battery #5.

As they withdrew the Polish cavalry operating with Bertrand's IV Corps threw itself through the skirmish line and attacked the formed infantry behind them. The Prussian 4th Reserve Regiment, under Major von Uttenhofen, formed square, as did the 2/, 3/, 4/3rd East Prussian Landwehr Regiment. The Poles then passed on and were engaged by Tauentzien's cavalry, which stood on Thümen's left flank.[28] The 1st Leib Hussar Regiment also joined the attack. The Poles were crushed, losing nine officers, including Colonel Clouet, 93 men, and 50 horses. The remaining Poles withdrew towards Wölmsdorf, where they passed in front of Krafft. Krafft's artillery fired on them as they went by. Ney reputedly sent orders for the nearest cavalry brigade to support the brave Poles. It was the Westphalian cavalry brigade. Its commander, seeing the danger, did not move. Ney is supposed to have sent him to Napoleon after "ripping off his epaulets".[29]

Two Prussian batteries had deployed as Thümen withdrew, and began to cover his retreat. However, the French advance was very quick and they were able to close on the batteries. The two Prussian batteries only just escaped being captured. Indeed, the French came so close that a number of gunners and horses were killed in 6pdr Battery #5 by French musketry.

The Prussian Leib Hussars' attack on Polish lancers at Dennewitz, by Knötel.

By the Uttenhofen farm, Thümen's forces also found themselves in trouble. On the hill by the farm the 3rd East Prussian Landwehr Regiment had arranged its three battalions in two lines. As it stood, defending its position, it found itself under heavy musketry fire from a screen of French skirmishers. The skirmishers and their supporting infantry caused the landwehr regiment to begin to waiver, but the fire from the 34 guns amassed by the Denkmalsberg began, about 2:00 p.m., to take the French under fire and drove them back. This was the two batteries of Spreuth (6pdr Foot battery #16) and Baumgarten (6pdr Foot battery #19) in front of Wölmsdorf and the batteries of Meyer (12pdr Foot battery #4), Ludwig (6pdr Foot battery #6) , and Dietrichs (Russian Position Battery #7), which were north of Nieder-Görsdorf. The batteries by Nieder-Görsdorf were covered by two battalions of the 4th East Prussian Regiment.[30]

Prussian Artillery Action

With the French assault stopped and recoiling, 12pdr Battery #4 (Meyer) and 6pdr Battery #5 (Glasenapp) advanced across the watercourse and began to fire on the French again. They took up positions by the Nieder-Görsdorf wind mill. The Russian guns had risen to 18 pieces with the arrival of Schluter's 12pdr Position Battery #21 and they took up a position 800 paces from the Prussian guns. This brought the number of guns on the Denkmalsberg, on right flank of the 6th Brigade's batteries, to 24 guns.

The French assault had spelt misfortune for Spreuth's 6pdr Foot Battery #16 as well. It had been detached from Krafft's brigade and was posted by Wölmsdorf. It had fired for some time on Dennewitz, but as Devaux's brigade appeared, Spreuth switched his fire to that new target. The

French response to this was fatal for the isolated Prussian battery and four guns were dismounted in 10 minutes. It also suffered heavy losses in men and horses. The devastating fire appears to have come from Devaux's brigade battery who, by Devaux's position, must have had a flanking position on the battery. Similar fire must have come from Defrance's divisional horse artillery, as well as that of the Saxons.

Spreuth's 6pdr Foot Battery #16 continued to suffer and shortly it had only two guns. The French fire shifted to the half battery under Baumgarten (6pdr Foot Battery #19) and the Fus/4th East Prussian Regiment under Major von Clausewitz, which had moved to Spreuth's position from the Denkmalsberg.

Behind them, in Wölmsdorf the Polish cavalry, who were later defeated by the 1st Leib Hussars, had overrun the Prussian munitions column posted there. A battalion of the 3rd Neumärk Landwehr Regiment turned and fired on them. The misdirected landwehr fire inflicted further casualties on Spreuth's battery.

Thümen's Counterattack

Thümen organized a counterattack with the sixteen battalions of the 3rd, 4th, and 6th Brigades. The 3/9th Reserve Regiment was ordered to seize Nieder-Görsdorf. The remainder of the assault was organized as follows:

Ludwig's 6pdr Foot Battery #6 stood on the right. The 1/, 2/4th East Prussian Regiment followed behind the right wing as a reserve with a Russian battery. The 1st Leib Hussars were to make contact with the 4th Army Corps. The schützen of the 1/, 2/4th East Prussian Regiment moved against the right bank of the river as it flowed through Dennewitz. Their attack was supported by the fire of a 12pdr cannon.[31] It was about 2:30 p.m., and Durutte's 32nd Division was beginning to arrive on the field.

Thümen's counterattack rolled forward, driving the French before it. As the French withdrew back into the pine woods, the 2/Brandenburg Dragoon Regiment pursued them. Moving at a trot the squadron encountered a French battalion in square. They broke into a gallop at a range of 150 paces and at 30 paces the square delivered its volley. Dead and wounded Prussians dropped from their saddles from the single volley. The Prussians lost 7 men and 23 horses dead, 21 men and 18 horses wounded or missing, and the squadron was reduced to 80 men.

The Prussian battery on the Denkmalsberg became the center of attention, as the more than 40 guns the French had across their line by Dennewitz turned their attention on them. The Italians and Württembergers poured a flanking fire into the position as well. As a result, the 3/4th Reserve Regiment and the 1/, 2/, 3/, 4/5th Reserve Regiment were ordered forward to engage them.

The Prussians began a bayonet attack on the middle of the Italian/Württemberg line. The Prussians pushed into the pine woods that the Italians occupied. Polczinski's battalion (3/4th Reserve), supported by 50 landwehr cavalry, struck at a company of the 2/4th Württemberg Regiment which was deployed in the woods as skirmishers. The Prussians broke it, taking several prisoners. The remainder of the 1/9th Württemberg was pushed back on Morand's division. General Stockmayer, beset by the cloud of Prussian skirmishers from Tauentzien's corps,[32] found himself obliged to withdraw his brigade. The Prussian skirmishers were supported by the 1/, 2/3rd Pomeranian Landwehr Cavalry Regiment. This force pushed through the Württembergers and quickly encountered the 7th Württemberg Regiment, also part of Stockmayer's brigade, formed in square. The Pomeranian cavalry attacked and at 60 paces received the defensive fire from the square and withdrew.

Polczinski's battalion (3/4th Reserve Regiment) completely deployed as skirmishers, closed on the 7th Württembergers, supported by the guns from Jenichen's Horse Battery #6 and Gleim's

6pdr Battery #17. The two batteries began to fire canister on the huddled mass of Württembergers, breaking the square and inflicting heavy casualties on it. The square was broken with 15 officers and 516 men being lost. Only 70 escaped back to their division. A total of 230 were captured and the rest were killed or wounded.[33] The 2nd Württemberg Regiment found itself trapped in the same manner and it too was destroyed.[34]

It was 4:00 p.m., and the combined effects of this attack were to break the French flank. Its flank compromised, Morand's 12th Division began to pull back from the woods. Ney threw forward his last reserve, two Württemberg battalions with four horse guns that had been standing in the streets of Dennewitz. Fontanelli's division and Morand's divisions began to pull back towards Rohrbeck.

Actions before Jüterbogk

Bertrand sent two battalions of Stockmayer's brigade forward over the Nuthe and placed them on the heights on the northern bank by Rohrbeck. They pushed Spreuth's battery from the ridge and secured Franquemont's flank from threat by Major Kleist's three battalions and Mathais' 6pdr Foot Battery #27.

Kleist's flanks had been unsupported until about noon, when Tauentzien moved Kosposth's battalion (5/1st Silesian Landwehr) and Lent's half battery (12pdr Battery #5) to Kappan. Mathais accidentally had his battery fire on Gleim's battery, which stood on the road to Dennewitz. After firing 24 shots at a range of 1,300 to 1,400 paces, he discovered his error and began firing on the Württemberg infantry, which stood at the same distance before him.

Before Rohrbeck stood a pine forest, in which the Württembergers had posted some artillery and cavalry. Facing them across the Agger stream stood the 2/2nd Neumärk Landwehr Infantry Regiment (Grolmann's Battalion) and the 1/, 2/, 4/5th Kurmärk Landwehr Regiment. Tauentzien's left wing extended towards Major Kleist's position. The battle raging across the northern face of the battlefield consisted mostly of a skirmish fight. Unfortunately, Tauentzien's artillery had expended its ammunition and suddenly found itself faced by the arrival of the Saxon cavalry brigade about 3:30 p.m. the 2/2nd Neumärk Landwehr (Grolmann), the 3rd Pomeranian Landwehr Cavalry Regiment, and the Illowaiski #3 Cossack Pulk were sent towards Rohrbeck to engage them. The Württemberg skirmishers still stood in the pine forest before the village. The 3rd Neumärk Landwehr Cavalry Regiment drove them back, but lost 12 men and 22 horses.

Finally, the Russian 12pdr Battery #7, Dietrichs, arrived, and established itself at a distance of 900 paces from Rohrbeck, and began to bombard the French forces occupying it. It was about 5:00 p.m., as this bombardment began, which is also the time that Bertrand received the order to begin withdrawing from the battlefield.[35]

The Württembergers began to withdraw back across the Agger, covered by Stockmayer's artillery. Stockmayer pulled his brigade into Rohrbeck, but found himself soon beset by the skirmishers of the 3rd East Prussian Infantry Regiment, supported by the battalions of Kemphen (Fus/4th East Prussian Infantry) and Friccius (3/3rd East Prussian Landwehr).

Oudinot and the XII Corps

Until about noon, Oudinot's XII Corps remained in and around Seyda, despite the sound of artillery to the west. At noon, Ney sent Oudinot an order to advance. When the XII Corps began to move, around 1:00 p.m., Pacthod (13th Division) and Guilleminot (14th Division) moved from Seyda down the main road to Dennewitz. The Bavarians (29th Division) stood behind the cavalry, by Gudesgast, and Oudinot's headquarters was in Seyda. Oudinot's advance was not a mad dash forward to join the battle, but was rather a normal day's marching pace. There appeared to be little eagerness to join the battle.

Reynier Arrives

The VII Corps (Reynier) had begun moving down the Ohna-Rohrbeck road about 1:00 p.m., in response to the same order from Ney. Defrance's 4th Heavy Cavalry Division accompanied the VII Corps.

Reynier's Corps, at this time, contained 16,278 men and 59 guns. They were distributed as follows:

24th Division – Lecoq	5,136 men	16 guns[1]
25th Division – von Sahr	3,981	20
32nd Division – Durutte	4,600	10
Polish Infantry – Dombrowski	1,200	2
Polish Cavalry	?	–
26th Light Cavalry Brig – Lindenau	1,361	9

Note
1   von Boyen, *Darestellung*, p.34.

As they closed on the battlefield, one of Nev's adjutants arrived with word that Reynier was to detach a force to support Morand's left wing. Durutte's 32nd Division was pulled from the middle of the march column and sent north. It arrived about 2:00-2:30 p.m. Jarrv's brigade passed over the stream by the mill and relieved the Württembergers, and Devaux's Brigade positioned itself to support the guns on the heights southwest of Göhlsdorf, near the stream.

Reynier then saw the Prussians to the west, and swung his two Saxon divisions to meet them. The Saxon cavalry and horse artillery moved to Rohrbeck, where it encountered Tauentzien's Cossacks.

The 1/Niesemeuschel Regiment was detached to cover the road and left in Ohna.[36] As Durutte's 32nd Division moved to its assigned position, it became entangled with Lecoq's 24th Division, delaying its march. The 25th Division (von Sahr) found itself set upon by Voronzov's and Czernichev's Cossacks, which had come from Zahna into the rear of the French army. Lecoq's 24th Division received its orders. Mellentin's 2nd Brigade was ordered to seize Göhlsdorf and von Brause's 1st Brigade was ordered to move to his right and cover a 12pdr battery, that was to be positioned on the Windmühlberg. The 25th Division was to move behind Mellentin and support its attack.

Defrance's 4th Heavy Cavalry Division was also closing up and passed between Dennewitz and Göhlsdorf to take a position on the low hills behind the guns facing Wölmsdorf. It stood behind the crest of the low hill running from Göhlsdorf and Dennewitz, where it was concealed from the view of the Prussians.

Durutte's Attack

About 3:00 p.m., Jarry and Devaux led their brigades forward against Nieder-Görsdorf, where Clausewitz stood with three battalions, two from the 4th East Prussian Regiment. They stood on the left bank of the stream. The 3/9th Reserve Regiment (from Krafft's Brigade) and a number of schützen stood on the right bank of the stream.[37]

Jarry's assault pushed the 2/4th East Prussian Regiment back into the now burning village. Behind the village it rallied with the other battalion and found itself assaulted from the south by Defrance's cavalry. The 4th East Prussian Regiment then withdrew to the heights, where it joined Thümen's 4th Brigade.

The Final Phase of the Battle

At 3:30 p.m., the Prussian forces on the battlefield were deployed such that Major Kleist still stood before Jüterbogk with three battalions[38] and Mathias' 6pdr Foot Battery #27. The 2nd Neumärk Landwehr Cavalry Regiment and the Illowaiski #3 Cossack Pulk stood on the Agger facing Rohrbeck. Tauentzien stood with his forces extending from Jüterbogk to the west, where they joined Thümen. Tauentzien's forces were deployed in a line. The 12pdr Foot Battery #5 (Lent)[39] and Kospoth's Battalion (5/1st Silesian Landwehr Regiment), stood on the road behind Kappan. To the west on the road, 800 paces from Lent's battery and on the edge of the woods, stood the 3rd East Prussian Landwehr Cavalry Regiment. Grolmann's Battalion (2/2nd Neumärk Landwehr Regiment) stood in the forest and the 3rd Pomeranian Landwehr Cavalry Regiment stood on the western edge of the forest.

Extending to the west were the Mellerski (4/5th Kurmärk) and Treskow Battalions (1/5th Kurmärk) and the Wittich (2nd), Welling (1st), and Rango (3rd) Battalions of the 3rd Reserve Regiment. Behind the 3rd Reserve Regiment was half of 6pdr Foot Battery #30 Hertig and 6pdr Foot Battery #17 Gleim. To the west of the artillery stood Lemke's Battalion, 2/1st Silesian Landwehr.

Thümen's 4th Brigade and Hessen-Homburg's 3rd Brigade appear to have become totally mixed. This combined force, under Thümen's direction, extended from Nieder-Görsdorf to Tauentzien's division. The 3/4th Reserve Regiment stood in the pine forest, on the road from Jüterbogk to Neider-Görsdorf. Behind it, also in the forest, was the Fus/4th East Prussian Regiment. On the western edge of the forest were the 1/, 2/Elbe Infantry Regiment. Extending to their right was the massed artillery of Hessen-Homburg's 3rd Brigade, Thümen's 4th Brigade and the Prussian reserve. Behind the artillery in the first line, from east to west, were three battalions of the 5th Reserve Regiment, and the 2/, 1/4th Reserve Regiment.

On their left, behind the end of the line, stood the two squadrons and jägers of the Brandenburg Dragoon Regiment. Behind the dragoons, in the second line, stood the 2/, 3/, 4/3rd East Prussian Landwehr Regiment and the Leib Hussars.

Running southwest from Neider-Görsdorf to Wölmsdorf, was Krafft's 6th Brigade. His first line, east to west, was the 2/, 1/9th Reserve Regiment, 2/Colberg Regiment, two howitzers of 12pdr Foot Battery #5, 6pdr Foot Battery #16 Spreuth, and half of Russian 12pdr Position Battery #21. Behind Spreuth's battery stood two squadrons of the 2nd West Prussian Dragoon Regiment.

Borstell's 5th Brigade was marching towards Göhlsdorf, in two lines with its artillery in the lead and his cavalry on his right flank. Oppen's reserve cavalry was posted to the southwest of Göhlsdorf.

The French were deployed such that Franquemont's Württembergers (38th Division) stood to the north of Denmewitz, facing Tauentzien. Fontinelli's Italians (15th Division) were marching to Rohrbeck to cover the French rear from the Prussian cavalry. To their rear, yet still north of Dennewitz, Morand's 12th Division faced northwest, directly opposite Thümen's division. Behind him was Lorge's 5th Light Cavalry Division. To Morand's left stood Devaux's 1st Brigade, 32nd Division. In front of Devaux was his artillery. Jarry's brigade, 32nd Division, stood south of Dennewitz, behind Devaux. The Württemberg cavalry (24th Light Cavalry Brigade) stood behind

Bavarians from Raglovich's Division at Dennewitz, by Zimmer.

Jarry's Brigade. To their right, behind Rohrbeck stood the Saxon 26th Light Cavalry Brigade. Daring's brigade (38th Division) stood south of Dennewitz, half way to Ohna.

To Devaux's left stood Brause's 1st Saxon Brigade, 24th Division. Brause's left flank touched the village of Göhlsdorf. Defrance's 4th Heavy Cavalry Division stood behind them.

Mellentin's 2nd Brigade, 24th Division stood in the eastern edge of Göhlsdorf, contesting possession of the village with the Prussians. Behind him, and to Defrance's left, stood the 25th (Saxon) Division, under GL von Sahr.

Behind von Sahr, advancing from Ohna, was the XII Corps. Guilleminot's 14th Division led, followed by Pacthod's 13th Division, Wolf's 29th Light Cavalry Brigade, and Raglovich's (29th Bavarian) Division. Raglovich's division was moving on the road from Zahna to Ohna, to the southwest of the rest of the XII Corps. Fournier's 6th Light Cavalry Division marched to the west of Guilleminot.

The Assault on Göhlsdorf

As Revnier's forces deployed, Lecoq's 24th Division swung to the west facing Göhlsdorf and began to advance towards the Prussians. Brause's brigade assumed a position on the north flank of the village, while Mellentin's brigade moved into and occupied the eastern half of the village. To face this movement the Fus/3rd East Prussian Regiment, under Major von Gleisenberg, moved through the western gardens of the village and occupied the village before Mellentin's brigade arrived. On the Windmühlberg stood Spreuth's 6pdr Foot Battery #16. The pressure of the Saxon attack was such that Spreuth was obliged to withdraw back behind Wölmsdorf. However, the fusiliers remained to fight for the possession of the village.[40]

The Saxon schützen, supported by the Saxon Grenadier Battalion Spiegel, advanced into the village and pushed the Prussian fusiliers out. The Prussians quickly regrouped and came back into the village with a bayonet assault and threw the Saxons back in their turn.

The Saxons renewed the effort by sending in a battalion of the Steindel Infantry Regiment and one other. The Prussians pulled back into the cemetery and assumed a position behind an earthen wall, about 100 paces from the village.

The Prussian fusiliers were shortly joined by the schützen of the 9th Reserve Regiment under Captain von Petzhold and supported by the remainder of the battalion of the 9th Reserve Regiment. Bülow, seeing the developing battle for Göhlsdorf, ordered Hessen-Homburg's 3rd Brigade forward to contest the village with the Saxons.[41]

Brause had placed his Saxon brigade on the north of Göhlsdorf, along the road running from Göhlsdorf to Dennewitz. The 2nd Saxon 6pdr battery stood before his infantry, a 12pdr battery stood on right and a French horse battery was slightly further to his right. Von Sahr's 25th Division closed behind Brause's brigade and sent its artillery forward to the right of Brause's artillery. His other battery moved to the south of Göhlsdorf, where it could bombard Oppen's reserve cavalry, which stood on the plains to the south of Göhlsdorf.

The Prussians moved Spreuth's (6pdr Foot Battery #16), Baumgarten's (6pdr Foot Battery #19) and the half battery of Steinwehr (Horse Battery #6) forward to face the Saxon 12pdr batteries. Steinwehr's battery was quickly driven back by skirmishers coming from the north end of the village and Spreuth lost four guns. The Saxon artillery drove Oppen's reserve cavalry back behind Wölmsdorf.

The Saxon pressure was heavy and Krafft was ordered to withdraw. Once he was disengaged from the Saxons, he was reinforced by the arrival of three battalions. A second attack was prepared, with the battalions of the first line being deployed, in order to minimize their losses to the French artillery. The second line of battalions advanced in columns 300 to 400 paces behind the first.[42]

The first Prussians to move against Göhlsdorf was the Fus/3rd East Prussian Infantry regiment under Major von Gleisendorf. They were followed quickly by the 2nd East Prussian Grenadier Battalion and the 1/3rd East Prussian Regiment. Behind them was the 1/3rd East Prussian Landwehr Regiment. This force was commanded by brigade commander Major von Sjöholm.

The Prussian assault was covered on the flank by the remaining guns of Spreuth's Battery (6pdr Foot Battery #16) and half Russian 12pdr Position Battery #7, Dietrichs, on the right. On the right side of the village, by the reserve cavalry, stood Horse Battery #5, Neindorff, and 6pdr Foot Battery #5, Glasenapp. The Prussian artillery began a furious barrage to support the Prussian advance. A special effort was made to suppress the flanking fire from the French and Saxon batteries to the north of Göhlsdorf.

Gleisenberg's battalion (Fus/3rd East Prussian) struck into the village supported by the fire of Neindorff and Glasenapp's batteries. As these Prussians drove forward, the first Swedish forces appeared on the field. A Swedish horse battery supported by the Morner Hussar Regiment arrived and joined Borstell, assuming a position on the left flank.[43]

The first Prussian assault was pushed back. A second assault started, when the 1/, Fus/Colberg Regiment were ordered forward to assist the first wave and attack Gohlsberg.

The battalions of Hecken, Graben,[44] and Zäune pushed down the main street of the village. The 1/Colberg Regiment moved into the northern edge of the village under the command of Oberst von Zastrow. The 2nd East Prussian Grenadier Battalion, under Oberstleutnant von Sjöholm, and the 1/3rd East Prussian Infantry Regiment, under Major von Bülow, moved into the southern part of the village. The reserve, following the assault, consisted of 1/1st Neumärk Landwehr Regiment and the 1/3rd East Prussian Landwehr Regiment. Spreuth's battery and the half Russian battery advanced and continued their fire on the northern side of the village, while on the south the batteries of Neindorff and Glasenapp continued their fire.

The 2/Colberg and the 1st Neumärk Landwehr Regiment were drawn from the reserve and ordered to move against the Windmühlberg.

The battle in the village ceased to be a formal Battle of volley fire and became a house to house bayonet fight. On the northern end of the village, the Saxon Prinz Friedrich Infantry Regiment had positioned itself in the church and defended itself with the greatest tenacity.[45] They were facing the 1/3rd East Prussian Regiment. In an effort to push the Prussians out, the Saxons charged forward in column. Major von Bülow swung his right wing and fired on the Saxons at a range of 60–80 paces. Despite the Saxon defense, the Prussians were to prevail, taking 300–400 Saxons prisoners.[46]

With his forces pushed out, Oudinot turned his artillery loose on Göhlsdorf, determined to pound the offending Prussians into submission. The Prussians were obliged to withdraw, surrendering the village once again to the Saxons.

Borstell brought his 5th Brigade forward to renew the attack. He advanced with his eight battalions in two lines on Göhlsdorf. His first line consisted of 1/, 2/2nd Kurmärk Landwehr Regiment, 12 guns in the middle, and the 1/, 2/2nd Reserve Regiment. The second line consisted of the 1st Pomeranian Grenadier Battalion, the 1/1st Pomeranian Regiment, the 4/2nd Kurmärk Landwehr Regiment, and the 3/2nd Landwehr Regiment. The three squadrons of the East Prussian Uhlans and the Pomeranian Hussars covered the right flank along with two horse guns.[47]

As the Prussians attacked, the 2/, 3/2nd Reserve Regiment supported the attack, with the 4/2nd Kurmärk Landwehr Regiment striking the right of the village and the 2/2nd Reserve Regiment (von Hovel) and the Pomeranian Grenadier Battalion striking the left. The artillery stood on the heights to the right of the village. The remainder of the battalions formed themselves on the flank of the Saxon position. A reserve was formed from the Fus/, 2/1st Pomeranian Regiment,[48] the 3/2nd Kurmärk Landwehr Regiment, 3/West Prussian Uhlan Regiment, and two horse batteries.[49] The northern end of the village was taken under fire by the Swedish battery and the Russian half-battery.[50]

The 2nd Reserve Regiment made the first attack on the village, with the Pomeranian Grenadier Battalion supporting their attack. The other battalions advanced to the heights below the village. The Saxons fought desperately to hold their positions. Major von Hovel, who led the 2/2nd Reserve, moved against a battery by the village, only to be driven back by its fire and that of its supporting infantry. The 2/2nd Reserve Regiment suffered massive losses.

The Saxons responded by counterattacking with six battalions. This was more than the Prussians could stand and they were pushed back in their turn.[51]

As Borstell advanced, Oppen's reserve cavalry moved to the south of the field and the batteries of Neindorff (Horse Battery #5) and Glasenapp (6pdr Foot Battery #5), which had earlier been on the south of the village, moved to the right.

Reynier continued to support his right flank with a strong battery on the Windmühlberg heights. His left flank extended to the XII Corps. Having no instructions from Ney, Oudinot detached Gruyer's 1st Brigade, Guilleminot's 14th Division, to move towards Göhlsdorf and support the Saxons.

After the attack by the 2/2nd Reserve fell back, the Prussians renewed their artillery bombardment. The battery was reinforced by the arrival of Horse Battery #5, Neindorff. The Fus/Colberg Infantry Regiment, the 2nd East Prussian Grenadier Battalion, the 1/3rd East Prussian Infantry Regiment and the 1st Neumärk Landwehr Regiment had joined themselves to Borstell's brigade after their attacks. In addition, two companies of the 2/Colberg Regiment joined him as well. The 5th Brigade had organized itself with the six companies of the Colberg Regiment and the 1/, 2/2nd Reserve in its first line. The second line was reformed with the Pomeranian Grenadiers and the three landwehr battalions. As a reserve, the 3/2nd Reserve Regiment formed behind the left wing.[52]

The 1/1st Pomeranian Infantry Regiment (Major Podewils) advanced against the Windmühlberg, attacking a 12pdr battery supported by a battalion of the Anton Infantry Regiment. The battery defended itself at 60 paces with canister, followed by a volley fire from the Anton Infantry Regiment, which killed or wounded 90 men.[53] Under such punishment the Pomeranians fell back. Elsewhere, however, the battle went better for the attacking Prussians and the *Leibfahn* (principal standard) of the Saxon 2/König Regiment was captured. The Saxons were unable to stand the overall effect of this final attack. They collapsed and fell back only to be saved from total destruction by the timely intervention of Defrance's 4th Heavy Cavalry Division and his 11 dragoon squadrons. The Prussian advance stalled and Ney's situation was at its critical phase.

It was also during this phase of the battle, that Maréchal Ney had ordered the XII Corps to withdraw from battle around Göhlsdorf, and assume a position behind Rohrbeck.

The XII Corps' Fateful Maneuver

Around 4:00 p.m., the XII Corps arrived on the field and deployed to the left of the VII Corps and the action renewed. Faced with the repulse to the north, Ney committed the XII Corps in the center. Bülow was thrown back by the attacks of the French left (VII and XII Corps) and forced to abandon Wölmsdorf and Dalichow.

Ney found himself with his entire force committed and no reserve on hand to administer the coup de grace to the allies. To do this, he withdrew the XII Corps from the action and ordered it to fall behind the IV and VII Corps where it would form a reserve. The Prussians, perceiving this as a withdrawal, quickly reoccupied Nieder-Göhlsdorf.

If Ney had not been with the IV Corps, personally leading an attack, but had remained in central control, this probably would not have happened.

It was as the XII Corps fell back, that Borstell arrived in Eckmansdorf. Borstell assumed a position on the right of Bülow, and the Prussians began a renewed attack. Shortly after this, the heads of Bernadotte's Swedish and Russian columns appeared near Eckmansdorf, but of them, only the Russian hussars were to take part in the battle. The French found themselves obliged to withdraw.

Bertrand's Renewed Attacks – 4:30 p.m.

Ney now organized a major assault, using the rest of Morand's and Fontinelli's divisions, plus a force of cavalry. They advanced behind a swarm of skirmishers, until they were within 80 paces of the 4th East Prussian Regiment. The East Prussians were deployed in line and received them with heavy musket fire. The 1/, 2/5th Reserve Regiment (Thümen's Brigade) stood with them, pouring volley after volley into the French assault.

On their left, a battery and two squadrons of the 1st Leib Hussars stopped the French cavalry. The 3rd East Prussian Landwehr Regiment advanced from the rear and joined the battle. This, combined with supporting artillery fire from the Prussian center left, drove the French attack back.

The result of the abandonment of Göhlsdorf by the XII Corps and the failure of Bertrand's attack had changed the tactical situation of the battle to the point where Ney's position was rapidly becoming untenable. The Saxons were not destroyed, but they continued their withdrawal. Ney and Reynier tried to rally the Saxons as they fell back. They would collide with the XII Corps and carry them away as well. It was into this that Bülow would launch yet another attack.

Bülow's Exploitation

As the XII Corps withdrew to become a tactical reserve, Bülow ordered General von Oppen to support the attack of the 5th Brigade, with his entire cavalry reserve. Oppen moved to Borstell's right wing and sent forward half of Horse Battery #6 (Steinwehr) supported by the Königin Dragoon Regiment. They were quickly engaged by a Saxon howitzer battery.

This force was quickly joined by the Swedish battery under Colonel Cardel, and two Russian batteries under Captain Grabowski which had been behind Wölmsdorf. Two Russian Hussar Regiments, led by GM von Pahlen, and two Russian jager Battalions moved to the vicinity of Wölmsdorf and joined in the last attack of the 6th Brigade. The Russian hussars joined the Prussian hussars in a sharp engagement against a French cavalry regiment and threw it back capturing eight cannons.[54] By Ohna, the Pomeranian Hussars charged a force of French infantry capturing 1,200 infantry and three cannons.

Pahlen, by G. Dawe.

His troops were fatigued, so General von Borstell sent one last attack forward towards Körbitz and Wölsikendorf, supported by Oppen's cavalry. This attack consisted of his three landwehr regiments and the Pomeranian National Cavalry Regiment. Their attack was successful and they captured a large quantity of baggage. The West Prussian Uhlans moved against Schönewalde and captured one howitzer and two cannons.

The 1/, 2/4th East Prussian Regiment was then ordered to take the heights by Dennewitz, as well as to take the village. This assault was successful, though the standard of the 1st Battalion was shot down.

Rohrbeck remained in French hands, but the 4th Brigade was sent forward. Thümen brought forward Dietrichs' 12pdr Russian Position Battery #7, which took the village under fire and set it ablaze. The schützen of the 5th Kurmärk Landwehr Regiment, which had moved into the woods before Rohrbeck, moved into the village led by Lieutenants Kalisch and Klingner. They captured two French guns in the village.

The 2/, 3/3rd East Prussian Landwehr Cavalry Regiment drove through the village and encountered two groups of French cavalry. One force consisted of 11 squadrons and the other of 8. The Prussian cavalry struck the smaller group, which was already engaged. The French broke and withdrew from the field.

Thümen's forces moved between Rohrbeck and Dennewitz. The Fus/4th East Prussian Regiment was the first to cross the main road and found only French cavalry before it. The Brandenburg Dragoons and the 2nd Kurmärk Landwehr Cavalry Regiment followed the French cavalry back between Kötlitz and Wölsikendorf, where they joined the Prussian cavalry from the right wing. The last of Ney's forces withdrew from the battlefield, leaving it to the allies.

The Withdrawal from the Battle

Ney was forced to order his forces to withdraw towards Dahme, but the convoys advancing down that road became entangled with the withdrawing forces, causing tremendous confusion. Ney,

A French staff officer is captured by a Prussian hussar at Dennewitz, by Knötel.

with the IV Corps, moved on Dahme, where he engaged Wobeser's division coming from Luckau in the streets of Dahme itself. Wobeser ordered an immediate attack and sent Oberst Jeanneret forward with the bulk of his cavalry. Inside Dahme, the 3/, 4/1st West Prussian Landwehr Infantry Regiment moved from Rosenthal street, right to Baruther Street, while the 1/, 2/1st West Prussian Landwehr Infantry Regiment, supported by two cannons, stood on both sides of the Steindammes facing the Luckau Gate. The first two battalions moved towards the Schlof Gate. The French of Bertrand's IV Corps were, at first, delayed by cutting their way through the undergrowth and crossing the ditches outside Dahme. They encountered the Prussians and slowly fed in more and more forces.[55]

The 1/2nd Neumärk Landwehr Regiment stood on the left wing and had a break in the wall before them, which they defended stoutly. At the same time, a French battalion moved against the church taking it quickly. The Prussians countered with their cavalry taking a number of prisoners.[56]

As brave as the Prussian defense may have been, it could not stand before the weight of three full French corps, and it soon withdrew, allowing Ney to pass. The last Prussians out of his way, Ney felt obliged to withdraw on Torgau, which he reached on 7 September, after making a 40 kilometer march without halting.

On 7 September, the VII Corps arrived in Annaberg and at noon, it encountered the XII Corps in Kreischau, which had come by way of Schönewalde. From there Reynier and Oudinot took the road to Torgau.

Results of the Battle of Dennewitz

The French losses at Dennewitz were estimated by Ney to be about 8,000 men, but he also lost 53 cannons and 412 vehicles in the tangled roads. Records indicate that the 38th Württemberg

Division lost 2,259 men killed, wounded and missing out of a strength of around 4,000 men.[57] The Saxons lost 16 officers and 1,082 men killed or wounded, while they also appear to have lost 12 officers and about 2,000 men as prisoners. In addition, they lost 12 guns and 40 wagons to the allies.[58] The heaviest fighting was done by France's German allies, who lost 5,357 men.

The Swedes, because of their minimal involvement in the battle, lost 2 officers and 14 men killed or wounded. The Prussians, on the other hand, suffered rather heavily. Their losses were:

	Killed		Wounded		Missing	
	Officers	Men	Officers	Men	Officers	Men
IV Prussian Army Corps						
1st Brigade	3	187	10	770	1	257
2nd Brigade	4	170	27	943	1	761
Artillery Reserve: total 17 officers and men killed, wounded or missing						
III Prussian Army Corps						
3rd Brigade	6	219	36	840	0	390
4th Brigade	3	236	34	1,074	0	277
5th Brigade	5	110	17	647	0	81
6th Brigade	6	186	61	1,317	0	290
Reserve Cavalry	5	31	24	99	0	62
Artillery Reserve: 1 officer, 47 men total						
A total of 9,255 killed, wounded & missing for both Prussian corps						

Bernadotte, however, took little profit from his victory. His pursuit was leisurely and did not arrive before Torgau until the morning of 8 September. From there he moved to Jüterbogk, on 12 September, to Zerbst on 15 September, and eventually reaching Blücher, with whom he would begin coordinating his operations. The Army of the North stood on the Elbe for several days, preparing its crossing at a leisurely pace.

If the Battle of Dennewitz raised the morale of the allies, it completely destroyed that of the French. Ney submitted his resignation, asking to be a simple grenadier, rather than a général en chef leading several divisions.

After the action at Dennewitz and the withdrawal of the three French corps to Torgau, this force was reorganized. The XII Corps was dissolved and its forces distributed to the other two corps, except for Raglovich's Bavarians, which were sent to Dresden to form part of the city's garrison.

It is difficult to say why Dennewitz turned out as it did. The principal problem on the French side of the battle was a lack of a clear, overall plan of battle. Ney is often accused of getting too closely involved in the battle and losing the overall vision of what was happening. On the other hand, Oudinot is also accused of sour grapes at having his command given to another after his defeat at Gross-Beeren. Certainly Ney was known to be impulsive and to get distracted into the micromanagement of a battle. He did this on several occasions and was probably out of his element as the commander of an independent army.

As for Oudinot's supposed deliberate failure to fully support Ney, this accuation is not without some substance. He and most of Napoleon's other marshals at one time or another showed themselves to be little more than overgrown children squabbling over a favorite toy or pouting because their egos were bruised. This is not to say that the allied generals were not an equally immature bunch, as they certainly intrigued against one another to the detriment of their armies on more than one occasion between 1792 and 1815.

The situation in question is when Ney ordered Oudinot to march to his right and Reynier begged him to leave one division to complete the French success at Göhlsdorf. Oudinot had orders and it can be argued that he felt that there were sufficient forces on hand for Göhlsdorf to fall to the French without his corps. It is also possible to argue that Oudinot assumed that Ney's request was the result of a more urgent threat than the surrender of Göhlsdorf. It would seem preferable to lay the blame on Ney's poor management of the battle than Oudinot's deliberate, malicious obedience knowing that to do so the battle would be lost. One must also remember that Oudinot must have recognized that his position depended on Napoleon's overall success and that any defeat of French forces did reduce Oudinot's prospects to continue in his position as an Imperial duke.

Epilogue:
September Silence:
The End of the August Campaign

August 1813 had been a whirlwind of action. So much so that the guns of August did not stopped firing until after the Battle of Dennewitz on 7 September. The allies had arrived at an agreement on tactics that had proven its worth and caused the allies to chalk up victory after victory against Napoleon's armies. In the one instance where the allies stood their ground against Napoleon he again proved to them that he was the greatest general of his age, thrashing them soundly, and driving them from the waterlogged Dresden battlefield with cold steel and cannon. Unfortunately, Napoleon's single victory at Dresden did not begin offset his losses at Katzbach, Hagelberg, Gross-Beeren, Dennewitz, Löwenberg, and Kulm.

In August the allies had seized and retained the strategic initiative. Napoleon and his armies had been ground down steadily, with some of his allies' contingents being almost totally obliterated. An example was the Württemberg army. By 8 September its 20 battalions had been reduced by combat losses to four combined infantry battalions with about 1,500 men. Its four cavalry regiments, originally about 2,000 men, totalled about 100 men.

The myth of French invincibility was seriously shaken, but not yet dead. Though Napoleon was still the terror of the battlefield, the allies had come to believe that he might yet succumb to a series of blows against his generals, followed by a crushing blow against Napoleon's main army. However, this assumed they could coordinate all their forces against his central army and deliver the blow before Napoleon struck them.

The allies had chosen a plan that would lead them down a very dangerous path. During September and October they would continue to operate on external lines of communication in dispersed armies against the still formidable Napoleon, who stood in central Saxony. Had the old Napoleon reawakened in this situation he might well have turned his army against one of the three principal allied armies operating against him and forced them into a decisive battle.

Napoleon had tired this repeatedly during August, but the old Napoleon was no longer at the helm. The allies had succeeded, with the exception of the Battle of Dresden, in staying one step ahead of the hammer's blow. Napoleon's principal fault lay in the terrain he felt obliged to defend. By holding Dresden and engaging the allies there, the Army of Bohemia did not have a particularly long march to make in order to withdraw into the fastness of the Erzgebirg Mountains. If the battle site had been another day's march north of those mountains, Napoleon's hard marching infantry might have been able to outpace the Austrians and inflict on them a second crushing defeat, driving Austria from the allied camp and ending the war. Even if the French had been unable to catch the Austrians, a second day's pursuit might well have inflicted sufficient losses on the Army of Bohemia during its retreat to shift the strategic situation.

Napoleon's operations in August 1813 lacked the elegant maneuvers of his spring campaign when he marched his newly formed armies across Germany to collide with the allies at Lützen. In bringing about that battle, and in the subsequent battle at Bautzen, Napoleon implemented sophisticated battle plans. These consisted of a pinning force to hold the allies in place and one or more sweeping pincer movements designed to strike and the flanks and rear of his enemies.

The subtle and elegant maneuvers had vanished over the summer and all that remained was the sledge hammer and fire brigade approach. Napoleon's one battle, Dresden, was a toe-to-toe slug fest that resulted after he ran his central army back and forth in an effort to catch one of the allied armies. Indeed, it was the allies who were attempting the carefully crafted envelopments, not Napoleon.

Why had Napoleon replaced the rapier with the bludgeon? It is hard to say. One can only speculate that it was a combination of causes, for no single event or illness particularly stands out.

Napoleon certainly appears to have felt that Saxony had to be defended. His letters and memorandums on the fortification of Dresden are substantial. He provisioned it heavily, he turned it into an "entrenched camp," and he defended it with a substantial garrison. It was the *point d'appui*, or point of support around which he executed all his maneuvers. His correspondence in late summer speaks of his hopes that it could withstand an allied assault, unsupported, for ten to twelve days, while he moved from Pirna to strike at the rear of the Army of Bohemia.

Napoleon's correspondence also gives a clear indication that he did not trust the Saxons and felt that he had to maintain a close eye on them or they would defect. This can be readily seen in the comments he made about ensuring that key Saxon fortresses had

Napoleon, by Delaroche.

French contingents of garrisons substantially larger than the Saxon contingents in them. This is the same approach he took to the seizure of the Spanish fortresses in 1808.

One potential reason for this was that he may have feared his German allies and empire would fall away from him should Dresden fall and Saxony be lost. His fear may have been real, but the probability of a mass defection while his armies were still whole was slim. It is true that his German allies were shaky. However, the Cossacks had roamed all across Western Germany that spring in an effort to ferment revolution and were still wandering about with little success in September. Both Dresden and Leizpig had been occupied by the allies the spring of 1813. Neither situation had caused Napoleon's German allies to fall away.

It is true that by August the members of the Confederation of the Rhine had rebuilt their armies and could now take some sort of military action. It is possible that Napoleon felt that by controlling Saxony he could keep his allies in line and would not have to fight the armies of a defecting German ally. Then again, if Napoleon felt the presence of armed Confederation contingents as potential support from a defecting ally, he should have placed them in the forefront of the August battles and burnt them out so they could not support a defection at home. It is arguable that this is what he did with the Saxon and Württemberg contingents, but not the Bavarian contingent, the most dangerous of them. There was ample opportunity for this, and to a degree Napoleon pursued this policy. Both the Württemberg and Saxon armies suffered very heavily in August, but the Bavarian and Westphalian armies were never engaged. As things would work out the Württembergers were faithful until the end, the Saxons finally defected the last day of the Battle of Leipzig, the Bavarians defected a few days before the Battle of Leipzig, and the Westphalians started deserting when the campaign began and never stopped.

If this was a major force driving Napoleon's operations it is neither supported by his actions nor the actions of his allied armies.

It has been suggested that Napoleon chose to defend Saxony in order to defend its ability to supply his troops. This would suggest that Napoleon felt no other part of Germany was rich enough to support his army or that the Cossack raiding parties would be more disruptive to the movement his supplies elsewhere.

Simply put, Germany was as capable as ever of supporting Napoleon's armies. Napoleon's correspondence is filled with discussions of heavy convoys of material and food stuffs coming into Germany from France, indicating that the French Army was not dependent on German supplies. In addition, the further east Napoleon stood the more spread out he was, giving the Cossacks more miles of his supply lines to harass. Dresden was as far east as Napoleon could advance his armies.

Historically Napoleon had repeatedly shown little regard for his lines of communications and though the main East-West road ran through Erfurt, Weimar, Leipzig, and Dresden, it was constantly overrun by Cossacks in the Fall of 1813. Indeed, he made very clear statements in June and July 1813 in his correspondence that if the allies were to march on Leipzig he would be delighted and would respond by marching on Prague and their lines of communication. His own lines of communication were not his principal concern.

The more easterly position did offer Napoleon two advantages. First, it put him closer to the enemy's heart, Berlin and Vienna. These strategic goals were well within striking distance. Napoleon's plans in early August envisioned Davout with 30,000 men and Oudinot with 80,000 men moving against Berlin. Girard, Oudinot, and Ney did eventually march against Berlin with disastrous results for all three. However, it is interesting to note that Napoleon had not sent anyone against Vienna as he had done in the 1805 and 1809 campaigns.

The second value of the more easterly position was that it offered Napoleon a position that was much closer to large garrisons of troops that had been cut off behind the allied lines. Napoleon's early plans had envisioned a movement through Berlin and on to liberate Danzig.

However, if any of these points were of major significance it would be reasonable to assume that Napoleon would have led the advance himself, not one of his lieutenants. As it was, Napoleon limited his personal movements to the direct defense and support of Dresden, the capitol of Saxony and the seat of its government. This suggests that Napoleon's actions were driven either by the need to control of Saxony or by the principal threat to that city, the Army of Bohemia.

The Saxon army was not a major player. It had been chewed up in Russia, and though it was rebuilt in early 1813, it had again been chewed up and cut almost to insignificance at Gross-Beeren and Dennewitz. It is, as a result, highly unlikely that the status of the Saxon army drove Napoleon's actions.

The political condition of Saxony is a possible driving force for Napoleon's actions. In contrast, in 1814, once France was invaded, Napoleon raced his army back and forth across France, leaving his vulnerable capitol totally uncovered, as he struck at allied army after allied army. Whereas in 1813, many of his movements were against the Army of Bohemia, driving it back into Bohemia and keeping it away from Dresden. It is apparent that, for some unknown reason, Napoleon felt obliged to literally sit on Saxony.

But why should this be? The King of Saxony was a weak ally and Napoleon in the Spring of 1813 was almost forced into kidnapping him in order to drive him back to Dresden. Despite that, during the Spring Napoleon maneuvered his armies with the goal of destroying his enemy's armies, not of acting from fixed positions to defend geographical landmarks.

In the political arena, the King of Saxony did not have any particular following amongst the other rulers of the Confederation of the Rhine. Indeed, the only significant sway the King of

Saxony held over another country was what he held as the nominal monarch of the Grand Duchy of Warsaw. Yet, the Poles were completely loyal to Napoleon even when their country was overrun and occupied by the allies. Their loyalty to Napoleon was such that it is unlikely that Napoleon felt he needed the support of the King of Saxony in order to regain control over the Grand Duchy of Warsaw.

Napoleon's actions can arguably attributed to a desire to ensure that the allies did not break Saxony away from his control. It is apparent that he felt he could not accept its being out of his control for even the shortest period. If the control of Saxony was not central to him, he would have certainly abandoned Leizpig and Dresden to the Army of Bohemia and turned his main force against Bernadotte's Army of the North or against Blücher's Army of Silesia. As it was, he sent Oudinot and Ney to execute a task beyond their abilities.

It remains that Napoleon felt that Saxony was the key to his hopes for success or that its loss would cause him irreparable damage. As it was, he destroyed his army to hold it.

There is a school of thought that suggests that Napoleon had, in fact, undergone an emotional and philosophical change of roles. This school argues that Napoleon had changed from Napoleon the general to Napoleon the emperor. It also argues that the Emperor could not tolerate the loss of any more of his German empire. The argument runs that after Malet's abortive coup in 1812 Napoleon did not feel secure enough on his throne to tolerate the collapse of his confederation of German puppet states. It is also possible that the Emperor's ego would not accept a further diminution of his empire. The loss of Germany would push France back to the borders it had when Napoleon became Emperor. With no territorial gains there was no glory. Either situation leads to the same result.

As the Emperor and not the general, political considerations intervened and surpassed military considerations. Surely the old "General" Napoleon would have ignored his lines of communication and moved to destroy the true strength of his enemies, their armies. Napoleon assuredly knew that a march on Berlin would force a battle and he had hoped that Oudinot, and later Ney, would be up to the task. But instead of going himself to ensure it was done right, in August and September Napoleon sent boys to do a man's job. Obviously Napoleon no longer considered the destruction of the enemy's army the primary goal, and instead chose to hold the important terrain.

As for sending Ney and Oudinot, there is some basis for suggesting that Napoleon felt that the Prussians were not a significant enemy worthy of his sword. Indeed, they had been crushed in 1806 as Napoleon had crushed no other army in his military career. Napoleon also knew that their army was over one third landwehr (militia) and another third were reservists, who he probably held in equally low regard. The qualitative improvements in the Prussian army and the "liberation" mentality of the Prussians were not in Napoleon's equation and upset Napoleon's calculations.

This mindset obviously changed in 1814 when Napoleon ignored lines of communications and concentrated on the destruction of the allied armies, as he had in the Spring of 1813. What occurred between 1 June and 15 August 1813 must have caused this change of mind set.

There is another possibility as to why Napoleon was so tied to Dresden. Though the impact of the Cossack raids on his lines of communications has already been minimized, the provisioning of his army may yet have been the major consideration.

Napoleon's correspondence from June to August is filled with directives on the movement of supplies and the Cossack threat to those supplies. Over the summer Napoleon established two major forward supply depots, Magdeburg and Dresden. It was his intention to support his armies from those two depots. Of the two, Dresden was by far, the largest. If Dresden and its supplies were lost the impact of the Cossack raids on Napoleons supply lines might have been such that Napoleon would have been forced to either 1.) disperse his army to feed it, 2.) keep it concentrated and ravage allied Saxony in the process, thereby increasing its internal dissent, or 3.) fall back on the French borders where the French system could supply his army.

Dispersal could easily result in further defeats at the hands of the allies. Their cavalry superiority would allow them to monitor the French and maneuver unobserved with larger forces against any isolated army corps they chose. This was to happen on a much smaller scale in September 1813 when GB Pécheux and slightly more than a thousand Frenchmen were caught by General Wallmoden's 14,000 man corps and scattered.

If Napoleon chose to remain concentrated in Saxony his troops would soon ravage the countryside, stripping it of everything edible. This would undermine both Napoleon's grasp on his German empire, but increase his military problems by generating a hostile population.

The option of withdrawing to the French border would have lost Napoleon his German empire and would be a de facto acceptance of the peace terms proffered by the Austrians. Napoleon had already rejected them out of hand. He was hardly likely to surrender to such terms without a fight.

Instead, he tried to use Dresden as a point of maneuver, much as he had used Manuta in his earlier Italian campaign. His goal was to crush the Allied armies one by one as they came within reach.

Unfortunately, the Allies had developed a superior strategy and postponed the decisive battle until they had weakened Napoleon sufficiently for their eventual victory at Leipzig. August 1813 was like a bullfight. Each allied army, like a matador, advanced to attract the French bull. Seeing his enemy, the Grande Armée, like a bull charging a cape, charge across Saxony only to have the cape pulled away before it could be caught. Again and again Napoleon drove his ever wearier army back and forth across Saxony, never quite coming to grips with any of his antagonists. Eventually, the Grande Armée, like the bull, grew weaker and weaker. Finally, it stood and waited the approach of its antagonists. Once the Grande Armée was sufficiently weakened, the allies, like the matador, came in for the kill.

Why Napoleon chose this campaign plan, we will never know. Circumstantial evidence supports every one of aforementioned scenarios as having some impact on Napoleon's thinking. Even if the plan was not defective, Napoleon's command structure failed him, giving him only one victory – Dresden, which was more than offset by the defeats at Katzbach, Hagelberg, Gross-Beeren, Dennewitz, Löwenberg, and Kulm.

Appendix I

Extension of the Armistice to 10 June 1813

His Majesty, the Emperor of the French, King of Italy, etc., and His Majesty, the Emperor of Austria, etc., united in their equal desire to seek a reestablishment of the peace, and having to this effect, said Emperor of Austria, offers his mediation for the general peace, and, at his want, for the peace of the continent; and His Majesty, the Emperor of the French, having manifested his intention to accept the aforementioned mediation, having judged, acceptable, certifies said offer and said acceptance by a convention; in consequence, their majesties have named for their pleni- potentiaries: His Majesty the Emperor of the French, Monsieur Hughes-Bernard, Count Maret, Duke of Bassano, etc.; His Majesty the Emperor of Austria, Herr Graf Clément Wenceslas von Metternich-Winnebourg-Ochsenhausen, Knight of the Golden Fleece, etc., his minister of foreign affairs, who, after having exchanged their respective powers, have concluded the following articles:

Article 1.
His Majesty, the Emperor of Austria offers his mediation for the general or continental peace.

Article 2.
His Majesty, the Emperor of the French, accepts said mediation.

Article 3.
The French, Russian, and Prussian plenipotentiaries shall gather prior to 5 July in the city of Prague.

Article 4.
In view of the insufficient time which remains until 20 July the term fixed for the armistice signed at Pleiswitz on 4 June, His Majesty, the Emperor of the French, engages himself not to denounce said armistice prior to 10 August, and His Majesty, the Emperor of Austria to obtain such an agreement from Russia and Prussia.

Article 5.
This convention shall not be made public.

The convention shall be ratified and the ratifications shall be exchanged in Dresden after a term of four days.

Made and Signed in Dresden on 30 June 1813

Signed: Duke de Bassano
Signed: Count von Metternich

Appendix II

Instructions Given to the Prussian Partisan Corps in 1813

1. When the partisan corps arrive in a region where the enemy may find them or where they are exposed to be attacked by superior forces, or taken in the rear, they shall march at night, led by guides, and sleep in during the day in locations a distance from the main routes or in woods. No one shall know where to find the detachment. The guide shall be held to prevent him signalling the enemy, if they are encountered during the transit of the areas through which he is used.

2. The detachment shall never engage a superior enemy force; its mission consists above all to surprise and destroy munition and provisions columns, the small detachments of enemy cantoned or moving, to take couriers, etc.; in brief, to disquiet without respite the main routes. They shall watch the main and secondary routes in such a manner that nothing shall pass unobserved.

3. At times, the detachment shall send an advanced guard to several points, requesting provisions for a large force and taking all the measures necessary to cause the enemy to believe that the detachment is a considerably larger force. But, during the night, the detachment shall briskly change its direction in order to vanish without a trace.

4. The detachment shall not cross rivers on the main bridges in the cities or villages, but shall cross at the smaller bridges, ferries, or fords. They shall endeavor to avoid all points where they may be observed in detail, as well as the important centers of population where they may be counted.

5. The officers and non-commissioned officers of the detachment shall know all the passages, the roads, the hills which are on their line of retreat in order to permit them to escape in case of check.

6. If the enemy arrives in force on several sides and there is no chance of escape, the detachment shall disperse in an effort to escape in small groups.

7. One shall indicate to small detached groups and to flying patrols several points where they can rally to the main body in order to retain the greatest degree of freedom.

8. In day marches, the detachment shall be preceded at a great distance, a quarter or half hour, by scouts or advance runners, in order to be free in its movements and to prevent ambushes.

9. It is very important to send, in addition to flying patrols, peasants in several directions. One shall find these latter by preference in isolated cabins and mills, etc.; the detachment, during these times, shall remain at a distance, hidden in a woods or in a concealed location. One shall send these men on horse or on foot, treating them well, but threatening to burn their houses if they betray the detachment.

10. When the detachment remains in a location for an extended region, it shall never establish itself in a fixed position nor shall it seek to guard itself with advanced posts or patrols, for it shall expose itself to surprise by a superior force and be destroyed. It shall, in contrast, constantly change its location and at times give the impression of having evacuated the region. During this time, the flying patrols of three men, the peasants posted in vigil, the men which

one attaches to the detachment in one manner or another, shall continue to observe, without raising suspicion, the roads, the important river passages, etc.

11. The corps of partisans or very distant advanced posts shall never pass more than a single night in one location, never sleep in a village, nor feed their horses in villages. If the topographical disposition of the position exists where they may sleep near a village, they shall constantly move their position around the village such that no one shall know where they will spend the night.

12. The commander of the detachment shall cause his projects to be misinterpreted, misunderstood, or remain secret.

13. He shall equally establish relations with the priests, forest agents, etc., etc., through out the region with the goal of obtaining through these men, news of the enemy and word of approaching convoys.

14. These few regulations which have proceeded on the subject of the partisan corps or detached posts are to indicate to their commander the spirit in which he should act. The topography of the region, particular circumstances, the reports on the spirit of the population, etc., shall be evaluated by him to show the means to achieve his goal.

Everyone knows what one learns from distant patrols. We are content to observe, to this end, that if the enemy is very distant, patrols shall render the greatest service in the form of a grand reconnaissance.

They shall never follow the main roads, but the back roads, passing through the woods; they shall never approach a village by the normal rout, but shall stop at distant houses where they shall seek word of the presence of the enemy in the villages. If they are obliged to pass through villages or cities, they shall endeavor to do so at night. It is necessary that they never pass repeatedly by the same route and that if they are obliged to retrace their steps, that they do so by another route than the one by which they came.

Orders of Battle
Table of Contents

How to Read the Orders of Battle

Formation Seniority

The unit closest to the left margin is the senior formation and all units listed immediately below it and indented are part of that command.

Strengths

The French strength figures drawn from the archives are "men under arms," not the effective strength, which includes various categories of individuals not present, often including those in hospital etc. If strength figures drawn from other sources are "men under arms" or "effective strength" is not known.

If one number appears in parenthesis after the unit's name it is a total strength figure, which may or may not include the officers. If two appear they are the number of officers and men. If more than two figures are presented, there will be a footnote to explain the numbers. This footnote applies only to that particular order of battle and all similar numerical notations should be read in the same manner.

The following illustrates the general formation of the orders of battle and explains how to read them.

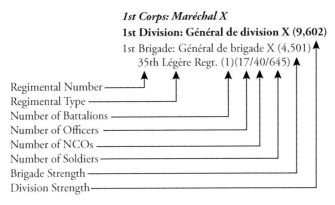

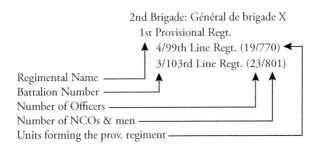

260

Cavalry

Cavalry was organized with regiments and squadrons. Its notations are as follows:

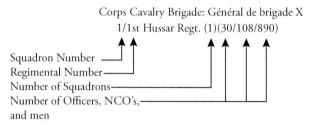

Corps Cavalry Brigade: Général de brigade X
1/1st Hussar Regt. (1)(30/108/890)

Squadron Number
Regimental Number
Number of Squadrons
Number of Officers, NCO's,
and men

Artillery

The Artillery was organized by regiments and companies. Their notations are:

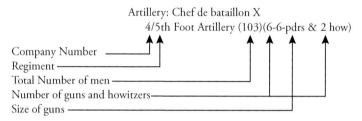

Artillery: Chef de bataillon X
4/5th Foot Artillery (103)(6-6-pdrs & 2 how)

Company Number
Regiment
Total Number of men
Number of guns and howitzers
Size of guns

Train and Support Units

These formations were organized by battalion and company. Their notations are:

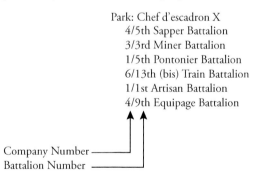

Park: Chef d'escadron X
4/5th Sapper Battalion
3/3rd Miner Battalion
1/5th Pontonier Battalion
6/13th (bis) Train Battalion
1/1st Artisan Battalion
4/9th Equipage Battalion

Company Number
Battalion Number

General Notes on Artillery

Where documents have indicated the actual numbers and types of guns in the various armies they are provided. There are, however, standard equipment allocations and these should be assumed unless otherwise noted.

The French divisional foot batteries were normally organized with six 6pdr cannon and two howitzers. The type of howitzer could and did vary, but the 24pdr was the most common. The corps reserve foot batteries were equipped with six 12pdrs and two 6" howitzers, though this too could vary. Horse batteries were equipped with four 6pdrs and two 24pdr howitzers. The Imperial Guard varied slightly from this and the howitzers were generally 5.7" howitzers.

The Russian position batteries were always equipped with four medium 12pdr guns, four short 12pdr guns, and four 20pdr licornes. The Cossacks, horse, and light batteries were always organized with eight 6pdr guns and four 10pdr licornes. The licorne was a cross between a cannon and a howitzer that was unique to the Russian army. Its barrel was longer than the typical howitzer, but much shorter than a cannon's barrel. It served the same function as a howitzer, firing explosive shells, but was significantly more accurate.

The Prussian batteries had six guns and two howitzers each. The 6pdr foot battery or a horse battery had six 6pdrs and two 7pdr howitzers, while the 12pdr foot battery had six 12pdrs and two 10pdr howitzers.

The Austrian position batteries had four 12pdrs or four 6pdrs and two howitzers. The brigade batteries had six 6pdrs and two 8pdr howitzers. The light foot batteries had six 6pdrs and 8pdr howitzers.

The Württemberg artillery varied. Those batteries taking the field in 1813 were organized as follows: the 1st Horse Battery and the 1st Light Battery had four 6pdrs and two 7pdr howitzers, and the 1st Heavy Battery had four 12pdrs and two heavy howitzers.

The Bavarian Horse Battery and the light foot batteries had six 6pdrs and two 7pdr howitzers. The single 12pdr battery had six 12pdrs and two 7pdr howitzers.

The single horse battery from Cleves-Berg had four 6pdrs and two 24pdr howitzers. The Hesse-Darmstadt foot battery consisted of six 6pdrs and two 7pdr howitzers.

Orders of Battle

THE ARMIES AT THE BEGINNING OF THE CAMPAIGN

I
FRENCH ARMY 1 AUGUST 1813

Commander-in-Chief: Napoleon Bonaparte

Imperial Guard: Marshal Mortier
Old Guard Division: Général de division Friant 5,000 men
1st Brigade: Général de division Curial
  1/1st Chasseur à Pied Regiment (23/648)
  2/1st Chasseur à Pied Regiment (14/599)
  1/2nd Chasseur à Pied Regiment (26/414)
  2/2nd Chasseur à Pied Regiment (14/195)
2nd Brigade: Général de brigade Michel
  1/1st Grenadier à Pied Regiment (25/625)
  2/1st Grenadier à Pied Regiment (17/587)
  1/2nd Grenadier à Pied Regiment (25/461)
  2/2nd Grenadier à Pied Regiment (8/333)
  Velites of Turin (15/438)
  Velites of Florence (25/403)
Artillery: Chef de bataillon Courin
  1st Old Guard Foot Battery (3/112)
  (6–6pdrs & 2–5.7" howitzers)
  6/1st Guard Train Battalion (1/100)
1st Infantry Division: Général de division Dumoustier
1st Brigade: Général de brigade Mouton-Duvernet
  1/Fusilier-Chasseur Regiment (21/697)
  2/Fusilier-Chasseur Regiment (16/722)
  1/Fusilier-Grenadier Regiment (23/586)
  2/Fusilier-Grenadier Regiment (18/604)
2nd Brigade: Général de brigade Tindal
  1/1st Voltigeur Regiment (19/527)
  2/1st Voltigeur Regiment (11/498)
  1/2nd Voltigeur Regiment (21/144)
  2/2nd Voltigeur Regiment (12/458)
3rd Brigade: Général de brigade Lanusse
  1/3rd Voltigeur Regiment (19/704)
  2/3rd Voltigeur Regiment (13/672)
  1/6th Voltigeur Regiment (20/665)
  2/6th Voltigeur Regiment (17/655)
  1/7th Voltigeur Regiment (19/620)
  2/7th Voltigeur Regiment (12/577)
Artillery: Chef de bataillon Levic
  1st Young Guard Foot Battery (3/116)

(6–6pdrs & 2–5.7 howitzers)
2nd Young Guard Foot Battery (3/120)
(6–6pdrs & 2–5.7" howitzers)
8th Young Guard Foot Battery (2/111)
(6–6pdrs & 2–5.7 howitzers)
4/1st Guard Train Battalion
3/2nd Guard Train Battalion
Total Train (3/283)
2/5th Sapper Battali (3/127)
1st Guard Equipage Train Company (2/124)
2nd Young Guard Division: Général de division Barrois
(strength as of 10 August)
1st Brigade: Général de brigade Rothemberg
  1/1st Tirailleur Regiment (24/523)
  2/1st Tirailleur Regiment (12/489)
  1/2nd Tirailleur Regiment (18/459)
  2/2nd Tirailleur Regiment (11/445)
2nd Brigade:
  1/3rd Tirailleur Regiment (18/512)
  2/3rd Tirailleur Regiment (13/551)
  1/6th Tirailleur Regiment (19/483)
  2/6th Tirailleur Regiment (12/471)
  1/7th Tirailleur Regiment (19/658)
  2/7th Tirailleur Regiment (11/517)
3rd Brigade: Général de brigade Boyeldieu
  1/Flanquer-Chasseur Regiment (18/601)
  2/Flanquer-Chasseur Regiment (12/578)
  1/Flanquer-Grenadier Regiment (23/681)
  2/Flanquer-Grenadier Regiment (12/661)
Artillery: Chef de bataillon Lefrancois
  3rd Young Guard Foot Battery (3/89)
  (6–6pdrs & 2–5.7" howitzers)
  4th Young Guard Foot Battery (2/100)
  (6–6pdrs & 2–5.7" howitzers)
  12th Young Guard Foot Battery (1/108)
  (6–6pdrs & 2–5.7" howitzers)
  9/1st Guard Train Battalion
  9/2nd Guard Train Battalion
  Total Train (2/288)
  3/7th Sapper Battalion (3/137)
  7th Guard Equipage Train Company (1/115)
3rd Young Guard Division: Général de division Roguet
1st Brigade: Général de brigade Gros
  1/4th Voltigeur Regiment (19/649)
  2/4th Voltigeur Regiment (13/594)
  1/5th Voltigeur Regiment (23/696)
  2/5th Voltigeur Regiment (12/694)
2nd Brigade: Général de brigade Combelle

1/8th Voltigeur Regiment (19/703)
2/8th Voltigeur Regiment (11/667)
1/9th Voltigeur Regiment (21/717)
2/9th Voltigeur Regiment (11/685)
1/10th Voltigeur Regiment (18/725)
2/10th Voltigeur Regiment (12/711)
3rd Brigade: Général de brigade Dulong
1/11th Voltigeur Regiment (19/556) (en route)
2/11th Voltigeur Regiment (9/550) (en route)
1/, 2/12th Voltigeur Regiment (forming in Mainz)
Artillery: Chef de bataillon Faivre
5th Young Guard Foot Battery (3/96)
(6–6pdrs & 2–5.7 howitzers)
6th Young Guard Foot Battery (2/92)
(6–6pdrs & 2–5.7" howitzers)
7th Young Guard Foot Battery (3/90)
(6–6pdrs & 2–5.7 howitzers)
1/2nd Guard Train Battalion
2/2nd Guard Train Battalion
Total Train (2/257)

4th Young Guard Division: Général de division Friant
1st Brigade: Général de brigade Boyer de Rebeval
1/4th Tirailleur Regiment (21/610)
2/4th Tirailleur Regiment (10/599)
1/5th Tirailleur Regiment (17/653)
2/5th Tirailleur Regiment (12/593)
2nd Brigade:
1/8th Tirailleur Regiment (19/652)
2/8th Tirailleur Regiment (13/624)
1/9th Tirailleur Regiment (16/650)
2/9th Tirailleur Regiment (12/566)
1/, 2/10th Tirailleur Regiment (29/1,545)
3rd Brigade: Général de brigade Pelet
1/, 2/11th Tirailleur Regiment (28/1,277) (en route)
1/, 2/12th Tirailleur Regiment (forming in Paris)
Artillery: Chef de bataillon Oudin
9th Young Guard Foot Battery (2/102)
(6–6pdrs & 2 5/7" howitzers)
10th Young Guard Foot Battery (1/104)
(6–6pdrs & 2 5/7" howitzers)
11th Young Guard Foot Battery (1/103)
(6–6pdrs & 2 5/7 howitzers)
4/Guard Train Battalion Battalion
5/Guard Train Battalion Battalion
Total Train (2/325)

Guard Cavalry Division: Général de division Count Walther
Général de division Ornano
Generaux de brigade Colbert, Letort, Krasinski, Lyon & Castex.
1–7/1st Chevauléger-lancier Polonaise (83/1,300/1,459)
1–10/2nd Chevauléger-lancier (70/1,506/1,606)
1/, 3/, 4/Chevauléger of Berg (31/568/663)
5/Chevauléger of Berg (9/226/253)
6/Chevauléger of Berg (9/226/241)
1–10/Chasseurs à Cheval de la Garde (90/1,747/1,945)

1–6/Empress Dragoon Regiment (64/1,301/1,461)
1–6/Grenadiers à Cheval de la Garde (63/1,209/1,380)
1/, 2/Gendarmerie d'elite (17/493/536)
Artillery: Chefs d'escadron Dolesnud & Bosselier
1st Old Guard Horse Battery (3/90)
(4–6pdrs & 2–5.7" howitzers)
2nd Old Guard Horse Battery (3/85)
(4–6pdrs & 2–5.7" howitzers)
3rd Old Guard Horse Battery (3/87)
(4–6pdrs & 2–5.7" howitzers)
4th Old Guard Horse Battery (2/89)
(4–6pdrs & 2–5.7" howitzers)
1/Guard Train Battalion Battalion (1/140)
12/Guard Train Battalion Battalion (1/139)
à la suite
1/1st Gardes d'Honneur (11/254/276) (en route Gotha)
2/1st Gardes d'Honneur (3/236/242) (in Gotha 8/14)
3/1st Gardes d'Honneur (5/240/252) (in Gotha 8/24)
4/1st Gardes d'Honneur (5/245/255) (in Mainz 8/29)
5/1st Gardes d'Honneur (8/238/253) (in Mainz 9/18)
1/2nd Gardes d'Honneur (4/250/265) (en route Gotha)
2/2nd Gardes d'Honneur (4/252/260) (in Gotha 8/15)
3/2nd Gardes d'Honneur (8/247/262) (in Mainz 9/5)
4/2nd Gardes d'Honneur (4/239/247) (in Mainz 9/5)
5/2nd Gardes d'Honneur (2/247/252) (in Mainz 9/15)
1/3rd Gardes d'Honneur (4/226/234) (en route Gotha)
2/3rd Gardes d'Honneur (6/243/252) (in Gotha 9/8)
3/3rd Gardes d'Honneur (4/236/246) (in Gotha 9/8)
4/3rd Gardes d'Honneur (4/245/255) (in Mainz 9/24)
5/3rd Gardes d'Honneur (3/247/253) (in Mainz 10/1)
1/4th Gardes d'Honneur (2/246/257) (en route Gotha)
2/4th Gardes d'Honneur (5/118/128) (in Gotha 8/16)
3/4th Gardes d'Honneur (6/289/305) (in Mainz 8/31)
4/4th Gardes d'Honneur (4/238/248) (in Mainz 9/23)
5/4th Gardes d'Honneur (2/239/243) (in Mainz 9/23)

Guard Reserve and Grand Park: Général de brigade Drouet (60 guns)
2nd Old Guard Foot Battery (3/116)
(6–12pdrs & 2–6" howitzers)

3rd Old Guard Foot Batten, (3/115)
(6–6pdrs & 2–5.7" howitzers)
4th Old Guard Foot Battery (4/122)
(6–6pdrs & 2–6" howitzers)
5th Old Guard Foot Battery (3/124)
(6–6pdrs & 2–6" howitzers)
6th Old Guard Foot Battery (3/115)
(6–6pdrs & 2–6" howitzers)
5th Old Guard Horse Battery (3/88)
(4–6pdrs & 2–5.7" howitzers)
6th Old Guard Horse Battery (2/85)
(4–6pdrs & 2–5.7" howitzers)
13th Young Guard Foot Battery (2/116)
(4–6pdrs & 2–5.7" howitzers)
(enroute from Frankfurt)
14th Young Guard Foot Battery (2/116)
(4–6pdrs & 2–5.7" howitzers)
(enroute from Frankfurt)
15th Young Guard Foot Battery (2/115)
(4–6pdrs & 2–5.7" howitzers)
16th Young Guard Foot Battery (2/110)
(4–6pdrs & -5.7" howitzers)
6/, 7/, 8/, 9/, 10/, 11/, 12/2nd Guard Train Battalion
Total Train (21/1,010)
Berg Horse Artillery Battery (4/88)
(4–6pdrs & 2–5.7" howitzers)
Berg Train Company (3/122)
1st Pontooneer Artisan Company (4/128)
1st Guard Sapper Company (4/219)
3/Guard Marine Battalion (3/71)
2nd Italian Guard Marine Company (3/103)
1st Neapolitian Guard Marine Company (3/58)
1st Guard Engineering Train Company (1/39)
1–12/Guard Equipage Train Battalion (20/1,246)
3rd Guard Administrative Worker Company
  (17/577)
General Park
  10/1st Foot Artillery (2/91)
  21/1st Foot Artillery (2/56)
  6/5th Foot Artillery (1/34)
  2/6th Foot Artillery (2/115)
  5/7th Foot Artillery (2/77)
  24/7th Foot Artillery (2/76)
  25/7th Foot Artillery (2/71)
  4/8th Foot Artillery (2/60)
  5/8th Foot Artillery (3/87)
  15/8th Foot Artillery (1/69)
  16/8th Foot Artillery (2/55)
  12/9th Foot Artillery (2/77)
  14/9th Foot Artillery (1/52)
  17/9th Foot Artillery (2/70)
  21/9th Foot Artillery (2/71)
  4/2nd Horse Artillery (3/95)
  2/3rd Horse Artillery (3/90)
  2/6th Horse Artillery (2/91)
  Det/6th Principal Train Battalion (0/21)
  Det/10th (bis) Train Battalion (2/116)
  Det. 3/1st Principal Train Battalion (0/10)
  Det. 1/5th Principal Train Battalion (0/20)

Det. 2/6th Principal Train Battalion (0/19)
Det. 2/, 4/9th Principal Train Battalion (0/39)
4/9th Principal Train Battalion (3/134)
Det. 7/7th (bis) Train Battalion (0/32)
Det. 4/9th (bis) Train Battalion (0/19)
Det. 2/11th (bis) Train Battalion (0/21)
Det. 4/13th (bis) Train Battalion (0/28)
Det. 4th Principal Train Battalion (0/12)
Det. 7th Principal Train Battalion (3/147)
Det. 8th Principal Train Battalion (2/104)
Det. 9th Principal Train Battalion (0/12)
Det. 12th Principal Train Battalion (0/2)
Det. 14th Principal Train Battalion (0/18)
Det. 5th (bis) Train Battalion (0/9)
Det. 8th (bis) Train Battalion (0/51)
Det. 11th (bis) Train Battalion (2/100)
Det. 13th (bis) Train Battalion (0/18)
5th Artillery Artisan Company (1/60)
6th Artillery Artisan Company (2/105)
10th Artillery Artisan Company (2/135)
14th Artillery Artisan Company (1/24)
16th Artillery Artisan Company (2/76)
17th Artillery Artisan Company (1/52)
18th Artillery Artisan Company (1/60)
1/1st Pontooneer Battalion (2/136)
3/1st Pontooneer Battalion (3/136)
5/1st Pontooneer Battalion (3/139)
7/1st Pontooneer Battalion (3/137)
8/1st Pontooneer Battalion (3/134)
9/1st Pontooneer Battalion (2/118)
1/3rd Pontooneer Battalion (3/130)
2/3rd Pontooneer Battalion (3/132)
4/3rd Pontooneer Battalion (2/131)
2nd Naval Artisan Battalion (6 cos) (18/789)
8th Naval Artisan Battalion (6 cos) (18/871)
2nd Artillery Artisan Company (1/49)
Det/1st Armorer Company (0/7)
5/1st Sapper Battalion (2/135)
5/5th Sapper Battalion (3/114)
6/5th Sapper Battalion (3/116)
6/1st Miner Battalion (3/120)
2/2nd Miner Battalion (3/96)
Engineering Workers (1/65)
1/Engineering Train Battalion (3/120)
5/Engineering Train Battalion (3/112)

I Corps: Général de division Vandamme
1st Division: Général de division Philippon
1st Brigade: Général de brigade Pouchelon
  1/7th Légère Regiment (32/708)
  2/7th Légère Regiment (17/630)
  3/7th Légère Regiment (15/682)
  4/7th Légère Regiment (19/658)
  1/12th Line Regiment (39/821)
  2/12th Line Regiment (18/698)
  3/12th Line Regiment (17/781)
  4/12th Line Regiment (18/618)
2nd Brigade: Général de brigade Fezensac
  1/17th Line Regiment (32/775)

2/17th Line Regiment (18/536)
3/17th Line Regiment (17/629)
4/17th Line Regiment (15/650)
3/36th Line Regiment (21/680)
4/36th Line Regiment (20/453)
Artillery: Chef de bataillon Ferrary
  8/2nd Foot Artillery (2/82) (6–6pdrs & 2–24pdr
    howitzers)
  15/9th Foot Artillery (4/59) (6–6pdrs & 2–24pdr
    howitzers)
  Det/4th Principal Train Battalion (0/28)
  3/9th Principal Train Battalion (1/127)
2nd Division: Général de division Dumonceau
1st Brigade: Général de brigade Dunesme
  1/13th Légère Regiment (25/744)
  2/13th Légère Regiment (22/587)
  3/13th Légère Regiment (18/820)
  4/13th Légère Regiment (17/648)
  1/25th Line Regiment (33/760)
  2/25th Line Regiment (17/589)
  3/25th Line Regiment (18/750)
  4/25th Line Regiment (17/715)
2nd Brigade: Général de brigade Doucet
  3/51st Line Regiment (24/705)
  4/51st Line Regiment (17/723)
  1/57th Line Regiment (36/799)
  2/57th Line Regiment (30/699)
  3/57th Line Regiment (16/750)
  4/57th Line Regiment (22/725)
Artillery: Chef de bataillon Fourgeon
  23/3rd Foot Artillery (4/63) (6–6pdrs & 2–24pdr
    howitzers)
  24/3rd Foot Artillery (2/57) (6–6pdrs & 2–24pdr
    howitzers)
  1/1st Principal Train Battalion (2/153)
  Det/8th (bis) Train Battalion (0/28)
23rd Division: Général de division Teste
1st Brigade: Général de brigade O'Meara
  1/21st Line Regiment (29/617)
  2/21st Line Regiment (18/599)
  3/21st Line Regiment (15/342)
  3/21st Line Regiment (5/478)
  (*These detachments of the main battalion were
    incompletely organized and generally lacking
    equipment, uniforms, etc.*)
  4/21st Line Regiment (18/365)
  1/33rd Line Regiment (24/689)
  2/33rd Line Regiment (21/697)
  3/33rd Line Regiment (15/459)
  4/33rd Line Regiment (24/681)
2nd Brigade: Général de brigade Quiot
  1/85th Line Regiment (24/681)
  2/85th Line Regiment (19/673)
  3/85th Line Regiment (13/550)
  3/85th Line Regiment (6/274) (arrived Dessau
    8/27/13)
  4/85th Line Regiment (25/645)
  3/55th Line Regiment (19/531)
  4/55th Line Regiment (22/741)

Artillery
  5/4th Foot Artillery (3/55) (6–6pdrs & 2–24pdr
    howitzers)
  21/4th Foot Artillery (3/72) (6–6pdrs & 2–24pdr
    howitzers)
  Det/9th Principal Train Battalion (1.79)
  Det/1st (bis) Train Battalion (1/109)
27th Division: Général de division Dombrowski
1st Brigade: Général de brigade Zotowski
  1/2nd Polish Infantry Regiment (31/369)
  2/2nd Polish Infantry Regiment (21/340)
  1/14th Polish Infantry Regiment (30/383)
  2/14th Polish Infantry Regiment (23/245)
Cavalry Brigade: Général de brigade Krustowecki
  1/2nd Polish Uhlan Regiment (14/170/204)
  (*Figures on the cavalry regiments with only three
    numbers are officers, men, total horses.*)
  2/2nd Polish Uhlan Regiment (7/146/160)
  3/2nd Polish Uhlan Regiment (5/143/154)
  4/2nd Polish Uhlan Regiment (9/145/153)
  1/4th Polish Chasseur à Cheval Regiment
    (17/158/214)
  2/4th Polish Chasseur à Cheval Regiment
    (6/129/142)
  3/4th Polish Chasseur à Cheval Regiment
    (7/141/152)
  4/4th Polish Chasseur à Cheval Regiment
    (8/141/160)
Artillery: Chef de bataillon Schewrin
  Polish Horse Battery (8/88) (4–6pdrs & 2–24pdr
    howitzers)
  Polish Train Company (0/70)
Corps Cavalry
  1/9th Chevauléger-lancier Regiment (8/154/178)
  2/9th Chevauléger-lancier Regiment (9/179/208)
  1/Anhalt Jäger zu Pferd Regiment (12/243/258)
  2/Anhalt Jäger zu Pferd Regiment (7/233/242)
Artillery Reserve & Park: Chef de bataillon Coisy
  6/7th Foot Artillery (3/88) (6–12pdrs & 2–6"
    howitzers)
  9/8th Foot Artillery (3/105) (6–12pdrs & 2–6"
    howitzers)
  2/4th Horse Artillery (4/92) (4–6pdrs & 2–24pdr
    how.)
  5/6th Horse Artillery (3/93) (4–6pdrs & 2–24pdr
    how.)
  Det. 4/7th Principal Train Battalion (1/15)
  Det. 1/9th Principal Train Battalion (1/129)
  2/13th (bis) Train Battalion (1/158)
  5/3rd Sapper Battalion (3/126)
  7/3rd Sapper Battalion (3/125)
  Det/13th Equipage Battalion (1/51)
  4/14th Equipage Battalion (3/139)
Troops En Route to I Corps:
  7th Légère Regiment (1/111) (in Erfurt)
  13th Légère Regiment (2/250) (in Magdeburg)
  17th Line Regiment (1/62) (in Magdeburg)
  25th Line Regiment (1/54) (in Erfurt)
  33rd Line Regiment (2/115) (in Magdeburg)

36th Line Regiment (2/216) (in Mainz)
36th Line Regiment (4/103) (in Magdeburg)
55th Line Regiment (1/237) (in Magdeburg)
57th Line Regiment (1/196) (in Wittemberg)
85th Line Regiment (2/71) (in Erfurt)

II Corps: Marshal Victor
4th Division: Général de division Dubreton
Brigade: Général de brigade Ferrière
  1/24th Légère Regiment (23/775)
  2/24th Légère Regiment (21/591)
  3/24th Légère Regiment (21/820) (in Magdeburg)
  4/24th Légère Regiment (21/542)
  1/19th Line Regiment (28/746)
  2/19th Line Regiment (17/607)
  3/19th Line Regiment (19/740) (in Magdeburg)
  3/19th Line Regiment (3/137) (arrived 8 August)
  4/19th Line Regiment (18/596)
Brigade: Général de brigade Brune
  1/37th Line Regiment (32/576)
  2/37th Line Regiment (16/465)
  4/37th Line Regiment (15/318)
  1/56th Line Regiment (25/737)
  2/56th Line Regiment (21/606)
  3/56th Line Regiment (20/805) (in Magdebourg)
  4/56th Line Regiment (21/587)
Artillery: Chef de bataillon Risser
  7/2nd Foot Artillery (3/92) (6–6pdrs & 2–24pdr howitzers)
  11/4th Foot Artillery (3/99) (6–6pdrs & 2–24pdr howitzers)
  Det. 1/11th Principal Train Battalion (1/89)
  Det. 3/12th Principal Train Battalion (0/21)
  Det. 2/3rd (bis) Train Battalion (1/79)
5th Division: Général de division Dufour
Brigade: Général de brigade Estko
  1/26th Légère Regiment (17/722)
  2/26th Légère Regiment (16/572)
  3/26th Légère Regiment (21/820) (in Magdeburg)
  4/26th Légère Regiment (18/667)
  1/46th Line Regiment (23/648)
  2/46th Line Regiment (21/455)
  4/46th Line Regiment (23/491)
Brigade: Général de brigade Prince von Reuss
  1/72nd Line Regiment (20/693)
  2/72nd Line Regiment (21/644)
  4/72nd Line Regiment (20/572)
  1/93rd Line Regiment (22/817)
  2/93rd Line Regiment (20/519)
  3/93rd Line Regiment (20/804)
  4/93rd Line Regiment (21/669)
Artillery:
  13/5th Foot Artillery (3/59) (6–6pdrs & 2–24pdr howitzers)
  12/8th Foot Artillery (4/58) (6–6pdrs & 2–24pdr howitzers)
  Diverse Train Battalion Detachments (1/180)
6th Division: Général de division Vial
1st Brigade: Général de brigade Valory

1/11th Légère Regiment (29/689)
2/11th Légère Regiment (18/500)
4/11th Légère Regiment (21/579)
1/2nd Line Regiment (31/688)
2/2nd Line Regiment (18/533)
4/2nd Line Regiment (17/544)
2nd Brigade: Général de brigade Bronikowski
  1/4th Line Regiment (29/710)
  2/4th Line Regiment (16/594)
  4/4th Line Regiment (18/470)
  1/18th Line Regiment (24/777)
  2/18th Line Regiment (21/595)
  3/18th Line Regiment (18/809) (in Magdeburg)
  4/18th Line Regiment (19/576)
Artillery:
  25/3rd Foot Artillery (3/64) (6–6pdrs & 2–24pdr howitzers)
  26/3rd Foot Artillery (3/72) (6–6pdrs & 2–24pdr howitzers)
  Det. 4/12th Principal Train Battalion (0/15)
  Det. 3/14th Principal Train Battalion (1/107)
  Det. 3/1st (bis) Train Battalion (0/25)
  Det. 1/11th (bis) Train Battalion (0/22)
Light Cavalry Brigade: Général de brigade v. Hammerstein
  1/, 2/, 3/1st Westphalian Hussar Regiment (27/392/461)
  I/, 2/, 3/2nd Westphalian Hussar Regiment (22/340/413)
Artillery Reserve and Park: Chef de bataillon Jucqueau
  9/2nd Foot Artillery (3/76) (6–12pdrs & 2–6" howitzers)
  10/6th Foot Artillery (3/93) (6–12pdrs & 2–6" howitzers)
  1/2nd Horse Artillery (3/82) (4–6pdrs & 2–24pdr how.)
  4/3rd Horse Artillery (2/90) (4–6pdrs & 2–24pdr how.)
  Det. 3/1st Principal Train Battalion (1/25)
  Det. 2/9th Principal Train Battalion (1/58)
  Det. 2/14th Principal Train Battalion (1/114)
  Det. 3/3rd (bis) Train Battalion (1/59)
  Det. 1/, 2/11th (bis) Train Battalion (1/63)
  2/2nd Sapper Battalion (3/137)
  3/3rd Sapper Battalion (3/118)
  3/5th Sapper Battalion (3/114)
Troops En Route to II Corps
  11th Légère Regiment (1/50) (in Magdeburg)
  26th Légère Regiment (2/105) (in Mainz)
  4th Line Regiment (3/22) (in Mainz)
  18th Line Regiment (3/173) (in Dresden)
  19th Line Regiment (3/161) (in Magdeburg)
  24th Line Regiment (4/621) (in Mainz)
  26th Line Regiment (4/155) (in Mainz)
  93rd Line Regiment (1/131) (in Mainz)

III Corps: Maréchal Ney
8th Division: Général de division Souham
Brigade: Général de brigade Brayer
  6th Provisional Légère Regiment
    2/6th Légère Regiment (21/670)
    3/25th Légère Regiment (20/532)
  10th Provisional Regiment
    3/16th Légère Regiment (21/734)
    1/28th Légère Regiment (21/734)
  14th Provisional Regiment
    4/34th Line Regiment (24/402)
    3/40th Line Regiment (22/389)
  19th Provisional Regiment
    6/32nd Line Regiment (22/464)
    2/58th Line Regiment (21/560)
Brigade: Général de brigade Charrière
  1/22nd Regiment (21/481)
  3/22nd Regiment (17/443)
  4/22nd Regiment (14/492)
  21st Provisional Regiment
    3/59th Line Regiment (19/651)
    4/69th Line Regiment (22/496)
  24th Provisional Regiment
    3/88th Line Regiment (21/354)
    3/103rd Line Regiment (17/433)
Artillery: Chef de bataillon Tripp
  10/2nd Foot Artillery (2/70) (6–6pdrs & 2–24pdr
    howitzers)
  5/9th Foot Artillery (1/55) (6–6pdrs & 2–24pdr
    howitzers)
  Det. 3/9th Principal Train Battalion (2/98)
  Det. 4/3rd (bis) Train Battalion (1/60)
9th Division: Général de division Delmas
1st Brigade: Général de brigade Anthing
  2nd Provisional Regiment
    3/2nd Légère Regiment (19/402)
    3/4th Légère Regiment (22/393)
    1/29th Légère Regiment (21/369)
    2/29th Légère Regiment (18/376)
    1/136th Line Regiment (25/523)
    2/136th Line Regiment (21/495)
    3/136th Line Regiment (30/518)
2nd Brigade: Général de brigade Vergez
  1/138th Line Regiment (23/519)
  2/138th Line Regiment (19/486)
  3/138th Line Regiment (21/462)
  1/145th Line Regiment (32/573)
  2/145th Line Regiment (18/612)
  3/145th Line Regiment (28/591)
Artillery: Chef de bataillon Chasvel
  2/9th Foot Artillery (3/61) (6–6pdrs 2–24pdr
    howitzers)
  11/9th Foot Artillery (3/50) (6–6pdrs & 2–24pdr
    howitzers)
  Det. 4/3rd (bis) Train Battalion (1/41)
  Det. 4/6th Principal Train Battalion (2/116)
  Det. 7/10th Principal Train Battalion (0/12)
10th Division: Général de division Albert
1st Brigade: Général de brigade Vandedem

4th Provisional Regiment
  4/5th Légère Regiment (24/476)
  4/12th Légère Regiment (23/252)
  1/139th Line Regiment (28/626)
  2/139th Line Regiment (25/624)
  3/139th Line Regiment (25/653)
2nd Brigade: Général de brigade Suden
  1/140th Line Regiment (28/447)
  2/140th Line Regiment (15/461)
  3/140th Line Regiment (16/473)
  1/141st Line Regiment (24/334)
  2/141st Line Regiment (21/525)
  3/141st Line Regiment (22/308)
Artillery: Chef de bataillon Gagneur
  3/7th Foot Artillery (3/81) (6–6pdrs & 2–24pdr
    howitzers)
  4/7th Foot Artillery (2/62) (6–6pdrs & 2–24pdr
    howitzers)
  Det. 4/1st Principal Train Battalion (1/129)
  Det. 7/10th Principal Train Battalion (0/17)
11th Division: Général de division Richard
1st Brigade: Général de brigade Tarayre
  3/9th Légère Regiment (20/370)
  4/9th Légère Regiment (20/304)
  17th Provisional Regiment
    4/43rd Line Regiment (19/470)
    3/75th Line Regiment (21/396)
    3/50th Line Regiment (29/509)
    4/50th Line Regiment (21/467)
    4/65th Line Regiment (19/294)
2nd Brigade: Général de brigade Dumoulin
  1/142nd Line Regiment (35/481)
  2/142nd Line Regiment (18/478)
  3/142nd Line Regiment (19/496)
  1/144th Line Regiment (33/556)
  2/144th Line Regiment (18/549)
  3/144th Line Regiment (27/636)
Artillery: Chef de bataillon de Larue
  19/7th Foot Artillery (3/82) (6–6pdrs & 2–24pdr
    howitzers)
  5/9th Foot Artillery (2/42) (6–6pdrs & 2–24pdr
    howitzers)
  Det. 7/10th Principal Train Battalion (0/33)
  Det. 7/11th Principal Train Battalion (1/42)
  Det. 4/13th (bis) Train Battalion (1/105)
39th Division Général de division Marchand
1st Brigade: Général de brigade Stockhorn
  1/1st Baden Infantry Regiment (15/660)
  2/1st Baden Infantry Regiment (11/593)
  1/3rd Baden Infantry Regiment (15/462)
  2/3rd Baden Infantry Regiment (13/512)
2nd Brigade: Prince Emil of Hesse
  1/Hessian Fusilier Guards (17/502)
  2/Hessian Fusilier Guards (15/522)
  1/2nd Hessian Leib Infantry Regiment (21/503)
  2/2nd Hessian Leib Infantry Regiment (12/502)
  1/Hessian Leibgarde Regiment (17/518)
  2/Hessian Leibgarde Regiment (16/517)

Artillery: Capitaine Muller
  1st Baden Foot Battery (3/120) (5–6pdrs &
    1–24pdr howitzer)
  1st Hessian Foot Battery (6/226) (5–6pdrs &
    1–24pdr howitzer)
**23rd Light Cavalry Brigade: Général de brigade
Beurmann**
  1/10th French Hussar Regiment (15/191/226)
  2/10th French Hussar Regiment (7/184/195)
  3/10th French Hussar Regiment (7/172/186)
  4/10th French Hussar Regiment (8/178/191)
  5/10th French Hussar Regiment (7/157/184)
  6/10th French Hussar Regiment (2/115/118)
  6/10th French Hussar Regiment (3/124/130) (in
    Dresden)
  1/Baden Dragoon Regiment (5/81/125)
  2/Baden Dragoon Regiment (2/89/104)
  3/Baden Dragoon Regiment (2/96/111)
  4/Baden Dragoon Regiment (3/8/108)
  5/Baden Dragoon Regiment (2/110/118)
Corps Artillery Reserve
  8/4th Foot Artillery (3/79) (6–12pdrs & 2–24pdr
    howitzers)
  21/7th Foot Artillery (2/79) (6–12pdrs & 2–24pdr
    howitzers)
  6/3rd Foot Artillery (3/65) (no guns)
  15/4th Foot Artillery (3/91) (no guns)
  5/1st Horse Artillery (3/102) (4–6pdrs & 2–24pdr
    howitzers)
  1/3rd Horse Artillery (3/72) (4–6pdrs & 2–24pdr
    howitzers)
  2/1st Principal Train Battalion (2/138)
  3/1st Principal Train Battalion (1/102)
  4/1st Principal Train Battalion (0/17)
  Det. 7/5th Principal Train Battalion (2/77)
  Det. 2/6th Principal Train Battalion (1/91)
  Det. 4/8th Principal Train Battalion (1/16)
  Det. 3/10th Principal Train Battalion (1/102)
  Det. 7/10th Principal Train Battalion (1/29)
  Det. 3/3rd (bis) Train Battalion (1/54)
  Det. 2/9th (bis) Train Battalion (1/94)
  1/Spanish Sapper Battalion (5/152)
  2/Spanish Sapper Battalion (3/128)
  3/Spanish Sapper Battalion (3/117)
  4/Spanish Sapper Battalion (2/149)
  1/6th Equipage Train Battalion (4/31)
  2/6th Equipage Train Battalion (2/120)
  3/6th Equipage Train Battalion (1/28)
  4/6th Equipage Train Battalion (1/37)
  5/6th Equipage Train Battalion (1/121)
  6/6th Equipage Train Battalion (1/40)
  Det. Imperial Gendarmes (2/44/50)
Troops En Route to III Corps:
  16th Légère Regiment (2/75) (en route)
  136th Line Regiment (1/130) (en route)
  138th Line Regiment (3/364) (in Dresden)
  136th Line Regiment (2/148) (in Dresden)
  139th Line Regiment (3/162) (in Erfurt)

  139th Line Regiment (2/53) (in Mainz)
  140th Line Regiment (2/164) (en route)
  140th Line Regiment (4/376) (in Erfurt)
  141st Line Regiment (6/366) (en route)
  141st Line Regiment (4/306) (in Erfurt)
  142nd Line Regiment (2/233) (in Erfurt)
  142nd Line Regiment (1/157) (en route)
  144th Line Regiment (4/357) (in Mainz)
  145th Line Regiment (5/46) (en route)
  145th Line Regiment (2/249) (in Dresden)
  10th Hussar Regiment (1/69/71) (in Dresden)
  10th Hussar Regiment (0/35/37) (in Mainz)

IV Corps: Général de division Count Bertrand
12th Division: Général de division Morand
1st Brigade: Général de brigade de Belair
  2/8th Légère Regiment (20/681)
  4/8th Légère Regiment (20/677)
2nd Brigade: Général de brigade Toussaint
  1/13th Line Regiment (28/693)
  2/13th Line Regiment (18/617)
  3/13th Line Regiment (16/642)
  4/13th Line Regiment (17/674)
  6/13th Line Regiment (18/606)
  Artillery Det./13th Line Regiment (2/46)
3rd Brigade: Général de brigade Hulot
  1/23rd Line Regiment (30/589)
  2/23rd Line Regiment (11/537)
  4/23rd Line Regiment (14/587)
  6/23rd Line Regiment (14/593)
  Artillery Det./23rd Line Regiment (2/23)
Artillery: Chef de bataillon Foulguier
  1/2nd Foot Artillery (3/70) (6–6pdrs & 2–24pdr
    howitzers)
  3/2nd Foot Artillery (4/67) (6–6pdrs & 2–24pdr
    howitzers)
  1/7th (bis) Train Battalion (1/117)
  2/7th (bis) Train Battalion (1/111)
15th Division: Général de division Fontanelli
1st Brigade: Général de brigade Martel
  3/1st Italian Line Regiment (22/581)
  4/1st Italian Line Regiment (19/524)
  2/4th Italian Line Regiment (32/459)
  3/4th Italian Line Regiment (22/421)
  4/4th Italian Line Regiment (22/435)
2nd Brigade: Général de brigade Saint-Andrea
  2/1st Italian Légère Regiment (27/755)
  3/1st Italian Légère Regiment (18/723)
  4/1st Italian Légère Regiment (21/700)
  3/6th Italian Line Regiment (27/467)
  4/6th Italian Line Regiment (16/460)
3rd Brigade: Général de brigade Moroni
  1st Milan Guard Battalion (23/547)
  2/7th Italian Line Regiment (28/434)
  3/7th Italian Line Regiment (18/404)
  4/7th Italian Line Regiment (19/414)
Artillery: Colonel Armandi
  1st Italian Foot Battery (5/103) (6–6pdrs &
    2–24pdr howitzers)

13th Italian Foot Battery (5/103) (6–6pdrs &
  2–24pdr howitzers)
Italian 5th Train Company (3/131)
Italian 6th Train Company (2/131)
Det. Italian 6th (bis) Train Company (0/13)

38th Division: Général de division Franquemont
1st Brigade: Generalmajor von Stockmayer
  1/9th Württemberg Light Regiment (13/494)
  1/10th Württemberg Light Regiment (12/521)
  1/7th Württemberg Line Regiment (11/372)
  2/7th Württemberg Line Regiment (10/352)
2nd Brigade: Generalmajor von Spitzenberg
  1/1st Württemberg Line Regiment (12/460)
  2/1st Württemberg Line Regiment (11/431)
  1/2nd Württemberg Line Regiment (12/484)
  2/2nd Württemberg Line Regiment (4/280)
Artillery:
  1st Württemberg Foot Battery (3/112)
  (4–6pdrs & 2–7pdr howitzers)

24th Light Cavalry Brigade: Generalmajor von Jett
  1/, 2/, 3/4/lst Württemberg Chevaulégers "Prince
    Adam" (18/384/77/332)*
  1/, 2/, 3/4/3rd Württemberg Chevaulégers "Duke
    Louis" (14/347/70/300)
  1st Württemberg Horse Battery – "von Bürgi"
    (3/114)
  (4–6pdrs & 2–7pdr howitzers)

Corps Artillery Reserve: Colonel Menoire
  24/2nd Foot Artillery (3/81) (6–12pdrs & 2–6"
    howitzers)
  26/2nd Foot Artillery (3/62) (6–12pdrs & 2–6"
    howitzers)
  25/4th Foot Artillery (3/79) (6–12pdrs & 2–6"
    howitzers)
  8/4th Horse Artillery (3/89) (4–6pdrs & 2–24pdr
    howitzers)
  5/7th (his) Train Battalion (1/109)
  6/7th (his) Train Battalion (1/152)
  7/7th (bis) Train Battalion (1/145)
  4/11th (bis) Train Battalion (1/134)
  Det. 13th Artillery Artisan Company (1/27)
  2/1st Sapper Battalion (3/133)
  8/1st Sapper Battalion (4/140)
  8th Italian Sapper Company (3/104)
  3rd Italian Marine Artisan Company (2/69)
  Det/Engineering Train Company (0/7)
  5/9th Equipage Train Battalion (2/79)
  7/9th Equipage Train Battalion (2/74)
  5th Italian Transport Company (2/114)

Troops En Route to IV Corps:
  13th Line Regiment (2/178) (in Dresden)
  1st Italian Line Regiment (3/148) (in Dresden)
  4th Italian Line Regiment (3/201) (in Dresden)
  6th Italian Line Regiment (1/95) (in Dresden)
  7th Italian Line Regiment (2/201) (in Dresden)

V Corps: Général de division Lauriston
(strengths as of 8/15)
16th Division: Général de division Count Maison
Brigade: Général de brigade Penne
  1/, 2/, 3/151st Line Regiment (detached to Glogau)
  1/152nd Line Regiment (30/733)
  2/152nd Line Regiment (22/765)
  3/152nd Line Regiment (20/782)
Brigade: vacant
  1/153rd Line Regiment (33.771)
  2/153rd Line Regiment (17/741)
  3/153rd Line Regiment (16/759)
  1/154th Line Regiment (20/718)
  2/154th Line Regiment (19/669)
  3/154th Line Regiment (18/676
Artillery: Chef de bataillon Vandidon
  1/1st Foot Artillery (3/62) (6–6pdrs & 2–24pdr
    howitzers)
  3/1st Foot Artillery (2/87) (6–6pdrs & 2–24pdr
    howitzers)
  7/6th Horse Artillery (2/83) (4–6pdrs & 2–24pdr
    howitzers)
  7/1nd Principal Train Battalion (2/90)
  2/4th (bis) Train Battalion (0/111)
17th Division: Général de division Puthod
Brigade: Général de brigade Penne
  1/134th Line Regiment (28/585)
  2/134th Line Regiment (23/527)
  1/146th Line Regiment (43/718)
  2/146th Line Regiment (27/644)
  3/146th Line Regiment (27/674)
  1/3rd Foreign Regiment (20/218)
  2/3rd Foreign Regiment (2/248)
Brigade: Général de brigade Siblet
  1/147th Line Regiment (41/662)
  2/147th Line Regiment (26/637)
  3/147th Line Regiment (25/658)
  1/148th Line Regiment (42/667)
  2/148th Line Regiment (19/647)
  3/148th Line Regiment (23/611)
Artillery: Chef de bataillon Bonafos
  1/5th Foot Artillery (3/102) (6–6pdrs & 2–24pdr
    howitzers)
  11/5th Foot Artillery (3/92) (6–6pdrs & 2–24pdr
    howitzers)
  1/11th Principal Train Battalion (1/115)
  Det. 7/11th Principal Train Battalion (0/59)
19th Division: Général de division Rochambeau
Brigade: Général de brigade Harlet
  1/135th Line Regiment (37/726)
  2/135th Line Regiment (17/674)
  3/135th Line Regiment (17/606)
  1/149th Line Regiment (46/777)
  2/149th Line Regiment (17/746)
  3/149th Line Regiment (16/728)
Brigade: Général de brigade Lafitte
  1/150th Line Regiment (42/904)
  2/150th Line Regiment (18/876)

3/150th Line Regiment (18/949)
1/155th Line Regiment (37/712)
2/155th Line Regiment (19/673)
3/155th Line Regiment (20/667)
Artillery: Chef de bataillon Richard
12/5th Foot Artillery (3/86) (6–6pdrs & 2–24pdr howitzers)
17/5th Foot Artillery (3/53) (6–6pdrs & 2–24pdr howitzers)
Det. 1st & 4/4th Principal Train Battalion (1/157)
Reserve and Park: Chef de bataillon Châteaubrun
15/1st Foot Artillery (3/72) (no guns)
16/1st Foot Artillery (1/73) (6–12pdrs & 2–6" howitzers)
17/1st Foot Artillery (2/88) (6–12pdrs & 2–6" howitzers)
2/5th Horse Artillery (3/86) (4–6pdrs & 2–24pdr howitzers)
7/3rd Principal Train Battalion (1/137)
Det 1/12th Principal Train Battalion (1/155)
5/5th (bis) Train Battalion (2/143)
4/8th (bis) Train Battalion (1/126)
4/9th (bis) Train Battalion (0/60)
1/6th Sapper Battalion (4/57)
2/6th Sapper Battalion (3/104)
3/6th Sapper Battalion (3/93)
Troops En Route to V Corps:
134th Line Regiment (2/50) (in Magdeborg)
147th Line Regiment (2/310) (in Mainz)
148th Line Regiment (1/138) (in Dresden)
149th Line Regiment (3/245) (in Dresden)
149th Line Regiment (2/154) (in Mainz)
149th Line Regiment (0/42) (in Mainz)
152nd Line Regiment (1/200) (in Dresden)
153rd Line Regiment (1/125) (in Erfurt)
154th Line Regiment (1/46) (in Dresden)
155th Line Regiment (0/122) (in Mainz)

VI Corps: Maréchal Marmont, Duke of Ragusa
20th Division: Général de division Compans
1st Brigade: Général de brigade Pelleport
2/32nd Légère Regiment (27/427)
3/32nd Légère Regiment (19/461)
1/1st Marine Regiment (34/547)
2/1st Marine Regiment (18/514)
3/1st Marine Regiment (19/517)
4/1st Marine Regiment (18/545)
5/1st Marine Regiment (13/705)
2nd Brigade: Général de brigade Joubert
20th Provisional Regiment
5/66rd Line Regiment (24/451)
3/122th Line Regiment (20/443)
25th Provisional Regiment
3/47th Line Regiment (24/586)
3/86th Line Regiment (22/563)
1/3rd Marine Regiment (26/736)
2/3rd Marine Regiment (17/699)
3/3rd Marine Regiment (16/703)

Artillery: Chef de bataillon Ocler
16/5th Foot Artillery (3/106) (6–6pdrs & 2–24pdr howitzers)
10/8th Foot Artillery (3/91) (6–6pdrs & 2–24pdr howitzers)
Det. 7/4th (bis) Train Battalion (2/123)
Det. 4/1st (bis) Train Battalion (1/121)
21st Division: Général de division Lagrange
1st Brigade: Général de brigade Jamin
1/37th Légère Regiment (30/647)
2/37th Légère Regiment (20/592)
3/37th Légère Regiment (20/567)
4/37th Légère Regiment (20/570)
1/4th Marine Regiment (29/676)
2/4th Marine Regiment (17/679)
3/4th Marine Regiment (17/596)
1/Joseph Napoleon Regiment (13/470)
2nd Brigade: Général de brigade Buquet
1/2nd Marine Regiment (29/570)
2/2nd Marine Regiment (16/535)
3/2nd Marine Regiment (18/543)
4/2nd Marine Regiment (19/527)
5/2nd Marine Regiment (20/520)
6/2nd Marine Regiment (20/555)
Artillery: Chef de bataillon Picard
10/4th Foot Artillery (2/118) (6–6pdrs & 2–24pdr howitzers)
18/5th Foot Artillery (3/78) (6–6pdrs & 2–24pdr howitzers)
Det. 1/8th Principal Train Battalion (0/30)
Det. 2/8th Principal Train Battalion (1/167)
Det. 1/10th (bis) Train Battalion (2/79)
22nd Division: Général de division Frederichs
1st Brigade: Général de brigade Coehorn
11th Provisional Regiment
4/1st Line Regiment (21/397)
2/62nd Line Regiment (19/460)
13th Provisional Regiment
3/14th Line Regiment (23/731)
4/16th Line Regiment (21/564)
3/23rd Légère Regiment (19/307)
4/23rd Légère Regiment (18/287)
3/15th Line Regiment (24/460)
4/15th Line Regiment (17/409)
2nd Brigade: Général de brigade Bacheler
16th Provisional Regiment
4/26th Line Regiment (22/428)
6/82nd Line Regiment (19/279)
3/121st Line Regiment (20/406)
4/121st Line Regiment (20/426)
3/70th Line Regiment (22/385)
4/70th Line Regiment (17/375)
Artillery:
14/4th Foot Artillery (2/119)
(6–6pdrs & 2–24pdr howitzers)
22/9th Foot Artillery (2/100)
(6–6pdrs & 2–24pdr howitzers)
3/8th Principal Train Battalion (2/160)
2/10th (bis) Train Battalion (1/98)

Light Cavalry Brigade: Général de brigade Normann
1/2nd Württemberg Chevauléger Regiment (6/121/134)
2/2nd Württemberg Chevauléger Regiment (3/109/112)
3/2nd Württemberg Chevauléger Regiment (4/110/114)
4/2nd Württemberg Chevauléger Regiment (4/109/113)
1/4th Württemberg Chevauléger Regiment (6/113/127)
2/4th Württemberg Chevauléger Regiment (3/105/108)
3/4th Württemberg Chevauléger Regiment (3/107/110)
4/4th Württemberg Chevauléger Regiment (3/100/106)
3rd Württemberg Horse Battery "Bruhaupt" (4–6pdrs & 2 7pdr howitzers)

Reserve and Park: Chef de bataillon Moran
3/5th Foot Artillery (2/41) (no guns)
18/5th Foot Artillery (3/102) (6–12pdrs & 2–6" howitzers)
26/5th Foot Artillery (3/96) (6–12pdrs & 2–6" howitzers)
1/1st Horse Battery (3/101) (4–6pdrs & 2–24pdr howitzers)
3/4th Horse Battery (3/91) (4–6pdrs & 2–24pdr howitzers)
Det. 4/12th Principal Train Battalion (1/107)
4/6th (bis) Train Battalion (2/122)
6/6th (bis) Train Battalion (2/126)
7/6th (bis) Train Battalion (1/142)
7/10th (bis) Train Battalion (2/103)
6/2nd Sapper Battalino (3/125)
2/4th Sapper Battalion (3/114)
9/4th Sapper Battalion (4/117)
4/7th Sapper Battalion (4/68)
Imperial Gendarmes (2/37/41)

Troops En Route to VI Corps:
4th Marine Regiment (I/277) (in Dresden)
4th Marine Regiment (1/380) (in Dresden)
23rd Légère Regiment (1/36) (in Dresden)
37th Légère Regiment (2/150) (in Dresden 8/18)
37th Légère Regiment (1/46) (in Erfurt 9/2)

VII Corps: Général de division Reynier
24th Division: Generalleutenant Lecoq (Saxon)
(Strength figures as of 8/15)
1st Brigade: Oberst von Brause
1/Saxon Guard Grenadier Battalion (13/710)
1/1st Saxon Light Infantry Regiment (14/617)
2/1st Saxon Light Infantry Regiment (12/604)
1/Maximilian Infantry Regiment (11/568)
2/von Rechten Infantry Regiment (12/597)
1st Jäger Company (3/133)

2nd Brigade: Generalmajor Mellentin
Converged Saxon Grenadier Battalion Spiegel (10/658)
1/Friederich Infantry Regiment (9/369)
2/Friederich Infantry Regiment (11/462)
1/Steindel Infantry Regiment (16/575)
2/Steindel Infantry Regiment (15/546)
Artillery: Major von Roth
1st Saxon Foot Battery "Dietrich" (4/168) (6–6pdrs & 2–8pdr howitzers)
2nd Saxon Foot Battery "Zandt" (4/179) (6–6pdrs & 2–8pdr howitzers)
Saxon Train Det. (2/95)

25th Division: Generalleutenant von Sahr
1st Brigade: Oberst von Bosch
Converged Saxon Grenadier Battalion Kleist (12/668)
1/2nd Saxon Light Regiment (14/598)
2/2nd Saxon Light Regiment (10/545)
2/König Infantry Regiment (12/489)
1/Niesmeuschel Infantry Regiment (9/545)
2nd Brigade: Generalmajor von Ryssel
1/Löw Infantry Regiment (12/547)
2/Löw Infantry Regiment (11/519)
1/Anton Infantry Regiment (12/541)
2/Anton Infantry Regiment (12/520)
Artillery: Major Gau
3rd Saxon Foot Battery "Kühnel" (4/104) (6–6pdrs & 2–8pdr howitzers)
4th Saxon Foot Battery "Rouvroy II" (3/173) (6–6pdrs & 2–8pdr howitzers)
Saxon Train Det. (2/73)

32nd Division: Général de division Durutte
(strengths as of 8/1/13)
1st Brigade: Général de brigade Devaux
1/35th Légère Regiment (21/889) (en route to Luckau)
Det. 2/35th Légère Regiment (3/90) (en route to Luckau)
4/35th Légère Regiment (18/680) (enroute from Erfurt)
1/132nd Line Regiment (17/870) (enroute from Erfurt)
Det. 2/132nd Line Regiment (2/91) (en route from Luckau)
3/132nd Line Regiment (20/691) (en route to Luckau)
4/132nd Line Regiment (20/697) (en route to Luckau)
2nd Brigade: Général de brigade Jarry
1/36th Légère Regiment (17/786) (enroute to Dresden)
Det. 3/36th Légère Regiment (2/72) (en route to Luckau)
4/36th Légère Regiment (22/724) (en route to Luckau)
1/131st Line Regiment (15/989) (enroute to Dresden)

2/131st Line Regiment (20/760) (en route to Luckau)

3/131st Line Regiment (19/758) (en route to Luckau)

3rd Brigade: Général de brigade Menu

Det. 2/133rd Line Regiment (2/54) (en route to Luckau)

3/133rd Line Regiment (22/615) (en route to Luckau)

4/133rd Line Regiment (24/687) (en route to Luckau)

2/Würzburg Infantry Regt (21/463) (en route to Luckau)

3/Würzburg Infantry Regt (17/460) (en route to Luckau)

Artillery: Chef d'escadron Simonin

12/1st Foot Artillery (3/88) (6–6pdrs & 2 howitzers)

13/8th Foot Artillery (3/89) (6–6pdrs & 2 howitzers)

Det. 2/9th (bis) Train Battalion (2/105)

Det. 2/, 4/9th Principal Train Battalion (1/148)

26th Light Cavalry Brigade: Oberst von Lindenau

1–8/Saxon Hussar Regiment (23/702/56/692)

1–5/Prinz Clemens Lancer Regiment (24/773/65/800)

Artillery:

1st Saxon Horse Battery "Birnbaum" (3/90) (4–6pdrs & 2–8pdr howitzers)

2nd Saxon Horse Battery "Probsthayn" (1/66) (4–6pdrs & 2–8pdr howitzers)

Reserve and Grand Park: Chef de bataillon Rabe

Saxon 12pdr Foot Battery "Rouvroy I" (3/118) (6–12pdrs & 2–8pdr howitzers)

1 Sapper Company (3/71)

Saxon Train Det. (0/89)

Troops En Route to VII Corps

131st Line Regiment (0/60) (in Dresden)

132nd Line Regiment (0/80) (in Dresden)

131st Line Regiment (2/166) (in Mainz)

133rd Line Regiment (1/67) (in Mainz)

VIII Corps: Prince Poniatowski
(strength as of 7/6/13)

26th Division: Général de division Kaminiecki

1st Brigade: Général de brigade Sierawski

1/1st Polish Infantry Regiment (30/528)

2/1st Polish Infantry Regiment (24/512)

1/16th Polish Infantry Regiment (31/538)

2/16th Polish Infantry Regiment (24/528)

1/, 2/Vistula Regiment (detached to Wittenberg)

2nd Brigade: Général de brigade Malachowski

1/8th Polish Infantry Regiment (29/549)

2/8th Polish Infantry Regiment (24/530)

1/15th Polish Infantry Regiment (31/542)

2/15th Polish Infantry Regiment (24/523)

Artillery: Orzinski

5th Polish Foot Artillery (7/132) (4–6pdrs & 2–24pdr howitzers)

7th Polish Foot Artillery (6/129) (4–6pdrs & 2–24pdr howitzers)

18th Polish Foot Artillery (6/133) (4–6pdrs & 2–24pdr howitzers)

27th Division:

2nd Brigade: Général de brigade Grabowski

1/, 2/4th Polish Infantry Regiment (detached to Wittenberg)

1/12th Polish Infantry Regiment (32/560)

2/12th Polish Infantry Regiment (24/549)

Artillery: Chef de bataillon Weisflog

10th Polish Foot Artillery (6/136)

Det 14th Polish Foot Artillery (3/61)

27th Light Cavalry Brigade: Général de brigade Uminski

1/14th Cuirassier Regiment (8/147)

2/14th Cuirassier Regiment (1/83)

1/Krakus Regiment (17/208)

2/Krakus Regiment (8/195)

3/Krakus Regiment (9/199)

4/Krakus Regiment (4/114)

Artillery Park: Colonel Bontemps

11th Polish Foot Artillery (6/129) (4–6pdrs & 2–24pdr howitzers)

Det. 14th Polish Foot Artillery (3/62)

1st Polish Sapper Company (5/135)

Polish Military Equipage (9/98)

Polish Gendarmes (4/90)

IX Corps: Maréchal Augereau (forming)

51st Division: Général de division Turreau

1st Brigade: Général de brigade Lagarde

32nd Provisional Demi-brigade

2/25th Légère Regiment

4/32nd Légère Regiment

1/, 2/, 3/, 4/113rd Line Regiment

2nd Brigade: Général de brigade Aymard

33rd Provisional Demi-brigade

2/27th Line Regiment

2/63rd Line Regiment

34th Provisional Demi-brigade

3/10th Légère Regiment

2/21st Légère Regiment

35th Provisional Demi-brigade

3/32nd Line Regiment

2/58th Line Regiment

Artillery

22/1st Foot Artillery (6–6pdrs & 2–24pdr howitzers)

5/2nd Foot Artillery (6–6pdrs & 2–24pdr howitzers)

21/2nd Foot Artillery (6–6pdrs & 2–24pdr howitzers)

Train Battalion Detachment

52nd Division: Général de division Semele

1st Brigade: Général de brigade Bagneria

36th Provisional Demi-brigade

2/24th Line Regiment

2/39th Line Regiment

37th Provisional Demi-brigade
  2/17th Légère Regiment
  4/29th Légère Regiment
38th Provisional Demi-brigade
  2/54th Line Regiment
  2/95th Line Regiment
2nd Brigade:
39th Provisional Demi-brigade
  2/8th Line Regiment
  4/28th Line Regiment
  2/88th Line Regiment
40th Provisional Demi-brigade
  6/15th Line Regiment
  6/70th Line Regiment
Artillery
  21/2nd Foot Artillery (6–6pdrs & 2–24pdr
    howitzers)
  27/7th Foot Artillery (6–6pdrs & 2–24pdr
    howitzers)
  2nd Train Company
Reserve and Grand Park
  28/5th Foot Artillery (6–12pdrs & 2–6" howitzers)
  3/6th Horse Artillery (4–6pdrs & 2–24pdr
    howitzers)
  1/4th Sapper Battalion
  Det/16th Artillery Artisan Company
  Train Battalion Det.

X Corps: Général de division Rapp (Garrison of Danzig)
7th Division: Général de division Grandjean
Brigade: Général de brigade Radzwill
  1/, 2/, 3/, Art/5th Polish Infantry Regiment
    (63/1,731)
  1/, 2/, 3/, Art/10th Polish Infantry Regiment
    (61/1,697)
  1/, 2/, 3/, Art/11th Polish Infantry Regiment
    (62/1,435)
Brigade: Général de brigade Bachelu
  1/, 2/, Art./1st Westphalian Infantry Regiment
    (34/1,004)
  1/, 2/, Art./13th Bavarian Infantry Regiment
    (41/1,132)
30th Division: Général de division Heudelet
Brigade: Général de brigade Husson
  1st Provisional Demi-brigade
    4/2nd Légère Regiment (21/791)
    4/4th Légère Regiment (19/632)
    4/17th Légère Regiment (18/649)
  6th Provisional Demi-brigade
    4/16th Légère Regiment (17/575)
    4/21st Légère Regiment (16/673)
    4/28th Légère Regiment (16/679)
  7th Provisional Demi-brigade
    4/8th Line Regiment (15/611)
    4/14th Line Regiment (15/642)
    4/94th Line Regiment (18/552)
Brigade: Général de brigade Grissand
  8th Provisional Demi-brigade

    4/54th Line Regiment (16/555)
    4/88th Line Regiment (20/418)
    4/95th Line Regiment (20/479)
  9th Provisional Demi-brigade
    4/24th Line Regiment (22/521)
    4/45th Line Regiment (20/618)
    4/59th Line Regiment (21/555)
  17th Provisional Demi-brigade
    4/6th Légère Regiment (20/575)
    4/25th Légère Regiment (23/555)
    4/39th Légère Regiment (20/782)
Brigade: Général de brigade Gault
  1 Co., 3rd Line Regiment (1/13)
  1/29th Line Regiment (26/214)
  1 Co., 105th Line Regiment (strength unknown)
  2 Cos., 113rd Line Regiment (20/210)
  1 Co., Prince Primate (Frankfurt) Regiment (5/34)
  1 Co., 4th Rhinbund Regiment (14/90)
  1 Co., 5th Rhinbund Regiment (22/159)
  1 Co., 6th Rhinbund Regiment (12/281)
Artillery: Colonel Gusskel
  7/7th Foot Artillery (3/90) (6–6pdrs & 2–24pdr
    howitzers)
  17/7th Foot Artillery (2/95) (6–6pdrs & 2–24pdr
    howitzers)
  18/9th Foot Artillery (2/90) (6–6pdrs & 2–24pdr
    howitzers)
  4/12th Principal Train Battalion (1/98)
  5/8th Principal Train Battalion (1/23)
  1/7th Sapper Battalion (2/92)
33rd Division: Général de division Destrees
Brigade: Général de brigade Rossarol
  1/, 2/5th Neapolitan Infantry Regiment (41/1,315)
  1/, 2/6th Neapolitan Infantry Regiment (32/1,258)
  1/, 2/7th Neapolitan Infantry Regiment (27/1,345)

XI Corps: Maréchal Macdonald
(Strength figures for 1 August)
31st Division: Général de division Ledru
Brigade: Général de brigade Fressinet
  11th Provisional Demi-Brigade
    4/27th Légère Regiment (21/601)
    6/20th Line Regiment (19/510)
    4/102nd Line Regiment (19/622)
  13th Provisional Demi-Brigade
    4/5th Line Regiment (20/516)
    4/11th Line Regiment (18/598)
    4/79th Line Regiment (20/613)
Brigade: Generalmajor d'Henin
  1/Westphalian Fusilier-Garde Regiment (24/448)
  2/Westphalian Fusilier-Garde Regiment (17/456)
  1/8th Westphalian Line Regiment (21/439)
  2/8th Westphalian Line Regiment (19/450)
  4th Westphalian Light Battalion (22/682)
Brigade: Général de brigade Macdonald
  1/Neapolitan Elite Regiment (20/609)
  2/Neapolitan Elite Regiment (14/251)
  1/4th Neapolitian Light Regiment (14/436)
  2/4th Neapolitian Light Regiment (12/418)

Artillery: Chef de bataillon Grosse
  20/5th Foot Artillery (3/91) (6–6pdrs & 2–24pdr howitzers)
  20/8th Foot Artillery (3/70) (6–6pdrs & 2–24pdr howitzers)
  1st Westphalian Foot Battery (4/69)
  Det. 1/, 4/8th Principal Train Battalion (1/177)
  Det. 1/3rd (his) Train Battalion (1/39)
  1st Westphalian Train Battalion (2/201)

5th Division: Général de division Gérard
Brigade: Général de brigade Lesenecal
  3/6th French Line Regiment (22/484)
  4/6th French Line Regiment (22/502)
  7/6th French Line Regiment (20/464)
  Artillery Co./6th French Line Regiment (2/45)
  1/112th French Line Regiment (23/487)
  2/112th French Line Regiment (17/526)
  3/112th French Line Regiment (18/522)
  4/112th French Line Regiment (23/562)
  Artillery Det./112th French Line Regiment (2/47)
Brigade: Général de brigade Zucchi
  3/2nd Italian Légère Regiment (20/426)
  4/2nd Italian Légère Regiment (21/421)
  Artillery Det./2nd Italian Légère Regiment (2/36)
  1/5th Italian Line Regiment (23/538)
  2/5th Italian Line Regiment (21/521)
  3/5th Italian Line Regiment (23/518)
  4/5th Italian Line Regiment (20/483)
  Artillery Det./5th Italian Line Regiment (3/72)
Artillery: Chef de bataillon Riva
  6/1st Foot Artillery (2/102) (6–6pdrs & 2–24pdr howitzers)
  3rd Italian Horse Battery (3/92) (6–6pdrs & 2–24pdr how.)
  Det. 1/11th (bis) Train Battalion (1/37)
  3rd Italian Train Battalion (1/99)
  4th Italian Train Battalion (2/110)

16th Division: Général de division Charpentier
Brigade: Général de brigade Simmer
  1/22nd Légère Regiment (25/593)
  2/22nd Légère Regiment (18/562)
  3/22nd Légère Regiment (19/557)
  4/22nd Légère Regiment (21/606
  Artillery Det./22nd Légère Regiment (2/36)
  4/10th Line Infantry Regiment (21/429)
  6/10th Line Infantry Regiment (18/458)
Brigade: Général de brigade Meunier
  3/14th Légère Regiment (20/548)
  4/14th Légère Regiment (23/574)
  7/14th Légère Regiment (22/532)
  Artillery Det./3rd Légère Regiment (2/69)
  3/3rd Légère Regiment (19/502)
  4/3rd Légère Regiment (23/559)
Artillery:
  5/1st Foot Artillery (2/80) (6–6pdrs & 2–24pdr howitzers)
  19/2nd Foot Artillery (3/82) (6–6pdrs & 2–24pdr howitzers)
  Det. 1/7th Principal Train Battalion (2/60)

2/12th Principal Train Battalion (2/172)
28th Light Cavalry Brigade: Général de brigade Montbrun
  1–4/2nd Neapolitan Chasseur à Cheval Regiment (28/659/78/656)
  4th Italian Chasseur à Cheval Regiment (2) (17/281/36/284)
  1/Würzburg Chevauléger Regiment (11/158/20/150)
Artillery: Major Gargant
  13/2nd Foot Artillery (3/97) (6–12pdrs & 2–6" howitzers)
  22/5th Foot Artillery (3/117) (6–12pdrs & 2–6" howitzers)
  15/5th Foot Artillery (3/87) (no guns)
  8/9th Foot Artillery (3/110)
  6/6th Horse Artillery (3/78) (4–6pdrs & 2–24pdr howitzers)
  Neapolitan Horse Battery (5/48) (4–6pdrs & 2–24pdr howitzers)
  14th Artillery Artisan Company (0/9)
  Dets. 3/, 4/7th Principal Train Battalion (3/243)
  Det. 2/8th (bis) Train Battalion (0/19)
  Det. 2/8th Principal Train Battalion (1/65)
  Det. 1/13th (his) Train Battalion (1/104)
  7/5th Sapper Battalion (3/113)
  2/7th Sapper Battalion (4/99)
  9th Italian Sapper Company (3/33)
  1/, 2/12th Equipage Train Battalion (2/126)

XII Corps: Marshal Oudinot
(strength as of 8/10)
13th Division: Général de division Pacthod
1st Brigade: Général de brigade Bardet
  4/1st Légère Regiment (20/483)
  3/, 4/7th Line Regiment (40/655)
  4/42nd Line Regiment (20/407)
2nd Brigade: Général de brigade Cacault
  3/, 4/67th Line Regiment (40/1,003)
  2/, 3/, 4/101st Line Regiment (59/1,464)
Artillery: Capitaine Lamy (strength as of 8/15)
  4/4th Foot Artillery (3/70) (6–6pdrs & 2–24pdr howitzers)
  20/4th Foot Artillery (4/77) (6–6pdrs & 2–24pdr howitzers)
  Det. 2/4th Principal Train Battalion (1/89)
  Det. 3/7th Principal Train Battalion (1/77)
14th Division: Général de division Guilleminot
1st Brigade: Général de brigade Grayer
  2/, 6/18th Légère Regiment (45/908)
  1/, 2, /3, /156th Line Regiment (84/2,680)
2nd Brigade: Général de brigade Brun de Villeret
  2/Illyrian Regiment (26/473)
  3/, 4/52nd Line Regiment (36/1,032)
  1/, 2/, 3/137th Line Regiment (83/1,811)
Artillery: Chef de bataillon Lyon
  2/4th Foot Artillery (3/93) (6–6pdrs & 2–24pdr howitzers)
  1/8th Foot Artillery (4/71) (6–6pdrs & 2–24pdr howitzers)

Det. 1/9th (bis) Train Battalion (0/56)
Det. 4/3rd (bis) Train Battalion (0/19)
Det. 1/4th Principal Train Battalion (1/59)
Det. 5/7th Principal Train Battalion (3/37)

29th (Bavarian) Division: Generallieutenant Raglovich

(Strengths as of 8/15)

Brigade: Generalmajor Beckers
  1st Light Batalion (14/452)
  2/Prinz Carl #3 Bavarian Infantry Regiment (13/360)
  Res/13th Bavarian Infantry Regiment (12/364)
  1/Isenburg #4 Bavarian Infantry Regiment (10/387)
  2/Herzog Pius #8 Bavarian Infantry Regiment (18/432)
Brigade: Generalmajor Maillot
  2nd Light Batalion (16/419)
  2/Preysing #5 Bavarian Infantry Regiment (11/439)
  7th Bavarian Infantry Regiment (18/606)
  2/#9 Bavarian Infantry Regiment (17/517)
  2/Junker #10 Bavarian Infantry Regiment (20/645)
Artillery: Major Marabini
  1st Bavarian Foot Battery (2/60)
  (6–6pdrs & 2–7pdr howitzers)
  2nd Bavarian Foot Battery (2/60)
  (6–6pdrs & 2–7pdr howitzers)
  Bavarian Reserve Foot Battery (2/280)
  (6–12pdrs & 2–7pdr howitzers)
  Bavarian Train Company (6/190)

29th Light Cavalry Brigade: Général de brigade Beaumont
  1/, 2/, 3/, 4/Westhphalian Garde Chevauléger Regiment (35/482/545)
  1/, 2/, 3/Combined Bavarian Light Dragoon Regiment (16/394/421)
  1/, 2/, 3/Hesse-Darmstadt Light Dragoon Regiment (12/248/283)

Park: Major Michel
  1/4th Foot Artillery (1/73)
  18/4th Foot Artillery (4/82)
  3/5th Horse Artillery (3/90)
  1/4th Principal Train Battalion (1/1 02)
  Det. 2/4th Principal Train Battalion (0/89)
  Det. 4/12th Principal Train Battalion (0/6)
  Det. 1/3rd (bis) Train Battalion (0/11)
  Det. 3/3rd (bis) Train Battalion (0/9)
  Det. 3/7th (bis) Train Battalion (1/4)
  Det. 4/7th (bis) Train Battalion (1/88)
  Det. 5/7th (bis) Train Battalion (0/17)
  4/2nd Sapper Battalion (3/100)
  4/6th Sapper Battalion (3/92)
  1/7th Equipage Train Battalion (1/75)
  2/7th Equipage Train Battalion (1/66)
  3/7th Equipage Train Battalion (1/130)
  Imperial Gendarmes à Cheval (2/34)

Troops En Route to XII Corps
  137th Line Regiment (1/90)
  156th Line Regiment (1/70)

XIII Corps: Maréchal Davout, Prince of Eckmuhl

3rd Division: Général de division Loison

1st Brigade: Général de brigade Mielzinski
  1/15th Légère Regiment (20/699)
  2/15th Légère Regiment (20/561)
  3/15th Légère Regiment (20/777)
  4/15th Légère Regiment (21/526)
  3/44th Line Regiment (19/727)
  4/44th Line Regiment (13/649)
2nd Brigade: Général de brigade Leclerc
  1/48th Line Regiment (20/738)
  2/48th Line Regiment (20/454)
  3/48th Line Regiment (19/568)
  4/48th Line Regiment (16/632)
  1/108th Line Regiment (24/698)
  2/108th Line Regiment (21/652)
  3/108th Line Regiment (19/560)
  4/108th Line Regiment (21/633)
Artillery: Chef de bataillon Mathieu
  3/8th Foot Artillery (3/83) (6–6pdrs & 2–24pdr howitzers)
  17/8th Foot Artillery (3/90) (6–6pdrs & 2–24pdr howitzers)
  Det. 1/6th Principal Train Battalion (1/74)
  Det. 5/7th Principal Train Battalion (0/45)

40th Division: Général de division Thiebault

1st Brigade: Général de brigade Delcambre
  3/33rd Légère Regiment (22/597)
  4/33rd Légère Regiment (19/806)
  1/61st Line Regiment (24/759)
  2/61st Line Regiment (15/734)
  3/61st Line Regiment (19/767)
  4/61st Line Regiment (18/714)
2nd Brigade: Général de brigade Gengoult
  1/30th Line Regiment (23/719)
  2/30th Line Regiment (20/758)
  3/30th Line Regiment (17/774)
  4/30th Line Regiment (18/697)
  1/111th Line Regiment (25/662)
  2/111th Line Regiment (21/551)
  3/111th Line Regiment (23/717)
  4/111th Line Regiment (20/551)
Artillery: Chef de bataillon Grosjean
  12/2nd Foot Artillery (3/72) (detached) (6–6pdrs & 2–24pdr howitzers)
  21/9th Foot Artillery (3/97) (6–6pdrs & 2–24pdr howitzers)
  18/8th Foot Artillery (3/148) (6–6pdrs & 2–24pdr howitzers)
  Det. 7/2nd (bis) Train Battalion (1/16)
  Det. 3/8th (bis) Train Battalion (1/99)

Danish Auxillary Division: Prince Frederich von Hesse

Advanced Guard: Colonel von Waldeck
  2/Schleswig Jager Regiment) (15/485)
  1/, 2/Holstein Jager Regiment) (33/925)
  2/, 6/Jutland Hussar Regiment) (13/216/27/282)
  Artillery & Train (5/113)

1st Brigade: Général de brigade Schulemburg
  1/Queen's Infantry Regiment (32/824)
  1/, 2/, 3/, 4/Oldenburg Infantry Regiment
    (74/2,400)
  1/, 2/, 3/, 4/Holstein Cavalry Regiment
    (32/467/33/563)
  Artillery & Train (5/140)
2nd Brigade: Général de brigade de Lasson
  1/Fionie Infantry Regiment (23/774)
  3/, 4/Holstein Infantry Regiment (38/1,419)
  1/, 2/Schleswig Infantry Regiment (29/1,042)
  1/, 2/, 3/, 4/Jutland Dragoon Regiment
    (24/457/48/576)
  Artillery & Train (6/184)
**30th Light Cavalry Brigade: Général de brigade
Lallemand**
  1/, 2/, 3/17th Polish Uhlan Regiment
    (62/391/174/576)
  1/, 2/28th Chasseurs à Cheval Regiment (18/305)
**Reserve and Grand Park: Chef de bataillon
Allouier**
  5/5th Foot Artillery (3/78) (detached)
  2/8th Foot Artillery (3/102) (detached)
  4/5th Horse Artillery (3/90)
    (4–6pdrs & 2–24pdr howitzers)
  8/4th Sapper Battalion (2/127)
  Artillery Artisan Det. (1/56)
  Det. 4/5th (bis) Train
  Det. 1/6th (bis) Train
  Det. 3/6th (bis) Train
  Det. 1/6th Principal Train Battalion
  Total Train – (2/121)
  12th Equippaige Train Battalion (4 cos) (12/478)
Troops En Route to XIII Corps: (as of 8/15)
  48th Line Regiment (3/77) (in Wesel on 8/25)
  108th Line Regiment (3/120) (in Hamburg on 9/7)
  30th Line Regiment (2/115) (in Hamburg on 9/10)
  111th Line Regiment (2/239) (in Magdeburg on
    7/15)
  61st Line Regiment (0/53) (in Magdeburg on 7/15)

XIV Corps: Marshal St. Cyr
(Strength figures for 1 August)
42nd Division: Général de division Dupas
1st Brigade: Général de division Reuss
  Provisional Demi-brigade
    2/4th Légère Regiment (20/725)
    3/12th Légère Regiment (22/709)
  4th Provisional Demi-brigade
    6/9th Légère Regiment (20/743)
    3/28th Légère Regiment (16/620)
  Provisional Demi-brigade
    4/10th Légère Regiment (22/741)
    3/21st Légère Regiment (21/713)
2nd Brigade: Général de brigade Creutzer
  Provisional Demi-brigade
    3/27th Line Regiment (24/804)
    3/63rd Line Regiment (18/792)
  16th Provisional Demi-brigade

  4/40th Line Regiment (20/556)
  3/43rd Line Regiment (20/825)
    (last detachments arrived 8/8 and 8/21)
  2/76th Line Regiment (21/780)
  3/76th Line Regiment (19/819)
  2/96th Line Regiment (18/800) (arrived 8/25)
  3/96th Line Regiment (17/803) (half arrived 8/20)
  Artillery: Chef de bataillon Lalombardière
    1/7th Foot Artillery (3/108) (6–6pdrs & 2–24pdr
      howitzers
    9/7th Foot Artillery (2/104) (6–6pdrs & 2–24pdr
      howitzers)
    Det. 6/1st (bis) Train Battalion (1/90)
    Det. 7/1st (bis) Train Battalion (1/46)
    Det. 5/11th Principal Train Battalion (1/136)
43rd Division: Général de division Claparède
Brigade: Général de brigade Butrand
  2/27th Légère Regiment (20/819)
  3/27th Légère Regiment (18/711)
  Provisional Demi-brigade
    2/29th Légère Regiment (15/742) (arrived 8/21)
    3/65th Line Regiment (17/805) (arrived 8/20)
    2/100th Line Regiment (20/760)
    3/100th Line Regiment (23/786)
    4/100th Line Regiment (21/746)
Brigade: Général de brigade Meunier
  2/45th Line Regiment (15/775)
  3/45th Line Regiment (20/733)
  2/103rd Line Regiment (21/762) (Erfurt 8/21)
  3/103rd Line Regiment (20/780)
  4/103rd Line Regiment (20/665)
  21st Provisional Demi-brigade
    2/59th Line Regiment (?/556)
    3/94th Line Regiment (24/684)
  Artillery: Chef de bataillon Paraviccini
    2/7th Foot Artillery (3/119) (6–6pdrs & 2–24pdr
      howitzers)
    4/6th Foot Artillery (2/107) (6–6pdrs & 2–24pdr
      howitzers)
    Det. 6/1st (bis) Train Battalion (1/49)
    Det. 7/1st (bis) Train Battalion (1/46)
    Det. 4/10th Principal Train Battalion (1/43)
    6/12th Principal Train Battalion (1/124)
44th Division: Général de division Berthezène
1st Brigade: Général de brigade Paillard
  1/8th Légère Regiment (17/575)
  3/8th Légère Regiment (13/696) (det. left Mainz
    8/23)
  34th Provisional Demi-brigade
    2/16th Légère Regiment (21/585)
    1/18th Légère Regiment (10/820)
    3/64th Line Regiment (19/712)
    4/64th Line Regiment (20/820)
2nd Brigade: Général de brigade Letellier
  Provisional Demi-brigade
    3/54th Line Regiment (21/689)
    3/95th Line Regiment (19/582)
  19th Provisional Demi-brigade
    2/50th Line Regiment (18/577) (half arrived 8/21)

2/75th Line Regiment (20/593) (half arrived 8/21)
Provisional Demi-brigade
   3/24th Line Regiment (20/783)
   3/39th Line Regiment (23/820)
Artillery:
   4/1st Foot Artillery (1/115) (6–6pdrs & 2–24pdr
     howitzers)
   15/7th Foot Artillery (2/106) (6–6pdrs & 2–24pdr
     howitzers)
   Det. 3/11th Principal Train Battalion (0/53)
   Det. 7/1st (bis) Train Battalion (1/45)
   Det. 4/11th (bis) Train Battalion (0/29)
   3/11th Principal Train Battalion (1/131)
   Det. 6/12th Principal Train Battalion (0/12)

45th Division: Général de division Razout
1st Brigade: Général de brigade Goguet
Provisional Demi-brigade
   3/6th Légère Regiment (15/607) (half arrived 7/9)
   4/60th Line Regiment (22/693)
26th Provisional Demi-brigade
   3/5th Line Regiment (18/750)
   3/11th Line Regiment (19/688)
Provisional Demi-brigade
   3/8th Line Regiment (19/718)
   2/28th Line Regiment (21/655) (det. arrived 8/26)
2nd Brigade: Général de brigade d'Esclevin
Provisional Demi-brigade
   4/32nd Line Regiment (19/686)
   4/58th Line Regiment (22/688)
18th Provisional Demi-brigade
   3/34th Line Regiment (21/757)
   3/69th Line Regiment (21/775)
27th Provisional Demi-brigade
   3/79th Line Regiment (22/720) (det. arrived 9/7)
   6/81st Line Regiment (15/687) (det. arrived 9/7)
Artillery: Chef de bataillon Auge
   21/5th Foot Artillery (2/113) (6–6pdrs & 2–24pdr
     howitzers)
   18/1st Foot Artillery (3/120) (6–6pdrs & 2–24pdr
     howitzers)
   Det. 5/12th Principal Train Battalion (1/126)
   Det. 4/11th (bis) Train Battalion (2/140)

**10th Light Cavalry Division: Général de division
Pajol**
16th Light Cavalry Brigade: Général de brigade
Jacquet
   1/, 2/, 3/, 4/14th Hussar Regiment (20/750/69/821)
   1/, 2/, 3/, 4/2nd Italian Chasseur à Cheval Regiment
     (35/704/115/704)
34th Light Cavalry Brigade: Général de brigade
Stedman
   1/, 2/, 3/, 4/7th Chevauléger Regiment (29/566)
   (half en route from Magdeburg)
Corps Artillery Reserve:
   10/7th Foot Artillery (3/120) (6–12pdrs & 2–6"
     howitzers)
   5/6th Foot Artillery (2/104) (6–12pdrs & 2–6"
     howitzers)

7/3rd Horse Artillery (2/96) (4–6pdrs & 2–24pdr
   howitzers)
5/2nd Horse Artillery (3/92) (4–6pdrs & 2–24pdr
   howitzers)
6/1st Horse Artillery (3/96) (4–6pdrs & 2–24pdr
   howitzers)
Det. 3/, 6/4th Principal Train Battalion (0/95)
4/10th Principal Train Company (2/128)
Det 8/1st (bis) Train Battalion (2/97)
6/4th Principal Train Battalion (1/78)
5/3rd Pontooneer Battalion (3/133)
8/2nd Sapper Battalion (3/145)
5/4th Sapper Battalion (3/145)
6/4th Sapper Battalion (3/144)
7/4th Sapper Battalion (3/129)
6th Engineering Train Company (3/143)
6/2nd Equipage Train Battalion (1/95)
Troops En Route to XIV Corps:
   7th Chevauléger Regiment (2/40/45) (in Leipzig
     8/23)
   28th Line Regiment (2/94) (in Erfurt 8/26)
   75th Line Regiment (1/53) (in Erfurt 8/26)

Reserve Cavalry:
I Cavalry Corps: Général de division
* Latour-Maubourg*
**1st Light Cavalry Division: Général de division
  Corbineau**
1st Brigade: Général de brigade Pire
   1/, 2/6th Hussar Regiment (21/337/395)
   1/7th Hussar Regiment (15/186/234)
   2/7th Hussar Regiment (9/156/174)
   3/7th Hussar Regiment (5/105/115)
   1/8th Hussar Regiment (12/180/212)
   2/8th Hussar Regiment (8/159/173)
   3/8th Hussar Regiment (7/196/208)
2nd Brigade: Général de brigade Montmarie
   1/, 2/1st Chevauléger-lancier Regiment (27/426/526)
   1/, 2/3rd Chevauléger-lancier Regiment
     (24/390/435)
   1/, 2/16th Chasseur à Cheval Regiment
     (16/280/323)
3rd Brigade: Général de brigade Piquet
   1/, 2/5th Chevauléger-lancier Regiment
     (24/370/430)
   1/, 2/8th Chevauléger-lancier Regiment
     (20/346/424)
   1/1st Italian Chasseur à Cheval Regiment
     (17/198/236)
   2/1st Italian Chasseur à Cheval Regiment
     (7/162/174)
   3/1st Italian Chasseur à Cheval Regiment
     (8/166/182)
   4/1st Italian Chasseur à Cheval Regiment
     (8/169/182)
**3rd Light Cavalry Division: Général de division
  Chastel**
4th Brigade: Général de brigade Vallin
   1/, 2/8th Chasseur à Cheval Regiment (22/393/447)

1/, 2/9th Chasseur à Cheval Regiment (17/361/395)
1/, 2/25th Chasseur à Cheval Regiment
(24/407/441)
5th Brigade: Général de brigade van Merlen
1/1st Chasseur à Cheval Regiment (16/149/180)
2/1st Chasseur à Cheval Regiment (10/212/228)
3/1st Chasseur à Cheval Regiment (4/114/128)
1/19th Chasseur à Cheval Regiment (8/133/157)
2/19th Chasseur à Cheval Regiment (8/224/258)
3/19th Chasseur à Cheval Regiment (8/252/265)
4/19th Chasseur à Cheval Regiment (7/252/262)
6th Brigade: Général de brigade Dermoncourt
1/, 2,'2nd Chasseur à Cheval Regiment
(26/297/360)
1/, 2/3rd Chasseur à Cheval Regiment (26/419/469)
1/, 2/, 3/6th Chasseur à Cheval Regiment
(25/494/525)

**1st Cuirassier Division: Général de division
Bordesoulle**
Brigade: Général de brigade Berkheim
1/, 2/2nd Cuirassier Regiment (18/302/346)
1/, 2/3rd Cuirassier Regiment (21/265/316)
1/, 2/6th Cuirassier Regiment (17/222/251)
Brigade: Général de brigade Bessières
1/, 2/, 3/9th Cuirassier Regiment (28/423/499)
1/, 2/, 3/11th Cuirassier Regiment (16/332/389)
1/, 2/12th Cuirassier Regiment (22/288/333)
Brigade: Generalmajor Lessing
1/Saxon Leib-Cuirassier Regiment (11/175/216)
2/Saxon Leib-Cuirassier Regiment (4/149/160)
3/Saxon Leib-Cuirassier Regiment (6/158/170)
4/Saxon Leib-Cuirassier Regiment (3/159/166)
1/Saxon Zastrow Cuirassier Regiment (7/148/186)
2/Saxon Zastrow Cuirassier Regiment (5/142/161)
3/Saxon Zastrow Cuirassier Regiment (4/143/161)
4/Saxon Zastrow Cuirassier Regiment (5/143/161)

**3rd Cuirassier Division: Général de division
Doumerc**
Brigade: Général de brigade d'Audenarde
1/, 2/, 3/4th Cuirassier Regiment (28/376/450)
1/, 2/, 3/7th Cuirassier Regiment (20/271/308)
1/, 2/14th Cuirassier Regiment (12/230/239)
1/Napoleon (Italian) Dragoon Regiment
(15/176/223)
2/Napoleon (Italian) Dragoon Regiment
(3/140/150)
3/Napoleon (Italian) Dragoon Regiment
(5/132/153)
4/Napoleon (Italian) Dragoon Regiment
(4/142/148)
Brigade: Général de brigade Reiset
1/, 2/7th Dragoon Regiment (24/286/350)
1/, 2/, 3/23rd Dragoon Regiment (21/341/387)
1/, 2/28th Dragoon Regiment (25/333/392)
1/, 2/30th Dragoon Regiment (26/355/339)
Artillery:
3/1st Horse Artillery (4/85) (4–6pdrs & 2–24pdr
howitzers)

6/3rd Horse Artillery (3/100) (4–6pdrs & 2–24pdr
howitzers)
1/4th Horse Artillery (3/100) (4–6pdrs & 2–24pdr
howitzers)
1/6th Horse Artillery (3/68) (4–6pdrs & 2–24pdr
howitzers)
4th Italian Horse Artillery (4/90)
(4–6pdrs & 2–24pdr howitzers)
3rd Saxon Horse Battery (3/77)
(4–6pdrs & 2–8pdr howitzers)
Det. 1/16th Principal Train Battalion
Det. 2/16th Principal Train Battalion
Det. 2/8th (bis) Train Battalion
Det. 5/8th (bis) Train Battalion
Det. 5/8th (bis) Train Battalion
1st Saxon Train Battalion
6th Italian Train Battalion

Troops En Route to I Cavalry Corps
6th Hussar Regiment (6/128/142)
7th Hussar Regiment (1/24/26)
8th Hussar Regiment (4/63/74)
16th Chasseur à Cheval Regiment (7/125/143)
1st Chevauléger Regiment (12/310/336)
3rd Chevauléger Regiment (8/195/215)
5th Chevauléger Regiment (13/319/357)
8th Chevauléger Regiment (5/99/125)
1st Chasseur à Cheval Regiment (3/80/86)
2nd Chasseur à Cheval Regiment (3/114/122)
3rd Chasseur à Cheval Regiment (1/30/34)
6th Chasseur à Cheval Regiment (6/113/124)
8th Chasseur à Cheval Regiment (5/68/79)
19th Chasseur à Cheval Regiment (4/130/146)
25th Chasseur à Cheval Regiment (6/72/87)
2nd Cuirassier Regiment (6/109/121)
3rd Cuirassier Regiment (4/106/L15)
4th Cuirassier Regiment (8/93/103)
6th Cuirassier Regiment (4/111/123)
7th Cuirassier Regiment (3/61/67)
9th Cuirassier Regiment (2/103/107)
11th Cuirassier Regiment (4/118/125)
12th Cuirassier Regiment (10/228/240)
14th Cuirassier Regiment (8/159/185)
7th Dragoon Regiment (5/81/94)
23rd Dragoon Regiment (2/22/26)
3rd Cuirassier Regiment

II Cavalry Corps: Général de division Sébastiani
2nd Division: Général de division Roussel
7th Brigade: Général de brigade Gérard
1/9th Hussar Regiment (13/205/255)
2/9th Hussar Regiment (8/203/222)
3/9th Hussar Regiment (7/202/223)
4/9th Hussar Regiment (8/210/226)
1/, 2/, 3/2nd Chevauléger-lancier Regiment
(21/421/477)
1/4th Chevauléger-lancier Regiment (16/163/205)
2/4th Chevauléger-fancier Regiment (12/226/251)
3/4th Chevauléger-lancier Regiment (4/114/129)

8th Brigade: Général de brigade Dommanget
  1/, 2/, 3/llth Chasseur à Cheval Regiment
  (26/456/517)
  1/, 2/, 3/12th Chasseur à Cheval Regiment
  (23/416/467)
  1/5th Hussar Regiment (17/153/199)
  2/5th Hussar Regiment (8/174/188)
  3/5th Hussar Regiment (5/123/136)
4th Division: Général de division Exelmans
9th Brigade: Général de brigade Maurin
  1/, 2/6th Chevauléger-lancier Regiment
  (23/351/408)
  1/, 2/4th Chasseur à Cheval Regiment (18/276/321)
  1/7th Chasseur à Cheval Regiment (14/207/249)
  2/7th Chasseur à Cheval Regiment (7/167/180)
  3/7th Chasseur à Cheval Regiment (15/199/231)
10th Brigade: Général de brigade Walthier
  1/20th Chasseur à Cheval Regiment (14/201/235)
  2/20th Chasseur à Cheval Regiment (9/157/177)
  3/20th Chasseur à Cheval Regiment (8/170/189)
  4/20th Chasseur à Cheval Regiment (4/76/85)
  1/23rd Chasseur à Cheval Regiment (14/182/220)
  2/23rd Chasseur à Cheval Regiment (7/137/147)
  3/23rd Chasseur à Cheval Regiment (8/170/189)
  4/23rd Chasseur à Cheval Regiment (4/76/85)
  1/24th Chasseur à Cheval Regiment (10/110/149)
  2/24th Chasseur à Cheval Regiment (4/84/91)
  3/24th Chasseur à Cheval Regiment (7/159/164)
  1/, 2/11th Hussar Regiment (19/220/281)
**2nd Cuirassier Division: Général de division
  Walthier**
1st Brigade: Général de brigade d'Augeranville
  1/, 2/1st Carabinier Regiment (21/328/381)
  1/, 2/2nd Carabinier Regiment (24/348/409)
  1/, 2/1st Cuirassier Regiment (22/301/352)
2nd Brigade: Général de brigade Thiry
  1/5th Cuirassier Regiment (19/165/197)
  2/5th Cuirassier Regiment (7/158/1670
  3/5th Cuirassier Regiment (4/82/93)
  1/, 2/8th Cuirassier Regiment (18/221/267)
  1/, 2/10th Cuirassier Regiment (25/339/408)
Artillery:
  7/1st Horse Artillery (4/103) (4–6pdrs & 2–24pdr
  howitzers)
  7/4th Horse Artillery (3/94) (4–6pdrs & 2–24pdr
  howitzers)
  8/6th Horse Artillery (3/84) (4–6pdrs & 2–24pdr
  howitzers)
  Det. 2/11th (bis) Train Battalion (1/62)
  Det. 4/11th (bis) Train Battalion (1/133)
  Det. 3/13th (bis) Train Battalion (0/57)
Troops En Route to II Cavalry Corps:
  11th Chasseur à Cheval Regiment (0/6/6)
  12th Chasseur à Cheval Regiment (2/18/22)
  5th Hussar Regiment (15/263/296)
  9th Hussar Regiment (0/51/51)
  11th Hussar Regiment (4/120/128)
  2nd Chevauléger Regiment (5/119/143)
  4th Chevauléger Regiment (3/136/144)

  6th Chevauléger Regiment (8/198/214)
  4th Chasseur à Cheval Regiment (6/130/144)
  20th Chasseur à Cheval Regiment (0/14/14)
  23rd Chasseur à Cheval Regiment (1/40/42)
  24th Chasseur à Cheval Regiment (14/345/387)
  1st Carabinier Regiment (3/127/131)
  2nd Carabinier Regiment (4/98/107)
  1st Cuirassier Regiment (2/117/119)
  5th Cuirassier Regiment (0/4/4)
  8th Cuirassier Regiment (0/11/11)
  10th Cuirassier Regiment (1/49/51)
  7th Dragoon Regiment (2/30/35)
  23th Dragoon Regiment (1/17/19)
  28th Dragoon Regiment (0/9/9)

III Cavalry Corps: Général de division Arrighi
**5th Light Cavalry Division: Général de division
  Lorge**
12th Brigade: Général de brigade Jacquinot
  1st Combined Regiment
    3/, 4/5th Chasseur à Cheval Regiment
    (19/451/50/458)
    3/, 4/10th Chasseur à Cheval Regiment
    (12/276/29/285)
  2nd Combined Regiment
    5/, 6/13th Chasseur à Cheval Regiment
    (17/366/48/373)
    3/, 4/14th Chasseur à Cheval Regt
    (12/339/29/346)
13th Brigade: Général de brigade Merlin
  Combined Regiment
    4/15th Chasseur à Cheval Regiment
    (9/218/22/226)
    3/21st Chasseur à Cheval Regiment
    (8/219/19/226)
  Combined Regiment
    3/, 4/22nd Chasseur à Cheval Regt
    (13/459/32/463)
    3/, 4/26th Chasseur à Cheval Regt
    (10/178/22/168)
**6th Light Cavalry Division: Général de division
  Fournier**
14th Light Cavalry Brigade: Général de brigade
Mouriez
  Combined Regiment
    4/29th Chasseur à Cheval Regiment
    (6/222/13/226)
    4/27th Chasseur à Cheval Regiment
    (10/267/28/229)
  Combined Regiment
    4/37th Chasseur à Cheval Regiment
    (9/222/22/232)
    4/1st Hussar Regiment (5/197/18/198)
15th Light Cavalry Brigade: Général de brigade Ameil
  Combined Regiment
    3/2nd Hussar Regiment (9/241/22/240)
    3rd Hussar Regiment (15/374/42/374)
  Combined Regiment
    5/4th Hussar Regiment (4/209/9/213)

4/12th Hussar Regiment (9/228/22/241)

4th Heavy Cavalry Division: Général de division Defrance

1st Brigade: Général de brigade Avice
Combined Dragoon Regiment
  2nd Dragoon Regiment (1) (11/154/31/168)
  3/5th Dragoon Regiment (8/205/20/205)
  3/12th Dragoon Regiment (9/166/22/169)
Combined Dragoon Regiment
  13th Dragoon Regiment (1) (12/177/32/165)
  3/14th Dragoon Regiment (8/155/19/156)

2nd Brigade: Général de brigade Quinette
Combined Dragoon Regiment
  17th Dragoon Regiment (1) (14/208/39/205)
  19th Dragoon Regiment (1) (7/93/15/72)
Combined Dragoon Regiment
  4th Dragoon Regiment (1) (6/111/13/119)
  6th Dragoon Regiment (1) (9/151/22/148)
  20th Dragoon Regiment (1) (9/165/23/176)

5th Heavy Cavalry Division: Général de division L'Heritier

1st Brigade: Général de brigade Collaert
Combined Dragoon Regiment
  11th Dragoon Regiment (106/117/15/131)
  15th Dragoon Regiment (1) (8/183/18/185)
  4/16th Dragoon Regiment (1) (4/105/7/103)
Combined Dragoon Regiment
  18th Dragoon Regiment (1) (5/89/12/91)
  21st Dragoon Regiment (1) (9/138/27/144)

2nd Brigade: Général de brigade Lamotte
Combined Dragoon Regiment
  22nd Dragoon Regiment (11(8/137/18/187)
  24th Dragoon Regiment (1) (1/82/3/82)
  25th Dragoon Regiment (1) (8/201/22/201)
Combined Dragoon Regiment
  26th Dragoon Regiment (1) (1/94/2/93)
  27th Dragoon Regiment (1) (5/68/11/68)
5/13th Cuirassier Regiment (5/171/15/178)

Artillery: Colonel Chauveau
1/5th Horse Artillery (3/93) (4–6pdrs & 2–24pdr howitzers)
5/5th Horse Artillery (2/100) (4–6pdrs & 2 24pdr howitzers)
5/1st (bis) Train Battalion (2/136)
2/1st Horse Artillery (3/92) (4–6pdrs & 2 24pdr howitzers)
4/6th Horse Artillery (2/89) (4–6pdrs & 2 24pdr howitzers)
6/4th Train Battalion (2/140)
Det. ? Train Battalion (0/65)

Troops En Route to III Cavalry Corps:
5th Chasseur à Cheval Regiment (7/185/197)
10th Chasseur à Cheval Regiment (1/129/131)
13th Chasseur à Cheval Regiment (2/61/66)
15th Chasseur à Cheval Regiment (2/125/130)
21st Chasseur à Cheval Regiment (4/126/136)
22nd Chasseur à Cheval Regiment (3/125/133)
31st Chasseur à Cheval Regiment (4/124/132)
1st Hussar Regiment (5/125/136)

2nd Hussar Regiment (6/250/264)
12th Hussar Regiment (2/201/204)
4th Dragoon Regiment (4/53/62)
5th Dragoon Regiment (0/2/2)
14th Dragoon Regiment (3/109/115)
14th Dragoon Regiment (2/105/1060
14th Dragoon Regiment (2/100/105)
16th Dragoon Regiment (0/66/66)
17th Dragoon Regiment (1/20/22)
21st Dragoon Regiment (0/18/18)
26th Dragoon Regiment (2/83/88)
27th Dragoon Regiment (3/150/154)
13th Cuirassier Regiment (2/68/72)

IV Corps:
(Strength as of 6 July 1813)

7th Light Cavalry Division: Général de division Sokolnicki
Brigade: Général de brigade Krustowski (Detached to I Corps)
  2nd Polish Uhlan Regiment
  4th Polish Chasseur à Cheval Regiment
Brigade: Général de brigade Tolinski
  1/3rd Polish Uhlan Regiment (19/208/276)
  2/3rd Polish Uhlan Regiment (8/195/232)
  3/3rd Polish Chian Regiment (9/199/237)
  4/3rd Polish Uhlan Regiment (4/144/112)
  1/13th Polish Hussar Regiment (19/164/221)
  2/13th Polish Hussar Regiment (7/102/109)
  3/13th Polish Hussar Regiment (8/105/120)
  4/13th Polish Hussar Regiment (8/127/138)

8th Light Cavalry Division:
Brigade: Général de brigade Ominski
  1/1st Polish Chasseur à Cheval Regiment (20/181/262)
  2/1st Polish Chasseur à Cheval Regiment (7/119/140)
  3/1st Polish Chasseur à Cheval Regiment (8/141/163)
  4/1st Polish Chasseur à Cheval Regiment (11/98/106)
  1/6th Polish Uhlan Regiment (20/182/272)
  2/6th Polish Uhlan Regiment (8/141/166)
  3/6th Polish Uhlan Regiment (9/148/168)
  4/6th Polish Uhlan Regiment (11/126/87)
Brigade: Général de brigade Weissenhoff
  1/8th Polish Uhlan Regiment (20/231/298)
  2/8th Polish Uhlan Regiment (11/167/202)
  3/8th Polish Uhlan Regiment (11/170/203)
  4/8th Polish Uhlan Regiment (15/164/161)
  1/16th Polish Uhlan Regiment (19/193/262)
  2/16th Polish Uhlan Regiment (11/130/159)
  3/16th Polish Uhlan Regiment (11/118/143)
  4/16th Polish Uhlan Regiment (12/129/162)
Artillery:
  1st Polish Horse Battery (8/161)
  (4–6pdrs & 2–24pdr howitzers)

V Cavalry Corps: (Strength as of 25 August 1813)
9th Light Cavalry Division: Général de brigade Klicky
Brigade:
  3/, 4/3rd Hussar Regiment (14/374/417)
  3/, 4/27th Chasseur à Cheval Regiment (10/207/257)
Brigade:
  3/, 4/14th Chasseur à Cheval Regiment (12/337/377)
  3/, 4/26th Chasseur à Cheval Regiment (14/283/319)
  1/13th Hussar Regiment (7/200/211)
  3/13th Hussar Regiment (7/145/169)
  4/13th Hussar Regiment (7/132/195)
5th Heavy Cavalry Division: Général de brigade Collaert
Brigade:
  3/2nd Dragoon Regiment (11/157/201)
  3/, 4/6th Dragoon Regiment (14/267/306)
Brigade:
  3/, 4/11th Dragoon Regiment (12/209/248)
  3/13th Dragoon Regiment (12/178/214)
  3/15th Dragoon Regiment (8/182/203)
6th Heavy Cavalry Division: Général de brigade Lamotte
Brigade:
  3/18th Dragoon Regiment (6/89/105)
  3/19th Dragoon Regiment (10/202/205)
  3/20th Dragoon Regiment (9/167/199)
Brigade:
  3/22nd Dragoon Regiment (8/185/207)
  3/25th Dragoon Regiment (9/201/225)
Artillery Park:
  5/3rd Horse Artillery (3/92) (4–6pdrs & 2–24pdr howitzers)
  5/11th Principal Train Battalion (1/82)
  5/4th Principal Train Battalion (1/66)
Troops En Route to V Cavalry Corps
  3rd Hussar Regiment (3/173/179)
  27th Chasseur à Cheval Regiment (14/375/399)
  14th Chasseur à Cheval Regiment (4/130/138)
  26th Chasseur à Cheval Regiment (5/181/190)
  2nd Dragoon Regiment (7/80/95)
  6th Dragoon Regiment (6/158/171)
  11th Dragoon Regiment (5/90/100)
  15th Dragoon Regiment (3/126/130)
  18th Dragoon Regiment (6/91/102)
  19th Dragoon Regiment (3/98/104)
  20th Dragoon Regiment (0/34/34)
  25th Dragoon Regiment (3/126/134)

Hamburg Garrison:
50th Division: Generaux de brigade Avril & Osten
  Det. 1/33rd Légère Regiment (15/83)
  2/33rd Légère Regiment (17/539)
  Det. 5/33rd Légère Regiment (2/86)
  Art/33rd Légère Regiment (3/107)
  Det. 2/3rd Line Regiment (3/210)

Det. 3/3rd Line Regiment (2/210)
Det. 4/3rd Line Regiment (3/208)
Det. 5/3rd Line Regiment (3/113)
Art/3rd Line Regiment (2/80)
2/29th Line Regiment (24/552)
3/29th Line Regiment (18/714)
4/29th Line Regiment (18/635)
Det. 5/29th Line Regiment (4/199)
Artillery Co/29th Line Regiment (2/87)
2/105th Line Regiment (2/216)
3/105th Line Regiment (2/210)
4/105th Line Regiment (3/390)
5/105th Line Regiment (5/245)
Artillery Co/105th Line Regiment (2/87)
Provisional Cuirassier Brigade: Général de brigade Duboise
1st Provisional Cuirassier Regiment
  4/1st Cuirassier Regiment (9/120/26)
  4/2nd Cuirassier Regiment (8/138/26)
  4/3rd Cuirassier Regiment (6/197/22)
  4/4th Cuirassier Regiment (9/220/18)
2nd Provisional Cuirassier Regiment
  4/5th Cuirassier Regiment (6/220/14)
  4/6th Cuirassier Regiment (7/188/17)
  4/7th Cuirassier Regiment (4/180/8)
  4/8th Cuirassier Regiment (9/142/19)
3rd Provisional Cuirassier Regiment
  4/9th Cuirassier Regiment (6/206/14)
  4/10th Cuirassier Regiment (6/120/13)
  4/11th Cuirassier Regiment (6/120/12)
  4/12th Cuirassier Regiment (7/176/16)
Hamburg Regiment de Marche
  2nd Cuirassier Regiment (3/41/39)
  3rd Cuirassier Regiment (3/92/96)
  5th Cuirassier Regiment (1/20/22)
  6th Cuirassier Regiment (5/102/111)
  7th Cuirassier Regiment (2/58/59)
  8th Cuirassier Regiment (1/20/16)
  11th Cuirassier Regiment (4/20/16)
  14th Cuirassier Regiment (3/102/92)
  13th Dragoon Regiment (1/31/33)
  23th Dragoon Regiment (0/13/13)
  28th Dragoon Regiment (0/8/8)
  30th Dragoon Regiment (2/70/73)
  2nd Chasseur à Cheval Regiment (3/99/106)
  16th Chasseur à Cheval Regiment (1/32/32)
  7th Chevauléger Regiment (2/122/126)
  13th Dragoon Regiment (3/91/8)
  28th Dragoon Regiment (1/20/15)
  30th Dragoon Regiment (0/21/0)
  7th Chevauléger Regiment (1/46/2)
  16th Chasseur à Cheval Regiment (2/56/17)
  16th Chasseur à Cheval Regiment (1/38/2)
  20th Chasseur à Cheval Regiment (3/80/11)
  9th Hussar Regiment (1/45/2)
  3/28th Chasseur à Cheval Regiment (8/481/0)
  5/28th Chasseur à Cheval Regiment (28/148/72)
  17th Lithuanian Uhlan Regiment (6/66/24)
  13th Veterans Battalion (13/450)

Mounted & Foot Customs Guards (9/472/8)
Imperial Gendarmes (10/245/219)
1/2nd Sapper Battalion (4/1430 5/5th Foot Artillery
(2/109)
Det. 12th Equipage Battalion (4/62)

Garrisons on the Elbe and Oder
Danzig: Général de division Rapp: See X Corps,
above
Modlin: Général de division Daendels
18th Lithuanian Infantry Regiment (54/824)
19th Lithuanian Infantry Regiment (22/22)
20th Lithuanian Infantry Regiment (39/891)
21st Lithuanian Infantry Regiment (23/575)
22nd Lithuanian Infantry Regiment (12/53)
3rd Polish Infantry Regiment (unknown)
17th Polish Infantry Regiment (unknown)
Saxon 1/Niesmeuschel Infantry Regiment (12/414)
4/Würzburg Infantry Regiment (17/361)
1/133rd Line Regiment (17/402)
18/7th Foot Artillery (3/103)
2/5th Foot Artillery (1/23)
8/9th Foot Artillery (0/7)
Stettin: Général de division Grandeau
10th Provisional Demi-brigade (91/2,316)
  4/27th Line Regiment
  4/63rd Line Regiment
  4/76th Line Regiment
  4/96th Line Regiment
12th Provisional Demi-brigade (49/1,950)
  3/123rd Line Regiment
  4/124th Line Regiment
  4/134th Line Regiment
Miscellaneous Infantry Detachments (95/2,133)
  12th Line Regiment
  17th Line Regiment
  21st Line Regiment
  1st & 2nd Co., 5/25th Line Regiment
  30th Line Regiment
  33rd Line Regiment
  48th Line Regiment
  57th Line Regiment
  61st Line Regiment
  3rd Co,5/108th Line Regiment
  111th Line Regiment
  7th Légère Regiment
  13th Légère Regiment
  15th Légère Regiment
5th Bataillon de marche (6/460)
2nd Compagnie de marche (3/253)
Det. 6th Rhinbund Regiment (0/77)
1st Provisional Dragoon Regiment (0/22/26)
2/1st Foot Artillery (3/112)
11/3rd Foot Artillery (2/51)
7/6th Foot Artillery (2/112)
4/8th Foot Artillery (3/97)
8/8th Foot Artillery (3/53)
3/9th Foot Artillery (2/63)
Artillery Train (6/84)

1/1st Pontooneer Battalion (4/44)
Det/5th Armorer Company (0/33)
Det/7th Artillery Artisan Company (0/8)
Det/12th Equipage Battalion (0/21)
Custrin: Général de division Fournier d'Albe
2/4th Westphalian Regiment
2/5th Westphalian Regiment
Total Westphalian Infantry (47/953)
3/128th Line Regiment (21/507)
Miscellaneous Infantry Detachments (79/212)
  1st & 2nd Co, 2nd Line Regiment
  1st & 2nd Co, 19th Line Regiment
  1st & 2nd Co, 37th Line Regiment
  1st & 2nd Co, 56th Line Regiment
  1st & 2nd Co, 11th Légère Regiment
  1st & 2nd Co, 26th Légère Regiment
  1st Co, Depot/1st Swiss Line Regiment
  1st Co, Depot/2nd Swiss Line Regiment
1/3rd Foot Artillery (3/27)
13/3rd Foot Artillery (3/56)
14/7th Foot Artillery (2/87)
20/9th Foot Artillery (1/57)
Det. 5th Armorer Company (0/15)
8/5th Sapper Battalion (2/66)
Glogau: Général de division Laplane
3/151st Line Regiment (75/2,310)
1/, 2/1st Provisional Croatian Line Regiment
  (24/1,107)
1/, 2/2nd Provisional Croatian Line Regiment (21/474)
1/, 2/Frankfurt Regiment (35/855)
8/3rd Foot Artillery (2/64)
16/4th Foot Artillery (4/103)
7/8th Foot Artillery (2/77)
9th Saxon Foot Artillery (2/93)
9/5th Sapper Battalion (3/73)
3/1st Miner Battalion (2/86)
Depot of Isolated Individuals (1/240)
Joseph Napoleon (Spanish) Regiment (5/135)
Construction Workers (4/71)
Magdeburg: Général de division Lemarois
3/134th Line Regiment (17/439)
5/134th Line Regiment (23/1190)
6/134th Line Regiment (3/678)
4th Provisional Carabinier Regiment
  4/1st Carabinier Regiment (4/185)
  4/2nd Carabinier Regiment (8/178)
  4/14th Cuirassier Regiment (1/98/27)
1/9th Foot Artillery (3/92)
16/9th Foot Artillery (2/103)
11th Artillery Artisan Company (2/121)
Det/5th Armorer Company (1/16)
Det. 3/1st Miner Battalion (1/26)
Det/4th Sapper Battalion (0/15)
Italian Naval Workers (2/43)
Imperial Gendarmes (1/9)
Wittenberg: Général de division Lapoype
2/Vistula Regiment (65/676)
2/4th Polish Line Regiment (47/339)
2/123rd Line Regiment (15/584)

2/124th Line Regiment (21/318)
Det. Polish Uhlans (4/52/62)
16/7th Foot Artillery (2/95)
1/7th Sapper Battalion (4/92)
1/Spanish Pioneer Battalion (3/164)
Erfurt: Général de brigade Dalton
6/1st Marine Regiment (8/656) (arrived 9/2/13)
8/2nd Marine Regiment (13/103) (arrived 9/12/13)
8/1st Foot Artillery (1/104)
7th Artillery Artisan Company (2/45)
Det/11th Principal Train Battalion (0/20)
1/3rd Sapper Battalion (2/145)
Würzburg:
2/127th Line Regiment (20/409)
2/128th Line Regiment (21/417)
8/5th Foot Artillery (2/69)
17th Artillery Artisan Company (0/16)

---

*French Archives, Cartons C²– 537, 538, 539, 540, 541,
542, 543, 544, and C²–708.*

THE ALLIED ARMIES 10 AUGUST 1813

II
ARMY OF BOHEMIA

Commander-in-Chief: Feldmarschall Fürst Carl zu
  Schwarzenberg
Chief of Staff: Feldmarschal-leutnant Graf Radetzky
General Quartermasters: Generalmajor Baron
  Langenau,
Generalmajor Baron Trapp
Chief of Artillery: Feldmarschal-leutnant Reiszner
General-Intendant: Feldmarschal-leutnant Prohaska

1st Eintheilung
1st Light Division: Feldmarschalleutnant Fürst Moritz Liechtenstein
Brigade: Generalmajor Haugwitz
  Jäger Battalion #1
  Jäger Battalion #2
  Kaiser Chevauléger Regiment (6)
  3pdr Brigade Battery
Brigade: Generalmajor Scheither
  Broder Grenz Regiment (1)
  Jäger Battalion #7
  St. Vincent Chevauléger Regiment (6)
2nd Light Division: Feldmarschal-leutnant Bubna
Brigade: Generalmajor Baron Zechmeister
  Peterswardeiner Grenz Regiment (1)
  Jäger Regiment #6
  Liechtenstein Hussar Regiment (6)
  3pdr Brigade Battery

Brigade: Generalmajor Graf Neipperg
  Jäger Battalion #5
  Kaiser Hussar Regiment (6)
  Blankenstein Hussar Regiment (6)
  6pdr Cavalry Battery

1st Army Abteilung: Feldzeugmeister Graf H. Colloredo
1st Division: Feldmarschal-leutnant Schneller
Brigade: Generalmajor von Hessen-Homburg
  Deutsch-Banat Grenz Regiment (2)
  Hessen-Homburg Hussar Regiment (6)
  Riesch Dragoon Regiment (6)
  6pdr Cavalry Battery
2nd Division: Feldmarschal-leutnant Wimpfen
Brigade: Generalmajor Torry
  Froon Infantry Regiment (3)
  Devaux Infantry Regiment (3)
Brigade: Generalmajor Czerwenka
  Argenteau Infantry Regiment (2)
  Erbach Infantry Regiment (3)
  2 6pdr Brigade Batteries
3rd Division: Feldmarschal-leutnant Greth
Brigade: Generalmajor Mumb
  de Ligne Infantry Regiment (2)
  Czartorisky Infantry Regiment (2)
Brigade: Generalmajor Quasdannovich
  Albert Gyulai Infantry Regiment (2)
  Reuss Paulen Infantry Regiment (3)
  2 6pdr Brigade Batteries
Artillery Reserve:
  1 6pdr Position Battery
  2 12pdr Foot Batteries

2nd Army Abteilung: GdK Graf Merveldt
1st Division: Feldmarschal-leutnant Ignatz Lederer
Brigade: Generalmajor Sorenberg
  Gradiscaner Grenz Regiment (1)
  Kienmeyer Hussar Regiment (6)
  Johann Dragoon Regiment (6)
  2 6pdr Brigade Batteries
Brigade: Generalmajor Giffing
  Strauch Infantry Regiment (2)
  Bellegarde Infantry Regiment (2)
2nd Division: Feldmarschal-leutnant Fürst Liechtenstein
Brigade: Generalmajor Klopstein
  Kaunitz Infantry Regiment (2)
  W. Colloredo Infantry Regiment (2)
Brigade: Generalmajor Meszerev
  Vogelsang Infantry Regiment (2)
  Reuss Graitz Infantry Regiment (2)
  3pdr Brigade Battery
Artillery Reserve:
  1 6pdr Position Battery
  2 12pdr Foot Batteries

*3rd Army Abteilung: Feldzeugmeister Graf I.
    Gyulai*
1st Division: Feldmarschal-leutnant Crenneville
Brigade: Generalmajor Hecht
  Warasdiner Kreuzer Grenz Regiment (1)
  St. George Grenz Regiment (1)
  Klenau Chevauléger Regiment (6)
  Rosenberg Chevauléger Regiment (6)
  1 6pdr Cavalry Battery
2nd Division: Feldmarschal-leutnant Murray
Brigade: Generalmajor Herzogenberg
  Erzherzog Ludwig Infantry Regiment (2)
  Grossherzog von Würzburg Infantry Regiment (2)
Brigade: Generalmajor Reichling
  Weidenfeld Infantry Regiment (2)
  Ignatz Infantry Regiment (2)
  2 6pdr Brigade Batteries
3rd Division: Feldmarschal-leutnant Weissenwoif
Brigade: Generalmajor Czollich
  Kottulinsky Infantry Regiment (2)
  Kaiser Infantry Regiment (2)
Brigade: Generalmajor Grimmer
  Kollowrath Infantry Regiment (2)
  Frohlich Infantry Regiment (2)
Artillery Reserve
  1 6pdr Position Battery
  2 12pdr Foot Batteries

*3rd Army Abteilung: General der Kavallerie Graf
    J. Klenau*
1st Division: Feldmarschal-leutnant Freiherr Mohr
Brigade: Generalmajor Paumgarten
  1st Wallachen Grenz Regiment (1)
  Wallachen-Illyrian Grenz Regiment (2)
  Hohenzollern Chevauléger Regiment (6)
  Palatinal Hussar Regiment (6)
  Erzherzog Ferdinand Hussar Regiment (6)
  6pdr Cavalry Battery
**2nd Division: Feldmarschal-leutnant Fürst
    Hohenlohe-Bartenstein**
Brigade: Generalmajor Schaffer
  J. Colloredo Infantry Regiment (2)
  Zach Infantry Regiment (3)
Brigade: Generalmajor Splenyi
  Herzog Württemberg Infantry Regiment (3)
  Lindeneau Infantry Regiment (2)
  2 6pdr Brigade Batteries
3rd Division: Feldmarschal-leutnant Mayer
Brigade: Generalmajor Abele
  Alois Liechtenstein Infantry Regiment (3)
  Coburg Infantry Regiment (3)
Brigade: Generalmajor Pest
  Erzherzog Carl Infantry Regiment (2)
  Obrist Salis Infantry Regiment (2)
  Kerpen Infantry Regiment (2)
  2 6pdr Brigade Batteries

Artillery Reserve
  1 6pdr Position Battery
  2 12pdr Foot Batteries

*Army Reserve: General der Kavallerie Erbprinz
    von Hessen-Homburg*
**1st Division: Feldmarschal-leutnant Graf
    Weissenwolf**
Brigade: Generalmajor Fürstenwarther
  Grenadier Battalion Czarnotzky
  Grenadier Battalion Ohermever
  Grenadier Battalion Berger
  Grenadier Battalion Oklopsia
Brigade:
  Grenadier Battalion Habinay
  Grenadier Battalion Portner
  Grenadier Battalion Fischer
  Grenadier Battalion Rüber
  2 6pdr Brigade Batteries
2nd Division: Feldmarschal-leutnant Bianchi
Brigade: Generalmajor Prinz P. von Hessen-Homburg
  Hiller Infantry Regiment (2)
  H. Colloredo Infantry Regiment (2)
  Hessen-Homburg Infantry Regiment (2)
Brigade: Generalmajor Quallenberg
  Simbischen Infantry Regiment (2)
  Esterhazy Infantry Regiment (2)
  Davidovich Infantry Regiment (2)
  2 6pdr Brigade Batteries

*Cuirassier Corps: Feldmarschal-leutnant Graf
    Nostitz*
1st Division: Feldmarschal-leutnant Hardegg
Brigade: Generalmajor Rothkirch
  Erbprinz Franz Cuirassier Regiment (4)
  Kronprinz Ferdinand Cuirassier Regiment (4)
Brigade: Generalmajor Raigencourt
  Hohenzollern Cuirassier Regiment (4)
  Sommariva Cuirassier Regiment (4)
2nd Division: Feldmarschal-leutnant Civallart
Brigade: Generalmajor Dufours
  Kaiser Cuirassier Regiment (6)
  O'Reilly Chevauléger Regiment (6)
Brigade: Generalmajor Kuttalck
  Herzog Albert Cuirassier Regiment (4)
  Lothringen Cuirassier Regiment (4)
  3 6pdr Cavalry Batteries

Russo-Prussian Troops:
  Commander-in-Chief: General of Infantry Barclay
    de Tolly
  Chief of Staff: Generallieutenant Sabanejev
  General Quartermaster: Generalmajor Diebitsch II
  Chief of Artillery: Generallieutenant Jachwill
  General-Intendant: Generalmajor Kankerin
  Chief of Engineers: Generalmajor Count Sievers
  General of the Day: Generalmajor Oldekop

Right Wing: General of Cavalry Count Wittgenstein
1st Russian Corps: Generallieutenant Count Gortschakov
5th Division: Generalmajor Mezentzov
Brigade: Generalmajor Lukov
  23rd Jager Regiment (2)
  Perm Infantry Regiment (2)
  Mohilev Infantry Regiment (2)
Brigade: Generalmajor Vlassov
  24th Jager Regiment (2)
  Sieversk Infantry Regiment (1)
  Kalouga Infantry Regiment (2)
  Grand Duchess Catherine Battalion (1)
14th Division: Generalmajor Helfreich
Brigade: Generalmajor Laelin
  Tenguinsk Infantry Regiment (2)
  Estonia Infantry Regiment (2)
Brigade: Generalmajor Roth
  25th Jager Regiment (2)
  26th Jager Regiment (2)
Artillery:
  Position Battery #3
  Light Battery #6

2nd Corps: Generallieutenant Prince Württemberg
3rd Division: Generalmajor Schachafskoy
Brigade: Colonel Ivanov
  20th Jager Regiment (2)
  Mourman Infantry Regiment (2)
  Revel Infantry Regiment (2)
Brigade: Colonel Baron Wolff
  21st Jager Regiment (1)
  Tschernigov Infantry Regiment (2)
  Selenguinsk Infantry Regiment (2)
4th Division; Generalmajor Pischnitzky
Brigade: Colonel Treffurt
  4th Jager Regiment (2)
  Tobolsk Infantry Regiment (2)
  Minsk Infantry Regiment (2)
Brigade: Colonel Mononov
  34th Jager Regiment (1)
  Volhynie Infantry Regiment (2)
  Krementchug Infantry Regiment (2)
Artillery:
  Position Battery #33
  Light Battery #27

Cavalry Corps: Generallieutenant Count Pahlen III
1st Line: Generalmajor Millesinov
Brigade: Generalmajor Illowaiski
  Illowaiski #12 Don Cossack Regiment
  Ataman Don Cossack Regiment
  Rabinov #2 Cossack Regiment
1st Hussar Division: Generallieutenant Count Pahlen III
Brigade: Generalmajor Rudinger
  Grodno Hussar Regiment (6)

  Soum Hussar Regiment (6)
Brigade: Colonel Schufanov
  Loubnv Hussar Regiment (2)
  Olivopol Hussar Regiment (4)
2nd Line: Generalmajor Lissanevich
Brigade: Generalmajor Knorring
  Tartar Uhlan Regiment (4)
  Serpuchov Uhlan Regiment (6)
  Tchougouiev Uhlan Regiment Horse Battery #7

Left Wing: Generallieutenant von Kleist
9th Brigade: Generalmajor von Klüx
Brigade: Oberst von Schumalensee
  1/, 2/, Fus/1st West Prussian Infantry Regt (61/196/2,447)
  1/, 2/, 3/6th Reserve Infantry Regiment (57/180/2,067)
  1/, 2/Silesian Schützen Battalion (13/30/370)
  1/, 2/, 3/, 4/7th Silesian Landwehr Regt (6/202/2,369)
Attached
  Neumärk Dragoon Regiment (4) (26/56/501)
    Freiwilliger Jäger Co. (3/5/62)
  6pdr Foot Battery #7 (4/11/126)
10th Brigade: Generalmajor Pirch I
Brigade: Oberst von Jagow
  1/, 2/, Fus/2nd West Prussian Infantry Regt (67/180/2,913)
    Freiwilliger Jäger Co. (2/30/346)
  1/, 2/, 3/7th Reserve Infantry Regiment (64/180;'2,233)
  1/, 2/, 3/, 4/9th Silesian Landwehr Regt (68/202/2,275)
Attached:
  2nd Silesian Landwehr Cavalry Regiment (4) (22/59/489)
  6pdr Foot Battery #14 (4/12/126)
11th Brigade: Generalmajor Ziethen
Brigade: Oberst von Jagow
  1/, 2/, Fus/1st Silesian Infantry Regiment (67/180/2,473)
    Freiwilliger Jäger Co. (2/6/60)
  1/, 2/, 3/10th Reserve Infantry Regiment (66/180/2,223)
  3/, 4/Silesian Schützen Battalion (7/27/370)
  1/, 2/, 3/, 4/8th Silesian Landwehr Regt (71/217/2,220)
Attached:
  1st Silesian Hussar Regiment (4) (32/68/584)
    Freiwilliger Jäger Co. (1/0/55)
  6pdr Foot Battery #9 (4/12/125)
12th Brigade: Generallieutenant Prince August von Preussen
Brigade: Oberst von Funk
  1/, 2/, Fus/2nd Silesian Infantry Regiment (66/180/2,233)
    Freiwilliger Jäger Co. (2/8/90)
  1/, 2/, 3/11th Reserve Infantry Regiment (56/180/2,223)

1/, 2/, 3/, 4/10th Silesian Landwehr Regt
(67/210/1,920)
Attached:
  1st Silesian Landwehr Cavalry Regiment (4)
  (23/48/405)
  6pdr Foot Battery #13 (4/11/125)
Cavalry Reserve: Generalmajor von Röder
Brigade: Oberst von Wrangel
  East Prussian Cuirassier Regiment (4) (23/60/554)
    Freiwilliger Jäger Co. (4/9/76)
  Silesian Cuirassier Regiment (4) (30/59/562)
    Freiwilliger Jäger Co. (1/2/29)
  Brandenburg Cuirassier Regiment (4) (23/60/533)
    Freiwilliger Jäger Co. (5/11/92)
Brigade: Oberst von Starkenfels
  Silesian Uhlan Regiment (4) (26/60/555)
    Freiwilliger Jäger Co. (1/0/24)
  Silesian National Cavalry Regiment (4) (11/22/196)
    Freiwilliger Jäger Co. (3/?/47)
  2nd Silesian Hussar Regiment (4) (16/34/302)
    Freiwilliger Jäger Co. (0/4/43)
Brigade: Oberst von Mutius
  7th Silesian Landwehr Cavalry Regiment (4)
  (24/60/494)
  8th Silesian Landwehr Cavalry Regiment (4)
  (22/50/378)
Artillery:
  Horse Battery #7 (4/9/133)
  Horse Battery #8 (4/12/134)
Reserve Artillery: Oberst von Braun
  12pdr Foot Battery #3 (4/12/174)
  12pdr Foot Battery #6 (4/14/194)
  6pdr Foot Battery #8 (4/10/125)
  6pdr Foot Battery #11 (4/10/126)
  6pdr Foot Battery #21 (4/13/150)
  7pdr Howitzer Battery #1 (4/10/154)
  Horse Battery #9 (4/12/134)
  Horse Battery #10 (4/13/134)
  Munition Column #7 (2/4/39)
  Munition Column #8 (2/4/39)
  Munition Column #9 (2/6/39)
  Munition Column #10 (2/6/39)
  Munition Column #11 (2/6/39)
  Artisan Column #2 (1/1/11)
  7th Feldjäger Company

Reserve Army:
  Commander-in-Chief: Grand Duke Constantine
  Chief of Staff: Generalmajor Kurutta
  Quartermaster: Colonel Baron Crossard
  General du Jour: Generalmajor Patepov
  Infantry Commander: General of Infantry
    Miloradovich
  Chief of Staff: Colonel Sipaegin
  Quartermaster: Colonel Niedhardt II

3rd (Grenadier) Corps: Generalmajor Raevsky
1st Division: Generalmajor Sulima
Brigade: Generalmajor Zwielikov
  Ekaterinoslav Grenadier Regiment (2)
  Count Arakcheyev Grenadier Regiment (2)
Brigade: Colonel Acht
  Tauride Grenadier Regiment (2)
  St. Petersburg Grenadier Regiment (2)
Brigade: Colonel Yemelianov
  Pemau Infantry Regiment (2)
  Kexholm Infantry Regiment (2)
2nd Division: Generalmajor Tchoglokov
Brigade: Colonel Pissarev
  Kiev Grenadier Regiment (2)
  Moscow Grenadier Regiment (2)
Brigade: Colonel Colovin
  Astrakhan Grenadier Regiment (2)
  Fangoria Grenadier Regiment (2)
Brigade: Colonel Hesse
  Siberia Grenadier Regiment (2)
  Little Russian Grenadier Regiment (2)

5th (Guard) Corps: Generallieutenant Yermolov
**1st Guard Infantry Division: Generalmajor Baron
Rosen**
Brigade: Generalmajor Potemkin
  Preobragenski Guard Infantry Regiment (3)
  Semenovski Guard Infantry Regiment (3)
Brigade: Generalmajor Krapovitzsky
  Ismailov Guard Infantry Regiment (3)
  Guard Jager Regiment (2)
  Guard Equipage Battalion (2 coys)
Prussian Guard Brigade: Oberst von Alvensleben
  1/1st Garde zu Fuss Regiment (24/42/777)
  2/1st Garde zu Fuss Regiment (18/55/745)
  Fus/1st Garde zu Fuss Regiment (22/49/755)
    1st Freiwilliger Co. (3/15/189)
    2nd Freiwilliger Co. (3/15/182)
    3rd Freiwilliger Co. (3/15/181)
  1/2nd Garde zu Fuss Regiment (21/57/750)
  2/2nd Garde zu Fuss Regiment (19/60/747)
  Fus/2nd Garde zu Fuss Regiment (19/60/751)
    1st Freiwilliger Co. (3/15/185)
    2nd Freiwilliger Co. (3/15/162)
  1/, 2/Garde Jager Battalion (12/26/371)
2nd Guard Division: Generalmajor Udom I
Brigade: Colonel Krishanovsky
  Lithuanian Guard Infantry Regiment (3)
  Finland Guard Infantry Regiment (3)
Brigade: Scheltuchin II
  Leib-Garde Guard Infantry Regiment (2)
  Pavlov Guard Grenadier Regiment (2)
Artillery: Generalmajor Euler
  Guard Position Battery #2
  Guard Light Battery #1
  Guard Light Battery #2
  Pioneer Company of Captain Föliakov
  Worker's Battalion of Major Ratinikov

Reserve Cavalry: Generallieutenant Count Gallitzin V

1st Cuirassier Division: Generalmajor Depreradovich

Brigade: Generalmajor Arseniev
  Chevalier Guard Regiment (6)
  Horse Guard Regiment (6)
Brigade: Generalmajor Baron Rosen
  Leibgarde Cuirassier Regiment (3)
  Empress Cuirassier Regiment (4)

Prussian Guard Cavalry Brigade:

Brigade: Oberst von Werder
  Garde du Corps Regiment (4) (40/62/547)
    Guard Volunteer Cossack Sqn (5/112/110)
  Guard Light Cavalry Regiment (4) (43/55/592)
    Guard Volunteer Cossack Sqn (11/24/220)
  Guard Horse Battery (#4) (4/12/134)

2nd Cuirassier Division: Generalmajor Kretov

Brigade: Generalmajor Karatiev
  Astrakhan Cuirassier Regiment (4)
  Ekaterinoslav Cuirassier Regiment (4)
Brigade: Generalmajor Leontiev
  Gluchov Cuirassier Regiment (4)
  Pskov Cuirassier Regiment (4)

3rd Cuirassier Division: Generalmajor Duka

Brigade:
  Military Order Cuirassier Regiment (4)
  Starodoub Cuirassier Regiment (4)
Brigade: Generalmajor Levaschoff
  Novgorod Cuirassier Regiment (4)
  Little Russia Cuirassier Regiment (4)

Guard Light Cavalry Division: Generalmajor Chevich

Brigade: Generalmajor Tchailikov
  Guard Hussar Regiment (6)
  Guard Uhlan Regiment (6)
  Guard Dragoon Regiment (6)
Attached:
  Don Guard Cossack Regiment (3)
  Guard Black Sea Cossack Sotnia (1)

Artillery: Generalmajor Kosen

  Guard Horse Battery #1
  Guard Horse Battery #2

Reserve Artillery: Generalmajor Hüne

  Guard Position Battery #1 (6 guns)
  Position Battery #1 (12 guns)
  Position Battery #2 (12 guns)
  Position Battery #10 (12 guns)
  Position Battery #14 (12 guns)
  Horse Battery #1 (2 guns)
  Horse Battery #3 (12 guns)
  Horse Battery #10 (6 guns)
  Horse Battery #23 (12 guns)
  Guard Marine Equipage Battery (2 guns)

Cossack Corps: General of Cavalry Count Platov

Brigade: Generalmajor Count Kudashov
  Grekov #21 Cossack Regiment

  Illowaiski #10 Cossack Regiment
  Koschkin Cossack Regiment
Brigade: Colonel Bergmann
  1st Black Sea Cossack Regiment
  Shaltonoshka Cossack Regiment
  Gorin #1 Cossack Regiment
  Elmursin Cossack Regiment
Brigade: Generalmajor Count Scherbatov
  Jagodin Cossack Regiment
  1st Teptar Cossack Regiment
  3rd Orenburg Cossack Regiment
  3rd Ural Cossack Regiment
Brigade:
  Rebrejev Cossack Regiment
  Don Cossack Horse Artillery Company #1

Detached Corps:

Attached to Army Headquarters of Barclay de Tolly
  3rd Bug Cossack Regiment
  Tabunzikov Don Cossack Regiment
  Kireva Don Cossack Regiment
  1st Tula Cossack Regiment
Attached to Army Headquarters of Count Wittgenstein
  Ingremannland Dragoon Regiment (3)
  2nd Bug Cossack Regiment
  Olonetz Opolochenie Battalion
  Vologda Opolochenie Battalion
In Transit: Generalmajor Kankerin
  Little Russia Opolochenie Cossack Regiment
  Tschernigov Opolochenie Cossack Regiment
  2nd Pultava Opolochenie Cossack Regiment
Transporting Prisoners
  2nd Bashkir Regiment
  11th Bashkir Regiment

III
ARMY OF SILESIA

Commander-in-Chief: General der Kavallerie Blücher
Chief of Staff: Generalmajor von Gneisenau
Quartermaster: Oberst von Müffling
General Intendent: von Ribbentrop

Right Wing: Generallieutenant Baron Sacken
11th Corps:
10th Infantry Division: Generalmajor Count Lieven III
Brigade: Generalmajor Agatin
  Jaroslav Infantry Regiment (2)
  Kursk Infantry Regiment (1)
Brigade: Colonel Sass
  Crimea Infantry Regiment (1)
  Bieloserk Infantry Regiment (2)
Brigade: Colonel Achlestishev
  8th Jager Regiment (2)
  39th Jager Regiment (2)

Detached from 16th Division:
Brigade: Generalmajor Repninsky
  Okhotsk Infantry Regiment (2)
  Kamtchatka Infantry Regiment (2)
27th Division: Colonel Stavitzky (General Neverovsky)
Brigade: Colonel Levandskoy
  Odessa Infantry Regiment (2)
  Vilna Infantry Regiment (2)
Brigade: Colonel Alexejev
  Tarnopol Infantry Regiment (1)
  Simbrisk Infantry Regiment (1)
Brigade: Colonel Kollogribov
  49th Jager Regiment (2)
  50th Jager Regiment (2)
Artillery:
  Position Battery #13
  Position Battery #28
  Light Battery #24
  Light Battery #35

Cavalry Corps: Generallieutenant Vassil'shikov
3rd Dragoon Division:
Brigade: Generalmajor Pantschulid
  Courland Dragoon Regiment (2)
  Smolensk Dragoon Regiment (2)
2nd Hussar Division: Generalmajor Tschaplitz
Brigade: Colonel Vassil'shikov
  Akhtyrsk Hussar Regiment (4)
  Marioupol Hussar Regiment (4)
Brigade: Generalmajor Kaslovsky
  Alexandria Hussar Regiment (4)
  White Russia Hussar Regiment (4)
Artillery:
  Horse Battery #18
Light Troops: Generalmajor Karpov II
  Semenschenko Cossack Regiment
  Kutainikov #4 Cossack Regiment
  Tcharnusubov #4 Cossack Regiment
  Loukoffkin Cossack Regiment
  Karpov #2 Cossack Regiment
  4th Ukrainian Cossack Regiment
  St. Petersburg Cossack Regiment
  2nd Kalmuck Regiment
  Popov #13 Cossack Regiment
  Unknown Cossack Regiment

1st Prussian Army Corps: Generallieutenant von Yorck
1st Brigade: Oberst von Steinmetz
Detachment: Oberst von Hiller
  1st East Prussian Grenadier Battalion (17/58/744)
    Freiwilliger Jäger Co. (1/3./47)
  Leib Grenadier Battalion (20/56/814)
    Freiwilliger Jäger Co. (3/13/166)
  West Prussian Grenadier Battalion (19/59/745)
    Freiwilliger Jäger Co. (3/6/85)
  Silesian Grenadier Battalion (20/57/745)
    Freiwilliger Jäger Co. (2/3/92)

  1/, 3/East Prussian Jäger Battalion (10/22/369)
Detachment: Oberst von Losthin
  1/, 2/, 3/, 4/5th Silesian Landwehr Regt (68/212/2,140)
  1/, 2/, 3/, 4/13th Silesian Landwehr Regt (74/204/2,302)
Attached:
  2nd Leib Hussar Regiment (4)
  6pdr Foot Battery #2 (4/13/126)
2nd Brigade: Generalmajor Prinz Carl von Mecklenburg-Strelitz
Detachment: Oberstleutnant von Lobenthal
  1/, 2/, Fus/1st East Prussian Infantry Regt (53/177/2,203)
    Freiwilliger Jäger Co. (3/9/174)
  1/, 2/, Fus/2nd East Prussian Infantry Regt (54/180/2,233)
    Freiwilliger Jäger Co. (0/1/43)
  1/, 2/, 3/, 4/6th Silesian Landwehr Regt (66/201/2,131)
Attached:
  Mecklenburg Strelitz Hussar Regiment (4) (20/44/406)
    Freiwilliger Jäger Co. (0/8/42)
  6pdr Foot Battery #1 (4/12/126)
7th Brigade: Generalmajor von Horn
Brigade: Oberst von Zepelin
  1/, 2/, Fus/Leib Infantry Regiment (58/180/2,203)
    Freiwilliger Jäger Co. (6/29/359)
  Thüringian Battalion (14/55/569)
  3/, 4/Guard Jager Battalion (11/30/378)
Landwehr Brigade: Colonel Weltzien
  1/, 2/, 3/, 4/4th Silesian Landwehr Regt (70/199/2,004)
  1/, 2/, 3/, 4/15th Silesian Landwehr Regt (73/212/2,310)
Attached:
  Brandenburg Hussar Regiment (2)
  3rd Silesian Landwehr Cavalry (2)
  6pr Foot Battery #3 (4/13/124)
8th Brigade: Generalmajor von Hünerbein
Brigade: Oberstleutnant Bork
  1/, 2/Brandenburg Infantry Regiment (43/120/1,492)
  Fus/Brandenburg Infantry Regiment (20/60/741)
  1/, 2/, Fus/12th Reserve Infantry Regt (52/176/22,191)
  1/, 2/, 3/, 4/14th Silesian Landwehr Regt (69/198/1,809)
Attached:
  Brandenburg Hussar Regiment (2)
  3rd Silesian Landwehr Cavalry (2)
  6pr Foot Battery #15 (4/14/126)
Cavalry Reserve: Generalmajor Jürgass
Brigade: Oberst von Henckel von Donnersmark
  1st West Prussian Dragoon Regiment (4) (23/60/541)
    Freiwilliger Jäger Co. (1/1/13)
  Lithuanian Dragoon Regiment (4) (23/58/672)

Freiwilliger Jäger Co. (5/15/159)
Brigade: Oberst von Katzeler
  Brandenburg Uhlan Regiment (4) (19/60/541)
  East Prussian National Cavalry Regiment (4)
    (15/60/485)
  Frewilliger Jager Co. (2/11/113)
Brigade: Major von Bieberstein
  1st Neumärk Landwehr Cavalry Regiment (4)
    (19/32/342)
  5th Silesian Landwehr Cavalry Regiment (4)
    (27/65/456)
  10th Silesian Landwehr Cavalry Regiment (4)
    (19/50/319)
Artillery:
  Horse Battery #1 (4/13/134)
  Horse Battery #2 (5/13/134)
Reserve Artillery: Oberst von Schmidt
  12pdr Foot Battery #1 (4/13/222)
  12pdr Foot Battery #2 (4/12/184)
  6pdr Foot Battery #11 (4/10/126)
  6pdr Foot Battery #24 (4/18/109)
  3pdr Foot Battery #1 (3/10/87)
  Horse Battery #3 (4/13/134)
  Horse Battery #12 (4/14/134)
Park Column
  Park Column #1 (1/2/30)
  Park Column #3 (1/3/31)
  Park Column #5 (1/3/29)
  Park Column #13 (1/2/30)
  Artisan Column #1 (1/1/11)
  1st Field Pioneer Co. (2/8/73)
  2nd Field Pioneer Co. (2/8/73)

Left Wing: General of Infantry Count Langeron
6th Corps: Generalmajor Scherbatov
7th Division: Generalmajor Tallisin
Brigade: Colonel Kirschnitzkv
  Pskov Infantry Regiment (2)
  Moscow Infantry Regiment (2)
Brigade: Colonel Augustov
  Sofia Infantry Regiment (1)
  Libau Infantry Regiment (2)
Brigade: Colonel Dietrich
  11th Jager Regiment (2)
  36th Jager Regiment (1)
18th Division: Generalmajor Bernodossov
Brigade: Lt. Colonel Blagovenzenko
  Vladimir Infantry Regiment (1)
  Dnieper Infantry Regiment (1)
Brigade:
  Tambov Infantry Regiment (1)
  Kostroma Infantry Regiment (1)
Brigade: Generalmajor Mescherinov
  32nd Jager Regiment (2)
  28th Jager Regiment (2)
Artillery:
  Position Battery #15
  Light Battery #28
  Light Battery #12

9th Corps: Generallieutenant Alsusiev
9th Division: Generalmajor Udom II
Brigade: Colonel Poltaratzky
  Nacheburg Infantry Regiment (1)
  Apcheron Infantry Regiment (2)
Brigade: Lieutenant Colonel Ogriumov
  Iakout Infantry Regiment (1)
  Riajsk Infantry Regiment (2)
Brigade: Major Grimbladt
  10th Jager Regiment (1)
  36th Jager Regiment (1)
15th Division: Generallieutenant Rudsevich
Brigade: Colonel Tern
  Vitebsk Infantry Regiment (1)
  Kozlov Infantry Regiment (1)
Brigade: Lt. Colonel Anensur
  Kourin Infantry Regiment (2)
  Kolvvan Infantry Regiment (1)
Brigade: Colonel Tichanovsky
  12th Jager Regiment (2)
  22nd Jager Regiment (1)
Artillery:
  Position Battery #18
  Light Battery #25
  Light Battery #34

10th Corps: Generallieutenant Kapzevich
8th Division: Generalmajor Count Urussov
Brigade: Lt. Colonel Schindshin
  Archangel Infantry Regiment (2)
  Old Ingremannland Infantry Regiment (2)
Brigade: Colonel Rerin
  Schusselburg Infantry Regiment (1)
  7th Jager Regiment (1)
  37th Jager Regiment (2)
22nd Division: Generalmajor Turtshaninov
Brigade: Generalmajor Schapskov
  Viatka Infantry Regiment (2)
  Staroskol Infantry Regiment (2)
  Olonetz Infantry Regiment (1)
Brigade: Colonel Durnov
  29th Jager Regiment (2)
  45th Jager Regiment (2)

1st Cavalry Corps: Generallieutenant Baron Korff
Brigade: Generalmajor Berdaeev
  Tver Dragoon Regiment (2)
  Kinbourn Dragoon Regiment (2)
1st Chasseur à Cheval Division: Generalmajor
Pantschulid
  Tschernigov Chasseur à Cheval Regiment (3)
  Sieversk Chasseur à Cheval Regiment (2)
  Arasmass Chasseur à Cheval Regiment (2)
Detached from 2nd Chasseur à Cheval Division:
Brigade: Generalmajor Count Pahlen II
  Dorpat Chasseur à Cheval Regiment (2)
  Lithuanian Chasseur à Cheval Regiment (2)
  Light Troops: Generalmajor Grekov VIII
Brigade: Generalmajor Count de Witte

1st Ukrainian Cossack Regiment
2nd Ukrainian Cossack Regiment
3rd Ukrainian Cossack Regiment
Attached:
1st Teptar Cossack Regiment
Zikilev Cossack Regiment
Isaeva #2 Cossack Regiment
Selivanov #2 Don Cossack Regiment
Kutainikov #8 Cossack Regiment

Reserve Artillery:
Position Battery #10
Light Battery #29
Pontoon Company #4
75th Marine (or Ships) Equipage
Pioneer Company Lt. Colonel Gebenera

Detached Corps: Generallieutenant Pahlen I
8th Corps: Generallieutenant Count St. Priest
11th Division: Generallieutenant Count Gurgalov
Brigade: Kartvenkov
Jeletz Infantry Regiment (2)
Polotsk Infantry Regiment (2)
Brigade: Colonel Turgenev
Ekaterinburg Infantry Regiment (2)
Rilsk Infantry Regiment (2)
Brigade: Generalmajor Bistrom II
1st Jager Regiment (2)
33rd Jager Regiment (2)
17th Division: Generalmajor Pillar
Brigade: Colonel Kern
Riazan infantry Regiment (2)
Bieloserk Infantry Regiment (2)
Brigade: Colonel Schertov I
Brest Infantry Regiment (1)
Wilmanstrand Infantry Regiment (1)
Brigade: Major Charitanov
30th Jager Regiment (2)
48th Jager Regiment (2)
1st Dragoon Division: Generalmajor Borosdin
Brigade:
Kargopol Dragoon Regiment (4)
Mitau Dragoon Regiment (5)
Brigade:
Moscow Dragoon Regiment (3)
New Russia Dragoon Regiment (4)
Detached from 4th Dragoon Division:
Brigade:
Karkov Dragoon Regiment (5)
Kiev Dragoon Regiment (5)
Light Troops:
Grekov #21 Don Cossack Regiment
Gzov #3 Don Cossack Regiment
Stavrapol Kalmuck Regiment
3rd Black Sea Cossack Regiment

IV
ARMY OF THE NORTH

Commander-in-Chief: Bernadotte, Crown Prince of
Sweden
Chief of Staff: Generallieutenant Baron Adlerkreutz
Assist. CoS: Generallieutenants Count Lowenhielm,
Count Sparre, Baron Tawast
General Intendant: von Billherg
General Field Surgeon: Welzten
General Auditeur: Thurstell
Field Post Master: Rydberg
Russian Liaison: Generalmajor Pozzo di Borgo
Austrian Liaison: Feldmarschal-Lieutenant Baron St.
Vincent
Prussian Liaison: Generalmajor Baron von Krusemark

Royal Swedish Army:
Commander-in-Chief: Fieldmarshal Graf Stedingk
Chief of Staff: Generalmajor Count Lagerbring
Quartermaster: Colonel Bionstierna
Chief of Artillery: Generalmajor Surmaine
Chief of Engineers: Colonel Baron Sparre

1st Infantry Division: Generallieutenant Posse
1st Brigade: Generalmajor Schützenheim
Svenska Guard Regiment (1)
2nd Guard Regiment (1)
Lifregimentet Grenadier Regiment (1)
Lifgrenadierregementets (2)
Drottningen Regiment (1)
2nd Brigade: Colonel Reuterskjold
Upland Regiment (2)
Sodermanland Regiment (3)
Nord Schonen Regiment (1)
Pomeranian Foot Legion (100)
Artillery:
2 6pdr Foot Batteries (Gothland Regiment)
2nd Division: Generallieutenant Sandels
3rd Brigade: Generalmajor Brandstroem
Vestgotadals Regiment (2)
Vestmanlands Regiment (3)
Nerike Regiment (2)
4th Brigade: Generalmajor Posse
Skaraborg Regiment (3)
Elfshorg Regiment (3)
Vermlands Faltjägerbataljon (Field Jager Battalion)
(1)
Artillery:
2 6pdr Foot Batteries (Swedish Regiment)
3rd Division: Generalmajor Baron Boyen
5th Brigade: Generalmajor Boize
Kronoborg Regiment (3)
Kalmar Regiment (3)
Sud Schonen Regiment (1)
6th Brigade: (detached)
Smaländ Regiment (1)
Nord Schonen Regiment (1)

Drottningen Regiment (1)
Engelbrecht Regiment (2)
Schonen Regiment (2)
Schonen Carabinier Regiment (4)
Artillery:
  2 6pdr Foot Batteries (Wenden Regiment)
Cavalry Division:
Lifregiment Dragoncorps (5)
Smaländ Dragoon Regiment (6)
Pomeranian Horse Legion (1)
Guard Cuirassier Corps (4)
Schonen Hussar Regiment (6)
Mörner Hussar Regiment (6)
Artillery Reserve: Generalmajor Cardell
1 12pdr Foot Battery (8 guns)
2 Horse Battery (12 guns)
Artillery Park

***Russian Corps: Generallieutenant Baron
  Winzingerode***
Chief of Staff: Generalmajor Renny
Quartermaster: Colonel Count Wolchonsky
Chief of Artillery: Generalmajor Merlin

12th Corps: Generalmajor Laptiev
21st Division:
Brigade: Colonel Rudinger
  Neva Infantry Regiment (1) (526)
  44th Jager Regiment (2) (996)
Brigade: Colonel Rosen
  Petrovsk Infantry Regiment (1) (652)
  Podolsk Infantry Regiment (1) (665)
  Lithuania Infantry Regiment (1) (525)
Artillery:
  46th Light Battery (73)
  42nd Light Battery (58)
  31st Position Battery (182)
Cavalry:
Brigade: Generalmajor Manteufel
  St. Petersburg Dragoon Regiment (3) (324)
  Elisabethgrad Hussar Regiment (5) (510)
  4th Horse Battery (8 guns) (120)
  9th Horse Battery (12 guns) (150)
Cossack Brigade: Generalmajor Stahl I
  Illowaiski #11 Cossack Regiment (401)
  Barbantchikov Cossack Regiment (186)
  Rebrejev Cossack Regiment (246)
  Grekov #18 Cossack Regiment (220)
  Pantelev #21 Cossack Regiment (358)
Brigade: Generalmajor Prendel
  1st Bug Cossack Regiment (318)
  4th Orel Cossack Regiment (287)
Cossack Brigade:
  Jachontov Opolochenie Cossack Regiment (198)

Russian Corps: Generallieutenant Count Voronsov
14th Division: Generalmajor Harpe
Sieversk Infantry Regiment (1) (481)
Toula Infantry Regiment (1) (430)

Navaguinsk Infantry Regiment (1) (618)
Converged Grenadiers of the 9th, 15th & 18th
  Divisions
  Bn of Lt. Col. Filatov (553)
  Bn of Lt. Col. Sokolov (529)
  Bn of Lt. Col. Fischer II (535)
21st Position Battery (2 guns) (28)
28th Position Battery (10 guns) (199)
26th Light Battery (12 guns) (159)
Cavalry: Generalmajor Orurk
Brigade: Colonel Schevachov
  Pavlovgrad Hussar Regiment (6) (856)
  Volhynie Uhlan Regiment (4) (513)
Brigade: Generalmajor Zagriajski
  Nijine Chasseur à Cheval Regiment (2) (178)
  Polish Uhlan Regiment (2) (298)
Brigade: Generalmajor Balk
  Riga Dragoon Regiment (2) (165)
  Finland Dragoon Regiment (2) (207)
Brigade: Generalmajor Baron Pahlen
  Isoum Hussar Regiment (3) (398)
  Converged Hussar Regiment (3) (301)
Artillery:
  Horse Battery #1 (8 guns) (74)
  Horse Battery #11 (12 guns) (240)
  Horse Battery #13 (12 guns) (183)

Cossack Corps: Generalmajor Czernichev
Brigade: Lt. Colonel Count Lapuchin
  Illowaiski #4 Cossack Regiment (310)
  Diatchkin Cossack Regiment (312)
  Grekov #9 Cossack Regiment
Brigade: Generalmajor Illowaiski IX
  Vlassov #3 Don Cossack Regiment (319)
  Balbin #2 Cossack Regiment (280)
  Rebrejev Cossack Regiment (296)
Brigade: Colonel Melnikov V
  Melnikov #4 Cossack Regiment (345)
  Melnikov #5 Cossack Regiment (313)
Brigade: Colonel Benkendorf
  Sisava Cossack Regiment (355)
  Girova Cossack Regiment (298)
  Grekov #18 Cossack Regiment (334)
Brigade: Generalmajor Narishkin
  Lotchilin #1 Cossack Regiment (370)
  Andreinov #2 Cossack Regiment (352)

***Russian Corps: Generallieutenant Count
  Wallmoden***
Brigade: Generalmajor Tettenborn
  2nd Jager Regiment (1) (247)
  Grekov #1 Cossack Regiment (336)
  Komissarov Cossack Regiment (368)
  Sulima #9 Cossack Regiment (314)
**Russo-German Legion: Generalmajor von
Arentschildt**
Brigade: Generalmajor von Arentschildt
  1st RGL Hussar Regiment (4)
  2nd RGL Hussar Regiment (4)

1st RGL Horse Battery
1/, 2/1st RGL Infantry Regiment
1/, 2/, 3/2nd RGL Infantry Regiment
6pdr Foot Battery
Total 4,250 men
Swedish Division: Generallieutenant Vegesack
1/, 2/1st Mecklenburg-Schwerin Regiment (1600)
Mecklenburg-Schwerin Freiwilliger Jäger Battalion
  (4 coys) (500)
Brigade: Generalmajor von Fallois
Mecklenburg-Schwerin Freiwilliger Mounted Jäger
  Regiment (4) (500)
Artillery:
Mecklenburg-Schwerin Foot Battery (150)
Swedish Pomeranian Troops: (4,000 men)
6th Brigade: Generalmajor Engelbrecht
  Smaländ Regementet (1)
  Nord Schonen Regementet (1)
  Drottningen Regimentet (1)
  Engelbrechtenska Regementet (2)
  Schonen Regementet (2)
  Schonen Carabinierregementet (4)
Reserve: Crown Prince of Mecklenburg-Schwerin
  Chief of Staff: Swedish Colonel Count Lagerbielke
Brigade: Colonel von Hinzenstern
  1st Mecklenburg Landwehr Battalion
  2nd Mecklenburg Landwehr Battalion
  3rd Mecklenburg Landwehr Battalion
  4th Mecklenburg Landwehr Battalion
  5th Mecklenburg Landwehr Battalion
  6th Mecklenburg Landwehr Battalion
Hanseatic Troops: Generalmajor von Dornberg
(2,450 men)
  Hamburg Infantry Battalions (2)
  Lubeck Infantry Battalion (1)
  Prussian Infantry (200)
  Hamburg Mounted Troopers (6 sqn)
  Lubeck Mounted Troopers (2 sqn)
  Horse Artillery (6 guns)
  Foot Artillery (6 guns)
Hanoverian Troops:
  Razeburger Infantry Battalion
  Hanoverian Sharpshooter Battalion
  Lüneburg Jager Battalion
  Hanoverian Infantry-Jäger Battalion
Brigade: Colonel von Essdorf
  Lüneburg Hussar Regiment (3)
  Bremen-Verden Hussar Regiment (2)
British Troops:
Major General Gibbs and Major General Lyon
Brigade: Major General Lyon (3,000 men)
  3rd KGL Light Dragoon Regiment
  73rd (British) Regiment of Foot
  Half KGL Battalion Holtzermann
  Rocket Battery (4 launchers)
  Duchy of Dessau Infantry Battalion (583)
  Bremen Infantry Battalion
  Bremen Cavalry Squadron
  Bremen Jäger Company

Prussian 3rd Corps: Generallieutenant Bülow
Chief of Staff: Oberst von Boyen
Quartermaster: Oberst von Holtzendorf
3rd Brigade: Generalmajor Prinz Ludwig von
  Hessen-Homberg
Brigade: Oberst von Sicholm II
  1/3rd East Prussian Infantry Regiment (23/63/873)
  2/3rd East Prussian Infantry Regiment (23/60/843)
  Fus/3rd East Prussian Infantry Regiment
    (20/60/787)
    Freiwilliger Jäger Co. (4/16/183)
    Freiwilliger Jäger Co. (4/13/144)
  1/4th Reserve Infantry Regiment (21/60/773)
  2/4th Reserve Infantry Regiment (18/60/746)
  3/4th Reserve Infantry Regiment (18/60/743)
  1/4th East Prussian Landwehr Regiment
    (25/60/741)
    Freiwilliger Jäger Co. (0/1/14)
  2/4th East Prussian Landwehr Regiment (17/60/741)
  3/4th East Prussian Landwehr Regiment
    (23/60/741)
  4/4th East Prussian Landwehr Regiment
    (23/60/741)
Attached:
  1st Leib Hussar Regiment (4) (2664/567)
  Freiwilliger Jäger Co. (5/14/181)
  6pdr Foot Battery #5 (4/14/131)
4th Brigade: Generalmajor von Thümen
  1/4th East Prussian Infantry Regiment (23/64/843)
  2/4th East Prussian Infantry Regiment (22/51/777)
  Fus/4th East Prussian Infantry Regiment
    (19/61/890)
  1/5th Reserve Infantry Regiment (18/60/745)
    Freiwilliger Jäger Co. (0/8/33)
  2/5th Reserve Infantry Regiment (15/60/740)
  3/5th Reserve Infantry Regiment (17/50/735)
  2/, 4/East Prussian Jager Battalion (9/30/353)
  Elbe Infantry Regiment (2)
Attached:
  Pomeranian National Cavalry Regiment (4)
    (21/42/453)
  6pdr Foot Battery #6 (4/12/151)
5th Brigade: Generalmajor von Borstell
  1/, 2/, Fus/Pomeranian Infantry Regiment
  1/2nd Reserve Infantry Regiment (17/60/746)
  2/2nd Reserve Infantry Regiment (15/62/748)
  3/2nd Reserve Infantry Regiment (16/60/776)
  1/2nd Kurmärk Landwehr Infantry Regiment
    (21/61/728)
  2/2nd Kurmärk Landwehr Infantry Regiment
    (18/63/731)
  3/2nd Kurmärk Landwehr Infantry Regiment
    (22/64/733)
  4/2nd Kurmärk Landwehr Infantry Regiment
    (21/64/727)
Attached:
  Pomeranian Hussar Regiment (4) (25/60/556)
    Freiwilliger Jäger Co. (6/7/105)
  6pdr Foot Battery #10 (4/12/127)

6th Brigade: Generalmajor von Krafft
1/Colberg Infantry Regiment (24/60/845)
2/Colberg Infantry Regiment (20/60/817)
Fus/Colberg Infantry Regiment (20/60/833)
  Freiwilliger Jäger Co. (3/15/170)
  Freiwilliger Jäger Co. (3/9/108)
1/9th Reserve Infantry Regiment (19/60/750)
2/9th Reserve Infantry Regiment (19/60/741)
3/9th Reserve Infantry Regiment (19/60/741)
1/1st Neumärk Landwehr Regiment (14/56/625)
2/1st Neumärk Landwehr Regiment (17/56/588)
3/1st Neumärk Landwehr Regiment (19/48/561)
4/1st Neumärk Landwehr Regiment (19/60/760)
Attached:
  1st Pomeranian Landwehr Cavalry Regt (4)
    (15/32/256)
  6pdr Foot Battery #16 (4/14/126)
Cavalry Reserve: Generalmajor von Oppen
Brigade: Oberst von Treskow
    Brandenburg Dragoon Regiment (4) (21/64/570)
    Freiwilliger Jäger Co. (1/7/91)
    Koningin Dragoon Regiment (4) (27/60/586)
    2nd West Prussian Dragoon Regiment (4)
      (37/60/684)
    Freiwilliger Jäger Co. (3/5/49)
Brigade: Oberst von Hobe
  West Prussian Uhlan Regiment (4) (25/60/500)
  2nd Silesian Hussar Regiment (4)
Brigade: Oberst von Malzahn
  2nd Pomeranian Landwehr Cavalry Regt (4)
    (15/39/300)
  2nd Kurmärk Landwehr Cavalry Regt (4)
    (17/48/335)
  4th Kurmärk Landwehr Cavalry Regiment (4)
    (19/44/337)
Artillery:
  Horse Battery #5 (4/10/138)
  Horse Battery #6 (4/11/138)
Artillery Reserve: Oberst von Holtzendorf
12pdr Foot Battery #4 (4/13/184)
12pdr Foot Battery #5 (4/13/188)
6pdr Foot Battery #6
Horse Battery #11 (4/12/136)
Munition Train
  Munition Column #1 (1/2/30)
  Munition Column #3 (1/3/31)
  Munition Column #4 (1/3/30)
  Munition Column #6 (2/3/40)
  Field Pioneer Company #4 (2/7/88)
  Field Pioneer Company #5 (2/8/74)
Cossacks:
  Illowaiski #3 Don Cossack Regiment
  Illowaiski #5 Don Cossack Regiment
  Bihalov #1 Cossack Regiment
  Kutainikov #6 Cossack Regiment
  Position Battery #7 Dietrich
  Position Battery #14

Prussian 4th Corps:
Generallieutenant Count von Tauentzien
  Chief of Staff: Major von Rothenburg
  Chief of Artillery: Major von Meander

1st Brigade: Generalmajor von Dobschütz
1/, 2/, 3/3rd Reserve Infantry Regiment
  (54/180/2,233)
4/3rd Reserve Infantry Regiment (17/64/740)
  Freiwilliger Jäger Co. (4/16/183)
  Freiwilliger Jäger Co. (4/13/144)
1/1st Kurmärk Landwehr Infantry Regiment
  (17/64/736)
2/1st Kurmärk Landwehr Infantry Regiment
  (16/39/515)
3/1st Kurmärk Landwehr Infantry Regiment
Attached:
  2nd Neumärk Landwehr Cavalry Regiment (4)
  3rd Neumärk Landwehr Cavalry Regiment (4)
  2nd East Prussian Landwehr Cavalry Regt (4)
    (23/48/436)
  3rd East Prussian Landwehr Cavalry Regt (4)
    (18/36/278)
  1/2 English 6pdr Foot Battery von Hertig
2nd Brigade: Generalmajor von Lindenau
1/2nd Neumärk Landwehr Infantry Regt
  (20/52/537)
2/2nd Neumärk Landwehr Infantry Regt
  (18/52/537)
3/2nd Neumärk Landwehr Infantry Regt
  (14/52/536)
4/2nd Neumärk Landwehr Infantry Regt
  (13/52/530)
1/5th Kurmärk Landwehr Infantry Regiment
  (22/56/653)
2/5th Kurmärk Landwehr Infantry Regiment
  (21/56/652)
3/5th Kurmärk Landwehr Infantry Regiment
  (20/56/651)
4/5th Kurmärk Landwehr Infantry Regiment
  (21/56/653)
1st Silesian Landwehr Infantry Regiment (1)
1/, 2/, 3/, 4/4th Silesian Landwehr Regt
  (70/199/2,010)
Attached:
  Illowaiski #4 Don Cossack Regiment
  Berlin Landwehr Cavalry Regiment (2)
  7th Kurmärk Landwehr Cavalry Regiment (2)
    (18/?/90)
  1st Kurmärk Landwehr Cavalry Regiment (4)
    (11/27/247)
  3rd Pomeranian Landwehr Cavalry Regt (4)
    (14/40/295)
  6pdr Heavy Iron Foot Battery Lt. Gleim
Reserve Artillery: Oberst von Strampf
½ 6pdr Foot Battery Lt. von Schuler
½ 8pdr Foot Battery Lt. von Protel
English 6pdr Horse Battery Lt. von Matthias

Corps of the Oder: Generalmajor von Wobeser
Infantry: Obersteutnant von Plötz
  1/1st West Prussian Landwehr Regiment
    (18/50/531)
  2/1st West Prussian Landwehr Regiment
    (18/50/454)
  3/1st West Prussian Landwehr Regiment
    (15/46/390)
  4/1st West Prussian Landwehr Regiment (9/29/352)
  1/2nd West Prussian Landwehr Regiment
    (15/32/366)
  2/2nd West Prussian Landwehr Regiment
    (19/56/321)
  3/2nd West Prussian Landwehr Regiment
    (19/53/346)
  1/, 2/, 3/3rd West Prussian Landwehr Regiment
    (42/111/1,187)
  1st Silesian Landwehr Infantry Regiment (3)
Brigade: Oberst von Jeanneret
  1st West Prussian Landwehr Cavalry Regt (4)
    (12/26/194)
  2nd West Prussian Landwehr Cavalry Regt (4)
    (9/27/181)
  3rd West Prussian Landwehr Cavalry Regt (4)
    (8/?/177)
Artillery:
  6pdr Foot Battery #22 (3/9/131)
Corps besieging Magdeburg: Generalmajor von Hirschfeld
  1/, 2/, 3/, 4/1st Reserve Infantry Regiment
    (53/177/2,203)
    Freiwilliger Jäger Co. (1/3/50)
  1/6th Kurmärk Landwehr Infantry Regiment
    (22/56/653)
  2/6th Kurmärk Landwehr Infantry Regiment
    (21/56/653)
  3/6th Kurmärk Landwehr Infantry Regiment
    (22/56/653)
  4/6th Kurmärk Landwehr Infantry Regiment
    (20/56/653)
  1/7th Kurmärk Landwehr Infantry Regiment
    (22/56/653)
  2/7th Kurmärk Landwehr Infantry Regiment
    (20/56/650)
  3/7th Kurmärk Landwehr Infantry Regiment
    (20/49/551)
  4/7th Kurmärk Landwehr Infantry Regiment
    (9/30/409)
Brigade: Oberst von Bismark
  5th Kurmärk Landwehr Cavalry Regiment
    (0/18/40/288)
  6th Kurmärk Landwehr Cavalry Regiment (4)
    (17/40/288)
  ½ 6pdr Foot Battery #20
  ½ 6pdr Foot Battery Lt. von Zollner
Corps of the Lower Elbe: Generalmajor von Puttlitz
  1/3rd Kurmärk Landwehr Infantry Regiment
    (20/65/713)

  2/3rd Kurmärk Landwehr Infantry Regiment
    (22/65/700)
  3/3rd Kurmärk Landwehr Infantry Regiment
    (21/65/712)
  4/3rd Kurmärk Landwehr Infantry Regiment
    (20/65/746)
  1/4th Kurmärk Landwehr Infantry Regiment
    (24/64/669)
  2/4th Kurmärk Landwehr Infantry Regiment
    (21/59/673)
  3/4th Kurmärk Landwehr Infantry Regiment
    (23/60/661)
  4/4th Kurmärk Landwehr Infantry Regiment
    (21/30/135)
  3rd Kurmärk Landwehr Cavalry Regt (4) (15/498/327)
  ½ 6pdr Foot Battery #32

V
PRUSSIAN RESERVE AND GARRISON FORCES

Reserve and Garrison Troops in Prussia
In Brandenburg: Inspecteur Oberst von Witzleben
  Guard Invalid Battalion (17/48/516)
  1st Guard Garrison Company (4/15/185)
  Garrison Battalion/Leib Infantry Regiment
    (14/60/374)
  Garrison Bn./Brandenburg Infantry Regt
    (17/60/741)
  1st Brandenburg Brigade – Garrison Battalion
    (17/60/741)
    Freiwilliger Jäger Det. (0/1/23)
  2nd Brandenburg Brigade – Garrison Battalion
    (17/60/741)
  Reserve Battalion/lst Garde zu Fuss Regt
    (11/46/795)
    Freiwilliger Jäger Co. (0/6/105)
  Reserve Battalion/2nd Garde zu Fuss Regt
    (11/46/755)
  Ersatz Battalion/Leib Infantry Regiment (8/24/624)
  Ersatz Battalion/Brandenburg Infantry Regiment
    (not formed until September)
  Ersatz Company/Garde Jager Battalion (3/14/156)
  Ersatz Company/East Prussian Jager Battalion
    (2/8/106)
In Pommerania: Inspecteur Oberst von Herwarth
  Garrison Bn./Ist Pomeranian Infantry Regt
    (15/60/741)
  Garrison Battalion/Colberg Infantry Regt
    (15/60/741)
  1st Pomeranian Brigade – Garrison Battalion
    (17/60/741)
  2nd Pomeranian Brigade – Garrison Bn. (17/60/741)
  Ersatz Bn./lst Pomeranian Infantry Regt (9/36/760)
  Ersatz Battalion/Colberg Infantry Regiment
    (8/60/779)

In Silesia: Inspecteur Generalmajor von Kessel
Garrison Bn/lst West Prussian Infantry Regt
(22/60/641)
Garrison Bn/2nd West Prussian Infantry Regt
(17/60/741)
Garrison Battalion/1st Silesian Infantry Regt
(15/60/741)
Garrison Battalion/2nd Silesian Infantry Regt
(23/80/839)
1st Lower Silesian Brigade – Garrison Bn.
(19/60/741)
2nd Lower Silesian Brigade – Garrison Bn.
(13/60/734)
1st Upper Silesian Brigade – Garrison Bn.
(12/60/837)
Freiwilliger Jäger Co. (0/0/9)
2nd Upper Silesian Brigade – Garrison Bn.
(17/60/737)
Ersatz Bn./lst West Prussian Infantry Regt
(9/60/741)
Ersatz Bn./2nd West Prussian Infantry Regt
(9/60/741)
Ersatz Bataillon/1st Silesian Infantry Regiment
(9/60/741)
Ersatz Bataillon/2nd Silesian Infantry Regt
(9/60/741)
Ersatz Company/Silesian Schutzen Battalion
(4/15/185)
In Prussia: Inspecteur Oberst von Below
Garrison Bn./lst East Prussian Infantry Regt
(17/56/745)
Garrison Bn./2nd East Prussian Infantry Regt
(17/56/745)
Garrison Bn./3rd East Prussian Infantry Regt
(17/56/745)
Garrison Bn./4th East Prussian Infantry Regt
(17/56/745)
1st West Prussian Brigade – Garrison Battalion
(17/60/741)
Freiwilliger Jäger det. (0/1/23)
2nd West Prussian Brigade – Garrison Bn.
(17/60/741)
Ersatz Bn./1st East Prussian Infantry Regt
(9/56/745)
Ersatz Bn./2nd East Prussian Infantry Regt
(9/56/745)
Ersatz Bn./3rd East Prussian Infantry Regt
(9/56/745)
Ersatz Bn./4th East Prussian Infantry Regt
(9/56/745)
**Reserve Squadrons in the Mark: Inspecteur
Generalmajor von Zawadtzky**
5/Garde du Corps Regiment (5/16/124)
5/East Prussian Cuirassier Regiment (5/15/210)
5/Brandenburg Cuirassier Regiment (5/15/90)
5/Brandenburg Hussar Regiment (5/13/141)
5/Brandenburg Uhlan Regiment (6/15/146)
5/West Prussian Uhlan Regiment (4/15/214)
5/Guard Light Cavalry Regiment (5/11/142)

**Reserve Squadrons in Prussia: Inspecteur
Generalmajor von Towardowsky**
5/Lithuanian Dragoon Regiment (4/11/223)
5/1st Leib Hussar Regiment (5/15/308)
5/2nd Leib Hussar Regiment (5/15/135)
5(Depot)/East Prussian National Cavalry Regt
(3/15/135)
**Reserve Squadrons in Silesia: Inspecteur
Generalmajor von Corswandt**
5/Silesian Cuirassier Regiment (5/12/138)
5/1st West Prussian Dragoon Regiment (5/14/136)
5/Neumärk Dragoon Regiment (5/12/138)
5/1st Silesian Hussar Regiment (5/12/138)
5/2nd Silesian Hussar Regiment (5/15/135)
5/Silesian Uhlan Regiment (5/12/138)
3(Depot)/Silesian National Hussar Regiment
(3/0/50)
**Reserve Squadrons in Pommerania: Inspecteur
Oberst Diezelsky**
5/Königin Dragoon Regiment (5/15/110)
5/2nd West Prussian Dragoon Regiment (3/11/134)
5/Brandenburg Dragoon Regiment (5/15/127)
5/Pomeranian Hussar Regiment (5/15/135)
4(Depot)/Pomeranian National Hussar Regt
(1/0/61)

*Plotho, C. Der Krieg in Deutschland und Frankreich
in den Jahren 1813 und 1814, Carl Friederich, Berlin,
1817.*

THE BATTLE OF GROSS-BEEREN
23 AUGUST 1813

VI
ALLIED FORCES

*Army of the North:
Bernadotte, Crown Prince of Sweden*

*3rd Prussian Army Corps: Generallieutenant
Bülow*
3rd Brigade: Generalmajor L. Hesse-Homburg
2nd East Prussian Grenadier Battalion (20/1,004)
1/, 2/, Fus/3rd East Prussian Infantry Regiment
(65/2,397) (includes 2 jäger dets)
1/, 2/, 3/4th Reserve Infantry Regiment (49/2,127)
8/, 11/, 12/, 20/3rd East Prussian Landwehr
Regiment
1/, 2/, 3/, 4/lst Leib Hussar Regiment (27/691) (+jägers)
6pdr Foot Battery #5 "Glassenapp" (4/109)
4th Brigade: Generalmajor Thümen
1/, 2/, Fus/4th East Prussian Infantry Regiment
(68/2,481)
I/, 2/, 3/, 4/5th Reserve Infantry Regiment
(56/2,825)

1/, 2/Elbe Infantry Regiment (34/1,686)
2/, 4/East Prussian Jager Battalion (8/350)
1/, 2/, 3/Pomeranian National Cavalry Regt (14/361)
6pdr Foot Battery #6 "Ludwig" (3/101)

5th Brigade: Generalmajor Borstell
Pomeranian Grenadier Battalion (25/943)
1/, 2/, Fus/1st Pomeranian Infantry Regiment (68/2,622)
1/, 2/, 3/2nd Reserve Infantry Regiment (41/2,150)
2/, 4/2nd Kurmärk Landwehr Regiment (29/710)
1/, 2/, 3/, 4/Pomeranian Hussar Regiment (29/710) (+jägers)
1/, 2/, 3/, 4/West Prussian Uhlan Regiment (16/575)
6pdr Foot Battery #10 "Magenhöfer" (3/111)

6th Brigade: Generalmajor Krafft
1/, 2/, Fus/Colberg Infantry Regiment (68/2,627) (2 jäger detachments)
1/, 2/, 3/9th Reserve Infantry Regiment (45/2,210)
1/, 2/, 3/, 4/1st Neumärk Landwehr Regiment (65/2,730)
1/, 2/, 3/, 4/1st Pomeranian Landwehr Cavalry Regiment (15/270)
6pdr Foot Battery #16 "Spreuth" (4/119)

Reserve Cavalry: Generalmajor Oppen
1/, 2/, 3/, 4/Königin Dragoon Regiment (+jäger) (21/676)
1/, 2/, 3/, 4/Brandenburg Dragoon Regiment (+jäger) (22/613)
1/, 2/, 3/, 4/2nd West Prussian Dragoon Regiment (+jäger) (19/598)
3/, 4//2nd Silesian Hussar Regiment (14/430)
1/, 2/, 3/, 4/2nd Kurmärk Landwehr Cavalry Regt (15/316)
1/, 3/, 4/, 5/4th Kurmärk Landwehr Cavalry Regt (19/356)
Horse Battery #5 "Neindorff" (4/126)
Horse Battery #6 "Steinwehr" (4/128)

Artillery Reserve: Oberst Holtzendorf
12pdr Foot Batteries #4 "Meyer" & #5 "Condradi" (4/353)
6pdr Foot Battery #19 "Baumgarten/Liebermann" (4/108)
2 Russian 12pdr Batteries #7 "Dietrich/Zaweski" & #21 "Schluter" (18/500)
Prussian Feld Pioneer Companies #4 & #5 (3/152)

4th Prussian Army Corps: Generallieutenant Tauentzien

1st Brigade: Generalmajor Dobschütz
1/, 2/, 3/3rd Reserve Infantry Regiment (49/2,405)
1/, 2/1st Kurmärk Landwehr Regiment (37/1,426)
1/, 3/2nd Neumärk Landwehr Cavalry Regiment (8/164)
1/, 2/, 3/, 3rd East Prussian Landwehr Cav. Regt (15/295)
1/2 6pdr Foot Battery #20 "Papendick" (2/52)

2nd Brigade: Oberst Graf Lindenau
I/, 2/, 3/, 4/5th Kurmärk Landwehr Regiment (86/2,790)
1/, 2/, 3/, 4/2nd Neumärk Landwehr Regiment (50/1,520)
1/, 2/, 5/1st Silesian Landwehr Regiment (61/2,010)
2/, 6/Berlin Landwehr Cavalry Regiment (2) (8/176)
1/, 2/1st Kurmärk Landwehr Cavalry Regiment (9/136)
1/, 2/, 3/, 4/3rd Pomeranian Landwehr Cavalry Regiment (12/315)
1/, 2/7th Kurmärk Landwehr Cavalry Regiment (7/157)
1/2 6pdr Foot Battery #30 "Hertig" (2/79)

Artillery Reserve: Oberstleutnant von Strampf
6pdr Foot Batteries #17 "Gleim" & #27 "Matthias" (4/157)
Horse Battery #11 "Borchard" (2/79)

Detached Corps: General von Wobeser
1/, 2/, 3/, 4/1st West Prussian Landwehr Regt (62/1,770)
1/, 2/, 3/2nd West Prussian Landwehr Regt (68/1,860)
1/, 2/, 3/, 4/3rd West Prussian Landwehr Regt (64/1,950)
4/1st East Prussian Landwehr Regiment
1/, 2/, 3/1st West Prussian Landwehr Cav. Regt (10/198)
1/, 2/, 3/2nd West Prussian Landwehr Cav. Regt (9/168)
1/, 2/3rd West Prussian Landwehr Cavalry Regt (9/153)
6pdr Foot Battery #22 "Wegner" (3/122)

Detached Corps: General von Hirschfeldt
1/, 2/, 3/, 4/1st Reserve Infantry Regiment (82/2,800)
1/, 2/, 3/, 4/3rd Kurmärk Landwehr Regiment (80/1,860)
1/, 2/, 3/4th Kurmärk Landwehr Regiment (68/1,800)
1/, 2/, 3/, 4/6th Kurmärk Landwehr Regiment (80/2,400)
1/, 2/, 3/7th Kurmärk Landwehr Regiment (68/1,800)
1/, 2/, 3/, 4/3rd Kurmärk Landwehr Cavalry Regt (14/320)
1/, 2/, 3/, 4/5th Kurmärk Landwehr Cavalry Regt (14/320)
1/, 2/, 3/, 4/6th Kurmärk Landwehr Cavalry Regt (14/320)
Russian Light Battery #26 "Chamborand" (10 guns) (6/190)

Fabry, G. Etude stir les Operations de Mareckal Ouidinot, du 15 Aôut an 4 Septembre – Gross-Beeren. Recueil des Plans de Combats et de Batailles Liorees par l'Armée Prussienne pendant les Campagnes des Annes 1813, 14 et 15.

VII
FRENCH FORCES

French Army of Berlin: Maréchal Oudinot
IV Corps: Général de division Bertrand
15th (Italian) Division: Général de division Fontenelli
Brigade: Général de brigade Martel
  2/, 3/, 4/1st Italian Légère Regiment
  1/Milan Guard Regiment
Brigade: Général de brigade Saint Andrea
  3/, 4/1st Italian Line Regiment
  2/, 3/, 4/4th Italian Line Regiment
Brigade: General de brigde Moroni
  3/, 4/6th Italian Line Regiment
  2/, 3/, 4/7th Italian Line Regiment
Artillery:
  1st Italian Foot Artillery (6–6pdrs & 2–24pdr howitzers)
  13th Italian Foot Artillery (6–6pdrs & 2–24pdr howitzers)
  5th Italian Artillery Train Company
  6th Italian Artillery Train Company
  Det/6th (bis) Italian Artillery Train Company
12th Division: Général de division Morand
Advanced Guard:
  2/8th Légère Regiment
  4/8th Légère Regiment
Brigade: Général de brigade Belair
  1/, 2/, 3/, 4/, 6/3th Line Regiment
  Regimental Artillery
Brigade: Général de brigade Hulot
  1/, 2/, 4/, 6/23rd Line Regiment
  Regimental Artillery
Artillery:
  1/2nd Foot Artillery (6–6pdrs & 2–24pdr howitzers)
  3/2nd Foot Artillery (6–6pdrs & 2–24pdr howitzers)
  1/7th (bis) Train Battalion
  2/7th (bis) Train Battalion
38th (Württemberg) Division: Generallieutenant Franquemont
Brigade: Generalmajor Spitzemberg
  1/, 2/1st Line Regiment "Prinz Paul"
  1/, 2/2nd Line Regiment "Herzog Wilhelm"
Brigade Generalmajor Döring
  1/, 2/4th Line Regiment
  1/, 2/6th Line Regiment
Brigade: Generalmajor Stockmeyer
  1/, 2/7th Line Regiment
  1/9th Light Regiment
  1/10th Light Regiment
Artillery:
  1st Württemberg Heavy Battery (4–12pdrs & 2 heavy how.)
  1st Württemberg Light Battery (4–6pdrs & 2–7pdr how.)

24th Light Cavalry Brigade: Général de brigade Briche
(Generalmajor Jett)
  1/, 2/, 3/, 4/3rd Württemberg Chasseur Regiment "Herzog Ludwig"
  1/, 2/, 3/, 4/lst Württemberg Chevauléger Regiment "Prinz Adam"
  1st Württemberg Horse Battery – "von Burgi" (4–6pdrs & 2–7pdr howitzers)
Park & Reserve:
  24/2nd Foot Artillery (6–12pdrs & 2 6" howitzers)
  26/2nd Foot Artillery (6–12pdrs & 2 6" howitzers)
  26/4th Foot Artillery (6–12pdrs & 2 6" howitzers)
  8/4th Horse Artillery (4–6pdrs & 2–24pdr howitzers)
  13th Artillery Ouvriers
  3/7th (bis) Artillery Train Battalion
  4/7th (bis) Artillery Train Battalion
  5/7th (bis) Artillery Train Battalion
  6/7th (bis) Artillery Train Battalion
  7/7th (bis) Artillery Train Battalion
  4/11th Principal Artillery Train Battalion
Engineers:
  2/1st Sapper Battalion
  8/1st Sapper Battalion
  8/1st Italian Sapper
  Battalion 3/Italian Marine Artisian
  Battalion Engineering Train Squad
Military Equipage:
  5/9th Military Equipage Battalion
  6/9th Military Equipage Battalion
  7/9th Military Equipage Battalion
  Italian Transport

VII Corps: Général de division Reynier
24th (Saxon) Division: Generallieutenant Le Coq
Brigade: Oberst von Brause
  1/, 2/1st Light Infantry Regiment "LeCoq"
  1/Maximilian Infantry Regiment
  1st Jäger Company
  1/Guard Grenadier Regiment
  2/Von Rechten Regiment
Brigade: Oberst von Mellentin
  Converged Grenadier Battalion "Spiegel"
  1/, 2/Prinz Frederich August Infantry Regiment
  1/, 2/von Steindel Infantry Regiment
Artillery: Major von Roth
  1st Saxon Foot Battery "Dietrich" (6–6pdrs & 2–8pdr how.)
  2nd Saxon Foot Battery "Zandt" (6–6pdrs & 2–8pdr how.)
  Saxon Train Det.
25th (Saxon) Division: Generallieutenant von Sahr
Brigade: Oberst von Bose
  Converged Grenadier Battalion "Sperl"
  1/, 2/2nd Light Infantry Regiment "von Sahr"
  2/König Infantry Regiment
  1/Niesemeuschel Infantry Regiment

Brigade: Oberst von Ryssel
  1/, 2/Prinz Anton Infantry Regiment
  1/, 2/von Löw Infantry Regiment
Artillery: Major Gau
  3rd Saxon Foot Battery "Kühnel" (6–6pdrs &
    2–8pdr howitzers)
  4th Saxon Foot Battery "Rouvroy II" (6–6pdrs &
    2–8pdr howitzers)
  Saxon Train Det.
32nd Division: Général de division Durutte
Brigade: Général de brigade Jarry
  1/36th Légère Regiment
  Det/3/36th Légère Regiment
  4/36th Légère Regiment
  1/, 3/, 4/131st Infantry Regiment
Brigade:
  Det/133rd Infantry Regiment
  3/, 4/133rd Infantry Regiment
  2/, 3/Würzburg Infantry Regiment
**26th Light Cavalry Brigade: Generalmajor von
  Gablenz**
  (Oberst Lindenau)
  1–8/Saxon Hussar Regiment
  1–5/Prinz Clemens Uhlan Regiment
  1st Saxon Horse Battery "Birnbaum" (4–6pdrs &
    2–8pdr howitzers)
  2nd Saxon Horse Battery "Probsthavn" (4–6pdrs &
    2–8pdr howitzers)
Park & Reserves:
  Saxon 12pdr Foot Battery "Rouvroy I"
    (6–12pdrs & 2–8pdr howitzers)
  Saxon Sapper Company
  Saxon Park
  Saxon Train

XII Corps: Maréchal Oudinot
13th Division: Général de division Pacthod
Brigade: Général de brigade Bardet
  4/1st Légère Regiment
  3/, 4/7th Infantry Regiment
  4/42nd Infantry Regiment
Brigade: Général de brigade Cacault
  3/, 4/67th Infantry Regiment
  2/, 3/, 4/101st Infantry Regiment
Artillery:
  4/4th Foot Artillery (6–6pdrs & 2–24pdr howitzer)
  20/4th Foot Artillery (6–6pdrs & 2–24pdr
    howitzer)
  2/4th Principal Train Battalion
  3/7th (bis) Train Battalion
14th Division: Général de division Guilleminot
Brigade: Général de brigade Brun de Villeret
  2/, 6/18th Légère Regiment
  1/, 2/, 3/156th Infantry Regiment
Brigade: Général de brigade Gruyère
  2/Illyrian Infantry Regiment (26/486)
  3/, 4/52nd Infantry Regiment
  1/, 2/, 3/137th Infantry Regiment
  Illyrian Chasseurs

Artillery:
  2/4th Foot Artillery (6–6pdrs & 2–24pdr howitzer)
  1/8th Foot Artillery (6–6pdrs & 2–24pdr howitzer)
  1/9th (bis) Train Battalion
  4/3rd (bis) Train Battalion
  1/4th Principal Train Battalion
  5/7th Principal Train Battalion
**29th (Bavarian) Division: Generallieutenant
  Raglovitch**
Brigade: Generalmajor Maillot de la Treille
  1st Bavarian Light Infantry Battalion
  2/3rd Bavarian Infantry Regiment
  1/13th Bavarian Infantry Regiment
  1/4th Bavarian Infantry Regiment
  2/8th Bavarian Infantry Regiment
Brigade: Generalmajor Wolf
  2nd Bavarian Light Infantry Battalion
  2/5th Bavarian Infantry Regiment
  2/7th Bavarian Infantry Regiment
  2/9th Bavarian Infantry Regiment
  2/10th Bavarian Infantry Regiment
Artillery:
  1st Bavarian Foot Artillery (6–6pdrs & 2–7pdr
    howitzers)
  2nd Bavarian Foot Artillery (6–6pdrs & 2–7pdr
    howitzers)
  1st Bavarian Reserve Artillery (6–12pdrs & 2–7pdr
    how.)
  1st Bavarian Train Battalion

*III Cavalry Corps: Général de division Duke of
  Padua (Arrighi)*
**5th Light Cavalry Division: Général de division
  Lorge**
12th Light Cavalry Brigade: Général de brigade
Jacquinot
  3/, 4/5th Chasseur à Cheval Regiment
  3/, 4/10th Chasseur à Cheval Regiment
  5/, 6/13th Chasseur à Cheval Regiment
13th Light Cavalry Brigade: Général de brigade
Merlin
  4/15th Chasseur à Cheval Regiment
  3/21st Chasseur à Cheval Regiment
  3/, 4/22nd Chasseur à Cheval Regiment
**6th Light Cavalry Division: Général de division
  Fournier**
14th Light Cavalry Brigade: Général de brigade
Mouriez
  4/29th Chasseur à Cheval Regiment
  4/31st Chasseur à Cheval Regiment
  4/1st Hussar Regiment
15th Light Cavalry Brigade: Général de brigade Ameil
  3/, 4/2nd Hussar Regiment
  5/4th Hussar Regiment
  4/12th Hussar Regiment
**4th Heavy Cavalry Division: Général de division
  Defrance**
1st Brigade: Général de brigade Avice
  4/4th Dragoon Regiment

3/5th Dragoon Regiment
3/12th Dragoon Regiment
3/14th Dragoon Regiment
4/24th Dragoon Regiment
2nd Brigade: Général de brigade Quinette
4/16th Dragoon Regiment
3/17th Dragoon Regiment
3/21st Dragoon Regiment
4/26th Dragoon Regiment
5/27th Dragoon Regiment
5/13th Cuirassier Regiment

Artillery
1/5th Horse Artillery (4–6pdrs & 2–7pdr howitzers)
5/5th Horse Artillery (4–6pdrs & 2–7pdr howitzers)
2/1st Horse Artillery (4–6pdrs & 2–7pdr howitzers)
4/6th Horse Artillery (4–6pdrs & 2–7pdr howitzers)
Det. 5/1st (bis) Artillery Train
Det. 5/4th Principal Artillery Train

Fabry, G. Etude sur les Operations de Maréchal Oudinot, du 15 Août au 4 Septembre – Gross-Beeren. Recueil des Plans de Combats et de Batailles Livrees par l'Armée Prussienne pendant les Campagnes des Annes 1813, 14 et 15. French Archives, Carton C²–708

VIII
CASUALTIES

Losses for the Army of the North:
III Prussian Army Corps: Generallieutenant Bülow

3rd Brigade: Generalmajor L. Hesse-Homburg
2nd East Prussian Grenadier Battalion (0/8/2/38/0/0)
Jäger Detachment (0/3/0/3/0/0)
1/3rd East Prussian Infantry Regiment (0/15/3/64/0/12)
Jager 1/3rd East Prussian Infantry Regt (0/3/0/12/0/0)
2/3rd East Prussian Infantry Regiment (0/19/2/60/0/13)
Fus/3rd East Prussian Infantry Regt (1/2/0/10/0/16)
Jägers Fus/3rd East Prussian Infantry Regt (0/1/0/4/0/4)
1/4th Reserve Infantry Regiment (1/6/2/34/0/0)
2/4th Reserve Infantry Regiment (0/2/0/15/0/7)
3/4th Reserve Infantry Regiment (0/1/0/21/0/8)
8/3rd East Prussian Landwehr Regiment (0/5/0/7/0/0)
11/3rd East Prussian Landwehr Regiment (0/4/0/18/0/0)
12/3rd East Prussian Landwehr Regiment (0/1/0/7/0/5)
Jäger, 20/3rd East Prussian Landwehr Regt (0/0/0/1/0/0)
1st Leib Hussar Regiment (0/10/0/31/0/6)
Jägers/1st Leib Hussar Regiment (0/1/1/4/0/0)

6pdr Foot Battery #5 (0/3/0/13/0/0)
4th Brigade: Generalmajor Thümen
1/4th East Prussian Infantry Regiment (0/0/0/0/0/0)
2/4th East Prussian Infantry Regiment (0/0/0/0/0/0)
Fus/4th East Prussian Infantry Regiment (0/0/0/0/0/0)
1/5th Reserve Infantry Regiment (0/0/0/0/0/0)
2/5th Reserve Infantry Regiment (0/1/0/3/0/6)
3/5th Reserve Infantry Regiment (0/26/1/44/0/0)
4/5th Reserve Infantry Regiment (0/0/0/0/0/0)
2/Elbe Infantry Regiment (0/5/0/0/0/10)
East Prussian Jagers (not engaged)
Pomeranian National Cavalry Regiment (0/0/0/0/0/0)
6pdr Foot Battery #6 (1/2/0/5/0/0)
5th Brigade: Generalmajor Borstell
Pomeranian Grenadier Battalion (0/0/0/0/0/0)
1st Pomeranian Infantry Regiment (0/0/0/0/0/0)
2nd Reserve Infantry Regiment (0/0/0/0/0/0)
1/2nd Brandenburg Landwehr Regiment (0/0/0/0/0/0)
4/2nd Brandenburg Landwehr Regiment (0/0/0/0/0/0)
1/, 3/Pomeranian Hussar Regiment (0/0/0/4/0/)
West Prussian Uhlan Regiment (0/0/0/4/0/0)
6pdr Foot Battery #10 (0/0/0/0/0/0)
6th Brigade: Generalmajor Krafft
Colberg Infantry Regiment (0/0/1/15/0/8)
9th Reserve Infantry Regiment (0/2/0/8/0/0)
1/1st Neumdrk Landwehr Regiment (0/0/0/0/0/0)
2/1st Neumärk Landwehr Regiment (3/31/4/88/1/31)
4/1st Neumärk Landwehr Regiment (0/0/0/5/0/0)
1st Pomeranian Landwehr Cavalry Regt (0/3/0/4/0/6)
6pdr Foot Battery #16 (0/1/0/3/0/0)
Reserve Cavalry: Generalmajor Oppen
Königin Dragoon Regiment (0/0/0/8/0/0)
Jagers/Königin Dragoon Regiment (0/4/0/9/0/3)
Brandenburg Dragoon Regiment (0/1/1/4/0/1)
Jagers/Brandenburg Dragoon Regiment (0/0/0/0/0/0)
2nd West Prussian Dragoon Regiment (0/1/1/11/0/0)
2nd Silesian Hussar Regiment (not engaged)
2nd Kurmärk Landwehr Cavalry Regiment (0/0/0/0/0/0)
4th Kurmärk Landwehr Cavalry Regiment (0/0/0/1/0/1)
Horse Battery #5 (0/1/0/2/0/0)
Horse Battery #6 (0/0/0/0/0/)/0)
Artillery Reserve: Oberst Holtzendorf
Prussian 12pdr Foot Battery #4 (0/1/0/3/0/0)
Russian 12pdr Foot Batteries #7 & #21 (0/10/1/15/0/0)
6pdr Foot Battery #19 (0/1/0/7/0/1)
Horse Battery #11 (0/0/0/0/0/0)

Swedish and Russian Losses:
Horse Battery (3/3/1/3/0/0)
3rd (Russian) Jager Regiment (0/0/0/24/0/0)
Varmland Jager Regiment (0/0/0/0/0/0)

French Losses
VII Corps: Général de division Reynier
24th Division: Le Coq (Saxon)
Brigade: Oberst von Brause
1/, 2/lst Light Infantry Regiment (0/0/0/1/0/1)
1/Maximilian Infantry Regiment (unknown)
1st Jager Company (0/0/0/3/0/4)
1/Guard Grenadier Regiment (0/0/0/0/1/0)
2/Von Rechten Regiment (0/2/1/19/0/54)
Brigade: Oberst von Mellentin
1st Converged Grenadier Battalion (0/0/0/0/0/3)
1/, 2/Prinz Frederich August Inf. Regt
  (0/4/0/15/0/12)
1/, 2/von Steindel Infantry Regiment (0/0/0/0/0/3)
Artillery:
1st Saxon Foot Company (0/0/0/0/1/1/)
2nd Saxon Foot Company (0/0/0/1/0/0)
Park (0/0/0/0/0/0)
25th Division: Sahr (Saxon)
Brigade: Oberst von Bose
Converged Grenadier Battalion (0/0/I/12/1/202)
1/, 2/von Sahr Infantry Regiment (0/44/0/47/0/82)
2/König Infantry Regiment (0/0/1/0/0/77)
1/Niesemenschel Infantry Regiment (unknown)
Brigade: Oberst von Russel
1/, 2/Prinz Anton Infantry Regiment
  (0/13/0/36/0/252)
1/, 2/von Löw Infantry Regiment (0/37/1/97/0/695)
Artillery:
3rd Saxon Foot Company (0/3/1/12/1/42)
4th Saxon Foot Company (0/6/0/2/0/25)
Park (0/0/0/0/0/2)
26th Light Cavalry Brigade: Lindenau
Saxon Hussar Regiment (0/1/2/12/0/0)
Prinz Clemens Uhlan Regiment (0/2/3/4/2/61)
1st Saxon Horse Artillery (0/10/1/1/0/8)
2nd Saxon Horse Artillery (0/1/0/1/1/53)
Park & Reserves:
Saxon Reserve Artillery (0/0/0/0/0/10)
Saxon Park (0/0/0/0/0/8)
Saxon Sapper Detachment (0/1/0/0/0/1)
Division: Général de division Durutte
16 officers and 1,122 men from 133nd Line and
  Würzburg
Regiment. 59 dead & 236 missing from 36th
  Légère.

Numbers are officers dead, enlisted men dead, officers wounded, enlisted wounded, officers missing, enlisted missing von Quistorp, B., Geschichte der Nord-Armee im Jahre 1813 Berlin, 1894.

THE REAR AREAS

IX
FRENCH WITTENBERG AND MAGDEBURG
DIVISIONS MID-AUGUST 1813
(ALSO KNOWN AS THE MIDDLE CORPS)

Commanding Officer: General de division Baron Girard
Wittenberg Division: General de division Dombrowski
Brigade: Général de brigade Zoltowski
1/, 2/2nd Polish Infantry Regiment
1/, 2/4th Polish Infantry Regiment
Brigade: Général de brigade Krukowiecki
1/, 2/, 3/, 4/2nd Uhlan Regiment
1/, 2/, 3/, 4/4th Chasseur à Cheval Regiment
Artillery: Lieutenant Colonel von Schwerin
Polish Horse Battery "Zwiecicki" (4 guns)
Polish Foot Battery "Zwan" (4 guns)
Sapper Company
  Total 2,600 infantry & 1,200 cavalry

Magdeburg Division: Général de division Lanusse
Brigade: Général de brigade Sennegon
3/24th Légère Infantry Regiment
3/26th Légère Infantry Regiment
3/18th Line Infantry Regiment
3/19th Line Infantry Regiment
1/9th Westphalian Line Infantry Regiment
2/1st Croatian Infantry Regiment
Brigade: Général de brigade Baville
3/, 6/134th Line Infantry Regiment
3/56th Line Infantry Regiment
3/72nd Line Infantry Regiment
1/, 2/Saxon Ducal House Infantry Regiment
Attached:
1/, 3/, 4/13th French Hussar Regiment
1 Escadron de marche (Heavy Cavalry)
1 Escadron de marche (Light Cavalry)
Artillery:
1/9th Foot Artillery
16/9th Foot Artillery Total – 15 guns
Unknown Train Detachment

von Quistorp, B., Geschichte der Nord-Armee im Jahre 1813 Berlin, 1894, & French Archives, Carton C²=-708

X
RUSSIAN RESERVE ARMY
24 AUGUST 1813

Commander-in-Chief: General of Cavalry Bennigsen
Chief of Staff: Generallieutenant Oppermann
General-Quartermaster: Generalmajor Insov
Chief of Artillery: Generalmajor Resvov
War Commissary: Generalmajor Petrovsky
General-Intendant: Generalmajor Santv
General-Provision-Master: Generalmajor Parogskv

Advanced Guard: Generallieutenant Markov III
16th Division: Generalmajor Bulatov
Brigade: Generalmajor Sucharev
  1/, 2/, 3/Neutchlot Infantry Regiment (45/1,805)
  1/, 2/, 3/27th Jager Regiment (59/2,199)
  I/, 2/, 3/43rd Jager Regiment (47/1,597)
13th Division: Generalmajor Ivanov
Brigade: Colonel Ivanov
  1/, 2/, 3/Saratov Infantry Regiment (56/2,026)
  1/, 2/, 3/Pensa Infantry Regiment (29/1,373)
Cavalry: Generalmajor Dechterev
Brigade: Generalmajor Diadkov
  Orenburg Uhlan Regiment (2) (18/202)
  Vladimir Uhlan Regiment (3) (19/385)
Brigade: Colonel Baron Bennigsen
  1st Hussar Regiment (5) (33/824)
  1st Uhlan Regiment (5) (21/695)
Cossacks: Generalmajor von Bagration
  Vlassov #2 Cossack Regiment (5) (12/358)
  Platov #5 Cossack Regiment (5) (10/502)
  Andreinov #3 Cossack Regiment (5) (13/502)
  Shamschev Cossack Regiment (5) (13/419)
  4th Ukrainian Cossack Regiment (5) (8/233)
  9th Bashkir Regiment (15/314)
  11th Bashkir Regiment (15/340)
  14th Bashkir Regiment (25/340)
  15th Bashkir Regiment (14/302)
Artillery:
  Position Battery #16 (7/249)
  Light Battery #56 (6/183)
  1/2 Horse Battery #10 (2/105)
  Horse Battery #30 (4/133)
  Sapper Company of Capt. Shteender (3/105)
Opolochenie:
  Sibirsk Cossack Regiment (19/494)
  Peizenski Cossack Regiment (13/446)

Right Wing: General of Infantry Docturov
  Chief of Staff: Lt. Colonel Teuner
12th Division: Generalmajor Count Chovansky
Brigade: Generalmajor Sanders
  1/, 2/Smolensk-Viburg Infantry Regiment
    (53/1,388)
  1/, 2/Narva Infantry Regiment (44/1,439)
Brigade: Generalmajor Scheltuchin I
  1/, 2/Alexopol Infantry Regiment (39/1,399)

  New Ingremannland Infantry Regiment (32/1,398)
Brigade: Generalmajor Glebov
  1/, 2/6th Jager Regiment (53/1,671)
  1/, 2/41st Jager Regiment (41/1,172)
26th Division: Generalmajor Paskievich
Brigade: Colonel Tshomshushnikov
  1/, 2/Nivegorod Infantry Regiment (39/1,473)
  1/, 2/Orel Infantry Regiment (45/1,277)
Brigade: Generalmajor Savoyna
  1/, 2/Lagoda Infantry Regiment (61/1,341)
  1/, 2/Poltava Infantry Regiment (46/1,546)
Brigade: Lt. Colonel Kovrigin
  1/, 2/5th Jager Regiment (39/1,467)
  1/, 2/42nd Jager Regiment (31/1,230)
Artillery:
  Position Battery #26 (5/258)
  Position Battery #45 (9/254)
  Light Battery #1 (5/150)
  Light Battery #47 (4/157)
  Horse Battery #2 (7/302)
  Pioneer Company of Lt. Col. Asanassiev III (3/71)
**Reserve Infantry Brigade of 13th Division:
  Generalmajor Lindfors**
Brigade: Generalmajor Rossi
  1/, 2/, 3/Veliki-Loutzk Infantry Regiment
    (58/2,146)
  1/, 2/Galitz Infantry Regiment (36/977)
Cavalry Division: Generallieutenant Pushkin
Brigade: Generalmajor Repninsky
  Converged Dragoon Regiment (5) (13/760)
  1st Converged Chasseur à Cheval Regiment (4)
    (14/524)
  2nd Converged Chasseur à Cheval Regiment (4)
    (9/616)
Brigade: Generalmajor Baron Kreutz
  2nd Converged Uhlan Regiment (4) (15/552)
  Taganrog Uhlan Regiment (4) (24/622)
  Siberian Uhlan Regiment (2) (20/174)
  Jitomir Uhlan Regiment (2) (13/176)
Reserve Artillery: Colonel Kolotinsky
  Position Battery #22 (7/274)
  Light Battery #18 (8/159)
  Light Battery #48 (5/171)
  Light Battery #53 (5/175)
  Horse Battery #9 (5/287)
  Pioneer Company #1 (unknown)
  Pioneer Company #7 (5/171)

Left Wing: Generallieutenant Tolstoy
Opolochenie Corps: Generalmajor Muromoc
  1/, 2/, 3/1st Nishegorod Opolochenie Regiment
    (34/1,276)
  1/, 2/, 3/2nd Nishegorod Opolochenie Regt
    (34/1,374)
  1/, 2/, 3/3rd Nishegorod Opolochenie Regiment
    (35/1,400)
  1/, 2/, 3/4th Nishegorod Opolochenie Regiment
    (34/1,090)
  Position Battery #52 (6/237)

Horse Battery #22 (8/222)
Opolochenie Corps: Generalmajor Titov
Brigade: Generalmajor Kashansky
1/, 2/, 3/1st Pensa Opolochenie Regiment (43/1,182)
1/, 2/, 3/2nd Pensa Opolochenie Regiment
(44/1,556)
1/, 2/, 3/3rd Pensa Opolochenie Regiment (31/1,162)
Brigade: Generalmajor Tshishkin
1/, 2/, 3/1st Riazan Opolochenie Regiment
(41/1,373)
1/, 2/, 3/3rd Riazan Opolochenie Regiment
(46/1,182)
Artillery:
Light Battery #64 (5/131)
½ Pensa Opolochenie 6pdr Foot Battery (4 guns)
(2/52)
Cavalry: Generallieutenant Tschlapitz
Nishegorod Opolochenie Cossack Regiment (5)
Kostroma Opolochenie Cossack Regiment (5)
(25/471)
Riazan Opolochenie Cossack Regiment (5) (23/515)
Kasan Opolochenie Cossack Regiment (2) (6/216)
5th Ural Cossack Regiment (5) (18/435)

_____

*Bogdanovich,M.I., Istorich Vloin 1813 Goda Za
Nezavicimost Gernianii Po Dostonern'm' Istochnikam',
St. Petersburg, 1863.*

THE BATTLE OF THE KATZBACH
26 AUGUST 1813

XI
THE ARMY OF SILESIA

Commander-in-Chief: General der Kavallerie Blücher
Chief of Staff: Generalmajor von Gneisenau
Quartermaster: Oberst von Müffling
General Intendent: von Ribbentrop

Right Wing: Generallieutenant Baron Sacken
11th Corps: Generallieutenant Vassil'shikov
**10th Infantry Division: Generalmajor Count
Lieven III (3,778 men)**
Brigade: Generalmajor Agatin
Jaroslav Infantry Regiment (2)
Brigade: Colonel Sass
Crimea Infantry Regiment (1)
Bieloserk Infantry Regiment (2)
Brigade: Colonel Achlestishev
8th Jager Regiment (2)
39th Jager Regiment (2)
Detached from 16th Division:
Brigade: Generalmajor Repninsky (1,182 men)
Okhotsk Infantry Regiment (1)
Kamtchatka Infantry Regiment (1)

27th Division: General Neverovsky (3,424 men)
Brigade: Colonel Levandskoy
Odessa Infantry Regiment (1)
Vilna Infantry Regiment (1)
Brigade: Colonel Alexejev
Tarnopol Infantry Regiment (1)
Simbrisk Infantry Regiment (1)
Brigade: Colonel Kollogribov
49th Jager Regiment (2)
50th Jager Regiment (1)
Artillery:
Position Battery #13
Position Battery #28
Light Battery #24
Light Battery #35

Cavalry Corps: Generallieutenant Tschaplitz
(3,170 men)
3rd Dragoon Division:
Brigade: Generalmajor Pantschulid
Courland Dragoon Regiment (2)
Smolensk Dragoon Regiment (2)
2nd Hussar Division: Generalmajor Tschaplitz
Brigade: Colonel Vassil'shikov
Akhtyrsk Hussar Regiment (4)
Marioupol Hussar Regiment (4)
Brigade: Generalmajor Kaslovsky
Alexandria Hussar Regiment (4)
White Russia Hussar Regiment (4)
Artillery:
Horse Battery #18
Cossacks: Generalmajor Karpov II (4,348 men)
Karpov #2 Cossack Regiment (5)
Loukoffkin Cossack Regiment (5)
Tcharnusubov #3 Cossack Regiment (5)
Kutainikov #4 Cossack Regiment (5)
Semenschenko Cossack Regiment (5)
Grekov #2 Cossack Regiment (5)
4th Ukrainian Cossack Regiment (5)
2nd Kalmuck Regiment (5)
2nd Bashkir Regiment (5)

Center
*1st Prussian Army Corps: Generallieutenant von
Yorck*
1st Brigade: Oberst von Steinmetz (9,178 men)
Detachment: Oberst von Hiller
East Prussian Grenadier Battalion
Leib Grenadier Battalion Silesian Grenadier
Battalion
West Prussian Grenadier Battalion
3/, 4/East Prussian Jäger Battalion
Detachment: Oberst von Losthin
5th Silesian Landwehr Regiment
1st Battalion – Mumm
2nd Battalion – Borwitz
3rd Battalion – Seidlitz
4th Battalion – Kossecky
13th Silesian Landwehr Regiment

1st Battalion – Walter von Cronegk
2nd Battalion – Larisc
3rd Battalion – Rekowsky
4th Battalion – Martitz
Attached:
2nd Silesian Hussar Regiment (5)
6pdr Foot Battery #2

2nd Brigade: Generalmajor Prinz Carl von Mecklenburg-Strelitz
(7,588 men)
Detachment: Oberstleutnant von Lobenthal
1/, 2/Fus/lst East Prussian Regiment
1/, 2/Fus/2nd East Prussian Regiment
Landwehr:
6th Silesian Landwehr Regiment
1st Battalion – Fischer
2nd Battalion – Kempsky
3rd Battalion – Rostke
4th Battalion – Dobrowolsky
Attached:
Mecklenburg-Strelitz Hussar Regiment (5)
6pdr Foot Battery #1

7th Brigade: Generalmajor von Horn (8,241 men)
Detachment: Oberstleutnant von Zepelin
1/, 2/, Fus/Leib Infantry Regiment
Thüringian Battalion
3/, 4/Guard Jager Battalion (2 coys)
Attached:
4th Silesian Landwehr Regiment
1st Battalion – Courbiere
2nd Battalion – Kotulinsky
3rd Battalion – Reichenbach
4th Battalion – Knorr
15th Silesian Landwehr Regiment
1st Battalion – Sommerfeld
2nd Battalion – Pottinghofer
3rd Battalion – Reibnitz
4th Battalion – Wedell
Brandenburg Hussar Regiment (3)
3rd Silesian Landwehr Cavalry Regiment (2)
6pdr Foot Battery #3

8th Brigade: Generalmajor von Hünerbein (7,209 men)
Detachment: Oberstleutnant von Bork
1/, 2/Fus/Brandenburg Infantry Regiment
1/, 2/Fus/12th Reserve Infantry Regiment
Attached:
14th Silesian Landwehr Regiment
1st Battalion – Kempsky
2nd Battalion – Thiele
3rd Battalion – Brixen
4th Battalion – Gfug
3/, 4/Brandenburg Hussar Regiment
3rd Silesian Landwehr Cavalry Regiment (2)
6pdr Foot Battery #15

Cavalry Reserve: Generalmajor Jürgass (4,198 men)
Brigade: Oberst von Henckel von Donnersmark
1st West Prussian Dragoon Regiment (4)

Lithuanian Dragoon Regiment (5)
Brigade: Oberst von Katzeler
Brandenburg Uhlan Regiment (4)
East Prussian National Cavalry Regiment (5)
Brigade: Major von Bieberstein
1st Neumärk Landwehr Cavalry Regiment (4)
5th Silesian Landwehr Cavalry Regiment (4)
10th Silesian Landwehr Cavalry Regiment (4)
Artillery:
Horse Battery #1
Horse Battery #2

Reserve Artillery: Oberstleutnant Schmidt (1,231 men)
12pdr Foot Battery #1
12pdr Foot Battery #2
6pdr Foot Battery #12
6pdr Foot Battery #24
3pdr Foot Battery #1
Horse Battery #3
Horse Battery #12 Park Column
Park Column #1
Park Column #3
Park Column #5
Park Column #13
Artisan Column #1
Field Pioneer Company #1 Field Pioneer Company #2

Left Wing: General of Infantry Count Langeron
6th Corps: Generalmajor Scherbatov
7th Division: Generalmajor Tallisin (4,920 men)
Brigade: Colonel Kirschnitzky
Pskov Infantry Regiment (2)
Moscow Infantry Regiment (2)
Brigade: Colonel Augustov
Sofia Infantry Regiment (1)
Libau Infantry Regiment (2)
Brigade: Colonel Dietrich
11th Jager Regiment (2)
36th Jager Regiment (1)

18th Division: Generalmajor Bernodossov (3,368 men)
Brigade: Oberstleutnant Blagovenzenko
Vladimir Infantry Regiment (1)
Dnieper Infantry Regiment (1)
Brigade:
Tambov Infantry Regiment (1)
Kostroma Infantry Regiment (1)
Brigade: Generalmajor Mescherinov
32nd Jager Regiment (1)
28th Jager Regiment (1)
Artillery:
Position Battery #15
Light Battery #28
Light Battery #17

9th Corps: Generallieutenant Alsusiev
9th Division: Generalmajor Udom II (2,839 men)
Brigade: Colonel Poltaratzky
  Nacheburg Infantry Regiment (1)
Brigade: Lieutenant Colonel Ogriumov
  Iakout Infantry Regiment (1)
  Riajsk Infantry Regiment (2)
Brigade: Major Grimbladt
  10th Jager Regiment (1)
  36th Jager Regiment (1)
15th Division: Generalmajor Rudsevich (3,703 men)
Brigade: Colonel Tern
  Vitebsk Infantry Regiment (1)
  Kozlov Infantry Regiment (1)
Brigade: Lt. Colonel Anensur
  Kourin Infantry Regiment (2)
  Kohvvan Infantry Regiment (1)
Brigade: Colonel Tichanovskv
  12th Jager Regiment (2)
  22nd Jager Regiment (1)
Artillery:
  Position Battery #18
  Light Battery #29
  Light Battery #34

10th Corps: Generallieutenant Kapzevich
8th Division: Generalmajor Count Urussov (3,672 men)
Brigade: Lt. Colonel Schindshin
  Archangle Infantry Regiment (2)
  Old Ingremannland Infantry Regiment (2)
Brigade: Colonel Rerin
  Schusselburg Infantry Regiment (1)
  7th Jager Regiment (2)
  37th Jager Regiment (1)
22nd Division: Generalmajor Turtshaninov (3,940 men)
Brigade: Generalmajor Schapskov
  Viatka Infantry Regiment (2)
  Staroskol Infantry Regiment (2)
  Olonetz Infantry Regiment (1)
Brigade: Colonel Durnov
  29th Jager Regiment (2)
  45th Jager Regiment (2)

1st Cavalry Corps: Generallieutenant Baron Korff (4,009 men)
Brigade: Generalmajor Berdaeev
  Tver Dragoon Regiment (2)
  Kinhourn Dragoon Regiment (2)
1st Chasseur à Cheval Division: Generalmajor Pantschulid I
  Tschernigov Chasseur à Cheval Regiment (3)
  Sieversk Chasseur à Cheval Regiment (2)
  Arasmass Chasseur à Cheval Regiment (2)
  (Arasmass was the Headquarters Guard)

Detached from 2nd Chasseur à Cheval Division:
Brigade: Generalmajor Count Pahlen II
  Dorpat Chasseur à Cheval Regiment (2)
  Lithuania Chasseur à Cheval Regiment (2)
Artillery:
  Horse Battery #6
Light Troops: Generalmajor Grekov VIII
Brigade: Generalmajor Count de Witte
  1st Ukrainian Cossack Regiment
  2nd Ukrainian Cossack Regiment
  3rd Ukrainian Cossack Regiment
Don Cossacks Attached: Generalmajor Grekov III (2,372 men)
This force joined after the battle was over.
  Selivanov #2 Don Cossack Regiment (5)
  Kutainikov #8 Cossack Regiment (5)
  Isaeva #2 Cossack Regiment (5)
  Zikilev Cossack Regiment (5)
  Grekov #8 Cossack Regiment (5)
  3rd Black Sea Cossack Regiment (5)
  1st Teptar Cossack Regiment (3)
  Don Cossack Horse Battery #2
Reserve Artillery:
  Position Battery #11
  Position Battery #34
  Position Battery #39
  Light Battery #3
  Pontoon Company #4
  75th Marine (or Ships) Equipage
  Pioneer Company Lt. Colonel Gebenera

Detached Corps: Generallieutenant Pahlen I (later St. Priest)
8th Corps: Generallieutenant Count St. Preist
11th Division: Generallieutenant Count Gurgalov (4,107 men)
Brigade: Kartvenkov
  Jeletz Infantry Regiment (1)
  Polotsk Infantry Regiment (1)
Brigade: Colonel Turgenev
  Ekaterinburg Infantry Regiment (2)
  Rilsk Infantry Regiment (1)
Brigade: Generalmajor Bistrom II
  1st Jager Regiment (1)
  33rd Jager Regiment (2)
17th Division: Generalmajor Pillar (4,422 men)
Brigade: Colonel Kern
  Riazan Infantry Regiment (2)
  Bieloserk Infantry Regiment (2)
Brigade: Colonel Schertov I
  Brest Infantry Regiment (2)
  Wilmanstrand Infantry Regiment (2)
Brigade: Major Charitanov
  30th Jager Regiment (2)
  48th Jager Regiment (2)
1st Dragoon Division: Generalmajor Borosdin (2,561 men)
Brigade:
  Kargopol Dragoon Regiment (4)

Mitau Dragoon Regiment (4)
Brigade:
  Moscow Dragoon Regiment (2)
  New Russia Dragoon Regiment (4)
Detached from 4th Dragoon Division:
Brigade:
  Karkov Dragoon Regiment (2)
  Kiev Dragoon Regiment (5)
Light Troops: (1,114 men)
  Grekov #21 Don Cossack Regiment
  Gzov #3 Don Cossack Regiment
  Stavrapol Kalmuck Regiment
Reserve Artillery: (1,007 men)
  Position Battery #32
  Light Battery #32
  Light Battery #33
  Horse Battery #7
  Pontooneer Company #4
  Pontooneer Company #5

---

*Plotho, C., Der Kreig in Deutschland and Frankreich
in den Jahren 1813 and 1814, Carl Friedrich, Berlin,
1817, Vol II.
Prussian General Staff, Plane der Schlachten and
Treffen welche von der preussischen Armee in den
feldzügen der Jahre 1813, 14, and 15 geliesert worden,
G.Reimer, Berlin, 1821, Vol II.*

XII
FRENCH FORCES

Commander-in-Chief: Maréchal MacDonald, Duke
  of Tarente

III Corps Général de division Souham
8th Division: Général de brigade Brayer
1st Brigade:
  6th Provisional Regiment
    2/6th Légère Regiment
    3/25th Légère Regiment
  10th Provisional Regiment
    3/16th Légère Regiment
    1/28th Légère Regiment
  14th Provisional Regiment
    4/34th Line Regiment
    3/40th Line Regiment
  19th Provisional Regiment
    6/32th Line Regiment
    2/58th Line Regiment
2nd Brigade: General de brigade Charrière
  1/, 3/, 4/22nd Line Regiment
  21st Provisional Regiment
    3/59th Line Regiment
    4/69th Line Regiment
  24th Provisional Regiment
    3/88th Line Regiment
    3/103rd Line Regiment

Artillery:
  10/2nd Foot Artillery (6–6pdrs & 2–24pdr
    howitzers)
  5/9th Foot Artillery (6–6pdrs & 2–24pdr
    howitzers)
  Det. 3/9th Principal Train Battalion
  Det. 4/3rd (bis) Train Battalion
9th Division: Général de division Delmas
1st Brigade:
  2nd Provisional Regiment
    3/2nd Légère Regiment
    3/4th Légère Regiment
  1/, 2/29th Légère Regiment
  1/, 2/, 3/136th Line Regiment
2nd Brigade: General de brigade Vergez
  1/, 2/, 3/138th Line Regiment
  1/, 2/, 3/145th Line Regiment
Artillery:
  2/9th Foot Artillery (6–6pdrs & 2–24pdr
    howitzers)
  11/9th Foot Artillery (6–6pdrs & 2–24pdr
    howitzers)
  Det. 4/3rd (bis) Train Battalion
  Det. 4/6th Principal Train Battalion
  Det. 7/10th Principal Train Battalion
10th Division: Général de division Albert
1st Brigade: Général de brigade Vandedem
  4th Provisional Regiment
    4/5th Légère Regiment
    4/12th Légère Regiment
  1/, 2/, 3/139th Line Regiment
2nd Brigade: Général de brigade Suden
  1/, 2/, 3/140th Line Regiment
  1/, 2/, 3/141st Line Regiment
Artillery:
  3/7th Foot Artillery (6–6pdrs & 2–24pdr howitzers)
  4/7th Foot Artillery (6–6pdrs & 2–24pdr
    howitzers)
  Det. 4/1st Principal Train Battalion
  Det. 7/10th Principal Train Battalion
11th Division: Général de division Ricard
1st Brigade:
  3/, 4/9th Légère Regiment
  17th Provisional Regiment
    4/43rd Line Regiment
    3/75th Line Regiment
  3/, 4/50th Line Regiment
  4/65th Line Regiment
2nd Brigade: Général de brigade Dumoulin
  1/, 2/, 3/142nd Line Regiment
  1/, 2/, 3/144th Line Regiment
Artillery:
  19/7th Foot Artillery (6–6pdrs & 2–24pdr
    howitzers)
  5/9th Foot Artillery (6–6pdrs & 2–24pdr
    howitzers)
  Det. 7/10th Principal Train Battalion
  Det. 7/11th Principal Train Battalion
  Det. 4/13th (bis) Train Battalion

39th Division: Général de division Marchand
1st Brigade: Generalmajor Stockhorn
  1/, 2/1st Baden Infantry Regiment
  1/, 2/3rd Baden Infantry Regiment
2nd Brigade: Prince Emil of Hesse
  1/, 2/Hessian Fusilier Guards
  1/, 2/2nd Hessian Leib Infantry Regiment
  1/, 2/Hessian Leib Guard Regiment
Artillery:
  1st Baden Foot Battery
  1st Hessian Foot Battery
  Train Battalion Det.
23rd Light Cavalry Brigade: General de Brigade Beurmann
  1/, 2/, 3/, 4/, 5/, 6/10th French Hussar Regiment
  1/, 2/, 3/, 4/, 5/Baden Dragoon Regiment
Reserve and Grand Park
  8/4th Foot Artillery (6–12pdrs & 2–24pdr howitzers)
  21/7th Foot Artillery (6–6pdrs & 2–24pdr howitzers)
  6/3rd Foot Artillery (no guns)
  15/4th Foot Artillery (no guns)
  5/1st Horse Artillery (4–6pdrs & 2–24pdr howitzers)
  1/3rd Horse Artillery (4–6pdrs & 2–24pdr howitzers)
  4 Companies Spanish Sappers
  Det. 2/1st Principal Train Battalion
  Det. 3/1st Principal Train Battalion
  Det. 4/1st Principal Train Battalion
  Det. 7/5th Principal Train Battalion
  Det. 2/6th Principal Train Battalion
  Det. 4/8th Principal Train Battalion
  Det. 3/10th Principal Train Battalion
  Det. 7/10th Principal Train Battalion
  Det. 3/3rd (bis) Train Battalion
  Det. 9/3rd (bis) Train Battalion
  1/, 2/, 3/, 4/, 5/, 6/6th Equipage Train Battalion

V Corps: Général de division Lauriston
16th Division: Général de division Maison
Brigade: Général de brigade Penne
  1/, 2/, 3/151st Line Regiment
  1/, 2/, 3/152nd Line Regiment
Brigade:
  1/, 2/, 3/153rd Line Regiment
  1/, 2/, 3/154th Line Regiment
Artillery: Chef de bataillon Vandidon
  1/1st Foot Artillery (3/62) (6–6pdrs & 2–24pdr howitzers)
  3/1st Foot Artillery (2/87) (6–6pdrs & 2–24pdr howitzers)
  7/6th Horse Artillery (2/53) (4–6pdrs & 2–24pdr howitzers)
  7/2nd Principal Train Battalion (2/90)
  4/lst (bis) Train Battalion (0/110)
19th Division: Général de division Rochambeau
Brigade: Général de brigade Harlet

1/, 2/, 3/135th Line Regiment
1/, 2/, 3/149th Line Regiment
Brigade: Général de brigade Lafitte
  1/, 2/, 3/150th Line Regiment
  1/, 2/, 3/155th Line Regiment
Artillery: Chef de Bataillon Richard
  12/5th Foot Artillery (3/86) (6–6pdrs & 2–24pdr howitzers)
  17/5th Foot Artillery (3/53) (6–6pdrs & 2–24pdr howitzers)
  Det. 1st & 4/4th Principal Train Battalion (1/157)
6th Light Cavalry Brigade: Général de brigade Dermoncourt
  1/, 2/2nd Chasseur à Cheval Regiment
  1/, 2/3rd Chasseur à Cheval Regiment
  1/, 2/, 3/6th Chasseur à Cheval Regiment
Corps Reserve Artillery: Chef de bataillon Châteaubrun
  15/1st Foot Artillery (3/71) (no guns)
  16/1st Foot Artillery (1/73) (6–12pdrs & 2–6' howitzers)
  17/1st Foot Artillery (2/88) (6–12pdrs & 2–6" howitzers)
  2/5th Horse Artillery (3/86) (4–6pdrs & 2–24pdr howitzers)
  7/3rd Principal Train Battalion
  Det 1/12th Principal Train Battalion
  5/5th (bis) Train Battalion (2/143)
  4/8th (bis) Train Battalion (1/126)
  4/9th (bis) Train Battalion (0/60)
  1/6th Sapper Battalion
  2/6th Sapper Battalion
  3/6th Sapper Battalion

XI Corps
  Commander-in-Chief: Maréchal MacDonald, Duke of Tarente
  (Général de division Gérard – acting)
  Chief of Staff: Général de brigade Grundler
  Artillery Commander: Colonel Sautereau
  Commander of Engineers: Chef de bataillon Marion
35th Division: Général de brigade d'Henin (acting)
1st Brigade: General de Brigade Senecal
  3/, 4/, 7/6th Line Regiment
  1/, 2/, 3/, 4/112nd Line Regiment
2nd Brigade: General de Brigade Zucchi
  3/, 4/2nd Italian Légère Regiment
  1/, 2/, 3/, 4/5th Italian Line Regiment
Artillery:
  6/1st Foot Artillery (6–6pdrs & 2–24pdr howitzers)
  3rd Italian Horse Battery (4–6pdrs & 2–24pdr howitzers)
  Det. 1/11th (bis) Train Battalion
  3/, 4/Italian Train Battalion
36th Division: Général de division Charpentier
1st Brigade: General de Brigade Simmer
  1/, 2/, 3/, 4/22nd Légère Regiment
  4/, 6/10th Line Regiment

2nd Brigade: General de Brigade Meunier
  3/, 4/3rd Légère Regiment
  3/, 4/, 7/14th Légère Regiment
Artillery:
  5/1st Foot Artillery (6–6pdrs & 2–24pdr howitzers)
  19/2nd Foot Artillery (6–6pdrs & 2–24pdr howitzers)
  Det. 1/7th Principal Train Battalion
  Det. 2/12th Principal Train Battalion
Corps Cavalry Brigade:
  1/, 2/4th Italian Chasseurs
  1/Würzburg Chevaulégers
  1/, 2/, 3/, 4/2nd Neapolitian Chasseurs
Reserve and Grand Park
  13/2nd Foot Artillery (6–12pdrs & 2–6" howitzers)
  22/5th Foot Artillery (6–12pdrs & 2–6" howitzers)
  15/5th Foot Artillery (no guns)
  8/9th Foot Artillery (6–12pdrs & 2–6" howitzers)
  Det. 3/7th Principal Train Battalion
  Det. 4/7th Principal Train Battalion
  Det. 2/8th Principal Train Battalion
  Det. 2/8th (bis) Train Battalion
  Det. 1/13th (bis) Train Battalion
  6/6th Horse Artillery (4–6pdrs & 2–24pdr howitzers)
  1st Neapolitan Horse Battery (4–6pdrs & 2–24pdr howitzers)
  7/5th Sapper Battalion
  2/7th Sapper Battalion
  9th Italian Sapper Company

II Cavalry Corps: (10,304 men)
  Commander-in-Chief: Général de division Sébastiani
  Chief of Staff: Adjutant Commandant Lascours
  Commander of Artillery: Colonel Colin
2nd Light Cavalry Division: Général de division Roussel d'Hurbal
7th Light Cavalry Brigade: Général de brigade Gérard
  1/, 2/, 3/, 4/9th Hussar Regiment
  1/, 2/, 3/4th Chevauléger-lancier Regiment
  1/, 2/, 3/5th Hussar Regiment
8th Light Cavalry Brigade: Général de brigade Domanget
  1/, 2/, 3/2nd Chevauléger-lancier Regiment
  1/, 2/, 3/11th Chasseur à Cheval Regiment
  1/, 2/, 3/12th Chasseur à Cheval Regiment
4th Light Cavalry Division: Général de division Exelmans
9th Light Cavalry Brigade: Général de brigade Maurin
  1/, 2/6th Chevauléger-lancier Regiment
  1/, 2/4th Chasseur à Cheval Regiment
  1/, 2/, 3/7th Chasseur à Cheval Regiment
10th Light Cavalry Brigade: Général de brigade Wathiez
  1/, 2/, 3/, 4/20th Chasseur à Cheval Regiment
  1/, 2/, 3/, 4/23th Chasseur à Cheval Regiment
  1/, 2/, 3/24th Chasseur à Cheval Regiment

  1/, 2/l lth Hussar Regiment
2nd Heavy Cavalry Division: Général de division Saint-Germain
1st Brigade: Général de brigade d'Augeranville
  1/, 2/1st Carabinier Regiment
  1/, 2/2nd Carabinier Regiment
  1/, 2/1st Cuirassier Regiment
2nd Brigade: Général de brigade Thiry
  1/, 2/, 3/5th Cuirassier Regiment
  1/, 2/8th Cuirassier Regiment
  1/, 2/10th Cuirassier Regiment
Artillery:
  7/1st Horse Artillery (4–6pdrs & 2–24pdr howitzers)
  7/4th Horse Artillery (4–6pdrs & 2–24pdr howitzers)
  8/6th Horse Artillery (4–6pdrs & 2–24pdr howitzers)
  Det. 2/11th (bis) Train Battalion
  Det. 4/11th (bis) Train Battalion
  Det. 3/13th (bis) Train Battalion

Friederich, R., Die Schlacht and der Katzbach, Ernst Siegfried Mittler and Sohn, Berlin, 1913.
Prussian General Staff, Plane der Schlachten and Treffen welche von der preussischen Armee in den feldzugen der Jahre 1813, 14, and 15 geliesert worden, G.Reimer, Berlin, 1821, Vol II. C. Rousset, La Grande Armée de 1813, Paris, 1892
Frederichs, Geschichte des Herbstfeltzuges 1813, Berlin, 1903. Clément, G., Campagne de 1813, H. Charles-Lavauzelle, Paris, date unknown.
French Archives, Cartons C² 538, 540, 543, & 544

THE BATTLE OF DRESDEN
26/27 AUGUST 1813

XIII
ARMY OF BOHEMIA

Commander-in-Chief: Feldmarschall Fürst Carl zu Schwarzenberg
Chief of Staff: Feldmarschall-lieutenant Graf Radetzky
General Quartermasters: Generalmajor Baron Langenau,
Generalmajor Baron Trapp
Russian General Quartermaster: Generalmajor Baron Toll
Chief of Artillery: Feldmarschall-lieutenant Reiszner
General-IntendantFeldmarschall-lieutenant Prohaska

Austrian Troops
Right Wing: General der Kavallerie Erbprinz F. von Hessen-Homburg
1st Light Division: Feldmarschall-lieutenant Fürst Moritz Liechtenstein
Brigade: Generalmajor Hardegg

1st Jäger Battalion (638)
2nd Jäger Battalion (663)
Kaiser Chevauléger Regiment #1 (6) (674)
Brigade: Generalmajor Scheither
7th Jäger Battalion (446)
1/Broder Grenz Regiment #7 (1,193)
Vincent Chevauléger Regiment #4 (6) (785)
2–6pdr Cavalry Batteries (14 guns)

1st Line Division: Feldmarschall-lieutenant Graf Colloredo

Brigade: Generalmajor Chiesa
1/, 2/Froon Infantry Regiment #54 (2,068)
1/, 2/Devaux Infantry Regiment #25 (2,020)
Brigade: Generalmajor Drechel
1/, 2/Argenteau Infantry Regiment #35 (2,026)
1/, 2/Erbach Infantry Regiment #42 (2,110)
Brigade: Generalmajor von Andrasy
1/, 2/, 3/de Ligne Infantry Regiment #30 (3,282)
1/, 2/Czartorisky Infantry Regiment #9 (2,331)

3rd Line Division: Feldmarschall-lieutenant Graf Civalart

Brigade: Generalmajor Quasdanovich
1/, 2/Albert Gyulai Infantry Regiment #21 (2,331)
1/, 2/Reuss Plauen Infantry Regiment #17 (2,282)
6pdr Brigade Battery (6 guns)
Brigade: Generalmajor Giffing
1/, 2/Strauch Infantry Regiment #24 (1,126)
1/, 2/Bellegarde Infantry Regiment #44 (1,509)
6pdr Brigade Battery (6 guns)
Brigade: Generalmajor Reichlin-Meldegg
1/, 2/Weidenfeld Infantry Regiment #37 (1,904)
1/, 2/Ignatz Gyulai Infantry Regiment #60 (1,457)
6pdr Brigade Battery (6 guns)

1st Reserve Division: Feldmarschall-lieutenant Marquis Chasteler

Brigade: Generalmajor Freiherr Koller
Grenadier Battalion Czarnotzky (788)
Grenadier Battalion Obermeyer (780)
Grenadier Battalion Berger (731)
Grenadier Battalion Oklopsia (758)
6pdr Brigade Battery (6 guns)
Brigade: Generalmajor Graf Murray
Grenadier Battalion Habinay (517)
Grenadier Battalion Portner (819)
Grenadier Battalion Fischer (614)
Grenadier Battalion Rüber (800)
6pdr Brigade Battery (6 guns)

2nd Reserve Division: Feldmarschall-lieutenant Bianchi

Brigade: Generalmajor Prinz P. von Hessen-Homburg
1/, 2/Hiller Infantry Regiment #2 (1,979)
1/, 2/H. Colloredo Infantry Regiment #33 (1,700)
6pdr Brigade Battery (6 guns)
Brigade: Generalmajor von Mariassy
1/, 2/Simbischen Infantry Regiment #48 (1,864)
1/, 2/Hessen-Homburg Infantry Regiment #19 (1,599)
6pdr Brigade Battery (6 guns)

Brigade: Generalmajor Quallenberg
1/, 2/Esterhazy Infantry Regiment #32 (1,924)
1/, 2/Davidovich Infantry Regiment #34 (1,577)
6pdr Brigade Battery (6 guns)

1st Cavalry Division: Feldmarschall-lieutenant Nostitz

Brigade: Generalmajor Rothkirch
Erbprinz Franz Cuirassier Regiment #2 (4) (614)
Kronprinz Ferdinand Cuirassier Regiment #4 (4) (636)
Brigade: Generalmajor Kroyher
Hohenzollern Cuirassier Regiment #8 (4) (577)
Sommariva Cuirassier Regiment #5 (4) (645)

3rd Cavalry Division Feldmarschall-lieutenant Schneller

Brigade: Generalmajor von Zechmeister
O'Reilly Chevauléger Regiment #3 (4) (367)
Hohenzollern Chevauléger Regiment #2 (5) (632)
Brigade: Generalmajor Prinz G. von Hessen-Homburg
Kienmayer Hussar Regiment #8 (6) (605)
Hessen-Homburg Hussar Regiment #4 (6) (732)

Attached: (744 men)

8 Pioneer Companies
1 Pontooneer Company

Left Wing: Feldzeugmeister Graf I. Gyulai

2nd Line Division: Feldmarschall-lieutenant Weissenwolf

Brigade: Generalmajor Czollich
1/, 2/, 3/Kottulinsky Infantry Regiment #41 (2,764)
1/, 2/, 3/Kaiser Infantry Regiment #1 (2,910)
6pdr Brigade Battery (6 guns)
Brigade: Generalmajor Grimmer
1/, 2/Kollowrath Infantry Regiment #36 (2,071)
1/, 2/Frohlich Infantry Regiment #28 (1,143)
6pdr Brigade Battery (6 guns)
Brigade: Generalmajor Herzogenberg
1/, 2/Würzburg Infantry Regiment #7 (1,696)
1/, 2/Erzherzog Ludwig Infantry Regiment #8 (1,839)
6pdr Brigade Battery (6 guns)

4th Line Division: Feldmarschal-leutnant Fürst A. Liechtenstein

Brigade: Generalmajor von Seethal
1/, 2/Kaunitz Infantry Regiment #20 (1,764)
1/, 2/W. Colloredo Infantry Regiment #56 (1,848)
6pdr Brigade Battery (6 guns)
Brigade: Generalmajor Mecserey
1/, 2/Vogelsang Infantry Regiment #47 (2,238)
1/, 2/Reuss-Greiz Infantry Regiment #18 (2,285)
6pdr Brigade Battery (6 guns)
Brigade: Generalmajor Mumb von Muhlheim
1/, 2/Erzherzog Rainer Infantry Regiment #11 (2,190)
1/, 2/Lusignan Infantry Regiment #16 (2,189)
6pdr Brigade Battery (6 guns)

3rd Reserve Division: Feldmarschal-leutnant Graf Crenneville
Brigade: Generalmajor Greth
  1/Walachisch-Illyrian Grenz Regiment #13 (1,244)
  1/Gradiscaner Grenz Regiment #8 (1,126)
  1/Deutsch-Banat Grenz Regiment #12 (1,256)
  1/Warasdiner-Kreuzer Grenz Regiment #5 (978)
  1/Warasdiner-St. George Grenz Regiment #6 (744)
  3pdr Battery (6 guns)
Brigade: Generalmajor Haecht
  Klenau Chevauléger Regiment #5 (6) (768)
  Rosenberg Chevauléger Regiment #6 (6) (888)
2nd Cavalry Division: Feldmarschal-leutnant Freiherr Lederer
Brigade: Generalmajor Desfours
  Kaiser Cuirassier Regiment #1 (4) (557)
  Erzherzog Johann Dragoon Regiment #1 (4) (561)
Brigade: Generalmajor Raigecourt
  Levenehr Dragoon Regiment #3 (4) (598)
  Reisch Dragoon Regiment #6 (6) (892)

Army Corps: General der Kavallerie Graf Klenau
3rd Light Division: Feldmarschall-Lieutenant Mesko
Brigade: Generalmajor Paumgartten
  1/1st Walachisch Infantry Regiment #16 (989)
  2/Deutsch-Banater Infantry Regiment #12 (1,266)
  2/Walachisch-Illyier Infantry Regiment #13 (1,171)
  Palatinal Hussar Regiment #12 (6) (641)
  3pdr Battery (6 guns)
Brigade: Generalmajor Szecsen
  1/, 2/, 3/Beaulieu Infantry Regiment #58 (1,791)
  Erzherzog Ferdinand Hussar Regiment #3 (6) (785)
  6pdr Brigade Battery (6 guns)
1st Line Division: Feldmarschall-lieutenant Mayer
Brigade: Generalmajor Haugwitz
  1/, 2/, 3/A. Liechtenstein Infantry Regiment #12
    (3,021)
  1/, 2/Koburg Infantry Regiment #22 (1,937)
  6pdr Brigade Battery (6 guns)
Brigade: Generalmajor de Best
  1/, 2/Erzherzog Karl Infantry Regiment #3 (2,104)
  1/, 2/Kerpen Infantry Regiment #49 (2,206)
  6pdr Brigade Battery (6 guns)
Brigade: Generalmajor Czerwenka
  1/, 2/Saint Julien Infantry Regiment #61 (1,597)
  1/, 2/Vacquant Infantry Regiment #62 (1,390)
  6pdr Brigade Battery (6 guns)
2nd Line Division: Feldmarschall-lieutenant Hohenlohe-Bartenstein
Brigade: Generalmajor Schaffer
  1/, 2/J. Colloredo Infantry Regiment #57 (2,048)
  1/, 2/Zach Infantry Regiment #15 (2,159)
  6pdr Brigade Battery (6 guns)
Brigade: Generalmajor F. Splenyi
  1/, 2/Württemberg Infantry Regiment #40 (2,021)
  1/, 2/Lindenau Infantry Regiment #29 (2,155)
  6pdr Brigade Battery (6 guns)

Cavalry Division:
Brigade: Generalmajor Kuttalek
  Albert Cuirassier Regiment #3 (4) (609)
  Lothringen Cuirassier Regiment #7 (4) (628)
Artillery Reserve
  1 Cavalry Battery (6 guns)
  2 6pdr Position Batteries
  3 12pdr Position Batteries
  1 Pioneer Company
Other
  Medical Troops (532)
  Staff Infantry (248)

Russian-Prussian Troops:
  Commander-in-Chief: General of Infantry Barclay
    de Tolly
  Chief of Staff: Generallieutenant Sabanejev
  General Quartermaster: Generalmajor Diebitsch II
  Chief of Artillery: Generallieutenant Jachwill
  General-Intendant: Generalmajor Kankerin
  Chief of Engineers: Generalmajor Count Sievers
  General of the Day: Generalmajor Oldekop

Attached to Army Headquarters of Barclay de Tolly
  3rd Bug Cossack Regiment
  Tabunzikov Don Cossack Regiment
  Kireva Don Cossack Regiment
  1st Tula Cossack Opolochenie Regiment

Right Wing: General of Cavalry Count Wittgenstein
Attached to Headquarters of Count Wittgenstein
  Ingermannland Dragoon Regiment (3)
  2nd Bug Cossack Regiment
  Olonetz Opolochenie Battalion
  Vologda Opolochenie Battalion

Advanced Guard: Generalmajor Roth
  20th Jager Regiment (3) (1,762)
  21st Jager Regiment (1) (570)
  24th Jager Regiment (2) (1,370)
  25th Jager Regiment (2) (1,362)
  26th Jager Regiment (2) (1,418)
  Selenginsk Infantry Regiment (2) (800)
  Light Battery #6 (12 guns) (186)

1st Russian Corps: Generallieutenant Count Gortschakov
5th Division: Generalmajor Mezentzov
Brigade: Generalmajor Lukov
  Perm Infantry Regiment (2) (1,390)
  Mohilev Infantry Regiment (2) (1,524)
  23rd Jager Regiment (2) (1,450)
Brigade: Generalmajor Vlassov
  Kalouga Infantry Regiment (2) (1,343)
  Sieversk Infantry Regiment (2) (1,212)
Artillery:
  Position Battery #3 (12 guns) (256)
  Light Battery #7 (12 guns) (196)

Left Wing: Generallieutenant von Kleist
II Prussian Corps: Generallieutenant von Kleist
9th Brigade: Generalmajor von Klüx
Brigade: Oberstlieutenant von Schumalensee 1/, 2/,
  Fus/lst West Prussian Infantry Regiment (2,379)
1/, 2/, 3/6th Reserve Infantry Regiment (2,116)
1/, 2/Silesian Schützen Battalion (383)
1/, 2/, 3/, 4/7th Silesian Landwehr Infantry Regt
  (2,481)
Attached:
1/, 3/Nieumärk Dragoon Regiment (310)
1/,2/1st Silesian Landwehr Cavalry Regiment (217)
6pdr Foot Battery #7 (8 guns) (135)
10th Brigade: Generalmajor Pirch I
Brigade: Oberstlieutenant von Jagow
1/, 2/, Fus/2nd West Prussian Infantry Regiment
  (2,550)
1/, 2/, 3/7th Reserve Infantry Regiment (2,404)
1/, 2/, 3/, 4/9th Silesian Landwehr Infantry Regt
  (2,468)
Attached:
2/, 4/Neumärk Dragoon Regiment (252)
3/, 4/1st Silesian Landwehr Cavalry Regiment (222)
6pdr Foot Battery #8 (8 guns) (128)
11th Brigade: Generalmajor Ziethen
Brigade: Oberstlieutenant von Carnall
1/, 2/, Fus/lst Silesian Infantry Regiment (2,504)
1/, 2/, 3/10th Reserve Infantry Regiment (2,364)
3/, 4/Silesian Schützen Battalion (394)
1/, 2/, 3/, 4/8th Silesian Landwehr Infantry Regt
  (2,400)
Attached:
1/, 2/, 3/, 4/1st Silesian Hussar Regiment (648)
1/, 2/2nd Silesian Landwehr Cavalry Regiment
  (300)
6pdr Foot Battery #9 (8 guns) (133)
**12th Brigade: Generallieutenant Prince August
von Preussen**
Brigade: Oberstlieutenant von Funk
1/, 2/, Fus/2nd Silesian Infantry Regiment (2,369)
1/, 2/, 3/11th Reserve Infantry Regiment (2,347)
1/, 2/, 3/, 4/10th Silesian Landwehr Infantry Regt
  (2,094)
Attached:
3/, 4/2nd Silesian Landwehr Cavalry Regiment
  (228)
6pdr Foot Battery #13 (8 guns) (134)
Cavalry Reserve: Generalmajor von Röder
Brigade: Oberst von Wrangel
1/, 2/, 3/, 4/East Prussian Cuirassier Regiment (623)
1/, 2/, 3/, 4/Silesian Cuirassier Regiment (589)
1/, 2/, 3/, 4/Brandenburg Cuirassier Regiment (671)
Brigade: Oberst Laroche von Starkenfels
1/, 2/, 3/, 4/Silesian Uhlan Regiment (577)
1/, 2/Silesian National Cavalry Regiment (189)
1/, 2/2nd Silesian Hussar Regiment (319)
Brigade: Oberst von Mutius
1/, 2/, 3/, 4/7th Silesian Landwehr Cavalry
  Regiment (562)

1/, 2/, 3/, 4/8th Silesian Landwehr Cavalry
  Regiment (435)
Artillery:
Horse Battery #7 (8 guns) (139)
Horse Battery #8 (8 guns) (143)
Reserve Artillery: Major von Lehmann I
12pdr Foot Battery #3 (8 guns) (176)
12pdr Foot Battery #6 (8 guns) (205)
6pdr Foot Battery #8 (8 guns) (131)
6pdr Foot Battery #14 (8 guns) (140)
6pdr Foot Battery #21 (8 guns) (159)
7pdr Howitzer Battery #1 (8 guns) (163)
Horse Battery #9 (8 guns) (135)
Horse Battery #10 (8 guns) (142)
Munition Column #7
Munition Column #8
Munition Column #9
Munition Column #10
Munition Column #11
Total munitions columns – 203
6th Field Pioneer Company (77)
7th Field Pioneer Company (78)

Russian-Prussian Guard & Reserves:
Commander-in-Chief: Grand Duke Constantine
Chief of Staff: Generalmajor Kurutta
Quartermaster: Colonel Baron Crossard
General du Jour: Generalmajor Patepov

Infantry Forces: General of Infantry Miloradovich
Chief of Staff: Colonel Sipaegin
Quartermaster: Colonel Niedhardt II

3rd (Grenadier) Corps: Generalmajor Raevsky
1st Division: Generalmajor Tschoglokov
Brigade: Generalmajor Zwielikov
Ekaterinoslav Grenadier Regiment (2) (1,209)
Count Arakchevev Grenadier Regiment (2) (1,225)
Brigade: Colonel Acht
Tauride Grenadier Regiment (2) (1,179)
St. Petersburg Grenadier Regiment (2) (1,189)
Brigade: Colonel Yemelianov
Pernau Grenadier Regiment (2) (1,171)
Kexholm Grenadier Regiment (2) (1,234)
Artillery:
Position Battery #33 (12 guns) (250)
Light Battery #14 (12 guns) (132)

5th (Guard) Corps:
2nd Guard Division: Generalmajor Udom I
Brigade: Colonel Krishanovsky
Lithuanian Guard Infantry Regiment (3) (865)
Finland Guard Infantry Regiment (3) (1,349)
Brigade: Generalmajor Scheltuchin II
Leib-Garde Guard Infantry Regiment (2) (1,349)
Pavlov Guard Grenadier Regiment (2) (1,222)
Artillery: Generalmajor Euler
Guard Light Battery #2 (12 guns) (175)
Prussian Guard Brigade: Oberstlieutenant von

Alvensleben
1/, 2/, Fus/1st Garde zu Fuss Regiment (2,617)
1/, 2/, Fus/2nd Garde zu Fuss Regiment (2,330)
1/, 2/Garde Jager Battalion (399)
6pdr Guard Foot Battery #4 (8 guns) (139)

Cavalry Forces: Grand Duke Constantine
Reserve Cavalry Corps: GL Count Gallitzin V
1st Cuirassier Division: Generalmajor
 Depreradovich
Brigade: Generalmajor Arseniev
 Chevalier Guard Regiment (6) (757)
 Horse Guard Regiment (6) (814)
Brigade: Generalmajor Baron Rosen
 Leibgarde Cuirassier Regiment (3) (409)
Artillery: Generalmajor Kosen (389 men)
 Guard Horse Battery #1 (8 guns)
 Guard Horse Battery #2 (8 guns)
2nd Cuirassier Division: Generalmajor Kretov
Brigade: Generalmajor Leontiev
 Gluchov Cuirassier Regiment (5) (617)
 Pskov Cuirassier Regiment (3) (510)
Brigade: Generalmajor Karatiev
 Astrakhan Cuirassier Regiment (3) (378)
 Ekaterinoslav Cuirassier Regiment (3) (355)
3rd Cuirassier Division: Generalmajor Duka
Brigade: Generalmajor Gudovich
 Military Order Cuirassier Regiment (4) (520)
 Little Russia Cuirassier Regiment (4) (571)
Brigade: Generalmajor Levaschoff
 Novgorod Cuirassier Regiment (4) (484)
 Starodoub Cuirassier Regiment (4) (571)
Guard Light Cavalry Division: Generalmajor
 Chevich
Brigade: Generalmajor Tchailikov
 Guard Hussar Regiment (6) (713)
 Guard Dragoon Regiment (6) (677)
Attached: Generalmajor Orlov-Denisov
 Don Guard Cossack Regiment (4) (475)
Cossack Brigade: Generalmajor Illowaiski XII
 Ataman Cossack Regiment (796)
 Illowaiski #12 Cossack Regiment (457)
 Rebrejev #3 Cossack Regiment (382)
 Don Cossack Horse Artillery Company #1 (12
 guns) (167)
Prussian Guard Cavalry Brigade: Oberst von
 Werder
1/, 2/, 3/, 4/, Cossack/Garde du Corps Regiment
 (683)
1/, 2/, 3/, 4/, 1Jag,2Jag//Leichtes Garde-Kavallerie-
 Regiment (790)
 Guard Horse Battery #4 (8 guns) (133)
Reserve Artillery: Generalmajor Hüne
 Guard Position Battery #1 (12 guns) (281)
 Position Battery #1 (12 guns) (259)
 Position Battery #14 (12 guns) (266)
 Position Battery #29 (12 guns) (223)
 Position Battery #30 (12 guns) (232)
 Guard Marine Artillery (2 guns) (29)

 Horse Battery #1 (2 guns) (57)
 Horse Battery #3 (12 guns) (172)
 Horse Battery #23 (12 guns) (266)
 Horse Battery #10 (6 guns) (98)
 Engineers (289 men)
 Pioneer Company of Captain Zotov
 Pioneer Company of Colonel Miller
 Pioneer Company of Captain Gerua
Headquarters Staff Guard:
 Platov #4 Don Cossack Regiment
 Popov #3 Don Cossack Regiment

Detached Units:
Escort Intendant-General: Generalmajor Kankerin
 Little Russia Opolochenie Cossack Regiment
 Tschernigov Opolochenie Cossack Regiment
 2nd Pultava Opolochenie Cossack Regiment
Transporting Prisoners:
 2nd Bashkir Regiment
 11th Bashkir Regiment

Army Detachment: Generallieutenant
 Osterman-Tolstoy
(by Pirna & Königstein – facing Vandamme):
Cavalry Brigade: Generalmajor Prinz L. Saxe-Coburg
 Empress Cuirassier Regiment (4) (448)
 Guard Uhlan Regiment (6) (680)
 Tartar Uhlan Regiment (6) (552)
 Olivopol Hussar Regiment (2) (283)

5th (Guard Corps): Generallieutenant Yermolov
1st Guard Infantry Division: Generalmajor Baron
 Rosen
Brigade: Generalmajor Potemkin
 Preobragenski Guard Infantry Regiment (3) (1,793)
 Semenovski Guard Infantry Regiment (3) (1,826)
Brigade: Generalmajor Krapovitzskv
 Ismailov Guard Infantry Regiment (3) (1,759)
 Guard Jager Regiment (3) (1,751)
 Guard Equipage Battalion (1) (596)
Artillery:
 Guard Position Battery #2 (12 guns) (269)
 Guard Light Battery #1 (12 guns) (188)
14th Division: Generalmajor Helfreich
Brigade: Generalmajor Laelin
 Tenguinsk Infantry Regiment (2) (1,182)
 Estonia Infantry Regiment (2) (1,249)
 Grand Duchess Catherine Battalion (1) (503)
Artillery:
 Light Battery #6 (6 guns)

2nd Corps: Generallieutenant Prince Eugen von
 Württemberg
3rd Division: Generalmajor Schachafskoy
Brigade: Colonel Salfinski
 Revel Infantry Regiment (2) (1,013)
 4th Jager Regiment (2) (1,501)
Brigade: Colonel Baron Wolff
 Mourman Infantry Regiment (2) (1,203)

Tschernigov Infantry Regiment (2) (1,250)
4th Division; Generalmajor Pischnitzky
Brigade: Colonel Treffurt
  Tobolsk Infantry Regiment (2) (983)
  Minsk Infantry Regiment (2) (581)
Brigade: Colonel Mononov
  Volhynie Infantry Regiment (2) (771)
  Krementchug Infantry Regiment (2) (1,050)
Brigade: Colonel Volkov II
  34th Jager Regiment (1) (484)
Artillery: Colonel von Wachten
  Position Battery #5 (12 guns) (267)
  Light Battery #13 (12 guns) (191)
  Light Battery #27 (12 guns) (178)

Cavalry Corps: Generallieutenant Count Pahlen III
Uhlan Brigade: Generalmajor Lisanevic
  Tchougouiev Uhlan Regiment (6) (925)
  Serpuchov Uhlan Regiment (4) (463)
Cossack Brigade:
  Rabinov #2 Cossack Regiment (396)
  Jagodin #2 Don Cossack Regiment (362)
  Gorin #2 Don Cossack Regiment (399)
  Illowaiski #10 Don Cossack Regiment (443)
1st Hussar Division: Generalmajor Milesinov
Brigade: Generalmajor Rudinger
  Grodno Hussar Regiment (6) (872)
  Soum Hussar Regiment (7) (816)
Brigade: Colonel Schufanov
  Loubnv Hussar Regiment (4) (659)
Corps Artillery
  Horse Battery #6 (8 guns) (172)
  Horse Battery #7 (12 guns) (266)
Attached:
  Kanatcikov Pioneer Company (73)

Detached Force facing Zittau & Frontier Border
2nd Light Division: Feldmarschall-lieutenant Bubna
Brigade: Generalmajor Graf Klebelsberg
  6th Jäger Battalion (629)
  1/Peterswardeiner Grenz Regiment #9 (1,255)
  Liechtenstein Hussar Regiment #7 (6) (657)
Brigade: Generalmajor Graf Neipperg
  5th Jäger Battalion (531)
  Kaiser Hussar Regiment #1 (6) (697)
  Blankenstein Hussar Regiment #6 (6) (661)
  2 6pdr Cavalry Batteries (12 guns)

Detached Force at Melnik & Prague
2nd Grenadier Division: Generalmajor Sulima
Brigade: Generalmajor Zwielinov
  Kiev Grenadier Regiment (2) (1,132)
  Moscow Grenadier Regiment (2) (1,096)
Brigade: Colonel Baron de Damas
  Astrakhan Grenadier Regiment (2) (1,024)
  Fangoria Grenadier Regiment (2) (1,166)
Brigade: Colonel Hesse

Siberia Grenadier Regiment (2) (1,192)
Little Russian Grenadier Regiment (2) (1,146)

Fabry, G. Journal des Campagnes du Prince du Wurtemberg. Paris: Librairie Militaire R. Chapelot et Cie, 1907.
Friederich, R. Geschichte des Herbstfeldzuges 1813. 3 vols. Berlin: Ernst Siegfried Mittler and Sohn, 1904.
Plotho, C. Der Kreig in Deutschland and Frankreich in den Jahren 1813 and 1814. Vol II. Berlin: Carl Friedrich, 1817.
Prussian General Staff. Plane der Schlachten and Treffen welche von der preussischen Armee in den feldzügen der Jahre 1813, 14, and 15 geliesert worden. Vol II. Berlin: G.Reimer, 1821. von Quistorp, B. Geschichte der Nord Armée im Jahre 1813. Berlin: E.S.Mittler and Sohn, 1894.
Simon, G. Die Kriegeserignisse zzvischen Teplitz and Pirna in August and September des Jahres 1813. Die Schlacht bei Kulm am 29. and 30. August 1813 and das Gefecht bei Arbesau am 17. September 1813; Nach verlaszlichen Quellen Bearbeitet. Teplitz-Schönau: Emil Seewald, 1911.

XIV
FRENCH FORCES

Imperial Guard: Maréchal Mortier (58,191 men)
Old Guard:
1st Division: Général de division Friant
Brigade: Général de brigade Michel
  1/, 2/1st Grenadier à Pied Regiment (1,505)
  1/, 2/2nd Grenadier à Pied Regiment (1,253)
  Velites of Turin Battalion (295)
  Velites of Florence Battalion (195)
Brigade: Général de division Curial
  1/, 2/1st Chasseur à Pied Regiment (1,575)
  1/, 2/2nd Chasseur à Pied Regiment (1,130)
Artillery:
  1st Old Guard Foot Battery (6–6pdrs & 2–5.7" howitzer)

Young Guard: Maréchal Mortier
1st Division: Général de division Dumoustier
  Wounded on 8/26 and replaced by Général de division Curial
Brigade: Colonel Rousseau
  1/, 2/Fusilier-Chasseur Regiment
  1/, 2/Fusilier-Grenadier Regiment
Brigade: Général de brigade Tindal
  1/, 2/1st Voltigeur Regiment
  1/, 2/2nd Voltigeur Regiment
Brigade: Colonel Couloumy
  1/, 2/3rd Voltigeur Regiment
  1/, 2/6th Voltigeur Regiment
  1/, 2/7th Voltigeur Regiment
Artillery:

1st Young Guard Battery (6–6pdrs & 2–5.7"
 howitzer)
2nd Young Guard Battery (6–6pdrs & 2–5.7"
 howitzer)
8th Young Guard Battery (6–6pdrs & 2–5.7"
 howitzer)
2nd Division: Général de division Barrois
Brigade: Général de brigade Rottembourg (LtC.
Vionnet)
 1/, 2/1st Tirailleur Regiment
 1/, 2/2nd Tirailleur Regiment
Brigade: Général de brigade Poret de Morvan
 1/, 2/3rd Tirailleur Regiment
 1/, 2/6th Tirailleur Regiment
 1/, 2/7th Tirailleur Regiment
Brigade: Général de brigade Boyeldieu
 1/, 2/Flanqueur-Chasseur Regiment
 1/, 2/Flanqueur-Grenadier Regiment
Artillery:
 3rd Young Guard Battery (6–6pdrs & 2–5.7"
 howitzer)
 4th Young Guard Battery (6–6pdrs & 2–5.7"
 howitzer)
 12th Young Guard Battery (6–6pdrs & 2–5.7"
 howitzer)
3rd Division: Général de division Delaborde
 Wounded on 8/25, replaced by Decouz
Brigade: General de brigade
 1/, 2/4th Voltigeur Regiment
 1/, 2/5th Voltigeur Regiment
Brigade: Général de brigade Combelle
 1/, 2/8th Voltigeur Regiment
 1/, 2/9th Voltigeur Regiment
 1/, 2/10th Voltigeur Regiment
Artillery:
 5th Young Guard Battery (6–6pdrs & 2–5.7"
 howitzer)
 6th Young Guard Battery (6–6pdrs & 2–5.7"
 howitzer)
 7th Young Guard Battery (6–6pdrs & 2–5.7"
 howitzer)
4th Division: Général de division Roguet
Brigade: Général de brigade Boyer de Rebeval
 1/, 2/4th Tirailleur Regiment
 1/, 2/5th Tirailleur Regiment
Brigade: Général de brigade Pelet
 1/, 2/8th Tirailleur Regiment
 1/, 2/9th Tirailleur Regiment
 1/, 2/10th Tirailleur Regiment
Artillery:
 9th Young Guard Battery (6–6pdrs & 2–5.7"
 howitzer)
 10th Young Guard Battery (6–6pdrs & 2–5.7"
 howitzer)
 11th Young Guard Battery (6–6pdrs & 2–5.7"
 howitzer)

Guard Cavalry: Général de division Nansouty
1st Division: Général de division Ornano
 1/, 3/, 4/, 5/Berg Lancer Regiment
 1/, 2/, 3/, 4/, 5/, 6/, 7/, 8/, 9/, 10/2nd Guard Lancer
 Regt
 5/, 6/Empress Dragoon Regiment
**2nd Division: Général de division
Lefevre-Desnouëttes**
 1/, 2/, 3/, 4/, 5/, 6/, 7/1st Guard Lancer Regiment
 7/, 8/, 9/, 10/Guard Chasseur à Cheval Regiment
 5/, 6/Guard Grenadiers à Cheval Regiment
3rd Division: Général de division Walther
 1/2/1st Gardes d'Honneur
 1/, 2/2nd Gardes d'Honneur
 1/3rd Gardes d'Honneur
 1/4th Gardes d'Honneur
 1/, 2/, 3/, 4/Empress Dragoon Regiment
 1/, 2/, 3/, 4/Guard Grenadiers à Cheval Regiment
 1/, 2/, 3/, 4/, 5/, 6/Guard Chasseur à Cheval
 Regiment
Artillery:
 1st Old Guard Horse Battery (4–6pdrs & 2–5.7"
 howitzer)
 2nd Old Guard Horse Battery (4–6pdrs & 2–5.7"
 howitzer)
 3rd Old Guard Horse Battery (4–6pdrs & 2–5.7"
 howitzer)
 4th Old Guard Horse Battery (4–6pdrs & 2–5.7"
 howitzer)

Guard Reserve Artillery:
 2nd Old Guard Foot Battery (6–6pdrs & 2–5.7"
 howitzer)
 3rd Old Guard Foot Battery (6–12pdrs & 2–6"
 howitzer)
 4th Old Guard Foot Battery (6–12pdrs & 2–6"
 howitzer)
 5th Old Guard Foot Battery (6–12pdrs & 2–6"
 howitzer)
 6th Old Guard Foot Battery (6–12pdrs & 2–6"
 howitzer)
 14th Young Guard Battery (6–6pdrs & 2–5.7"
 howitzer)
 5th Old Guard Horse Battery (4–6pdrs & 2–5.7"
 howitzer)
 6th Old Guard Horse Battery (4–6pdrs & 2–5.7"
 howitzer)
 Berg Foot Battery (4–6pdrs & 2–5.7" howitzer)
 Sappers of the Guard (159)
 2/5th Sapper Battalion (23)
 3/7th Sapper Battalion (47)
 3/Guard Marine Battalion (111)
 Pontooneers (1 co)
 Total Guard Artillery – 218 guns

I CORPS
23rd Division: Général de division Teste
Brigade: Général de brigade O'Meara
1/, 2/, 3/, 4/21st Line Regiment
1/, 2/, 3/, 4/33rd Line Regiment
Artillery:
21/4th Foot Artillery (6–6pdrs & 2–24pdr howitzers)
Det. 1/9th Principal Train Battalion
Det. 1/1st (bis) Train Battalion

II Corps: Maréchal Victor (25,158 men)
4th Division: Général de division Dubreton
Brigade: Général de brigade Ferrière
1/, 2/, 4/24th Légère Regiment
1/, 2/, 4/19th Line Regiment
Brigade: Général de brigade Brun
1/, 2/, 4/37th Line Regiment
1/, 2/, 4/56th Line Regiment
Artillery:
7/2nd Foot Artillery (6–6pdrs & 2–24pdr howitzers)
11/4th Foot Artillery (6–6pdrs & 2–24pdr howitzers)
2/3rd (bis) Train Battalion
Det. 1/11th Principal Train Battalion
3/12th Principal Train Battalion
Det. 1/14th Principal Train Battalion (0/11)
5th Division: Général de division Dufour
Brigade: Général de brigade d'Estko
1/, 2/, 4/26th Légère Regiment
1/, 2/, 4/93rd Line Regiment
Artillery:
13/5th Foot Artillery (6–6pdrs & 2–24pdr howitzers)
12/8th Foot Artillery (6–6pdrs & 2–24pdr howitzers)
Det. 4th Principal Train Battalion
Det. 3/11th (bis) Train Battalion
Det. 12th Principal Train Battalion
6th Division: Général de division Vial
Brigade: Général de brigade Valorv
1/, 2/, 4/11th Légère Regiment
1/, 2/, 4/2nd Line Regiment
Brigade: Général de brigade Bronikowski
1/, 2/, 4/4th Line Regiment
1/, 2/, 4/18th Line Regiment
Artillery:
25/3rd Foot Artillery (6–6pdrs & 2–24pdr howitzers)
26/3rd Foot Artillery (6–6pdrs & 2–24pdr howitzers)
Det. 3/1st (bis) Train Battalion
Det. 1/11th (his) Train Battalion
Det. 4/11th (bis) Train Battalion
3/14th Principal Train Battalion
Ambulance (0/12)
22nd Light Cavalry Brigade: Oberst Hammerstein
1/1st Westphalian Hussar Regiment

2/2nd Westphalian Hussar Regiment
Artillery Reserve:
10/6th Foot Artillery (8–12pdr cannons)
2/14th Principal Train Battalion
1/2nd Horse Battery (4–6pdrs & 2–24pdr howitzers)
Det. 2/11th (bis) Train
Det. 3/11th (bis) Train
2/2nd Sapper Battalion
3/3rd Sapper Battalion
3/5th Sapper Battalion
Artillery Park:
9/2nd Foot Artillery
Det. 3/3rd (bis) Train Battalion
Det. 3rd (bis) Train Battalion
Det. 4th Principal Train Battalion
Det. 4/8th Principal Train Battalion
2/9th Princpal Train Battalion
Det. 11th Principal Train Battalion
Det. 7/11th Principal Train Battalion
Det. 2/14th Principal Train Battalion

VI Corps: Maréchal Marmont, Duke of Ragusa
20th Division: Général de division Compans
1st Brigade: Général de brigade Pelleport
2/, 3/32nd Légère Regiment
1/, 2/, 3/, 4/5/1st Marine Regiment
2nd Brigade: Général de brigade Joubert
20th Regiment Provisoire
5/66rd Line Regiment
3/122th Line Regiment
25th Regiment Provisoire
3/47th Line Regiment
3/86th Line Regiment
1/, 2/, 3/3rd Marine Regiment
Artillery: Chef de bataillon Ocler
16/5th Foot Artillery (6–6pdrs & 2 howitzers)
10/8th Foot Artillery (6–6pdrs & 2 howitzers)
Det. 7/4th (bis) Train Battalion
Det. 4/1st (bis) Train Battalion
21st Division: Général de division Lagrange
1st Brigade: Général de brigade Jamin
1/, 2/, 3/, 4/37th Légère Regiment
1/, 2/, 3/4th Marine Regiment
1/Joseph Napoleon Regiment
2nd Brigade: Général de brigade Buquet
1/, 2/, 3/, 4/, 5/, 6/2nd Marine Regiment
Artillery: Chef de bataillon Picard
10/4th Foot Artillery (6–6pdrs & 2 howitzers)
18/5th Foot Artillery (6–6pdrs & 2 howitzers)
Det. 1/8th Principal Train Battalion
Det. 2/8th Principal Train Battalion
Det. 1/10th (bis) Train Battalion
22nd Division: Général de division Frederichs
1st Brigade: Général de brigade Coehom
11th Regiment Provisoire
4/1st Line Regiment
2/62nd Line Regiment
13th Regiment Provisoire

3/14th Line Regiment
4/16th Line Regiment
3/, 4/23rd Légère Regiment
3/, 4/15th Line Regiment
2nd Brigade: Général de brigade Bachelet
16th Regiment Provisoire
6/26th Line Regiment
6/82nd Line Regiment
3/, 4/121st Line Regiment
3/, 4/70th Line Regiment
Artillery:
14/4th Foot Artillery (6–6pdrs & 2 howitzers)
22/9th Foot Artillery (6–6pdrs & 2 howitzers)
3/8th Principal Train Battalion
2/10th (his) Train Battalion
25th Light Cavalry Brigade: Général de brigade Normann
1–4/2nd Württemberg Chevauléger Regiment
1–4/4th Württemberg Chevauléger Regiment
3rd Württemberg Horse Battery "Bruhaupt"
(4–6pdrs & 2 7pdr howitzers)
Reserve and Park: Chef de bataillon Moran
3/5th Foot Artillery (no guns)
18/5th Foot Artillery (6–12pdrs & 2–6" howitzers)
26/5th Foot Artillery (6–12pdrs & 2–6' howitzers)
1/1st Horse Battery (4–6pdrs & 2 how)
3/4th Horse Battery (4–6pdrs & 2 how)
Det. 4/12th Principal Train Battalion
4/6th (bis) Train Battalion
6/6th (bis) Train Battalion
7/6th (bis) Train Battalion
7/10th (bis) Train Battalion
6/2nd Sapper Battalion
2/4th Sapper Battalion
9/4th Sapper Battalion
4/7th Sapper Battalion
Imperial Gendarmes

XIV Corps: Maréchal St. Cyr (26,149 men)
43rd Division: Général de division Claperède
Brigade: Général de brigade Godard
2/, 3/27th Légère Regiment
3/29th Légère Regiment
2/, 3/, 4/100th Line Regiment
Brigade: Général de brigade Butrand
2/, 3/45th Line Regiment
3/65th Line Regiment
2/, 4/103rd Line Regiment
21st Provisional Demi-brigade
2/59th Line Regiment
3/94th Line Regiment
Artillery:
2/7th Foot Artillery (6–6pdrs & 2–24pdr howitzers)
4/6th Foot Artillery (6–6pdrs & 2–24pdr howitzers)
Det. 4/10th Principal Train Battalion
Det. 6/12th Principal Train Battalion
Det. 6/1st (bis) Train Battalion

Det. 7/1st (bis) Train Battalion
44th Division: Général de division Berthezène
Brigade: Général de brigade Paillard
1/, 3/8th Légère Regiment
3/, 4/64th Line Regiment
34th Provisional Demi-brigade
2/16th Légère Regiment
1/18th Légère Regiment
Brigade: Général de brigade Letellier
19th Provisional Demi-brigade
2/50th Line Regiment
2/75th Line Regiment
Provisional Demi-brigade
3/24th Line Regiment
3/39th Line Regiment
Provisional Demi-brigade
3/54th Line Regiment
3/95rd Line Regiment
Artillery:
4/1st Foot Artillery (6–6pdrs & 2–24pdr howitzers)
15/7th Foot Artillery (6–6pdrs & 2–24pdr howitzers)
Det. 7/1st (bis) Train Battalion
Det. 3/11th Principal Train Battalion
Det. 6/12th Principal Train Battalion
45th Division: Général de division Razout
Brigade: Général de brigade Goguet
3/6th Légère Regiment
26th Provisional Demi-brigade
3/5th Line Regiment
3/11th Line Regiment
Provisional Demi-brigade
3/8th Line Regiment
2/28th Line Regiment
Brigade: Général de brigade d'Esclevin
Provisional Demi-brigade
4/32nd Line Regiment
4/58th Line Regiment
7th Provisional Demi-brigade
3/79th Line Regiment
6/81st Line Regiment
18th Provisional Demi-brigade
6/34th Line Regiment
3/69th Line Regiment
4/60th Line Regiment
Artillery:
21/5th Foot Artillery (6–6pdrs & 2–24pdr howitzers)
Det. 5/12th Principal Train Battalion
Det. 4/11th Principal Train Battalion
Reserves and Grand Park
15/7th Foot Artillery (6–12pdrs & 2–24pdr howitzers)
5/6th Foot Artillery (6–12pdrs & 2–24pdr howitzers)
5/2nd Horse Artillery (4–6pdrs & 2–24pdr howitzers)
3/6th Horse Artillery (4–6pdrs & 2–24pdr howitzers)

5/3rd Pontooneer Battalion
8/2nd Sapper Battalion
5/4th Sapper Battalion
6/4th Sapper Battalion
7/4th Sapper Battalion
4/10th (bis) Train Battalion
Det. 3/4th Principal Train Battalion
Det. 6/4th Principal Train Battalion
Det. 3/1st (bis) Train Battalion
Engineering Train Detachment
Equipage Train Detachment
10th Light Cavalry Divison: Général de division Pajol
16th Light Cavalry Brigade: Général de brigade Jacquet
  1/, 2,3/, 4/14th Hussar Regiment
  1/, 2/, 3/, 4/2nd Italian Chasseur à Cheval Regiment
31st Light Cavalry Brigade: Général de brigade Stedmann
  1/, 2,3/, 4/7th Chevauléger-lancier Regiment

I Cavalry Corps: Latour-Marbourg (16,537 men) (at Pirna)
3rd Light Division: Général de division Chastel
4th Light Cavalry Brigade: Général de brigade Vallin
  1/, 2/, 3/1st Chasseur à Cheval Regiment
  1/, 2/, 3/, 4/19th Chasseur à Cheval Regiment
5rd Light Cavalry Brigade: Général de brigade Van Merlen
  1/, 2/8th Chasseur à Cheval Regiment
  1/, 2/9th Chasseur à Cheval Regiment
  1/, 2/25th Chasseur à Cheval Regiment
1st Heavy Division: General de divison Bordesoulle
Brigade: Général de brigade Berckheim
  1/, 2/2nd Cuirassier Regiment
  1/, 2/3rd Cuirassier Regiment
  1/, 2/6th Cuirassier Regiment
Brigade: Général de brigade Bessières
  1/, 2/, 3/9th Cuirassier Regiment
  1/, 2/, 3/11th Cuirassier Regiment
  1/, 2/12th Cuirassier Regiment
Brigade: Generalmajor von Lessing
  1/, 2/, 3/, 4/Saxon Garde du Corps
  1/, 2/, 3/, 4/Saxon Zastrow Cuirassier Regiment
3rd Heavy Division: Général de division Doumerc
Brigade: Général de brigade d'Audenarde
  1/, 2/, 3/4th Cuirassier Regiment
  1/, 2/, 3/7th Cuirassier Regiment
  1/, 2/, 3/14th Cuirassier Regiment
  1/, 2/, 3/, 4/Italian Napoleon Dragoon Regiment
Brigade: Général de brigade Reiset
  1/, 2/7th Dragoon Regiment
  1/, 2/, 3/23rd Dragoon Regiment
  1/, 2/28th Dragoon Regiment
  1/, 2/30th Dragoon Regiment
Corps Artillery:
  3/1st Horse Artillery (4–6pdrs & 2–24pdr Howitzers)

  6/3rd Horse Artillery (4–6pdrs & 2–24pdr Howitzers)
  1/4th Horse Artillery (4–6pdrs & 2–24pdr Howitzers)
  1/6th Horse Artillery (4–6pdrs & 2–24pdr Howitzers)
  1st Westphalian Horse Artillery "Wissel" (4–6pdrs & 2–24pdr Howitzers)
  4th Saxon Horse Battery (4–6pdrs & 2–24pdr Howitzers)
  Det. 4/9th Principal Train Battalion
  1/1st (bis) Train Battalion
  2/1st (bis) Train Battalion
  2/8th (bis) Train Battalion
  Det. 5/8th (bis) Train Battalion
  1st Saxon Train Battalion
  Westphalian Train Battalion

V Cavalry Corps: Général de division l'Heritier (3,000)
9th Light Cavalry Division: Général de brigade Klicky
33rd Light Cavalry Brigade:
  3/, 4/14th Chasseur à Cheval Regiment (14/284)
  3/, 4/26th Chasseur à Cheval Regiment (13/230)
5th Dragoon Division: Général de brigade Collaert
Brigade:
  3/2nd Dragoon Regiment (11/148)
  3/, 4/6th Dragoon Regiment (19/246)
Brigade:
  3/, 4/11th Dragoon Regiment 10/156)
  3/13th Dragoon Regiment (10/154)
  3/15th Dragoon Regiment (11/147)
6th Dragoon Division: Général de brigade Lamotte
Brigade:
  3/18th Dragoon Regiment (2/40)
  3/19th Dragoon Regiment (3/31)
  3/20th Dragoon Regiment (7/150)
Brigade:
  3/22nd Dragoon Regiment (8/172)
  3/25th Dragoon Regiment (11/190)
Artillery:
  5/2nd Horse Artillery (4–6pdrs & 2 Howitzers) (3/94)
  5/11th Principal Train Battalion (1/71)
  5/4th Principal Train Battalion (unknown)

Dresden Garrison: (strengths as of 22 August)
Brigade: Général de brigade Gros
  1/, 2/11th Voltigeur Regiment (1,304)
  1/, 2/11th Tirailleur Regiment (1,395)
  13th Young Guard Foot Battery (6–6pdrs & 2–5.7" how)
Brigade: Général de brigade Bernard
  1st Westphalian Light Battalion (580)
  1/, 2/3rd Westphlian Line Regiment (1,125)
  Westphalian Foot Battery "Orges" (129)
  Westphalian Train (113)

Attached:
  2/Saxon Guard Grenadier Regiment (614)
  Saxon Foot Battery (143)
  Saxon Artillery Train (109)
  Saxon Sappers (41)
  French Sappers (830)
  French Gendarmes (55)
  Infantry Depot Battalion (715)
  Infantry Depot Battalion (890)
  Guard Depot Battalion (744)
  Cavalry Depot (4,393)
  Guard Artillery (99)
  Guard Train (103)
  French Foot Artillery (645)
  13th Young Guard Battery (6–6pdrs & 2–5.7
    howitzers)
  French Artillery Train (429)

Detached at Pirna
*I Corps: Général de division Vandamme (33,298
  men)*
1st Division: Général de division Philippon
Brigade: Général de brigade Pouchelon
  1/, 2/, 3/, 4/7th Légère Regiment
  1/, 2/, 3/, 4/12th Line Regiment
Brigade: Général de brigade Fezensac
  1/, 2/, 3/, 4/17th Line Regiment
  3/, 4/36th Légère Regiment
Artillery:
  8/2nd Foot Artillery (6–6pdrs & 2–24pdr
    howitzers)
  15/9th Foot Artillery (6–6pdrs & 2–24pdr
    howitzers)
  Det. 4th Principal Train Battalion
  3/9th Principal Train Battalion
2nd Division: Général de division Dumonceau
Brigade: Général de brigade Dunesme
  1/, 2/, 3/, 4/13th Légère Regimen
  1/, 2/, 3/, 4/25th Line Regiment
Brigade: Général de brigade Doucet
  1/, 2/, 3/, 4/57th Line Regiment
  3/, 4/51st Line Regiment
Artillery
  23/3rd Foot Artillery (6–6pdrs & 2–24pdr
    howitzers)
  24/3rd Foot Artillery (6–6pdrs & 2–24pdr
    howitzers)
  1/1st Principal Train Battalion
  Det. 2/8th (bis) Train Battalion
23rd Division
Brigade: Général de brigade Quiot
  1/, 2/, 3/, 4/85th Line Regiment
  3/, 4/55th Line Regiment
**21st Light Cavalry Brigade: Général de brigade
  Gobrecht**
  1/, 2/9th Chevauléger-lancier Regiment
  1/, 2/Anhalt Jäger zu Pferd Regiment

Reserve and Park
  9/8th Foot Artillery (6–12pdrs & 2–24pdr
    howitzers)
  6/7th Foot Artillery (6–12pdrs & 2–24pdr
    howitzers)
  2/4th Horse Artillery (4–6pdrs & 2–24pdr
    howitzers)
  5/6th Horse Artillery (4–6pdrs & 2–24pdr
    howitzers)
  5/3rd Sapper Battalion
  7/3rd Sapper Battalion
  Det. 4/7th Principal Train Battalion
  Det. 1/9th Principal Train Battalion
  2/13th (bis) Train Battalion
  Equipage Train detachment
II Corps – 5th Division
Brigade: Général de brigade Prinz Reuss
  1/, 2/, 4/46th Line Regiment
  1/, 2/, 4/72nd Line Regiment
**XIV Corps – 42nd Division: Général de division
  Mouton-Duvernet**
Brigade:
  22nd Provisional Demi-brigade
    2/4th Légère Regiment
    3/12th Légère Regiment
  4th Provisional Demi-brigade
    6/9th Légère Regiment
    3/28th Légère Regiment
  3rd Provisional Demi-brigade
    4/10th Légère Regiment
    3/21st Légère Regiment
Brigade: Général de brigade Creutzer
  17th Provisional Demi-brigade
    3/27th Line Regiment
    3/63rd Line Regiment
  16th Provisional Demi-brigade
    4/40th Line Regiment
    3/43rd Line Regiment
  2/, 3/76th Line Regiment
  2/, 3/96th Line Regiment
Artillery:
  1/7th Foot Artillery (6–6pdrs & 2–24pdr howitzers)
  9/7th Foot Artillery (6–6pdrs & 2–24pdr howitzers)
  Det. 6/16th (bis) Train Battalion
  Det. 7/16th (bis) Train Battalion
  Det. 1/6th Principal Train Battalion

I Cavalry Corps
1st Light Division: Général de division Corbineau
2nd Light Cavalry Brigade: Général de brigade
Montmarie
  1/, 2/, 3/16th Chasseur à Cheval Regiment
  1/, 2/, 3/1st Chevauléger-lancier Regiment
  1/, 2/3rd Chevauléger-lancier Regiment
3rd Light Cavalry Brigade: Général de brigade
Heimrodt
  1/, 2/, 3/5th Chevauléger-lancier Regiment
  1/, 2/8th Chevauléger-lancier Regiment
  1/, 2/, 3/, 4/1st Italian Chasseur à Cheval Regiment

V Cavalry Corps – 9th Light Cavalry Division
32nd Light Cavalry Brigade: Colonel Rosseau
  3/, 4/3rd Hussar Regiment
  3/, 4/27th Chasseur à Cheval Regiment

Detached toward Leipzig
I Cavalry Corps – 1st Cavalry Division
1st Light Cavalry Brigade: Général de brigade Pire
  1/, 2/6th Hussar Regiment
  1/, 2/, 3/7th Hussar Regiment
  1/, 2/, 3/8th Hussar Regiment

Frederichs, R. Geschichte des Herbstfeldzuges 1813. Berlin: 1903 French Archives, Cartons C² 538, 540, 543, 544 & 708

THE BATTLE OF HAGELBERG
27 AUGUST 1813

XV
PRUSSIAN FORCES

Commanding Officer: Generalmajor von Hirschfeld
Advanced Guard: Major von Langen
  1/, 2/, 3/1st Reserve Infantry Regiment
    1st Battalion – Reckow
    2nd Battalion – Lemcke
    3rd Battalion – Romig
  (all 4 battalions of 1st Reserve had 82/2,800)
Right Wing Brigade: Generalmajor von Puttlitz
  4/1st Reserve Infantry Regiment – Rembow
  1/, 2/, 3/, 4/6th Kurmärk Landwehr Regiment
  (80/2,400)
    1st Battalion – von Bonigke
    2nd Battalion – von Streit
    3rd Battalion – von Delitz
    4th Battalion – von Woisky
  2/7th Kurmärk Landwehr Regiment – von Held
  (all 3 battalions of 7th had 68/1,800)
Left Wing Brigade: Oberst von Boguslavsky
  2/3rd Kurmärk Landwehr Regiment – von
    Bornstedt
  2/, 3/4th Kurmärk Landwehr Regiment
    2nd Battalion – von Liewen
    3rd Battalion – von Schwerin
  (all 3 battalions of 4th had 68/1,800)
Reserve Brigade: Oberstleutnant von der Marwitz
  1/, 3/, 4/3rd Kurmärk Landwehr Regiment
    1st Battalion – von Zschi.ischen
    3rd Battalion – Laviere
    4th Battalion – von Schönholz
  (all 4 battalions had 80/1,860)
Detachment: Oberstleutnant von Reuss
  1/4th Kurmärk Landwehr Regiment – von Grolman

1/7th Kurmärk Landwehr Regiment – von Osarowsky
1/Elbe Infantry Regiment – von Stutterheim (~850
  men)
3rd Kurmärk Landwehr Cavalry Regiment (1 sqn) –
  von Bornstadt
Prussian 6pdr Foot Battery #6 – Tiehsen (1 howitzer)
Cavalry: Oberst von Bismark
  3rd Kurmärk Landwehr Cavalry Regiment –
    Teschen (3 sqns) (all 4 squadrons had 14/320)
  5th Kurmärk Landwehr Cavalry Regiment –
    Uckermann (4 sgns) (14/320)
  6th Kurmärk Landwehr Cavalry Regiment – Jagow
    (4 sgns) (14/320)
  Russian Light Battery #26 – Captain Chamboran
    (10 guns) (6/190)
  Total Strength 10,350 infantry and 960 cavalry

Cossacks under Czernichev
  Sisava #3 Cossack Regiment
  Grekov #18 Don Cossack Regiment
  Vlassov #3 Don Cossack Regiment
  Rebrejev Don Cossack Regiment
  Pantelev Cossack Regiment

Prussian General Staff, Plane der Schlachten and Treffen welche von der preussischen Armee in den feldzügen der Jahre 1813, 14, and 15 geliesert worden, G.Reimer, Berlin, 1821.

XVI
FRENCH FORCES

Commanding Officer: General de division Baron Girard
Magdeburg Division: Général de division Lanusse
Brigade: Général de brigade Sennegon
  3/24th Légère Infantry Regiment
  3/26th Légère Infantry Regiment
  3/18th Line Infantry Regiment
  3/19th Line Infantry Regiment
  1/9th Westphalian Line Infantry Regiment
  2/1st Croatian Infantry Regiment
Brigade: Général de brigade Baville
  3/, 6/134th Line Infantry Regiment
  3/56th Line Infantry Regiment
  3/72nd Line Infantry Regiment
  1/, 2/Saxon Ducal House Infantry Regiment
Attached:
  1/, 3/, 4/13th French Hussar Regiment (21/504)
  1 Escadron de marche (Heavy Cavalry)
  1 Escadron de marche (Light Cavalry)
Artillery:
  1/9th Foot Artillery
  16/9th Foot Artillery
  Total – 15 guns
  Unknown Train Detachment
Total 8,000 infantry and 900 cavalry

THE BATTLE OF KULM
30 AUGUST 1813

XVII
ALLIED FORCES AT

Austrian Troops
**1st Infantry Division: Feldmarschall-lieutenant
Graf H. Colloredo-Mansfeld**
Brigade: Oberst Abele
  1/, 2/Erbach Infantry Regiment #42
  1/, 2/Argenteau Infantry Regiment #35
Brigade: Generalmajor Chiesa
  1/, 2/De Vaux Infantry Regiment #25
  1/, 2/Froon Infantry Regiment #54
Brigade: Oberst Kolb
  1/, 2/, 3/De Ligne Infantry Regiment #30
  1/, 2/Czartorisky Infantry Regiment #9
Artillery:
  3 Brigade Batteries
**1st Reserve Division: Feldmarschall-lieutenant
Bianchi**
Brigade: Generalmajor Quallenberg
  1/, 2/Davidovich Infantry Regiment #34
  1/, 2/Esterhazv Infantry Regiment #32
Brigade: Generalmajor Mariassv
  1/, 2/Hessen-Homburg Infantry Regiment #19
  1/, 2/Simbischen Infantry Regiment #48
Brigade: Generalmajor Prinz Phillip von
Hessen-Homburg
  1/, 2/Hiller Infantry Regiment #2
  1/, 2/H.Colloredo-Mansfield Infantry Regiment #33
Artillery:
  3 Brigade Batteries
Cavalry Brigade: Generalmajor Sorbenberg
  Kaiser Cuirassier Regiment #1 (2)
  Erzherzog Johann Dragoon Regiment #1 (4)

Russian Troops
5th (Guard) Corps: Generallieutenant Yermolov
1st Guard Division: Generalmajor Rosen
Brigade: Generalmajor Potemkin
  1/, 2/, 3/Preobragenski Guard Regiment
  1/, 2/, 3/Semenovski Guard Regiment
Brigade: Generalmajor Krapovitzskv
  1/, 2/, 3/Ismailov Guard Regimen
  1/, 2/, 3/Guard Jager Regiment
Artillery:
  Guard Light Battery #1
  Guard Heavy Battery #2
  Guard Horse Battery #1
2nd Guard Division: Generalmajor Udom I
Brigade: Generalmajor Kryschanovski
  1/, 2/, 3/Lithuanian Guard Regiment
  1/, 2/Guard Leib Grenadier Regiment
Brigade: Generalmajor Scheltuchin
  1/, 2/, 3/Finland Guard Regiment

  1/, 2/Pavlov Guard Regiment

3rd (Grenadier) Corps: Generallieutenant Raevsky
1st Grenadier Division: Generalmajor Pissarev
Brigade: Generalmajor Kniasnin
  Arakchevev Grenadier Regiment (2)
  Ekaterinoslav Grenadier Regiment (2)
Brigade: Colonel Ocht
  Tauride Grenadier Regiment (2)
  St. Petersburg Grenadier Regiment (2)
Brigade: Colonel Yemelianov
  Kexholm Grenadier Regiment (2)
  Pernau Grenadier Regiment (2)

*2nd Corps: Generallieutenant Herzog Eugen von
  Württemberg*
3rd Division: Generalmajor Schachofskoi
Brigade: Oberst Wolff
  Murmon Infantry Regiment (2)
  Tschernigov Infantry Regiment (2)
Brigade: Oberst Schellwinski
  Revel Infantry Regiment (2)
  4th Jager Regiment (2)
4th Division: Generalmajor Puschnitzki
Brigade: Colonel Treffurt
  Tobolsk infantry Regiment (2)
  Minsk Infantry Regiment (1)
Brigade: Colonel Mononov
  Volhynie Infantry Regiment (2)
  Krementchug Infantry Regiment (2)
Attached Artillery:
  Position Battery #5 (12 guns)
  Light Battery #13 (12 guns)

1st Corps – 14th Division: Generalmajor Helfreich
Brigade:
  Tenguinsk Infantry Regiment (2)
  Estonia Infantry Regiment (2)
  Grand Duchess Catherine Battalion (1)
  Light Battery #6 (6 guns)
**Guard Light Cavalry Division: Generallieutenant
Chevich**
  Russian Guard Hussar Regiment (6)
  Russian Guard Dragoon Regiment (6)
  Russian Guard Uhlan Regiment (6)
Cavalry Division: Generalmajor Knorring
  Empress Cuirassier Regiment (4)
  Tartar LThlan Regiment (6)
  Illowaiski #12 Cossack Pulk
  Loubnv Hussar Regiment (2)
  Serpuchov Uhlan Regiment (3)
**1st Cuirassier Division: Generallieutenant
Depreradovich**
1st Brigade Generalmajor Arseniev
  Gardes du Corps Regiment (6)
  Chevalier Garde Regiment (6)
2nd Brigade: Generalmajor Rosen
  Emperor Cuirassier Regiment (4)

2nd Cuirassier Division: Generalmajor Kretov
1st Brigade: Generalmajor Karatiev
  Astrakhan Curiassier Regiment (3)
  Ekaterinoslav Curiassier Regiment (3)
2nd Brigade:
  Pskov Curiassier Regiment (3)
  Gluchov Curiassier Regiment (5)
3rd Cuirassier Division: Generalmajor Duka
1st Brigade: Generalmajor Gudovich
  St. George Curiassier Regiment (4)
  Little Russia Curiassier Regiment (4)
2nd Brigade: Generalmajor Levaschoff
  Starodoub Curiassier Regiment (4)
  Novgorod Curiassier Regiment (4)
Artillery:
  Horse Battery #3

Prussian Troops
II Corps: Generallieutenant von Kleist
9th Prussian Brigade: (detachment only)
  1/, 2/Silesian Schützen Battalion
  Fus/1st West Prussian Infantry Regiment
  1/, 2/, 3/6th Reserve Infantry Regiment
  1/, 3/Neumärk Dragoon Regiment
10th Brigade: Generalmajor von Pirch I
  1/, 2/, F/2nd West Prussian Infantry Regiment
  1/, 2/, 3/7th Reserve Infantry Regiment
  1/, 2/, 3/, 4/9th Silesian Landwehr Regiment
  2/, 4/Neumärk Dragoon Regiment
  3/, 4/1st Silesian Landwehr Cavalry Regiment
  6pdr Foot Battery #8 (8 guns)
11th Brigade: Generalmajor von Ziethen
  3/, 4/Silesian Schützen Battalion
  1/, 2/, F/1st Silesian Infantry Regiment
  1/, 2/, 3/10th Reserve Infantry Regiment
  1/, 2/, 3/, 4/8th Silesian Landwehr Infantry
    Regiment
  1/, 2/, 3/, 4/1st Silesian Hussar Regiment
  1/, 2/2nd Silesian Landwehr Cavalry Regiment
  6pdr Foot Battery #9 (8 guns)
**12th Brigade: Generalmajor Prinz August von
Preussen**
  1/, 2/, F/2nd Silesian Infantry Regiment
  1/, 2/, 3/11th Reserve Infantry Regiment
  1/, 2/, 3/, 4/l0th Silesian Landwehr Infantry
    Regiment
  3/, 4/2nd Silesian Landwehr Cavalry Regiment
  6pdr Foot Battery #13 (8 guns)
Reserve Cavalry: Generalmajor von Röder
Brigade: Oberst von Laroche
  1/, 2/, 3/, 4/Silesian Uhlan Regiment
  1/, 2/Silesian National Cavalry Regimen
  1/, 2/2nd Silesian Hussar Regiment
Brigade: Oberst von Wrangel
  1/, 2/, 3/, 4/East Prussian Cuirassier Regiment
  1/, 2/, 3/, 4/Silesian Cuirassier Regiment
  1/, 2/, 3/, 4/Brandenburg Cuirassier Regiment
Brigade: Oberst von Mutius
  1/, 2/, 3/, 4/7th Silesian Landwehr Cavalry Regiment

  1/, 2/, 3/, 4/8th Silesian Landwehr Cavalry
    Regiment
Artillery:
  Horse Battery #7 (8 guns)
  Horse Battery #8 (8 guns)
Reserve Artillery: Oberst von Braun
  12pdr Foot Battery #3 (8 guns)
  12pdr Foot Battery #6 (8 guns)
  6pdr Foot Battery #9 (8 guns)
  6pdr Foot Battery #14 (8 guns)
  6pdr Foot Battery #21 (8 guns)
  7pdr Howitzer Battery #1 (8 guns)
Horse Battery #9 (8 guns)
Horse Battery #10 (8 guns)

---

*K. and K. Kreigsarchivs. Befreiungskrieg 1813
and 1814, Einzeldarstellung der entscheidenden
Kriegsereignisse. IV. Band, Schlacht bei Kulm, by
Maximilian Ehni. Vienna: L.W. Seidel & Sohn, 1913.
Plotho, K. Der Kreig in Deutschland und Frankreich in
den Jahren 1813 and 1814. Berlin: 1817.
Prussian General Staff. Plane der Schlachten and
Treffen welche von der preussischen Armee in den
feldzugen der Jahre 1813, 14, and 15 geliefert warden,
Vol II. Berlin: G.Reimer, 1821. von Quistorp, B.
Geschichte der Nord Armée im jahre 1813, Berlin:
E.S.Mittler und Sohn, 1894.
Simon, G. Die Kriegeseregnisse zwischen Teplitz and
Pirna in August and September des jahres 1813. Die
Schlacht bei Kulm am 29. and 30. August 1813 and
das Gefecht bei Arbesau am 17. September 1813; Nach
verlaszlichen Quellen Bearbeitet, Teplitz-Schönau: Emil
Seewald, 1911.*

XVIII
FRENCH FORCES

*Commanding Officer: Général de division
Vandamme (taken prisoner)*

Advanced Guard:
5th Division:
Brigade Reuss: Général de brigade Reuss
  1/, 2/, 4/46th Line Regiment
  1/, 2/, 4/72nd Line Regiment
**42nd Division: Général de division
Mouton-Duvernet**
1st Brigade:
  4th Demi-brigade provisoire
    3/28th Légère Regiment
  3rd Demi-brigade provisoire
    4/10th Légère Regiment
    3/21st Légère Regiment
2nd Brigade: Général de brigade Creutzer
  17th Demi-brigade provisoire
    3/27th Line Regiment
    3/63rd Line Regiment

16th Demi-brigade provisoire
  4/40th Line Regiment
  3/43rd Line Regiment
  2/, 3/96th Line Regiment
Artillery:
  1/7th Foot Artillery (6–6pdrs & 2–24pdr howitzers)
  9/7th Foot Artillery (6–6pdrs & 2–24pdr howitzers)
  Detachment 6/16th (bis) Artillery Train
  Detachment 7/16th (bis) Artillery Train
  Detachment 1/6th Principal Artillery Train

I Corps: General de Division Vandamme
1st Division: Général de division Philippon
1st Brigade: Général de brigade Pouchelon (wounded)
  1/, 2/, 3/, 4/7th Légère Regiment
  1/, 2/, 3/, 4/12th Line Regiment
2nd Brigade: Général de brigade Fezensac
  1/, 2/, 3/, 4/17th Line Regiment
  3/, 4/36th Line Regiment
Artillery:
  8/2nd Foot Artillery Company
  15/9th Foot Artillery Company
  Detachment 4th Principal Artillery Train
  3/9th Principal Artillery Train
2nd Division: Général de division Dumonceau
1st Brigade: Général de brigade Dunesme (killed)
  1/, 2/, 3/, 4/13th Légère Regiment
  1/, 2/, 3/, 4/25th Line Regiment
2nd Brigade: Général de brigade Doucet
  1/, 2/, 3/, 4/57th Line Regiment
  3/, 4/51st Line Regiment
Artillery:
  23/3rd Foot Artillery (6–6pdrs & 2–24pdr
    howitzers)
  24/3rd Foot Artillery (6–6pdrs & 2–24pdr
    howitzers)
  1/1st Principal Artillery Train
  Detachment 2/8th (bis) Artillery Train
23nd Division:
2nd Brigade: Général de brigade Quiot (wounded &
captured)
  1/, 2/, 3/, 4/85th Line Regiment
  3/, 4/55th Line Regiment
Artillery:
  21/4th Foot Artillery Company (6–6pdrs &
    2–24pdr how)
  Detachment 1/9th Principal Artillery Train
  Detachment 1/1st (bis) Artillery Train
**21st Light Cavalry Brigade: Général de brigade
  Gobrecht**
  1/, 2/9th Chevaulégers-lanciers Regiment
  1/, 2/Anhalt Jäger zu Pferd
Artillery Reserve & Park: Chef de bataillon Coisy
  6/7th Foot Artillery (6–12pdrs & 2–24pdr
    howitzers)
  9/8th Foot Artillery (6–12pdrs & 2–24pdr
    howitzers)
  2/4th Horse Artillery (4–6pdrs & 2 howitzers)
  5/6th Horse Artillery (4–6pdrs & 2 howitzers)

Det. 4/7th Principal Train Battalion
Det. 1/9th Principal Train Battalion
2/13th (bis) Train Battalion
Det/13th Equipage Battalion
4/14th Equipage Battalion

**1st Light Cavalry Division: Général de division
  Corbineau**
2nd Light Cavalry Brigade: Général de brigade
Montmarie
  1/, 2/1st Chevauléger-lancier Regiment
  1/, 2/3rd Chevauléger-lancier Regiment
  1/, 2/16th Chasseur à Cheval Regiment
3rd Light Cavalry Brigade: Général de brigade
Heimrodt (*killed*)
  1/, 2/5th Chevauléger-lancier Regiment
  1/, 2/8th Chevauléger-lancier Regiment
  1/, 2/, 3/, 4/1st Italian Chasseur à Cheval Regiment
Artillery:
  unknown Horse Artillery (4–6pdrs & 2–24pdr
    Howitzers)

**Detachment at Aussig: General de Brigade
  Creutzer**
  5/3rd Sapper Battalion
  7/3rd Sapper Battalion
  ?/57th Line Regiment
  6/9th Légère Regiment
42nd Division
  22nd Demi-brigade provisoire
    2/4th Légère Regiment
    3/12th Légère Regiment
  2/, 3/76th Line Regiment
9th Light Cavalry Division:
32nd Light Cavalry Brigade: Colonel Rosseau
  3/, 4/3rd Hussar Regiment
  3/, 4/27th Chasseur à Cheval Regiment

---

*Simon, G. Die Kriegeserignisse zwischen Teplitz und
Pirna in August and September des Jahres 1813. Die
Schlacht bei Kuhn am 29. and 30. August 1813 and
das Gefecht bei Arbesau am 17. September 1813; Nach
verläszlichen Quellen Bearbeitet, Teplitz-Schönau: Emil
Seewald, 1911.*
*French Archives, Cartons C²–538, 540, 543, 544 &
708*

SMALLER FRENCH FORMATIONS

XIX
DIVISION D'OBSERVATION DE MINDEN
31 AUGUST 1813

Commanding officer: Général de division Lemoine
Battalions detached from the II Corps:
  3/11th Légère Regiment (16/726)
  3/2nd Line Regiment (15/571)
  3/2nd Line Regiment (6/98) (arrived 9/6/13)
  3/4th Line Regiment (20/800)
  3/37th Line Regiment (18/583)
  3/37th Line Regiment (1/147) (arrived 9/20/13)
  3/40th Line Regiment (10/500)
  3/40th Line Regiment (6/274) (arrived 9/7/13)
  3/40th Line Regiment (2/93) (arrived 9/15/13)
  3/93rd Line Regiment (19/758)
Attached:
  2/Joseph Napoleon Regiment (20/800)
  Transient Battalion (4/300)
  Det/20th Dragoon Regiment (5/96/100)
  (*Numbers are officers, men, & horses*)
  Det/23rd Chasseur à Cheval Regiment (2/25/30)
  Det/6th Cuirassier Regiment (1/15/17)
  Det/2nd Chasseur à Cheval Regiment (1/24/26)
  26/8th Foot Artilerv (3/115) (6–6pdrs & 2
    howitzers)
  Transient Gunners (1/40)
  6/5th Horse Artillery (3/92) (4–6pdrs & 2
    howitzers)
  6/14th Equipage Battalion (1/86)

French Archives, Cartons C²–708

XX
DIVISION D'OBSERVATION DE MAGDEBURG
1 SEPTEMBER 1813

Commanding General: Général de division Girard
Brigade: Général de brigade Baville
  3/18th Line Regiment (15/850)
  3/19th Line Regiment (22/910)
  3/56th Line Regiment (21/816)
  3/72nd Line Regiment (20/910)
  Det. 2/1st Croatian Regiment (12/500)
  Provisional Cavalry Regiment (14/806/32/400)
  1/9th Westphalian Regiment (14/400)
  21/1st Foot Artillery (2/93)

French Archives, Cartons C²–542

THE EFFECT OF THE CAMPAIGN ON NAPOLEON'S VITAL CAVALRY

XXI
FRENCH I, II, III, AND V RESERVE CAVALRY
CORPS 1 SEPTEMBER 1813

I Cavalry Corps: Général de division
Latour-Maubourg
  1st Light Cavalry Division: (detached)
3rd Light Cavalry Division: Général de division
  Chastel
  4th Light Cavalry Brigade: Général de brigade Vallin
    Staff/8th Chasseur à Cheval Regiment (4/5/17/2)
    1/8th Chasseur à Cheval Regiment (11/152/24/146)
    2/8th Chasseur à Cheval Regiment (8/163/17/155)
    Staff/, 1/, 2/9th Chasseur à Cheval Regt
      (18/274/43/262)
    Staff/25th Chasseur à Cheval Regiment (5/4/22/6)
    1/25th Chasseur à Cheval Regiment (3/155/9/150)
    2/25th Chasseur à Cheval Regiment (8/190/18/188)
    3/25th Chasseur à Cheval Regiment (3/26/7/29)
  5th Light Cavalry Brigade: Général de brigade van
  Merlen
    Staff/1st Chasseur à Cheval Regiment (6/8/20/7)
    1/1st Chasseur à Cheval Regiment (9/175/18/168)
    2/1st Chasseur à Cheval Regiment (10/183/20/174)
    3/1st Chasseur à Cheval Regiment (9/181/16/177)
    4/1st Chasseur à Cheval Regiment (3/47/6/43)
    Staff/19th Chasseur à Cheval Regiment (4/6/15/5)
    1/19th Chasseur à Cheval Regiment (4/71/10/71)
    2/19th Chasseur à Cheval Regiment (6/123/15/123)
    3/19th Chasseur à Cheval Regiment (8/150/15/150)
    4/19th Chasseur à Cheval Regiment (8/130/15/130)
1st Cuirassier Division: Général de division
  Bordesoulle
  1st Brigade: Général de brigade Berckheim
    1/, 2/2nd Cuirassier Regiment (20/298/53/295)
    1/, 2/3rd Cuirassier Regiment (20/224/56/220)
    1/, 2/6th Cuirassier Regiment (17/209/33/198)
  2nd Brigade: Général de brigade Bessières
    1/, 2/, 3/9th Cuirassier Regiment (27/343/82/330)
    1/, 2/, 3/11th Cuirassier Regiment (26/264/52/258)
    1/, 2/12th Cuirassier Regiment (27/259/64/255)
  3rd Brigade: Generalmajor Lessing
    1/, 2/, 3/, 4/Saxon Guard Cuirassier Regt
      (23/521/62/521)
    1/, 2/, 3/, 4/Saxon Zastrow Cuirassier Regt
      (21/462/61/452)
3rd Cuirassier Division: Général de division
  Doumerc
  1st Brigade: Général de brigade d'Audenarde
    Staff/4th Cuirassier Regiment (17/82/44/79)
    1/4th Cuirassier Regiment (5/184/10/156)
    2/4th Cuirassier Regiment (5/68/12/63)
    Staff/7th Cuirassier Regiment (5/6/20/2)
    1/7th Cuirassier Regiment (9/92/25/95)

2/7th Cuirassier Regiment (4/53/7/48)
3/7th Cuirassier Regiment (4/40/9/42)
Staff/14th Cuirassier Regiment (4/7/10/1)
1/14th Cuirassier Regiment (7/142/16/145)
2/14th Cuirassier Regiment (5/36/11/29)
3/14th Cuirassier Regiment (0/9/0/4)
Staff/Italian Napoleon Dragoon Regiment
 (9/11/30/6)
1/, 2/Italian Napoleon Dragoon Regiment
 (3/81/7/79)
3/Italian Napoleon Dragoon Regiment
 (5/130/11/136)
4/Italian Napoleon Dragoon Regiment
 (9/193/20/186)
2nd Brigade: Général de brigade Reiset
 Staff/7th Dragoon Regiment (6/3/26/3)
 1/7th Dragoon Regiment (8/113/18/113)
 2/7th Dragoon Regiment (unknown)
 3/7th Dragoon Regiment (9/80/18/80)
 Staff, 1/23rd Dragoon Regiment (12/152/37/148)
 2/23rd Dragoon Regiment (8/113/8/108)
 Staff/28th Dragoon Regiment (6/7/26/3)
 1/28th Dragoon Regiment (10/146/22/142)
 2/28th Dragoon Regiment (9/129/21/125)
 Staff/30th Dragoon Regiment (7/8/31/3)
 1/30th Dragoon Regiment (6/78/14/70)
 2/30th Dragoon Regiment (6/76/16/75)
 3/30th Dragoon Regiment (6/65/14/73)
Artillery:
 3/1st Horse Artillery (3/80) (4–6pdrs & 2–24pdr
  Howitzers)
 6/3rd Horse Artillery (3/105) (4–6pdrs & 2–24pdr
  How)
 1/4th Horse Artillery (3/97) (4–6pdrs & 2–24pdr
  How)
 1/6th Horse Artillery (4/80) (4–6pdrs & 2–24pdr
  How)
 1st Westphalian Horse Artillery (2/64) (4–6pdrs &
  2–24pdr Howitzer)
 4th Italian Horse Battery (4/62) (4–6pdrs &
  2–24pdr How)
 Det. 4/9th Principal Train Battalion (0/79)
 1/1st (bis) Train Battalion (1/80)
 2/1st (bis) Train Battalion (1/84)
 2/8th & Det. 5/8th (bis) Train Battalion (1/154)
 6/2nd Italian Artillery Train (3/112)
 Westphalian Artillery Train (1/65)

II Cavalry Corps: Général de division Sébastiani
**2nd Light Cavalry Division: Général de division
 Roussel d'Hurbal**
 (Total 2,294 men)
7th Light Cavalry Brigade: Général de brigade
F.Gérard
 1/, 2/, 3/4th Chevauléger-lancier Regiment
 1/, 2/, 3/5th Hussar Regiment
 1/, 2/, 3/, 4/9th Hussar Regiment
8th Light Cavalry Brigade: Général de brigade
 Dommanget

1/, 2/, 3/2nd Chevauléger-lancier Regiment
1/, 2/11th Chasseur à Cheval Regiment
1/, 2/, 3/12th Chasseur à Cheval Regiment
**4th Light Cavalry Division: Général de division
 Exelmans**
 (Total – 2,295 men)
9th Light Cavalry Brigade: Général de brigade
Maurin
 1/, 2/, 3/6th Chevauléger-lancier Regiment
 1/, 2/4th Chasseur à Cheval Regiment
 1/, 2/, 3/7th Chasseur à Cheval Regiment
 1/, 2/, 3/, 4/20th Chasseur à Cheval Regiment
10th Light Cavalry Brigade: Général de brigade
Wathiez
 1/, 2/11th Hussar Regiment
 1/, 2/, 3/, 4/23rd Chasseur à Cheval Regiment
 1/, 2/, 3/24th Chasseur à Cheval Regiment
**2nd Cuirassier Division: Général de division
 St-Germain**
 (Total – 2,201 men)
1st Brigade: Général de brigade d'Augeranville
 1/, 2/1st Carabinier Regiment
 1/, 2/2nd Carabinier Regiment
 1/, 2/1st Cuirassier Regiment
2nd Brigade: Général de brigade Thiry
 1/, 2/, 3/5th Cuirassier Regiment
 1/, 2/8th Cuirassier Regiment
 1/, 2/10th Cuirassier Regiment
Artillery: Colin
 7/1st Horse Artillery (3–6pdrs & 1–24pdr
  Howitzer)
 7/4th Horse Artillery (3–6pdrs & 1–24pdr
  Howitzer)
 8/6th Horse Artillery (3–6pdrs & 1–24pdr
  Howitzer)
 Total artillery – 262 men
 3/13th (bis) Train Battalion
 Det 8th (bis) Train Battalion
 Total train – 233 men

III Cavalry Corps:
Général de division Arrighi, Duke of Padua
**5th Light Cavalry Division: Général de division
 Lorge Staff**
 (9/0/52/0)
12th Light Brigade: Général de brigade Jacquinot
 3/, 4/5th Chasseur à Cheval Regiment
  (22/560/56/548)
 3/, 4/10th Chasseur à Cheval Regiment
  (13/266/33/267)
 5/, 6/13th Chasseur à Cheval Regiment
  (18/384/41/382)
13th Light Brigade: Général de brigade Merlin
 4/15th Chasseur à Cheval Regiment (7/192/17/193)
 3/21st Chasseur à Cheval Regiment (8/203/19/198)
 3/, 4/22nd Chasseur à Cheval Regiment
  (11/390/27/398)

6th Light Cavalry Division: Général de division
Fournier Staff
(6/0/41/0)
14th Light Brigade: Général de brigade Mouriez
4/29th Chasseur à Cheval Regiment (8/133/25/132)
4/31th Chasseur à Cheval Regiment
(11/230/25/234)
4/1st Hussar Regiment (11/287/24/287)
15th Light Brigade: Général de brigade Ameil
3/, 4/2nd Hussar Regiment (15/415/31/412)
5/4th Hussar Regiment (4/40/11/39)
4/12th Hussar Regiment (8/289/20/298)
**4th Heavy Cavalry Division: Général de division
Defrance Staff**
(6/0/44/0)
1st Brigade: Général de brigade Avice
4/4th Dragoon Regiment (8/142/19/140)
3/5th Dragoon Regiment (12/267/31/265)
3/12th Dragoon Regiment (9/161/22/160)
3/14th Dragoon Regiment (11/191/24/184)
4/24th Dragoon Regiment (2/77/25/76)
2nd Brigade: Général de brigade Quinette
4/16th Dragoon Regiment (4/137/7/138)
3/17th Dragoon Regiment (14/249/41/243)
3/21st Dragoon Regiment (8/141/17/141)
4/26th Dragoon Regiment (3/98/5/97)
4/, 5/27th Dragoon Regiment (8/129/19/125)
5/13th Cuirassier Regiment (7/162/16/160)
Artillery:
1/5th Horse Artillery (3/94) (4–6pdrs & 2–24pdr
Howitzer)
5/5th Horse Artillery (2/101) (4–6pdrs & 2–24pdr
Ho)
4/6th Horse Artillery (2/84) (4–6pdrs & 2–24pdr
Howitzer)
5/1st (bis) Artillery Train (2/165)
5/4th Principal Train Battalion (1/97)

V Cavalry Corps: Général de division L'Heriter
Chief of Staff: Adjutant Commandant Souverian
**9th Light Cavalry Division: Général de brigade
Klicky**
32nd Light Cavalry Brigade: Colonel Rousseau
(*This brigade was detached to Mouton-Duvernet's
division*)
3/, 4/3rd Hussar Regiment (-)
3/, 4/27th Chasseur à Cheval Regiment (-)
33rd Light Cavalry Brigade: Colonel Miller
3/, 4/14th Chasseur à Cheval Regiment
(12/223/28/226)
3/, 4/26th Chasseur à Cheval Regiment
(13/222/32/222)
1/, 3/, 4/13th Hussar Regiment (-) (detached to
Magdcburg)
**5th Heavy Cavalry Division: Général de brigade
Collaert**
1st Brigade: Colonel Holinayor
3/2nd Dragoon Regiment (11/147/31/152)

3/, 4/6th Dragoon Regiment (16/260/36/254)
2nd Brigade: Colonel Boudinhon
3/, 4/11th Dragoon Regiment (10/151/25/153)
3/13th Dragoon Regiment (10/153/21/158)
3/15th Dragoon Regiment (11/142/31/152)
**6th Heavy Cavalry Division: Général de brigade
Lamotte**
1st Brigade: Colonel Desargues
3/18th Dragoon Regiment (3/41/7/41)
3/19th Dragoon Regiment (2/42/4/41)
3/20th Dragoon Regiment (7/148/18/159)
2nd Brigade: Colonel Montigny
3/22nd Dragoon Regiment (8/165/19/167)
3/25th Dragoon Regiment (9/186/27/185)
Artillery:
2/3rd Horse Artillery
Det. 12th Principal Train Battalion

---

*Numbers are officers, men, officers' horses, men's horses
French Archives, Carton C²–543 & 544, Xᵖ-3*

BATTLE OF DENNEWITZ
6 SEPTEMBER 1813

XXII
PRUSSIAN FORCES

Prussian Commander: Generallieutenant Bülow

*4th Prussian Corps: Generallieutenant Count von
Tauentzien*
Division: Generalmajor von Lindenau
3rd Reserve Infantry Regiment
Battalion – Rango
Battalion – Willing
Battalion – Wittich
1st Kurmärk Landwehr Infantry Regiment
Battalion – Klöden
Battalion – Dullack
2nd Neumärk Landwehr Infantry Regiment
3rd Battalion – Steinmetz
4th Battalion – Paczkowski
Battalion – Grollmann
5th Kurmärk Landwehr Infantry Regiment
2nd Battalion – Havellander
Battalion – Treskow
Battalion – Mellersky
1st Silesian Landwehr Infantry Regiment
1st Battalion – Kospoth
2nd Battalion – (Bonin) Lemke
3rd Battalion – Wins
Other:
Illowaiski #3 Don Cossack Regiment
Berlin Landwehr Cavalry Regiment (2)
2nd Neumärk Landwehr Cavalry Regiment (2)

1/, 2/, 3/, 4/3rd East Prussian Landwehr Cavalry
Regiment
1/, 2/, 3/, 4/3rd Pomeranian Landwehr Cavalry Regt
1/2 6pdr Horse Battery #6 – Jenichen
1/2 6pdr Horse Battery #11 – Borchard
1/2 6pdr Foot Battery #30 – von Hertig
Heavy 6pdr Iron Foot Battery #17 – Gleim
6pdr Foot Battery #27 – von Matthias

3rd Prussian Corps
Arriving about 12:00 p.m.
4th Brigade: Generalmajor von Thümen
Infantry: Oberst von Stutterheim
1/, 2/, 3/4th East Prussian Infantry Regiment
Fus/4th East Prussian Infantry Regt – Major
Gleisenberg
1/5th Reserve Infantry Regiment – Major Bentheim
2/5th Reserve Infantry Regiment – Major Puttlitz
3/5th Reserve Infantry Regiment – Major von
Wedell
4/5th Reserve Infantry Regiment – Major von
Clausewitz
1/, 2/Elbe Infantry Regiment
2/, 3/East Prussian Jager Battalion (2 coy)
Attached:
Brandenburg Dragoon Regiment (3)
1st Leib Hussar Regiment
6pdr Foot Battery #6 – Ludwig
Russian 12pdr Position Battery #7 – Dietrich
12pdr Foot Battery #4 – Meyer
3rd Brigade: Generalmajor Hesse-Homburg
Infantry Oberstleutnant von Siöholm II
2nd East Prussian Grenadier Battalion
1/3rd East Prussian Infantry Regiment – Major von
Bülow
2/3rd East Prussian Infantry Regiment -
Fus/3rd East Prussian Infantry- Regt – Major v.
Gleisenberg
1/, 2/4th Reserve Regiment
Fus/4th Reserve Regiment – Major Polczinskv
Attached:
1/, 2/, 3/, 4/3rd East Prussian Landwehr Infantry
Regiment
1/, 2/, 3/, 4/1st Leib-Hussar Regiment
6pdr Foot Battery #5 – Glasenapp
6th Brigade: Oberst von Krafft
Infantry: Oberstleutnant von Zastrow
1/, 2/, Fus/Colberg Infantry Regiment
1/, 2/, 3/9th Reserve Infantry Regiment
1/, 2/, 3/1st Neumärk Landwehr Infantry Regiment
4/1st Neumärk Landwehr Regt – Major von
Reckow
Attached:
1/, 2/, 3/, 4/1st Pomeranian Landwehr Cavalry
Regiment
West Prussian Dragoon Regiment (2)
12pdr Foot Battery #5 (2 howitzers) – Lt Conradi
6pdr Foot Battery #16 – Spreuth

Russian 12pdr Position Battery #21 – Schlüter (6
guns)
Cavalry Reserve: Generalmajor von Oppen
1/, 2/, 3/, 4/Königin Dragoon Regiment
1/, 2/, 3/, 4/2nd West Prussian Dragoon Regiment
2nd Kurmärk Landwehr Cavalry Regiment (3)
4th Kurmärk Landwehr Cavalry Regiment (3)
2nd Pomeranian Landwehr Cavalry Regiment (3)
Pomeranian National Cavalry Regiment (3)
Artillery:
Horse Battery #5 – Neindorff
1/2 Horse Battery #6 – Steinwehr
Artillery Reserve:
6pdr Foot Battery #19 – Baumgarten
Munitions Column 3,4,& 6
Field Pioneer Company #4
Field Pioneer Company #5

Arriving about 4:00 p.m.
5th Brigade: Generalmajor von Borstell
Infantry: Oberstleutnant von Schoon
Pomeranian Grenadier Battalion (1)
1/, 2/, 3/1st Pomeranian Infantry Regiment
1/2nd Reserve Infantry Regiment – von Hövel
2/2nd Reserve Infantry Regiment
Fus/2nd Reserve Infantry Regiment
Attached:
1/, 2/, 3/, 4/2nd Kurmärk Landwehr Infantry
Regiment
1/, 2/, 3/, 4/Pomeranian Hussar Regiment
6pdr Foot Battery #10 – Magenhöfer
Swedish Forces
Mörner Hussar Regiment (6)
Swedish Horse Battery (6 guns)
Detached as Bagggage Guard
2nd Pomeranian Landwehr Cavalry Regiment (1)

Arriving about 6:00 p.m.
Russian Corps
Lead Elements
44th Jager Regiment (2)
Brigade: Generalmajor Baron Pahlen
Isoum Hussar Regiment (3)
Converged Hussar Regiment (3)

*von Boyen, Col., Darestellung der Vorgang in der
Schlacht von Dennewitz,Julius Sittenfeld, Berlin, 1895.
Prussian General Staff, Plane der Schlachten and Tref
fen welche von der preussischen Armee in den feldzugen
der Jahre 1813, 14, and 15 geliesert worden, G.Reimer,
Berlin, 1821.*

XXIII
FRENCH FORCES

French Army of Berlin: Maréchal Ney
IV Corps: Général de division Count Bertrand
Chief of Staff: Général de brigade Delort
Artillery Commander: Général de division Traviel
12th Division: Général de division Morand
1st Brigade: Général de brigade Belair
   2/, 4/8th Légère Regiment
2nd Brigade: Général de brigade Toussaint
   1/, 2/, 3/, 4/, 6/13th Line Regiment
3rd Brigade: Général de brigade Hulot
   1/, 2/, 4/, 6/23rd Line Regiment
Artillery:
   1/2nd Foot Artillery Company
   3/2nd Foot Artillery Company
   1/7th (bis) Artillery Train
   2/7th (bis) Artillery Train
15th Division: Général de division Fontanelli
1st Brigade: Général de brigade Martel
   3/, 4/1st Italian Line Regiment
   2/, 3/, 4/4th Italian Line Regiment
2nd Brigade: Général de brigade Saint-Andrea
   2/, 3/, 4/1st Italian Légère Regiment
   3/, 4/6th Italian Line Regiment
3rd Brigade: Général de brigade Moroni
   1st Milan Guard Battalion
   2/, 3/, 4/7th Italian Line Regiment
Artillery:
   1/1st Italian Foot Battery
   13/1st Italian Foot Battery
   Italian 5th Train Company
   Italian 6th Train Company
   Detachment Italian 6th (bis) Train Company
38th Division: Generalleutnant de Franquemont
1st Brigade: Generalmajor von Stockmayer
   1/9th Württemberg Light Regiment
   1/10th Württemberg Light Regiment
   1/, 2/7th Württemberg Line Regiment
2nd Brigade: Generalmajor von Spitzenberg
   1/, 2/1st Württemberg Line Regiment
   1/2nd Württemberg Line Regiment
3rd Brigade: Generalmajor Döring
   1/, 2/4th Württemberg Line
   1/, 2/, 6th Württemberg Line
Artillery:
1st Württemberg Foot Battery
24th Light Cavalry Brigade: Generalmajor Jett
   1–4/1st Württemberg Chevauléger Regt "Prince
   Adam"
   1–4/3rd Württemberg Jäger zu Pferd Regt "Duke
   Louis"
   1st Württemberg Horse Battery
27th Division: Général de division Dombrowski
Brigade: Général de brigade Zoltowski
   1/, 2/2nd Polish Infantry Regiment (Attached to
   32nd Division)

   1/, 2/4th Polish Infantry Regiment
18th Light Cavalry Brigade: Général de brigade
Krukowski
   1/, 2/, 3/, 4/2nd Polish Uhlan Regiment
   1/, 2/, 3/, 4/4th Polish Chasseur à Cheval fRegiment
Reserve and Grand Park
   24/2nd Foot Artillery Company
   26/2nd Foot Artillery Company
   25/4th Foot Artillery Company
   8/4th Horse Artillery Company
   2/1st Sapper Battalion
   8/1st Sapper Battalion
   8th Italian Sapper Company
   Detachment of 3rd Italian Marine Artisan
      Company
   3/7th (bis) Artillery Train
   /7th (bis) Artillery Train
   5/7th (bis) Artillery Train
   6/7th (bis) Artillery Train
   7/7th (bis) Artillery Train
   4/11th Artillery Train
   5/9th Equipage Train Battalion
   6/9th Equipage Train Battalion
   7/9th Equipage Train Battalion
   Italian Military Transport
   Engineering Train Detachment
   13th Artillery Artisan Company

VII Corps: Général de division Count Reynier
   Chief of Staff: Général de brigade Gressot
   Artillery Commander: Colonel Verpeau
24th Division: Generalleutnant Lecoq (Saxon)
1st Brigade: Oberst von Brause
   1/Saxon Guard Grenadier Battalion
   1/, 2/1st Saxon Light Infantry Regiment
   1/Maximilian Infantry Regiment
   2/von Rechten Infantry Regiment
   1st Jäger Company
2nd Brigade: Generalmajor Mellentin
   Converged Saxon Grenadier Battalion Spiegel
   1/, 2/Friederich August Infantry Regiment
   1/, 2/Steindel Infantry Regiment
Artillery:
   1st Saxon Foot Battery
   2nd Saxon Foot Battery
   Saxon Train Detachment
25th Division: Generalleutnant von Sahr (Saxon)
1st Brigade: Oberst von Bosch
   Converged Saxon Grenadier Battalion Kleist
   1/, 2/2nd Saxon Light Regiment
   2/König Infantry Regiment
   1/Niesemeuschel Infantry Regiment
2nd Brigade: Generalmajor von Rissel
   1/, 2/Low Infantry Regiment
   1/, 2/Anton Infantry Regiment
Artillery:
   3rd Saxon Foot Battery
   4th Saxon Foot Battery
   Saxon Train Detachment

32nd Division: Général de division Durutte
1st Brigade: Général de brigade Devaux
  1/, 4/35th Légère Regiment
  1/132nd Line Regiment
  3/, 4/132nd Line Regiment
2nd Brigade: Général de brigade Jarry
  1/, 4/36th Légère Regiment
  4/36th Légère Regiment
  1/, 3/, 4/131st Line Regiment
3rd Brigade: Général de brigade Menu
  3/, 4/133rd Line Regiment
  2/, 3/Würzburg Infantry Regiment
Artillery:
  12/1st Foot Artillery Company
  13/8th Foot Artillery Company
  Detachment 2/9th (bis) Artillery Train
  Detachment 2/9th Principal Artillery Train
  Detachment 4/9th Principal Artillery Train
26th Light Cavalry Brigade: Oberst von Lindenau
  1–8/Saxon Hussar Regiment
  1–5/Prinz Clemens Lancer Regiment
Artillery:
  1st Saxon Horse Battery
  2nd Saxon Horse Battery
Reserve and Grand Park
  1st Saxon 12pdr Foot Battery
  1 Saxon Sapper Company
  Saxon Train Detachment

XII Corps: Maréchal Oudinot, Duke of Reggio
  Chief of Staff: Général de division Lejeune
  Artillery Commander: Général de brigade Nourry
  Commander of Engineers: Général de brigade Blein
13th Division: Général de division Pacthod
1st Brigade: Général de brigade Bardet
  4/1st Légère Regiment
  3/, 4/7th Line Regiment
  4/42nd Line Regiment
2nd Brigade: Général de brigade Cacault
  3/, 4/67th Line Regiment
  3/, 4/101st Line Regiment
Artillery:
  4/4th Foot Artillery Company
  20/4th Foot Artillery Company
  Detachment 2/4th Principal Artillery Train
  Detachment 3/7th Principal Artillery Train
14th Division: Général de division Guilleminot
1st Brigade: Général de brigade Graver
  2/, 6/18th Légère Regiment
  1/, 2/,3/,156th Line Regiment
2nd Brigade: Général de brigade Brun de Villeret
  2/Illyrian Regiment
  3/, 4/52nd Line Regiment
  1/, 2/, 3/137th Line Regiment
Artillery:
  2/4th Foot Artillery Company
  1/8th Foot Artillery Company
  Detachment 1/9th (bis) Artillery Train
  Detachment 4/3rd (bis) Artillery Train

  Detachment 1/4th Principal Artillery Train
  Detachment 5/7th Principal Artillery Train
29th Division: Generalleutnant Raglovich (Bavarian)
1st Brigade: Generalmajor von Beckers
  2/3rd Bavarian Line
  1/4th Bavarian Line
  2/8th Bavarian Line
  Res/13th Bavarian Line
  1st Jäger Battalion
2nd Brigade:
  2/5th Bavarian Line
  2/7th Bavarian Line
  2/9th Bavarian Line
  2/10th Bavarian Line
  2nd Jäger Battalion
Artillery:
  1st Bavarian Foot Battery
  2nd Bavarian Foot Battery
  Bavarian Train Detachment
Corps Cavalry: Général de division Beaumont
29th Light Cavalry Brigade: Général de brigade Wolff
  1/, 2/, 3/, 4/Westphalian Chevauléger-lancier
    Regiment
  1/, 2/, 3/, 4/Hessian Chevauléger Regiment
  1/, 2/, 3/Bavarian Chevauléger Regiment
Reserve and Grand Park
  1/4th Foot Artillery Company
  18/4th Foot Artillery Company
  3/5th Horse Artillery Company
  4/2nd Sapper Battalion
  4/9th Sapper Battalion
  Detachment 1/4th Principal Artillery Train
  Detachment 2/4th Principal Artillery Train
  Detachment 4/12th Principal Artillery Train
  Detachment 1/3rd (bis) Artillery Train
  Detachment 3/3rd (bis) Artillery Train
  Detachment 3/7th (bis) Artillery Train
  Detachment 4/7th (bis) Artillery Train
  Detachment 5/7th (bis) Artillery Train
  1/7th Equipage Train Battalion
  2/7th Equipage Train Battalion
  3/7th Equipage Train Battalion

III Cavalry Corps:
Général de division Arrighi, Duke of Padua
  Chief of Staff: Adjutant Commandant Salel
  Artillery Commander: Colonel Chauveau
5th Light Cavalry Division: Général de division Lorge
12th Light Cavalry Brigade: Général de brigade Jacquinot
  3/, 4/5th Chasseur à Cheval Regiment
  3/, 4/10th Chasseur à Cheval Regiment
  5/, 6/13th Chasseur à Cheval Regiment
13th Light Cavalry Brigade: Général de brigade Merlin
  4/15th Chasseur à Cheval Regiment
  3/21st Chasseur à Cheval Regiment

3/, 4/22nd Chasseur à Cheval Regiment
6th Light Cavalry Division: Général de division Fournier
14th Light Cavalry Brigade: Général de brigade Mouriez
  4/29th Chasseur à Cheval Regiment
  4/31th Chasseur à Cheval Regiment
  4/1st Hussar Regiment
15th Light Cavalry Brigade: Général de brigade Ameil
  3/, 4/2nd Hussar Regiment
  5/4th Hussar Regiment
  4/12th Hussar Regiment
4th Heavy Cavalry Division: Général de division Defrance
1st Brigade: Général de brigade Axamitowski
  4/4th Dragoon Regiment
  3/5th Dragoon Regiment
  3/12th Dragoon Regiment
  3/14th Dragoon Regiment
  4/24th Dragoon Regiment
2nd Brigade: Général de brigade Quinette
  4/16th Dragoon Regiment
  3/17th Dragoon Regiment
  3/21st Dragoon Regiment
  4/26th Dragoon Regiment
  4/, 5/27th Dragoon Regiment
  5/13th Cuirassier Regiment
Artillery
  1/5th Horse Artillery
  5/5th Horse Artillery
  2/1st Horse Artillery
  4/6th Horse Artillery
  Detachment 5/1st (bis) Artillery Train
  Detachment 5/4th Principal Artillery Train

*von Boyen, Col., Darestellung der Vorgang in der Schlacht von Dennewitz, Julius Sittenfeld, Berlin, 1895.
C. Rousset, La Grande Armée de 1813, Paris, 1892.
Friederich, R. Geschichte des Herbstfeldzuges 1813, Ernst Siegfried Mittler and Sohn, Berlin, 1904.
Plotho, C., Der Kreig in Deutschland and Frankreich in den Jahren 1813 and 1814, Carl Friedrich, Berlin, 1817.*

XXIV
CASUALTIES

Army of the North: Bernadotte, Crown Prince of Sweden
III Prussian Army Corps: Generallieutenant Bülow
3rd Brigade: Generalmajor Bortel
2nd East Prussian Grenadier Battalion (0/20/3/105/0/12)
Jägers/2nd East Prussian Grenadier Bn. (0/2/0/20/0/5)
1/3rd East Prussian Infantry Regiment (0/35/3/122/0/36)

2/3rd East Prussian Infantry Regiment (1/3/2/30/0/4)
Fus/3rd East Prussian Infantry Regt (1/11/2/70/0/30)
Jägers/3rd East Prussian Infantry Regt (0/0/0/12/0/6)
1/4th Reserve Infantry Regiment (0/9/4/114/0/29)
2/4th Reserve Infantry Regiment (0/9/3/93/0/26)
3/4th Reserve Infantry Regiment (0/42/2/18/0/61)
1/3rd East Prussian Landwehr Regt (2/55/4/43/0/58)
2/3rd East Prussian Landwehr Regt (1/11/5/47/0/29)
3/3rd East Prussian Landwehr Regt (0/1/1/34/0/13)
4/3rd East Prussian Landwehr Regt (1/12/3/91/0/69)
Jägers/3rd East Prussian Landwehr Regt (0/4/0/16/0/12)
1st Leib Hussar Regiment (0/2/2/30/0/3)
Jägers/1st Leib Hussar Regiment (0/2/0/7/0/3)
6pdr Foot Battery #5 (0/1/2/0/0/0)
4th Brigade: Generalmajor Thuemen
1/4th East Prussian Infantry Regiment (0/47/5/249/0/0)
Jägers/4th East Prussian Infantry Regt (0/2/2/20/0/0)
2/4th East Prussian Infantry Regiment (0/38/3/93/0/0)
Fus/4th East Prussian Infantry Regiment (0/11/2/71/037)
1/5th Reserve Infantry Regiment (1/4/3/70/0/18)
2/5th Reserve Infantry Regiment (1/3/5/147/0/100)
3/5th Reserve Infantry Regiment (0/5/5/132/0/3)
4/5th Reserve Infantry Regiment (0/15/2/152/0/12)
1/Elbe Reserve Infantry Regiment (0/88/6/94/0/25)
Jagers/Elbe Reserve Infantry Regiment (0/5/0/8/0/4)
2/Elbe Infantry Regiment (0/16/1/24/0/78)
East Prussian Jagers (2 coys) (1/0/0/0/0/0)
Pomeranian National Cavalry Regiment (0/0/0/6/0/0)
6pdr Foot Battery #6 (0/2/0/8/0/0)
5th Brigade: Generalmajor Hesse-Homberg
Pomeranian Grenadier Battalion (0/16/4/121/0/0)
Jägers/Pomeranian Grenadier Battalion (0/2/0/12/0/0)
1/1st Pomeranian Infantry Regiment (2/9/2/86/0/0)
Jägers/1st Pomeranian Infantry Regt (0/4/0/10/0/0)
2/1st Pomeranian Infantry Regt (2 cos) (0/11/1/92/0/0)
1/2nd Reserve Infantry Regiment (0/12/2/45/0/12)
2/2nd Reserve Infantry Regiment (1/27/0/99/0/38)
3/2nd Reserve Infantry Regiment (0/2/1/31/0/9)
1/2nd Brandenburg Landwehr Regiment (0/6/0/7/0/0)
2/2nd Brandenburg Landwehr Regiment (1/7/3/58/0/0)
4/2nd Brandenburg Landwehr Regt (0/10/3/56/0/6)
Pomeranian Hussar Regiment (1/3/1/15/0/15)
West Prussian Uhlan Regiment (0/1/0/2/0/0)
6pdr Foot Battery #10 (0/0/0/13/0/1)

6th Brigade: Generalmajor Krafft
  1/Colberg Infantry Regiment (1/19/6/148/0/0)
  Jäger, 1/Colberg Infantry Regiment (0/4/1/20/0/0)
  2/Colberg Infantry Regiment (2/46/9/215/0/88)
  Fus/Colberg Infantry Regiment (1/15/6/108/0/60)
  Jäger, Fus/Colberg Infantry Regiment
    (0/1/0/29/0/10)
  1/9th Reserve Infantry Regiment (0/100/6/162/0/0)
  2/9th Reserve Infantry Regiment (0/25/4/190/0/7)
  3/9th Reserve Infantry Regiment (0/1/0/66/0/21)
  1/1st Neumärk Landwehr Regiment
    (0/22/12/180/0/20)
  2/1st Neumärk Landwehr Regiment (2/15/5/89/0/2)
  3/1st Neumärk Landwehr Regiment
    (0/21/7/61/0/24)
  4/1st Neumärk Landwehr Regiment
    (0/15/5/44/0/58)
  1st Pomeranian Landwehr Cavalry Regt
    (0/0/0/0/0/0)
  6pdr Foot Battery #16 (0/2/0/5/0/0)
Reserve Cavalry: Generalmajor Oppen
  Königin Dragoon Regiment (0/1/3/14/0/18)
  Brandenburg Dragoon Regiment (2 sqns)
    (2/8/2/25/0/5)
  Jagers/Brandenburg Dragoon Regiment
    (1/7/0/12/0/0)
  2nd West Prussian Dragoon Regiment
    (0/3/8/12/0/11)
  Jagers/2nd West Prussian Dragoon Regt
    (1/0/3/5/0/0)
  2nd Pomeranian Landwehr Cav. Regt (0/0/0/2/0/0/)
  2nd Brandenburg Landwehr Cav. Regt
    (0/9/8/16/0/27)
  4th Brandenburg Landwehr Cav. Regt (1/1/0/6/0/1)
  Horse Battery #5 (0/0/0/0/0/0)
  1/2 Horse Battery #6 (0/2/0/6/0/0)
  1/2 HorseBattery #11 (0/0/0/1/0/0)
Artillery Reserve: Oberst Holtzendorf
  12pdr Foot Battery #4 (0/1/0/6/0/0)
  12pdr Foot Battery #5 (0/0/0/9/0/1)
  6pdr Foot Battery #19 (0/1/0/4/0/0)
  2 Russian 12pdr Batteries #7 & #21 (1 officer, 25
    men total)
  Prussian Pioneer Companies #4 & #5 (unknown)

IV Prussian Army Corps: Generallieutenant
  Tauentzien
1st Brigade: Dobschuetz
  3rd Reserve Infantry Regiment (2/153/7/634/1/150)
  1st Brandenburg Landwehr Regiment
    (1/28/3/114/0/98)
  2nd Neumärk Landwehr Cavalry Regt
    (0/6/0/17/0/8)
  3rd East Prussian Landwehr Cavalry Regt
    (0/0/0/5/0/1)

2nd Brigade: Count Lindenau
  5th Brandenburg Landwehr Regt
    (0/108/11/649/0/188)
  2nd Neumärk Landwehr Regiment
    (1/24/7/188/1/226)
  1st Silesian Landwehr Regiment (0/18/2/34/0/218)
  1st Brandenburg Landwehr Cavalry Regt
    (0/6/1/30/0/42)
  3rd Pomeranian Landwehr Cavalry Regt
    (2/8/2/22/0/30)
  7th Brandenburg Landwehr Cavalry Regt
    (1/0/2/0/0/34)
  1/2 Brandenburg Dragoon Regiment
    (0/6/2/20/0/23)
Artillery Reserve: Oberstlieutenant von Strampf
  6pdr Foot Battery #17 (0/3/1/3/0/0)
  6pdr Foot Battery #27 (0/0/0/0/0/0)
  6pdr Foot Battery #30 (0/0/0/1/0/0)
  1/2 Horse Battery #6 (0/2/0/3/0/0)
  1/2 Horse Battery #11 (0/2/0/2/0/0)
Swedes:
  Artillery (1 officer & 11 men)
  Schonen Hussars (1 officer & 3 men

French Army of Berlin:
IV Corps: Général de division Bertrand
15th Division: Général de division Fontanelli
  (Italian)
  (casualties unknown)
12th Division: Général de division Morand
  8th Légère Regiment (2/117/5/341/1/3)
  13th Line Regiment (6/131/2/275/18/629)
  23rd Line Regiment (2/42/8/440/10/783)
Artillery:
  1/2nd Foot Artillery (unknown)
  3/2nd Foot Artillery (unknown)
  1/7th (bis) Train Battalion (unknown)
  2/7th (bis) Train Battalion (unknown)
38th Division: Franquemont (Württemberg)
  1st Line Regiment Prinz Paul (0/1/0/2/0/161)
  2nd Line Regiment Herzog Wilhelm (531 total
    losses)
  4th Line Regiment (0/7/2/23/3/385)
  6th Line Regiment (0/3/1/30/1/361)
  7th Line Regiment (648 total losses)
  9th Line Regiment (0/1/1/3/0/10)
  10th Line Regiment (0/1/0/1/1/85)
Artillery:
  Württemberg Foot Battery (0/1/0/3/0/4)
  Württemberg Horse Battery (0/2/0/2/0/1)
24th Light Cavalry Brigade: Jett
  3rd Württemberg Jäger zu Pferd (0/0/2/15/2/35)
  1st Württemberg Chevauléger (1/0/0/9/0/67)
  Park & Reserve: (casualties unknown)

VII Corps: Général de division Reynier
24th Division: Le Coq (Saxon)
Brigade: Oberst von Brause
  1/, 2/lst Light Infantry Regiment
    (1/46/3/104/5/200)
  1st Jäger Company (0/1/0/3/0/31)
  1/Guard Grenadier Regiment (0/4/1/45/0/82)
  2/Von Rechten Regiment (0/33/0/88/0/98)
Brigade: Oberst von Mellentin
  1st Converged Grenadier Battalion
    (0/12/1/80/1/137)
  1/, 2/Frederick August Infantry Regt
    (0/16/3/164/0/218)
  1/, 2/von Steindel Infantry Regiment
    (1/7/2/159/0/267)
Artillery:
  Saxon 12pdr Foot Company (0/1/0/3/0/34)
  2nd Saxon Foot Company (0/0/0/12/0/38)
  Park (0/0/0/0/0/0)
  Saxon Sapper Detachment (0/0/0/3/0/4)
25th Division: Sahr (Saxon)
Brigade: Oberst von Bose
  Converged Grenadier Battalion (0/0/1/58/2/156)
  1/, 2/von Sahr 2nd Light Infantry Regt
    (0/3/1/22/1/252)
  2/Koenig Infantry Regiment (0/0/1/13/0/119)
  1/Niesemeuschel Infantry Regiment (0/0/0/3/1/69)
Brigade: Oberst von Ryssel
  1/, 2/Prinz Anton Infantry Regiment
    (0/58/0/109/0/248)
  1/, 2/von Löw Infantry Regiment (0/0/0/0/0/164)
Artillery:
  1st Saxon Foot Company (0/0/0/4/1/24)
  4th Saxon Foot Company (0/0/0/3/0/15)
  Park (0/0/0/0/0/0)
32nd Division: Général de division Durutte
  36th Légère Regiment (1/9/0/29/0/31)
  131st Infantry Regiment (0/51/0/0/3/28)
  133rd Infantry Regiment (2/190/0/0/0/5)
  35th Légère Infantry Regiment (0/8/0/0/2/83)
26th Light Cavalry Brigade: Lindenau
  Saxon Hussar Regiment (0/1/0/4/0/14)

Prinz Clemens Uhlan Regiment (0/0/1/2/0/6)
1st Saxon Horse Artillery (0/0/0/0/0/0)
2nd Saxon Horse Artillery (0/0/0/0/0/0)
Park & Reserves:
Saxon Reserve Artillery (0/0/0/0/0/0)
Saxon Park (0/0/0/0/0/0)
Saxon Train (0/0/0/0/0/0)

XII Corps: Maréchal Oudinot
13th Division: Général de division Guillemont
Brigade: Général de brigade Bardet
  1st Légère Regiment (0/38/0/79/0/113)
  67th Infantry Regiment (1/14/2/35/3/34)
  101st Infantry Regiment (0/87/1/89/2/29/4)
Artillery:
  4/4th Foot Artillery (unknown)
  20/4th Foot Artillery (unknown)
  2/4th Principal Train Battalion (unknown)
  3/7th (bis) Train Battalion (unknown)
14th Division: Guilleminot
  156th Infantry Regiment (8/240/13/1,409)
  52nd Infantry Regiment (4/22/6/301/0/7)
  137th Infantry Regiment (5/289/8/394/1/72)
Artillery:
  2/4th Foot Artillery (unknown)
  1/8th Foot Artillery (unknown)
  1/9th (bis) Train Battalion (unknown)
  4/3rd (bis) Train Battalion (unknown)
  1/4th Principal Train Battalion (unknown)
  5/7th Principal Train Battalion (unknown)
**29th Division: Generallieutenant Raglovich
(Bavarian)**
Total losses 2,251 men
29th Light Cavalry Brigade: Wolff
Total losses 844 men

---

*Fabry, Etude stir les Operations de Maréchal Ouidinot,
du 15 Aout an 4 Septembre – Gross-Beeren
Recueil des Plans de Combats et de Batailles Livrees par
l'Armée Prussienne pendant les Campagnes des Annes
1813, 14 et 15. von Quistorp, B., Geschichte der Nord-
Armes im Jahre 1813, Berlin, 1894.*

Notes

1 The Summer Armistice 8 June–10 August 1813

1   Fain, Baron, *Manuscrit de Mil Huit Cent Treize*, Vol II, p.35.
2   Galli, H. *L'Allemagne en 1813, pg 165 & Fain, Baron, Manuscrit de Mil Huit Cent Treize*, Vol II, p.36.
3   Fain, Baron, *Manuscrit de Mil Huit Cent Treize*, Vol II, p.41.
4   Fain, Baron, *Manuscrit de Mil Huit Cent Treize*, Vol II, p.45.
5   Fain, Baron, *Manuscrit de Mil Huit Cent Treize*, Vol II, p.73.
6   Fain, Baron, *Manuscrit de Mil Huit Cent Treize*, Vol II, pp. 90.
7   Galli, H. *L'Allemagne en 1813*, p.171.
8   Galli, H. *L'Allemagne en 1813*, p.172.
9   Dodge, T.A., *Napoleon*, Vol IV, p.97.
10 Maude, Col. F.N., The Leipzig Campaign 1813, p.161.
11 Dodge, T.A., *Napoleon*, Vol IV, pp.98–100.

2 The Armies Refit 8 June–1 August 1813

1   Friederich, *Geschichte des Herbstfeldzuges 1813*, pp.38-41.
2   Friederich, *Geschichte 1813*, p.41.
3   Schlosser, Ad., *Geschichte des Lützowschen Freikorps*, pp.56-57.
4   The infantry totalled 2,800 men. The 1st and 3rd Battalions each had 4 musketeer companies and a jäger detachment. The 2nd Battalion had three musketeer companies, a "Tyrolian" jäger company, and a jäger detachment. The cavalry had 480 men organized into two hussar and two uhlan squadrons and a mounted jäger detachment. The artillery had 4 – 3pdr guns, 1 – 7pdr howitzer, and 3 iron 2.25pdr cannons. Half of the guns were foot artillery and the other half horse artillery.
5   Hofschröer, P., *Prussian Landwehr and Landsturm*, 1813–1815, p.1.
6   Friederich, *Geschichte 1813*, p.43.
7   Maude, Col. F.N., *The Leipzig Campaign, 1813*, pp.151-2.
8   Friederich, *Geschichte 1813*, p.8.
9   Gayda, M., & Krijitsky, A., *L'Armée Russe*, p.11.
10 Friederich, *Geschichte 1813*, pp.52-53.
11 F riederich, *Geschichte 1813*, p.57.
12 Friederich, *Geschichte 1813*, p.58.
13 Friederich, *Geschichte des Herbstfeldzuges 1813*, p.58.
14 French National Archives, Carton AFIV* 1342.
15 French Archives, Château Vincennes, Cartons C²-37, 538, 539, 540, 541, 542, 543, 544, and C²-708.
16 Fain, Baron, *Manuscrit de Mil Huit Cent Treize*, Vol II, p.51.

3 Blücher Advances: The Battles on the Bober 18–23 August 1813

1   Clément, *Campagne de 1813*, p.315.
2   Sporschil, *Grosse Chronik*, Vol I, pg 484.
3   Prussian General Staff, *Plane* Vol II, pg 3.
4   Lobenthal's advanced guard consisted of the Fusilier Battalions of the 1st East Prussian, 2nd East Prussian, Leib and Brandenburg Infantry Regiments, the Kosecky (4/5th Silesian) and Sommerfeld (1/15th Silesian) Landwehr Battalions, 1/2nd Leib Hussar Regiment, 1/Mecklenburg Hussar Regiment, the Brandenburg

Uhlan Regiment (4 sqns), two squadrons of Landwehr cavalry under Major von Falkenhausen, a foot battery and a horse battery.

5   Fabry, *Wurtemberg*, p.LXXIX.

6   Clément, *Campagne de 1813*, p.318.

7   Prussian General Staff, *Plane* Vol II, p.4.

8   Prussian General Staff, *Plane* Vol II, p.5.

9   Prussian General Staff, *Plane* ,Vol II, pp.5-6.

10   The source does not indicate if these were the integral skirmishers of the fusilier battalion or a freiwilliger jäger detachment.

11   Plotho, *Krieg in Deutschland*, Vol II, p.94.

12   Plotho, *Krieg in Deutschland*, Vol II, p.95.

13   Prussian General Staff, *Plane*, Vol II, p.7.

14   The 4th Light Cavalry Division of Général de Division Exelmans consisted of: 9th Light Cavalry Brigade: Général de Brigade Maurin – 6th Chevauléger-lancier Regiment (2), 4th Chasseur à Cheval Regiment (3), 7th Chasseur à Cheval Regiment (3); 10th Light Cavalry Brigade: Général de Brigade Wathiez – 20th Chasseur à Cheval Regiment (4), 23th Chasseur à Cheval Regiment (4), 24th Chasseur à Cheval Regiment (3), 11th Hussar Regiment (2).

15   These two battalions were the 4/5th Légère and the 4/12th Légère Regiments.

16   Fabry, *III et V Corps en 1813*, pp.46-47.

17   Fabry, *III et V Corps en 1813*, p.47.

18   Fabry, *III et V Corps en 1813*, p.48.

19   Fabry, *III et V Corps en 1813*, p.48.

20   Beitzke, *Deutschen Freiheitskriege*, Vol V, p.135.

21   Fabry, *Maréchal Macdonald*, p.1.

22   The 6th Provisional Regiment was formed with the 2/6th and 3/25th Légère Regiments.

23   The 19th Provisional Regiment was formed by the 6/32nd and 2/58th Line Regiments.

24   Fabry, *III et V Corps en 1813*, pp.49-50.

25   Fabry, *III et V Corps en 1813*, p.50.

26   Fabry, *Maréchal Macdonald*, p.3.

27   Prussian General Staff, *Plane*, Vol II, p.11.

28   Fabry, *III et V Corps en 1813*, p.51.

29   Prussian General Staff, *Plane*, Vol II, p.9.

30   Prussian General Staff, *Plane*, Vol II, p.10.

31   Prussian General Staff, *Plane*, Vol II, p.11.

32   Fabry, *Maréchal Macdonald*, p.4.

33   Fabry, *Maréchal Macdonald*, p.6.

34   Fabry, *Maréchal Macdonald*, p.7.

35   Fabry, *Maréchal Macdonald*, p.8.

36   Major Golz commanded the 2/Brandenburg, 1/,2/12th Reserve Infantry Regiment and the Kottulinsky Landwehr Battalion (2/4th Silesian Regiment), Gfug Landwehr Battalion (4/14th Silesian Regiment), and Reibnitz Landwehr Battalion (3/15th Silesian Regiment).

37   Prussian General Staff, *Plane*, Vol II, p.12.

38   Clément, *Campagne de 1813*, p.320.

39   The garrison consisted of the 15th Silesian Landwehr Regiment – 3rd Battalion (Rebinitz) with 3 companies in the Selzer Gate suburbs and the 4th Battalion at the gate. The 1/12th Reserve stood at the Ober Gate. The 3/12th Reserve stood in skirmish formation at the Friedrichs Gate. The 2/Brandenburg had 1 ½ companies in the buildings of the Nieder Gate suburb, one company at the gate, and 1 ½ companies in the Nicolai cemetery. Four Russian guns were also in the cemetery. The 2/14th Silesian Landwehr Regiment was in the main square, the 4/14th (Gfug) and 1/14th Silesian Landwehr (Kempsky II), and 3pdr Foot Battery #6 (Lt. Anders) was in Flensberg.

40   Fabry, *Maréchal Macdonald*, pg.4.

41   Fabry, *Maréchal Macdonald*, p.17.

42   Fabry, *Maréchal Macdonald*, pp.18-19.

43　Fabry, *Maréchal Macdonald*, pp.29-30.

44　GL Count Pahlen II and Count Pahlen III were different men. They were brothers.

45　Friederich, *Herbstfeldzuges*, Vol I, p.276.

46　Friederich, *Herbstfeldzuges* , Vol I, p.276.

47　Fabry, *Maréchal Macdonald*, p.32.

48　Prussian General Staff, *Plane*, Vol II, p.13; Friederich, *Herbstfeldzuges*, Vol I, p.276.

49　Beitzke, *Deutschen Freiheitskriege*,Vol V, p.145.

50　Friederich, *Herbstfeldzuges*, Vol I, p.278.

51　Fabry, *Maréchal Macdonald*, p.33.

52　Friederich, *Herbstfeldzuges*, Vol I, p.279.

53　Turning about by platoons.

54　*Denkwürdigkeiten des Meklenburg-Strelitzischen Husaren-Regiments*, p.65.

55　Fabry, *Maréchal Macdonald*, p.33.

56　Friederich, *Herbstfeldzuges*, Vol 1, p.282.

57　Fabry, *Maréchal Macdonald*, p.34.

58　Prussian General Staff, *Plane*, Vol II, p.16.

59　Prussian General Staff, *Plane*, Vol II, p.15.

60　Fabry, *Maréchal Macdonald*, p.35.

61　Friederich, *Herbstfeldzuges*, Vol I, pg.82.

62　The right wing consisted of General Lanskoi's forces, which were in Haynau and the road to Liegnitz.

63　Fabry, *Maréchal Macdonald*, p.36.

64　Prussian General Staff, *Plane*, Vol II, p.17.

4 Macdonald goes to War: The Battle of the Katzbach 24–26 August 1813

1　The Thüringian Battalion was formed from soldiers from the Saxon Ducal Houses of Saxe-Meiningen, -Weimar, -Hildburghausen and -Coburg. They had been organized as a new battalion for the 4th Rheinbund Regiment, but were captured in the spring and joined Prussian service.

2　These were the 3/5th Silesian and 1/14th Silesian Landwehr Regiments.

3　Prussian General Staff, *Plane*, Vol II, p.17; Fabry, *Macdonald*, p.42.

4　Friederich, *Herbstfeldzuges*, Vol I, p.299.

5　Plotho, *Der Kreig*, Vol II, p.108.

6　Friederich, *Herbstfeldzuges*, Vol I, p.302.

7　Clément, *Campagne de 1813*, p.324.

8　Fabry, *Macdonald*, pp.52-53.

9　Clément, *Campagne de 1813*, pp.325-6.

10　Lauriston to Macdonald – Report on the affair of 26 August and the following days: Fabry, *Macdonald*, Appendices, p.23.

11　Beitzke, *Freiheitskriege*, Vol V, p.158.

12　Müller-Leobnitz, *Katzbach*, p.31.

13　Plotho, *Der Kreig*, Vol II, p.108.

14　Müller-Leobnitz, *Katzbach*, p.32.

15　Müller-Leobnitz, *Katzbach*, p.32.

16　Müller-Leobnitz, *Katzbach*, p.33.

17　Müller-Leobnitz, Katzbach, pg 34.

18　Prussian General Staff, *Plane*, Vol II, p.21.

19　Prussian General Staff, *Plane*, Vol II, p.27; Plotho, *Der Kreig*, Vol II, p.110.

20　Fabry, *Macdonald*, p.69.

21　Plotho, *Der Kreig*, Vol II, p.110.

22　Prussian General Staff, *Plane* Vol II, p.27; Fabry, *Macdonald*, p.70.

23　Prussian General Staff, *Plane* Vol II, p.27.

24　Apparently the Thüringian battalion had deployed the third rank of every company as skirmishers and was now in a two rank formation.

25 Fabry, *Macdonald*, p.73. The Prussian General Staff work, *Plane* Vol II, p.19, describes the deployments as follows: The East Prussian Jager Company and a detachment of 300 men from the Silesian Grenadier Battalion, the 1/Brandenburg Infantry Regiment and the Thüringian Battalion, under the command of Major von Klüx, occupied the villages of Crayn, Kroitsch, Wultsch and Schimmelwitz. The Thüringian Battalion stood in Ober- and Nieder-Weinberg. Three companies of the 1/Brandenburg stood on the bridge in Nieder-Crayn and one company guarded the mill at Weinberg. Supporting this line were two squadrons of the Lithuanian Dragoon Regiment and the Brandenburg Uhlan Regiment, which was in and behind Kroitsch. The remaining troops were on the Weinberg Heights.

26 The 7th Light Cavalry Brigade was commanded by Général de Brigade Gérard, while Général de Division Gérard commanded the XI Corps.

27 Gérard to Macdonald – Report on the operations of the XI Corps from 26 August to 31 August: Fabry, *Macdonald*, appendices, p.28.

28 Friederich, *Katzbach*, p.22.

29 Fabry, *Macdonald*, p.75.

30 Fabry, *Macdonald*, p.75.

31 Fabry, *Macdonald*, p.76.

32 Fabry, *Macdonald*, p.77.

33 Fabry, *III et V Corps*, p.55.

34 Fabry, *Macdonald*, p.80.

35 Fabry, *Macdonald*, pp.81-82: Column formed on the center means that the battalions were formed in column such that the 4th and 5th platoons were the leading elements of the column. Behind the 4th platoon stood the 3rd, 2nd and 1st platoons (in that order) and behind the 5th platoon stood the 6th, 7th, and 8th platoons (in that order).

36 Prussian General Staff, *Plane* Vol II, p.30; Fabry, *Macdonald*, p.82.

37 Fabry, *Macdonald*, p.83.

38 Friederich, *Katzbach*, p.24.

39 Müller-Leobnitz, *Katzbach*, p.34.

40 Friederich, *Herbstfeldzuges*, Vol I, p.306.

41 The West Prussian and Lithuanian Dragoons, supported by some Prussian artillery.

42 Friederich, *Herbstfeldzuges*, Vol I, p.306.

43 Brayer's old brigade consisted of the 6th, 10th, 14th, and 19th Regiments Provisoires and had a total of eight battalions.

44 Fabry, *III et V Corps*, p.56.

45 The latter was the Prussian regiment, not to be confused with the Russian Chasseur à Cheval Regiment or the Lithuanian regiments serving in the French army.

46 Fabry, *Macdonald*, p. 87.

47 Müller-Leobnitz, *Katzbach*, p.36.

48 Friederich, *Katzbach*, p.24.

49 Gérard to Macdonald – Report on the Operations of the XI Corps from 26 August to 31 August: Fabry, *Macdonald*, appendices, p.29.

50 Report from Sébastiani to Macdonald – Report on the day of 26 August: Fabry, Macdonald, *Appendices*, p.21.

51 Lanskoy commanded 2nd Hussar Division of which the Achtyrsk and White Russian Hussar Regiments formed a brigade.

52 The Alexandria and Marioupol Hussar Regiments.

53 Prussian General Staff, *Plane*, Vol II, p.32.

54 Fabry, *Macdonald*, pgp.88-89.

55 Fabry, Macdonald, p.90.

56 Fabry, *Macdonald*, p.94. & Prussian General Staff, *Plane*, Vol II, p.33.

57 Weil, *Campagne de 1813, La Cavalerie des Armées Allies*, p.110.

58 The destruction of the 17th Division is discussed in the next chapter.

59 Clément, *Campagne de 1813*, p.239.

60 Friederich, *Katzbach*, p.25.

5 Macdonald's Flanking Corps 22 August–4 September 1813

1   Fabry, *Macdonald*, p.100.
2   An analysis of Martinien's *Tableaux par Corps et par Batailles des Officiers rues et Blesses* indicates that it was the 150th Regiment. The actual regiment involved is not identified by Prussian General Staff, *Plane der Schlachten and Treffen*.
3   Prussian General Staff, *Plane* Vol II, p.35.
4   Fabry, *Macdonald*, p.102.
5   The 3rd Foreign Regiment was also known as the Irish Legion. Though this unit served in Spain for many years, this was to be its first and last action.
6   Prussian General Staff, *Plane* Vol II, p.37; Fabry, *Macdonald*, p.120.
7   Fabry, *Macdonald*, pg.34.
8   Prussian General Staff, *Plane*, Vol II, p.38.
9   Beitzke, *Freiheitskriege*, Vol V, p.180.
10 Chuquet, *Inedits Napoleniens*, Vol II, #2476, p.212.
11 Prussian General Staff, *Plane*, Vol II, p.39.
12 Prussian General Staff, *Plane*, Vol II, p.40.
13 Prussian General Staff, *Plane*, Vol II, p.40.
14 Fabry, *Macdonald*, p.144.
15 Fabry, *Macdonald*, p.144.
16 Fabry, *Macdonald*, p.145.
17 Beitzke, *Freiheitskriege*, Vol V, p.183.
18 Prussian General Staff, *Plane*, Vol II, p.42.
19 Fabry, Macdonald, pp.146.
20 Fabry, Macdonald, pp.148-149.
21 Prussian General Staff, *Plane*, Vol II, p.43.
22 Fabry, *Macdonald*, p.152.
23 Fabry, *Macdonald*, p.155.
24 Fabry, *Macdonald*, p.156.
25 Poniatowski, *Correspondence*, Vol V p.387.
26 Fabry, *Macdonald*, p.157.
27 Poniatowski, *Correspondence*, Vol V, p.390.
28 Poniatowski, *Correspondence*, Vol V, p.392.
29 Bonaparte, *Correspondence*, Paris, #20512.
30 Poniatowski, *Correspondence*, Vol V, p.395.
31 Fabry, *Macdonald*, p.181.
32 Fabry, *Macdonald*, p.182.
33 Fabry, *Macdonald*, p.183.
34 Fabry, *Macdonald*, p.186.
35 Fabry, *Macdonald*, pg.87.
36 Though not identified other than "black uhlans" this is probably the East Prussian National Cavalry Regiment. It wore a dark blue uniform and carried lances.
37 Fabry, *Macdonald*, p.98.
38 Fabry, *Macdonald*, p.199.
39 Fabry, *Macdonald*, p.205.

6 Oudinot's Advance on Berlin: The Prelude to the Battle of Gross-Beeren 20–23 August 1813

1   Clément, *Campagne de 1813*, p.379.
2   Prussian General Staff, *Plane*, Vol I, p.37.
3   Prussian General Staff, *Plane*, Vol I, p.38; Fabry, *Oudinot*, p.78.
4   Fabry, *Oudinot*, p.78.
5   Fabry, *Oudinot*, p.80.

6   Quistorp, *Nord Armée*, Vol I, p.245.
7   Quistorp, *Nord Armée*, Vol I, p.247.
8   Fabry, *Oudinot*, p.92.
9   Quistorp, *Nord Armée*, Vol I, p.249.
10 Quistorp, *Nord Armée*, Vol I, p.250.
11 The normal allocation of ammunition was 30 to 40 rounds per man. This firefight was a tremendous affair, with men whose ammunition was expended going to the rear three or four times to replenish their ammunition supplies. This also indicates a very disciplined group of soldiers, who did not take the opportunity this provided to desert or shirk their duties.
12 Prussian General Staff, *Plane*, Vol II, p.38.
13 Oppen had with him 17 squadrons and 14 guns from the 2nd West Prussian and Königin Dragoons, the 2nd and 4th Kurmärk Landwehr Cavalry Regiments, 4/2nd Pomeranian Landwehr Cavalry, and 6pdr Horse Batteries #5 and #6, less the two guns remaining in Blankenfelde.
14 A "colonise serrée" is a column closed up into a dense mass, such that there are only 3 feet between each company.
15 This was, apparently, Steinwehr's Horse Battery #6 supported by the Jagers of the Königin Dragoons and the 4/2nd Pomeranian Landwehr Regiment.
16 Fabry, *Oudinot*, pp.94-95.
17 Quistorp, *Nord Armée*, Vol I, p.252.
18 Fabry, *Oudinot*, p.96.
19 The Landwehr Battalions Kemphen and Wedell and the 2/Elbe Infantry Regiment.
20 Quistorp, *Nord Armée*, Vol I, p.255.
21 Quistorp gives the French losses as follows: 35th Légère – 94 men, 131st Line – 94 men, 132nd Line – 380 men, but provides no details on the Saxon losses.
22 3/2nd Neumärk and 6pdr Foot Battery #17.
23 Fabry, *Oudinot*, p.97.
24 Prussian General Staff, *Plane*, Vol I, p.42.
25 Quistorp, *Nord Armée*, Vol I, p.259.
26 Fabry, *Oudinot*, p.97.
27 Prussian General Staff, *Plane*, Vol II, p.41.

7 Oudinot's Advance on Berlin: The Battle of Gross-Beeren 23 August–25 August 1813

1   Quistorp, *Nord Armée*, Vol I, p.273.
2   Plotho, *Der Kreig*, Vol II, pp.13-139.
3   Dullack commanded the 1/1st Kurmärk and Klöden commanded the 2/1st Kurmärk.
4   Prussian General Staff, *Plane*, Vol I, p.44.
5   Quistorp, *Nord Armée*, Vol I, p.274.
6   Papendick commanded 6pdr Foot Battery #20. Blankenburg appears to have temporarily commanded either 6pdr Battery #17 or #27.
7   Quistorp, *Nord Armée*, Vol I, p.276.
8   Prussian General Staff, *Plane*, Vol I, p.45.
9   Mackensen, *Schwarz Husaren*, p.411.
10 Fabry, *Oudinot*, p.114.
11 von Quistorp, *Nord Armée*, Vol I, p.283.
12 The Sperl Grenadier Battalion was formerly the Anger Grenadier Battalion.
13 This deployment and references to Devaux's and Jarry's brigades in the battle would indicate that Menu's 3rd Brigade was not present, but this is not confirmed or denied by *any* of the sources consulted.
14 Quistorp, *Nord Armée*, Vol I, p.284.
15 Prussian General Staff, *Plane*, Vol I, p.48.
16 During the morning of 23 August, the 1/2nd Kurmärk (Borstell's Brigade), and with two squadrons of the Brandenburg Dragoons from the cavalry reserve, and 6pdr Foot Battery #20 had been detached by Bülow and sent to join Dobschütz's brigade.

17   Prussian General Staff, *Plane*, Vol I, pp.46-8; Fabry, *Oudinot*, p.117.
18   Prussian General Staff, *Plane*, Vol I, p.49.
19   Fabry, *Oudinot*, p.118; Prussian General Staff, *Plane*, Vol I, p.50.
20   Prussian General Staff, *Plane*, Vol I, p.50; Quistorp, *Nord Armée*, p.288.
21   Prussian General Staff, *Plane*, Vol I, p.50.
22   Quistorp, *Nord Armée*, Vol I, p.286.
23   Quistorp, *Nord Armée*, Vol I, p.291.
24   Prussian General Staff, *Plane*, Vol I, p.51.
25   Quistorp, *Nord Armée*, Vol I, p.292.
26   Fabry, *Oudinot*, p.122.
27   Prussian General Staff, *Plane*, Vol I, p.52.
28   Fabry, *Oudinot*, pp.123-124.
29   Prussian General Staff, *Plane*, Vol I, p.53.
30   Mackensen, *Schwarz Husaren,*, p.412.
31   The separation of the eagle bearers from their regiments clearly indicates the disintegration that had occurred in the 131st Line and 36th Légère Regiments.
32   Fabry, *Oudinot*, p.127.
33   Schuster & Francke, *Sächsischen Armee*, Vol II, p.357.
34   Fabry, *Oudinot*, p.128.
35   Schuster & Francke, *Sächsischen Armee*, Vol II, p.357.

8 Oudinot's Withdrawal and the Other Northern Corps 25 August–5 September 1813

1   These were the 4/3rd West Prussian, 3/3rd West Prussian and 4/1st West Prussian Landwehr Regiments respectively.
2   Prussian General Staff, *Plane*, Vol I, p.57.
3   Fabry, *Oudinot* , p.136.
4   Quistorp, *Nord Armée*, Vol I, p.329.
5   Fabry, *Oudinot*, p.137.
6   Rossler, *Tagebucher*, p.331.
7   The Douglas (2/2nd West Prussian Landwehr) and Schmude (3/2nd West Prussian Landwehr) Battalions, of the 2nd West Prussian Landwehr Regiment, the Bennigsen Battalion, 1/1st West Prussian Landwehr Regiment, 6pdr Foot Battery "Wegner" #22, and 3rd West Prussian Landwehr Cavalry Regiment.
8   The 1/9th and 1/10th Light Regiments were the reorganized light infantry of the Württemberg army and though they were listed with the line, they continued the Württemberg army's only light formations.
9   Fabry, *Oudinot*, p.143.
10 Rossler, *Tagebucher*, p.333.
11 Prussian General Staff, *Plane*, Vol I, p.94.
12 Fabry, *Oudinot*, p.82.
13 Prussian General Staff, *Plane*, Vol I, pp.95-96.
14 Prussian General Staff, *Plane*, Vol II, p.96.

9 The Battle of Hagelberg 27 August 1813

1   Forming a column on the middle means that the column was formed on the middle of battalion when it was in line. In an attack column, this would put the 5th and 4th half companies in the front of the column. The 3rd, 2nd and 1st half companies would then stand in that sequence behind the 4th half company and the 6th, 7th, and 8th half companies would stand behind the 5th half company. Though normally the 1st and 2nd half companies would form the 1st Company, in this situation the 1st and 8th half companies stand adjacent to one another at the end of the battalion column. Similarly, forming a column on the left means that the battalion formed behind the left most company of the battalion when the battalion was in line. This puts the 7th and 8th half companies (or the 4th Company) in the front rank the 5th and 6th half companies (3rd Company) immediately behind them, etc.

2   Quistorp, *Nord Armée*, Vol I, p.407; Plotho, *Der Kreig*, Vol II, p.151.

3   Quistorp, *Nord Armée*, Vol I, p.407; Friederich, *Herbstfeldzuges*, Vol I, p.428.

4   Prussian General Staff, *Plane*, Vol I, p.100.

5   Prussian General Staff, *Plane*, Vol I, p.100.

6   Friederich, *Herbstfeldzuges*, Vol I, p.428.

7   Quistorp, *Nord Armée*, Vol I, p.410.

8   Plotho, *Der Kreig*, Vol II, p.151.

9   Prussian General Staff, *Plane*, Vol I, p.100.

10 Quistorp, *Nord Armée*, Vol I, p.411; Friederich, *Herbstfeldzuges*, Vol I, p.429.

11 Quistorp, *Nord Armée*, Vol I, p.412.

12 Prussian General Staff, *Plane*, Vol II, p.101.

13 Friederich, *Herbstfeldzuges*, Vol I, p.429.

14 Quistorp, *Nord Armée*, Vol I, p.413.

15 Friederich, *Herbstfeldzuges*, Vol I, p.429.

16 Quistorp, *Nord Armée*, Vol I, p.414.

17 Friederich, *Herbstfeldzuges*, Vol I, p.430.

18 Quistorp, *Nord Armée*, Vol I, p.414; Friederich, *Herbstfeldzuges*, Vol I, p.430.

19 Quistorp, *Nord Armée*, Vol I, p.415.

20 Friederich, *Herbstfeldzuges*, Vol I, p.430.

21 Friederich, *Herbstfeldzuges*, Vol I, p.430.

22 Friederich, *Herbstfeldzuges*, Vol I, p.430.

23 Friederich, *Herbstfeldzuges*, Vol I, p.431.

24 Friederich, *Herbstfeldzuges*, Vol I, p.430.

25 Prussian General Staff, *Plane*, Vol II, p.105.

26 The Prussians claim to have captured 33 officers and 1,320 men, but Martinien's *Tableaux par Corps et par Batailles des Officiers Tues et Blesses* does not support this. Indeed, it shows fewer than a dozen officers killed or wounded in all the infantry formations present in the battle.

27 It is unusual to report a landwehr battalion operating in skirmish formation inasmuch as that the landwehr was generally considered a militia and the ability of its officers to control the militia men would have been very poor. It is probable, however, that this regiment was still motivated by a high level of nationalism and patriotism and did not lose a significant number of men to desertion with the loosening of control that occurs when a unit deploys into skirmish formation.

28 Friederich, *Herbstfeldzuges*, Vol I, p.432.

29 Quistorp, *Nord Armée*, Vol I, p.421.

30 Friederich, *Herbstfeldzuges*, Vol I, p.433; Martinien, *Tableaux*, 1984, p.15; Prussian General Staff, *Plane*, Vol. II, p.107.

31 Martinien, *Tableaux*, p.15. & Prussian General Staff, *Plane*, Vol II, p.107.

32 Quistorp, *Nord Armée*, Vol I, p.422.

33 Friederich, *Herbstfeldzuges*, Vol I, p.433; Quistorp, *Nord Armée*, Vol I, p.425.

34 Quistorp, Nord Armée, Vol I, p.427.

35 Plotho, *Der Kreig*, Vol II, p.155.

36 Prussian General Staff, *Plane*, Vol II.

37 Boppe, *Croatie Militaire*, p.133.

38 Sauzey, *Allemands sous les Aigles Francaises, Le Regiment des Duches de Saxe*, p.172.

39 This is based on the assumption that Girard's battalions averaged 500 men and his squadrons averaged 100 men. The theoretical strength of a battalion was 840 men and that of a squadron was 250 men.

10 The Army of Bohemia Advances on Dresden 12–25 August 1813

1   Dodge, *Napoleon*, Vol IV, p.123.

2   Bonaparte, *Correspondence*, 20390.

3   Bonaparte, *Correspondence*, 20381.

4   Bonaparte, *Correspondence*, 20398.

5   Bonaparte, *Correspondence*, 20398.
6   The title "fürst" translates from the German as "prince".
7   The main Austrian army consisted of:
     9 Infantry Regiments (3 bns ea) = 27 battalions
     31 Infantry Regiments (2 bns ea) = 62 battalions
     8 Grenadier Battalions = 8 battalions
     5 Jager Battalions = 5 battalions
     10 Grenz Battalions = 10 battalions
     Total = 99,000 infantry
     7 Cuirassier Regiments = 28 squadrons
     6 Chevauléger Regiments = 36 squadrons
     3 Dragoon Regiments = 8 squadrons
     7 Hussar Regiments = 2 squadrons
     Total = 24,000 cavalry
     45 Artillery Batteries (280 guns) = 6,750 artillerists, etc.
8   Sporschil, *Grosse Chronik*, Vol I, pp.394-7.
9   Plotho, *Der Kreig*, Vol II, p.18.
10   Plotho, *Der Kreig*, Vol II, p.19.
11   Plotho, *Der Kreig*, Vol II, p.19.
12   Streifkorps were raiding parties formed of mostly of Cossacks, some line cavalry, and light infantry, i.e.
     jägers or fusiliers.
13   Sporschil, *Grosse Chronik*, Vol I, pp.394-7.
14   Bonaparte, *Correspondence*, 20397; Friederich, Herbstfeldzuges Vol I, p.115.
15   Friederich, *Herbstfeldzuges*, Vol I, p.162.
16   Sporschil, *Grosse Chronik*, Vol I, pp.400-401.
17   Sporschil, *Grosse Chronik*, Vol I, pp.402-403.
18   Plotho, *Der Kreig*, Vol II, p.27.
19   Fabry, *Wurtemberg*, p.90.
20   Wolf commanded the Mourmon and Tschernigov Infantry Regiments.
21   Chelvinski commanded the Revel Infantry Regiment and 4th Jager Regiment.
22   Treuffurt commanded the Tobolsk and Minsk Infantry Regiments.
23   Mamonov commanded the Volhynie and Krementchug Infantry Regiments.
24   Fabry, *Wurtemberg*, p.90.
25   Mesenzov's 5th Division was formed with the 23rd and 24th Jager Regiment Perm, Mohilev, Sievesk and
     Kalouga Infantry Regiments.
26   The Toula and Navajinsk Infantry Regiments were transferred to the Army of the North and the 25th and
     26th Jager Regiments under Roth, were with the advanced guard. The 14th Division, at this time, contained
     only the Tenginsk and Estonian Infantry Regiments and the Grand Duchess Catherine Battalion, which was
     transferred from the 5th Division for this battle.
27   Fabry, *Wurtemberg*, p.91; Plotho, *Der Kreig*, Vol II, p.28.
28   St. Cyr, *Memoires*, Vol II, p.79.
29   Fabry, *Wurtemberg*, pp.91-92.
30   Fabry, *Wurtemberg*, pp.91-92.
31   Plotho, *Der Kreig*, Vol II, p.29.
32   Fabry, *Wurtemberg*, pp.92-93.
33   Clément, *Campagne de 1813*, p.349.
34   Plotho, *Der Kreig*, Vol II, pp.34-35.
35   Fabry, *Wurtemberg*, p.96.
36   Clément, *Campagne de 1813*, p.350.
37   Fabry, *Wurtemberg*, p.CCIII.
38   Fabry, *Wurtemberg*, p.CCIII.
39   Fabry, *Wurtemberg*, p.CCI.
40   Fabry, *Wurtemberg*, p.CCVII.

41 Fabry, *Wurtemberg*, p.CCVIII.
42 "Colonnes serrées par division" are columns formed by three divisions of infantry (a division is two companies in a line) at a close interval (serrées), or at a distance of about 3 feet one behind the other.
43 Fabry, *Wurtemberg*, p.CCIX.
44 Fabry, *Wurtemberg*, p.CCXI.
45 The 1st Guard Division consisted of the Preobragenski, Semeovsky, and Ismailov Guard Infantry Regiments and the Guard Jager Regiment. In addition, it was accompanied by the five and a half squadrons of the Guard Hussar Regiment, the four squadrons of the Tartar Uhlan Regiment and three Guard artillery batteries – 36 guns.
46 Fabry, *Wurtemberg*, p.CCXII.
47 Pires brigade had been sent back to Dresden.
48 Fabry, *Wurtemberg*, p.CCXV.

11 The Battle of Dresden 26–27 August 1813

1   Bonaparte, *Correspondence*, Paris, #20356.
2   Plotho, *Der Kreig*, Vol II, p.42.
3   Plotho, *Der Kreig*, Vol II, p.42.
4   Plotho, *Der Kreig*, Vol II, p.43.
5   St. Cyr, *Memoires*, Vol II, pp.95-98.
6   St. Cyr, *Memoires*, Vol II, pp.100-101.
7   Consisting of two Russian batteries (24 guns), three Prussian batteries (24 guns) and eight Austrian batteries (64 guns).
8   Plotho, *Der Kreig*, Vol II, pp.44-45.
9   K. and K. Kriegsarchivs, *Befreiungskrieg*, Vol III, p.213.
10 Friederich, *Herbstfeldzuges*, Vol I, p.452.
11 K. and K. Kriegsarchivs, *Befreiungskrieg*, Vol III, p.214.
12 Plotho, *Der Kreig*, Vol II, p.45; Friederich, *Herbstfeldzuges*, Vol I, p.457.
13 Friederich, *Herbstfeldzuges*, Vol I, p.457.
14 St. Cyr, *Memoires*, Vol II, p.105.
15 Friederich, *Herbstfeldzuges*, Vol I, p.458.
16 Friederich, *Herbstfeldzuges*, Vol I, p.459.
17 Dumoustier was wounded on 26 August and replaced that evening by Curial.
18 St. Cyr, *Memoires*, Vol II, p.105.
19 K. and K. Kriegsarchivs, *Befreiungskrieg*, Vol III, p.203.
20 Plotho, *Der Kreig*, Vol II, p.46.
21 Plotho, *Der Kreig*, Vol II, p.46.
22 K. and K. Kriegsarchivs, *Befreiungskrieg*, Vol III, pp.204-205.
23 Beitzke, *Deutschen Freiheitskriege*, p.47.
24 Friederich, *Herbstfeldzuges*, Vol I, p.460.
25 K. and K. Kriegsarchivs, *Befreiungskrieg*, Vol III, p.215.
26 Friederich, *Herbstfeldzuges*, Vol I, p.461.
27 Friederich, *Herbstfeldzuges*, Vol I, pp.453-454, 462.
28 Friederich, *Herbstfeldzuges*, Vol I, p.463.
29 Friederich, *Herbstfeldzuges*, Vol I, p.463.
30 Plotho, *Der Kreig*, Vol II, p.47.
31 St. Cyr, *Memoires*, Vol II, p.106.
32 K. and K. Kriegsarchivs, *Befreiungskrieg*, Vol III, p.185.
33 K. and K. Kriegsarchivs, *Befreiungskrieg*, Vol III, p.186.
34 K. and K. Kriegsarchivs, Befreiungskrieg, Vol III, p.187.
35 Plotho, *Der Kreig*, Vol II, p.48.
36 K. and K. Kriegsarchivs, *Befreiungskrieg*, Vol III, p.189.
37 K. and K. Kriegsarchivs, *Befreiungskrieg*, Vol III, p.190.
38 Friederich, *Herbstfeldzuges*, Vol I, p.465.

39   K. and K. Kriegsarchivs, *Befreiungskrieg*, Vol III, p.217.

40   Quallenberg commanded the Esterhazy and Davidovich Infantry Regiments.

41   K. and K. Kriegsarchivs, *Befreiungskrieg*, Vol III, p.220.

42   Plotho, *Der Kreig*, Vol II, p.49.

43   Plotho, *Der Kreig*, Vol II, p.49; K. and K. Kriegsarchivs, Befreiungskrieg, Vol III, p.222.

44   K. and K. Kriegsarchivs, *Befreiungskrieg*, Vol III, p.223.

45   The 7th Chevauléger Regiment was formed of Poles and had been part of the Vistula Legion prior to being absorbed into the French line establishment.

46   K. and K. Kriegsarchivs, *Befreiungskrieg*, Vol III, p.231.

47   Plotho, *Der Kreig*, Vol II, p.51.

48   St. Cyr, *Memoires*, Vol II, p.107.

49   K. and K. Kriegsarchivs, *Befreiungskrieg*, Vol III, p.228.

50   Abele commanded the Erbach and Argenteau Infantry Regiments.

51   K. and K. Kriegsarchivs, *Befreiungskrieg*, Vol III, p.230.

52   K. and K. Kriegsarchivs, *Befreiungskrieg*, Vol III, p.235.

53   Sachsen-Coburg commanded the Empress Cuirassier Regiment (4 squadrons), the Russian Guard Uhlan Regiment (6 squadrons), and the Tartar Uhlan Regiment (4 squadrons).

54   Plotho, *Der Kreig*, Vol II, p.54.

55   Simon, *Kriegeserignisse*, p.17.

56   Plotho, *Der Kreig*, Vol II, p.54.

57   Plotho, *Der Kreig*, Vol II, p.56.

58   Simon, *Kriegeserignisse*, p.17.

59   Plotho, *Der Kreig*, Vol II, p.56.

60   Friederich, *Herbstfeldzuges*, Vol I, p.481.

61   Curial had taken command of the 1st Young Guard Division after the wounding of Dumoustier in the previous day's battle.

62   Plotho, *Der Kreig*, Vol II, p.56.

63   K. and K. Kriegsarchivs, *Befreiungskrieg*, Vol III, p.258.

64   Friederich, *Herbstfeldzuges*, Vol I, p.486.

65   Friederich, Herbstfeldzuges, Vol I, p.487.

66   A *"Divisionsmasse"* was a uniquely Austrian formation where two companies broke into four half companies, aligned themselves one behind the other, and closed their ranks up to about 3 feet between the half companies. This was, principally, an anti-cavalry formation.

67   K. and K. Kriegsarchivs, *Befreiungskrieg*, Vol III, p.261.

68   Friederich, *Herbstfeldzuges*, Vol I, p.485.

69   Weissenwolf and A. Liechtenstein commanded the 2nd and 4th Line Infantry Divisions of Gyulai's Corps. Meszko's 3rd Light Division belonged to Klenau's Corps, the bulk of which was not to arrive until later in the battle.

70   K. and K. Kriegsarchivs, *Befreiungskrieg*, Vol III, p.276.

71   K. and K. Kriegsarchivs, *Befreiungskrieg*, Vol III, p.277.

72   K. and K. Kriegsarchivs, Befreiungskrieg, Vol III, p.278.

73   O'Meara commanded the only brigade of Teste's 23rd Division that participated in the Battle of Dresden.

74   K. and K. Kriegsarchivs, *Befreiungskrieg*, Vol III, p.279.

75   Plotho, *Der Kreig*, Vol II, p.58.

76   K. and K. Kriegsarchivs, *Befreiungskrieg*, Vol III, p.280.

77   Friederich, *Herbstfeldzuges*, Vol I, p.492; Plotho, *Der Kreig*, Vol II, p.58.

78   Friederich, *Herbstfeldzuges*, Vol I, p.492.

79   Friederich, *Herbstfeldzuges*, Vol I, p.493.

80   Schuster & Francke,.*Sächsischen Armee*, Vol II, p.362.

81   K. and K. Kriegsarchivs, *Befreiungskrieg*, Vol III, p.280.

82   K. and K. Kriegsarchivs, *Befreiungskrieg*, Vol III, p.281.

83   K. and K. Kriegsarchivs, *Befreiungskrieg*, Vol III, p.282.

84   K. and K. Kriegsarchivs, *Befreiungskrieg*, Vol III, p.283.

85   K. and K. Kriegsarchivs, *Befreiungskrieg*, Vol III, p.284.
86   K. and K. Kriegsarchivs, *Befreiungskrieg*, Vol III, p.286.
87   K. and K. Kriegsarchivs, *Befreiungskrieg*, Vol III, p.286.
88   K. and K. Kriegsarchivs, *Befreiungskrieg*, Vol III, p.286.
89   Plotho, *Der Kreig*, Vol II, p.59.
90   K. and K. Kriegsarchivs, *Befreiungskrieg*, Vol III, p.287.
91   This was probably the 1/Kottulinsky Infantry Regiment.
92   Klenau's corps, at this time, consisted of the divisions of Mayer and Hohenlohe. Normally, Meszko's light division was assigned to this corps, but it had been detached earlier for other duties and was already on the battlefield.
93   K. and K. Kriegsarchivs, *Befreiungskrieg*, Vol III, p.288.
94   K. and K. Kriegsarchivs, *Befreiungskrieg*, Vol III, p.289.
95   K. and K. Kriegsarchivs, *Befreiungskrieg*, Vol III, p.290.
96   K. and K. Kriegsarchivs, *Befreiungskrieg*, Vol III, p.291.
97   K. and K. Kriegsarchivs, *Befreiungskrieg*, Vol III, p.291.
98   K. and K. Kriegsarchivs, *Befreiungskrieg*, Vol III, pp.261-262.
99   Friederich, *Herbstfeldzuges*, Vol I, p.483.; K. and K. Kriegsarchivs, *Befreiungskrieg*, Vol III, p.262.
100 K. and K. Kriegsarchivs, *Befreiungskrieg*, Vol III, pp.272–273.
101 Friederich, *Herbstfeldzuges*, Vol I, p.489.
102 K. and K. Kriegsarchivs, *Befreiungskrieg*, Vol III, p.273.
103 Allied propaganda later would report that Napoleon had personally the gun that killed his revolutionary rival for power in France. This was, however, not true.
104 Friederich, *Herbstfeldzuges*, Vol I, p.494.
105 Friederich, *Herbstfeldzuges*, Vol I, p.482.
106 K. and K. Kriegsarchivs, *Befreiungskrieg*, Vol III, p.262.
107 K. and K. Kriegsarchivs, *Befreiungskrieg*, Vol III, p.263.
108 K. and K. Kriegsarchivs, *Befreiungskrieg*, Vol III, p.268.
109 Friederich, *Herbstfeldzuges*, Vol I, p.482.
110 Friederich, *Herbstfeldzuges*, Vol I, p.488.
111 Weil, *Campagne de 1813*, pp.97i98; Martinien, *Tableaux*, p.86.
112 Plotho, *Der Kreig*, Vol II, p.60.
113 Clément, *Campagne de 1813*, p.359.
114 Plotho, *Der Kreig*, Vol II, p.61.

12 The French Pursuit After Dresden 27–28 August 1813

1   Fabry, *Wurtemberg*, p.CCXVIII.
2   Fabry, *Wurtemberg*, p.CCXIX.
3   Fabry, *Wurtemberg*, p.CCXXIII.
4   Fabry, *Wurtemberg*, p.CCXXXIV.
5   Fabry, *Wurtemberg*, p.CCXXXVI.
6   Fabry, *Wurtemberg*, p.CCXXXVI.
7   Fabry, *Wurtemberg*, p.CCXL.
8   Simon, *Kriegeserignisse*, p.20.
9   Fabry, *Wurtemberg*, p.CCXLII.
10   Fabry, Wurtemberg, p.CCXLII.
11   Fabry, *Wurtemberg*, p.CCXLIV.
12   At this time Pischnitzkywas leading only the Volhynie and Krementchug Infantry Regiments.
13   Fabry, Wurtemberg, p.CCXLVII.
14   Simon, Kriegeserignisse, p.21.
15   Clément, *Campagne de 1813*, p.365.
16   Marmont, *Memoires*, Vol V, p.159.
17   Marmont, *Memoires*, Vol V, p.160.
18   This is most certainly an exaggeration by a Marshal who was to fall into ill repute after his betrayal of

Napoleon in 1814 and was, no doubt, attempting to rebuild his reputation. The French word "*Raguser*" – to betray – originated from Marmont's title "Duc de Raguse".

19   Fabry, *Wurtemberg*, p.CCXLVII.
20   Fabry, *Wurtemberg*, p.CCLII.
21   Fabry, *Wurtemberg*, p.CCLV.
22   Fabry, Wurtemberg, p.CCLVIII.
23   Fabry, *Wurtemberg*, p.CCLIX.
24   The four squadrons of the 1st Silesian Hussars and half of Horse Battery #7 led the column. The 10th Brigade was joined by 6pdr Foot Battery #8,12pdr Foot Battery #3, and half of Horse Battery #7. The cavalry reserve was joined by Horse Battery #8, the 11th Brigade was joined by 6pdr Batteries #11 and #12, the 12th Brigade was joined by 6pdr Battery #13 and 12pdr Battery #6, and the three battalions of the 9th Brigade were joined by 6pdr Battery #21 and part of Horse Battery #9.
25   Fabry, *Wurtemberg*, p.CCLIX.
26   Simon, *Kriegeserignisse*, pp.25-6.
27   Fabry, *Wurtemberg*, p.CCLXVII.
28   Fabry, Wurtemberg, p.CCLXVII.
29   Fabry, Wurtemberg, p.CCLXX.
30   Martinien, Tableaux, p.24.& Fabry, Wurtemberg, p.CCLXX.

13 The Battle of Kulm 29 August–5 September 1813

1   Fabry, *Wurtemberg*, p.CCLXXIII.
2   Simon, *Kriegeserignisse*, pp.30-31; Fabry, *Wurtemberg*, p.CCLXXIII.
3   Simon, *Kriegeserignisse*, p.32.
4   Gobrecht commanded the 9th Chevaulégers-lanciers Regiment (2 sqns) and Anhalt Jäger zu Pferd (2 sqns).
5   Fabry, *Wurtemberg*, p.CCLXXV.
6   Plotho, *Der Kreig* Vol II, p.71.
7   Friederich, *Herbstfeldzuges*, Vol I, p.519.
8   Pouchelon's brigade consisted of the 7th Légère Regiment (4 bns) and 12th Line Regiment (4 bns).
9   Montesquiou-Fezensac commanded the 17th Line Regiment (4 bns) and 36th Line Regiment (2 bns).
10   Fabry, *Wurtemberg*, pp.CCLXXV-CCLXXVI.
11   The French artillery no doubt consisted of the 8/2nd & 15/9th Foot Artillery from 1st Division. It is possible, but unlikely, that some artillery from the corps reserve or horse battery from the I Cavalry Corps artillery reserve might have accompanied Corbineau and been on the field by this time.
12   Simon, *Kriegeserignisse*, p.37.
13   Plotho, *Der Kreig*, Vol II, p.71.
14   This is the same Diebitsch who affected the Treaty of Tauroggen between the Prussian Helfkorps and the Russians in December 1813.
15   Simon, *Kriegeserignisse*, p.38.
16   Fabry, *Wurtemberg*, p.CCLXXVII.
17   Plotho, *Der Kreig*, Vol II, p.72.
18   Clément, *Campagne de 1813*, p.369.
19   Dunesme commanded the 13th Légère Regiment (4 bns) and 25th Line Regiment (4 bns).
20   Doucet's brigade contained the 57th Line Regiment (4 bns) and 51st Line Regiment (2 bns).
21   Creutzer's brigade consisted of two provisional Demi-brigades, each with two battalions, and the 76th Line Regiment (2 bns) and 96th Line Regiment (2 bns).
22   The 1/7th Foot Artillery and 9/7th Foot Artillery, plus train units.
23   K. and K. Kriegsarchivs, *Befreiungskrieg* Vol IV, p.130.
24   Fabry, *Wurtemberg*, p.CCLXXXIV.
25   K. and K. Kriegsarchivs, *Befreiungskrieg* Vol IV, p.130.
26   Simon, *Kriegeserignisse*, pp.53–54.
27   K. and K. Kriegsarchivs, *Befreiungskrieg* Vol IV, p.131.
28   Fabry, *Wurtemberg*, p.CCLXXIX.

29   Simon, *Kriegeserignisse*, pp.42-43.
30   Mononoff commanded, at this time, only the Volhynie and Krementchug Infantry Regiments.
31   P. Hessen-Homburg's brigade consisted of the Hiller and Colloredo-Mansfeld Infantry Regiments.
32   Fabry, *Wurtemberg*, p.CCLXXXVIII.
33   Plotho, *Der Kreig*, Vol II, p.77.
34   Prussian General Staff, *Plane*, Vol II, pp.48-49.
35   K. and K. Kriegsarchivs, *Befreiungskrieg* Vol IV, p.132.
36   K. and K. Kriegsarchivs, *Befreiungskrieg* Vol IV, p.133.
37   K. and K. Kriegsarchivs, *Befreiungskrieg* Vol IV, p.135.
38   Plotho, *Der Kreig*, Vol II, p.76.
39   K. and K. Kriegsarchivs, *Befreiungskrieg* Vol IV, p.136.
40   K. and K. Kriegsarchivs, *Befreiungskrieg* Vol IV, p.137.
41   K. and K. Kriegsarchivs, *Befreiungskrieg* Vol IV, p.138.
42   Fabry, *Wurtemberg*, p.CCLXXXIX.
43   K. and K. Kriegsarchivs, *Befreiungskrieg* Vol IV, p.139.
44   Fabry, *Wurtemberg*, p.CCLXXXIX.
45   Fabry, *Wurtemberg*, p.CCXC.
46   Simon, *Kriegeserignisse*, p.55.
47   K. and K. Kriegsarchivs, *Befreiungskrieg* Vol IV, p.140.
48   K. and K. Kriegsarchivs, *Befreiungskrieg* Vol IV, p.141.
49   The Erbach Regiment was assigned to Wimpffen's division of Colloredo's Corps.
50   Chapuis, *Observations*, pp.23-24.
51   K. and K. Kriegsarchivs, *Befreiungskrieg* Vol IV, p.142.
52   K. and K. Kriegsarchivs, *Befreiungskrieg* Vol IV, p.143.
53   K. and K. Kriegsarchivs, *Befreiungskrieg* Vol IV, p.145.
54   Fabry, *Wurtemberg*, p.CCXCI.
55   K. and K. Kriegsarchivs, *Befreiungskrieg* Vol IV, p.149.
56   The 9th Chevau-legers had formerly been the 30th Chasseur-Lancier Regiment, sometimes known as the Red Lancers because of their unique, baggy red breeches.
57   Fabry, *Wurtemberg*, p.CCXCV.
58   K. and K. Kriegsarchivs, *Befreiungskrieg* Vol IV, p.146.
59   K. and K. Kriegsarchivs, *Befreiungskrieg* Vol IV, p.149.
60   K. and K. Kriegsarchivs, *Befreiungskrieg* Vol IV, p.150.
61   K. and K. Kriegsarchivs, *Befreiungskrieg* Vol IV, p.152.
62   K. and K. Kriegsarchivs, *Befreiungskrieg* Vol IV, p.151.
63   Fabry, *Wurtemberg*, p.CCXCV.
64   This force consisted of the 3/8th Silesian Cavalry Landwehr, I/1st Silesian Landwehr Cavalry, and two squadrons of the 2nd Silesian Landwehr Cavalry Regiment.
65   Fabry, *Wurtemberg*, p.CCXCVI.
66   Simon, *Kriegeserignisse*, p.63.
67   K. and K. Kriegsarchivs, *Befreiungskrieg* Vol IV, p.153
68   Fabry, *Wurtemberg*, p.CCC.
69   K. and K. Kriegsarchivs, *Befreiungskrieg* Vol IV, p.154.
70   Chapuis, *Observations*, p.29.
71   K. and K. Kriegsarchivs, *Befreiungskrieg* Vol IV, p.155.
72   Fabry, *Wurtemberg*, p.CCCI.
73   Fabry, *Wurtemberg*, p.CCCII.
74   French Archives, Carton C^2–538.
75   Numbers are officers, men, horses.
76   Fabry, Wurtemberg, p.CCCV. Because of the proximity to the Battle of Dresden and the improbability that a muster was run between Dresden and Kulm, these figures should be viewed as the combined losses of Kleist's command in both battles.
77   Chapuis, *Observations*, p.34.

14 Ney Takes an Independent Command. The Battle of Dennewitz 2–7 September 1813

1   Prussian General Staff, *Plane*, Vol I, p.60.
2   There is more than a modest amount of confusion about how many of Dombrowski's Poles joined Ney. Zoltowski states only one battalion of the 2nd Regiment, while Kukasiewicz states two regiments. Zoltowski states 600 cavalry, Lewell speaks of one squadron of the 4th Uhlans and Gembarzewski speaks of three squadrons of the 2nd Uhlans and later mentions the presence of the 4th Uhlans. Prussian sources indicate a regiment and record the loss of its colonel. Though the 4th Polish cavalry regiment was, in fact, a chasseur regiment, they often carried lances, so this distinction is not a decisive, clarifying distinction. My analysis of these facts leads me to the conclusion that it was a full regiment and that it was probably the 2nd Uhlans.
3   Prussian General Staff, *Plane*, Vol I, p.60.
4   Prussian General Staff, *Plane*, Vol I, p.61.
5   Prussian General Staff, *Plane*, Vol I, p.63.
6   Quistorp, *Nord Armée*, Vol I, p.453.
7   Prussian General Staff, *Plane*, Vol I, p.64.
8   Quistorp, *Nord Armée*, Vol I, p.453.
9   Clément, *Campagne de 1813*, p.398.
10   von Boyen, *Darestellung*, p.14.
11   Schmitterlöw's detachment consisted of the one squadron of the 2nd West Prussian Dragoon Regiment.
12   Prussian General Staff, Plane, Vol I, p.71.
13   The 24/2nd and 36/2nd Foot Artillery.
14   Rossler, Tagebücher, p.341.
15   Krukowiecki's 18th Light Cavalry Brigade consisted of the 2nd Uhlans and 4th Chasseur Regiments. The 4th Chasseurs were probably not present at Dennewitz. The brigade had been part of the Wittenberg garrison and was transferred to Ney's forces after the Battle of Gross-Beeren.
16   von Boyen, *Darestellung*, p.16.
17   The 1/, 2/, Jager/Brandenburg Dragoon Regiment were assigned to Oppen's cavalry reserve, part of Bülow's 3rd Corps.
18   Quistorp, *Nord Armée*, Vol I, p.490.
19   Prussian General Staff, *Plane*, Vol I, p.73.
20   Prussian General Staff, *Plane*, Vol I, p.74.
21   On that day Oppen commanded the Königin Dragoons, 2nd West Prussian Dragoons (both with 4 squadrons), Pomeranian National Cavalry Regiment, 2nd Pomeranian, 2nd and 4th Kurmärk Landwehr Cavalry Regiments (each with 3 squadrons). The 2nd West Prussian Dragoons, however, may not have been here, as they are also shown with Tauentzien's forces as a reserve.
22   Borstell's advance had been unhurried. He left posts in Kropstädt and another, under General von Ackercreutz, to watch the road. As Borstell arrived on the Dalichow heights, he quickly realized that he was no longer able to call those detachments back to his force and found himself less three battalions, five squadrons and two guns. He was then ordered to move to Eckmansdorf and from there to support Bülow, who was heavily engaged.
23   The term "denkmal" means "memorial" and this is, no doubt, a name applied to the hill sometime after the battle. Unfortunately, this site is not now identifiable by the presence of a memorial. The only two memorials on the battlefield are in the center of Dennewitz. Efforts to follow the original road from Dennewitz to Jüterbogk in 1993 failed and ended in an apparently abandoned military preserve surrounded with barbed wire and labeled with no trespassing signs marked "lebensgefahr" (dangerous to life).
24   Quistorp, *Nord Armée*, Vol I, p.494.
25   von Boyen, *Darestellung*, pp.18-19.
26   Prussian General Staff, *Plane*, Vol I, p.75.
27   Prussian General Staff, *Plane*, Vol I, p.76.
28   von Boyen, *Darestellung*, p.24.
29   This was probably Oberst Hammerstein. Much of this brigade had already deserted and the rest would desert before too long. It is hardly surprising that it failed to act in this instance.
30   von Boyen, *Darestellung*, p.39.
31   Prussian General Staff, *Plane*, Vol I, p.78.

32 These skirmishers were drawn from the following battalions: von Treskow (1/5th Kurmärk), von Mellerski (4/5th Kurmärk), and von Grolmann (2/2nd Neumärk).

33 von Boyen, *Darestellung*, p.31.

34 Rossler, *Tagebücher*, p.342.

35 von Boyen, *Darestellung*, p.43.

36 Quistorp, *Nord Armée*, Vol I, p.509.

37 von Boyen, *Darestellung*, p.40.

38 These were the landwehr battalions of Wins (1/1st Silesian Landwehr Regiment), Klöden (2/1st Kurmärk) and Dullack (1/1st Kurmärk Landwehr Regiment).

39 This may have been 6pdr Foot Battery #17 (Gleim). The sources consulted conflict.

40 Prussian General Staff, *Plane*, Vol I, p.79.

41 Prussian General Staff, Plane, Vol I, p.79.

42 The attacking force consisted of 1/Colberg Infantry Regiment, Fus/Colberg Infantry Regiment, 1/1st Neumärk Landwehr Regiment, 2nd East Prussian Grenadier Battalion, 1/3rd East Prussian Infantry Regiment, Fus/3rd East Prussian Infantry Regiment, 1/3rd East Prussian Landwehr Regiment, 6pdr Foot Battery #5, Glasenapp and the 6pdr Horse Battery #5, Neindorff.

43 von Boyen, *Darestellung*, p.61; Prussian General Staff, *Plane*, Vol I, p.80.

44 Graben was the commander of the Colberg Infantry Regiment.

45 von Boyen, *Darestellung*, p.50.

46 Prussian General Staff, *Plane*, Vol I, p.82.

47 Prussian General Staff, *Plane*, Vol I, p.83.

48 The Fusilier Battalion was commanded by von Cardell.

49 von Boyen, *Darestellung*, p.54.

50 Prussian General Staff, *Plane*, Vol I, p.83.

51 Prussian General Staff, *Plane*, Vol I, p.84.

52 Prussian General Staff, *Plane*, Vol I, p.84.

53 von Boyen, *Darestellung*, p.59.

54 Prussian General Staff, *Plane*, Vol I, pp.85-86.

55 Prussian General Staff, *Plane*, Vol I, p.90.

56 Prussian General Staff, *Plane*, reports the 23rd Line lost 1 colonel, 17 officers, and 2,800 men, however, French records of show that on 15 August the regiment had only 2,286 men. Also, Martinien indicates only 13 officers and men killed or wounded in the Battle of Dennewitz and none at Dahme.

57 Rossler, *Tagebücher*, p.346.

58 Schuster & Francke, *Sächsischen Armee*, Vol II, p.359.

Bibliography

d'Amonville, Cpt. *Les Cuirassiers du Roy, Le 8e Cuirassiers, Journal Historique du Régiment 1638-1892* (Paris: Lahure, 1892).

Anonymous, *Campagne de Prince Eugène en Italie Pendant les Annees 1813 et 1814* (Paris: Plancher, 1817).

Anonymous, *Denkwürdigkeiten des Mecklenburg-Strelitzischen Husaren-Régiments in den jahren des Befreiungskampfes 1813 bis 1815* (Neubrandenburg: C. Brünslow, 1854).

Anonymous, *Geschichte des Magdeburgischen Husaren-Regiments Nr. 10* (Berlin, A. Duncker, 1863).

Anonymous, *Historique du 2ème Régiment d'Artillerie* (Grenoble: Librairie Dauphinoise, 1899).

Anonymous, *Historique du 3e Régiment de Cuirassiers, ci-devant du Commissaire Général 1645-1892* (Paris: Boussod, Valadon & Cie., 1893).

Anonymous, *Historique du 4e Régiment de Cuirassiers, 1643-1897* (Paris: Lahure & Cie., 1893).

Anonymous, *Historique du 127e Régiment d'Infanterie* (Valenciennes: P.& G.Girard, 1897).

Anonymous, "Premier Siège de Glogau, Mars 1813 a Juin 1813," *Le Spectateur Militaire* Vol 1905.

von Ardenne, *Geschichte des Husaren-Regiments von Zieten (Brandenburgisches) Nr. 3* (Berlin: Mittler & Sohn, 1905).

Arthur, R., *A Legiao Portuguesa ao servico de Napoleo 1808-1813* (Lisbon: Livraria Ferin, 1901).

d'Artois, P.H., *Rélation de la Defense de Danzig en 1813 par le 10e corps de l'Armée Francaise, contre l'Armée combine Russe et Prussienne* (Paris: Ladrange, 1820).

Atteridge, A.H., *Joachim Murat* (New York: Brentano's, 1911).

Arvers, P., *Historique du 82e Régiment d'Infanterie de Ligne et du 7e Régiment d'Infanterie Légère, 1684-1876* (Paris: Tyopgrahie Lahure, 1876).

Aubier, Lt., *Un Régiment de Cavalerie Légère de 1793 à 1815* (Paris, Berger-Levrault & Cie., 1888).

Augoyat, *Relation de la défense de Torgau par les troupes francaises en 1813* (Paris: Chez Leneveu, 1840).

Austro-Hungrian (K. u. K.) Kriegsarchiv, *Befreiungskrieg 1813 and 1814* (Vienna, Verlag von L.W.Seidel & Sohn, 1913).

Bagés, Cdt. G., *Le Siege de Glogau 1813-1814* (Paris: H.Charles-Lavauzelle, date unknown).

von Barsewisch, *Geschichte des Grossherzoglich Badischen Leib-Grenadier-Regiments (1803-1872)* (Karlsruhe: Chr. F. Müller, 1893).

de Behaine, Cdt L., *La Campagne de France, Napoleon et les Allies sur la Rhin* (Paris: Perrin & Cie., 1913).

Beitzke, Dr. H., *Geschichte der Deutschen Freiheitskriege in den Jahren 1813 and 1814* (Berlin: Dunker & Humblot, 1864).

Belhomme, Lt. Col., *Histoire de l'lnfanterie en France* (Paris: H. Charles-Lavauzelle, 1893-1902).

Bigge, W., *Geschichte des Infanterie-Régiments Kaiser Wilhelm* (2. Grossherzoglich Hessisches) Nr. 116 (Berlin: Mittler & Sohn, 1893).

Bleibtreu, C., *Maschalle, Generale, Soldaten, Napoleons I* (Berlin: A. Schall, unknown date).

Bleibtreu, C., *Die Völkerschlacht bei Leipzig* (Leipzig: T.Thomas, 1907).

Blond, G., *La Grande Armée* (Paris: R. Laffont, 1979).

Bogdanovich, M.I., *Istoria Bojny 1813 Goda, Za Nezavisimost' Germanii po Dostobernym' Istochnikam' Sostabdena po Bysochayshchemy Pobeleniju* (St. Petersburg: 1863).

Bogdanovich, M.I., *Istorich Voin 1813 Goda Za Nezavicimost' Germanii Po Dostovern'm' Istochnikam'* (St. Petersburg: 1863).

Bogdanovich, M.I., *Istorich Voin 1814 Goda Vo Frantsii i Nizlozhenich Napoleona I* (St. Petersburg: 1865).

von Bonin, U., *Geschichte des Ingenieurkorps and der Pioniere in Preussen* (Wiesbaden: LTR Verlag, 1981).

Bonaparte, N., *Correspondance de Napoléon 1er* (Paris: H. Plon, 1868).

Bonnières de Wierre, Cpt. A., *Historique du 3e Régiment de Dragons* (Nantes: Bourgeois, 1892).

Boppe, A., *Les Espagnols dans la Grande Armée; Le Division Romana (1808-1809); Le Régiment Joseph Napoleon (1809-1813)* (Paris: Berger-Levrault & Cie., 1899).

Boppe, A., *La Legion Portuguese (1808-1813)* (Paris: Berger-Levrault & Cie., 1897).

Bory, J.R. *Régiments Suisses au Service de France* (Freiburg: Collection "Le Shako", 1975).

Bouchard, S., *Historique du 28e Régiment de Dragons* (Paris: Berger-Levrault & Cie., 1893).

Boucquoy, E.L., *Les Gardes d'honneur du Premier Empire* (Paris: A. Crépin-Leblond, 1908).

Boucquoy, E.L., *La Garde Impériale; Troupes a Pied* (Paris, J. Grancher, 1977).

Boucquoy, E.L., *La Garde Impériale; Troupes à cheval* (Paris, J. Grancher, 1977).

Boucquoy, E.L., *La cavalerie légère (les hussards, les chasseurs à cheval)* (Paris, J. Grancher, 1980).

Boucquoy, E.L., *L'infanterie* (Paris, J. Grancher, 1979).

Boucquoy, E.L., *Les Cuirassiers* (Paris, J. Grancher, 1978).

Boucquoy, E.L., *Dragons et Guides d'Etat-major* (Paris, J. Grancher, 1980).

Bourgue, Lt. M., *Historique du 3e Régiment d'Infanterie (ex-Piémont) 1569-1891* (Paris: Henri Charles-Lavauzelle, 1894).

von Boyen, Col., *Darstellung der Vorgang in der Schlacht von Dennewitz: Nach den Geschichten der betreffenden Regimenter Mit besonderer Berücksichtigung der Errinerungen des damaligen Generalstabschefs* (Berlin: Julius Sittenfeld, 1893).

Breton de la Martinière, M, *Campagnes de Buonaparte en 1812,1813, et 1814 jusqu'a son Abdication* (Paris: J.Dentu, 1814).

Brett-James, A., *Europe Against Napoleon* (New York: McMillian, 1970).

Burghersh, Lord, *Memoir of the Operations of the Allied Operations under Prinz Schwarzenburg and Marschal Blücher During the Latter End of 1813 and the Year 1814* (London: J. Murray, 1822).

Burturlin, D., *Tableau de la Campagne d'Autome de 1813 en Allemagne, Depuis la Rupture de l'Armistice jusqu'au Passage du Rhin par l'Armée Francais* (Paris: A. Bertrand & Magimel, Anselin & Pochard, 1817).

Calmon-Maison, J.J.R, *Le Général Maison et le 1er Corps de la Grande Armée: Campagne de Belgique (decembre 1813-avril 1814)* (Paris: 1870).

Camon, Col., *La guerre Napoléonienne, Les Batailles, Vol IV* (Paris: Librairie Militaire R. Chapelot, 1910).

du Casse, A., *Mémoires et Correspondance Politique et Militaire du Prince Eugene* (Paris: Michel Lévy Frères, 1859).

Cathcart, G., *Commentaries on the War in Russia and Germany in 1812 and 1813* (London: J. Murray, 1850).

Chandler, D., *Dictionary of the Napoleonic Wars* (New York: MacMillan, 1979).

Chandler, D., *The Campaigns of Napoleon* (New York: MacMillan, 1966).

Chandler, D., *Napoleon's Marshals* (New York: MacMillan, 1987).

Chapuis, Col., *Observation sur les Combats de Culm, des 29 et 30 Aôut 1813* (Paris: L. Martinet, 1853).

Charras, Lt. Col., *Historie de la Guerre de 1813 en Allemagne* (Paris: 1870).

Chuquet, A., *Inédits Napoléoniens* (Paris: Ancienne Librairie Fontemoing et Cie., 1914-1919).

Chuquet, A., *Ordres et Apostilles de Napoleon* (Paris: Librarie Ancienne Honoré Champion, 1912).

Chavane, J., *Historie du 11e Cuirassiers* (Paris: C. Charavay, 1889).

Clément, G., *Campagne de 1813* (Paris: H. Charles-Lavauzelle, date unknown).

Clerc, *Historique du 79e Régiment d'Infanterie* (Paris: Berger-Levrault & Cie., 1896).

von Conrady, C., *Geschichte des Königlich Preussischen Sechsten Infanterie-Regiments von seiner Stiftung im Jahr 1773 zu Ende des Jahres 1865* (Glogau: C. Flemming, 1857).

Corda, H., *Le Regiment de la Fère et le 1er Régiment d'Artillerie* (Paris, Berger-Levrault & Cie., 1906).

Cosse-Brissac, R., *Historique du 7e Régiment de Dragoons 1673-1909* (Paris: Leroy, 1909).

Diamant-Berger, M., *Le 19e Régiment du Chasseurs à cheval 1792-1826, 1872-1919* (Paris, Librairie Courtot, date unknown).

Drexl, Dr. F., *Die Befreiungskriege 1813-1815* (Regensberg: F. Habbel, 1913).

Dupre, Chef de Bataillon, *Les Fastes du 14e Régiment de Ligne* (Paris, Librairie Militaire d'Anselin, 1956).

Dupuy, Cmdt. R., *Historique du 12e Régiment de Chasseurs de 1788 à 1891* (Paris: E. Person, 1891).

Duroisel, Cpt. G., *Historique du 93 Régiment d 'Infanterie Ancien Enghien et 18e Légère* (La Roche-sur-Yon: Ivonnet & Filles, 1893).

von Eck, *Geschichte des 2. Westfälischen Husaren-Régiments Nr. 11 and seiner Stammtruppen von 1807-1893* (Mainz: H. Kusittich, 1893).

d'Eckmuhl, *Le Maréchal Davout, Prince d'Eckmuhl, Correspondence inedite 1790-1815* (Paris: Perrin & Cie., 1887).

Esposito, Gen., *A Military History and Atlas of the Napoleonic Wars* (New York: AMS Press, 1978).

Fabry, G., *Journal des Operations des III et V Corps en 1813* (Paris: Librairie Militaire R. Chapelot et Cie., 1902).

Fabry, G., *Journal des Campagnes du Prince du Wurtemberg* (Pairs: Librairie Militaire R. Chapelot et Cie., 1907).

Fabry, G., *Étude sur les Operations du Maréchal Oudinot du 15 aout au 4 septembre 1813* (Paris: Librairie Militaire R. Chapelot et Cie., 1910).

Fabry, G., *Étude sur les Operations de 1'Empereur 5 Septembre au 21 Septembre 1813* (Paris: Librairie Militaire R. Chapelot & Cie., 1913).

Fain, Baron, *Manuscrit de Mil Huit Cent Treize, Contenant le precis des Evénemens de cette Année Pour Servir à 1'Histoire de l'Empereur Napoléon* (Paris: Delaunay Librairie, 1824).

Fiffre, E., *Histoire des Troupes Étrangeres au Service de France* (Paris: Librairie Militaire, 1854).

Foucart, Cmdt., *Une Division de Cavalerie Légère en 1813* (Paris: Librairie Militaire Berger-Levrault et Cie., 1891).

von Freytag-Loringhoven, *Kriegslehren nach Clausewitz aus den Feldzügen 1813 and 1814* (Berlin: E.S. Mittler and Sohn., 1908).

Friederich, E., *Die Befreiungskriege 1813-1815* (Berlin: Ernst Siegfried Mittler & Sohn., 1913).

Friederich, R., *Die Schlacht an der Katzbach* (Berlin, E.Siegfried Mittler & Sohn., 1913).

von Fritz Kersten & Ortenberg, G., *Hessisches Militär zur Zeit des Deutschen Bundes* (Beckum: Deutschen Gesellschaft für Heereskunde e. V., 1984).

Galli, *L'Allemagne en 1813* (Paris: Garnier Freres., 1889).

Gasiorowski, M.W., *Mémoires militaires de Joseph Grabowski, Officier à l'état-major imperial de Napoléon 1er 1812-1813-1814* (Paris, Librairie Plon., 1907).

Giesse, K., *Kassel-Moskau-Küstrin 1812-1813* (Leipzig: Verlag der Dykschen Buchlandlung, 1912).

Gilardone, G., *Bayerns Anteil am Herbstfeldzuge 1813, Darstellungen aus der Bayerischen Kriegs- and Herresgeschichte* (Munich: K. B. Kriegsarchiv, 1913).

Gleich, *Die ersten 100 Jahren des Uhlanen-Régiments König Wilhelm (2 Württemberger) Nr. 20* (Stuttgart: Uhland'schen Buchdruckerei, G.m.b.h., date unknown).

Grossen Generalstab Kriegsgeschichtliche Abteilung II Deutschland, *Urkundliche Beiträge and Forschung zur Geschichte des Preussischen Heeres: Die Gefechtsausbildung der Preussische Infanterie von 1806* (Wiesbaden: LTR-Verlag, 1982).

Grossen Generalstab Kriegsgeschichtliche Abteilung II Deutschland, *Urkundliche Beiträge and Forschung zur Geschichte des Preussischen Heeres: Der Preussische Kavalleriedienst von 1806* (Wiesbaden: LTR-Verlag, 1984).

Grossen Generalstab Kriegsgeschichtliche Abteilung II Deutschland, *Pläne der Schlachten and Treffen welche von der preussische Armee in den feldzügen der Jahre 1813, 14, and 15 geliefert worden* (Berlin: G.Reimer, 1821).

Guillon, E., *Napoleon et la Suisse, 1803-1815* (Paris: Librairie Plon, 1910).

Gumtau, C.F, *Die Jäger and Schützen des Preussischen Heeres* (Berlin: E.S. Mittler, 1835).

von Guttenberg, E., "Die bayerische Nationalgarde II Classe in den Befreiungskriegen", *Darstellungen aus der Bayerischen Kriegs- and Heeresgeschichte* (Munich: K. B. Kriegsarchiv, 1913).

Guye, A., *Le Bataillon de Neuchâtel, dit les Canaris au service de Napoleon* (Neuchâtel: A la Baconnière, 1964).

Henderson, E., *Blücher and the Uprising of Prussia against Napoleon 1806-1815* (New York: AMS Press, 1978).

Henke, C., *Davout and die Festung Hamburg-Harburg 1813-14* (Berlin, E.S. Mittler and Sohn, 1911).

Heuman, Lt. Col., *Historique du 148e Régiment d'Infanterie* (Paris: H. Charles-Lavauzelle, date unknown).

von Holleben, Gen. Maj., *Geschichte des Frühjahresfeldzuges 1813 and Vorgeschichte* (Berlin, E. Siegfried Mittler & Sohn, 1904).

von Holz, Col. Freiherr G., *1813-1815 Österreich in den Befreiungskriegen* (Vienna: A. Edlingers, 1912).

James, C., *An Universal Military Dictionary in English and French in which are explained the Terms of the Principal Sciences that are Necessary for the Information of an Officer* (London: T. Egerton, 1816).

Jerabek, R., *Die Kämpfe in Südkärnten 1813* (Vienna: Heeregeschichtliches Museum, 1986).

Jomini, Gen. Baron, *Historie Critique et Militaire des Campagnes de la Revolution Paisant suit au Traite des Grandes Operations militaires* (Paris: Chez Magimel, Anselin & Pouchard, 1816).

Jomini, Gen. Baron, *Réplique du Colonel Jomini à Lord Londonderry (General Stuart) sur Les evenements de la Campagne de Dresde en 1813* (date unknown, publisher unknown).

Jomini, Gen. Baron, *Traité des Grand Operations Militaires, Contenant l'Historie Critique des Campagnes de Frederic II, Comparées à celles de l'Emperor Napoléon* (Paris: Magimel, 1811).

de Juzancourt, G. *Historique du 7e Régiment de Cuirassiers (1659-1886)* (Paris: Berger-Levrault & Cie., 1887).

de Juzancourt, G. *Historique du 10e Régiment du Cuirassiers (1643-1891)* (Paris: Berger-Levrault & Cie., 1893).

Kircheisen, F., *Napoleon I. and das Zeitalter der Befreiungskriege in Bildern* (Munich: G.Müller: 1914).

Klessman, E., *Die Befreiungskriege in Augenzeugenberichten* (Düsseldorff: Karl Rauch Verlag, 1967).

von Knobelsdorff-Brenkenhoff, B.,*Briefe aus den Befreiungskriegen, Ein Beitrag zur Situation von Truppe and Heimat in den Jahren 1813/14* (Bonn:1981).

Königlich Bayerischen Kriegsarchiv, *Darstellungen aus der Bayerischen Kreigs- and Heeresgeschichte* (Munich: J. Lindauersche, Buchhandlung, 1900-1914).

K. and K. Kriegsarchivs, *Befreiungskrieg 1813 and 1814* (Vienna: Verlag von L.W. Seidel and Sohn, 1913).

Kraft, Heinz, *Die Württemberger in den Napoleonischen Kreigen* (Stuttgart: 1953).

von L.-G., B., *Aus Hannovers militärischer Vergangenheit* (Hannover: Buchdruckerei von Arnold Weichelt, 1880).

Lachouque, H., *The Anatomy of Glory* (Providence, RI: Brown University Press, 1962).

Leonard, K.C., *Geschichtliche Darstellung der Schlacht bei Hauau am 30. Oktober 1813* (Hanau: Fr. König's Buchhandlung, 1913).

Léfèbvre de Behaine, *La Campagne de France, L'Invasion (decembre 1813 - janvier 1814)* (Paris: Librarie Academique Perrin, 1934).

Lewinski & Brauchitsch, *Geschichte des Grenadier-Regiments König Wilhelm I (2. Westpreussischen) Nr. 7.* (Glogau: C. Flemming, 1897).

zur Lippe-Weissenfeld, *E. Graf Geschichte des Königlich Preussischen 6. Husaren-Regiments (ehedem 2. Schlesischen)* (Berlin: Königlichen Geheimen Ober-Hofbuchdruckerei, 1860).

Louvat, Cpt., *Historique du 7eme Hussards* (Paris: Pairault & Cie., 1887).

Lumbroso, A., *Correspondance du Joachim Murat* (Turin: Roux Frassati et Cie., 1899).

Lunsman, F., *Die Armee des Königreichs Westfalen 1807-1813* (Berlin: C. Leddihn, 1935).

M. de M****, *Le siège de Dantzig en 1813* (Paris: 1814).

Maag, Dr. A., *Geschichte der Schweizer Truppen in Französische Dienst vom Ruckzug aus Russland bis zum zweiten Pariser Freiden* (Basel: E. Kuhn, 1894).

Mackensen, *Schwarze Husaren, Geschichte des 1. Leib-Husaren-Regiments Nr. 1 and des 2. Leib-Husaren-Régiments Kaiserin Nr. 2* (Berlin: Ernst Siegfried Mittler and Sohn, 1892).

Madelin, L., *Histoire du Consulate et de l'Empire* (Paris: Librairie Hachette, 1950).

Marbot, Baron de, *Mémoires de Baron de Marbot* (Paris: Librairie Plon, 1892).

de Margon, Cmdt, *Historique du 8e Régiment de Chasseurs de 1788 à 1888* (Verdun: BenveLallemant, 1889).

de Martimprey, A., *Historique du 8e Régiment de Cuirassiers d'apres les Archives du Corps, celles du Depot de Guerre, et autres Documents* (Paris: Berger-Levrault, 1888).

de Marmont, A.F.L.V, *Mémoires du Maréchal Marmont, Duc de Raguse, de 1792 à 1841* (Paris: Perrotin, 1857).

Martinet, M., *Historique du 9e Régiment de Dragons* (Paris: H.T.Hamel, 1883).

Martinien, A., *Tableaux par corps et par batailles des Officières Tués et Blessés pendant les Guerres de l'Empire (1805-1815)* (Paris: Librairie L. Fournier, 1909).

Mason, F., *Cavaliers de Napoleon* (Paris: Librairie Ollendorff, date unknown).

Maude, F.N., *1813: The Leipzig Campaign* (New York: MacMillian, 1908).

de Mazade, Ch., *Correspondance du Maréchal Davout, Prince d'Eckmühl 1801-1815* (Paris: Librairie Plon, 1885).

McQueen, J., *The Campaigns of 1812, 1813, and 1814* (Glasgow: E. Khull & Co., 1815).

Mirus, R., *Das Treffen bei Wartenburg, am 3. Oktober 1813* (Berlin: E.S. Mittler and Sohn, 1863).

Mollard, J., *Historique du 63 Régiment d'Infanterie* (Paris: Berger-Levrault & Cie., 1887).

Müller-Leobnitz, *a.D., Die Schlacht an der Katzbach* (Liegnitz: Niederschlesische Tageszeitung, 1938).

Nafziger, G.F, *The Russian Army, 1800-1815* (Cambridge: Ont., RAFM, 1983).

Nafziger, G.F, *The Bavarian and Westphalian Armies, 1799-1815* (Cambridge: Ont., RAFM, 1981, 1983).

von der Oelsnitz, A.C., *Geschichte des Königlich Preussischen Ersten Infanterie-Regiments seit seiner Stiftung im Jahr 1619 bis zur Gegenwart* (Berlin: E.C. Mittler & Sohn, 1855).

Odeleben, O. von, *Napoleons Feldzug in Sachsen im Jahr 1813* (Meisenheim: Anton Hain K.G., 1970).

Ore, C., *1er Régiment de Chasseurs 1651-1903* (Châteaudun: Laussedat, 1903).

Paret, P., *Yorck and the Era of Prussian Reform 1807-1815* (Princeton, NJ: Princeton University Press, 1966).

Parquin, Cpt, *Souvenirs du Capitaine Parquin 1803-1814* (Paris: Boussod, Valadon, & Cie., 1892).

Paulig, F.R., *Geschichte der Befreiungskriege* (Frankfort: Frederich Paulig, 1891).

Pelet, General, *Des Principales Opérations de la Campagne de 1813* (Extracted from the *Spectateur Militaire*).

Petre, F.L., *Napoleon's Last Campaign in Germany – 1813* (New York: Hippocrene, 1974).

Pfister, A., *Aus dem Lager des Rheinsbundes 1812 and 1813* (Leipzig: Deutsche Verlags-Anstalt, 1897).

Pflug-Harttung, *1813-1815, Illustrierte Geschichte der Befreiungskriege* (Stuttgart: Union Deutsche Verlagsgeselleschaft, 1913).

Phillippart, J., *Napoleon's Campaign in Germany and France 1813-1814* (London: C.J. Barrington, 1814).

Phillippart, J., *Memoires and Campaigns of Charles John, Prince Royal of Sweden* (London: C.J. Barrington, 1814).

Pichard & Tuety, *Unpublished Correspondence of Napoleon I* (New York: Duffield & Co., 1913).

Pieron, Lt., *Histoire d'un Régiment, La 32me Demi-Brigade 1775-1890* (Paris: à le Vasseur et Cie., date unknown).

Pietsch, P., *Die Formations – and Uniformierungs Geschichte des Preussischen Heeres 1808-1914* (Hamburg: Verlag H.Gerhard Schulz, 1963).

Pitot, Lt., *Historique du 83e Régiment d'Infanterie 1684-1891* (Toulouse: Private Publication, date unknown).

de Place, R., *Historique du 12e Cuirassiers (1668-1888)* (Paris: Lahure, 18890.

Plotho, C., *Der Krieg in Deutschland and Frankreich in den Jahren 1813 and 1814* (Berlin: Carl Friedrich, 1817).

Plotho, *Relation de la Bataille de Leipzig (16, 17, 18, & 19 Octobre)* (Paris: J. Correard, 1840).

Poniatowski, J., *Correspondance du Prince Joseph Poniatowski avec la France* (Poznan: 1929).

von Quistorp, B. *Die Kaiserlich Russisch-Deutsch Legion Verlag* (Berlin: von Carl Heymann, 1860).

von Quistorp, B., *Geschichte der Nord Armée im Jahre 1813* (Berlin: E.S. Mittler and Sohn, 1894).

Rapp, Count, *Memoirs of General Count Rapp, First Aide-de-camp to Napoleon* (London: Henry Colburn & Co., 1823).

Rehtwisch, T., *Grossgörschen 2 May 1813* (Leipzig: Turm Verlag, 1912).

Rossler, *Tagebücher aus den zehen Feldzügen der Württemberger unter der Regierung Königs Friedrich* (Ludwigsberg: Friedrich Nast, 1820).

Rothwiller, Baron, *Historique du Deuxième Régiment de Cuirassiers ancien Royal de Cavalerie (1635-1876)* (Paris: Plon & Cie., 1877).

Roulin, Lt. Col., *125e Régiment d'Infanterie* (Orleans: George Jacob, 1890).

Rousset, C., *La Grande Armée de 1813* (Paris: Librairie Academique Didier, 1892).

Rousset, M.C., *Souvenirs du Maréchal Macdonald, Duc de Tarente* (Paris: Librairie Hachette & Cie., 1892).

Ruby, Col., & de Labeau, Cpt., *Historique du 2me Régiment de Cuirassiers (1668-1942)* (Marseille, Etablissements Moullot Fils Aine, 1944).

von Ruesch, von Lossow, von Gunther & von l'Estocq, *Geschichte des Königlichen Zweiten Ulanen-Régiments* (Potsdam: A. Stein., 1858).

St. Cyr, G., *Mémoires du Maréchal Gouvion Saint-Cyr 1812-1813* (Paris: Remanences, 1982).

von Salisch, G., *Geschichte des königlich Preussischen Siebenten Infanterie-Regiments von seiner Stiftung in Jahre 1797 bis zum lsten Juli 1854* (Glogau: C. Flemming, 1854).

Sauzey, Cpt., *Les Allemands sous les Aigles Françaises, essai sur les troupes de la Confédération du Rhin 1806-1814* (Paris: Librairie Militaire R. Chapelot et Cie, no date).

Savary, M., *Relation de la defense de Hambourg en 1813, et 1814* (Extracted from the *Spectateur Militaire*, July 1846).

von Schauroth, Freiherr W.F., *Im Rheinbund-Regiment der Herzoglich Sächsischen Kontingente Koburg-HildburghausenGotha-Weimar während der Feldzuge in Tirol, Spanien and Russland, 1809-1813* (Berlin: E.S. Mittler & Sohn, 1905).

Schmidt, C., *Le Grand-Duche de Berg (1806-1813): Étude sur la Domination Francaise en Allemagne sous Napoleon ler* (Paris: 1905).

Schmitt, Lt., *151e Régiment d'Infanterie* (Paris: 1901).

von Schöning, K.W., *Geschichte des Königlich Preussische Regiments Garde du Corps zu seinem hundertjährigen Jubelfest* (Berlin: 1840).

Schussler, A., *Geschichte des Lützowischen Freikorps, Ein Beitrag zur Kriegsgeschichte der Jahre 1813 and 1814* (Berlin:, E.S. Mittler, 1826).

Schuster, O. & Francke, F.A..*Geschichte der Sächsischen Armee von deren Errichtung bis auf die neuste Zeit* (Leipzig: Duncker und Humblot, 1885).

Schwertfeger, B., *Geschichte der Königlich Deutsch Legion 1803-1816* (Hannover: Hahn'sche Buchhandlung, 1907).

von Seidel, F., *Affair de Lindenau, Extracted from the Austrian Military Journal and translated by P. Himly* (Paris: J. Correard, 1840).

Shanahan, W.O., *Prussian Military Reforms 1786-1813* (New York: Columbia University Press, 1945).

von Sichart, A. and R., *Geschichte der Königlich-Hannoverschen Armee* (Hanover & Leipzig: Han'sche Buchhandlung, 1898).

Simon, G., *Die Kriegeserignisse zwischen Teplitz and Pirna im August and September des Jahres 1813. Die Schlacht bei Kulm am 29. and 30. August 1813 and Das Gefecht bei Arbeau am 17. September 1813; Nach verläszlichen Quellen Bearbeitet* (Teplitz-Schönau: Emil Seewald, 1911).

Simond, E., *Le 28e de Ligne, Historique du Régiment* (Rouen: Megard & Cie., 1889).

Sporschil, J, *Die Grosse Chronik, Geschichte des Krieges des Verbundeten Europas gegen Napoleon Bonaparte, in den Jähren 1813, 1814, and 1815* (Braunschweig: G. Westermann, 1841).

Stiegler, E., *Le Maréchal Oudinot Duc de Reggio* (Paris: Librairie Plon, 1894).

von Strotha, Adolf, *Die Königlich Preussische Reitende Artillerie von Jahre 1759 bis 1816* (Wiesbaden: LTR Verlag, 1981).

Suremain, Lt.Gen., *Memoirs du Lieutenant General Suremain (1794-1815)* (Paris: Plon-Nourrit et Cie., 1902).

Susane, Louis, *Histoire de la Cavalerie Francaise* (Paris: C. Terana, 1984).

Temaux-Compans, M., *Le Général Compans (1769-1845)* (Paris: Librairie Plon, 1912).

Thomas, J., *Un Régiment Rhénan sous Napoléon Premier* (Liege: H. Vaillant-Charmanne, 1928).

Tournes, R., *La Campagne de Printemps en 1813, Lützen* (Paris: Charles-Lavauzelle & Cie., 1931).

Vassal, Lt., *Historique du 11e Régiment d'Infanterie* (Montauban: Edouard Forestie, 1900).

de Vaudoncourt, Gen. G., *Histoire des Campagnes d'Italie en 1813 et 1814, Avec un Atlas Militaire* (London: T. Egerton, 1817).

de Vaudoncourt, Gen. G., *Histoire Politique et Militaire du Prince Eugène Napoléon, Vice-roi d'Italie* (Paris: Librairie Universelle de P. Mongie, 1828).

Vaupell, O., *Den Danske Haers Historie til nutiden Og Den Norske Haers Historie indtil 1814* (Copenhagen: 1872).

Venzky, G., *Die Russisch-Deutsche Legion in den Jahren 1811-1815* (Wiesbaden: Otto Harrassowitz, 1966).

Viger, Count, *Davout, Maréchal d'Empire* (Paris: P. Ollendorff ed, Imprierie H. Bouilant, 1898).

von Vitzthum, Eckstädt, *Die Hauptquartiere im Herbstfeldzuge 1813 auf dem Deutschen Kriegsschauplatze* (Berlin: E.S. Mittler & Sohn, 1910).

Vogel, F.L., *Theilnahme der König. Preuss. Artillerie an dem Kämpfe des Befreiungskriege* (Weisbaden: LTR Verlag, 1981).

Voigtlander, L., *Das Tagebuch des Johann Heinrich Lang aus Lübeck and die Feldzuge der Hanseaten in den Jahren 1813-1815* (Lubeck: Verlag Schmidt-Romhild, 1980).

Voisin, Ch., *Historique du 6e Hussards* (Libourne: G.Maleville, 1888).

Vollmer, U., *Die Bewaffnung der Armeen des Königsreichs Württemberg and des Grossherzogtums Baden* (Schwabisch Hall: Journal Verlag Schwend GmbH, 1981).

Wagner, A., *Recueil des Plans de Combat et de Batailles livrees par l'Armèe Prussienne pendant les campagnes des Annes 1813, 1814, et 1815 avec des eclaircissements Historiques* (Berlin: G.Reimer, 1821).

Weil, M.H, *Campagne de 1813, La Cavalerie des armées allies* (Paris: Librairie Militaire de L. Baudoin et Cie., 1886).

Wilhelm, Duke of Brunswick, *Geschichte des Magdeburgischen Husaren-Régiments, Nr. 10* (Berlin: A. Duncker, 1863).

Wolf, A., *Historique du 10e Régiment de Chasseurs à cheval depuis sa création jusqu'en 1890* (Paris: Librairie Militaire de L. Baudoin, 1890).

Wrangell, Baron G., *Mit Graf Pahlens Reiterei gegen Napoelon* (Berlin: Ernst Siegfried Mittler un Sohn, 1910).

Index

INDEX OF PEOPLE

INDEX OF PLACES